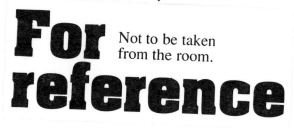
W9-BSJ-331

For
Not to be taken
from the room.
reference

Encyclopedia of
Women and Religion
in North America

Editorial Board

Encyclopedia of
Women and Religion
in North America

~

Edited by
Rosemary Skinner Keller
and
Rosemary Radford Ruether

Associate Editor
Marie Cantlon

VOLUME 3

INDIANA UNIVERSITY PRESS
Bloomington and Indianapolis

This book is a publication of

Indiana University Press
601 North Morton Street
Bloomington, Indiana 47404-3797 USA

http://iupress.indiana.edu

Telephone orders   800-842-6796
Fax orders   812-855-7931
Orders by e-mail   iuporder@indiana.edu

The paper used in this publication meets the minimum requirements of American National Standard for Information Sciences—Permanence of Paper for Printed Library Materials, ANSI Z39.48-1984.

Manufactured in the United States of America

Library of Congress Cataloging-in-Publication Data

The encyclopedia of women and religion in North America / Rosemary Skinner Keller and Rosemary Radford Ruether, editors ; Marie Cantlon, associate editor.
     p. cm.
 Includes bibliographical references and index.
  ISBN 0-253-34685-1 (cloth, set) — ISBN 0-253-34686-X (v. 1) — ISBN 0-253-34687-8 (v. 2) — ISBN 0-253-34688-6 (v. 3) 1. Women and religion—North America—Encyclopedias. 2. Women—Religious life—North America—Encyclopedias. 3. Women—Religious aspects—North America—Encyclopedias. I. Keller, Rosemary Skinner. II. Ruether, Rosemary Radford. III. Cantlon, Marie.
  BL458.E52   2006
  200.82'0973—dc22   2005032429

1 2 3 4 5 11 10 09 08 07 06

Contents

Part XI

~

Women, Religion, and Social Reform

NINETEENTH- AND TWENTIETH-CENTURY PROTESTANT SOCIAL REFORM MOVEMENTS IN THE UNITED STATES

Carolyn DeSwarte Gifford

FROM THE BIRTH of the United States as an independent nation, there has always been an emphasis on reform. Even during the colonial period, there were evidences of great enthusiasm for refining and deepening the moral dimensions of the American people's beliefs and values. A number of currents in religious and political thought provided an atmosphere hospitable to reform in the late eighteenth and early nineteenth centuries. Enlightenment thought, Scottish Common Sense philosophy, evangelical revivalism and perfectionism, Quaker humanitarianism, and Transcendentalism differed in many significant respects; yet together these ideas infused different segments of American society with exciting and optimistic notions about the nature of God and humanity and God's relation to creation.

These trends suggested that human beings were essentially good or, at least, that all could be saved that earnestly repented their sins and changed their ways. They further implied that God was concerned for human well-being and comfort as well as salvation. Many Americans fervently asserted that the country's newly won democratic form of government was God's instrument for carrying out the divine purpose in human society. Idealistic thought engendered hope that human ability could change society. The urgent duty of God's American children was to shape their nation in accord with the divinely inspired ideals of liberty and justice so recently enshrined in the documents that were to guide it: the Declaration of Independence, the Constitution, and the Bill of Rights. Americans understood the development of their country in accord with such ideals to be *the* grand reform on which all individual reform movements were predicated.

1800–1865

Historians have often referred to the antebellum period in U.S. history as "the Age of Reform." During the antebellum era, both women and men participated in a variety of reform efforts. These included temperance; moral reform (the elimination of prostitution and the sexual double standard for men and women); improved care for the ill, the insane, and the handicapped; prison reform and the elimination of capital punishment; charitable work among the poor, sometimes accompanied by the aim of eradicating poverty; the abolition of slavery; better treatment of American Indians; women's rights; and the promotion of peace. Some women became powerful and articulate national leaders in antebellum reforms, especially the women's rights movement, moral reform, and the antislavery crusade. Many more became grassroots workers who labored, sometimes for their entire lives, on behalf of causes in which they believed.

In order to carry out this mission of national reformation to which all Americans were called, they must be equipped with an intellectual and moral education, one that would teach them to reason and foster a virtuous character. Important as educational reform was for all, for women in particular it was central to their struggles over two centuries to gain credibility, power, authority, and equality. Essayist Judith Sargent Murray (1751–1820) definitely understood female education to be the necessary foundation for women's equality with men. She insisted, in her essay "On the Equality of the Sexes" (1790), that, given equal opportunity for education, women were men's intellectual equals, not their inferiors as many believed at the time. The serious public discussion of women's education during the era fostered the establishment of female academies, scattered through the settled regions of the country. However, such schools were, for the most part, local, ephemeral, and with little pedagogical basis underlying their attempts at education.

By the 1820s, however, three remarkable and determined women—Emma Hart Willard (1787–1870), Mary Lyon (1797–1849), and Catharine Esther Beecher (1800–1878)—joined the ranks of educational reformers, building enduring institutions that became influential models for women's education. Each of these women came to believe, early on in her work, that God had chosen her for a mission: to devise and provide the most thorough education possible at the time for young women. In carrying out this task, they became educational theorists, elaborating in their writings and speeches a convincing rationale and practice for female education. They also became formidable educational activists, enlisting vital financial support for their work by convincing sympathetic women and men of its crucial import for the nation.

Emma Willard opened Troy (New York) Female Seminary in 1821, with the intention of offering her young women students a secondary school education that would be equal to the best available to young men. Over the next decade, her institution became the standard to which female secondary schools aspired. The textbooks Willard wrote in geography and history became classics of their field, used by generations of students. Her school offered a combination of rigorous intellectual preparation in the classics, math and sciences, and modern languages, along with training in the social graces—

drawing, painting, and dancing—fitting for girls from the upper- and upper-middle-class families to whom the school catered. Willard herself gave students moral instruction with a broadly Protestant tone and taught them good manners, consciously preparing her graduates to make suitable marriages and be companions appropriate to their husbands' social and intellectual status.

Such intelligent wives could have great influence over the thoughts and opinions of the men of their social circle. They would also be competent to fill what Willard and most other women's educators of the time felt was their most important role, that of "republican mother" who would raise her sons to be thoughtful, moral citizens capable of acting responsibly in the public realm of politics and business. And she would train daughters who would, like her, be fit spouses for powerful upwardly mobile men. They, in turn, would become republican mothers, ensuring the production of succeeding generations of solid citizens.

A decade and a half after Troy Female Seminary began, Mary Lyon opened Mount Holyoke Female Seminary in Massachusetts. Like Emma Willard, Lyon was concerned about the higher education of women, but unlike her earlier counterpart, Lyon was steeped in evangelical beliefs and piety. The school she founded reflected this. Intellectual learning was important to Lyon, and she developed a respected curriculum. But central to the ethos of her school was an earnest Christian faith to be modeled by the staff and elicited from students through a round of prayer and missionary meetings, chapel services, and revivals (worship services with singing, prayers, and sermons, geared toward eliciting conversion experiences from participants) that defined the Mount Holyoke experience from its beginnings.

Mount Holyoke differed from Troy in a second important way. Lyon created her institution specifically to serve young women of more modest financial circumstances, who longed for a higher education but were unable to pay the tuition at schools like Emma Willard's. In order to keep tuition minimal, Lyon asked donors to give generously, teachers to work, as she would, for very small salaries, and students to perform domestic chores at the school so that servants would not have to be hired. Lyon aimed to train young women as teachers—whether of their own children or those of others. She believed that such a vocation was the most suitable and lofty field of action by which a young woman could evidence her faith. Nurturing and guiding generations of the nation's children was the highest calling Lyon and most of her contemporaries could imagine for an evangelical Protestant woman.

Catharine Beecher's work from the 1830s through the 1850s advanced the reform of women's education and, at the same time, contributed to a redefinition of the ideal of womanhood and woman's sphere. In an era when the United States was undergoing rapid economic and social change through industrialization and urbanization, women's and men's roles and relationships were also shifting and uncertain. In the mainly agricultural economy that characterized the country for its first two centuries, women's productive and reproductive work had been readily understood as necessary and valued accordingly. In the newly emerging economic pattern, with factories and businesses taking over many activities formerly performed in the household, women of the rising middle class saw some of their traditional duties disappearing. Beecher believed that women's self-worth and self-esteem were shrinking as well. She offered such women a new self-understanding and a strong sense of the important place they filled in the national mission of a powerful and aggressive Protestantism.

Beecher's writings and speeches, aimed specifically at recruiting hundreds of women for "the West" (the Old North West Territory, now the Middle West), delineated the key role she envisioned for aspiring Protestant middle-class women. Beecher saw women as responsible for the moral education of the young through mothering and teaching. She extended that responsibility far beyond Lyon's understanding, shifting virtually the total weight of shaping a national morality onto women. As she developed a new role for women over the course of three decades, Beecher became one of the most influential exponents of what women's historians have referred to as the "cult of true womanhood." The phrase denotes a reform ideal that has had profound implications for succeeding generations of women even up to the present day.

Beecher based her understanding of this ideal on the assumption of women's fundamental difference from men, a difference she believed was ordained by God and upheld by scripture and centuries of Christian teaching. Beecher described a woman's highest virtues as piety, purity, domesticity, and submissiveness. Although men's superiority over women was assumed in biblical gender arrangements, the relationship between male and female, would, nevertheless, be one of complementarity, each supplying what the other lacked and each presiding over a separate sphere of activity. Because women were understood to possess greater piety and purity than men, they were required in the ethical system that Beecher laid out to train children and youth in morality. Furthermore, they were to keep men moral. Women were ideally suited—indeed, had been created by God, Beecher believed—to be the moral guardians of the nation.

As Americans advanced westward, women would accept the duty of civilizing, Protestantizing, and moralizing the frontier, through their domination of the sphere of home/school/church, while men shouldered the responsibility for developing the spheres of economics and government. Because of their innate difference from men, women would carry out their duty with a peaceable demeanor, by indirect influence, gently persuading men to act morally in the governmental and economic spheres over which they ruled. As Beecher wrote in 1837:

> [I]t was designed [by God] that the mode of gaining influence and of exercising power should be altogether different and peculiar.... All the power, and all the conquests that are lawful to woman, are those only which appeal to the kindly, generous, peaceful and benevolent principles. Woman is to win everything by peace and love. ... [T]his is to be all accomplished within the domestic and social circle. (Beecher, 100–101)

The ideal of true womanhood flourished during the middle decades of the nineteenth century, becoming the dominant standard by which other notions of womanhood and woman's sphere were measured.

This ideal seemed in some ways to be highly appropriate to women's activity in an era when the predominant reform strategy was moral suasion—efforts to convince individuals to give up sinful behaviors. Motivated by their duty of moral guardianship, thousands of women became active in both charitable associations and reform groups of all kinds during the antebellum era, relying on their perceived moral superiority and employing their vast powers of persuasion. Women extended their domestic sphere of activity beyond their immediate families outward into the larger community, founding and staffing schools for poor children, teaching Sunday School, establishing homes for widows and orphans, and providing relief for the indigent populations of many towns and cities. Women took a leading role in the country's developing welfare system, during an era when municipal and state governments were often reluctant to devote more than minimum energy and funds to such work. They formed antislavery and temperance associations—parallel or auxiliary to men's—and raised money, wrote articles and tracts, circulated petitions, and spoke to women's groups, all activities accepted by most Americans as proper for women (although some, like Catharine Beecher, objected to women's petitioning as intruding too far into the male sphere of government). Yet, with such a circumscribed understanding of their nature and role, there were limits to women's ability to participate in reform movements.

As early as the 1830s, a few women antislavery reformers had begun to question the effectiveness and legitimacy of understanding both womanhood and reform based on gender difference. In a sharp exchange with Catharine Beecher in 1837, Quaker antislavery lecturer Angelina Grimké (1805–1879) defended women reformers' right and moral duty to fight aggressively against slavery in whatever way they could, disregarding any false notion of women's proper sphere or behavior. Like Beecher, Grimké and her sister Sarah (1792–1873), also an antislavery reformer, based their concept of womanhood and woman's moral responsibility on their interpretation of the Bible's teachings and Christian tradition. But they discerned in those sources a different message about woman than Beecher did. They believed that women were, equally with men, created by God to be responsible moral beings and endowed with consciences capable of being roused against injustice and oppression. When confronted with such clear examples of injustice as slavery and white racism, women as well as men must use any means consonant with the dictates of their consciences to oppose these evils. They must not be limited in their response to the demand for reform by fears of stepping beyond the behavioral bounds of true womanhood as defined by Beecher.

During the same decade, female moral reformers raised different issues than antislavery reformers, but ones no less critical of prevailing gender relationships. In 1834 a group of women met in a New York City Presbyterian church to discuss a subject that previously had been virtually taboo for women to raise: the plight of the city's prostitutes. Unlike most Americans at the time, these churchwomen did not view prostitutes as "Magdalenes" who lured men into vice. Instead they saw them as victims of male lust. Men's uncontrolled passion was, they believed, the result of a double sexual standard that prevailed in American society. Acting in their role as pious guardians of purity, they intended to hold men to the same high level of sexual behavior that the cult of true womanhood demanded for women. Underlying the sympathy that these women felt toward the prostitutes they wished to aid was dissatisfaction, even anger, at women's dependence on men, especially in sexual relationships.

The New York Female Moral Reform Society (FMRS) was founded with two goals: first, the rescue and rehabilitation of the city's prostitutes along with the closing of brothels and, second, a vigorous protest against the prevailing double sexual standard. The movement for female moral reform took hold throughout the northeastern states, with a network of local societies. In 1835 a weekly publication, *The Advocate of Moral Reform*, was launched and quickly circulated among large numbers of urban and rural women, building a strong sense of sisterhood among FMRS members. By 1839, a national organization formed, and during the next decade, members carried on a vigorous campaign to achieve their goals. Although FMRS women were mostly unsuccessful at reforming prostitutes, they did manage to give public voice to their dissatisfaction with male sexual behavior.

By the 1850s reformers also began to address the economic issues involved in female prostitution. They understood the limited and low-paying employment opportunities available to women who found it necessary to earn their own living. Prostitution, which promised higher pay and an easier life, was often the most viable job choice for women even though it carried with it a great social stigma. Although reformers did not really question the ideal of true womanhood, they did begin to look carefully at some of the consequences of the dichotomized male/female relationship and at what happened when the ideal failed to become a reality in the lives of some women.

By the 1840s, women's rights reformers joined the struggle over the meaning of womanhood, the extent of woman's sphere, and the implications for women's reform activism. At the 1848 Seneca Falls (New York) convention organized by antislavery activists Lucretia Coffin Mott (1793–1880) and Elizabeth Cady Stanton (1851–1902), the campaign for women's rights was officially launched. The convention issued a *Declaration of Sentiments and Resolutions* authored by Stanton and modeled on the Declaration of Independence that announced the God-given fundamental equality of women and men in all areas of life. Those attending the convention passed many resolutions addressing a wide range of women's educational, legal, and economic disabilities and their inequality in matters of religion. The only resolution that did not pass unanimously was one that demanded woman suffrage, the right that would claim, perhaps, the greatest concentration of women's reform energy for the next seven decades.

The issue of women's right to vote became more pressing as reform strategies, particularly in the antislavery and temperance movements, shifted from moral suasion to political measures such as the election of reform candidates, the creation of reform parties, and the passage of laws restricting or eliminating such evils as slavery and drunkenness. Woman suffragists believed that they should be able to vote on the basis of simple justice and equality. Even more important for the future of the reforms women championed, suffragists also demanded the vote so that they could have a direct impact on the political process at all levels. By the mid-nineteenth century, women understood that real power to reform no longer resided solely, or even mainly, in their womanly ability to achieve their goals by influence alone. If they were to carry out their duty of moral guardianship, women must become voters. In effect, they accepted Beecher's notion of women's national task

but rejected the circumscribed ideal of womanhood and women's sphere of action she proposed.

Like women in the antislavery movement, some women temperance reformers also chafed under the limitations of women's proper sphere. The temperance movement began in the United States by the 1820s. Since that time, thousands of women had been involved in temperance work at both the local and state level, but as in the case of antislavery women, the range of women's temperance activities was restricted by what was deemed appropriate for them as women. New York temperance women such as Susan B. Anthony (1820–1906) and Amelia Jenks Bloomer (1818–1894) gradually began to rebel at the gendered limitations placed on their work for the cause in which they believed.

Bloomer founded and edited the *Lily*, a temperance newspaper, in 1849 in order to disseminate the beliefs of a newly formed local New York Ladies' Temperance Society, of which she was an officer. She quickly turned the paper into a strong voice for a wide variety of women's rights reforms, from women's suffrage and dress reform to the right of a woman to divorce an alcoholic husband. As editor of a widely read and groundbreaking paper from 1849 to 1853, Bloomer help to shape women's thought about equality in the critical period at the movement's beginning. Many of the women who became leading women's rights reformers in the following decades first launched their ideas in the pages of her paper.

Although Bloomer espoused a range of reforms during her lifetime, temperance remained the one closest to her heart. As she and her husband moved westward across the country in the 1850s and 1860s, she allied herself with temperance organizations wherever she lived, a pattern typical of many other women who joined the Yankee migration into the Middle and Far West in the mid-1800s. Along with their cherished possessions, they brought their causes with them from their homes in the East. Before Bloomer and her husband moved west in 1853, she became a member of a local lodge of a brand-new temperance organization, the International Order of Good Templars (IOGT). She chose that organization over the Daughters of Temperance, a woman's auxiliary to the powerful Sons of Temperance, because the IOGT admitted women to membership on an equal basis with men, something the Sons of Temperance adamantly refused to do. When the Bloomers moved to Ohio, they quickly joined a local IOGT group, and in 1855, in their final move to western Iowa, Bloomer became an organizer for the IOGT in that state, once again combining her temperance work with a continued push for women's suffrage.

During the 1850s other temperance women joined Bloomer and her colleagues Anthony and Stanton in their suffrage activity. At the same time, a few women began to employ a novel strategy. Rather than merely trying to convince individuals to give up drinking, these women shifted their target, engaging in direct confrontation with saloon keepers and liquor dealers, whom they saw as implicated in the individual drunkard's sin. In what were at that point isolated and sporadic local attempts, bands of hymn-singing women marched from meetings in churches to saloons and drugstores, sometimes kneeling to pray that proprietors would voluntarily give up selling liquor. At other times, women dramatically broke up beer barrels or poured the contents of whisky bottles onto the street before the eyes of irate saloon owners and crowds of onlookers who gathered to see just how far these temperance women would go. Sometimes demonstrators were successful in persuading liquor dealers to give up their occupations, close down their saloons, and go into some other line of work. More often, the dealers waited until the demonstrations died down or were declared unlawful by local police chiefs and judges and went on with business as usual. Clearly in this instance the male-run justice system did not take women's plea for reform seriously. This new form of street demonstrations was not working. A more concerted and many-pronged effort to effect temperance reform would have to be developed in the future.

By the late 1850s, the entire nation's attention focused more and more exclusively on the issue of slavery and its consequences. War was imminent, and in 1861, when it was finally declared, Americans, northerners and southerners alike, threw their energy into the war effort. Many women trained in benevolent, charitable, and reform work redirected their skills toward needs generated by the war. Typical of these women was volunteer Mary Rice Livermore (1820–1905), active in benevolent and charitable work in Chicago before the war. She became codirector of the northwestern branch of the U.S. Sanitary Commission, a civilian group designated by President Abraham Lincoln to collect and distribute food, medicine, and other supplies to the Union armies. Livermore and her coworkers traveled throughout the Midwest, forming hundreds of local relief societies that sent a steady stream of supplies through a central Chicago depot to armies in the field.

For Livermore and many other women volunteers during the Civil War, the successful orchestration of a vast relief effort stretching across the northern United States and into the South presaged their postwar activity in new reform groups and networks that became truly national in scope. A new generation of women reformers joined with others who began their work before the war to take up again the causes that had been set aside during the Civil War years. With the exception of slavery, most of the reform issues that had engaged Americans during the antebellum period surfaced once more. Although slavery was now forbidden, the nation wrestled with the question of what forms freedom would take in the lives of former enslaved persons. Agencies of the federal government working with a number of Protestant organizations sought to provide education and economic and political rights to newly freed African Americans. Also pressing was the problem of how to ensure their protection in the face of growing white racism in both the South and North.

1865–1920

Even before the Civil War ended, northern Protestant clergy and laypersons went south to set up schools and relief centers for "contraband," the former enslaved persons under the protection of the Union armies. After the war, 5,000 teachers—the great majority young women—traveled under the auspices of denominational Freedmen's Aid organizations to the former Confederacy. They were inspired by a strong missionary spirit, one similar to that of the hundreds of teachers sent out to the West several decades earlier by Mary Lyon and Catharine Beecher. Wishing, above all, to be useful and self-sacrificing in the service of God, these northern teachers, mainly from abolitionist families, were imbued with an evangelical piety and middle-class morality based on individual self-control and hard work. They hoped to instill the same virtues in their African American students along with teaching them to read and write.

The northern teachers were filled with idealistic notions of lifting blacks out of the physical and moral degradation of slavery and substituting their own sober theology and worship for what they viewed as overly emotional religious practices. There was a certain amount of condescension and, thus, implicit racism in these goals, although the northerners usually failed to recognize it in themselves. But African American families saw and often resented the imposition of an uncongenial religious and moral system on them. They desperately wanted education but in the main rejected the attempted reform of the very values and institutions that had given them hope and strength during their centuries of enslavement. In order to ensure the cohesiveness of their communities and culture, African Americans often preferred teachers of their own race, to the bafflement of the white teachers.

Northern faculty and administrators also greatly underestimated the resentment and racism of many white southerners who began, as quickly as they could manage, to implement segregated state school systems and replace northern teachers with southerners. Yet for several years following the war, idealistic young northern women helped to provide African Americans with almost their sole opportunity for education. After 1870, most northern teachers returned home, just beginning to realize that Emancipation was only the first step in a long struggle to achieve true freedom for African Americans. A few teachers and administrators remained in the South their entire lives, serving in black higher education institutions and dedicating themselves to work for and with African Americans. They would be joined several decades later by some southern whites, especially women, who also dreamed of a "New South" based on justice and equality.

As the system of segregation and repression hardened in the South after the Reconstruction era ended, a small number of African Americans began to emigrate, leaving their homes and what few possessions they had and heading for the western plains states. They were aided by northerners like Laura Smith Haviland (1808–1898), who worked under the auspices of both the Michigan and Kansas Freedmen's Aid Commissions. Haviland exemplifies abolitionists whose commitment to African Americans was lifelong. Hers began in the 1830s when she and her husband helped to form the first antislavery society in Michigan and founded a preparatory school there that accepted both black and white pupils. After her husband's death, she became a guide on the Underground Railroad, participating in several daring rescues. During and after the Civil War, she traveled into the South to aid and protect former slaves. There she became a harsh critic of both northern Reconstruction policies, which she considered weak and finally ineffective, and southern obstructionist measures, which she condemned as segregationist in intent and terrorist in practice.

In her autobiography, Haviland recorded the despair among many African Americans by the late 1870s:

> The increasing intelligence among the four millions and a half of slaves, declared free by the nation's pen in the hand of her President, Abraham Lincoln, they found did not bring with it the glorious sunlight of freedom the proclamation promised in its dawn. After fifteen years of patiently hoping, waiting, and watching for the shaping of a government, they saw clearly that their future condition as a race must be submissive vassalage, a war of races, or emigration. (Haviland, 482)

Haviland's assessment starkly presented the choices, as she saw them, that African Americans had in the Jim Crow South. Given the discouraging situation, some blacks left for a life they hoped would be freer outside the South. But many stayed, determined to create freedom for themselves, a struggle that would continue into the next century.

Further evidences of white racism were visible in the treatment of American Indians. From colonial times, a small number of white Americans, particularly some Quakers and a few Protestant and Roman Catholic missionaries, had protested against the vicious attitudes and practices that too often characterized white people's relationships with the many Native American groups they encountered. But these reformers' concerns were mostly ignored. During the nineteenth century, the United States government's policies toward American Indian peoples were driven by three successive goals as white Americans pushed across the continent seeking land and wealth: the extermination of large numbers of Indians; the forced removal of others from lands traditionally theirs to reservations set aside for them; and, finally, their assimilation into the dominant white culture. Immediately after the Civil War, renewed interest in reform of whites' treatment of Indians occurred, spurred by the report of the Indian Peace Commission, issued in 1868. The report, which reflected the dominant opinion among thoughtful white people, favored the reservation system and the assimilation of native peoples as the best possible solutions to the "Indian question." But it also stressed humane treatment and justice toward Indians rather than the "pacification" process currently being conducted against them in the West, with its bloody wars and forced acceptance of white ways.

A small number of women took up the cause of reform in the treatment of American Indians. Lydia Maria Child (1802–1880), best known as an antislavery reformer, had also been keenly interested in Indian–white relationships from the time she wrote her first novel *Hobomok* (1824), a plea for racial and religious tolerance toward Indians. When the Indian Peace Commission's report appeared, Child endorsed its call for justice toward Indians and linked whites' racist behavior toward African Americans and American Indians. As she pointed out strongly in her pamphlet *An Appeal for the Indians* (1868): "Our relations with the red and black members of the human family have been one almost unvaried history of violence and fraud" (Meltzer and Holland, 479). Child differed from most reformers who believed that Indian assimilation (or "civilizing" as some termed the process) included "Christianizing" them. She saw value and strength in native peoples' own religious and ethical beliefs and felt that it was a mistake to insist on Indians' conversion to Christianity. Child's opinion was more akin to that of many American Indian reformers in the last third of the twentieth century than to reformers—both Indian and white—of her own time.

Sarah Winnemucca (c. 1844–1891) and Susette La Flesche (Tibbles) (1854–1903), two prominent Native American reformers, were, to some extent, products of the assimilation process carried out by the government and encouraged by missionaries and reformers alike. Winnemucca, a Piute Indian, learned English and served as a skilled interpreter of the Indians' position to sympathetic army officers. La Flesche identified herself as a member of the Omaha nation, who participated in traditional rituals and practices, but also attended mission schools where she was introduced to Christian teachings. Both women became powerful spokespersons for their people during the late 1870s and early 1880s. Winnemucca wrote and lectured on the situation of the Piutes and La Flesche toured the eastern United States and England to describe the plight of the Omaha and Ponca tribes. Each indicted the government for its consistent ill treatment of Indians, especially criticizing the rapacity of many Indian agents who were notorious for cheating the Indians out of their tribal lands. At the same time, they defended the assimilation of Indians into white culture as the best route for Indians to follow, given the overwhelming power of white America.

Both of these Indian women became inspirations for prominent white women supporters: Sarah Winnemucca for Boston educational reformer Elizabeth Peabody (1804–1894) and Susette La Flesche for writer Helen Hunt Jackson (1830–1885). Impressed by hearing Winnemucca lecture, Peabody arranged speaking engagements for her within the eastern reform community and lobbied government officials on behalf of Indian reform. After hearing La Flesche speak, Jackson undertook extensive research in government records and published *A Century of Dishonor* in 1881. Her volume was a detailed documentation of the U.S. government's lies to Indian peoples, the many treaties the government had broken over the course of its dealings with Indians, and its vicious practices of massacres. Continuing agitation on behalf of Indian reform, she published *Ramona* (1884), a novel she hoped would rouse the public's indignation against the unfair treatment of American Indians in the way that Harriet Beecher Stowe's *Uncle Tom's Cabin* had mobilized the American public against slavery three decades earlier. (Unfortunately, most readers understood the novel simply as a romance of early California and not as a vehicle for protest of injustice.) A few reformers continued into the twentieth century to work for changes that would alleviate the more onerous conditions Indians continued to experience on the reservations. For the most part, however, the policy of assimilation into white culture was pursued. Although some reformers honored the traditional cultures of Native American peoples as Lydia Maria Child had done earlier, sustained attempts to preserve and practice these distinctive ways would have to await the rise of the Native American protest movement during the last third of the twentieth century.

Along with the serious problem of white racism, Americans faced another equally daunting challenge by the last third of the nineteenth century: the interlinked processes of urbanization and industrialization that would come to characterize the modern era. Although these processes had begun by the early 1800s, their growth accelerated rapidly during the course of the century until the country was no longer mainly rural but predominantly urban. The rise of industrial capitalism meant an economic shift from small-scale producers and businesses to giant corporations run by a relatively few owners and managers employing large numbers of wage workers. This shift ushered in the "Gilded Age," an era of enormous, conspicuous wealth for a few and relentless, grinding poverty for many. It brought in its wake overcrowded, unhealthy living conditions; the exploitation of labor—including, by this time, growing numbers of women and children—through unsafe, poorly paid work; the manipulation of politics by big business; and strife between owners and workers. The great wave of immigration during the period exacerbated an increasingly grave situation, flooding the cities with several million more people in need of housing and jobs. Existing municipal and state governments and private religious and charitable organizations, normally responsible for alleviating such conditions, were ill-equipped to meet these new situations as the nation experienced the transformation of its economic structure.

To face the growing challenge of urban industrial modernity, some Protestant clergy and laity called for the development of new theological imperatives and methods of social action. Well before the turn of the century, they had begun to proclaim a "Social Gospel" taught by Jesus that emphasized a total salvation: not only the salvation of individual sinners but—equally important—the redemption of sinful social systems and structures, particularly economic and political ones. Under the rubric "the Fatherhood of God and the brotherhood of man," believers in the Social Gospel message analyzed the ills they perceived in American society and devised reform strategies that would bring their vision of the Kingdom of God—one that manifested social justice, economic equality, and political freedom—into reality. Both female and male reformers were deeply motivated by the tenets of the Social Gospel, bringing its ideas to bear on reform work within existing institutions or creating new ones that more adequately reflected their growing commitment to social salvation.

The last third of the nineteenth century also saw the rise of another new phenomenon: the exponential growth of regional and national women's associations and organizations, both religious and secular, African American and white. These included the Woman's Christian Temperance Union (WCTU); the Young Women's Christian Association (YWCA); the various denominational Women's Foreign and Home Missionary Societies (WFMS, WHMS); the General Federation of Women's Clubs (GFWC) and its member associations; the National and the American Woman Suffrage Associations (NWSA, AWSA, and by 1890, the merged NAWSA); along with a myriad of others. Some of the most powerful women's organizations were founded explicitly as reform groups, while others had strong reform components in their agendas.

Many of the national women's organizations that arose during the period of rapidly changing economic and social conditions fairly quickly turned their attention to the distresses caused by these changes and the measures needed to combat them. They continued to carry on benevolent work, as many women's organizations had done since the beginning of the century, but on an unprecedented scale, required by the human needs they encountered in the nation's cities. In order to combat extreme urban poverty, many women reformers drew upon the organizational skills developed to supply the military during the Civil War, systematizing relief and charitable work while still retaining a strong religious motivation as the basis for their efforts.

Implicitly or, in some cases, explicitly, many leaders and members of women's organizations espoused and applied Social Gospel principles. This meant that their struggles to relive suffering individuals and families were accompanied by a further struggle, one that sought to understand the causes of such vast misery in order to prevent further suffering. By the 1880s and 1890s, members of groups such as the WCTU, the YWCA, the GFWC, and the WHMSs, along with settlement house workers and Protestant deaconesses were educating themselves in the newly emerging academic disciplines of social science and political economy, bringing the theoretical knowledge they gained to bear on the actual situations of need they were encountering. The early history of the WCTU can serve as an example of the process by which many women's organizations gradually became strong advocates of the Social Gospel by the late nineteenth century. Details might differ, depending on the group, but the awakening of a sophisticated social conscience among women reformers is strikingly similar across the spectrum of organizations and individuals.

The WCTU quickly became the largest women's organization of the era, with membership numbering nearly 200,000 by the turn of the century. As its name implies, the WCTU was founded as a vehicle for temperance reform. Its formation came in the wake of the Women's Temperance Crusade that occurred during the winter and spring of 1873–1874. The Crusade was a series of hundreds of spontaneous churchwomen's demonstrations against liquor dealers similar to those that had occurred in the 1850s. They sprang up first in towns and cities in western New York and Ohio, then spread rapidly throughout the Midwest and beyond. Such demonstrations had waned during the Civil War but resurfaced in the late 1860s as liquor consumption rose (after having fallen off prior to the war). New production techniques and the possibility of national distribution gave impetus to the growth of a powerful liquor industry. The industry, a large source of revenue through taxes on individual liquor dealers, was encouraged by the federal government and supported by many politicians at local, state, and national levels who sought the backing of big business.

The liquor industry's expansion was the one manifestation of the growth of industrial capitalism probably most obvious to the Crusaders and their supporters. Their confrontations with local saloon keepers and their failure, in most cases, especially in the cities, to put them out of business, brought them face to face with the raw power of an arm of industrial capitalism and its influence over the nation's political and judicial structures. The Crusaders began to realize just what they were up against as they struggled, often fruitlessly, in local courts to get temperance laws enforced. This realization deepened as they tried to persuade the two main political parties—Democrats and Republicans—to choose temperance candidates and, then, appeal to the men of their communities to vote for them. To those Crusade women who chose to continue their efforts after the initial excitement of the demonstrations died down it became apparent that the battle against the liquor industry and its allies would be a long and difficult one.

The Crusade and its aftermath signaled a shift in the locus of power within temperance reform from male domination to the rise of female leadership. It also switched primary attention from the plight of male drunkards to their female and child victims. As the *Call* for the formation of a national women's temperance organization forcefully stated: "In the name of our Master [Jesus Christ]—in behalf of the thousands of women who suffer from this terrible evil—we call upon all to unite in an earnest, continued effort to hold the ground already won, and move onward together to a complete victory over the foes we fight" (*Woman and Temperance*, 126). The recognition, in this rallying statement, of women's vulnerable situation in the face of male irresponsibility pointed to a breakdown in the dominant ideal of gender relationships, in which men were to be women's protectors and women and their children were to be dependent on men. The wording of the *Call* suggests that, although some women were seen by temperance women as suffering, helpless victims, their rescuers were no longer understood to be men. They would, instead, be other women—a sisterhood of reform—united to challenge a powerful enemy—the liquor industry—in the name of women and children. In order to meet this formidable challenge, WCTU members must become strong, independent women who recognized no gendered limits to their sphere of action.

Under the leadership of Frances E. Willard (1839–1898), during her tenure as president of the WCTU from 1879 to her death, the organization became perhaps the most significant locus for the development of

Rather than merely trying to convince individuals to give up drinking, the Women's Temperance Crusade engaged in direct confrontation with saloon keepers and liquor dealers, whom they saw as implicated in the individual drunkard's sin. Bands of hymn-singing women marched from meetings in churches to saloons and drugstores, sometimes kneeling to pray that proprietors would voluntarily give up selling liquor. *Courtesy of the Library of Congress.*

a new American Christian womanhood, one that would supersede the mid-nineteenth century ideal of True Womanhood. The new ideal retained a key facet of the earlier one: the notion that women were more moral and nurturing than men. However, Willard understood these qualities in women to be the result of centuries of socializing and believed that men could eventually learn to be as pure and caring as women were seen to be. In the meantime, the new Christian woman intended to play a central reforming role in public life, bringing her mothering talents to bear on the problems of the nation.

Women reformers were well aware that they were still effectively barred from leadership in the male-dominated political, economic, and religious structures of society. Thus, many of them flocked to join the WCTU because it offered them a powerful national base from which to make an impact on those structures. During the last quarter of the nineteenth century, the or-

ganization functioned as a training ground for women reformers, a separate women's institution equipping thousands of women throughout the country with the skills to become effective agents of change. By 1887 Willard could declare that the WCTU's most important work was reconstructing the ideal of womanhood.

During the 1880s and 1890s, under the banner of the "Do Everything" policy, WCTU leaders moved the membership beyond a narrow focus on temperance toward a broad reform agenda that kept temperance as a central concern but added a whole spectrum of women's rights issues. The organization mounted a campaign for women's suffrage, using the slogan "The Ballot for Home Protection." Through its social purity department, the WCTU worked for an end to the sexual double standard and the protection of women and girls through a variety of means, including the successful campaign to raise the age of consent to sexual relations from as low as seven years in some states to eighteen years. It pushed for women's health and dress reform and called for equality in church governance including women's right to be ordained ministers. The mainly middle-class organization also championed the rising labor movement and attempted to form cross-class alliances with women labor union members in order to address the exploitation of workers—especially women and children—by owners and managers.

Like the leadership of several late-nineteenth-century women's organizations, many WCTU leaders embraced the Social Gospel with its concern for urban problems and indictment of sinful social systems. Local WCTUs in cities throughout the country worked to meet crises generated by the poverty and exploitation women and children endured. In doing so, they became adept at investigating and analyzing the problems that plagued cities. Willard observed in her 1888 Annual Address to the National WCTU:

> The general drift of the fortunate class toward a study of the unfortunate, with a helpful motive as its basis is the most hopeful feature of the times. Beside it must be placed the strongly growing tendency to study causes rather than effects. For the more we study the causes, the more certainly we find that justice, not charity, must be the watchword of the future. (Willard, 50)

Willard's own study of the conditions of the poor led her to reevaluate the link between intemperance and poverty. In her 1889 Annual Address, she rejected the explanation that intemperance caused poverty and insisted, instead, that in many instances poverty was a cause of intemperance. This was a stunning reversal of the traditional nineteenth-century explanation that placed the blame for the existence of poverty almost solely on the intemperate individual who would not or could not earn a living. Willard pointed to a much more complicated web of causes. She laid a good deal of the blame for the intemperance of the poor on unjust economic conditions that ground down workers—both male and female—whose desperation and exhaustion led them to seek relief through drinking.

As Willard pondered the growing gap between rich and poor, she became convinced of the necessity of a different, more equitable economic system. She was drawn to the ideals of Christian socialism, a movement that sought a peaceful restructuring of the economic system. Such a change would be achieved through elections rather than by the class warfare between capitalists and workers that Marxist socialists advocated at the time. In her socialist leanings, Willard was far ahead of her own organization as well as most other Americans of her day. The WCTU membership did not rush to endorse her view, as it had done with so many other new and daring ideas that she proposed during her presidency. Yet for the last decade of her life, she continued to speak out for Christian socialism because she believed that it promised true justice.

During the first decades of the twentieth century, women Social Gospelers echoed Willard's belief that justice, not mere charity, must be pursued. Such sentiment abounded in the writings and speeches of YWCA and Women's Home Missionary Society leaders, deaconesses, settlement workers, and civic reformers. Willard's championship of Christian socialism was carried on by such figures as Vida Scudder (1861–1954), radical Episcopal churchwoman, Wellesley professor, and settlement house movement leader; Ellen Gates Starr (1859–1940), cofounder of Chicago's Hull House, militant labor activist, and for most of her life, like Scudder, an Episcopalian; and Winifred Chappell (1879–1951), a Methodist deaconess and investigative reporter, who covered bitter clashes between workers and bosses in her position as research secretary for the Methodist Federation for Social Service. These women represented a new generation of reformers for whom *justice* did indeed become the watchword, as Frances Willard had predicted back in the 1880s.

Several trends in women's reform activity became apparent by the turn of the century, reflecting a broader scope of concerns and the tendency toward large-scale women's organizations. Cooperation between a variety of reform groups began to flourish, breaking down boundaries of religion, class, and gender. Interdenominational Protestant reform organizations had been a pattern since the beginning of the nineteenth century, as evidenced first by female moral reform, temperance, and antislavery societies and women's rights groups. By the 1880s and 1890s, some women's organizations began to reach beyond their Protestant bases to Catholic and Jewish women's groups, allying with them locally and nationally to pursue reform. Both secular and religious women's groups gathered under umbrella organizations such as the National Council of Women (founded in 1888) in order to combine their strengths and speak with a powerful united voice on a variety of women's issues.

By the late 1880s, some middle-class women reformers were able to effect tenuous cross-class alliances with working-class women in labor unions through the WCTU, local women's clubs, and settlement houses in order to address the poor treatment of women and child workers. The founding of the national Women's Trade Union League (WTUL) in 1903 gave working women and their middle-class allies a permanent base from which to organize. The WTUL attracted many Protestant reform women to its ranks because of its emphasis on workers' rights.

During the same period, women's organizations like the World's WCTU (founded in 1883) and the International Council of Women (founded in 1888) expanded their reform vision to encompass a global perspective. Delegates to international conventions educated each other on women's situation in many different countries, shared strategies and methods of reform, and banded together to demand attention to women's issues from the world's leaders. At the same time global concerns were brought home to the United States with the influx of millions of immigrants.

Women interested in reform continued to forge new alliances during the turn-of-the-century Progressive Era, a time marked by great efforts to come to terms with the ills of modern urban life. Progressive reformers, often motivated by Social Gospel ideals, sought to improve working and living conditions for vast numbers of new city dwellers, both immigrants from other countries and those from rural areas of the United States. They understood the necessity of creating new municipal institutions able to handle health and sanitation needs. They formed watchdog groups to fight corrupt city governments and monitored working conditions to ensure safety. Women worked alongside men in a variety of civic betterment projects and ad hoc community groups that sprang up in many U.S. cities to address various facets of urban reform.

Throughout the nineteenth century, when men and women worked together in an organization, the usual pattern was one of male leadership, with women providing much of the grassroots labor to effect reform. Some women reformers had not been satisfied with this arrangement. Disagreement over women's proper role in reform had a long history, stretching back to the antebellum period. However, after several decades of building strong, separate national women's organizations and directing their own activity, many women hoped for a more egalitarian partnership with men. They wished to become true colleagues, not merely relegated to carrying out plans and aims devised by male leaders. At times such collegiality occurred; more often it did not. Tension over gender roles in reform extended throughout the new century, making it continually necessary for women to assert their right and duty to share in shaping the direction of reform.

Women reformers did attempt, with varying success, to cross the barriers of class, religion, and gender. However, they mostly failed to come to terms with the white racism that pervaded the country at the close of the nineteenth century. During the Jim Crow era of hardening segregation and rising violence against African Americans, most women's reform organizations mirrored American society in its racist attitudes and structures. Although there had been some instances of cooperation between African American and white women

in antislavery societies, women's rights groups, and municipal charity associations, and other reform efforts during the antebellum period, by the 1880s and 1890s most women's suffrage organizations and women's clubs adamantly refused to admit African American members. Other groups simply did not entertain the possibility of black members, taking it for granted that segregation was the reigning pattern. A few organizations, the WCTU, for example, did encourage African American women to join and take part in their activities. The organization created a Department of Work among the Colored Women, led during the 1880s by noted author and club woman Frances E. W. Harper (1825–1911). But African American WCTU members worked almost exclusively in "colored" unions; thus the organization had created a problematic "separate but equal" status for its black membership.

Because of the segregationist attitude on the part of white women, middle-class African American women developed a parallel system of organizations including the National Association of Colored Women (NACW; founded in 1896) with its many local affiliate women's clubs, denominational women's organizations, settlement houses, and women's suffrage organizations. A strong cadre of leaders emerged from these groups during the 1890s, including such women as Josephine St. Pierre Ruffin (1842–1924), president of the Boston-based new Era Club; Ida B. Wells Barnett (1862–1931), antilynching activist and founder of an African American women's suffrage organization; Mary Church Terrell (1863–1954), first president of the NACW; and Nannie Helen Burroughs (1879–1961), corresponding secretary of the Women's Convention of the National Baptist Convention. African American women's organizations had some of the same reform goals as white women's groups. However, underlying their reform work was the constant and wearing effort required to combat systemic racism. African American women reformers struggled not only against gendered tensions in reform but also against racial ones.

Besides the tendency toward cooperation among different religious and secular groups in the pursuit of reform, another trend became increasingly apparent at the turn of the century: the desire to ground reform on a social scientific basis and develop what might be termed *professional reformers*. This process reflected, in part, a broader pattern of centralized, bureaucratized management developing throughout the business and academic sectors of society and within the Protestant denominational hierarchies as well. It also represented the rise of social scientific thought and discourse as a valid way of understanding and addressing many of the difficult issues of the time.

By the final decades of the nineteenth century, the discipline of sociology—the study of humans in community—was firmly established in many universities, theological seminaries, and deaconesses and missionary training schools. Frances Willard's call for study of urban situations during the 1880s anticipated the development of systematic attention to the improvement of society within academia, but her own generation of women had had little possibility of higher education. However, the daughters of that generation of reformers were college women, studying sociology and political economy with professors who imbued their academic subjects with a crucial ethical dimension. At the beginning of the twentieth century schools and departments were springing up in several universities in order to train social workers, especially preparing them to meet what reformers termed the "challenge of the city."

A 1912 series of articles in the *Deaconess Advocate*, a Methodist publication, clearly showed this trend. The author insisted that city workers in addition to possessing firm Christian beliefs must understand and utilize the language of social service and the work of professionals in the field of applied sociology. Many Protestant urban reformers saw science and faith as partners in facing the great urban challenge. Combining a deep Christian faith with scientific education enabling them to address social problems, this new breed of women often became paid professionals. They worked in a variety of situations from denominational women's missionary organizations, settlement houses, and interdenominational agencies to secular institutions. During the nineteenth century women's reform activity had been carried on almost entirely by volunteers. In the new century reform would still rely on voluntarism, but increasingly their work would be directed by specially trained professional women for whom reform was both a job and a Christian vocation.

Over the nineteenth century, a growing religious, ethnic, and cultural diversity became apparent in urban areas where vast numbers of Catholic, Jewish, and Eastern Orthodox immigrants brought into serious question the notion of the United States as an evangelical Protestant nation. This situation, along with the emerging professionalism of reform, made the new social service language appealing. Reform language became less dependent on the discourse of evangelical Protestantism, as had been the case for much of the nineteenth century. Instead, a secular reform language evolved, less threatening, more congenial to the ethnic and religious pluralism that would come to characterize the country during the twentieth century.

By the 1910s the nation's attention turned toward Europe with growing apprehension as that region prepared for war. A women's peace movement had already begun during the previous century, escalating in the 1880s and 1890s when an interest in settling conflicts between nations through arbitration drew support from such organizations as the WCTU and the International Council of Women. With World War I imminent, women's peace activity greatly increased. In 1915 the Woman's Peace Party was formed, a national organization chaired by Jane Addams (1862–1935), settlement movement leader and civic reformer. Playing on a familiar gendered theme, that women's maternal qualities made them more sensitive than men to the horror of war, women's peace groups opposed the United States' entry into the war.

American women joined with European women who were attempting, unsuccessfully, to find a peaceful solution to the conflict. In the superpatriotic atmosphere that prevailed once the United States entered the war, both female and male peace activists were reviled. Nevertheless, peace efforts continued. In 1919 the Women's International League for Peace and Freedom (WILPF) was founded in order to continue the ties formed before and during World War I among women from many countries. Jane Addams presided over WILPF, and Quaker Emily Greene Balch (1867–1961) was its first international secretary-treasurer. For their dedication to the cause of world peace, both women received the Nobel Peace Prize, Addams in 1931 and Balch in 1946.

In the immediate postwar period, temperance and women's rights reformers celebrated two long-awaited victories: one temporary, the other permanent. The passage of the Eighteenth Amendment to the U.S. Constitution in 1919 (repealed in 1933) ushered in the Prohibition Era, and the Nineteenth Amendment (passed in 1920) gave women throughout the country the right to vote. Women who had worked for the passage of these amendments for decades did not rest for long on the accomplishment of their aims. Temperance reformers immediately began the struggle to monitor the enforcement of Prohibition. Suffragists quickly organized groups such as the League of Women Voters (LVW) to educate women newly entering the political processes on key reform issues they saw surfacing during the 1920s.

1921–1970

At the close of World War I, politicians urged the nation back to "normalcy," but reformers resisted. They recognized many injustices still in need of redress. The United States' refusal to join the League of Nations prompted peace groups to step up efforts to seek alternatives to war. The entry of growing numbers of women into the workforce from the turn of the century on demanded attention to their working and living conditions. Race riots in several cities, continued instances of lynching, and increasing Ku Klux Klan activity dramatized the depth of the country's racism. Protestant women reformers tackled these and other situations that needed to be addressed, continuing to work through denominational and interdenominational organizations and cooperating with nonreligious groups, as they had during the height of the Progressive Era.

World War I was a catastrophe, resulting in huge loss of life, the creation of large refugee populations, and economic devastation on a vast scale. People were horrified at the extent of destruction that humans had wreaked on each other. They seemed to have forgotten the optimistic sentiments of global brotherhood and sisterhood that had been so popular at the turn of the century. Determined to put an end to all war, many Protestant women joined peace organizations such as Women's International League for Peace and Freedom; the Fellowship of Reconciliation (FOR), a nondenominational Christian pacifist group formed in the United States in 1915; and the American Friends Service Committee (AFSC), founded by Quakers in 1917. Women also formed new groups including the Women's Peace Society, the Women's Peace Union, and perhaps the most influential one, the national Committee on the Cause and Cure of War (CCCW), a coalition of large women's organizations led by suffragist Carrie Chapman Catt (1859–1947). Most women who became pacifists during the 1920s and 1930s were still motivated by the maternalist argument that had been the strongest foundation of women's peace activity from the movement's beginnings. Women as mothers, whether actual or potential, the argument went, had a particular interest and predisposition toward peace. As guardians of their own and other women's children, they had a responsibility to see that yet another whole generation of sons did not die in battle, as they had in World War I.

Women in the peace movement now began to undergird this gendered motivation with increasingly sophisticated analyses of the conditions that led to war. Under the umbrella of the CCCW, denominational churchwomen's societies and interdenominational groups, the National Council of Jewish Women, the YWCA, the General Federation of Women's Clubs, the WCTU, the Women's Trade Union League, the League of Women Voters, and others enthusiastically took up the study of global politics and economics, the causes of conflict, and methods of preventing war. The peace movement flourished, its ranks swelled during the early 1930s by many Protestant clergy, Catholic and Jewish peace activists, student peace groups, and some socialists and communists. Never before in the United States had there been such large numbers of people pledged to eradicate war.

As peace sentiments grew in the decades after World War I, so did concern about economic injustice. Women's organizations in particular worried about the welfare of the hundreds of thousands of women who comprised one-fifth of the total labor force by 1920. By then young single women made up over one-half of the total number of working women, and the YWCA took on this particular group of workers as one of its primary concerns. Under the leadership of Grace Hoadley Dodge (1856–1914), the "YW" focused its attention on "young women adrift" in the cities. In order to comprehend the situation of working women, Dodge and other YW staffers commissioned a landmark study, *Wage Earning Women* (1910), carried out by a team of professional women sociologists. Armed with exhaustive data on working women and an agenda of specific reforms, the YW made a large-scale commitment of leadership and resources to serve these young working women. Longtime professional YWCA workers Mabel Cratty (1868–1928), general secretary of the YW's National Board, and Florence Simms (1873–1923), industrial secretary, implemented this commitment.

Both women were steeped in the principles and aims of the Social Gospel with its emphasis on economic justice. In 1920 at their urging, the YWCA National Board formally adopted the "Social Ideals of the Churches," guidelines for a social ministry issued in 1912 by the Federal Council of Churches, an interdenominational organization of mainline Protestant churches formed to speak with a united voice on economic and social issues. These guidelines contained a long list of specific economic goals, including the regulation of working conditions for women, the right of employees to organize, and reforms in wages and working hours. The YW's program for young working women was conducted with these goals firmly in mind.

The immediate task was to develop a ministry to young women alienated from a Protestantism felt to be hopelessly middle class, unable to understand the realities of their lives as urban workers, and unwilling to care about them. In eloquent language, Mabel Cratty set forth the role she hoped that her organization could play in reaching out to these women:

The YWCA is in some sense, however imperfect, a visible expression in a community of the love of Christ, in a form and terms that any woman can understand. . . . [The YW] goes out to meet [the young working woman]. It begins its work where she is, it speaks her language. (Cratty, 186–188)

Her colleague Florence Simms created an appropriate venue for such a meeting, launching a program of industrial clubs, somewhat parallel to the YW groups that had already been established on college campuses.

The number of industrial and college clubs grew tremendously during the 1910s and 1920s, attesting to the real need they filled in young women's lives. Through these club networks with their Bible studies, discussion groups, and direct action on social and economic issues, the YWCA inspired a strong ethical concern in several generations of young women. YW staffers and industrial club members supported legislative measures to improve women's working conditions. They also established safe, inexpensive urban housing for working women. Many leaders in college clubs continued their commitment to social reform issues in later life, either as volunteers or as professionals working within religious or secular organizations (often choosing to become YW staff). By the late 1910s, the YWCA had also begun to create programs for African American women in both its community and student divisions. The organization made some headway toward integrating its programs from the 1920s on, usually under pressure from African American members and staff. For example, by the 1930s YW student leadership conferences were integrated everywhere but in the South, where the idea of segregation was most deeply entrenched in the culture.

Another group of southern women, however, did feel called to address the stubborn issue of white racism. At the turn of the century, under the leadership of its president Belle Harris Bennett (1852–1922) and a strong, devoted staff, the Woman's Home Missionary Society of the Southern Methodist Church (renamed the Woman's Missionary Council [WMC] in 1910) took the welfare of southern women and children—African American and white—as one of its special concerns. In doing so, Bennett noted, Southern Methodist women were well ahead of their male counterparts in the denomination. They were also in advance of the women's organizations of other white denominations in the South, a position they would maintain for many decades. Although the WMC's work with African Americans developed very slowly, its leadership was firmly committed to combating racism and finding ways to cooperate with African American women's groups. But in order for this to happen, insisted Lily Hardy Hammond (1859–1925), WMC leader and a prolific writer on race relations, white southerners would have to change their fundamental attitudes toward African Americans. They must rid themselves of prejudice and see blacks as persons made in the image of God, just as they understood themselves to be. Only then could African American and white southerners begin to work together to bring a just and egalitarian society into being.

Such beliefs reflected the Woman's Missionary Council leadership's embrace of a Social Gospel that identified racism as another sinful system to be eradicated, along with the movement's more familiar emphasis on economic sins. Nearly a decade earlier than the YWCA, the WMC had endorsed the "Social Ideals of the Churches" (1912), thus confirming their Social Gospel position. In order to carry out the broad social ministry called for by the Federal Council of Churches' guidelines, the WMC formed a Bureau of Social Service in 1915, led

during the 1920s and 1930s by Bertha Payne Newell (1867–1953). Through her position as director of the bureau, Newell was responsible for shaping a program that the WMC hoped would bring a dimension of social justice to the New South. The region was being viewed by investors and manufacturers from both North and South as a place ripe for profitable development, a rapidly industrializing region that might eventually rival the great urban centers of the North. Forging alliances with other women's groups such as the YWCA, the National Consumers' League, and the League of Women Voters, the WMC fought to secure legislation that protected workers from exploitation by owners through improving working conditions, raising wages, especially of women workers, and fighting abuses of child labor. The women's organizations also fought for legislation that would provide workmen's compensation, unemployment insurance, and other protective measures, thus anticipating New Deal programs enacted during the 1930s depression era. Although these alliances were not very successful in their push for industrial justice, they kept these economic reforms before the public and continued to agitate for a better life for southern families.

Beginning in the 1910s, the Woman's Missionary Council made further alliances with organizations working toward racial justice. Groups such as the Southern Sociological Congress (working in the 1910s) and the Commission on Interracial Cooperation (CIC—working from 1919 through the 1930s) looked to the Methodist women's organization to furnish both support and personnel for their efforts to bring about racial cooperation and integration. Although other Protestant women's organizations did take part in such efforts, Methodist women, through the WMC, were generally acknowledged to be in the vanguard of the struggle for the reform of racist attitudes and practices. For example, after more than a quarter century of preparation through study and active participation in race relations work, Methodist women responded most quickly to a call by Jessie Daniel Ames (1883–1972) to join a new group she was forming in 1930, the Association of Southern Women for the Prevention of Lynching (ASWPL).

Ames, the director of women's work for the Commission on Interracial Cooperation, was deeply disturbed by a rise in the incidence of lynching during the hard economic times of the early depression period. She saw an opportunity for southern white women to strike a blow at the key rationale for the vicious practice by dispelling, once and for all, the reigning myth that lynching was necessary to protect white womanhood from African American male sexual predators. Under Ames's direction, ASWPL members throughout the southern states carried out a decade-long campaign, working at the grassroots level among church groups and law enforcement officers, judges, and other leading citizens of southern towns. They challenged the notion that lynch mobs acted from chivalrous motives and showed, instead, that lynching was an effective means for preserving a culture of intimidation in which African Americans would "know their place" and not dare to step beyond it. The goal of the ASWPL was to create a climate throughout the South in which lynching was no longer acceptable.

Well before white women denounced lynching, African American women fought to end the practice, working since the 1890s through the black women's club movement, through denominational women's groups, and eventually through the YWCA and community organizations. Southern middle-class African American and white women had also been taking small, tentative steps toward cooperation since 1920, meeting together to become acquainted in a more egalitarian setting than was usually possible in the segregated South. Lugenia Burns Hope (1871–1945), founder of the Neighborhood Union, a community center in Atlanta, Charlotte Hawkins Brown (1883–1961), president of the North Carolina State Federation of Negro Women's Clubs and member of the board of directors of the National YWCA, and Margaret Murray Washington (c. 1865–1925), president of the National Association of Colored Women during the 1910s, along with other African American leaders, met with white Methodist leaders, including Carrie Parks Johnson (1866–1929), head of the Woman's Missionary Council's committee on race relations, and Sara Estelle Haskin (c. 1875–1940), a WMC officer and editor of its periodical. These initial meetings were painful. Black women attended them with great distrust, and white women came burdened with the cultural baggage of generations of negative stereotypes about African Americans. During the 1920s and 1930s some progress toward mutual understanding and cooperation between black and white women occurred at such interracial meetings. Though courageous for the times, the WMC's stance on race relations was decidedly moderate. The leadership did not oppose racial segregation in any thoroughgoing way, and substantial inroads against segregation would not be made until the civil rights movement of the late 1950s and 1960s. However, the earlier work of both African American and white women through decades of education and action helped create conditions in the South that made the later movement possible.

For the most part, the WMC also did not directly challenge owners and managers of the new southern industries on their unfair (and often illegal) labor practices or lend support to the union organizing going on in the region during the 1930s to 1950s. However, a few southern women did follow a more radical path to industrial justice. One of them, Lucy Randolph Mason (1882–1959), was a public relations director for the Congress of Industrial Organizations (CIO) in the southeast from 1937 to her retirement in 1953. A lifelong Episcopalian, Mason was raised in a family that took seriously Jesus' instructions in the gospels to feed the hungry, bring water to the thirsty, give clothes to those that lacked them, and visit the sick and prisoners. In Mason's autobiography, she remembered her parents teaching, through their own acts of kindness, that one served God by caring for God's children.

Her upbringing, plus her early career as a general secretary of the Richmond, Virginia, YWCA during the 1920s and as national head of the Consumers' League from 1930 to 1937, amply prepared her to be the CIO's "roving Ambassador" in the South. In each of these positions, she investigated the poor working situation that prevailed in industries all over the South, where hours were long, conditions poor, and labor legislation nearly nonexistent. In her YWCA work, she paid particular attention to women and child workers, at one point traveling on behalf of women's church groups to make the first thorough study of work conditions in the region. Because of her study, she became an expert and often was called to testify before Congress and various New Deal agencies attempting to reform the economic life of the country. In these activities, Mason was typical of a number of professional women during the first half of the twentieth century who were able to shape the newly developing welfare state through their leadership roles in reform organizations or within the government itself.

From her position in the CIO, Mason helped awaken Protestantism to a renewed responsibility for industrial justice. The CIO identified southern churches as mainly hostile to the labor movement. A crucial part of Mason's public relations task was to interpret the aims of unions and the hopes of their membership to this key group within southern communities. Another important aspect of her job was the protection of union members' civil rights during organizing campaigns and strikes. At a time when many Americans saw unions as subversive and controlled by communists, Mason defended the union viewpoint before national Protestant leadership as an Episcopal delegate to several industrial conferences sponsored by the Federal (later National) Council of Churches during the 1940s and early 1950s. Mason and others like her helped sustain the Social Gospel vision of economic justice well past the era when that movement was at its height.

While Lucy Randolph Mason was concentrating her efforts on behalf of workers in the South, Edith Elizabeth Lowry (1897–1970) created a national ministry that served another, far less visible part of the workforce: the migrant labor population. For nearly four decades, from 1927 until 1965, Lowry developed and led an ever-expanding number of migrant ministry programs, first for interdenominational women's and general mission organizations, then for the National Council of Churches (NCC). Lowry and her staff, augmented by thousands of volunteers, set up and maintained a whole range of social and educational services for migrants, as well as protecting their rights. Lowry studied the living and working patterns of migrant workers early in her career. She saw that too often they fell between the cracks of programs available from state-sponsored relief and welfare agencies because they followed the crops, never settling in one place long enough to meet the residency requirements for eligibility to receive such benefits. She devised an alternative agency model, one that traveled with the migrants. Her staff and volunteers set up day-care centers and sports facilities, provided family and economic counseling, community health clinics, and even occasionally brought portable altars and organs to remote camps for worship services.

As Lowry responded to these workers' needs, she also acquainted a generation of Americans with their plight through her speeches and writings. After retirement from the National Council of Churches in 1962, she spent several years in Washington, D.C., monitoring congressional action on issues affecting migrant workers for the National Council on Agriculture and Labor, a group of nongovernmental organizations lobbying for better treatment of farmworkers. Like Mason, Lowry became a nationally recognized expert on labor issues, acting out her Baptist faith in a lifelong social reform career. The ministry of Lowry and others who served migrant workers contributed to a growing awareness among many Americans of their responsibility to economically marginal groups that suffered in the midst of a nation becoming more and more prosperous by the 1950s. Their work helped prepare church people to sympathize with and join efforts on behalf of migrant workers led by the United Farm Workers of America (UFW) during the 1970s.

By the late 1930s, the threat of another war in Europe commanded much of the country's attention and energy. For many, the possibility of war was seen as a way to lift the United States out of its prolonged economic depression. It was also viewed as a just conflict, necessary to combat European fascism and Japanese imperialism. Pacifist voices were eclipsed by a growing patriotic clamor, ironically urging America to declare war on "the enemies of peace." When the United States entered the war in 1941, many peace activists, for example, American Friends Service Committee women, turned their efforts toward helping conscientious objectors. Others, such as Quaker Josephine Whitney Duveneck (1891–1978), AFSC leader in northern California, worked to aid thousands of Japanese Americans who were ordered by the U.S. government to leave their West Coast homes for internment camps in the country's interior as a security measure. Seeing this move as a grave injustice

against the civil rights of Japanese American citizens, AFSC members, church groups, members of the California Civil Liberties Union, and prominent community leaders vainly protested against internment.

Throughout the war, Duveneck organized volunteers to help set up a variety of social services at "relocation centers," making the internees as comfortable as possible in the stark conditions of the camps. Reflecting on the causes of the wartime treatment of Japanese Americans in her autobiography, Duveneck wrote:

It became evident that racial discrimination was at the root of the matter and that presented a greater threat to the American way of life than the war itself. To deplore the Nazi persecution of Jews in Europe and find ourselves guilty of similar unchristian tactics towards a minority group in our own country was a shock to many people previously unaware of what was going on.... [They] rallied to right a wrong that belied the foundations of democracy. (Duveneck, 237–238)

At the end of the war, Duveneck and the American Friends Service Committee helped former internees reintegrate into their communities, working to attack the race prejudice that she identified as a key cause of injustices. From the 1950s to her death in the late 1970s, Duveneck would champion Mexican migrant workers in California, joining with the United Farm Workers in its drive to unionize farmworkers.

The last third of the twentieth century brought a resurgence of social reform activity. Almost every kind of unjust situation that reform women had battled since the early 1800s surfaced again in new ways in contemporary society. Once more, women felt called to combat injustice. With the U.S. bombing of Hiroshima and Nagasaki at the close of World War II and the development of even greater potential for nuclear destruction in the postwar era, the search for peace that had begun before the Civil War intensified during the 1950s and 1960s. Coalitions of peace activists formed to protest the dangerous power of an unchecked American military industrial complex. During the late 1960s and early 1970s, the war in Vietnam generated enormous opposition by diverse groups mobilizing against U.S. policy in Southeast Asia. By then many Americans were becoming alarmed at the extent of their government's involvement in Central and South America and Africa as it shored up dictators who ignored human rights.

The establishment of the United Nations in 1945 set up an international forum for settling conflicts and addressing global humanitarian issues, one built on a firmer foundation than the League of Nations had been. Former First Lady Eleanor Roosevelt (1884–1962), U.S. delegate to the United Nations and a longtime social reformer, lobbied tirelessly for the passage of the UN Universal Declaration of Human Rights. In 1948 she and her colleagues produced a strong document that defined human rights and established guidelines for newly formed human rights organizations to invoke in their campaigns.

Racial injustice continued to plague the country, however, even though reformers had protested it since the antislavery movement in the mid-nineteenth century. A growing civil rights movement, begun in the early 1950s, intensified in the 1960s as it sought to bring an end to all forms of segregation of African Americans. The definition of racial equality broadened, extending to all people of color: to Hispanics, to Native Americans, and further, to the new wave of Asians flocking to the United States as immigration quotas were lifted in the mid-1960s. Reminiscent of the ideals and goals of the Social Gospel movement, the War on Poverty waged during the 1960s attempted to understand and correct the interlinked causes that created an "underclass" of the poor. The U.S. government in partnership with social service agencies and volunteers sought ways to address the poor health, unemployment, and homelessness of too many of its citizens. By the 1970s the problem of drug and alcohol addiction was viewed as a national and a global one, recalling the situation that organizations like the Woman's Christian Temperance Union had tried to reform nearly a century earlier.

By the late 1960s a second wave of feminism surged, echoing the first wave during the nineteenth and early twentieth centuries. The new women's rights reformers concentrated on a broad range of issues now including reproductive rights, the right to equal pay for equal work, the inclusion of women of color in the struggle for equality, and the recognition of the rights of lesbians. The women's liberation movement took on a global dimension as a host of secular and religious women's organizations around the world demanded that specific women's human rights be addressed. These demands resulted in new women's rights organizations protesting against the international sex trade, lobbying for the recognition of rape as a weapon of war, and condemning domestic violence and harmful practices such as female genital mutilation. At the same time these organizations continue to support more traditional women's educational, social, economic, political, and civil rights.

Protestant women continue to participate in all these areas of reform, whether as members of denominational and interdenominational groups or through participation in broader coalitions including both religious and secular organizations. Incorporating lessons learned during the course of two centuries of reform activity, they have become astute analyzers of the interlocking causes of injustice and adept agents of social change. Like their nineteenth-century sisters who were often characterized as "steadfast," a familiar biblical phrase, Protestant women in the late twentieth century and on into the twenty-first are unflagging in their pursuit of reform. Though the term *steadfast* might not be the one chosen in the twentieth century to describe their tenacity, they have been praised lately, in the words of the civil rights movement, for their ability to "keep on keeping on." That ability is sustained by the belief that a more just, merciful, and equitable world is God's will and their calling. The dying request of Lucy Stone (1818–1893), antislavery and women's rights reformer, epitomizes the ongoing motivating force of women reformers. With her family gathered round her in her final hours, Stone whispered: "Make the world better!" (Kerr, 245).

SOURCES: Sources on the history of social reform in the United States include Robert Abzug, *Cosmos Crumbling: American Reform and the Religious Imagination* (1994); Alice Felt Tyler, *Freedom's Ferment: Phases of Social History from the Colonial Period to the Outbreak of the Civil War* (1944); and Ronald G. Walters, *American Reformers, 1815–1860* (1978). For sources on women and American social reform, see Paul A. Cimbala and Randall Miller, eds., *Against the Tide: Women Reformers in American Society* (1997); Carolyn DeSwarte Gifford, "Women in Social Reform Movements," in *Women and Religion in America: A Documentary History*, vol. 1, *The Nineteenth Century*, ed. Rosemary Radford Ruether and Rosemary Skinner Keller (1981); Lori D. Ginsberg, *Women and the Work of Benevolence: Morality, Politics, and Class in the 19th-Century United States* (1990); Nancy A. Hewitt, *Women's Activism and Social Change: Rochester, New York, 1822–1872* (1984); Susan Hill Lindley, *"You Have Stept Out of Your Place": A History of Women and Religion in America* (1996), chaps. 9, 11, 21; Ann Firor Scott, *Natural Allies: Women's Associations in American History* (1993); and Caroll Smith-Rosenberg, *Disorderly Conduct: Visions of Gender in Victorian America* (1985). Sources on the history of specific reforms include Harriet Hyman Alonzo, *Peace as a Women's Issue: A History of the U.S. Movement for World Peace and Women's Rights* (1993); Ruth Bordin, *Woman and Temperance: The Quest for Power and Liberty, 1873–1900* (1981); Paula Giddings, *When and Where I Enter: The Impact of Black Women on Race and Sex in America* (1979); Jacquelyn Dowd Hall, *Revolt against Chivalry: Jessie Daniel Ames and the Women's Campaign against Lynching* (1979); Barbara Meil Hobson, *Uneasy Virtue: The Politics of Prostitution and the American Reform Tradition* (1990); Jacqueline Jones, *Soldiers of Light and Love: Northern Teachers and Georgia Blacks, 1865–1873* (1980); William Leach, *True Love and Perfect Union: The Feminist Reform of Sex and Society* (1980); Susan Lynn, *Progressive Women in Conservative Times: Racial Justice, Peace, and Feminism, 1945 to the 1960s* (1992); John Patrick McDowell, *The Social Gospel in the South: The Woman's Home Mission Movement in the Methodist Episcopal Church, South, 1866–1939* (1982); and Deborah Gray White, *Too Heavy a Load: Black Women in Defense of Themselves, 1894–1994* (1999). Sources for quotes that appear in the entry are Catharine Beecher, *An Essay on Slavery and Abolitionism with*

Reference to the Duty of American Females (1837), 99–100; Mabel Cratty, "Address to the World's Conference of the YWCA," quoted in Margaret E. Burton, *Mabel Cratty: Leader in the Art of Leadership* (1929), 186–188; Josephine Whitney Duveneck, *Life on Two Levels: An Autobiography* (1978), 137–138; Laura S. Haviland, *A Woman's Life Work: Including Thirty Years' Service on the Underground Rail-Road and in the War* (1902), 482; Andrea Moore Kerr, *Lucy Stone: Speaking Out for Equality* (1992), 245; Milton Meltzer and Patricia G. Holland, eds., *Lydia Maria Child: Selected Letters, 1817–1880* (1982); Frances E. Willard, "President's Annual Address," in *Minutes of the Woman's Christian Temperance Union at the Fifteenth Annual Meeting . . .* (1888), 50; and Jennie Fowler Willing, "Call" [from the chairman of the Woman's National Temperance Union], in Frances E. Willard, *Woman and Temperance: The Work and Workers of the Woman's Christian Temperance Union* (1883, 1986), 126.

ANTISLAVERY, ABOLITIONISM
Anna M. Speicher

IN MAY 1837 approximately 200 women gathered in New York City for an Anti-Slavery Convention of American Women. Although numerous local female antislavery societies had formed in the 1830s, this was the first time women had come together for a national assembly. Conscious of the momentousness of the occasion, the delegates moved immediately to assert the legitimacy of their cause. In their first substantive resolution they declared:

> A thorough investigation of the anti-slavery cause, in all its various aspects and tendencies, has confirmed us in the belief that *it is the cause of God*, who created mankind free, and of Christ, who died to redeem them from every yoke. Consequently it is the duty of *every human being* to labor to preserve, and to restore to all who are deprived of it, God's gift of freedom; thus showing love and gratitude to the Great Redeemer by treading in his steps. (*Proceedings of the Anti-Slavery Convention of American Women, Held in the City of New-York, May 9th, 10th, 11th, and 12th, 1837*, 7; emphasis added)

The delegates made two important claims in this resolution. First, they justified abolitionism—the movement to abolish the institution of slavery—primarily through their perceptions of God's will and Christian scripture, as opposed, for example, to secular claims regarding human rights. Second, in an era that highlighted women's domestic roles, these women justified their own participation in a political and public cause by claiming that antislavery activism was a religious and moral imperative for all human beings, not just for men.

The woman who introduced this resolution was Lydia Maria Child (1802–1880), who by 1837 already had acquired considerable experience in advocating and defending her abolitionist stance. Child was a well-known New England author, having achieved fame for her domestic advice book *The Frugal Housewife* (1829) and her popular children's magazine *The Juvenile Miscellany*. Child's family religious background was Congregationalist; as an adult she also lived for some years with her brother, a Unitarian pastor. In her personal religious quest she explored a variety of faiths, including Catholicism, Judaism, and Swedenborgianism, but she never allied herself with any organized religious group.

Child became an abolitionist in the early 1830s through reading the writings of William Lloyd Garrison, radical abolitionist and founder of the antislavery newspaper the *Liberator*. Radical abolitionists were those who believed in immediate, as opposed to gradual, abolition of slavery, who rejected the idea of any form of compensation to the former owners of freed slaves, and who tended to view antislavery as linked with other reforms such as nonresistance (to violence), women's rights, and reform of church hierarchies, policies, and practices.

Child's increasing dedication to the antislavery cause led her in 1833 to publish *An Appeal in Favor of That Class of Americans Called Africans*. This thoughtful and well-researched volume discussed the history of slavery and opposition to slavery, upheld the intellect and moral character of African Americans, and finally, defined and condemned racial prejudice. Child paid a heavy price for this act. Sales of her other books and subscriptions to her young people's magazine dropped sharply in both South and North. She felt, however, as she wrote in the conclusion of the *Appeal*, that "by publishing this book I have put my mite into the treasure. The expectation of displeasing all classes has not been unaccompanied with pain. But it has been strongly impressed upon my mind that it was a duty to fulfil this task; and earthly considerations should never stifle the voice of conscience" (207).

Slavery and Attitudes toward Slavery in North America

Child and her antislavery sisters believed that the nation had a considerable weight on its conscience. The American republic had been founded on principles of life, liberty, and the pursuit of happiness. Tentative steps had been taken toward abolition in the new nation. By 1804 all northern states had legislated the eventual emancipation of enslaved persons held within their boundaries. In 1807, Thomas Jefferson signed into law a prohibition (taking effect January 1, 1808) on the importation of slaves from abroad. Nonetheless, the American slave population continued to grow dramatically throughout the first two-thirds of the nineteenth century, mainly by means of new births but also because of international smuggling. In 1790, the U.S. Census recorded 697,624 slaves; by the time of the Civil War, that number had grown to nearly 4 million.

The increasing reliance on slave labor in the southern states in the nineteenth century was due largely to the invention of the cotton gin in 1793. This device automated the process of separating the seeds from the cotton fibers, and while it eliminated the need for humans to perform that task, it vastly increased the overall need for human labor in cultivation and processing. U.S. production of cotton increased from 2 million pounds in 1790 to 1 billion pounds in 1860, dominating the world market by mid-century. The national economy (not just the southern economy) was quite dependent on cotton by this time, which helps to explain both the aversion of southerners to giving up their slaves and the reluctance of northerners to tamper with the system.

In Canada, slavery was legal until 1834, when it was abolished throughout the British Empire, but it was never as profitable an institution there as in the American South. There never were more than a few thousand enslaved people in Canada. The biggest increase in the Canadian slave population was, in fact, due to the influx of American Loyalists who fled to Canada, bringing their slaves with them, after the American Revolution. After that time the slave population in Canada dwindled steadily until its total abolition. Throughout the American antebellum era, Canada was viewed as a haven for fugitive slaves due to its substantial free black population, the color-blindness of its laws, the lesser degree of racial prejudice there, and the reluctance of Canadian officials to extradite fugitive slaves to American slaveholders.

People of color in Canada were quite active in the American antislavery movement. Mary Ann Shadd Cary (1823–1893) was a freeborn American who immigrated to Canada in 1850. She cofounded and edited the *Provincial Freeman*, a newspaper that advocated abolition along with social and economic integration of white and black communities. During the Civil War she returned to the United States to recruit troops for the Union army. Mary Ellen Pleasant (c. 1814–1904), another American émigrée, lived in Canada in the 1850s. She led a colorful life, which allegedly included rescuing slaves held illegally in San Francisco, aiding fugitive slaves in Canada West as a member of the Chatham Vigilance Committee, and supporting John Brown's raid on Harpers Ferry. Pleasant was, in fact, so supportive of Brown that she asked that the words "she was a friend of John Brown's" be engraved on her tombstone.

In contrast to their reception in Canada, antislavery activists were generally unwelcome in both the southern and northern United States. Both South and North perceived themselves dependent on the economic benefits of slave labor. In addition, northern white laborers were not happy about the idea of the competition for jobs ensuing from a large influx of freed laborers. Racial prejudice was widespread: Most whites accepted the intellectual and moral inferiority of African Americans as a given and were disinclined to grant freedom and citizenship rights to such a population. And even northerners who believed that slavery was wrong often felt that abolitionists only stirred up anger and resentment rather than constructively helping to end slavery. Catharine Beecher (1800–1878), the well-known educator (daughter of the famous Congregational minister Lyman Beecher and sister of author Harriet Beecher Stowe), was one of those northerners. She claimed that the tactics of the antislavery societies "are not either peaceful or Christian in tendency, but they rather are those which tend to generate party spirit, denunciation, recrimination, and angry passions" (*An Essay on Slavery and Abolitionism, with Reference to the Duty of American Females*, 1837, 13–14).

Organized Religion and Slavery

There were few organized religious bodies that maintained an unequivocal stance against slavery throughout the colonial and antebellum eras. Quakers, along with Anabaptist sects, such as the Mennonites and Dunkers (later known as the Church of the Brethren), were among the earliest opponents. Mennonites, or Mennonite Quakers, produced the first public written statement against slavery in 1688, known as the "Germantown [Pennsylvania] Protest." By 1780 all six Friends yearly meetings (regional assemblies of local meetings), with the exception of the Virginia yearly meeting, moved to disown slaveholding members. The Quakers' aversion to mingling with the world, that is, non-Quakers, along with their dislike of the aggressive tactics of some abolitionists, however, prevented them as a body from supporting antislavery activism. In the nineteenth century, offshoots of the major denominations, such as the Free Will Baptists and some small Scottish Presbyterian sects, spoke out against slavery and barred slaveholders from membership.

John Wesley, the founder of Methodism, was ardently antislavery, and the original Methodist church not only opened itself to black members but actively opposed slavery. In the nineteenth century, however, the Methodist General Conference, like many other Protestant denominations, including Baptists, Presbyterians, Congregationalists, Unitarians, and Disciples of Christ, took a more equivocal stance, declining to censure slaveholders. The Presbyterian General Assembly passed a resolution in 1818 calling slavery "utterly inconsistent with the law of God," but they left its abolition in the hands of God. Lutherans, Episcopalians, and Roman Catholics took a neutral stance on the issue. Jews, particularly in the South, tended to support slavery and the Confederacy, although there were a few outspoken abolitionist Jews as well.

In the South, Christian groups not only refused to condemn slavery but also gradually began to endorse it as a positive good. They claimed publicly that slavery was the best means of Christianizing, or "civilizing," and providing for an inferior race. Their more subtle reasoning recognized that Christianity was useful as a means of behavior control. Beverly Jones, a woman enslaved in Virginia, recalled that although she and her fellow slaves had built a church and called a black preacher to serve their congregation,

> [t]hey wouldn't let us have no services lessen a white man was present. Most times the white preacher would preach, then he would set dere listenin' while the colored preacher preached. . . . Niggers had to set an' listen to the white man's sermon, but they didn' want to 'cause they knowed it by heart. Always took his text from Ephesians, the white preacher did, the part what said, "Obey your masters, be good servant."
>
> Can' tell you how many times I done heard that text preached on. They always tell the slaves dat ef he be good, an' worked hard fo' his master, dat he would go to heaven, an' dere he gonna live a life of ease. They ain' never tell him he gonna be free in Heaven. You see, they didn't want slaves to start thinkin' 'bout freedom, even in Heaven. (Berlin, 192)

In the mid-1840s and 1850s the largest Protestant denominations, the Methodists, Baptists, and Presbyterians, took more active stands against slavery. After doing so, all three suffered major internal dissension and, eventually, schism between northern and southern churches.

Enslaved Women as Antislavery Activists

The first Americans to oppose slavery were slaves themselves. While they could not petition for legislation to outlaw slavery, they could and did cast their votes against it by asserting their human worth in the face of devastatingly dehumanizing conditions, by resisting the demands put on them, by fighting back physically, and by running away and helping others to do so. According to most sources, young single men were most likely to be runaways. Women, partly because of physical limi-

tations, but mainly because of the obligation they felt toward their children and other family members, are thought to have been less likely to run away.

Still, there are many narratives of women who escaped their enslavement. Lear Green had herself crated into a box and shipped to Philadelphia. Ellen Craft and her husband William escaped from Georgia through an elaborate masquerade. She, a very light-skinned woman, posed as a white gentleman traveling with his slave valet—her husband—to Philadelphia. In the Crafts' memoirs, they recorded,

> When the time had arrived for us to start, we blew out the lights, knelt down, and prayed to our Heavenly Father mercifully to assist us, as he did his people of old, to escape from cruel bondage; and we shall ever feel that God heard and answered our prayer. Had we not been sustained by a kind, and I sometimes think special, providence, we could never have overcome the mountainous difficulties. (Raboteau, 305)

As an abused slave child in Maryland, Harriet Tubman "prayed to God to make me strong and able to fight." She fled to Philadelphia in 1849 and then became the most famous of all the Underground Railroad conductors, returning to the South at least fifteen times and assisting some 200 people to escape to the North. Tubman is quoted as having said, in response to a request to settle in Philadelphia: "There are three million of my people on the plantations of the south. I must go down, like Moses into Egypt, to lead them out" (Handing, 123).

Tubman also fought against slavery in many different capacities: She traveled and lectured, and during the Civil War she served as a spy, a military strategist, a scout, and a nurse.

Other women did not achieve the fame of Tubman or Craft. Most enslaved persons, knowing the slim odds of success, and the extreme consequences of failure, did not attempt to escape. Yet many resisted in subtle but significant ways. Religion was a key factor in their ability to assert their humanity and autonomy in the face of the inhumanities and infantilization imposed on them by those who called themselves their masters. Enslaved women and men adopted as their own the story of the Exodus, in which God leads an enslaved Israel out of bondage and punishes its Egyptian oppressors.

African Americans' conviction that they too were God's children kept them from succumbing to the view that they were somehow less than human. A slave named Polly told her mistress, "[W]e poor creatures have need to believe in God, for if God Almighty will not be good to us some day, why were we born? When

As an abused slave child in Maryland, Harriet Tubman "prayed to God to make me strong and able to fight." She fled to Philadelphia in 1849, and became the most famous Underground Railroad conductor, returning to the South at least fifteen times and assisting some 200 people to escape to the North. *Courtesy of the Library of Congress.*

I heard of [God's] delivering his people from bondage I know it means the poor African" (Raboteau, 310). And Lydia Adams said, "I've been wanting to be free ever since I was a little child. I said to them I didn't believe God ever meant me to be a slave" (309–310). During the Civil War, some slave owners asked their slaves to pray for the success of the Confederacy. Maria, an enslaved woman from Raleigh, North Carolina, was asked by her mistress, "M'ria, M'ria . . . what *does* you pray for?" to which Maria responded, "I prays, missus, that de Lord's will may be done." This alarmed the white woman, who told Maria, "But you mustn't pray that way. You must pray that our enemies may be driven back." "But, missus," Maria answered irrefutably, "if it's de Lord's will to drive 'em back, den they will go back" (309). The religious faith of such slaves enabled them to trust in an authority that outranked that of their owners—and that would eventually free them.

Woman's Sphere

White women and free black women faced a different set of challenges if they became abolitionists. While no antislavery activists in the United States could count on widespread support, women who opposed slavery had a double burden. In an age when they were expected to leave the conduct of public affairs to men, women had to justify their participation as well as their belief in a controversial cause. Although practice did not always reflect principle, women, white middle- and upper-class women in particular, were expected to conform to the notion of the "woman's sphere."

Woman's sphere, the realm of home and family, embraced domestic responsibilities such as housework and child rearing. It also involved religious activities such as going to church, fostering family moral and religious principles, and participating in benevolent activities, including relief for the poor and education. By this time women were believed to possess an innate and even superior capacity for religion, which made them good candidates for such work. They were expected, however, to do their good works unobtrusively and under male supervision. Proponents of women's limited sphere frequently quoted scripture to support their position. Paul's counsel in Ephesians that wives should be subject to their husbands was one key passage. His support for women's good works was heeded but was coupled with his admonition that woman was not "to teach, nor to usurp authority over the man, but to be in silence" (1 Timothy 2:10, 12, King James Version).

At the same time, the secular and political culture was sending women a similar message about their responsibilities. In what has become known as the ideal of "republican motherhood," the women of the new nation were encouraged to inculcate their children, particularly their sons, with the values of individualism and civic virtue. They were expected to have enough education adequately to instruct their children but not so much as to unfit them for their domestic roles.

Free African American women, in contrast to both their enslaved counterparts and their Euro-American peers, experienced relatively more liberty in terms of their social roles. The obstacles facing this community often made race more significant than gender and allowed women more access to the public sphere. Often, black women were already outside the domestic sphere by virtue of their families' need for their economic contributions.

This did not mean that black women's activism was accepted in whatever form it was offered. Jarena Lee (b. 1783) experienced a call to ministry that was initially discouraged by the African Methodist Episcopal hierarchy. At first she deferred to the church leadership but eventually accepted her sense of divine calling and became an itinerant preacher. Lee addressed mixed-race audiences and met with general approval. She noted in her memoirs one occasion in particular when she addressed a meeting that included a slaveholder who had claimed publicly that black people had no souls. Lee's preaching apparently so impressed that man that while he did not go so far as to free his slaves, he respected them more highly and treated them better thereafter.

While their economic contributions were often necessary, free black women were also expected to demonstrate virtue and piety by imitating middle-class white social conventions as much as possible. Like their white counterparts, black newspapers urged women to remain in proper domestic roles, respecting and serving their husbands and raising their children. Black women such as Maria W. Stewart (1803–1879) sometimes encountered the contradictions inherent in such mixed expectations.

Stewart was affiliated with the First African Baptist Church in Boston. In 1831, following a "born again" experience, she wrote *Religion And the Pure Principles Of Morality, The Sure Foundation On Which We Must Build*, an essay that included a strong defense of the black population in America. After that essay was published in 1831, Stewart began to deliver public lectures in Boston on the same themes. In so doing she became one of the first American women to speak publicly before audiences composed of men as well as women. Abolition was not the focus of her message, although Stewart had been converted to abolitionism by the words of the African American abolitionist David Walker, author of *An Appeal to the Coloured Citizens of the World* (1829). Stewart focused on the need she perceived for the free African American community to improve and demonstrate its education, industriousness, and moral virtue. She was harshly attacked when she dared to speak to the failings of the black community and of black men in particular. She delivered four speeches in Boston in 1832 and 1833 but then retired from public life because of the negative reaction to her presence and her message.

Antislavery Activism (Mostly) within Woman's Sphere: *Amistad*, a Case Study

Many women abolitionists continued to believe in the importance of women's domesticity and submissiveness. They preferred to work behind the scenes in support of the antislavery cause. While these women's names are not generally recorded in histories, they made substantial contributions by raising both money and sympathy for the antislavery cause.

The case of the *Amistad* incident is one example of how women worked effectively but relatively inconspicuously for the antislavery cause. In 1839 fifty-three illegally enslaved Africans who were being transported from Cuba revolted and seized control of the slave ship *Amistad*. They were taken into American custody off the New York coast and imprisoned in Hartford, Connecticut, pending the outcome of a court trial. The case eventually made it to the Supreme Court, where former president John Quincy Adams argued successfully that, having been enslaved despite the prohibition on the international slave trade, the *Amistad* rebels should be freed.

In 1840, Joanna W. Kingsbury, secretary of the Holliston (Massachusetts) Female Antislavery Society, wrote to the editor of the *Liberator* that the members of her group felt both gratitude and mourning as they ended the second year of their existence as an organization. They were happy for their achievements in creating a unified society and in successfully circulating antislavery petitions. They were unhappy, though, that so many people still did not agree that slavery was an evil and did not even respect the rights of persons who had been enslaved in violation of American law. This, Kingsbury wrote, was demonstrated by "the retention of Joseph Cinquez [sic] and his associates in prison, to be tried for life at our tribunals, after it is proved that they were kidnapped Africans—while their kidnappers were treated with complacency!" Kingsbury and the other members of the Holliston Society condemned this treatment as "a violation of every principle of justice, humanity and religion" (*Liberator*, January 10, 1840).

The Holliston women were doing what they felt they could to advance the cause of the *Amistad* captives while staying within the bounds of socially acceptable behavior. They were using their acknowledged superiority in the moral realm to make a statement about the immorality of slavery and the treatment of the *Amistad* captives and to convince others of their views, a process referred to as "moral suasion." This was a significant contribution in an age that deferred to religious authority in both public and private life.

Further, the Holliston women had unanimously agreed to protest slavery by buying products produced by free rather than slave labor whenever possible. This again was a public protest that was nonetheless within the bounds of social convention. Many other women's antislavery societies also adopted Free Produce resolutions as part of their work against slavery.

Women also made financial contributions to the *Amistad* campaign and to the antislavery cause in general. The *Amistad* Committee published lists of contributors to the cause in the monthly *American and Foreign Anti-Slavery Reporter*. Of the donors for whom it is possible to determine sex, women were prominently featured. Mrs. and Miss Buckingham of Putnam, Ohio, contributed $10.00. Hannah Hicks, "a poor colored woman" from Philadelphia, gave $.50. One issue included an entry of $1.00 that was contributed as "the widow's mite." Mary Hinsdale of New York City gave $5.00 on at least two different occasions, with the directive that the money be spent on education. Further, women's contributions were not always monetary; Mary Quinn, of England, made and contributed some clothes for the three female *Amistad* captives (*American Foreign and Anti-Slavery Reporter* [December 1840]: 88; [January 1841]: 120; [February 1841]: 128; [March 15, 1841 Extra]: 16).

Women raised as well as gave money to the antislavery cause. In 1834, the Boston Female Anti-Slavery Society, under the leadership of Maria Weston Chapman (1806–1885), held its first antislavery fair. Arts and crafts were sold, often inscribed with antislavery logos such as, "Am I not a woman and a sister?" This fair was so successful it became an annual event. Other female antislavery societies followed Boston's lead and helped raise a substantial amount of money for the antislavery cause.

The Philadelphia Female Anti-Slavery Society raised approximately $16,500 (about $384,000 in current dollars) between 1836 and 1853 in this way.

The *Amistad* was largely a political and legal campaign. It was conducted by lawyers and politicians, groups composed of men only. But women did make substantial contributions to the *Amistad* campaign, even though their efforts tended to be focused on moral suasion, not legislation or judicial procedure.

Beyond the Bounds of Woman's Sphere

The early proponents of women's religiosity and republican motherhood did not realize the implications of their ideas. However conservative their original intentions, granting women religious and moral authority in any domain made incursions into other realms inevitable. This view of women's moral authority was reinforced by the growing evangelical emphasis on individual spiritual autonomy and unmediated communication with the divine. Such changes in outlook encouraged even traditionally minded women to defy human authorities and social norms that would have proscribed some of their more public activities.

Even the Holliston women took a somewhat controversial step in their antislavery activism. Like many other women abolitionists, they went door to door, asking people to sign antislavery petitions, which would then be delivered to the U.S. Congress. Petitioning had long been an accepted way of requesting the government to take action on a particular issue. What was different in the 1830s was the great volume of antislavery petitions that were submitted to Congress, many of which had been collected by women. Women justified their petitioning with reference to divine will. In submitting a petition to the Kent County [Ohio] Female Anti-Slavery Society, Maria Sturges, a Presbyterian abolitionist, urged that "every petition . . . be baptized with prayer, and commended with weeping and supplication to Him in whose hands are the hearts of all men, that he would turn the channel of their sympathies from the oppressor to the oppressed. For God is our only hope" (Van Broekhoven, 182–183).

Proslavery members of Congress saw these petitions as a threat because each submitted petition offered opportunity for congressional debate on the subject of slavery. In 1836 the proslavery faction in the House of Representatives joined with those who simply did not want to debate the issue and succeeded in passing a gag rule, specifying that all petitions on the subject of slavery would be tabled automatically without debate. This gag rule remained in effect until 1844, when it was finally rescinded, largely due to the efforts of former President John Quincy Adams.

Despite the gag rule, abolitionists continued to flood

the Congress with antislavery petitions. This door-to-door work was valuable not only as a message to Congress but also as a means of raising public consciousness about the evils of slavery. Some felt, however, that women who engaged in collecting signatures had crossed the line into the public sphere and were, therefore, acting inappropriately. In her *Essay on Slavery and Abolitionism* (1837), Catharine Beecher wrote: "In this country, petitions to congress... seem, IN ALL CASES, to fall entirely without the sphere of female duty. Men are the proper persons to make appeals to the rulers whom they appoint" (104–105).

The delegates to the 1837 Female Anti-Slavery Convention defended themselves against charges such as Beecher's, claiming, as had Maria Sturges, that petitioning was not simply a political right but a religious obligation, "derived immediately from God, and guaranteed by the Constitution of the United States." It was in fact "the duty of every woman in the United States ... annually to petition Congress with the faith of an Esther, and the untiring perseverance of the importunate widow" in support of measures that were clearly within the jurisdiction of the federal government: the abolition of slavery in the District of Columbia and the Territory of Florida and the prohibition of the interstate slave trade (*Proceedings ... 1837*, 8).

Some women abolitionists challenged conventional ideas about women's roles more directly. We noted previously the pioneering lectures of Maria W. Stewart in Boston and Lydia Maria Child's shift from writing domestic advice literature to antislavery tracts. As time passed, the commitment of some women to abolitionism led them also to rethink the secular and scriptural assertions about women's place, which in turn brought them into conflict with church and clergy. The careers of two abolitionist sisters, Sarah and Angelina Grimké, illustrate these conflicts.

Sarah Moore Grimké (1792–1873) and Angelina Emily Grimké (1805–1879) were raised in an Episcopalian slaveholding family in Charleston, South Carolina. Both went through religious conversion experiences that eventually resulted in their moving to Philadelphia and becoming members of the Society of Friends. Both were wholeheartedly convinced that a work of ministry lay ahead of them. Sarah Grimké for years wrestled with a conviction that she was called to a preaching ministry within the Society of Friends; Angelina Grimké had an early apprehension that hers might have to do with slavery, which her personal experience had led her to oppose.

In 1835, after having resided in Philadelphia for nearly six years, Angelina Grimké penned a strong letter of support to William Lloyd Garrison for his abolitionist work. The publication of this letter in the *Liberator* brought condemnation upon Grimké from her ortho-

dox Quaker meeting. Quakers did not accuse her of acting in an unwomanly manner, for they were considerably more supportive of women's leadership than any other religious body and accepted women as well as men into the ministry. Instead, the elders of her meeting objected to her involvement in a cause that would bring her into association with the world and particularly with abolitionists, whose motives and actions were suspect. As her sister Sarah later wrote, Angelina was told that "the Meeting for Sufferings [the deliberative body of the Society of Friends] had the charge of this weighty matter, and that *whenever the way opened, they* would do all that friends could do"(Sarah Grimké to "My dear Friend" [Elizabeth Pease], 4th Month 10th 1839, William L. Clements Library, University of Michigan, Ann Arbor).

Grimké, still confident of her own spiritual mission, did not allow Quaker criticism to stop her. The following summer she drafted a tract titled *An Appeal to the Christian Women of the South* (1836) in which she encouraged her southern sisters to speak out against the sinfulness of slavery, thereby "obeying God, rather than man." She closed by saying that "I have appealed to your sympathies as women, to your sense of duty as *Christian women*" (Ceplair, 58, 79).

Sarah Grimké was slow to adopt her sister's radical views on abolition and religious authority but eventually embraced them wholeheartedly. In 1837 and 1838 they scandalized New England by conducting a hugely successful lecture tour in Massachusetts. They had been invited originally by the American Anti-Slavery Society to deliver a series of "parlor talks" for women, a socially acceptable activity. This format did not last long. The sisters, especially Angelina, were enormously popular speakers and soon were attracting large crowds. They moved their meetings to other sites, such as religious meetinghouses, and men as well as women began to attend their meetings. The Grimkés' willingness to speak on a political topic to "promiscuous" audiences (that is, those composed of men as well as women) brought down condemnation upon them. They were challenged not only for their antislavery message but also for transgressing the boundaries of woman's sphere.

Clerical condemnation was particularly harsh. In May 1837 the Congregationalist clergy of Massachusetts issued a pastoral letter, reprinted in the New England *Spectator*, that was clearly aimed at what they considered to be the misjudged and ungodly actions of the Grimkés in going beyond "the social influences which females use in promoting piety and the great objects of Christian benevolence" and "assum[ing] the place and tone of man as a public reformer." They warned, "If the vine, whose strength and beauty is to lean upon the trellis work and half conceal its clusters, thinks to assume the independence and the overshadowing nature of the elm, it will not only cease to bear fruit, but fall in shame and dishonor into the dust" (*Pastoral Letter from the General Association of Massachusetts to the Churches under Their Care*). Catharine Beecher's *Essay on Slavery*, mentioned above, was another response to Angelina Grimké's lecturing.

Both sisters responded in writing to these attacks. They had come to believe that if they were to be silenced on the topic of slavery because of their sex, then it was essential for them to defend their rights as women to speak publicly: that this too was a divinely inspired mission. Sarah Grimké began a series of *Letters on the Equality of the Sexes and the Condition of Woman* (1837), addressed to Mary Parker, president of the Boston Female Anti-Slavery Society. These letters stand as one of the earliest American feminist manifestos. Angelina Grimké in her turn composed a serial reply to Catharine Beecher's attack on abolitionism and women's antislavery activism (*Letters to Catherine [sic] E. Beecher, in reply to An Essay on Slavery and Abolitionism, addressed to A. E. Grimke*). Here she defended the "Christian character" of the abolitionists, as well as women's right and indeed responsibility to take action: "Whatever is *morally* right for a man to do . . . is *morally* right for a woman to do. I recognize no rights but *human* rights—I know nothing of men's rights and women's rights; for in Christ Jesus, there is neither male nor female."

Some abolitionists who had supported the Grimkés in their antislavery lecturing were unhappy about their women's rights advocacy, which they perceived as a diversion from the main cause. Yet the Grimkés defended their espousal of women's rights:

> Can you not see the deep laid scheme of the clergy against us as lecturers. They know full well that if they can persuade the people it is a *shame* for us to speak in public, and that every time we open our mouths for the dumb we are breaking a divine command, that even if we speak with the tongues of men and angels, we should have no hearers. They are springing a mine beneath our feet, and we shall very soon be compelled to retreat for we shall have no ground to stand on. If we surrender the right to *speak* to the public this year, we must surrender the right to petition next year and the right to *write* the year after and more. What *then* can woman do for the slave—when she is herself under the feet of man and shamed into silence. (Angelina Grimké to Theodore Weld and John Greenleaf Whittier, 20 August [1837], Clements Library)

The Grimkés did not succeed in converting all abolitionists to their point of view, but some, most often women, defended them. They received letters of support from numerous antislavery societies, the most striking of which came from the Buckingham (Massachusetts) Female Anti-Slavery Society. This society wrote:

> Dear Sisters! Being sensible that your vocation is rendered a far more difficult and delicate task since you have had to vindicate the rights and labor to elevate the condition of woman than it has heretofore been, and that this is indeed a task from which women would naturally be inclined to shrink and turn aside, but believing that when the truth has made any of us free, that we are not only free to labor for the emancipation of others, but that a propelling power is felt, which to resist were to quench the spirit of immutable truth which we are expressly commanded not to do. . . .
>
> We confess we have had some misgivings as to the *expediency* of having this subject agitated at present lest it might retard the AntiSlavery cause but when we reflect that the command has gone forth sanctioned by divine authority, to "let the oppressed go free and to break *every* yoke, it seems to us that [to] endeavour to set bounds to it and say thus far shalt thou go and no farther would be like [at]tempting to limit the Holy One. We would therefore say hold fast the form of sound words and keep to our first position that whatever is right must be expedient, for what can be more expedient than to do right. Let then, the right be done tho' all the associations of men be dissolved, and their glory laid low in the dust. (Buckingham Female Anti-Slavery Society to Angelina and Sarah Grimké, July 27, 1837, Center for American History, University of Texas at Austin)

Angelina Grimké also brought her view on the relatedness of religion, women's roles, and abolition before the larger body of antislavery women in the 1837 Anti-Slavery Convention of American Women. She proposed the following resolution:

> *Resolved*, That as certain rights and duties are common to all moral beings, the time has come for woman to move in that sphere which Providence has assigned her, and no longer remain satisfied in the circumscribed limits with which corrupt custom and a perverted application of Scripture have encircled her; therefore that it is the duty of woman, and the province of woman, to plead the cause of the oppressed in our land, and to do all that she can by her voice, and her pen, and her purse, and the influence of her example, to overthrow the horrible system of American slavery. (*Proceedings . . . 1837*, 9)

The convention proceedings note that this resolution "called forth an animated and interesting debate respecting the rights and duties of women" (9). Amendments were offered but defeated and the original resolution passed, but not unanimously. The following day, a motion was made to reconsider the resolution. Although it failed, proving that the majority of delegates supported the notion of women's expanded roles, the debate made clear that this was a controversial issue among the women present and undoubtedly would have been more so outside the confines of the convention.

Although the Grimkés were vilified in newspapers and church pulpits, they continued their tour, concluding with several addresses to the Massachusetts State Legislature and the general public in Boston. It has been estimated that in the twenty-three weeks of their lecture tour they visited sixty-seven towns, giving eighty-eight or more talks, and reaching over 40,000 people (Lerner, 227). In all their work, whether speaking out against slavery, defending women's right to public speech and action, or criticizing clerical authority, the Grimkés were sustained by their faith that they were pursuing a path to which they had received a divine call. As Angelina Grimké wrote to a friend, "I see not to what point, all these things are leading me, I wonder whether I shall make shipwreck of the faith—I cannot tell—but one thing comforts me, I do feel as tho' the Lord had sent us, and as if I was leaning on the arm of my beloved" (Angelina Grimké to Jane Smith, May 29, 1837, Clements Library).

Abolitionism and Faith Commitments

Faith conviction provided women other than the Grimkés with a powerful justification for assuming leadership in a public cause. The approval of the divine, such women felt, far outweighed human disapprobation. Lucretia Mott was one of those at the 1837 convention who spoke in favor of Angelina Grimké's resolution on women's roles. Mott (1793–1880) was born into a Quaker family in Nantucket. She was officially designated a minister by her meeting in 1821. She was frequently at odds, though, with the Friends' sectarian and hierarchical ways and referred to herself as "a kind of outlaw in my own society" ("I Am Not Here as a Representative of Any Sect," in Greene, 295). Mott was extraordinarily active in many reform movements throughout her life, including peace and women's rights causes as well as abolition. She declared that she had seen her antislavery mission clearly "when I consecrated myself to that gospel which anoints 'to preach deliverance to the captive,' 'to set at liberty them that are bruised' " (undated reminiscences dictated to Sarah J. Hale, Friends Historical Library, Swarthmore College).

Abby Kelley (1811–1887) was another Quaker who felt called to antislavery lecturing. A teacher from a Massachusetts farming family, she was initially hesitant to take on such a task and was discouraged by the negative response from her family, who felt that she was not capable of such work. But Kelley drew comfort from her reflection that some of the apostles of Jesus were simple fishermen. She became one of the most dedicated of the antislavery lecturers, female or male, and spent much of the following thirty years on the lecturing circuit.

Sallie Holley (1818–1890), who lectured in the 1850s and 1860s, also chose her work based on her feeling of divine call. Hearing Abby Kelley speak in a public forum and call for others to take up the work, Holley "felt called by a Divine Voice to plead her cause—and with instant yieldings to the hitherto undreamt-of command, said 'I will' " (Caroline Putnam to Samuel May, January 22, 1887, Massachusetts Historical Society). Holley had been raised in a religiously unorthodox household, but the way she combined her faith convictions with her antislavery stance made her a very popular speaker. One correspondent to the *Liberator* commented, "She [Holley] must be a great favorite with all, male and female, who think that the religious element in our nature should be often and perseveringly appealed to" (S.W.W., Letter to the editor, *Liberator*, January 28, 1853).

Sojourner Truth (c. 1799–1883) was a former slave whose tremendous presence bolstered both the antislavery and the women's rights causes. Known as Isabella, she had freed herself from her New York master with the help of friends at the end of 1826. She became an itinerant preacher and in 1843 renamed herself Sojourner Truth. In the 1850s she began to speak at women's rights and antislavery meetings as well; her religiosity continued to infuse her words and deeds.

The success of Harriet Beecher Stowe's (1811–1896) first novel, *Uncle Tom's Cabin*, catapulted her to the forefront of the antislavery movement in the 1850s. In it, Stowe contrasted the Christian pacifism of the slave Tom with the brutality of the reprobate slave owner Simon Legree. The book sold half a million copies in five years in the United States and was translated into thirty-seven languages. Stowe defended herself against the charges of having fabricated the type of events narrated in the novel by publishing *The Key to Uncle Tom's Cabin* in 1853. She also grounded the legitimacy of her work in a claim to having been "an instrument in [God's] hands." "I could not control the story. . . . The Lord himself wrote it," she often remarked, according to her son, Charles Edward Stowe (Stowe, 156).

The conviction that they were being faithful to God's will led these and other less prominent abolitionist women to challenge the church for its unwillingness to take a clear stand against slavery. The 1837 Anti-Slavery

Convention of American Women noted that "we have beheld with grief and amazement the death-like apathy of some northern churches on the subject of American slavery . . . and that as long as northern pulpits are closed against the advocates of the oppressed, whilst they are freely open to their oppressors, the northern churches have their own garments stained with the blood of slavery, and are awfully guilty in the sight of God" (*Proceedings . . . 1837*, 16).

In her sermons, Lucretia Mott frequently chastised church and clergy for thinking that creed and ritual could be more important that the sufferings of the enslaved. She asked

> that slavery shall be held up in every congregation, and before all sects, as a greater sin than erroneous thinking; a greater sin than Sabbath breaking. If any of you are seen on Sabbath day with your thimble on, performing some piece of needlework, the feelings of your neighbors are shocked on beholding the sight; and yet these very people may be indifferent to great sins. . . . To some, the sin of slaveholding is not so horrifying as certain deviations from established observances. ("One Standard of Goodness and Truth," in Greene, 256)

Comeouterism

Despite, or perhaps because of, the deep spiritual commitment of many of the antislavery activists, the gap between them and Christian churches continued to grow. Abolitionists deplored the generally tepid statements of the churches on the evils of slavery. They were disillusioned by the disinterest and indeed hostility of many members of the clergy and churches toward the antislavery cause. This led to a phenomenon they called "comeouterism," based on New Testament references to "come out from among them, and be ye separate, saith the Lord, and touch not the unclean thing; and I will receive you" (2 Corinthians 6:17); "Come out of her, my people, that ye be not partakers of her sins, and that ye receive not of her plagues" (Revelation 18:4); and "have no fellowship with the unfruitful works of darkness, but rather reprove them" (Ephesians 5:11). Comeouterism, the withdrawal from churches that even tacitly supported slavery, became a hotly debated issue within abolitionist circles. Most abolitionists retained their memberships, but some began to abandon their denominational affiliations because they believed the churches in America were not adhering to Christian principles.

Indeed, antislavery commitment and action became the fundamental principle by which some abolitionists judged Christian churches and individuals. They were unsympathetic to arguments that good could be accomplished while working within a proslavery church. The debate was at times vitriolic. In 1840 Abby Kelley was appalled when the Connecticut Anti-Slavery Society passed a resolution calling on its members not to support proslavery politicians but did not mention proslavery clergy. Kelley wrote a letter to the editor of the *Anti-Slavery Standard*, summarizing the action as tantamount to a declaration that "[t]hey must have a set of *politicians* whose hands are clear of the blood of the slave, but those whom they receive as ministers of Christ and *expounders of the* Scriptures, may have hands dripping with the blood of the mangled victim" (June 19, 1840; reprinted in the *Liberator*, July 10, 1840).

The issue of comeouterism was addressed at length at the Second Anti-Slavery Convention of American Women, held in 1838. Mary Grew, a Philadelphia abolitionist whose father was a Baptist minister, proposed:

> *Whereas*, The disciples of Christ are commanded to have no fellowship with the "unfruitful works of darkness"; and, whereas, union in His church is the strongest expression of fellowship between men; therefore,
>
> *Resolved*, That it is our duty to keep ourselves separate from those churches which receive to their pulpits and their communion tables, those who buy, or sell, or hold as property, the image of the living God. (*Proceedings of the Anti-Slavery Convention of American Women, Held in Philadelphia, May 15th, 16th, 17th and 18th, 1838*, 5)

As with the previous year's discussion on the province of women, this resolution called forth considerable debate. The dissenters agreed that slaveholders and apologists for slavery were guilty before God but also believed that "there is still moral power sufficient in the church, if rightly applied, to purify it" (6). The motion passed in spite of the opposition. For abolitionists such as Abby Kelley, comeouterism became the only conscionable action of a sincerely religious person. Other abolitionists, Lucretia Mott, for example, remained within their denominations, attempting to bring about change from within the church structure.

As is clear from the arguments employed by these women, their criticism of the churches and even comeouterism did not indicate a lack of religious conviction. Neither can it fairly be said that they used reform as a substitute for religion. In no case did any of these women imply that activism was identical to faith; rather, as Lucretia Mott stated, the "practical life" was "the highest *evidence* of a sound faith" (undated reminiscences, Friends Historical Library; emphasis added). Abby Kelley referred to abolitionism as Christianity *ap-*

plied to slavery, not the sum of Christianity, and claimed that reform movements in general were *inspired by* the doctrine of love to God and love to humankind.

Abolition and Racial Egalitarianism

Being antislavery did not necessarily mean that one favored racial egalitarianism. Unfortunately, the abolitionists themselves, while opposing the institution of slavery, often did not respect African Americans or treat them as equals. In fact, Sarah Mapps Douglass (1806–1882), an African American teacher and abolitionist who attended a Philadelphia Quaker meeting, commented that even among the Friends, "in proportion as we become intellectual and respectable, so in proportion does their disgust and prejudice increase" (Sarah Mapps Douglass to William Bassett, December 1837, Clements Library).

Douglass believed, rightly, that while abolitionists opposed slavery, most continued to view black Americans as inferior to white Americans. That made her particularly appreciative of the Grimkés, who not only spoke publicly against slavery but sat with their African American friends in the "negro seat"—the area in the meetinghouse designated for black attendees. The Grimkés helped to broaden the awareness that being antislavery meant more than simple abolition of the institution of chattel slavery.

The linkage of slavery and racial discrimination was not a new insight for black Americans. Free African Americans could clearly see that slavery and freedom were not polar opposites, but that they existed on a continuum, and that the racial prejudice and discrimination experienced by free northern blacks was an example of unfreedom. In 1832 Maria Stewart had argued passionately that the lack of education and economic opportunity for free African Americans left them little better than off than had they been enslaved. "Tell us no more of southern slavery," she demanded, "for with few exceptions . . . I consider our condition but little better than that. . . . [M]ethinks there are no chains so galling as those that bind the soul." She proposed breaking "the chains of slavery and ignorance" by uniting as a community and by "cultivat[ing] among ourselves the pure principles of piety, morality and virtue" ("Religion and the Pure Principles of Morality," in Richardson 1987, 30).

African Americans, while generally condemning northern hypocrisy on the topic of slavery and racial prejudice, did work hard for moral and economic uplift in their own communities. Black churches were often at the center of such benevolent activities. Women worked inside and outside of churches to improve conditions for themselves and others. In 1832 in Philadelphia, black women organized a Female Literary Association, de-

signed to advance the education of its members. Members held regular meetings at each other's homes and discussed various issues, including abolition. Black women were also involved in efforts to educate and train their members and provide for social uplift. Sarah Mapps Douglass was one who began teaching in Philadelphia in 1828 and continued teaching black students for forty-nine years. Through benevolence societies black women extended material aid to their poorer members. By 1841, there were over thirty black benevolent societies in the Northeast. These groups helped widows and orphans and other needy people.

Female antislavery societies, while not free from prejudice, were more likely to be racially integrated than their male counterparts and often assisted in projects such as schools for black children. Black women also founded their own antislavery societies; in fact, the first known female antislavery society was formed in February 1832 by African American women in Salem, Massachusetts.

The women's antislavery conventions also addressed this theme. In 1837, they declared that

> this Convention do firmly believe that the existence of an unnatural prejudice against our colored population, is one of the chief pillars of American slavery—therefore, that the more we mingle with our oppressed brethren and sisters, the more deeply are we convinced of the sinfulness of that anti-Christian prejudice which is crushing them to the earth in our nominally free states . . . and that we deem it a solemn duty for every woman to pray to be delivered from such an unholy feeling, and to act out the principles of Christian equality by associating with them as though the color of the skin was of no more consequence than that of the hair, or the eyes. (*Proceedings . . . 1837*, 13)

The convention also endorsed the establishment of schools and sabbath schools open to all, without regard to color of skin.

In contrast, a convention of male abolitionists held the same year put the onus for ending racial discrimination onto the African American community itself. Delegates resolved that

> this Convention rejoices in the efforts now making [*sic*] by our free colored brethren, to improve and elevate their intellectual, moral and religious character; and trust, while every encouragement and assistance should be given to these exertions, that every colored American will feel that a double responsibility is now laid upon him—that upon his conduct depends, not only his own welfare, but in a great degree, that of his race—and that all will,

therefore, endeavor, by constant well-doing, to put to silence the voice of prejudice and persecution. (*Proceedings of the Fourth New-England Anti-Slavery Convention, Held in Boston, May 30, 31, and June 1 and 2, 1837*, 123–124)

At the 1839 women's convention, Lucretia Mott described an encounter with the mayor of Philadelphia who had approached her beforehand to request that white women "should avoid unnecessary walking with colored people" at the convention (in order to avoid a riot such as had occurred the previous year, when the abolitionists' newly built meeting place, Pennsylvania Hall, had been burned to the ground). Mott replied that she and other white women "should do as we had done before—walk with them as occasion offered; . . . [that] it was a principle with us, which we could not yield, to make no distinction on account of color" and that she personally "was expecting delegates from Boston of that complexion, and should, probably, accompany them to the place of meeting" (*Proceedings of the Third Anti-Slavery Convention of American Women, Held in Philadelphia, May 1st, 2d and 3d, 1839*, 1839, 6).

The Intersection of Religion, Race, and Gender in the Antislavery Movement

Women made significant contributions to the antislavery movement. White women's involvement in the domestic realm, combined with an awareness of their own gender marginalization, may have made them more sensitive to the broader needs of African Americans; for their part, black women continued to work within their communities for educational, moral, and economic improvement.

Women's experiences in the antislavery movement brought them increasing awareness of other flaws in their society: of the injustice of their own supposed inferiority and necessary subordination to male authority and of their confinement to the domestic sphere. Their conviction that their participation in the antislavery movement was a divine mandate led them also to question the religious authority that attempted to deny them a role in that cause. Their conflicts with religious authorities further inspired women to examine the legitimacy of human religious authority and to question the authenticity of scripture as it had been translated.

Some women chose to struggle publicly on behalf of abolition by publishing antislavery manifestos and by public speaking. These women not only advanced the antislavery cause; they inspired a host of other people, women and men, to act as well. Among women they helped to create a sense of activist sisterhood that spread into other causes women adopted throughout the century.

Women who did not make a name for themselves nonetheless played important roles in the antislavery movement. Women's fund-raising was a critical element in sustaining the national and regional antislavery societies. Women's door-to-door petitioning raised consciousness at the grassroots and put pressure on Congress to consider the antislavery question. They provided aid to fugitives, ran Free Produce stores selling only goods produced by free labor, taught in schools for African Americans, and financially supported schools and other benevolent institutions.

In nearly every instance, the religious motivation for such actions is clearly evident. The conviction that slavery was a sin against God was the almost universal factor in prompting women to take an initial stand against slavery. Their belief that God, a higher authority than human beings, legitimated and supported their actions is what sustained them through the trials they faced as women working inside and outside the boundaries of "woman's sphere" on behalf of the antislavery cause.

SOURCES: There are increasing numbers of books and articles that deal with women and the antislavery movement; those mentioned here are a sample of those that specifically address religion as well as reform. The relationship of faith, antislavery activism, and women's rights for Sarah and Angelina Grimké, Lucretia Mott, Abby Kelley, and Sallie Holley is explored in *The Religious World of Antislavery Women: Spirituality in the Lives of Five Abolitionist Lecturers* (2000), by Anna M. Speicher, which also includes a bibliography of works relevant to women, religion, and antislavery and an appendix profiling sixteen other antislavery women lecturers. Deborah Van Broekhoven's article " 'Let Your Names Be Enrolled' " is one of a collection of significant essays found in *The Abolitionist Sisterhood: Women's Political Culture in Antebellum America*, ed. Jean Fagan Yellin and John C. Van Horne (1994). Many of Lydia Maria Child's writings can be found in *An Appeal in Favor of That Class of Americans Called Africans* (1833, 1996) and *A Lydia Maria Child Reader* (1997), both edited by Carolyn L. Karcher. Maria W. Stewart's essay *Religion and the Pure Principles of Morality*, along with the texts of her speeches, can be found in *Maria W. Stewart, America's First Black Woman Political Writer*, ed. Marilyn Richardson (1987). Edited versions of Sarah and Angelina Grimké's essays, along with the Pastoral Letter opposing women's activism, are accessible in *The Public Years of Sarah and Angelina Grimké: Selected Writings, 1835–1839*, ed. Larry Ceplair (1989). The most complete biography of the Grimké sisters remains Gerda Lerner's *The Grimké Sisters from South Carolina: Pioneers for Woman's Rights and Abolition* (1971). Lucretia Mott's sermons are collected in *Lucretia Mott: Her Complete Speeches and Sermons*, ed. Dana Greene (1980); another helpful volume is *Selected Letters of Lucretia Coffin Mott*, ed. Beverly Wilson Palmer (2002). Sources for African American history and religion include Vincent Harding's essay "Religion and Resistance among Antebellum Slaves, 1800–1860," in *African-American Religion: Interpretive Essays in History and Culture*, ed. Timothy E. Fulop and Albert J. Raboteau (1993); Albert J. Raboteau's *Slave Religion: The*

"Invisible Institution" in the Antebellum South (1978); and Remembering Slavery, ed. Ira Berlin (1998). See also Charles Edward Stowe, The Life of Harriet Beecher Stowe; Compiled from Her Letters and Journals (1889).

WOMEN AND PEACE MOVEMENTS IN NORTH AMERICA
Valarie Ziegler

THE WORK OF women in peace movements in North America has typically raised two strategic issues. The first poses the question of essentialism: Is there something about being a woman that naturally inclines one to detest violence and embrace harmony? In particular, does woman's biological role as mother predispose her toward pacifism? Or do men and women share a common nature, so that neither is innately more pacific than the other? The answer to that question is significant. If women have a unique capacity to instruct society on the blessings of peace, then it makes sense for them to band together, working apart from men, in the cause of peace. If, on the other hand, women share a common nature with men, then it is reasonable to work with men as their partners, since men can in theory eschew violence as easily as women.

The second issue that has marked women's involvement in peace movements poses a different strategic question: How can women effectively campaign for peace? Entering the arena of public debate has invariably obliged women to find ways to establish their right to a life outside the domestic sphere of home and family. Thus, publicly working for peace has invariably prompted women also to work for political equality with men. Ironically, however, working for women's political rights is not necessarily tied to working for peace. Contemporary women who have sought equal opportunity within the armed forces have found militarism, rather than pacifism, as a venue for seeking their political rights.

Early Organized Peace Movements

Organized peace movements in North America began in 1815, at the conclusion of the War of 1812. Prior to that, pacifism was most famously associated with several Protestant groups. Those of Anabaptist origin—such as the Mennonites, the Dunkers, and the Brethren—were historic peace churches that eschewed involvement with government. They believed that Christians were called to live according to the nonresistant love ethic outlined by Jesus in the Sermon on the Mount and that governments, based as they were upon the coercive threat in-nate to the state's police and military forces, were of necessity violent. Known as "the quiet in the land," these Anabaptist groups withdrew from the larger culture insofar as they could.

Far more influential were the Quakers, a British Christian pacifist group that was instrumental in the founding of Pennsylvania. Quakers believed in a source of inspiration they called "the inner light." Convinced that women as well as men had access to this inner light, when they gathered to worship, Quakers encouraged one another to speak as God's spirit led them. In thus inviting women to speak with authority before "promiscuous" audiences that contained men as well as women, Quakers were for their time astonishingly egalitarian. They were also notable for their early and persistent opposition to African American slavery. As a result, Quakers would play important roles in abolitionist and peace movements in the nineteenth century. Quaker women, accustomed to being afforded the spiritual authority to speak their minds in Quaker meetings, became important public advocates for peace, the abolition of slavery, and women's rights. Women such as Angelina and Sarah Grimké and Lucretia Mott became notable public advocates for these causes.

When, in 1815, David Low Dodge and Noah Worcester founded the first formal peace societies in American history (called, respectively, the New York Peace Society and the Massachusetts Peace Society), they had no intention of opening the cause of peace to women advocates. Rather, they hoped to persuade a wide range of Christian men that the cause of international peace demanded their immediate attention. They were convinced that obedience to the Sermon on the Mount was critical to Christianity, and they believed that nations, as well as individuals, should resolve to "turn the other cheek" and refuse to return evil for evil. If Christian nations refused to wage war, they reasoned, then war would go out of favor and cease to be an instrument of policy. In 1828, under the leadership of William Ladd, a national organization dubbed the American Peace Society was formed.

Like most other public organizations of its day, the American Peace Society enlisted only male members, but it eagerly solicited donations from women (particularly urging them to buy memberships for their ministers), and it also encouraged women to form auxiliary peace societies. The journal of the American Peace Society ran frequent articles reminding women that as mothers they held the key to peace education. The Society's annual report in 1837 noted that eight "Ladies peace societies" were in existence and that it had distributed 50 tracts titled Stories for Children and 110 titled Address to the Ladies in the previous year (The Advocate of Peace, no, 1 [June 1837]: 22, 35). In an 1836 work, William Ladd argued that the "subject of Peace is particularly adapted to the female mind." He urged women to pray for peace, to refuse to attend military balls and reviews, to teach their children to reject military displays, and to use their talents in writing poetry, music, and tracts for the cause of peace (Philanthropos, 6–30, 34–35).

Ladd's belief that women were by nature peaceful was thoroughly essentialist. In confining membership to men and in exiling women to auxiliary organizations, the American Peace Society ensured women's tangential status and left little room for them to develop a distinctive voice. Through the cause of abolitionism, however, women would go beyond the stereotypical roles of wife and mother to pioneer a new kind of peace advocacy. They were led by Angelina and Sarah Grimké, sisters who had abandoned their native South Carolina, moved to Pennsylvania, become Quakers, and joined other reformers in the emerging abolitionist movement.

Immediatist abolitionism (that is, antislavery efforts that demanded an immediate end to slavery) had begun in the early 1830s. It was marked by a commitment to nonviolence, to the Sermon on the Mount as the Christian statement of nonviolence par excellence, and to defining slavery as a form of coercive violence. In 1837, the Grimké sisters traveled to New England on an antislavery lecture tour. Though they had intended to honor the nineteenth-century convention that prohibited women from addressing promiscuous audiences of men and women, the Grimkés proved to be such powerful speakers that men began sneaking into their lectures. The Congregational clergy of Connecticut issued a pastoral letter condemning the Grimkés, and the two sisters were forced to defend their right to speak on behalf of the slave. One of the enduring literary works that resulted was Sarah Grimké's *Letters on the Equality of the Sexes and the Condition of Women*, published in 1838.

Many abolitionists feared that the Grimké sisters, by introducing the "extraneous" question of women's rights into the antislavery cause, would divert abolitionists from their main goal. The Grimkés disagreed vigorously. "*We* will settle *this right before* we go one step further," Angelina insisted, asking, "What *then* can *woman* do for the slave when she is herself under the feet of man and shamed in *silence*?" Indeed, she concluded, woman's right to speak publicly "*must* be firmly established . . . on the only firm basis of human rights, the Bible" (*Letters of Theodore Dwight Weld, Angelina Grimké Weld, and Sarah Grimké*, 1: 428). Sarah agreed: "I ask no favors for my sex. I surrender not our claim to equality. All I ask of our brethren is, that they will take their feet from off our backs and permit us to stand upright on that ground which God has designed us to occupy" (*Letters on the Equality of the Sexes*, 10).

Such claims predicated women's commitment to peace not to their femininity but to their humanity—to the God-given nature they shared, as part of the human race, with men. Most Americans disagreed and preferred the essentialist arguments typical of the American Peace Society. But a few reformers were delighted to welcome the Grimkés into their midst. The abolitionists led by William Lloyd Garrison were radical pacifists; terming themselves "nonresistants," they were dedicated to the immediate abolition of slavery, to the equality of men and women, and to the absolute rejection of all governments that fell below the perfection of the Sermon on the Mount. They were accustomed to being mobbed in the course of their antislavery lectures, and as early as 1835, one of their number, Maria Weston Chapman, had published *Right and Wrong in Boston*, a plea for abolitionists to regard women and men as moral and political equals. Garrison's weekly abolitionist paper, the *Liberator*, regularly challenged William Ladd and the American Peace Society to occupy the "higher ground" of nonresistant gender equality.

By 1838, the nonresistants had founded their own peace society: the New England Non-Resistance Society. Women joined as full members and were elected as officers. A number of women, such as Lydia Maria Child, Abby Kelley, and the Quaker Lucretia Mott, became prominent public figures on behalf of nonresistant abolitionism. Child went on to become editor of the influential *Anti-Slavery Standard*, and younger women such as Lucy Stone, Antoinette Brown Blackwell, Susan B. Anthony, and Elizabeth Cady Stanton received training that prepared them to become prominent leaders in the women's rights movement. They faced great opposition, even from other abolitionists. Catharine Beecher chastised the Grimkés for operating outside of the domestic sphere she believed appropriate to women, and a minister who belonged to the Connecticut Anti-Slavery Society was so distraught at the prospect of listening to a speech by Abby Kelley that he announced, "I will not sit in a meeting where the sorcery of a woman's tongue is thrown around my heart. I will not submit to PETTICOAT GOVERNMENT. No woman shall ever lord it over me" (Sterling, 107–109). Within their own community, however, egalitarian abolitionists celebrated women's freedom to speak. As one fan of Abby Kelley put it:

Miss Kelley of Lynn,
Some esteem it a sin
And a shame that thou darest to speak;
Quite forgetting that mind
Is to sex unconfined.
That in Christ is nor Gentile nor Greek,
Abby K!
That in Christ is nor Gentile nor Greek!
    (Sterling, 124)

In these ways, abolitionism, women's rights, and pacifism intertwined. Women who labored on behalf of one cause might easily work for all three. Ultimately, of course, political events drove a wedge into that alliance. The slaves would be freed not through peaceful means but through a devastating civil war. And with the passage of the Thirteenth Amendment after the war, freed male slaves would receive (at least in theory if not necessarily in practice) full citizenship rights, while the women who had dedicated themselves to the antislavery cause would remain disenfranchised. After the war, the cause of peace became even more strongly linked to woman suffrage, as well as to other reform efforts such as temperance and the woman's club movement. By the end of the nineteenth century, hundreds of thousands of American women would be pledged to the cause of peace.

From the Gilded Age to World War I

Interestingly, the most prominent women's reformers in this period used essentialist arguments as a platform for advocating women's rights. If it was the case—as most Victorian Americans assumed—that women were by nature less aggressive, more godly, and more inclined to self-sacrifice than men, then confining women to the domestic sphere meant that Americans' public life would be bereft of the leavening effect of women's pacific spirit. It was, in short, selfish for women to restrict themselves to the home; for the good of the nation, they needed to move into the public arena.

Women peace reformers combined that argument with a prevalent sociological theory of the origins of human civilization. This theory received scholarly attention in the works of a sociologist named Lester Ward and was given wide credence in popular culture as well. Briefly, the theory argued that human civilization's earliest forms were matriarchal. Since women had once ruled society, it was possible to argue that they should rule society again, or at least that human culture would remain skewed and underdeveloped so long as men alone controlled the public spheres of work, education, industry, literary arts, and government. Without women to balance men's natural aggression and selfishness, human civilization could never realize its full potential.

The woman who most prominently developed the theological implications of this theory for peace advocacy was an unlikely candidate: Julia Ward Howe, the author of the "Battle Hymn of the Republic." Howe became interested in woman suffrage in the late 1860s, and in 1870, as the Franco-Prussian war was under way in Europe, Howe pondered what she might do to make a witness for peace. Why, she wondered, did men persist in settling their political disagreements violently? And what could she, as a woman lacking even the right to vote, do about it? Feeling both politically marginal and morally outraged, she began to rethink what it meant to be a woman. "During the first two thirds of my life," she later explained,

I looked to the masculine ideal of character as the only true one. I sought its inspiration, and referred my merits and demerits to its judicial verdict. In an unexpected hour a new light came to me, showing me a world of thought and of character quite beyond the limits within which I had hitherto been content to abide. The new domain now made clear to me was that of true womanhood—woman no longer in her ancillary relation to her opposite, man, but in her direct relation to the divine plan and purpose, as a free agent, fully sharing with man every human right and every human responsibility. (*Reminiscences*, 372–373)

Borrowing from the evolutionary language popular in her time, Howe proposed that human development consisted of three stages. The first stage was that of primitive animal nature, in which individual men rose to power by brute force. The next stage was that of organized power, in which the "war-ideal, with its rules of loyalty and honor" surpassed the "savagery of primitive man." Thus, she claimed, "the savage individual gives way to the father-ideal, just and noble." Nevertheless, the age of the father-ideal celebrated masculine violence and needed to give way to divine love. "Now where," she asked, "do we find provided in Nature a counter-influence, a passion and power which shall be as conservative of human life as masculine influence is destructive of it?" The answer, of course, was in motherhood, "an organization," she said, "which gives . . . life through months of weariness, through hours of anguish and through years of labor—an organization in which suffering is the parent of love, and all that is endured receives its final crown in the life and love of something other than itself" ("The Woman's Peace Festival," 180). In short, Howe concluded, "The womanly power is that which links the divine to the human soul. God is born of a woman" (Julia Ward Howe Diaries, August 27, 1872). Thus, while God was both father and mother, there was a very real sense in which the maternal side of the divine was superior to the paternal side.

Having discovered these new ways of defining womanhood and motherhood, Howe was quick to put them into practice. In 1870 she called for mothers around the world to organize a crusade on behalf of peace. "My dream," she said, "was of a mighty and august Congress of Mothers, which should constitute a new point of departure for the regeneration of society" (Hall, 42). She held two well-attended meetings in New York City in 1870 to publicize the cause, then traveled to England in

1872, where she organized the first woman's peace congress. Beginning in 1873, she established the tradition of observing a Mothers' Day of Peace in early June. The first Mothers' Day was celebrated in eighteen American cities, as well as in Rome and Constantinople, and friends of peace in Philadelphia continued to observe her Mothers' Day for over fifty years, even forming a Julia Ward Howe Peace Band. She became a vice president of the American Peace Society and gave addresses to the International Peace Congress of 1904.

Howe did not labor alone. Rather, she worked in cooperation with other women to develop a common rhetoric about peace, so that it became second nature to argue that women's higher ethical sensibilities could take hold in American culture only if women were given equal political and social rights with men. Virtually every major reformer in the women's movement—such as Charlotte Perkins Gilman, Jane Addams, Frances Willard, Carrie Chapman Catt, or Anna Howard Shaw—used such language to create an essentialist feminist pacifist rhetoric. The Woman's Christian Temperance Union (WCTU) alone published two monthly peace journals and also had its own Department of Peace and Arbitration, headed by a Quaker named Hannah Bailey. By 1914, the 800,000 members of the Federation of Women's Clubs, plus the 100,000 women in the Council of Mothers, the 325,000 in the WCTU, the 161,000 in the Woman's Relief Corps, and hundreds of thousands in the National Council of Women, were all officially committed to promoting peace. Even the Daughters of the American Revolution (DAR) joined in.

As women began to create their own powerful reform organizations, they also began to find places alongside of men in the more traditional peace societies. The American Peace Society not only began to admit women as members but as early as 1871 allowed women to become officers. The Universal Peace Union, founded by Quaker Alfred Love at the conclusion of the Civil War, welcomed women as members and officers, so much so that by the 1890s half of the membership and one-third of the executive committee were women. Lucia Ames Mead became an important leader in the American Peace Society, and Belva Lockwood (now famous as the first woman to argue a case before the U.S. Supreme Court) served as a lobbyist for the Universal Peace Union. Fanny Fern Andrews, capitalizing on the common perception that the best way to convert people to the cause of peace was to train them in childhood, helped found the American School Peace League in 1908 and developed an extensive curriculum for grades one through twelve that allowed teachers in social studies and the humanities to incorporate peace studies into their everyday teaching.

There were other ways to crusade for peace as well. American women pacifists actively opposed imperialism and spoke out against the Spanish American War and the United States' annexation of the Philippines in the late 1890s. A conference on world peace at The Hague in 1899 sparked a plethora of responses from women reformers, as committees from suffrage groups, women's clubs, and even religious clubs sought to educate the American public about peace. In 1899, a suffrage organization called the International Council of Women (ICW) convened women from around the globe—including the United States and Canada—to focus on issues of peace, violence, and woman suffrage. In 1906 the internationally famous social worker Jane Addams published *Newer Ideals of Peace*, in which she argued that world peace would never come about by traditional pacifist appeals to conscience. Instead, she insisted, "more strenuous forces" must be applied; humanity had at its core an "ancient kindliness" that she called upon people to assert against military ambition and financial greed. What was needed, she said, was a "newer patriotism" that would impel people to unite across national borders in a heroic struggle for peace and social justice. What people needed, in short, was to crusade for peace as vigorously as they were accustomed to waging war. Then, and only then, would a new age arise (Addams, 16–18, 37). Addams believed that women would be in the vanguard of that movement, since they were, after all, the nurturers of every new generation, as well as naturally inclined to cooperate with others for good, rather to compete against them.

The outbreak of World War I in 1914 presented unique challenges and opportunities. On the one hand, it became easier than ever to argue that the "mother half" of humanity had unique capacities to rise above the war fever that infected the men of Europe. On the other hand, so long as Germany was successfully waging war in France, women's pleas for arbitration (the standard pacifist suggestion for adjudicating international tensions) seemed to favor German interests. The closer that the United States came to breaking relations with Germany and entering the war on the Allied side, the more precarious pacifist opposition to the war became. Pacifists risked appearing disloyal, and particularly since the cause of woman suffrage had been so closely tied to the cause of peace, there was real danger that public opposition to pacifism would also be directed at woman suffrage. Despite all the decades of peace advocacy, the reality was that most Americans would support President Woodnow Wilson if war was declared. For some suffrage supporters, it made sense to emphasize and even celebrate the important contributions that women could make to a war effort. If the American public believed that supporting woman suffrage meant supporting a strong national defense, then they would be inclined favorably toward extending to women the right to vote.

As a result, American women reformers did not present a united front during the Great War. To be sure, significant peace advocacy emerged from the beginning. On August 29, 1914—less than a month after war broke out—500 women dressed in mourning paraded down Fifth Avenue in New York City to protest the war. The parade was organized by Fanny Garrison Villard, aged daughter of William Lloyd Garrison. Villard was convinced that the time had come to embrace radical nonresistance, and in January 1915, women came together to form an exclusively female organization called the Woman's Peace Party, with Jane Addams as chair. In April 1915, an international group of women met at The Hague, called for mediation of the European conflict by neutral nations, demanded suffrage for women, and formed an ongoing organization called the International Committee of Women for Permanent Peace.

Reaction in the United States was not favorable. Theodore Roosevelt denounced the women's peace movement as "both silly and base," and the New York *Times* warned that this "mad plan" could only hurt the cause of woman suffrage (Degen, 70, 81). Repeated efforts to persuade President Wilson to serve as a neutral arbitrator failed, and finally in April 1917 (despite the negative vote of the only congresswoman, Jeannette Rankin of Montana), Congress declared war on Germany. In spite of opposition from more radical suffrage workers, as well as the pleas of her sister members of the Woman's Peace Party, Carrie Chapman Catt, leader of the National American Woman Suffrage Association (NAWSA), declared the NAWSA's support for the war and told the nation that the passage of woman suffrage would increase the morale of the hundreds of thousands of American women loyal to the war effort.

Women and men who resisted the war faced great public opposition. Nevertheless, after the armistice in November 1918, women around the globe returned to their efforts to sustain an international organization of women devoted to peace. In May 1919, women from the United States, France, Great Britain, Germany, and other Central Powers nations, as well as others from neutral countries, met in Zürich (with the peripatetic Jane Addams as president) to consider how best to continue their work. They lobbied for more generous terms of peace than those laid out in the Versailles Treaty, urged that the League of Nations include a Women's Charter, and established themselves as the Women's International League for Peace and Freedom (WILPF). The American Emily Greene Balch served as the first secretary-treasurer, and in 1923, the American Dorothy Detzer assumed that position. In 1920, woman suffrage became a reality in the United States, and women peace reformers embarked upon a new stage of peace advocacy.

From One Great War to the Next

Though women reformers continued to work with men in organizations like the American Peace Society, nothing that had happened in the Great War mitigated against the notion that women had a particular calling to resist war and establish peace. By 1924, there were four American peace organizations with exclusively female leadership: the Women's International League for Peace and Freedom, the National Committee on the Cause and Cure of War (NCCCW), the Women's Peace Society (WPS), and the Women's Peace Union (WPU). The latter two groups were more radical in their nonresistance and were thus predictably smaller and shorter lived. The NCCCW was founded in 1924 by Carrie Chapman Catt and shared with the WILPF a willingness to encourage any strategies that might lead to international peace. All four organizations suffered from harassment in the 1920s due to Red-baiting, as groups as wide ranging as the Daughters of the American Revolution, the American Legion, and the State Department suspected that efforts on behalf of international peace and racial equality were supportive of Bolshevism.

The New York branch of the WILPF recruited hundreds of public school teachers into its ranks. More and more, women peace activists were professional women, many active in social work and public school and university teaching. Socialist and labor workers were also attracted. Rose K. Edelman helped found a predominantly Jewish WILPF branch in Brooklyn in 1927, the same year that the United Order of True Sisters, a Jewish philanthropic organization of more than 12,000 members, decided to affiliate itself with the WILPF. The New York chapter of the WILPF also worked to recruit women of color, recognizing that even though the original delegation to Zürich in 1919 had included an African American named Mary Church Terrell, for the most part the work of peace advocacy had been a segregated affair. In the 1930s, the WILPF lobbied for antilynching legislation in Congress, worked to better the situation of southern sharecroppers, and pushed for racial integration of restaurants in Washington, D.C. By 1935–1936, the WILPF had chosen peace, freedom, and justice as its goals, arguing,

We believe that there can be neither peace nor freedom without justice, and that the existing economic system is a challenge to our whole position. It is shot through with force, injustice, and actual violence often employed in the name of public order. Our duty, therefore, and also our opportunity as pacifists, is to work for a better economic and social order by every non-violent means. (Foster, 161–166)

In particular, the league pointed to racial prejudice in American culture as an unethical and cruel form of covert violence.

This brief survey of the four groups with exclusively female leadership does not come close to exhausting women's involvement in peace movements following World War I, for a bewildering array of peace organizations blossomed in the postwar years. The Fellowship of Reconciliation, the War Resisters League, the Emergency Peace Campaign, the National Peace Conference, the Pacifist Action Committee, the National Council for Prevention of War—these names only began the list. Some groups sought to outlaw war, some worked with the League of Nations, some sought to create a World Court, some worked for disarmament, some were relief agencies, and some focused on education. Pacifism was never so attractive to mainline Protestant groups as at the conclusion of the Great War. Moreover, the historic American peace churches, such as the Quakers, the Mennonites, and the Brethren, were particularly active in war relief efforts in Europe, believing that sacrificial service on behalf of others was an essential part of Christian nonresistance. Another important Christian movement, begun in 1933 by Dorothy Day, was the Catholic Worker. Through its newspaper (*Catholic Worker*) and through a national web of Houses of Hospitality designed to serve the urban poor, the Catholic Worker publicized and epitomized a vision of Christian peace and social justice for decades to come.

Thus, unprecedented numbers of women as well as men committed themselves to work for peace in the years following World War I. Historian Charles Chatfield has calculated that by 1933 there were 12 international, 28 national, and 37 local peace societies in the United States, with another 2 international, 56 national, and 51 local groups promoting internationalism, and still another 120 organizations related to peace advocacy (Chatfield, 95). Women were involved at every level, from organizing Pan American conferences with women peace advocates from Latin America to serving as heads of major agencies that worked in coordination with agencies headed by men to serving as volunteers in the task of education and war relief efforts. In short, whether women pacifists believed that, as women, they had unique gifts to offer the cause, or whether they simply saw themselves as colleagues working alongside male pacifists, there had never been so many opportunities to labor on behalf of peace.

Ultimately, of course, the biggest challenge facing pacifists in this period was that of efficacy: Would peace reformers have the political acumen to create and sustain just social orders, or would they be at the mercy of military aggressors? For many pacifists, the answer to that question would be a sorrowful one; faced with the rise of European fascism and the Japanese invasion of Manchuria in the 1930s, they would sadly conclude that only military might could resist aggressor nations. Others were not convinced. They still believed it would be possible to labor for both peace and justice simultaneously; and in the 1950s, the burgeoning civil rights movement would employ just such tactics in its efforts to fight institutionalized racism. But for most American pacifists, World War II marked an unanswerable challenge to their peace convictions. Most Americans saw Allied war efforts as just and necessary, and even though Congresswoman Jeanette Rankin once again voted against American entry into war, most Americans agreed with President Roosevelt when he asked Congress to declare war in December 1941.

Just as in World War I, women were offered noteworthy opportunities for social and political advancement if they supported the national war effort. Not only were jobs in industry opened to women in unprecedented numbers (so that "Rosie the Riveter" entered into the national consciousness), but access to female corps in every major military branch was also available. The chance to do work previously reserved for men promised significant economic and social improvements for women. But pacifists like Dorothy Day urged women to see the new jobs in industry as a government scheme to enslave women to "work in the factories throughout the land to make the bombers, the torpedoes, the explosives, the tools of war" (Goosen, 4). The women of the Women's International League for Peace and Freedom (headed in the United States by Mildred Scott Olmstead, with Dorothy Detzer acting as Washington lobbyist) immediately went to work protesting the enforced removal of Japanese Americans into concentration camps on the West Coast. "I almost dread going down to the camp," one WILPF volunteer noted before a visit to provide supplies. "I keep thinking 'this is a nightmare.' It can't be that my country has put children and women behind barbed wires" (Foster, 299).

One important opportunity available to pacifists was the chance to seek a generous national policy on conscientious objection. The Selective Training and Service Act of 1940 promised to exempt from combat status men opposed to war "by reason of religious training and belief" and to assign them to "work of national importance under civilian direction." Such an act was a significant improvement in conscientious objection policy over that which reigned in World War I, but nevertheless more draftees than ever were denied conscientious objector (CO) status and sent to prison. The WILPF worked throughout the war to improve U.S. policy toward conscientious objection. Women were never subject to the draft—though occasionally that was threatened—but they found a way through the Civilian Public

Service (CPS) to serve as conscientious objectors. The CPS offered alternative service to men from historic peace churches. Wishing to make their own commitment to Christian nonresistance clear, and desiring to share in sacrificial humanitarian service alongside of Christian men, these women either joined their husbands at CO camps or entered volunteer service units themselves. "CO girls" worked as volunteers at mental hospitals and as dietitians, secretaries, and nurses at CPS camps (Goden, 44–93).

When World War II ended with the atomic conflagrations at Hiroshima and Nagasaki, it was predictable that women pacifists would protest the unthinkable destruction of nuclear warfare and that they would commit themselves to offering relief and solace to the many victims of the world's most extensive war. What remained to be seen was how women would find new techniques to work effectively for peace and social justice.

The 1950s and Beyond

The decade following the end of World War II was extraordinarily difficult for American pacifists. Continuing cold war pressures to build up the military, the outbreak of the Korean War in 1950, and widespread suspicions encouraged by McCarthyism that peace activism was pro communist combined to discourage peace advocacy. That Emily Greene Balch was awarded a Nobel Peace Prize in 1946 did not protect the Women's International League for Peace and Freedom from public apprehension that the organization was sympathetic to communism, and shorter-lived groups like the Congress of American Women (CAW) and American Women for Peace (AWP) that started in the 1950s faced considerable opposition. Even scientists who had helped create the nuclear bomb fell under suspicion when they lobbied for a reduction in the arms race. Nevertheless, women pacifists found ways even in these grim days to take action in the cause of peace, and with the atmospheric detonation of the hydrogen bomb in 1957, peace advocacy found renewed vigor.

Dorothy Day's Catholic Worker was one pacifist organization that maintained a relatively high profile even in the early 1950s. Though Federal Bureau of Investigation (FBI) agents regularly visited the *Catholic Worker* offices in New York, Day and her paper continued their support for peace. (After one visit, when the FBI interrogator displayed his pistol and declared his willingness to defend himself, Day later remarked, "How brave a man, defending himself with his gun against us unarmed women and children hereabouts" [Roberts, 17].) To oppose communist bashing, Catholic Workers regularly spoke at May Day rallies, and they looked for ways to

take direct action against militarism. Beginning in 1955, as civil defense planners began holding nationwide air raid drills to train Americans how to act in case of a nuclear attack, Day and other pacifists openly refused to cooperate, sitting calmly in public areas, while everyone around them scrambled to reach bomb shelters. Day said their actions were "an act of public penance for having been the first people in the world to drop the atom bomb, and to make the hydrogen bomb" (17).

For applied pacifism, however, nothing could top the burgeoning civil rights movement. Not so much a peace movement as a campaign that for ethical and strategic purposes adopted nonviolent direct action as its modus operandi, the civil rights movement of the 1950s and 1960s provided the clearest example in American history of the power of nonviolence to effect political and social change. Adhering to biblical principles of justice and love, hundreds of thousands of Americans marched, protested, boycotted, and worked in voter registration campaigns to extend full citizenship to African Americans. Though the most public figures in the civil rights movement were men—particularly clergy—the backbone consisted of women. From the working-class women who filled the ranks of marchers to the female students brave enough to integrate public elementary and high schools to the professional women of the Montgomery Women's Political Counsel who acted as "trailblazers" for the celebrated bus boycott of 1955–1956 to articulate college women like Diane Nash, whose work in the Student Nonviolent Coordinating Committee (SNCC) was pivotal in desegregating southern lunch counters and buses, women were absolutely pivotal in the work of what participants would come to call the "Movement." Particularly in the early 1960s, the Movement would bring into common cause an astonishing variety of people of different races, religions, educational attainments, regional backgrounds, and socioeconomic status.

The Student Nonviolent Coordinating Committee was the civil rights organization in which it was easiest for women to assume positions of leadership, but by 1965 tensions in the group were high. As early as 1964, Mary King and Casey Hayden (two white female SNCC staffers) had written that SNCC women were denied equal power with men. "The woman in SNCC," they argued, "is often in the same position as that token Negro hired in a corporation. The management thinks that it has done its bit. Yet, every day the Negro bears an atmosphere, attitudes and actions which are tinged with condescension and paternalism" (Evans, 86). By 1965, burned out by grueling work and unsure that the Movement was still effecting progress, SNCC staffers evidenced racial tensions, too, and it was no longer clear to all that nonviolent direct action was the best strategy for black liberation. In time, both in SNCC and in the larger civil rights movement, the coalition that had united whites and blacks in common cause fell apart. African American reform was headed in the direction of black nationalism and black power; white civil rights workers transferred their commitment to nonviolent social change to another target: the war in Vietnam.

Women in the mid-1960s who turned their attention to the war discovered that women peace activists before them had prepared the ground well. In November 1961—long before U.S. troop acceleration in Vietnam—50,000 American women belonging to an organization called Women Strike for Peace had walked out of their jobs and their homes to demand nuclear disarmament. The 1963 Soviet/American test ban treaty was in part an answer to the fears expressed in that walkout. Once American involvement in Vietnam became heated, Women Strike for Peace as well as other traditional women's pacifist groups like the WILPF protested American involvement in a variety of ways. They organized opposition to the draft as well as to the war itself. In this most unpopular of American conflicts, organized protests against war (at least to *this* war, if not all wars) reached a zenith. The list of significant persons in American religious life who contributed to the antiwar movement would run for pages.

One of the results was an abiding suspicion of what President Dwight D. Eisenhower had earlier coined "the military-industrial complex." Even after the end of the war in Vietnam, many women peace activists wanted to continue their witness for peace. By now, women's studies and peace studies were coming into their own as academic disciplines, and it was possible to talk more broadly about the relationship between gender and militarism. The innate hierarchy of the military, the phallocentric language used to describe its weaponry, its goals of mastery and domination, its celebration of violence—all of those factors characterized what many women pacifists came to call "patriarchy." For them, patriarchy described the reality of male-dominated cultures and institutions; militarism was just one example. Other examples included domestic violence against women, racial and gender discrimination, and the industrial abuse of the natural world. Simply to be a woman in the United States was to be subject to constant institutionalized violence. So long as patriarchy ruled, violence would thrive.

It was natural for such analysis to prompt women peace activists to turn to the arms race and to ecofeminism (a "convergence of feminism, ecology, and peace"). By the 1980s, women in both religious and secular organizations were pushing hard for a nuclear freeze—a moratorium on the development and production of nuclear weapons. These efforts were most spectacularly visible in the Women's Pentagon Action, a gathering of thousands of women who encircled the Pentagon in 1980 in an attempt to draw attention to the violence and abuse inherent in U.S. military policy.

> We are gathering at the Pentagon on Nov. 16 because we fear for our lives. We fear for the life of this planet, our Earth, and the life of the children who are our human future. . . . We have come to mourn and rage and defy the Pentagon because it is the workplace of the imperial power which threatens us all. . . . We want to know what anger in these men, what fear, which can only be satisfied by destruction, what coldness of heart and ambition drives their days. We want to know because we do not want that dominance which is exploitative and murderous in international relations, and so dangerous to women and children at home—we do not want that sickness transferred by this violent society through the fathers to the sons. (King, 284, 287)

Opposition to the arms race was furthered by a pastoral letter critical of militarism and condemnatory of nuclear war issued by the Catholic bishops of the United States in 1983. Bishops in the United Methodist Church wrote a pastoral letter sympathetic to the theological analysis of the Catholic bishops' letter. In some ways, it seemed as though the United States had never been so open to critique of the war system.

But other developments weakened those hopes. The end of the cold war in the 1980s was credited not to the efforts of peace advocates but to President Ronald Reagan's extraordinary military expenditures; ironically, the standoff between the United States and the USSR was resolved because the USSR drained its treasury and ruined its economy trying to keep pace in its arms race with the United States. Moreover, developing feminist theory did not always push women in peaceful directions. For some women who wished to achieve political equality with men, enhanced opportunity for military careers was one of the welcome developments of the 1980s and 1990s. NOW (the National Organization for Women), one of the most powerful women's groups, proclaimed its support for women in the military, and from time to time discussions arose about compulsory military service for women if the draft were ever reintroduced. At the end of the twentieth century, seeking equality with men could lead women to war as well as to peace.

Clearly, the final story on women and peace movements in North America has not been written. Nevertheless, a consistent pattern has emerged. From the start of organized North American peace movements in 1815,

During the 1970s to the mid-1980s, women in the United States made ecofeminist connections within environmental and feminist movements as well as from anti-militarist, peace, anti-nuclear, and anti-racist initiatives. For them, ecofeminism represented types of social action where gender and environment intersected. *Courtesy of Joan E. Biren.*

women peace activists used a variety of arguments against war. Often they argued as women and particularly as mothers, keeping alive the essentialist notion that, unlike men, women innately were pacific. At other times, women reformers abandoned essentialist notions and described peace as universal human possibility, not as a unique temperament peculiar to females. No matter what strategies women used, they faced a reality that emerged early on with the Grimké sisters: that is, that even in a democracy they were second-class citizens. If women wished to be heard—and certainly if they wished to be taken seriously—they would have to find ways to empower themselves politically so that their voices mattered. In a nation that assumed a strong military was crucial to prosperity, voices to the contrary, particularly if they were women's voices, would always have to struggle to be heard—perhaps never more so than at the beginning of the twenty-first century, when the model of women as warriors threatens to supersede the model of women as the peaceful mother half of humanity.

SOURCES: Relatively little work has been done on this topic. The archival collections at the Swarthmore College Peace Library, the Schlesinger Library of American Women's History at Radcliffe, and the Houghton Library at Harvard are teeming with unexplored documents and should be the first point of reference for primary source research on women and peace movements in North America. Sources cited in this essay include: for the American Peace Society, *The Advocate of Peace*, no. 1 (June, 1837); and for William Ladd, Philanthropos [William Ladd], *On the Duty of Females to Promote the Cause of Peace* (1836, repr. 1971). For the Grimké sisters, see Angelina Grimké in *Letters of Theodore Dwight Weld, Angela Grimké Weld, and Sarah Grimké, 1822–1824* (1934) and Sarah Grimké, *Letters on the Equality of the Sexes and the Condition of Woman* (1838). For debates over gender equality and slavery between the American Peace Society and immediatist abolitionists like William Lloyd Garrison and the members of the New England Non-Resistance Society, see Valarie H. Ziegler, *The Advocates of Peace in Antebellum America* (1992, 2001); Dorothy C. Bass, " 'In Christian Firmness and Christian Meekness': Feminism and Pacifism in Antebellum America," in *Immaculate and Powerful: The Female in Sacred Image and Social Reality*, ed. Clarissa W. Atkinson, Constance H. Buchanan, and Margaret R. Miles (1985); and Dorothy Sterling, *Ahead of Her Time: Abby Kelley and the Politics of Antislavery* (1991). For examples of Ward's evolutionary theories put to use to defend feminism and pacifism, see the works of Charlotte Perkins Gilman, especially *The Man-Made World: Or, Our Androcentric Culture* (1911), *Women and Economics: A Study of the Economic Relation between Men and Women as a Factor in Social Evolution*

(1898), and *His Religion and Hers: A Study in the Faith of Our Fathers and the Work of Our Mothers* (1923). For Julia Ward Howe, see Julia Ward Howe, *Reminiscences, 1819–1899* (1899); "The Woman's Peace Festival—Mrs. Howe's Address," *The Woman's Journal* 6.23 (June 5, 1875); Julia Ward Howe Diaries, August 27, 1872, Howe Family Papers, Houghton Library, Harvard University; Florence Howe Hall, *Julia Ward Howe and the Woman Suffrage Movement* (1913, 1969); and Valarie H. Ziegler, *Diva Julia: The Public Romance and Private Agony of Julia Ward Howe* (2003). For rich materials on Fanny Fern Andrews and the American School Peace League, consult the archives of the Schlesinger Library at Radcliffe College. Citations from Jane Addams come from her *Newer Ideals of Peace* (1906). For the Woman's Peace Party, see Mary Louise Degen, *The History of the Woman's Peace Party* (1939). For the WILPF, see Carrie A. Foster, *The Women and the Warriors: The U.S. Section of the Women's International League for Peace and Freedom, 1915–1946* (1996). For additional consideration of the interwar years, see Charles Chatfield, *For Peace and Justice: Pacifism in America, 1914–1941* (1971). Rachel Waltner Goosen's *Women against the Good War: Conscientious Objection and Gender on the American Home Front, 1941–1947* (1997) is the most comprehensive study of women and conscientious objection in World War II. Quotations from Dorothy Day are from Nancy L. Roberts, "Journalism and Activism: Dorothy Day's Response to the Cold War," *Peace & Change* 2.1–2 (1987): 13–27. Citations related to SNCC and feminism are from Sara Evans, *Personal Politics: The Roots of Women's Liberation in the Civil Rights Movement and the New Left* (1979). For the definition of ecofeminism and quotations from the Women's Pentagon Action, see Ynestra King, "If I Can't Dance In Your Revolution, I'm Not Coming," in *Rocking the Ship of State: Toward a Feminist Peace Politics*, ed. Adrienne Harris and Ynestra King (1991).

THE SETTLEMENT HOUSE MOVEMENT
Eleanor J. Stebner

THE SETTLEMENT HOUSE movement began in the final decades of the nineteenth century. Many women participated as it provided them a way to address a variety of concerns related to urbanization and industrialization, education and health, immigration and poverty, democracy and reform. In turn, the movement enabled women to develop leadership skills, networks, and independent living communities.

Although the movement waned after the first decades of the twentieth century, many of its methods and goals became incorporated within North American institutional systems. Settlement houses often developed into neighborhood and community centers. Volunteer (or leisured) settlement workers became paid social workers. And programs organized and operated by settlements were assumed by government or public agencies. The movement contributed to the formation of the so-called modern welfare state, the professionalization of social work, and the development of the academic discipline of applied sociology. Success in addressing issues such as the need for kindergartens, city parks, housing regulations, industrial health standards, and proper garbage collection may have contributed to the movement's own decline. Other factors, including the inability to fully support racial equality and integration in a timely fashion, also affected its viability in the post–World War I era. Settlement houses, however, continued to exist in the twenty-first century. The International Federation of Settlements and Neighbourhood Centres (IFS) is located in Toronto, Ontario, to facilitate the work of community-based, multipurpose organizations and connect houses and centers scattered throughout the world in voluntary associations. The federation is currently experiencing its fastest growth in eastern and central Europe.

One of the most famous settlement houses ever founded was Hull House, located in Chicago. Opened by Jane Addams and Ellen Gates Starr in 1889, Hull House developed into a huge institution, and Addams became one of the most well known women in North America. Few other settlement houses were as large and prestigious as Hull House. Indeed, most settlement houses were small, modest, and known only within their particular communities. Many were explicitly religious, even though such houses were not officially numbered within formal settlement statistics. Furthermore, dozens of settlement houses—unlike Hull House—did not endure for decades and did not become powerful institutions. Likewise, many of the workers who staffed them did not spend their entire adult lives associated with a particular house. The movement was broader and more diverse than exemplified by Hull House and Addams.

As a response to the tremendous crises of the late nineteenth and early twentieth century, the settlement house movement relied on the skills, energy, imagination, and leadership of women. While both women and men participated in it, the majority of settlement house workers were women; most also were white, Christian Protestant, and middle class. Particularly active in the movement was the first generation of college-educated women in North America. Thousands of unknown women and children, however, participated in settlement houses and were shaped by their experiences.

Settlement houses were not considered alternatives to religious institutions (such as churches, missions, or parishes) or religious practices (such as attending mass or worship). Yet many people understood them to be the practice grounds of religious life. In their creation of space for social and educational activities, the sharing of knowledge, and the advocacy of common concerns, settlement houses were said to encompass neighborliness. Early settlement leaders argued that neighborliness transcended religious divisions and embodied the root purpose of all religions. Whether or not such an interpretation is valid remains disputed, since some scholars argue that settlement houses—in their desire to form spaces free from religious dialogue or teachings—ultimately contributed to the secularizing of North American society.

Beginnings in England

While the settlement house movement came to thrive in North America and came to be staffed mostly by women, it started in England among university men. The first official settlement house in the English-speaking world was opened in 1884 in Whitechapel, one of the most impoverished areas of London. Named Toynbee Hall—in honor of an Oxford student who had studied the conditions resulting from the Industrial Revolution and laissez-faire capitalism—it was opened under the leadership of Samuel and Henrietta (Rowland) Barnett.

Samuel Barnett was appointed vicar of the St. Jude's parish in Whitechapel in 1873. A Christian socialist, he had been influenced by the philosophy of Thomas Carlyle, the economic ponderings of John Stuart Mill, and the social reform critique of John Ruskin. He was also influenced by the life and work of Edward Denison who, in 1865, lived in the slums of East London and published his insights. Denison, with the aid of Ruskin, first verbalized the idea of male university students living among the impoverished classes for the purpose of sharing their culture and providing them with education. Henrietta Rowland (1851–1936), before her marriage to Barnett, had worked with reformer Octavia Hill in addressing slum housing conditions. Like her husband, she was committed to ideals of social reform and proved an especially strong proponent of the movement through her writings, speaking engagements, and labor protests.

The Barnetts argued that the huge gap between the classes could be bridged by elite men settling among the poor. To this end, they established a residence near their parish and recruited Oxford and Cambridge students to live there for the length of their vacations or longer. Toynbee Hall became the home of about fifteen men, most of whom were graduate students or men of the leisure class (i.e., men who did not have to work because they possessed inherited or invested wealth). These men established a library, formed clubs, and gave lectures to working men.

Toynbee Hall did not offer charity or relief, welfare or handouts. It aimed instead to be a place where members of the educated and privileged classes would mingle with their lower-class neighbors, learn something of life from them, and transmit something of "higher culture" to them. The movement was based on an understanding of society as an organic whole that required all classes of people in order to function. Containing elements of Romanticism, it upheld beauty as innate to the natural order and necessary to human life and well-being. The movement did not aim to create social or economic equality but, rather, to increase interclass understandings and interclass cooperation.

Gender based, classist, and somewhat paternalistic from its beginnings, the movement upheld a hierarchical understanding of the world and advocated for gradual reform, not revolution. In the United States, Jane Addams argued that the goal of the movement was to extend democracy, which she upheld as the basis of social ethical order. She understood settlement houses as making democracy more democratic by expanding it beyond the simple (and symbolic) use of the ballot and incorporating it within social relationships. Most settlement workers viewed democracy not only as an ideal political system (although in need of some correction and requiring full participation) but as a social spirit. In theory, all citizens were to contribute to the democratic process and thereby advance the common good.

While settlement houses affirmed particular status quo views of society and social order, they also critiqued certain aspects of society, such as common charitable practices and the divisiveness of nineteenth-century religion. Although the practice of elite men going into slums was based in part on already existing patterns of college missions, and although the Barnetts understood Toynbee Hall as an extension of their Christian identity, they thought it best to separate the work of the settlement house from the official work of their parish. Not all participants agreed. Within weeks of the establishment of Toynbee Hall, a group of individuals broke away from it to found Oxford House, a house that offered religious instruction. The place of religion within settlement houses would prove to be an ongoing debate.

Growth of the Movement

From 1884, hundreds of settlement houses were founded in the United Kingdom, Europe, and North America. Distinctions were made in the early years between different kinds of houses. University settlements were founded and operated by university men. College settlements were founded and operated by women, many (though not all) of whom were college educated; these houses were also called women's settlements. Educational settlements became common in northern and middle Europe and were tied to the development of adult educational programs. Church settlements were founded by particular congregations or denominations and staffed and funded by proponents of them. The term *social settlement* was used to communicate the overarching purpose of these houses, as involving social or democratic concern.

In North America, the movement rapidly expanded during the last decade of the 1890s and the first decade of the twentieth century. According to official statistics, in 1890 there were 3 settlement houses; in 1900, over 100; and in 1910, more than 400. Hundreds of other settlements existed, however, that were not included in the 1911 *Handbook of Settlements* because they had explicit religious ties; this included about two dozen Roman Catholic settlements and innumerable settlements operated by black churches or black church–related institutions in the southern part of the United States.

Settlement houses were opened in medium-sized cities and in large cities. Allen F. Davis, an important scholar of the movement, stated that houses were mostly located in the Northwest and Midwest regions of the United States, with very few located in the South or on the West Coast; those located in the South, he argued, were mostly "modified missions" and therefore were of "very little importance" (Davis, 23). Elisabeth Lasch-Quinn, who reexamined the movement twenty-five years after Davis, argued that the movement was not nearly as "secular, urban, and northern" as many people—including early settlement leaders themselves—suggested; such a bias, however, worked to systematically exclude many southern black settlements from consideration (Lasch-Quinn, 7).

The movement expanded in the United States during the time period referred to as the Progressive Era. Between the end of the Civil War and the end of World War I (circa 1865 to 1920), urbanization, immigration, and industrialization resulted in tremendous societal changes. Middle-class women became involved in numerous social, religious, and cultural movements, including temperance, sabbatarianism, and suffrage. While settlement houses were part of an atmosphere indicative of unrest and discontent, they also marked a positive belief that society could be improved and individuals mobilized in the establishment of a better world. Such optimism fueled Progressivism. In Canada, where a political progressive movement did not emerge until the 1920s, settlement houses were tied to reform movements located mostly within Protestant churches, religious missions, and student organizations. In general, settlement houses in the United States were more politically involved than settlement houses in either Great Britain or Canada.

Although the movement was based on the establishment of local houses within specific communities, national, international, and civic links were established. The first informal gathering of North American settlement workers was held in 1892, and in 1908, twenty

settlement workers from New York, Chicago, and Boston gathered to discuss cooperative ventures. This latter meeting resulted in the 1911 formation of the National Federation of Settlements and the publication of the *Handbook of Settlements*. The first international gathering of settlement workers occurred in London in 1922 and resulted in the 1926 formation of the International Association of Settlements, precursor to the International Federation of Settlements (f. 1946). Settlement houses in metropolitan areas also formed alliances and associations through which they advocated for shared concerns.

The number of settlements remained relatively stable between the 1920s and the end of World War II, at which time the national federation dropped residency as a requirement for houses. This redefinition allowed the inclusion of neighborhood and community centers. It also, however, indicated a shift away from emphasizing interaction with neighbors to working with clients and the transition of settlement workers into social or community workers.

Residents and Residency

Settlement houses relied on middle- and upper-middle-class people moving into and establishing homes in poorer neighborhoods. Settling in poorer neighborhoods was intended to give people of privilege an enlarged perspective on life and facilitate informal interaction between them and the nonprivileged. Residency was deemed essential. Yet even in the early decades, not all people active in the movement lived in settlement houses. Furthermore, not all settlement residents interacted with their neighbors in an everyday fashion; the gulfs created by class, race, and education often limited such knowledge of one another. Yet residency made settlement houses unique from charitable organizations and Christian missions in the late nineteenth and early twentieth century and from the later-mid-twentieth-century neighborhood centers.

A particular house may have had only two or three residents, or it may have had twenty or thirty. Most residents worked at jobs outside of the house and paid room and board. Residents provided the major labor pool of the house; they planned the programs and staffed the clubs and engaged in social research and political lobbying. Usually one resident was named as head resident and assumed overall administrative responsibilities. The head resident exerted great influence in establishing the tone of the house and often was responsible for recruiting its residents. Settlement houses were hierarchical in structure, although some operated with a degree of mutual decision making among coresidents. While the head worker often reported to a board of directors—most of whom did not live in the neighborhood—neighborhood people held no formal representative voice in the organizational structure. Neither were the skills and talents of neighbors used in the programming elements of the house itself. Principles of self-direction and self-representation became common only in recent decades.

Despite such shortcomings, houses were experiments in collective living and were sought-after residencies, especially by young adult women. Indeed, settlement houses provided acceptable living locations for college-educated single women who desired not to live within a traditional nuclear household. While such houses may have replicated women's college dormitories, they provided a necessary, enjoyable, and financially reasonable living option in an era that lacked independent living spaces for women. Some houses also addressed the need for living facilities for the women in their neighborhood through establishing working women's cooperative apartments. By the time residency was dropped by settlement houses, professional, unmarried, and working women had a variety of housing alternatives unavailable to earlier generations.

Settlement Workers

Most settlement workers were under the age of thirty, and about 90 percent were university or college educated. Some of the men involved in the movement had studied theology and had originally intended to enter ordained Christian ministry. While most individuals were unmarried when they became active in settlement houses, some found their future marriage partners in settlement work. A substantial number of women active in settlement houses remained unmarried; as one scholar stated, "[W]omen married the settlement; men did not" (Kraus, 142). Single settlement women often established their most significant emotional and personal relationships with other women. Boston marriages—referring to two women living together in long-term unions—were rather common among career settlement women. Such relationships were probably both romantic and platonic and therefore cannot simply be classified as lesbian. Nevertheless, a significant percentage of settlement women established such partnerships.

Involvement in the movement gave participants a sense of importance and a sense of contributing to a cause greater than themselves. The first generation of settlement house workers were mostly Protestant in religious affiliation, and some participated in the movement as an alternative to the foreign missionary service of the previous generation. In a poll conducted in 1906, nearly all of the 339 settlement house workers questioned stated that religion was a major influence in their decision to join the movement. Many settlement workers upheld an ideal of service or usefulness and had been instilled with values that beckoned their social and political involvement. While residents exhibited a variety of motives—some were simply interested in the experience of "slumming" or desirous of an adventure beyond normative middle-class propriety—long-term residents exhibited strong elements of altruism.

Between 1889 and 1914, two-fifths of residents were women. Such women had limited employment opportunities beyond household work and grade school teaching. Settlement houses enlarged their employment possibilities and provided them with invaluable work experiences, which often enabled them to develop professional expertise in unique fields of interest. For black women, who had fewer choices for professional development than even white women, settlement work offered opportunities mostly unavailable in dominant white society. Most head residents were women. With the transition of settlement houses into neighborhood centers, head residents were replaced by executive directors; most executive director positions were then filled by men.

Activities and Programs of Settlement Houses

No predetermined agenda was set for settlement houses. Lea Taylor (1883–1975) of The Chicago Commons settlement wrote that since settlements signified a "way of life," their principles were more important than their activities or programs (Pacey, 245). Other settlement house folks verbalized the same idea, yet most houses became characterized by similar activities and programs. Most houses formed clubs for working men, young mothers, boys, and girls. Larger houses developed clubs based on shared interests in music, drama, sports, debate, philosophy, cooking, and politics. Clubs were central to settlement houses because they represented the method whereby individuals socialized and learned from one another; they also became the way white Anglo-Saxon culture was to be transmitted to new immigrants. Connected to clubs were lectures given by experts in particular topics.

Some settlement houses were founded with a particular focus. Henry Street Settlement, founded by Lillian Wald (1867–1940) and her friend Mary Brewster in 1893, for example, initiated the profession of home and community or public nursing, although it still organized a full slate of activities, including educational, vocational, and social programs. The Henry Street Settlement even opened the first public playground in the United States in 1902. Wald herself, in addition to being a nurse and head resident, was active in numerous committees and causes, including the movement to prohibit child labor. Like many settlement leaders, Wald argued that her involvement in broader social and political issues resulted from her settlement house ties and her desire to better the future lives of babies being born in her Manhattan neighborhood.

In comparison to settlement houses in Great Britain, North American houses tended to focus more intensively on women and children. As in Great Britain, problems related to industrialization and urbanization were a major concern of residents, yet in North America these issues were inevitably tied to immigration; and the majority of immigrants living in North American cities were women and children. North American houses also tended to place less emphasis on maintaining class structures than their English counterparts and were reputed to be places where reform was valued as highly as residency and any possible research findings resulting from residency. Indeed, much research regarding topics such as poverty and unemployment, alcoholism, and drug usage was first conducted by settlement house residents. The most well known publications include *Hull-House Maps and Papers* (1895), *City Wilderness* (edited by Robert A. Woods, 1898), and *My Neighbour* (by J. S. Woodsworth, 1911).

Settlement Houses and Religion

The words *sectarian* and *nonsectarian* were used to distinguish between religious and nonreligious houses. The 1911 guidelines of the movement excluded sectarian houses or houses that engaged in religious activities. While noting a difference between financial support provided by religious groups and the offering of religious programs, houses hosting religious programs were excluded from official status. Consequently, houses located in African American neighborhoods (which were often connected to congregations or industrial schools), those operated by the Roman Catholic Church in the United States, and those operated by the Presbyterian Church in Canada were not considered authentic settlements.

Many Protestant denominations, from the Unitarians to the Episcopalians to the Seventh Day Adventists, opened settlement houses. Of the 167 religious settlement houses listed in the *Handbook of Settlements*—meaning that they received church funding but did not engage in religious programs—31 were Methodist, 29 were Episcopalian, 20 were Presbyterian, and 10 were Congregational. Settlement houses were popular among certain Protestants because they augmented the Social Gospel movement. While the Social Gospel movement was dominated by white men, women settlement leaders were influenced by its ideals and became proponents of it. They embraced its goal of correcting both individual

and social sins and viewed their work as the application of Christianity; they believed that they were working to build the "kingdom of God," a major Social Gospel tenet.

It is hard to determine the number of sectarian versus nonsectarian houses founded. In New York City between the years 1886 and 1914, thirty-six nonsectarian settlements were founded, as were ten Roman Catholic houses and about thirty other sectarian houses. Jewish houses also existed, some of which were considered settlement houses because they offered cultural but not religious elements. (The Educational Alliance in New York City, upheld as one of the most important Jewish settlements by Jews, was excluded from the national federation because it was nonresidential.) Sectarian houses probably dominated the movement in the southern United States. Churchwomen's organizations, such as the Woman's Home Mission Society of the Methodist Episcopal Church South, sponsored settlement houses. Black and white women engaged in settlement work were often supported by organizations such as the Young Women's Christian Association and the National Urban League.

The lines between sectarian and nonsectarian houses —between missions and settlements—were blurred in the late nineteenth and early twentieth century. Official settlement spokespersons emphasized, however, their different purposes. Samuel Barnett stated that the object of missions is conversion, while the object of settlement houses is mutual knowledge, and that missions exist to create and support institutional structures, while settlement houses exist to facilitate interpersonal relations and human contact. Jane Addams argued that missions exist to convert people to a particular view, while settlements exist to identify the needs of a neighborhood and thereby improve social conditions. Mary Simkhovitch wrote that settlement houses are not "propagandist institution[s]" and that it is the role of churches—not settlements—to hold religious services (Holden, 192). Despite such defensive statements, nonsectarian houses were criticized by some religious leaders because of their attempt to be religiously neutral.

The irony was that settlement houses and missions often looked the same to neighbors; both usually offered educational classes, health programs, recreational activities, and so on. The formation of so-called institutional churches (local parishes that offered programming for neighborhood folks) added to the mix. Another irony loomed, however. Since many residents were Christian Protestant and held a Western worldview, suspicions lurked that even houses considered nonsectarian engaged in covert evangelism. Indeed, Roman Catholic priests and bishops suspected that settlement houses located in predominantly Roman Catholic immigrant neighborhoods engaged in proselytism, simply because most of their residents were Protestant. In response, the Roman Catholic Church opened hundreds of settlement houses, most of which were connected to schools and parishes; they sponsored numerous clubs and offered countless programs but also held catechism classes.

Nonsectarianism was stressed by official leaders of the movement because they saw religion as so divisive among the people in their neighborhoods. Religious antagonisms and prejudices existed between Christians and Jews, Protestants and Catholics, and between the various Protestant denominations. Religion was seen as inhibiting dialogue and the democratic process of settlement houses. The decision to deal with religious divisions by ignoring them may have resulted in the negation of religion for individual people and for society at large. While not the intent of the official policy or individual settlement leaders, their emphasis on nonsectarianism may have contributed to later secularization trends in society.

Houses and Leaders in the United States

The first settlement house opened in North America was Neighborhood Guild, later renamed University Settlement. Located in New York City, it was started in 1886 by Stanton Coit (after he had visited Toynbee Hall) as a house for university and neighborhood men. During 1888 and 1889, however, Jane E. Robbins and Jean Fine lived opposite the house and established activities for girls. In 1887 Vida Scudder took steps to establish the settlement house movement in North America. As a Smith College graduate who had studied in Oxford under John Ruskin, Scudder gathered with three other alumnae to discuss "the new economics, the new awakening of practical philanthropy in England, Toynbee Hall and the principles for which it stood" (Woods and Kennedy, 2). They decided to support the settlement house idea and prepared to organize and sponsor such work. Although the College Settlements Association was not formally organized until 1890, Scudder's network of alumnae from northeastern women's colleges opened College Settlement in New York City in 1889.

Located close to Neighborhood Guild, College Settlement drew upon the talent and presence of Jane Robbins and Jean Fine (Spahr). Robbins (1860–1946), who had attended Smith College and had taught school before studying medicine at the Woman's Medical College of the New York Infirmary, became one of the first residents of the house and, in 1894, its head worker. Fine (b. 1861), the first head worker at the settlement, was a college friend of Robbins and also a schoolteacher before becoming involved in the house. Robbins and Fine viewed their settlement house work as an extension of their Christian faith. The College Settlement was based

on the desire of several young privileged women who wanted to "approximate a 'more Christ-like life,'" Robbins stated (James, 3: 172).

Vida Scudder (1861–1954) was key in the establishment of the North American settlement idea and worked to form networks and financial support. She was also key in the 1893 founding of Denison House in Boston. Teaming with Helena Dudley (1858–1932), who became its head worker, Scudder was active in its everyday operations, even though she herself never lived in the house. Rather, Scudder lived for decades with her mother and taught English at Wellesly College. At the same time, her settlement house involvements became the basis of larger and increasingly radical political, religious, and social stances. The settlement house movement provided Scudder with a supportive community of peers and friends and was her major source of education regarding social realities.

Although their involvements varied, Vida Scudder, Jane Robbins, and Jean Fine remained connected to settlement houses for their entire lives. As reported in the 1894 College Settlements Association Fourth Report, they saw the establishment of settlement houses as a "great modern movement" that "touch[ed] them with a common sympathy, and inspire[d] them with a common ideal" (Woods and Kennedy, 2). They were drawn to its theoretical and theological foundations and its pragmatic (or hands-on) approach to social problems. They were also excited about participating in what they deemed a significant movement.

Such women were active in settlement houses, even though many of them still participated in church-related activities. The prohibitions on women's participation and leadership in Christian churches did not offer them as many opportunities for intense involvement. Although some Christian women became foreign or home missionaries and some trained and worked as deaconesses—the latter often within city missions or even settlement houses—many Christian women became settlement workers as a way to apply their Christian ideals of service and commitment. Settlement houses solicited their leadership skills and granted them opportunities largely unavailable in church work.

In 1889—the same year that College Settlement was opened in New York City—Jane Addams (1860–1935) and Ellen Gates Starr (1859–1940) rented space in a Chicago house and opened what they referred to as their Toynbee Experiment. The settlement became known as Hull House and expanded to include thirteen buildings. While the idea of opening a settlement was probably Addams's idea, without the support of Starr—and her church and society connections within the City of Chicago—Hull House may not have flourished as it did. Known as a "salon in the slums," it became a gathering place not only for thousands of neighborhood folks but also for the visitations of the rich and famous, who often stopped by the house to chat with residents and see what was happening.

Hull House attracted an amazing number and variety of residents. Although both women and men were residents (although housed in different buildings of the settlement), women remained its central leaders. Alice Hamilton (1869–1970) and Grace Abbott (1878–1939) are two such examples. Hamilton moved to Hull House in 1897 as a young medical doctor. She studied the typhoid epidemic and cocaine trade in the neighborhood and eventually became an expert in occupational (or work-related) diseases. Grace Abbott moved to Chicago in 1907 to pursue a master's degree in political science at the University of Chicago and became a resident at Hull House in 1908. Through her Hull House association, Abbott integrated her intellectual ideas with social analysis. She studied the abuses experienced by recent immigrants and wrote numerous reports, articles, and a book titled *The Immigrant and the Community* (1917). Neither Hamilton nor Abbott lived at Hull House for their entire lives. Hamilton moved on to become the first woman professor at Harvard University. Abbott accepted a position with the federal Children's Bureau (then headed by Julia Lathrop, another former Hull House resident) and eventually served as its head for thirteen years; she eventually returned to Chicago and taught public welfare in the School of Social Services Administration. Involvement in Hull House helped such women define and develop their own fields of professional expertise.

While Hull House was the first settlement house founded in Chicago, other settlement houses were soon established. These included university settlements, Christian Social Gospel settlements, Roman Catholic settlements, Jewish settlements, and African American settlements. The University of Chicago Settlement, for example, was opened in 1894 under the leadership of Mary McDowell (1854–1936). McDowell had previously worked for the Woman's Christian Temperance Union and had done a kind of internship at Hull House. In her years as head resident, McDowell became known as an intense advocate for her neighbors. She led a campaign against open garbage pits and creeks used as sewers. She became involved in establishing unions for women and was active in the Progressive Party in 1912. She was one of the founders of the National Association for the Advancement of Colored People (NAACP) and, in 1919, formed the Interracial Cooperative Committee, which brought together black and white women club members to advocate for shared concerns. McDowell, like other settlement workers, believed that the democratic process could correct the wrongs of injustice, but such a process demanded active involvement.

The Chicago Commons became another well-known Chicago social settlement. Opened in 1894 under the leadership of Graham Taylor, professor at the Chicago Theological Seminary, the Commons embodied an evangelical Social Gospel spirit. Seminary students were involved in it and from it researched social and theological issues. The Commons relied not only on the leadership of Taylor but on the presence and work of his wife, Leah (Demarest) Graham, and their four children. One of their children, Lea Demarest Taylor (1883–1975), became head resident of the Commons in 1922, a position she held for over thirty years. Leah Taylor has often been overlooked in favor of the leadership and writings of her more well known father, yet her contributions to the movement were significant. Few settlements in North America included husband and wife teams, and even fewer included traditional nuclear family units living in residency. Mary Simkhovitch, for example, who founded Greenwich House (New York City), did not share her work with her husband. And their two children mostly lived on a New Jersey farm where they were cared for by a governess.

Mary (Kingsbury) Simkhovitch (1867–1951) combined her roles as wife, mother, and settlement house leader. She became one of the most articulate spokespersons for the movement, successfully stating its aims as well as its theoretical foundations. Before opening Greenwich House in 1902, she was head worker at the College Settlement House and then at the Unitarian-sponsored Friendly Aid House in New York City. Her three years at the Friendly Aid House were frustrating, mostly because it operated more as a mission than as a settlement. As a response to this experience, Simkhovitch organized the Association of Neighborhood Workers and stated its principle of nonsectarianism. She argued that settlement houses were to develop community identity, nurture local leadership, and connect specific communities in larger social and political reform efforts. Referring to the settlement house as a family residing within an impoverished neighborhood, she argued that settlement houses were to engage in democratic cooperation and nourish community life.

While Simkhovitch understood her own work as rooted in religious conviction and did not disregard the personal faith of many residents, she was convinced that settlement houses needed to be working toward a "common faith," where all views and positions would be equally accepted. She claimed that Christianity is best expressed through actions or works, not through words or creeds, and asserted that the purpose of settlement houses was to enable the world to live in "loving association," so that the "faith of democracy and Christianity can be realized" (Pacey, 142). Like other settlement leaders, Simkhovitch emphasized the praxis (or practice) of Christianity over its doctrine (or creeds). Jane Addams, for example, considered settlement houses as a movement "toward [Christianity's] early humanitarian aspects" (Addams et al., 2).

Cities in the Midwest, as well as in the South and on the West Coast, also became early locations of settlement houses. In Indianapolis and Gary, for example, seven houses were opened between 1890 and 1930. In Minneapolis, the first settlement house was opened in 1897; by 1925, ten settlement houses existed. Kingsley House (New Orleans) opened in 1896 and became the first settlement house in the South. The Log Cabin Settlement (near Asheville, North Carolina) was founded in 1894 by an East Coast college alumna, Susan Chester, and was the first rural settlement opened.

The location of houses contributed to their size and style, yet other factors were important. Some houses were intentionally nonsectarian, while others were outgrowths of city missions and funded by religious denominations. Others were opened in cooperation with major industries in the areas and were seen as useful ways to ingrain workers with values upheld as crucial to the formation of good citizens. In such instances, settlement houses were viewed as socializing neighborhood people into obedient work ethics and middle-class white moral values. The teaching of English was deemed crucial in the process of forming citizens; Americanization became a more explicit goal in the post–World War I era.

Issues of race and integration also became more explicit in the post–World War I era. Despite official directives that stated that houses were to be neutral spaces crossing racial and religious lines, most white settlement house leaders interacted better with foreign immigrants than with black citizens. Christamore House in Indianapolis provides such an example, which was founded in 1905 by Edith Surbey (d. 1972) and Anna Stover (1870–1944). Stover and Surbey met while studying at Butler University and formed a primary relationship that was to last until Stover's death. Their intention in founding Christamore was to combine "practical help and spiritual uplift" (Crocker, 22). A Christian evangelical missionary approach grounded their vision of the house, as did their embedded racism; Christamore served only the white neighbors of their area, despite the fact that in 1910 half of their neighbors were black. Both resigned in 1911, when Christamore joined the national federation and therefore needed to eliminate its religious programs. The house also relocated to a primarily white neighborhood in an attempt to avoid interaction with—and integration with—black neighbors.

The first settlement houses founded in black neighborhoods depended on the leadership and financial support of white people. Flanner House (Indianapolis) and Steward House (Gary), for example, were founded through the cooperation of black and white leaders, even though they were opened for black neighbors. The Fred-

erick Douglass Center in Chicago was founded by white Unitarian minister Celia Parker Woolley (1848–1918), and its goal was to improve relations between white and black middle-class people and thereby show the possibility of interracial cooperation.

The first house opened by a black woman was Locust Street Settlement in Hampton, Virginia, by Janie Porter Barrett (1865–1948). Opened in 1890 in the house where she and her husband lived, the settlement initially focused on girls. But by 1902 a full slate of activities were offered for boys and girls, men and women. Barrett later got involved in many other organizations and worked for racial justice on state and national levels, yet the well-being of girls and women remained a primary focus throughout her life.

Leadership positions for black women in settlement houses mostly became available in the 1920s. The Phyllis Wheatley House opened in Minneapolis in 1924 and was headed by W. Gertrude Brown. Brown had strong connections with white women and was a close friend of Jane Addams. She had studied at the University of Chicago and graduated from Columbia University. She provided strong leadership to the house, even though the majority of board members were white. The house offered recreational, educational, musical, and dramatic programs for children and adults, yet perhaps its most significant role was to act as an "interpreter and translator of black culture and needs" in the city (Karger, 108). Brown resigned her position in 1937, after growing criticisms directed toward her by some of her white board members. Despite the problems encountered by Brown, the Phyllis Wheatley House nurtured black culture in a primarily white city. She—and the house—also reminded the North American movement of the presence of blacks within northern urban areas.

Other black women were attached to particular houses, even though they did not necessarily reside in them. Anna (Haywood) Cooper (c. 1859–1964), a graduate of Oberlin College and high school teacher for over forty years, was active in the Colored Social Settlement in Washington, D.C. A staunch Episcopalian and advocate of blacks gaining higher education, she viewed settlement houses as intermediary places where racial, social, and political inequalities could be addressed. Eartha White (1876–1974), who became a successful Floridan businesswoman, was influenced by Booker T. Washington and in 1900 became a charter member of the National Negro Business League. Active in many community organizations, White established in 1928 the Clara White Mission (named in honor of her adopted mother). White lived at the mission, which was "Jacksonville's counterpart to Chicago's Hull House" (James, 3: 726). The mission engaged in relief work (especially during the depression) and was the force behind the founding of maternity, orphanage, and tuberculosis homes and other social programs. White also was active in protesting job discrimination on the basis of race.

While some white settlement leaders were committed to racial equality and integration, Mary White Ovington was one of the strongest proponents. As a founder of the NAACP, Ovington (1865–1951) first studied the situation of blacks in Manhattan while working with Mary Simkhovitch at Greenwich House. She published her findings in a book titled *Half a Man: The Status of the Negro in New York* (1911). Ovington was a friend of W.E.B. DuBois and worked with the NAACP for almost four decades. Her dedication to black equality was exceptional among white settlement leaders.

In general, settlement houses worked better with ethnic immigrant populations than with African Americans. The Roman Catholic Church, which experienced astronomical growth due to European immigration, became especially apt in establishing connections with immigrants. Marion F. Gurney was one of the most dedicated of Roman Catholic settlement workers. As head resident at St. Rose's (New York City), one of the earliest Catholic houses opened in 1898, she worked primarily with Italians. In 1908, Gurney (then called Mother Marianne of Jesus) founded the Sisters of Our Lady of Christian Doctrine, whose purpose was to engage in urban settlement work. Roman Catholics also worked with Hispanics. Brownson House, founded in 1900 in Los Angeles, engaged with Mexican immigrants and relied on volunteer laypeople for its programs. Prior to World War I, Catholic laywomen—not religious sisters—provided most of the support needed for settlement houses and urban missions.

Houses and Leaders in Canada

Settlement houses founded in Canada were influenced by both American and English experiences. Evangelia, the first house founded in Canada, was opened in Toronto by Sara Libby Carson and her friend Mary Bell. Carson (d. 1928) had in 1897 cofounded Christodora House (New York City) with Christina Isobel MacColl (b. 1864). A graduate of Wellesley College, Carson had worked as a field secretary for the Young Women's Christian Association (YWCA) before she became convinced that settlement work was more useful than such explicit Christian work. At Christodora House, however, a Christian—although nondenominational—commitment was maintained. Having been familiarized with Canada through her YWCA work, Carson, with the cooperation of the Canadian YWCA and personal monies, organized the Young Women's Settlement in 1899, which became Evangelia in 1902.

Within the next decade, three more houses were opened in Toronto and exemplified the differences among the Canadian movement. University Settlement,

founded in 1910, was initially a men's settlement modeled after Toynbee Hall. Central Neighbourhood House, founded in 1911, employed Elizabeth B. Neufeld as its first head resident, a Jewish woman from Baltimore. St. Christopher House, opened in 1912, was organized by Carson but employed Helen Hart as its first head resident.

Born in the United States of Russian parents and educated at Warsaw (Poland) University, Elizabeth Neufeld was fluent in Yiddish, Russian, German, Polish, and English, which made communication possible with the majority of her Jewish neighbors. Central Neighbourhood House was intentionally nonsectarian, and its board members consisted of a Methodist, Presbyterian, Roman Catholic, Jew, and Plymouth Brother. Despite such precautions, Neufeld and the house were accused by some white Anglo-Saxon Protestant Torontonians as engaging in Jewish propagandism. Neufeld replied to such criticisms: "How could we be Judizers [*sic*]? We don't talk religion at all. We leave that to the ministers and rabbis. Citizenship is our gospel. Jane Addams is our John the Baptist and our Bible is the daily press when it knows enough to talk sense" (Toronto Association of Neighbourhood Services, 18).

Settlement house leaders were as concerned about the Canadianization of immigrants as were leaders in the United States concerned about Americanization. Yet Canadian houses were more closely aligned to Christian denominations than were most houses in either the United States or England. The Social Gospel movement was particularly present in the Canadian settlement house movement. This alliance became explicit when Carson was hired by the Presbyterian Church in Canada to set up a string of settlement houses across the country. Working during the next ten years with churchman John J. Shearer, Carson first organized St. Christopher House in 1912 and hired Helen Hart, a graduate of Mount Holyoke College, as its head resident. Shortly thereafter, St. Christopher became the field placement for students studying in the newly formed School of Social Work at the University of Toronto. Carson organized another five Presbyterian settlement houses, located from Montreal to Vancouver; she was called the Jane Addams of Canada.

Other settlement houses developed from city missions. In Winnipeg, a Methodist Sunday School aimed at educating immigrant children was started by Dolly Maguire (1866–1946) in 1889. It grew into All Peoples Mission, and by 1907, when Canadian Social Gospeller J. S. Woodsworth was hired as its superintendent, the mission operated as one of the most well known settlement houses in Canada. In Toronto, the Fred Victor Mission grew out of a Sunday School started by Mary Sheffield (1846–1937) in 1886. Influenced by the evangelical preaching of D. L. Moody, Sheffield studied in

In Canada, where a political progressive movement did not emerge until the 1920s, settlement houses, such as the St. Christopher House in Toronto, were tied to reform movements located mostly within Protestant churches, religious missions, and student organizations. In general, settlement houses in the United States were more politically involved than settlement houses in either Great Britain or Canada. *Courtesy of the Toronto City Archives.*

1893–1894 at the Chicago Bible Institute. While the mission initially emphasized charity, Canadianization, and Christianization, through the years it gained a social justice emphasis. Alexandra House in Vancouver grew out of an orphanage, which was initially founded by the Woman's Christian Temperance Society in 1891. Most early settlement houses in Canada were founded by women, often in connection with Christian organizations.

Settlements for blacks and Jews opened later in Canada than in the United States. In Montreal, for example, the Negro Community Centre was opened in 1925, while the Neighbourhood House, a settlement for Jewish children, was opened in 1927. Canada experienced major industrialization and immigration only in the first decades of the twentieth century, and numerous houses were opened during the depression. The Catholic Settlement (Toronto) was opened, for example, during the depression and closed in 1945. Simcoe Hall (Oshawa, Ontario) was opened during the depression by Mrs. R. S. MacLaughlin, wife of the manager of General Motors, as a way to help the families of laid-off autoworkers.

Settlement house leaders in Canada relied on their British and American counterparts, as exemplified by the fact that both Henrietta Barnett and Graham Taylor were guests of Canadian leaders. Influenced by the worldwide movement, the goal of Canadian leaders was to develop methods appropriate for their specific national context. In general, Canadian houses emphasized political reform less than did houses in the United States and deemed the orderly and peaceable interaction between peoples—and the facilitating of social services—as of primary importance.

Conclusion

The settlement house movement was significant within North American society. Although as embedded with racism and classism as was dominant society itself, settlement house leaders believed that democracy was best served by social interactions and a sense of social interdependence. While the early movement engaged in cultural assimilation better than in the nurturing of cultural pluralism, and worked better with European immigrants than with black citizens, it must be recognized that ideals upholding cultural distinctiveness and multiculturalism—and the black civil rights movement—did not emerge until later in the twentieth century.

Despite its shortcomings, the movement provided an amazing response to social problems and questions regarding individual and community development. Early settlement house leaders often engaged in their work out of their religious commitments, even though some felt that explicit religious practices were inappropriate within the houses themselves. Immensely successful in addressing a host of issues, the movement also provided (mainly but not exclusively) white middle-class women with significant personal ties and professional opportunities.

SOURCES: For primary source collections, see Robert A. Woods and Albert J. Kennedy, eds., *Handbook of Settlements* (1911); Jane Addams et al., *Philanthropy and Social Progress:*

Seven Essays (1970); Loren M. Pacey, ed., *Readings in the Development of Settlement Work* (1971); and Arthur C. Holden, *The Settlement Idea* (1922). For secondary overviews, see Allen F. Davis, *Spearheads for Reform: The Social Settlements and the Progressive Movement, 1890–1914* (1967); Elisabeth Lasch-Quinn, *Black Neighborhoods: Race and the Limits of Reform in the American Settlement House Movements, 1890–1945* (1993); and Judith Ann Trolander, *Professionalism and Social Change: From the Settlement House Movement to Neighborhood Centers, 1886 to the Present* (1987). For focused studies, see Harry P. Kraus, *The Settlement House Movement in New York City, 1886–1914* (1980); Ruth Hutchison Crocker, *Social Work and Social Order: The Settlement Movement in Two Industrial Cities, 1889–1930* (1992); Howard Jacob Karger, *The Sentinels of Order: A Study of Social Control and the Minneapolis Settlement House Movement, 1915–1950* (1982); and Allen Irving, Harriet Parsons, and Donald Bellamy, *Neighbours: Three Social Settlements in Downtown Toronto, 1888–1937* (1996). For locating the North American movement within the international context, see Toronto Association of Neighbourhood Services, *The Story of the Toronto Settlement House Movement, 1910–1985* (1986); Herman Nijenhuis, ed., *Hundred Years of Settlements and Neighbourhood Centres in North America and Europe* (n.d.); and Christian Johnson, *Strength in Community: An Introduction to the History and Impact of the International Settlement Movement* (1995). For biographical information on many of the women involved in settlement houses, refer to Edward T. James, ed., *Notable American Women: A Biographical Dictionary*, vols. 1–3 (1971), and Domenica M. Barbuto, *American Settlement Houses and Progressive Social Reform: An Encyclopedia of the American Settlement Movement* (1999). Autobiographies, biographies, and/or posthumous collections of letters and writings also are available for some settlement women.

THE SOCIAL GOSPEL
Susan Hill Lindley

THE SOCIAL GOSPEL refers to a North American Protestant form of a broad movement of social Christianity in the later decades of the nineteenth and the early decades of the twentieth century that attempted to apply the Christian gospel to particular social problems of the day. The focus of its best-known leaders, largely white men, and of its first generation of historians was the response to human problems and dislocations precipitated by urban industrialization. Its theological roots were in liberalism, particularly the emphasis on "the fatherhood of God," "the brotherhood of man," and the kingdom of God as the center of Jesus' teaching as these concepts were to be realized, at least in part, in the here and now. But the movement's roots were also found in the nineteenth-century American Protestant evangelicalism and perfectionism that fueled a range of social reforms. The Social Gospel's most striking contribution was its insistence that sin and salvation must be considered in their corporate and structural forms, not only as matters for the individual. Most earlier Christian reformers assumed that the task was to convert individuals; changed hearts would lead to changed actions, which in turn would result in a more "Christian" society. While Social Gospelers never denied the importance of individual conversion and responsibility, they were convinced that it was also crucial to address the social structures that impeded progress toward the kingdom of God for both individuals and society. The structures that seemed to them the least "Christianized" were economic, so their primary focus was on the capitalist system as it functioned in their time and on the needs of urban workers. Thus they made common cause with some secular reformers with similar concerns; the difference was in their theological motivation and vision and the religious justification they advanced for their beliefs and activities.

Given the time and location of the Social Gospel's acknowledged leadership and the movement's first generation of historians, it is perhaps not surprising that their attention to racism and sexism was limited. When they considered women and nonwhite men, they saw them primarily as victims, not as potential leaders or as Christians whose perspective on the imperatives of the gospel and unjust social structures might be different than their own. Yet revisionist historical scholarship, especially during the last quarter of the twentieth century, has suggested that white women and African American men and women shared core Social Gospel characteristics: They were motivated by a religious conviction that Jesus' preaching of the kingdom of God was an imperative for Christian action in this world and that progress was only possible by addressing structural issues as well as individual repentance and activity. These previously excluded actors—excluded at least in terms of perception and acknowledgment—often shared the white male leadership's focus on economic structures and urban labor, but they perceived additional areas of concern more visible and immediate to those not part of the culturally dominant white male elite.

Men like Walter Rauschenbusch raised significant, even radical questions about economic issues and structures at the turn of the twentieth century, but they were relatively conservative about political and familial structures. As Rauschenbusch argued in 1912, while four social orders were by no means perfected, they were well on their way to being "christianized": the church, education, political life, and "most Christian" of all, the family (Rauschenbusch, 128). The Christian family was the key to building a Christianized society and a pattern for other social relationships because of its principles of cooperation and self-sacrifice. It was the economic order of his time, Rauschenbusch insisted, that was most unchristian. Thus concern for women concentrated on the ways in which unjust economic structures prevented women from fulfilling their natural Christian roles as wives and mothers. Sympathy for women workers in the factories and for women driven to prostitution by economic desperation was real, but the men's preferred solution was a living wage for male workers that would make women's public economic activities unnecessary.

Temperance was another issue that claimed significant support from male Social Gospel leaders; thus they appreciated and supported women's temperance work, agreeing with most female temperance leaders that intemperance was largely a male problem but that women and children frequently suffered from the economic and moral consequences of men's drinking. Women's participation in the churches was also esteemed, even assumed, by male leaders, for they shared the cultural perception of women as naturally pious. The problems, they believed, were rather the dearth of men in the churches and the need for a more positive masculine image for Christian believers. Although Social Gospel leaders were not the most conservative religious leaders on matters of women's public activity—some endorsed woman suffrage, though not often as an issue of central importance—they typically most valued women for their familial roles, for their helping activities in the churches, and for their unassuming charitable work. They seldom viewed women as fellow-activists and partners in the Social Gospel movement.

Vida Dutton Scudder was one of the exceptions, a woman whom male Social Gospel leaders acknowledged as a fellow worker if not precisely an equal as she worked with the settlement movement, the labor movement, and church boards. She was born in 1861 in India. When her missionary father drowned while she was an infant, she and her mother returned to an extended New England family that was both long established and reasonably affluent. As she grew up, she traveled and studied in Europe as well as Boston, culminating her formal education at Smith College and a year's postgraduate work at Oxford. Shortly after her return from England, she accepted a teaching post in the English Department of Wellesley College, a position she held until her retirement in 1928. Yet Scudder had been radicalized at Oxford, and as much as she loved the English literature she taught, she also used her teaching position to promote social Christianity, especially in her favorite course, "Social Ideals in English Letters."

Nor did Scudder's attempt to influence her students end in the classroom. She was a founding member of the College Settlements Association (CSA), begun in 1887, which eventually supported three main settlements (in Boston, New York, and Philadelphia) as well as chapters on college campuses. Although Scudder herself was never a permanent settlement resident, she spent time at Denison House in Boston, was active in the governance of the CSA, and recruited her students for the movement. She was convinced that the experience would have a lasting influence even on those young women who went on to marriage or other careers, and thus it would make a contribution to social change as important as the settlements' direct work with the urban poor.

Scudder's contact with settlements contributed to her growing understanding of labor issues and particularly the problems of working women; thus she helped to organize the Women's Trade Union League (WTUL) in 1903. These concerns were reinforced by association with the radical wing of the Social Gospel. In 1889 she joined fellow Bostonian and Episcopalian W.D.P. Bliss as a charter member of his Brotherhood of the Carpenter, an Episcopal mission in Boston that espoused socialist principles. In the 1890s she became a member of the interdenominational Society of Christian Socialists and an Episcopal group, the Christian Social Union. In 1911, she joined the Socialist Party, writing later in her autobiography that "the ultimate source of my socialist convictions was and is Christianity. Unless I were a socialist, I could not honestly be a Christian" (Scudder, *On Journey*, 163). Scudder did not subordinate Christianity to socialism, but she believed it was the system most likely to advance the kingdom of God in her own time. In *Socialism and Character* (1912), she argued not only that socialism and Christianity were compatible but that only radical structural change in society could provide an environment in which *all* persons could hope to develop "character," religious virtues.

In addition to participation in organizations that were not explicitly religious like the CSA, the WTUL, and the Socialist Party, Scudder served on boards that promoted awareness of social justice in her own Episcopal Church. She helped to found its Church Socialist League in 1911 and was one of its vice presidents, and in 1918 she helped to organize the Church League for Industrial Democracy. Such groups gave her an opportunity to work with male Episcopal leaders, even though that church still denied her, as a woman, formal voice and vote in its deliberations. The Society of the Companions of the Holy Cross (SCHC), however, was an all-woman group in which Scudder found sisterly support and a platform for social concerns. Founded in 1884 by Emily Malbone Morgan, the society emphasized a blend of spirituality and action in the world, with a special concern for working women. Scudder joined in 1889, serving as its director of probationers from 1909 until 1942 and, unofficially, as leader of its radical activist wing. Despite the reservations of some members about the wisdom of public action by the SCHC as a whole,

Scudder and her supporters were able to pass petitions in 1907 and 1916 to the General Convention of the Episcopal Church calling for more social action.

Few other women in the Social Gospel were as theologically sophisticated as Scudder, but many shared her special concern for women's needs and potential. Theirs was frequently a "pragmatic" Social Gospel focused on action rather than social theory or constructive theology. But they were not unaware of theology, especially the Social Gospel's distinctive concern for the kingdom of God and the resultant stress on corporate identity and social structures in need of redemption. For many women, these convictions came as a result of reading or hearing the movement's male leadership. But the women's consciousness was also raised by their own experiences. Even women who did not begin work with a fully developed Social Gospel theology had strong religious motivations and a desire to show their faith in action and to be useful. They were also aware of the contemporary challenges of urbanization, industrialization, and immigration. The question was, Where could they go—what could they do *as women*?

Although few women had a literal pulpit from which to promote the Social Gospel, many employed the lectern and the pen to spread the word. Women gave speeches and wrote articles for church and club publications; they published accounts of their own lives and experiences; they wrote novels to defend social interpretations of Christianity, criticize current conditions, and suggest ways for female characters to act upon their convictions. Among woman-authored Social Gospel novels are Scudder's *A Listener in Babel* (1903), Florence's Converse's *The Burden of Christopher* (1900) and *The Children of Light* (1912), Katharine Pearson Woods's *Metzerott, Shoemaker* (1889), and Canadian Agnes Maule Machar's *Roland Graeme, Knight* (1892).

Women furthered the Social Gospel by acting as well as by writing. Some, like Scudder, worked with both religious and secular groups; others focused on one or the other but retained their religious motivation. Women's church groups were an important outlet for those who needed to combine their work with the responsibilities of marriage and motherhood. Such groups had been the seedbed for numerous benevolent and reform activities throughout the nineteenth century; women's service to the "less fortunate," especially women and children, was approved as a commendable extension of women's natural roles of nurture and self-sacrifice. But as women in the later decades of the nineteenth century carried out and supported home missions, many of them, especially Methodists in both North and South, began to realize that charity was insufficient to address the needs of the poor. Like their male pastors, the women were convinced that Christian homes were the crucial basis for a moral and Christian society, but how could the poor be expected to establish Christian homes when saloons tempted husbands and fathers to squander their meager wages, when economic need took children out of schools and into unhealthful factory work, when young girls were forced into prostitution by seduction or economic desperation, when minimal levels of decency were precluded by overcrowded housing and virtually nonexistent sanitation? Thus churchwomen turned from simple charity to begin questioning social, economic, and political structures and advocating change as they provided volunteer time, financial support, and publicity to educational ventures, settlements and neighborhood centers, and reform. The women's own experiences were complemented by study, as churchwomen's groups read works by Washington Gladden, Josiah Strong, or Rauschenbusch, or as colleges and training institutes introduced courses in the growing field of sociology. Meanwhile, the revelations of "muckrakers" opened middle-class eyes to contemporary conditions, and popular fiction like Charles Sheldon's bestselling Social Gospel novel *In His Steps* (1896) articulated a religious imperative for action—that Christians should act as Jesus would have in their particular situations—and suggested ways that women, too, could be involved, such as the settlement movement.

A young man who felt called by God to advance the Social Gospel most typically sought ordination and the leadership of a congregation, but the possibilities of official ordination among mainline Protestants for his similarly inspired sister were rare indeed. Instead, women who sought a full-time, religiously inspired vocation of social service, for a few years or for a lifetime, might become deaconesses. Deaconess institutes trained church workers and foreign missionaries, but they also sent young women into the cities with the dual goal of evangelism and social service to the poor, and some, like Lucy Rider Meyer's Chicago Training School, one of the most influential, included study of the new social sciences. For some deaconesses, the work retained an individualistic and charitable focus, but for others, contact with the complex realities of urban poverty led them to question the political and economic structures that produced such conditions. They thus began to gather data systematically and to ally themselves with urban reformers. They reported back to the churches to publicize the conditions they found and tried to build support for systemic change. Isabelle Horton, a Methodist deaconess, published *The Burden of the City* in 1904 to describe her own experiences. Evangelism is still critical, she insisted, but so are changes in things like child labor laws, courts' treatment of juveniles, the distribution of profits in industry, and public support of kindergartens for the poor. Another Methodist deaconess, Winifred Chappell, taught for several years at the Chicago Training School and later used her post with the Methodist Federation for Social Services to advocate a radical version of the Social Gospel.

Settlement houses attracted other young women fired with Social Gospel zeal, particularly if they discovered not only that they could not be ordained but also that their offer of service to the church was circumscribed and trivialized by a male pastor who was unsympathetic to the Social Gospel or who had strong conservative views on appropriate roles for women. While some settlements were directly sponsored or staffed by Protestant churches, others rejected a direct connection with Christianity and refused to engage in evangelism. Nevertheless, many young settlement workers were impelled by religious motives and remained active church members. Ellen Gates Starr, cofounder with Jane Addams of Hull House, was a devout Anglo-Catholic Episcopalian and member of the Society of the Companions of the Holy Cross (and in her later life, a convert to Roman Catholicism), but she was just as passionately committed to social causes. Her particular foci at Hull House were programs to make great art available to its immigrant neighbors and radical political work for urban labor. Scorning charity as a replacement for justice, she joined the WTUL and the Socialist Party and actively supported the strikes of urban textile workers. Helena Stuart Dudley was a close friend of Vida Scudder, another Episcopalian and SCHC member, who helped to found the College Settlement Association and made that her lifelong work as the head of Denison House in Boston. Her experiences convinced her that individual help through classes or services, while valuable, was insufficient without changes in industrial and economic structures, so she supported union causes and helped to found the WTUL. Another colleague of Scudder's, Mary Kingsbury Simkhovitch, was inspired by the Christian socialism of W.D.P. Bliss and the settlement movement. She founded Greenwich House in New York and worked particularly on issues of low-cost housing. Mary Eliza McDowell's social concern was rooted in a family antislavery tradition and a Methodist faith that emphasized practical Christianity. As a young woman she worked with the WCTU and spent some time at Hull House before she became director of a settlement sponsored by the University of Chicago near the stockyards. There she became involved in union organization and municipal politics, particularly concerned with issues of sanitation and pollution and with women workers.

While some women made settlement work or the political activism they began there lifelong careers, others spent only a few years before moving to other work or marrying but, as Scudder had hoped, they retained the impact of that experience, sometimes continuing to support settlements through financial donations and part-time work. Louise DeKoven Bowen was born into a wealthy Chicago family that impressed upon her the responsible stewardship of wealth. A lifelong Episcopalian, she first looked to her church for opportunities for social service. Her rector provided one—teaching Sunday School to a group of rowdy teenage boys, at which she was remarkably successful—but was reluctant to give a woman additional substantive work in the church. Thus it was through her association with Hull House that her mature work for social reform was inspired and implemented. Not only did she support the settlement financially and encourage wealthy friends to do likewise, but she was actively and personally involved in its programs, leading various clubs, working with Julia Lathrop to develop a Juvenile Court system in Chicago, and supporting Visiting Nurse services. She also used her social status to pressure business leaders like Cyrus McCormick to improve conditions for workers.

Settlement workers were among the early organizers of the Women's Trade Union League, along with women workers themselves and a few sympathetic male labor leaders. Founded in 1903 in Boston, the WTUL developed other major branches in New York and Chicago. Its membership was open not only to women laborers but also to sympathetic middle- or upper-class women—allies—in the hope that it might help bridge class differences among women. The WTUL's initial goal was to organize women workers, since male-dominated unions were, in general, uninterested or actively unsupportive of women, whom they regarded as short term and less skilled and, sharing the male cultural views of their day, belonged at home anyway. In time, the WTUL also offered financial, legal, and personal support to strikers, provided education in organization and leadership to working women, publicized the actual working conditions in factories and sweatshops to other women's groups, and promoted protective legislation, especially for women and children, and women's rights like suffrage and equal pay for equal work. Although its work was hurt at times by class differences, misunderstanding, and resentment among the women and by male resistance to women's participation in the union movement, the WTUL still made significant accomplishments on a number of fronts. The point is not, of course, that all or even a majority of WTUL members were advocates of the Social Gospel, any more than all settlement workers (or for that matter, all male Protestant ministers) were; rather, settlements and support of women workers in groups like the WTUL provided for some Social Gospel women a venue to address the particular economic and political structures that victimized women.

Between churchwomen's groups and deaconesses, on the one hand, and more "secular" options like settlement work and the WTUL, on the other, was a woman's organization that cut across denominational lines but was explicitly and self-consciously Christian in its orientation: the Woman's Christian Temperance Union (WCTU). The economic, political, and moral impact of the saloon was a serious concern for male Social Gospelers, but it was even more central for women. Frances Willard, leader of the WCTU during its most influential period, linked the cause of temperance to "home protection"—surely a legitimate concern for women. Thus she argued that women needed to vote to protect their homes and families from the devastations of liquor. Willard also allied herself openly with the cause of labor, joining the Knights of Labor, for unions, too, supported "home protection." Working men and women needed relief from long hours and unsafe, unhealthy working conditions so that they would not repair to the saloons for temporary relief. Single women needed a sufficient wage to resist the temptations of prostitution; men needed wages enough to support their families and work hours that allowed them to spend time at home. While Willard herself was more radical than many WCTU members, her leadership and the organization provided space for some women to expand their political awareness and activity. Beginning with a conviction that drunkenness was a personal moral problem, these women came, through observation and experience, to conclude that intemperance was affected by urban conditions that required broader institutional and structural reform, and they thus moved into political action and support of prison reform, especially for women and children, labor legislation, and public kindergartens or day nurseries for working women.

In Canada, Nellie L. McClung also found in the cause of temperance a centerpiece for a lifelong, wide-ranging career in the Social Gospel. She endorsed the WCTU and worked for many years for political enactment of prohibition, but she was by no means a single-issue reformer; rather, for her, religious conviction, social activism, and feminism were intrinsically related. Born in 1873, she grew up on farms in western Ontario and southwestern Manitoba. For McClung, marriage and motherhood (she had five children) were important but did not preclude a life of active participation in the public sphere as a writer, lecturer, reformer, and even politician: She served from 1922 to 1926 in the Legislative Assembly of Alberta, ran for other offices, and worked for many years behind the scenes in political party life. Like other Social Gospel leaders, she combined theological motivations and church activity with reform work. A Methodist laywoman, she participated in and lectured to women's church organizations and served as a delegate to the Ecumenical Methodist Conference in London in 1921. She also argued for greater leadership roles for women in the church, including ordination, chiding the church for its opposition or, at best, lukewarm official support for women's rights in church and society,

though she admitted that some individual ministers were more helpful. She took seriously the biblical injunction for Christ's followers to "Feed my sheep" but not simply through charity. Drawing on the parable of the Good Samaritan, she argued that women engaged in charitable work had begun to question the causes of poverty and suffering: "The road from Jerusalem to Jericho is here and now. Women have played the good Samaritan for a long time, and they have found many a one beaten and robbed on the road of life. They are still doing it, but the conviction is growing on them that it would be much better to go out and clean up the road!" (McClung, 126).

Nellie McClung's reform work was wide-ranging, including but going beyond typical Social Gospel causes. She was concerned about urban labor, once conducting the skeptical Conservative Premier Sir Rodmond Roblin on a tour of sweatshops in Winnipeg to see firsthand the conditions in which women and children worked. As a woman of rural background, however, her focus extended beyond urban factory workers as she also insisted that domestic workers and farmers were in need of political reform and protection. Indeed, her vision for Canada was that it might become "the Land of the Fair Deal" where neither class, ethnicity, nor gender would bar persons from equal opportunities. That meant McClung was an outspoken critic of prejudice against immigrants; it also meant that she saw "women's issues" like suffrage and equal pay for equal work as central, not peripheral, on a Social Gospel reform agenda.

If white women's work has been marginalized by traditional views of the Social Gospel, the work of African American women has been almost totally ignored, yet the need for reform was even more immediate and imperative to women whose lives were circumscribed by racism and, often, poverty. As the church was the religious, social, economic, and political center of black communities in the postbellum South, so black churchwomen's groups provided crucial charitable and educational services to those communities. But by the turn of the twentieth century, the beginnings of black migration to urban centers in the North, the growth of cities in the South, and the increasingly overt and repressive racism of Jim Crow and lynching moved more and more black women into questioning of structures and especially the impact of systemic racism as barriers to black advancement, no matter how moral or educated individual African Americans might be. Nannie Helen Burroughs, secretary of the Woman's Convention of the National Baptist Convention, was a leader in these Social Gospel directions.

Born in 1878 to former slaves, Burroughs was brought by her widowed mother to Washington, D.C., with hopes of better educational opportunities for her daughter. After graduating from high school but failing to find a teaching job, Burroughs worked for the Foreign Mission Board of the National Baptist Convention (NBC) until she was elected to her post in the Woman's Convention in 1900. For the next half century she rallied, inspired, and defended the black Baptist women who supported her and her causes, sometimes against the male leadership of the NBC. One of those causes was the National Training School for Women and Girls, established in 1909 in Washington, D.C., where young African American women could receive both classical and industrial education, as well as courses in black history to promote black pride. While Burroughs could be—and was—criticized for helping to promote a middle-class "politics of respectability" and acceptance of job segregation for blacks, she was also realistic enough to know where the vast majority of black women would find employment. Not only did she insist on the dignity of manual labor, but she encouraged black domestic workers to unionize. Under Burroughs's leadership, the Woman's Convention moved into other areas of social reform. A 1913 manifesto called for equality in accommodations and schools, equal protection in the courts, an end to lynching, and the vote for both African Americans and women; in the same year, the Woman's Convention founded a settlement house in Washington.

While many black women worked through their churches to advance a Social Gospel agenda, others chafed, as did white women, at male-imposed restrictions on their work and turned to secular reform organizations along with church work. Yet women's reform or service organizations dominated by white women, like the WCTU or the YWCA, were unwilling to welcome African American women as equals, typically offering only secondary or segregated status under the control of whites. Thus many black women looked instead or in addition to their own organizations where they could set their own agenda, free from male or white domination, and where their particular perspectives and concerns were central. The black women's clubs formed by middle- and upper-class black women and joined in the National Association of Colored Women (NACW) continued important benevolent work and social services but also moved into reform. Some issues like temperance and free kindergartens they shared with white women, but they also challenged the injustice of racist practices like Jim Crow, the convict lease system, and lynching. As the twentieth century moved into its second decade, the NACW expanded its work into issues like public health, treatment of juvenile offenders, and woman suffrage. Lugenia Burns Hope, the wife of the president of Atlanta Baptist (later Morehouse) College, was the driving force behind the Neighborhood Union (founded 1908), a group of black women determined to address the needs of black children in Atlanta. Alerted to a problem, the women conducted social research in their neighborhoods, presented their findings, and either responded themselves or sought another group who could, often working cooperatively with black ministers and black churches. Among the issues they addressed directly or through political pressure were education (and the grossly unequal opportunities for black children), public health, and inadequate housing.

Although the Neighborhood Union was not a single establishment, it functioned in many of its programs like a social settlement, and the settlement movement attracted other African American women as a venue for social reform. Some worked in black branches opened in northern cities by established settlements like Hull House in Chicago, South End House in Boston, or Henry Street in New York or in white-founded rural settlements in the South, but black women also founded their own settlements: The first was the Locust Street Settlement begun by Janie Porter Barrett in Hampton, Virginia, in 1890. The Colored Social Settlement in Washington, D.C., while initially founded by whites, gradually came under black control; it not only provided services to its neighbors but also worked with local government for better housing and education and the establishment of public playgrounds. Anna Julia Cooper, the black feminist and educator, most of whose life was spent in Washington, was a trustee and part-time worker at this settlement. In a 1913 essay, Cooper not only described the work of settlements but also rooted that work explicitly and decisively in Christian faith, a "Christianity that can save society" as it "sets about hammering down some of those hideous handicaps which hamper whole sections of a community through the inequalities of environment, or the greed of the great" ("The Social Settlement: What It Is, and What It Does," in *The Voice of Anna Julia Cooper*, 217).

With the emergence of the National Urban League and the National Association for the Advancement of Colored People, African American women found additional outlets for reform of American economic and political structures. When the National League on Urban Conditions among Negroes (later called the National Urban League) was formed in 1911 in response to growing black populations in urban centers and their economic and social needs, it merged a number of earlier reform organizations, including the National League for the Protection of Colored Women, a group focused on the need of young women migrants who came to the cities seeking work or were lured there by false promises of employment agents, only to be forced into prostitution. Women continued and expanded those services under the new organization. But as it spread geographically, the Urban League drew on the existing resources

Lugenia Burns Hope, wife of the president of Atlanta Baptist (later Morehouse) College, was the driving force behind the Neighborhood Union (founded in 1908), a group of black women determined to address the needs of black children in Atlanta. Alerted to a problem, the women conducted social research in their neighborhoods, presented their findings, and either responded themselves or sought another group who could, often working cooperatively with black ministers and black churches. *Courtesy of Robert W. Woodruff Library, Atlanta University Center.*

and programs of local reform groups and churches, many of which had been established and were supported by black women. In Atlanta, the Urban League was not only strengthened by affiliation with Lugenia Hope's well-organized and successful Neighborhood Union; it picked up some of her methods and used them in its own work in other cities. The central aims of the NAACP, founded in 1909 as an interracial group with substantial support from the settlement movement and the radical wing of black leadership, were legal and political. The organization used publicity, political means, and the courts to fight for the rights of blacks as citizens. Among its early important battles were antilynching and support of the vote for women and the restoration of suffrage for black men to whom it had been effectively denied in the South by Jim Crow laws and intimidation. A few black women, including Nannie Helen Burroughs, were part of the early leadership of the NAACP, and the NACW promoted its work. Black women played especially important roles in building the movement's breadth and base: They gave lectures to white and black groups, including churches; they wrote articles; they raised money; they organized and developed local branches; they served as early, often unofficial or unpaid, fieldworkers, investigating conditions and organizing support.

Just as it is important to note that not all women in organizations like the WCTU or in the settlement movement were part of the Social Gospel, neither were all supporters of the National Urban League or the NAACP (although Reverdy C. Ransom, a minister in the African Methodist Episcopal Church and leading male black proponent of the Social Gospel was also active in the NAACP). Rather, the point is that such "secular" reform organizations provided opportunities along with church and club work for black women to advance a Social Gospel agenda. Furthermore, the centrality of the church in black communities and women's multiple memberships in churches, clubs, and reform organizations make it likely that religion as one driving motive for these women was more the rule than the exception.

While women's Social Gospel activities overlapped central concerns of the traditional white male leadership, women made distinctive contributions in their perspectives on particular issues and in their emphasis on some reforms that were largely overlooked by male leaders. Men like Rauschenbusch publicly commended the family as the basis of Christian civilization, but their view of the family was both traditional and romantic, and their attention was thus sometimes indirect or superficial. Most Social Gospel women endorsed cultural assumptions about women's special—often morally superior—nature and women's special responsibility for the family. But they did not see concern for families in opposition to concern for women as women, nor did they limit women's concerns to their families. Moreover, their views were less romantic and their attention more direct as they realistically addressed social problems that impinged on families. Thus women's focus was most frequently on women and children in the urban labor force. They researched and publicized working conditions in factories and sweatshops; they urged governments to pass compulsory education laws and protective legislation to address the hours and conditions under which women and children could work. Using slogans like "home protection" and "housekeeping writ large," they pushed city governments on issues of sanitation and public housing and recreation: No Christian society could rise on building blocks of families for whom minimal levels of comfort, decency, and security were impossible.

Temperance, like urban labor, was a key issue for both male and female Social Gospelers, but again, women fought the saloon most consistently because of its impact on fathers, husbands, and sons. Not only was liquor a direct economic threat to the families of the poor, they argued, but so was it a temptation to their own sons and a danger to innocent bystanders: Matilda Carse became a leader in the Chicago WCTU after her young son was run over by a drunken cart driver. Women also worked for "purity reform." Beatrice Brigden, a Canadian Social Gospel proponent, spent six years early in her career as a lecturer advocating sex education and social reforms because of her concerns about the spread of venereal disease and the moral and economic implications of prostitution. Condemning the "double standard" of sexual morality then implied questions about culturally defined and restrictive gender roles.

One issue that received much more significant support from both black and white women than from men in the Social Gospel was woman suffrage. Scholars have sometimes distinguished between those who argued for woman suffrage as a justice issue—that is, women are equal persons and citizens who have a right to vote, not to be taxed without representation, nor forced to obey laws in whose formulation they have no voice—and those who promoted it on expedient and functional grounds—women, more moral by nature than men, should be able to vote so they could oppose liquor interests, "clean up" government, and promote educational and labor policies that helped women and children. Yet as women in the Social Gospel movement voiced concern for *both* families *and* for women as women, so they used both arguments for suffrage: It *was* a matter of justice and rights, but denying women the vote *also* robbed them of a crucial and direct political tool to address structural reforms like labor laws and public health issues. Moreover, if a key to the Social Gospel is its concern for changing structures, then surely challenge to the political structures that legally disenfranchised women was a Social Gospel concern. That was how the women saw it, even if most white male leaders did not. (There were exceptions, like Chicago-based Social Gospel teacher and writer Shailer Mathews, who were more outspoken in their support of women's issues like suffrage.)

A few women in the Social Gospel movement achieved public prominence or leadership at a national level, like Vida Scudder, Frances Willard, Nannie Helen Burroughs, and Nellie McClung, but more typically women acted at the grassroots level, building community support and addressing local needs, whether in church groups, WCTU projects, black women's clubs, NAACP branches, settlements, or neighborhood centers. They "spread the word" by arranging, giving, and attending lectures, by writing for periodicals and newsletters, by publishing novels or personal accounts. In that writing, women characteristically used vivid, specific personal examples to energize others about structural evils. Insisting on the futility of an individual's attempted flight from the world to achieve moral purity (and illustrating the nature of structural sin), Vida Scudder wrote,

For unless one retreated to a tropical climate . . . one would have to wear clothes. And every fibre of those clothes would sing persistently in the ear the modern Song of the Shirt: recalling the interminable array of men and women,—clerks, dressmakers, sewing-girls, weavers, back to the tenders of silkworms or gatherers of cotton, who have given life and labor, often under cruelly unjust conditions, that we may be clad. (Scudder, *Socialism and Character*, 41–42)

Women were less likely than men to engage in sophisticated theological construction or social analysis on a theoretical level, but they recognized in their own faith an imperative for action, in their concrete experiences the need for systemic change, and in their own communities an arena to act on the Social Gospel. In the process, they also effectively challenged the "structure" of those prevailing cultural images that limited their work on the basis of gender.

SOURCES: Primary sources include Walter Rauschenbusch, *Christianizing the Social Order* (1912); Vida Scudder, *On Journey* (1937) and *Socialism and Character* (1912); and Nellie McClung, *In Times Like These* (1915). A few books focus specifically on women and the Social Gospel, like Janet Forsythe Fishburn, *The Fatherhood of God and the Victorian Family: The Social Gospel in America* (1981); John Patrick McDowell, *The Social Gospel in the South: The Woman's Home Mission Movement in the Methodist Episcopal Church, South, 1886–1939* (1982); and Wendy J. Deichmann Edwards and Carolyn DeSwarte Gifford, eds., *Gender and the Social Gospel* (2003). Several articles in Christopher H. Evans, ed., *The Social Gospel Today* (2001), focus on women and the Social Gospel. Related works like Ruth Bordin, *Women and Temperance: The Quest for Power and Liberty, 1873–1900* (1981), and Evelyn Brooks Higginbotham, *Righteous Discontent: The Women's Movement in the Black Baptist Church, 1880–1920* (1993), provide helpful information about specific movements or groups, as do biographies of leading women Social Gospel advocates, like Randi R. Warne, *Literature as Pulpit: The Christian Social Activism of Nellie L. McClung* (1993), and Jacqueline Anne Rouse, *Lugenia Burns Hope: Black Southern Reformer* (1989). Susan Hill Lindley's *"You Have Stept Out of Your Place": A History of Women and Religion in America* (1996) includes a chapter on the Social Gospel.

WOMEN AND GARVEYISM

Anthea D. Butler

GARVEYISM IS A social movement associated with Marcus Mosiah Garvey (1887–1940). Garvey was a Jamaican-born leader of the Universal Negro Improvement Association (UNIA), founded in 1914 in Jamaica, with its first branch in the United States in 1917. Garvey's vision was to create a new "organization based on Pan-African principles to help the black peoples" to become self-sufficient, realize the greatness of their race, and focus on Mother Africa. Garvey organized thousands of African Americans and Caribbean blacks into an association that had its own newspaper, *The Negro World*, and its own church, the African Orthodox Church, complete with a black Christ and liturgy. Garvey supporter and chaplain of the movement Rev. George Alexander McGuire, a former Episcopalian, founded the African Orthodox Church in 1921. The church was the religious arm of the Garveyite movement, complete with its own catechism and liturgy, written by McGuire, titled *The Universal Negro Catechism* and *The Universal Negro Ritual*, published by the UNIA in 1921. McGuire's goal was to support Garvey's notion that Christianity, by focusing on a white representation of God and Christ, hampered the progress of the African people. Garvey wrote, "If the white man has the idea of a white God, let him worship his God as he desires, if the Yellow man's God is of his race, let him worship his God as he sees fit. . . . We as Negroes have found a new idea. . . . We have only now started out to see God through our own spectacles" (Garvey, 44). Pictures within the church portrayed both Mary and Jesus as black. Yet women were not allowed into the priesthood, holding office only in a later formed women's auxiliary organization.

Garvey's vision, of an economically powerful and secure black network of black-owned stores and businesses, culminated with the purchase of an ocean liner, named the *Yarmouth*, which was to be the flagship of Garvey's Black Star Line. Incorporated in 1919, the Black Star Line, composed of three ships, was to transport blacks from the United States and the Caribbean to Africa. Financial troubles from the Black Star Line, an ill-fated meeting with the Imperial Wizard of the Ku Klux Klan (KKK) in 1922, and charges of mail fraud and imprisonment eroded Garvey's and the UNIA's power. Garvey was convicted of mail fraud in 1923 and served twenty-two months in the Atlanta federal penitentiary. His wife Amy Jacques Garvey continued to promote the message of Garveyism while he was incarcerated and traveled and wrote on his behalf during this time. In 1927, upon his release from prison, he was deported to Jamaica, and the UNIA split into two conventions. He subsequently moved to London and died in June 1940. Garveyism is also considered to be the precursor to the Rastafarian movement in Jamaica.

Garvey's vision lasted because of the active participation of visible women, such as his wives, and the invisible work of the many women who joined the organization. Garveyism appealed to working-class women of African descent because of its political stance on the rights of the black man and woman and its reverence of black women as "Mothers of the Race." Women from both rural and urban areas were attracted to the Garveyite movement because of his explication of a black civil religion, one in which Africa and black women would play an important part. The combination of pan-African ideals, stressing the back to Africa movement, and black Zionism attracted many women in both the Caribbean and the United States to the movement.

Garvey's patriarchal viewpoint, on one hand, gave women a limited role as maternal figures, helpmeets, and keepers of the racial purity. Yet Garveyism also empowered black women by allowing them to take charge of organizations and work within the UNIA, speaking on behalf of the organization, and encouraging them to move beyond domestic work. The role of women in Garveyism, although largely defined by Garvey, was contested and redefined by the women in the movement. Also, at a time when black women were being castigated by the white press and their employers, Garveyism provided visibility, respectability, and protection for black women of the working class. *The Negro World* featured a women's column titled "Our Women and What They Think." Female members in the UNIA were able to express their opinions of the movement and of black men in the column, oftentimes finding themselves contradicting Garvey's ideology. Despite the patriarchal foundation of the UNIA as a Black Nationalist movement, the women of the UNIA transcended these limiting roles to become writers, leaders, teachers, and effective spokespersons for the movement. When the movement began to wane, women helped to hone much of the movement's persona and public presence when Garvey himself was unable to do so. Garveyism, and its tenets, could not have lasted as long as it did without the impetus and focus of the women who marched in the UNIA parades, served in the auxiliaries, and committed themselves to the furtherance of Black Nationalism.

Early Years: Women in the UNIA

Amy Ashwood Garvey, first wife of Garvey, was born in 1897 in Jamaica. She met Garvey in Jamaica just before the formation of the UNIA. The proximity of Ashwood and Garvey's marriage to the founding of the UNIA leads to referring to Ashwood as cofounder, but it is more probable that she was the first member. Ashwood served as the UNIA's executive secretary or "lady secretary" and worked with Garvey for a time in Jamaica before going to Panama in 1916. She rejoined Garvey in 1918 in New York City and began working earnestly with Garvey on *The Negro World*, the UNIA newspaper. Ashwood's childhood friend, Amy Euphemia Jacques, also from Jamaica, was introduced to Garveyism about this time as well. After being evicted from her apartment, Jacques met and roomed with Ashwood, assisting in the UNIA offices as executive secretary to Garvey.

Ashwood and Garvey culminated their relationship in marriage on Christmas Day 1919. Jacques served as the maid of honor, even traveling with the couple to Niagara Falls on their honeymoon. The honeymoon was short-lived. In the next few months, problems surfaced between Ashwood and Garvey, and accusations of infidelity, money mismanagement, and alcoholism surfaced. Ashwood left Garvey in the summer of 1921, claiming during their separation that Garvey had begun to live with Amy Jacques. Jacques claimed, however, that the romance began after he had made the decision to divorce Ashwood. Ashwood and Garvey were divorced in 1922 after an acrimonious battle. Soon after, Garvey married Amy Jacques, who took on a prominent role in the movement when Garvey was arrested on charges of mail fraud.

Roles of Women in the UNIA

From the beginning, women joined in large numbers and at one point comprised half the membership of the UNIA. Women who were members of the UNIA were primarily day workers and domestics. The roles of black women in Garveyism could best be summarized by a column written by Amy Jacques Garvey, in *The Negro World*, titled "The New Negro Woman." In the piece, "Our Women and What They Think," she defined the New Negro woman duties and aims: (1) work on par with men in the office and the platform, (2) practice thrift and economy, (3) teach constructive race doctrine to children, (4) demand absolute respect of the race from all men, and (5) teach the young to love the race first (Matthews, 5). These principles were the core of how women envisioned their roles and place within the movement.

These ideals of the New Negro woman clashed with Garvey's patriarchal viewpoint. Roles for black women in the UNIA were clearly defined in the Declaration of Rights and Constitution as complementary and gender specific. Men were encouraged to embrace traditional roles as breadwinners, while women were encouraged to be mothers first and then helpmeets. Structurally, the UNIA modeled these traditional gender roles—each local-level division with a male general president and a female president holding authority over all the women's auxiliaries and female members. Women were encouraged to step out of domestic service and become secretaries and nurses to combat the prevalent notions of black women as domestic workers. They were also encouraged to work within the UNIA organizational structure in positions such as dress and hat maker, restaurant worker, or officeworker at the Black Star line or *The Negro World*. However, they did not hold positions of authority in the early years of the newspaper or the shipping line. By 1920, the Women's Auxiliaries were

founded in the UNIA: Universal African Black Cross Nurses, the Motor Corps, and the Ladies of the Royal Court of Ethiopia.

The Universal African Black Cross Nurses, founded in 1920 in Philadelphia by national leader Henrietta Vinton Davis, were modeled after the Red Cross of World War I. The Black Cross Nurses were organized on the local city level within the UNIA. The local Nurses unit was composed of a president (matron), head nurse, secretary, and treasurer. The purpose of the group was to provide health and other services to their communities, working alone or in conjunction with other service agencies. Many of the women who joined were either trained nurses or had some knowledge of hygiene and diet. Members were expected to provide first aid and assistance, and they were also called upon to give public lectures on proper nutrition, care for the body, and women's health issues. The Nurses also assisted with infant and home health care and participated in social welfare duties such as distributing food and clothing. The uniform of the Black Cross Nurses is perhaps one of the most recognizable of the Garveyites. Dressed in long white robes with the emblem of a black Latin cross on their caps, the Nurses provided a striking presence in the many parades and presentations put on by Garvey and the UNIA. There was also a children's contingent to the Black Cross Nurses, and they had uniforms as well. The Nurses were an important link to and role model within the black community, especially to young mothers. They were recognized and respected within their communities.

The Universal African Motor Corps, unlike the Nurses, was associated with the Universal African Legion, an exclusively male arm of the UNIA. The Corps' purpose was training members in military discipline as well as automobile driving and repair. Heading the Corps was a woman brigadier general, but the commanders and officers of the units were men. The Motor Corps also participated in the UNIA parades, wearing a military-style outfit.

The Ladies of the Royal Court of Ethiopia was mostly a social group, arranging for such events as teas and beauty contests. Modeled after other African American fraternal and social organizations, it provided a social club for the working members of the UNIA. Other fraternal orders for both men and women existed as well, providing entertainment and networking opportunities for their members.

Ideology of the Movement

Underneath the UNIA structure was a very specific gender ideology that Garvey embraced. The purpose of this ideology was to promote black unity. Despite Amy Jacques Garvey's definition of the New Negro women and her role, Garvey had a highly structured patriarchal and religious vision of what he believed women's roles were in the movement. The vision may have stemmed from both his Roman Catholic background and his upbringing in the very traditionally gendered Jamaican society. According to Garvey, black women were considered to be of the highest stature, virtuous, and in need of protection from racial violence. Men were expected to be chivalrous, to provide for the women as the weaker sex, and to protect their virtue at all costs. Black women in the UNIA were supportive of this viewpoint, because of the prevalent notion of black women in American society as promiscuous and incapable of beauty. Garvey lauded the black woman and placed her upon a pedestal. Poems like "The Black Woman" and "The Black Mother," written by Garvey, helped to formulate the vision of womanhood in the UNIA. On one hand, these poems were complementary; on the other, they stood as an example of how women were expected to behave, as well as how they were to assist the black man in the quest for racial unity. To bolster these ideals, Garvey had images of the Madonna and child portrayed as the black Madonna and child in the church of the movement, the African Orthodox Church.

Motherhood was the highest ideal and stature that women could attain in the UNIA because of Garvey's quest for racial purity. Garvey, fascinated with eugenics, believed that the role of the black woman in preserving the race was tantamount to the success of the UNIA. Miscegenation was discouraged. Men were encouraged to be hardworking and protective and not to marry outside of the race when they gained wealth. Women were expected to embrace both biological and communal motherhood. This ideology of "race motherhood" permeated the Garveyite movement. Motherhood was cast in both a biological sense, to raise children, and in a movement sense to nurture the work of the UNIA. Still more emphasis was placed on the black woman's traditional role of wife and mother in the home, rather than caring for the community at large. Marriage was considered to be extremely important. Garvey even advocated not using birth control, considering it to be a sin. For Garvey, the two-parent family was the norm, and single parenthood was frowned upon. The emphasis on motherhood and marriage, therefore, was an attempt to control the sexuality of women and ensure their participation in the movement by linking their purpose to the race and its purity. Despite his strict views on women, Garvey praised black women like Madame C. J. Walker, who gave money to begin *The Negro World*, and Ida B. Wells Barnett, who spoke at meetings for the movement. The protection of black women in Garveyism, therefore, was counterbalanced by the notion that men had to be strong and chivalrous in order to protect their women. In a sense, the rhetoric of protection also helped to bolster the patriarchal backbone of the Garveyite movement and its nationalist rhetoric.

Women's reactions to the patriarchal ideology of Garveyites were varied. For some, these notions of "real or Negro" womanhood were a welcome respite from the harsh racial attitudes of white Americans. For others, it presented a challenge to their ability to be considered full partners and leaders in the UNIA. Garvey's emphasis on motherhood and virtue made the discourse between men and women in the association strained at times. On a practical level, the emphasis on motherhood seemed to lower the position of women within the movement. Women often did not get paid for the work that they did, and protests arose at several of the conventions of the UNIA to assert that the rights of women that were stated in the UNIA constitution should be observed. Though, on the one hand, the UNIA controverted the view of what black women should be and do in society, on the other, it oppressed the women within its ranks and set up a debate that would go on internally in the organization throughout the 1920s.

Despite Garvey's heavy-handed construction of black women's roles through his nationalist lens, women were integral to the UNIA and its visibility. Amy Jacques Garvey, second wife of Garvey, did not hold a formal position but became an outspoken leader and force during Garvey's incarceration. When Garvey was convicted of mail fraud in 1923, she traveled to division meetings and carried out Garvey's wishes for the movement. She also lobbied in Washington, D.C., for Garvey's release and published some of Garvey's writings in the book *Philosophy and Opinions*, a two-volume set. She became an associate at *The Negro World* and introduced the column called "Our Women and What They Think." Providing a public forum for the women in the column, she encouraged UNIA women to take on roles beyond the traditional ones of wife and mother, thus challenging her readers to think intelligently about their roles in the pan-African movement. Talented in her own right, she was often linked to Garvey in her role as wife rather than for her ability and intelligence. Using the column as a sounding board, she encouraged the women to step out of their traditional roles and lambasted the men of the UNIA at times for not holding up their share of the burdens. Accusing them of slothfulness, she was aggressive in her criticism, arguing that they were unable to "take care of their wives financially, content to be servants and lacked pluck" (Taylor, 116). She also encouraged women to be involved in their communities, even to the point of sacrificing their personal goals. However, her castigation of black men in her column ensured criticism. She wrote in 1925 as the UNIA power began to wane: "We are tired of hearing Negro men say, There is a better day coming, while they do nothing to usher in the day. . . . Mr. Black Man, watch your step! Ethiopia's

Women were expected to embrace both biological and communal motherhood. This ideology of "race motherhood" permeated the Garveyite movement. To bolster these ideals, Garvey had images of the Madonna and Child portrayed as the black Madonna and Child in the movement's African Orthodox Church.
Courtesy of Joe Cauchi estate.

Queens will reign again and her Amazons protect her shores and people. Strengthen your shaking knees and move forward, or we will displace you and lead on to victory and glory" (Sattler, 51). Men of the UNIA consistently challenged Jacques Garvey, stating she was not a part of the committee that had been chosen to run the organization while Garvey was incarcerated. This rejoinder prompted her to respond that she was not "helpless" in regards to her duties. Upon Garvey's deportation from the United States in 1927, she soon followed him to Jamaica, where she bore him two children, Marcus Jr. and Julius. Keeping the memory of Garvey alive after his death in 1940, she continued to publish materials on him, including a memoir of Garvey in 1963, *Garvey and Garveyism.*

Other women in the UNIA ascended to positions of prominence despite the prevalent definition of ideal women as helpmeets. Henrietta Vinton Davis, an assistant to Frederick Douglass as well as an actress and elocutionist, joined the UNIA in 1919. She traveled,

organizing local divisions and serving as one of the original directors of the Black Star Lines. In 1922, Davis was appointed fourth assistant president general, the first woman to be one of the main slate of officers in the UNIA; in this capacity she traveled to Liberia in 1924 along with other officers. Davis also traveled with another prominent Garveyite, Maymie De Mena, who assisted Garvey as an unofficial leader in the movement in the states after his deportation. When Garvey reorganized the UNIA after the split in 1929, De Mena briefly assumed directorship of *The Negro World* for a time and even started her own newspaper, the *Ethiopian World.*

The year that Davis was appointed to the slate of officers was also one of confrontation. During the 1922 UNIA convention, a series of five resolutions were bought to the floor when Garvey left the room. Represented by Victoria Turner from St. Louis, women requested that they be granted more authority as local officers, field representatives, delegates, and committee members. Additionally, the resolutions asked for more visibility for women in setting international policy so that all black women could function "without restriction from men." Several other women in the Black Cross Nurses and other divisions stood up to voice their dissatisfaction with the way that women had been treated within the organization. When Garvey returned to the meeting, he asserted that there was no need for the resolutions, as the concerns were covered by the UNIA constitution.

The stresses felt by women eventually led to an assassination. Laura Kofey, fiery speaker and organizer for the UNIA, began to work with the movement in 1927. Kofey soon became a success at organizing, and her popularity caused her to split with the UNIA and form her own organization, the African Universal Church and Commercial League, in 1928. A member of the UNIA's African Legion, who was loyal to Garvey, assassinated her in March 1928.

Despite the paternalism of Marcus Garvey, many women were highly visible participants in the UNIA. By encouraging black women to be more than just domestics, Garveyism appealed to the masses of working-class black women in the United States and Caribbean by focusing on the importance of black women to the furtherance of the race. For black women who were willing to put aside their own concerns for the advancement of the race, Garveyism provided positions of importance, influence, and recognition for those who otherwise lived lives of hardship and constant struggle. Despite the internal issues in the movement, women involved in Garveyism were able to make advances and become nascent womanists in their own right, fighting for the rights of black women and the black race as a whole.

SOURCES: Barbara Bair, "True Women, Real Men: Gender, Ideology and Social Roles in the Garvey Movement," in *Gendered Domains: Rethinking the Public and Private in Women's History*, ed. Dorothy O. Kelly and Susan M. Reverby (1992). Rupert Lewis and Patrick Bryan, eds., *Garvey: His Work and Impact* (1991). Mark D. Matthews, " 'Our Women and What They Think': Amy Jacques Garvey and the Negro World," *Black Scholar* (May–June 1979): 2–13. Beryl Sattler, "Marcus Garvey, Father Divine, and the Gender Politics of Race Difference and Race Neutrality," *American Quarterly* 48.1 (1996): 43–76. Ula Taylor, "Negro Women Are Great Thinkers as Well as Doers: Amy Jacques Garvey and Community Feminism in the United States, 1924–1927," *Journal of Women's History* 12.2 (2000): 104–206; and Amy Jacques Garvey, ed., *Philosophy and Opinions of Marcus Garvey* (1968).

THE CIVIL RIGHTS MOVEMENT
Rosetta E. Ross

THE CIVIL RIGHTS movement caused sweeping changes in public policies, social conventions, and morality in the United States. Deriving from religious and moral perspectives about what constitutes a good society, the civil rights movement sought to ensure recognition of all persons in the United States as members of the human community. The movement may be said to have been fueled by a norm of radical democracy. Political goals of the civil rights movement included full participation in the democratic processes of the country; equal access and equal rights to goods, services, and other benefits of citizenship; and an end to police brutality and all types of violence against and abuse of African Americans. Persons caught by the civil rights vision were motivated primarily by religious perspectives. However, a strong humanism also inspired movement participants. The shared sense of justice, the hope for a better society, and the commitment to equality that arose from religious and humanist perspectives motivated a willingness in civil rights participants to take risks that fueled major accomplishments of the era.

Many persons consider that the 1954 *Brown* decision and the 1955 Montgomery Bus Boycott marked the beginning of the civil rights movement. It certainly began an era of mass participation in what became civil rights practices. Yet the bus boycott was also a peak in an ongoing movement of peaks and valleys of the black struggle for freedom that predated the civil rights movement by several centuries. Historians and journalists recognize the gradually increasing legal victories of the National Association for the Advancement of Colored People (NAACP), protest of black veterans returning from World War II, and other protest activities, especially during the 1940s and early 1950s, as preparing for, if not beginning, the civil rights movement. After *Brown* and Montgomery, however, in fairly rapid succession a number of other "peak" events took place between which various ongoing forms of racial protest were themselves significant. The 1954 *Brown* decision, the 1955 Montgomery bus boycott, the 1960 sit-ins, the 1961 freedom rides, the 1963 March on Washington, the Birmingham campaigns, the 1964 Freedom Summer campaigns, the mid-1960s black entry into electoral politics connected with constant voter registration, school desegregation, and other efforts comprise the civil rights movement. Tens of thousands of people took up practices replicated around the country, but especially in the South, in order to achieve the movement's ends. Civil rights practices included mass meetings, voter registration drives, consciousness raising, teaching, boycotts, pickets, marches, fasts, group voting, networking, organizing, and many other activities. From the movement's beginning, women played important roles.

Women's contributions to the civil rights movement often derived from religion, religious values, and women's participation in religious institutions. Coupled with the use of organizational and interpersonal networks, many of which emerged as women entered public life through religious organizations, religious perspectives and religious institutions proved to be invaluable inspiration and support for women's civil rights work. In many cases, women's civil rights participation evolved from women's religious morality practices of the nineteenth and early twentieth centuries. This earlier work included black and white women's social reform work such as antislavery, temperance, and antilynching activism, advocacy for humane working conditions in emerging industrial centers, providing relief and support of persons moving to industrial centers from rural areas and small towns, and race relations work. Much of this work may be understood as Christian witness arising from the theological view of slavery and segregation as sin, a theological value affirming black survival and flourishing against white supremacy, and a moral perspective derived from the Christian scriptural norm of attending to the least. Though women participated in civil rights activism in myriad ways, it is possible to examine much of women's contributions through three broad categories: (1) in preparation, initiation, and support of the movement through early-twentieth-century activism that bridged nineteenth-century reform work with the civil rights movement, (2) as student workers whose civil rights activism pushed the movement forward with its intensity and focus on empowering local leaders, and (3) as grassroots activists whose leadership in their own communities helped sustain the movement by keeping it alive in diverse local areas.

Movement Preparation, Initiation, and Support

The civil rights movement did not spring up de novo. Both the tradition of practices to survive, oppose racism, and improve life in black communities (reflecting the affirmation of black life) and the experience of abolitionism and race relations activity in white communities (emerging as challenges to the "sins" of slavery and segregation) proved to be valuable work that prepared for and initiated emergence of the civil rights movement. African Americans' activities opposing racism and seeking to ameliorate their lives can be traced from the early slave era forward. Antebellum era slave women who led survival practices and rebellions, free black women who conducted abolitionist work, and black club women who practiced racial uplift work in the late nineteenth and early twentieth centuries demonstrated that women always were integral participants in activities seeking to improve black life. Physical *and* emotional affirmation of black persons evolved as an important religious value in the slave era, contributing significantly to the founding of independent black religious institutions. The religious work of affirming black persons physically and

emotionally continued well into the twentieth century as racism continued to menace black existence. More often than not, survival, racial uplift, and liberation practices originated in religious institutions, and long after initial emergence of these institutions, black women continued to develop religiously motivated quality-of-life practices. Around the turn of the eighteenth and nineteenth centuries, for example, black women organized clubs to address social issues such as the spread of lynching as a method of subjugating black persons through terror, the status of black women domestic workers, the difficulty African Americans faced as they migrated to urban areas seeking to improve their economic circumstances, and more. Some of the most well known efforts in this regard are those of Nannie Helen Burroughs and the National Baptist Women's Convention. However, there were many other religious black women and black women's groups that carried out this racial uplift work during this era. Ida B. Wells-Barnett was a newspaper editor and club woman who worked tirelessly promoting antilynching views. The Women's Political Council of Montgomery, Alabama, founded in 1946 and populated largely by college-educated women from Dexter Avenue Baptist Church, continued the tradition of black religious women's club work for improved quality of life by providing invaluable organizational assistance to make the historic Montgomery bus boycott work. Jo Ann Gibson Robinson, an Alabama State College English professor and Council president, led the Women's Political Council in communicating and mobilizing for the boycott's initial thrust.

Alongside church clubs, in the decades preceding the civil rights movement, black women worked to improve life for African Americans through programs of para-church groups like the Young Women's Christian Association (YWCA). Working in YWCA programs across the country, black women also fought racism within that organization as they sought to overcome the practice of segregated "Y" units. With the early-twentieth-century founding of the National Association for the Advancement of Colored People there developed a complementary alternative to strictly religious institutional work for racial progress. Though religious persons often populated its ranks, the NAACP became a pivotal mechanism for challenging formal structures of racial oppression through the courts. Black women were significant supporters and workers in these efforts.

Several black women whose preparatory activism continued into the civil rights era so significantly affected the movement that their activism may be said to have generated specific values and practices that made possible some important achievements. The women's activism, influenced by their education and relative social standing, paved the way for others to join and carry on their visions for society. They are most probably responsible for initiating, fostering, and nurturing what became the religious value of attending to the dignity of the least visible persons and the norm of empowering local people that permeated and fueled movement activity in rural areas. If there were architects of the civil rights movement, Ella Josephine Baker is among those persons. Having been involved in grassroots organizing campaigns for survival and fair treatment at least twenty years before the *Brown* decision, Baker developed a perspective on human dignity and human rights that shaped the civil rights movement as well as the character and direction of other New Left movements that originated in and evolved from the tumult of the 1960s. Influenced deeply by her mother's activity in Baptist women's groups and her Baptist minister grandfather, Baker's perspective on attending to the least emerged out of religiously motivated community activism she engaged as a child.

Baker began her own civic activism in the late 1920s and early 1930s as a volunteer at the Harlem YWCA following her graduation from Shaw University in Raleigh, North Carolina. After several years of community organizing, during which she worked for the New Deal Works Progress Administration, Baker joined the NAACP's national staff in 1942 as assistant national field secretary and later became national director of branches. Through her work in the 1940s, the organization's base of African American membership increased, not an insignificant accomplishment since these increases helped intensify work that ushered in the civil rights movement. In addition to her NAACP work, Baker participated directly in the origin of two other major civil rights organizations through whose programs structure of the movement developed—the Southern Christian Leadership Conference (SCLC) and the Student Nonviolent Coordinating committee (SNCC). When the Montgomery Bus Boycott began in the mid-1950s, Baker was a founding member of In Friendship, a northern group that raised funds and arranged other support for southern civil rights activities. After the bus boycott ended, Baker and her two primary associates at In Friendship (Stanley Levison and Bayard Rustin) supported Martin Luther King, Jr., and others in forming an organization to capitalize on the boycott's momentum by helping to sponsor the first meeting of what became the Southern Christian Leadership Conference. Drafted as the logical choice to get the new organization off the ground, Baker moved to Atlanta in 1957 and worked out of a hotel room until she orchestrated setting up the SCLC's office and getting its first major voting rights program under way. When black college students began almost spontaneously to sit in at lunch counters across the South in 1960, Baker convinced the SCLC to sponsor the Raleigh Conference over Easter weekend that brought together leaders of the sit-ins. Attended by over 200 students from the North and South, as well as by leaders of the major civil rights groups, the meeting culminated in the founding of SNCC. Baker's intervention prevented the student group's being annexed as a youth wing of the Congress on Racial Equality (CORE), NAACP, or SCLC. After SNCC's founding, Baker served as an adviser to the students, influencing them to adopt a group-centered style of operation as well as a focus on empowering persons in rural areas and training leaders indigenous to local communities. Baker helped determine evolution within the civil rights movement through her work with organizations.

Like Ella Baker, Septima Clark also focused on empowering local people. Clark was a consummate churchwoman who maintained active membership in local Methodist congregations throughout her life. Emphasizing the potential for improved quality of life through education, Clark understood volunteer literacy work as a means of fulfilling what she viewed as Christian duty to attend first to the most marginalized. As an eighteen-year-old teacher in her first job on Johns Island, off the coast of Charleston, South Carolina, Clark determined a method of relating the world of her students to the things she taught. In doing this, she both taught students to read and affirmed the life with which they were familiar. Clark used this method in her regular elementary classes and in her volunteer work with adults. In addition to teaching elementary school, Clark helped prepare for and initiate the movement through work with the NAACP and other civic groups throughout her life. In 1919, Clark began work with the NAACP, collecting signatures to help build a case for allowing black persons to teach in Charleston's public schools. Following the 1954 *Brown* decision, when South Carolina, like other states across the South, made NAACP membership illegal for state, county, and municipal employees, Clark lost her teaching post and pension after thirty-five years of work. Soon after her dismissal, Clark became Director of Workshops at the Highlander Folk School. Influenced by the Social Gospel movement, Myles Horton and his wife Zilphia founded and ran the Highlander Folk School in Monteagle, Tennessee. The school was an interracial laboratory designed to teach local people, especially the poor, how to cooperatively attend to social problems confronting them. At Highlander, Clark refined the teaching method she developed on Johns Island as it evolved into the civil rights movement Citizenship Education Program that became so important to increasing black voter registration across the South. Movement workers adopted and replicated her model to facilitate preparation for voter registration. Recognizing differences in barriers to enfranchisement from state to state, Clark developed curricula tailored to needs in each state. She also created a general workbook explaining election, registration, and voting laws; social security laws; tax laws; and other topics.

While Baker and Clark were exceptional examples of black women whose preparatory work helped usher in the movement, there were others who, though they influenced the movement less broadly, worked alongside them. Modjeska Monteith Simkins taught school in Columbia, South Carolina, until forced to resign when she married. Simkins directed "Negro Work" for the South Carolina Tuberculosis Association from 1929 to 1939. Following the example of her civic activist parents (members of the NAACP's predecessor organization, the Niagara Movement) Simkins worked with the Columbia NAACP and in 1939 joined leaders of other branches to form a state NAACP conference. From the State Conference's inception, Simkins was in the forefront of activities, which put her in touch with national leaders and activities. In 1942, after NAACP participation ended her Tuberculosis Association work, Simkins took up NAACP activism full-time. She helped organize the suit equalizing black and white teacher salaries in Columbia and contributed to the group's efforts to dismantle the state Democratic Party's whites-only primary. The most notable NAACP effort in which Simkins participated was the *Briggs v. Elliott* school desegregation case of Clarendon County, South Carolina. Briggs was one of five combined cases that culminated in the historic 1954 Supreme Court *Brown* decision. Beyond helping with legal preparation, Simkins organized relief for the Clarendon County families who suffered economic retaliation for involvement with the suit. This relief work helped sustain the case, and as retaliation persisted after the 1954 ruling, Simkins continued organizing relief.

In addition to the tradition of black women's activism opposing racism, there had been a long, persistent tradition of white Americans advocating and agitating in favor of social changes that could benefit African Americans. From the earliest abolitionists in the height of the slave era through reform work of club women during the late nineteenth and early twentieth centuries, some white women consistently worked to improve the circumstances of African Americans and race relations. Similar to black women social activists of the same period, many white club women also were churchwomen who saw their work as consistent with religious beliefs about the humanity of black people. Seeking initially to abolish slavery and later to ameliorate race relations, this activity eventually became sources of many white women's support of civil participation. Moreover, as white women's club work evolved into activity within denominational and local churchwomen's groups, the YWCA movement, and work in secular organizations, the women built on the nineteenth-century foundation of collaborative, though racially charged, social reform activity between black and white club women as they began to engage in mid-twentieth-century race relations work. Visionary women leaders were especially important to white women's twentieth-century race relations work.

Rooted in the Social Gospel that evolved near the turn of the nineteenth and twentieth-centuries and in traditional perspectives about mission work that developed in American Protestantism, white women's twentieth-century advocacy for African Americans often was tinged with paternalism and generally failed to overcome its embeddedness in the culture of white supremacy. It did, nevertheless, help prepare for and support ongoing progress of black people in the United States that reached a crescendo during the civil rights movement. Thelma Stevens was one churchwoman who began working toward ameliorating race relations in a local denominational community center in Augusta, Georgia, during the late 1920s. Focusing especially on issues of segregation in church and society, Stevens's activism as a churchwoman allowed her to continue this work directing the Department of Social Relations and Local Church Activities in the Women's Division of the Methodist Church in New York. Other white women completed similar race relations work through secular organizations. Lillian Smith and Frances Pauley in Georgia and Alice Spearman Wright in South Carolina helped found or directed humans relations councils in the 1940s and 1950s and led in other race relations work. Nineteenth-century club women's work in white communities also continued through some YWCA branches' work with women and youth that also helped prepare soil in which the civil rights movement thrived. While in many places the YWCA struggled to overcome its traditions of segregation, in other instances, particularly youth work, the Y provided safe spaces for white discussions of race relations and set the standard as examples of interracial work.

Virginia Durr and Anne Braden were two white women whose work preparing for and initiating the movement was particularly paradigmatic for others who followed them. Durr and Braden were exceptional in their unprecedented activity as southern white women opposing racism and conventional values of white supremacy (for which they were both severely excoriated). Younger women hailed both as models of courageous womanhood. Alabama native Virginia Foster Durr began premovement interracial work as early as the 1930s. In the unconventonal tradition of her Presbyterian minister father who was dismissed from his pulpit for failure to take the biblical story of Jonah literally, Durr broke with southern race conventions throughout much of her life. She was a founding member of the Southern Conference for Human Welfare (SCHW), an interracial group that fought segregation in Virginia. Durr worked with Eleanor Roosevelt in the Women's Division of the

National Democratic Party to help abolish the poll tax, one means by which white women and all African Americans were denied the franchise. When Red-baiting ended her national anti–poll tax work, Durr helped found the Progressive Party and ran unsuccessfully as its candidate for the U.S. Senate in 1948. In 1951, Virginia Durr and her husband Clifford returned to Alabama, as professional possibilities ended because Clifford would not take a loyalty oath. The Durrs participated in the Montgomery Human Relations Council, sponsored the Highlander Folk School, and supported the NAACP. Virginia Durr also worked with black women to organize prayer breakfasts. Though both previously had been labeled as communists, support of Highlander, which Clifford attempted to defend in court, and other interracial activity resulted in the Durrs' appearance before James Eastland's Senate Internal Security Subcommittee during the McCarthy Red Scare. Their activism eventually completely ended Clifford's law practice, as the family was ostracized by the local white community. Although involved in preparatory activity for almost two decades before the movement's heydey, Durr's prominence in the civil rights era began with the role she and Clifford played in the Montgomery bus boycott. Supportive of Rosa Parks's NAACP work, Virginia Durr recommended that Parks, whom she knew, attend workshops at Highlander Folk School. After Parks's arrest, the Durrs accompanied NAACP leader E. D. Nixon to post Parks's bail and participated in discussions as Parks contemplated becoming lead plaintiff for the NAACP's transportation desegregation case. The Durrs remained active allies throughout the boycott. When SNCC was founded in 1960, the Durrs supported and encouraged the students. In the work supporting SNCC, Virginia Durr collaborated with Ella Baker. Both women felt the students' energy helped prevent the movement from dying. The Durrs frequently housed SNCC as well as other movement workers en route to civil rights project work across the South.

Anne Braden of Kentucky is perhaps the most well known southern white woman of her generation who opposed racism. The moral value of Braden's activism is expressed in her identification of it as work for the "whole human race." Braden and her husband Carl, both newspaper reporters, became prominent for their unwavering stand against segregated housing in Louisville in 1954. Because race-based community covenants restricted home purchasing options for African Americans, the Andrew Wade family approached the Bradens, who purchased a house in an all-white suburb and then sold it to the Wades. Although they previously were active in unions and race relations work, white Louisville vilified and ostracized the Bradens when they helped the Wades. Both Bradens lost their newspaper jobs and were subjected to a grand jury investigation. Through the

"communist plot" hysteria often used to delegitimize challenges of oppressive racial conventions, Carl Braden was convicted of sedition, fined $5,000, and sentenced to fifteen years in prison. Carl served nine months of the term while Anne (whose trial was delayed) raised the phenomenal $40,000 bail. (The Supreme Court overturned the conviction in 1956.) This crisis propelled the Bradens' long-term civil rights activism. After Carl's release, since they had lost their jobs with the Louisville paper, the Bradens became organizers for the Southern Conference Educational Fund (SCEF). Devolved from interracial groups led by Eleanor Roosevelt, the SCEF provided financial and other support for civil rights and other human rights activities. Braden edited the SCEF journal, the *Southern Patriot*, and used her significant newspaper experience to double its circulation and to spotlight and support both civil rights causes. Anne Braden met Ella Baker in 1955. The two collaborated throughout the movement era. When Carl was jailed again in 1959, serving one year for contempt of Congress (after being called before the House Un-American Activities Committee), Anne continued her activism, especially opposing Red-baiting and later supporting SNCC work. As an early supporter of SNCC students, Braden helped broaden the group's work by raising funds to sponsor one of the earliest collaborations between black students who founded SNCC and white students who were supporters or who later became members of SNCC. Through her example of courage and tenacity, Braden became a particularly important example for white women students in SNCC.

Women Students and Civil Rights Activism

An important thrust of civil rights activism derived from the intensity of college students who often engaged in the movement with abandon. Their participation was a major vehicle in civil rights organizing and accomplishments, particularly in rural areas. Without the presence of college students, primarily working for SNCC, the breadth of civil rights practice might never have been so wide. Student activism began its intensity in 1960 following the February sit-down protest at a whites-only lunch counter in downtown Greensboro by four students from predominantly black North Carolina A&T College. As word of the protest spread, college students across the South followed the Greensboro example, and the sit-in movement began. Early on black women students were prominent participants in the sit-in protests, and as the students' activism evolved into SNCC, young women played crucial roles in shaping the organization's identity and practices. Following traditions of their elders in the movement, most student activism emerged from their religious, particularly Christian, understanding of the meaning of the civil rights movement. Like older African Americans, black students also saw advocacy for civil rights as consistent with their religious views about racial equity and flourishing in black life. This religious perspective was evident in what students said as they described and analyzed their work and in many documents they wrote. The SNCC founding statement, for example, asserted that students' work arose from the emphasis on love and justice of the "Judaic-Christian" tradition.

Diane Nash, reared Roman Catholic, was one black woman whose early activism helped shape SNCC's work. In Nashville, Tennessee, Nash, who attended workshops on nonviolent civil disobedience led by Reverend James Lawson, became a leader of the Nashville Student Movement. Identifying conventions of southern racial segregation as a "state of sin," Nash became tenacious in SNCC's early direct action work that she once identified as the work of the church. She coordinated successful sit-ins and other desegregation campaigns in Nashville and was a vocal leader in early sit-in collaborations across the South. She became nationally prominent when she coordinated and led the second leg of the freedom rides from Birmingham, Alabama, after James Farmer of the Congress on Racial Equality and the first freedom riders were brutalized and convinced by the Kennedy administration to give up. Nash, who insisted that the rides must go on, marshaled a group of new volunteers. After the freedom rides drew international attention to racial brutality in the South, Nash was one of several SNCC workers invited by the Kennedy administration to discuss use of voter registration instead of direct action. Among the holdouts, Nash preferred to continue direct action along with voter registration. Their position resulted in SNCC's developing two emphases focusing on both voter registration and direct action.

Spelman College student Ruby Doris Smith Robinson, once identified as the "heartbeat" of SNCC, was another black woman student who figured prominently in SNCC's work. An active youth participant in black church culture, Robinson also engaged student activism as Christian witness. After joining the second wave of sit-ins Robinson became a SNCC volunteer. By 1963, she rose to prominence as SNCC's administrative assistant. After James Forman's election as executive secretary, Robinson became the second most powerful person in SNCC, handling the group's budget and other resources, mediating day-to-day disagreements, attending to general administration, and communicating with fieldworkers. In this latter task Robinson's work was crucial since she served as a lifeline for activists in remote rural locations. During the summer of 1964 she initiated a discussion among some women in SNCC on the organization's failure to achieve gender equity. Following Forman's resignation from SNCC, Robinson served

briefly as the SNCC's executive secretary. This made her the first woman to lead SNCC or any major civil rights group. Unfortunately, Robinson's tenure was cut short by her illness and untimely death at age twenty-five. Other black women were prominent throughout SNCC's programs.

White women students also participated in SNCC's work and other civil rights activism. More often than not, their decisions to participate in the movement also were tied directly to religious belief. For many of these young women, "the movement was church." Often they sought to understand and realize the meaning of religious faith in practical life, especially as their beliefs began to conflict with conventional subordination and exclusion advocated and practiced in southern white communities. Their joining the black freedom movement meant letting go of traditional support from family and friends (who defended the traditional racist social order) and developing new support networks within the movement. When what some understood as an inevitable evolution of SNCC toward Black Nationalism occurred, many of these white women felt "loss and isolated" since they already had lost support of traditional family and friends. Many eventually left the Deep South. Participation by white students often was initiated and mediated by the YWCA and National Student Association (NSA), both of which by the 1950s had begun race relations discussions and work. In addition, young people who engaged social justice ideas in youth groups of Protestant denominations populated both groups.

The work of some YWCA chapters catapulted one group of young white women into deep and significant opposition to the country's racial conventions. Practice of these young white women civil rights activists went well beyond the normally patronizing traditions of white support for black people (denying conventional ideologies of white racial superiority and providing fertile ground for contemporary antiracist and antiwhite supremacy work). The students sometimes attempted to break down the racial hierarchy. In Austin, Texas, the local YWCA community nurtured the antiracist sentiments of two white women students, Sandra Cason (aka Casey Hayden) and Dorothy Dawson (Burlage), both of whom became SNCC activists. Other organizations that supported young people's exploration of race relations during the 1950s were denominational youth groups, the interdenominational Student Christian Movement, and civic organizations like the National Student Association. The Student Christian Movement explored political issues from the perspective of theology, fostered social justice thought and practice, and predisposed many white Christian youth for civil rights participation. In the late 1950s, the Methodist Student Movement developed a platform that asserted failure to promote Christian involvement in political affairs denies God's authority over all life. The same white students whose idealism and moral perspectives about race emerged in denominational and YWCA youth groups promoted interracial communication, collaboration, and work within the National Student Association. All of these youth groups contributed to white women students' participation in the civil rights movement. While she was in college, for example, Casey Hayden served as a national officer of the YWCA and explored race relations as a member of the burgeoning Student Christian Movement. Hayden initially began civil rights work as an assistant to Ella Baker at the Atlanta YWCA, where she filled a position funded by the Marshall Field Foundation to broaden support for race relations among southern white students. Mary King, who followed Hayden in the Field Foundation post, also worked with SNCC. The contribution of students to the civil rights movement had its greatest impact on rural communities. Most often it was students who ventured into rural communities to carry forward Ella Baker's vision of changing society by empowering local people.

Women's Grassroots Activism

The changes in rural communities are, perhaps, the most dramatic and in some ways the most important developments of the civil rights era. Challenges issuing from the civil rights movement devastated social and economic peonage of the sharecropping system that was the lingering hold of slavery on the lives of many southern blacks. The roles of rural leaders in the civil rights movement are especially heroic because they, more than others, were subjected to persistent and explicit retaliation for their participation. This retaliation included brutal violence as well as swift, sure economic reprisals. The role of violence as a means of countering civil rights work is significantly documented in movement literature, lore, and film. However, the economic sanctions were another powerful layer of opposition to movement goals. Many persons who became rural civil rights leaders were able to do so either because they had income sources that sufficiently insulated them from economic retaliation or because they and their communities determined means to overcome economic reprisals.

As rural activism rose, women often were leaders. More often than not the work of rural black women civil rights participants arose in connection to black Christian congregations, relationships among women church members, and black church networks. Frequently, civil rights leaders who went into rural communities made initial contact with local persons through church meetings. Later, as was true in cities and towns, persons who became rural leaders often interacted with pastors and congregations to spread the word and raise support for the movement and used church buildings as gathering places for movement mass meetings or strategy sessions. In rural communities, as in towns and cities, the black religious traditional value of affirming human life emerged as an impetus for many persons' participation in civil rights practices. Moreover, as was true for their counterparts in cities and towns, rural black women easily saw congruency of civil rights norms with their religious ideals. Proclamation of this congruence generally was evident throughout the rhetoric of rural black women civil rights leaders such as Fannie Lou Hamer, who declared that "Jesus means freedom," or Victoria Way DeLee, who asserted that "the Lord was in front leadin' all of us." Furthermore, as persons who felt themselves responsible for living in ways that reflected their faith and religious self-understanding, rural religious women civil rights participants—like many other religious civil rights activists—often understood civil rights practices as important to improving the lives of persons around them and as consonant with their responsibility to witness to their faith.

One of the most remarkable rural civil rights leaders was Fannie Lou Townsend Hamer, the youngest of twenty children born to sharecropping parents in Mississippi. Hamer became enmeshed in the sharecropping system of perpetual debt at age six when she was asked to try to pick thirty pounds of cotton in return for sweets from a plantation commissary store. As a young adult, she married Perry Hamer and worked with him as a tenant sharecropper and timekeeper on a Sunflower County Plantation for eighteen years. Fannie Lou Hamer first heard of civil rights in August 1962 at age forty-five when SNCC and SCLC workers visiting Williams Chapel Baptist Church in Sunflower County, Mississippi, held a meeting emphasizing the importance of voting. Hamer was one of seventeen volunteers who tried to register to vote. When Hamer returned to work at the plantation after attempting to register, she was fired and her family lost their home. Initially forced to leave not only her job but also the county to escape violence, Hamer returned to Sunflower County after several months to set up housekeeping for her family, aided by local residents and employed as a SNCC fieldworker. Although her first registration attempt was unsuccessful, as a SNCC worker Hamer attended citizenship education classes (that she later led) and completed her own voter registration in January 1963. That spring Hamer was among six persons ruthlessly beaten on the way back from one of Clark's citizenship education workshops. Led by Annell Ponder of the SCLC, the group was arrested at a bus station rest stop thirty miles outside Greenwood, Mississippi. Hamer was so badly injured that her fingers that she used to protect her head turned blue, and skin on her back swelled and hardened.

In 1964 Hamer was a founding member of the Mississippi Freedom Democratic Party (MFDP) and was an

As rural activism emerged, women often became leaders. More often than not the work of rural black women civil rights participants arose in black Christian congregations, relationships among women church members, and black church networks. Rural black women easily saw the congruency of civil rights norms with their religious ideals. This congruence generally was evident throughout the rhetoric of rural black women civil rights leaders, such as Fannie Lou Hamer, who declared that "Jesus means freedom." Copyright © Bettmann/CORBIS.

MFDP nominee for the U.S. Senate. Organized to challenge the segregated Mississippi Democratic Party at the Democratic National Convention (DNC) in Atlantic City, New Jersey, the MFDP called for rejection of the all-white state delegation. Hamer's passionate testimony became a focal point of the convention. Although MFDP delegates were not seated, their efforts brought dramatic changes to DNC delegate selection processes. Hamer inspired many through her passionate speeches relating civil rights activism to religious faith, her gospel singing, and her continued activism in Mississippi. She later started the Sunflower County Farm Cooperative, through which she helped persons produce their own food, and eventually empowered others to escape the desperation of sharecropping through home ownership.

Winson and Dovie Hudson are two other rural women who led civil rights activism in Mississippi. The Hudsons were siblings, two of fourteen children born to a minister and his "mission work–oriented" wife in Harmony, Mississippi. Harmony was an unusual town because since the turn of the nineteenth and twentieth centuries African Americans were landowners and had established their own school there. As literate landowners the Hudsons easily took on leadership roles in the community since economic reprisals did not completely devastate them. Although they could read and write, Winson and Dovie Hudson repeatedly were turned down for failing the literacy exam in their own efforts to register to vote. They were among the few rural Mississippi residents who initially housed civil rights workers, risking severe retaliation for assisting "outside agitators." However, the more they were challenged, the more determined the Hudsons became. Their courage made them role models for others. Winson Hudson (a mother of ten) was among the first group of African Americans to file suits to desegregate Mississippi public schools. Of an original fifty-two persons who petitioned the state, only six remained after retaliatory intimidation discouraged the others. Winson's sister Dovie Hudson led the group. As a result of her standing firm in support of the lawsuit, a local bank foreclosed a loan, taking all of the family's livestock and some furniture, notwithstanding that loan payments never were late. Moreover, her house was bombed and shot into repeatedly. In addition to their work with school desegregation, voter registration, and general local organizing, the Hudsons were instrumental in establishing preschool and nutrition programs in their community.

Another rural Mississippian whose work was significant to changes across the state was Annie Bell Robinson Devine. Born in Alabama, Devine moved to live with an aunt (a domestic and laundress) in Canton, Mississippi, at age two. Devine completed high school and as a young adult took several college courses. She worked a short while as a schoolteacher and eventually made a career for herself as an insurance salesperson. This work proved invaluable both to her family's support and to her civil rights activism. Devine's education provided her alternatives to the sharecropping life and gave her a measure of independence that, like the Hudsons, shielded her from economic reprisals when she engaged civil rights practices. Taking advantage of relationships built and skills learned in her insurance work, Devine soon became a full-time CORE employee. Through connections she already had and through her skills in relationship building, Devine worked across the state, encouraging blacks to register to vote. She also was an important strategist in establishing the Mississippi Freedom Democratic Party.

Like Mississippians, black women in other parts of the rural South also played significant roles in challenging conventions of southern repression. Victoria Way DeLee led similar work in Dorchester County, South Carolina, and across that state. Born into a tenant family supported by domestic work and farm labor, DeLee attended school through grade seven. Determined as a child to change social life, she began what became her career in civil rights work in 1947 at age twenty-two when she attained her enfranchisement after hearing her minister preach about voter registration. DeLee then encouraged others and began organized registration campaigns. By this time she was married with children. Her family escaped economic retaliation for her work because of her husband's federal employment in another county. This reprieve did not include retaliatory violence, however. Gunfire repeatedly pummeled their house. After she began school desegregation efforts in the county, arsonists completely destroyed the DeLee home. In 1969, DeLee was a founding member of the United Citizens Party (UCP) and in 1971 ran unsuccessfully as a UCP candidate for Congress. Although other UCP candidates also lost their races, the party succeeded in bringing major reforms to conventional and formal practices of the South Carolina State Democratic Party. Along with her other work, DeLee was instrumental in organizing a community center for economic development and became an advocate for Native American rights.

Other Women's Civil Rights Participation

In addition to these broad categories of women's participation as premovement activists, as student workers, and as grassroots activists, women played important roles in the civil rights movement in myriad other ways. Rosa Parks's role in the civil rights movement is so well known because her refusal to give her bus seat to a white male rider precipitated the Montgomery bus boycott, one of several marker events that catalyzed movement activity. Parks attended at least one weeklong workshop at Highlander, where she met Septima Clark. It is noteworthy that Parks was selected as lead plaintiff after Claudette Colvin was dropped as a plaintiff because she used profanity and was going to be a single parent. Addie Mae Collins, Denise McNair, Carole Robertson, and Cynthia Wesley, the four girls killed in the September 1963 bombing of 16th Street Baptist Church in Birmingham, were significant female figures in the civil rights movement. Their murder poignantly signaled to the nation and to the world the extent of southern intentions to secure white supremacy. Viola Luizzo was a thirty-nine-year-old Michigan housewife who recently had enrolled in college when in 1965 she heard about the second Selma to Montgomery, Alabama, march to protest violence against Selma civil rights activities. After the original Selma march—a demonstration in which clergy from around the country joined Martin Luther King in protesting the murder of Jimmie Lee Jackson—Boston Unitarian minister James Reeb was fatally beaten. Luizzo drove from Detroit to participate in the second march. Because officials limited the group to 300 marchers, Luizzo joined only the culminating walk through Montgomery to the state capitol. In addition, she used her car to transport volunteers and marchers between Selma and Montgomery before and after the march. During her last trip, Luizzo was shot and killed. "Wednesdays in Mississippi" was a collaboration of black and white religious women who traveled to Mississippi on Tuesday evenings and spent Wednesdays observing social practices and meeting with civil rights activists. When they returned to their home areas, the women supported the movement by reporting what they learned. Wednesdays in Mississippi participants included the American Federation of Jewish Women, Church Women United, and other religious women's groups.

Women in Civil Rights Organizations

As the movement went into full swing, women participated in the array of "civil rights" organizations that either prepared for or originated during the movement. Most major civil rights organizations were not conducive to or supportive of women's participation in formal leadership. The legacy of eighteenth- and nineteenth-century patriarchy and separate spheres of work for men and women affected black and white women quite differently. Nevertheless, the continuation of this legacy during the civil rights era often limited all women's roles as "formal" leaders in civil rights organizations. In spite of obstructions based on the predominant perspective that men should lead formally, women played major roles, serving as leaders in traditional and nontraditional ways and in some instances holding formal leadership positions.

In the oldest civil rights organization, the NAACP, black women's activism was decisive in local and state work. Hundreds of black women participated in efforts of the NAACP as state and local officers and as informal leaders and supporters of NAACP programs. Daisy Bates, who became so well known for the Central High School integration effort in Little Rock, was Arkansas state NAACP president. Rosa Parks was secretary and a youth worker in the NAACP's Montgomery branch at the time of her arrest. Modjeska Simkins was an officer in the South Carolina State Conference of NAACP Branches. Victoria DeLee was a local NAACP president in her civil rights leadership in Dorchester County, South Carolina. Many other black women were important leaders in local and state NAACP activities.

In spite of this significant work at local and state levels, men dominated the NAACP regional and national leadership, though there were a few exceptions. One exception was Ella Josephine Baker, who worked on the NAACP national staff in the New York office from 1941 to 1946. Baker's invaluable activity as a fieldworker and later as national director of branches yielded connections and support that later benefited the NAACP and other major civil rights organizations. As a national staff member, Baker emphasized training local leaders and challenged the organization's hierarchical practices. Ruby Hurley was another exception. Hurley served as NAACP national youth secretary and as a field representative. In this latter post Hurley helped investigate the Emmett Till murder in Mississippi in 1955. Later,

during the height of the movement, Hurley directed the NAACP's regional office in Atlanta. As regional director, Hurley worked with various NAACP desegregation efforts and, through her office, collaborated with the Southern Christian Leadership Conference and Student Nonviolent Coordinating Committee in other movement activity.

The Southern Christian Leadership Conference, primarily an organization of black male ministers, also limited women's participation as formal leaders. However, two women, Ella Baker and Septima Poinsette Clark, held primary responsibility for major SCLC programs and, in the case of Baker, contributed significantly to the organization's origin and existence. At the SCLC, Baker advocated education programs for black masses to expedite voter registration. In this she conflicted with the "clergy-led" body over its heavy dependence on charismatic leaders and on mobilizing instead of organizing. Yet Baker's initiative proved important to the SCLC's ongoing program since Baker was responsible for initiating the collaboration of Martin Luther King, Jr., and Myles Horton that resulted in Septima Clark and the Citizenship Education Program's move from Highlander to the SCLC. Clark directed workshops at Highlander for five years before joining the staff at the SCLC. Because of its interracial work, Tennessee state authorities revoked the school's charter and auctioned its property in December 1961. Anticipating the shutdown, Horton had conversations with King about transferring the Citizenship Program to the Southern Christian Leadership Conference. This cooperation resulted from a connection that Baker sought to make with the SCLC's voting rights program that came to fruition during the summer of 1961. Clark continued her work at the SCLC through funds the Marshall Field Foundation granted Highlander for the program. Moving about the South to set up citizenship classes, Clark instituted what became the civil rights Citizenship Education Program through which thousands of persons overcame the literacy tests that were intentional impediments to their enfranchisement. Through this work Clark served as a catalyst for transforming southern political life. While Baker and Clark led major portions of the SCLC's work, both women lamented that the SCLC never strongly affirmed women's leadership and often belittled ideas women brought to formal meetings.

Of all the major civil rights organizations, the Student Nonviolent Coordinating Committee was most conducive to women's participation and leadership. To a large extent, this is accounted for in the strong influence of Ella Baker on SNCC's structure that emphasized egalitarianism and consensual decision making. Baker's influence helped make way for more full participation by women in SNCC and contributed to the magnitude of

SNCC work in Mississippi, reputed to be the most difficult of the Deep South states. Mississippi was the site of the now-famous Freedom Summer when over 1,000 student volunteers from across the country converged on the state for a massive voter education and registration drive coordinated by SNCC and the Council of Federated Organizations (COFO), the unusual, but highly successful, collaboration of major civil rights groups working in Mississippi. Some of SNCC's most significant work arose through contacts Baker made when she worked for the NAACP in New York. Baker connected SNCC worker Bob Moses with longtime Mississippi activist Amzie Moore. The campaigns of college students in Mississippi during Freedom Summer, the Mississippi Freedom Democratic Party challenge at the 1964 Democratic Party Convention, the legacy of Fannie Lou Hamer, and much more originated from conversations of Moore and Moses and from Baker's ongoing influence on SNCC.

Beyond Ella Baker's role as adviser, women college students (and some who had completed college recently) also were important leaders and participants in SNCC programs from the time of its origin. In addition to Diane Nash and Ruby Doris Smith Robinson, other women students participated in SNCC's early protest activities and later—especially leading up to, during, and after Freedom Summer—were personnel for a number of SNCC projects intended to organize local people and build local leadership. In cases when women directed SNCC projects, they usually were African American, although Elaine DeLott Baker was a white woman who directed a farm cooperative in Panola County, Mississippi. Most white women student volunteers worked in offices (particularly during Freedom Summer). Office workers helped coordinate projects, attended to communications issues (within local areas and with the press), ran down information, and completed any number of other tasks that helped SNCC make its significant civil rights contribution. In the field, black and white women students recruited persons for and taught in freedom schools; canvassed, enlisted, and otherwise helped register voters; transported ballots during the Freedom Summer mock election; and completed many other tasks.

Other black women SNCC leaders included Prathia Hall, who worked with the southwest Georgia voter education project. Muriel Tillinghast and Cynthia Washington directed SNCC projects in Mississippi, organizing, registering voters, holding mass meetings, and coordinating other activities. Siblings and Mississippi natives Joyce and Dorie Ladner first became involved with civil rights work through the NAACP and later served as field secretaries for SNCC. Bernice Johnson Reagon joined SNCC as field staff in 1962 and became

a standout as a member of SNCC's Freedom Singers. The Singers, who helped shape some black spirituals as freedom songs, were an important fund-raising mechanism of SNCC.

Among white women who worked with SNCC, Constance Curry, who headed the National Student Association's Race Relations Project in Atlanta from late 1959 to 1964, became involved with SNCC through her acquaintance with Ella Baker. Baker invited Curry to the Raleigh meeting at which SNCC was founded. In her work for the NSA, Curry connected with Casey Hayden's race relations work and brought Dorothy Dawson into the movement through work on a voter registration project in North Carolina. All three women later participated with SNCC. After she completed work on the Raleigh, North Carolina, voting rights project, Dawson went to seminary in Massachusetts and formed a SNCC support group that became the first chapter of the Northern Students' Movement (NSM). Teresa Del Pozzo and Penny Patch (both born in New York) worked on SNCC projects in Mississippi and Georgia. Jane Stembridge, daughter of a Southern Baptist minister, who drove down to the Raleigh sit-in conference from Union Seminary in New York, was the first paid staff member of SNCC.

Throughout the heyday of the civil rights movement, the Congress on Racial Equality, a pre–civil rights era interracial group, was led nationally by James Farmer. Women's participation usually occurred as local CORE workers.

While not seen as mainstream civil rights organizations, several other groups emerged during and as a result of the civil rights movement and completed work that was beneficial to movement goals. Students for a Democratic Society (SDS), which focused more on analysis than activism, attended primarily to northern white students' perspectives about the civil rights movement and changing ideas about democracy that the movement brought. Casey Hayden participated with her husband Tom Hayden in founding the SDS. The Southern Student Organizing Committee (SSOC) was formed in 1964 to provide a space for southern white students interested in race relations work to collaborate with each other in their commitment to the black freedom struggle and to overcome the ostracism they experienced because of it. Sue Thrasher was a founder and leader of SSOC. Dorothy Dawson also was a significant leader in founding the group and worked with her future husband Rob Burlage, who wrote SSOC's founding statement, "We'll Take Our Stand," supporting the "Freedom Movement" and "true democracy in the South for all people." Like major civil rights organizations, the SDS and SSOC also were dominated by men, although women did most of the day-to-day work of traveling to campuses, talking with students, and setting up local chapters. Both groups became quasi-colleague organizations to SNCC. "Friends of SNCC," primarily northern white college students who learned of and agreed with SNCC, were groups that formed, advocated for SNCC programs, and raised financial and other support for SNCC work.

Women and Race in the Civil Rights Movement

The civil rights movement left two legacies of inter-action and cooperation between black and white women: one of a persistent, though halting, tradition of black and white women working together in cordial (though sometimes difficult) collaborations and another of black and white women working together amidst overt tensions, especially among college-aged women of SNCC. In the case of the former, the tradition of middle-class black and white women working together in cordial collaborations dated back to the antislavery movement and the late nineteenth century when on oc-casion black and white club women collaborated about social reform issues. Although conventions of white su-premacy prevented mutual recognition and solidarity among the women, the practice of a kind of civility and respectability related to class-consciousness often stifled tensions and made space for cooperation across race on social reform work. These efforts continued well into the early twentieth century, when they became more con-sistent, especially in race relations work by women's groups of Protestant denominations and in collaborative efforts of black and white units of the YWCA.

This work by older women's groups provided the foundation upon which black and white women stu-dents began more aggressive race work and interracial collaboration. Black and white women college students went much farther than their older women counterparts in cooperating for social reform work, especially related to overcoming devastations caused by racial oppression in black life. However, the students' interaction was more often and more generally affected by racial ten-sions. Conflict between black and white women of SNCC arose around leadership roles and gender rela-tions, especially sexual relationships. The blatant nature of this conflict is not surprising, as it resulted, quite naturally, from at least three dynamics of the context that contributed to the tension. First, black women stu-dents, like their foremothers, often took charge of what needed to be done to improve black life and, as a result, held formal and informal leadership roles in SNCC. Moreover, unlike their mothers and grandmothers, young black women of the civil rights era felt more lib-erty and a strong sense of black pride and identity. They did not feel constrained by conventions of cordiality to withhold expressing their negative perceptions of white

women's racism. Second, the intense and assertive na-ture of SNCC's interracial interaction released white women and black men from immediate experience and consciousness of violent repercussions for the tabooed heterosexual involvement of white women and black men. Finally, both these practices by black and white women occurred in the context of a still quite powerful national culture and sanctioning of white supremacy.

In spite of the difficulty of race relations, one im-portant legacy of black and white women's work in the civil rights movement is the contribution to develop-ment of the modern women's movement. During the civil rights movement women's practices included using, and sometimes acquiring, power and space in ways that promoted self-realization. The movement presented sig-nal opportunities both for women's creative and varied use of power they already possessed and for women to realize new personal and communal power that emerged as they worked to make the United States a more just society. Black women's civil rights participation often re-flected the take-charge attitude rooted in the legacy of practice by African Americans that opposed race op-pression and attended to black survival and quality of life. Female enactment of this tradition reached a sum-mit in black women's participation in the civil rights and Black Power movements. Correspondingly, white women's civil rights activism occurring as opposition to conventions of racism also conflicted with white male privilege on which many conceptions of white suprem-acy rest. These practices by black and white women per-sisted beyond civil rights settings and after the civil rights era. As a result of women's important roles in the civil rights movement, a more assertive women's move-ment unfolded, and black and white women, sometimes in distinctive ways, expressed more public claim to women's rights.

While the movement is hailed for its dramatic impact on U.S. society, its purpose was to make accessible to African Americans in particular and poor persons in general quite ordinary possibilities of life. These ordi-nary possibilities—being well fed, having meaningful work, having liberty to be educated, having opportunity to engage in and receive rewards of civic participation—often were taken for granted by a large segment of so-ciety who denied such possibilities to others. The legacy of changes in ordinary life left in the wake of the move-ment's challenges is a legacy that women's participation helped to bring about.

SOURCES: Anne Braden, *The Wall Between* (1999). Taylor Branch, *Parting the Waters: America in the King Years, 1954–63* (1988). Septima Poinsette Clark, *Echo in My Soul* (1962). Vicki Lynn Crawford, " 'We Shall Not Be Moved': Black Fe-male Activists in the Mississippi Civil Rights Movement, 1960–

1965" (Ph.D. diss., Emory University, 1987). Vicki L. Crawford, Jacqueline Anne Rouse, and Barbara Woods, eds., *Women in the Civil Rights Movement: Trailblazers and Torchbearers, 1941–1965* (1990). Constance Curry, Joan C. Browning, Dorothy Dawson Burlage, Penny Patch, Teresa Del Pozzo, Sue Thrasher, Elaine DeLott Baker, Emmie Schrader Adams, and Casey Hayden, *Deep in Our Hearts: Nine White Women in the Freedom Movement* (2000). Jonathan L. Entin, "Viola Luizzo and the Gendered Politics of Martyrdom," *Harvard Women's Law Journal* 23 (2000): 249–268. Sara Evans, *Personal Politics: The Roots of Women's Liberation in the Civil Rights Movement and the New Left* (1979). Joanne Grant, *Ella Baker: Freedom Bound* (1998). Cheryl Lynn Greenberg, *A Circle of Trust: Remembering SNCC* (1998). Rosemary Skinner Keller, ed., *Spirituality and Social Responsibility: Vocational Vision of Women in the United Methodist Tradition* (1993). Lynn Olson, *Freedom's Daughter's: Unsung Heroines of the Civil Rights Movement from 1830 to 1970* (2001). Belinda Robnett, *How Long? How Long? African-American Women in the Struggle for Civil Rights* (1997). Rosetta E. Ross, "From Civil Rights to Civic Participation," *Journal of the Interdenominational Theological Center* 28.1–2 (Fall 2000–Spring 2001): 39–77. Rosetta E. Ross, "Religious Responsibility and Community Service: The Activism of Victoria Way DeLee," in *Unspoken Worlds: Women's Religious Lives*, ed. Nancy Auer Falk and Rita M. Gross (2000). Rosetta E. Ross, *Witnessing and Testifying: Black Women, Religion, and Civil Rights* (2003). Bettye Collier Thomas and V. P. Franklin, *Sisters in the Struggle: African American Women in the Civil-Rights and Black Power Movements* (2001).

ENGAGED BUDDHIST WOMEN
Judith Simmer-Brown

ENGAGED BUDDHISM IS a loosely organized movement of social engagement that originated in Southeast Asia in the 1960s, applying the social teachings of Buddhism to the current realities of militarism, imperialism, globalization, and development in Asian countries. This movement has been likened to the Christian Liberation Theology movement, active especially in Latin America. The term *Engaged Buddhism* (*engagé* in French) is attributed to Thich Nhat Hanh, a Western-educated Vietnamese monk who published a book by that title in 1963 describing the inseparability of meditation and "merit work," or service to the poor. Women's influence is documented in the writing of Chan Khong, a social worker who eventually became a Buddhist nun and associate of Nhat Hanh. Upon meeting the famous teacher in 1959, she wrote, "I expressed concern that most Buddhists did not seem to care about poor people. I said that I did not believe that helping poor people was merely merit work. In fact, I did not feel that I needed any merit for my next life. I wanted to help free people from their suffering and be happy in the present moment" (Cao,

25). Nhat Hanh promised to support her work "according to the Buddhist spirit" through writing, teaching, and public speaking. During their long association, Sister Chan has worked tirelessly with the casualties of war in her country, providing food, medical care, and comfort to the many displaced people. Later, in exile in France, she proved to be a resourceful fund-raiser and supporter of refugees, an advocate for political change in her homeland, and a builder of community for Vietnamese and Western Buddhists at Plum Village in southern France.

The keystone for Engaged Buddhism is the interdependence of all things, so that the suffering of others is also one's own suffering, and the violence of others is also one's own violence. Social engagement is seen as a natural extension of this understanding; the inner work of meditation practice in inseparable from the outer work of alleviating the suffering of all sentient beings. The Engaged Buddhist movement relates directly to the ideal of the bodhisattva ("awakened-heart being"), whose spiritual path is dedicated to the happiness of all.

The Engaged Buddhism movement, active in many countries of Asian Buddhist heritage, communicates through the International Network of Engaged Buddhists founded by Sulak Sivaraksa of Thailand. In the late twentieth century, Engaged Buddhism was immeasurably enriched with the emergence of Buddhism in the West, where it became a broadly based ecumenical movement of Buddhists from many different traditions, cultural settings, and political approaches in order to integrate Buddhist meditation and ritual practices with social activism. The interaction of Asian and Western "convert" Buddhisms has created an environment of increasingly sophisticated approaches that integrate contemplative practice and social activism.

There is an ongoing debate among North American Buddhists about what constitutes "engagement." Some say that Buddhist practice is, by definition, engagement and that there is no such thing as disengaged Buddhism. Others question parameters of the definitions, suggesting that mindful livelihoods, child-raising, and community involvement are all "engaged." Still others claim that only social activism on global political issues is truly engaged. In this essay, the Engaged Buddhism movement in North America has three major areas. The first and the only highlighted area is social activism in the political sphere, covering issues of ecology, peacework, consumerism, and globalization. The second area, dominated by women, is spiritual caregiving for the infirm and dying, including victims of the AIDS (acquired immunodeficiency syndrome) epidemic as well as the homeless and inmate populations. And third, an often unrecognized area is "enlightened" community building within Buddhist organizations and communities, including activism that combats community racism, sexism, and homophobia.

Several characteristic North American networks support the work of Engaged Buddhists, such as the Buddhist Peace Fellowship (BPF), the Peacemaker Order (PO), and Naropa University. Many women have been pivotal in the development of these organizations. Buddhist Peace Fellowship, based in Berkeley, California, was founded in 1977 as a network of social activists of mostly Euro-American lay origin. With strong representation from West Coast Zen and Vipassana communities, its mission was to join the insight of Buddhist practice with skillful means of social activism. Current women leaders, such as Tova Green and Frances Peavy, facilitate activist and community projects in Asia and North America in concert with other Buddhist communities. The more recent Peacemaker Order was founded in the mid-1990s by Zen teachers Bernard Tetsugen Glassman, Roshi, and Sandra Jisshu Angyo Holms, Roshi, to foster a community in which the personal practice of inner penetration and outer healing could be joined to work with others. The PO began as a Buddhist organization but has expanded to form multicultural, ecumenical communities, Peacemaker Villages, based upon openness and healing. Colorado's Naropa University, founded in 1974 by Chogyam Trungpa, Rinpoche, is a fully accredited college and graduate school that trains students in Buddhist approaches to care of the elderly, mentally ill, and terminally ill; in environmental and community-based activism; in chaplaincy with prison and homeless populations; and in contemplative education of children and adults. Buddhism professor Judith Simmer-Brown developed an Master of Arts degree program in Engaged Buddhism in 1995, integrating each of the elements of activism, caregiving, and community building. Subsequently, she led the design of a Master of Divinity degree that integrates these components with Buddhist theology and meditation practice, training chaplains for hospitals, hospices, and prison work.

Examining Engaged Buddhist women in North America requires an understanding of a diversity of roles and styles. Several are Buddhist teachers who hold the transmission or lineage authorization to train dharma students but choose to be actively engaged as well. Some work within organizations they or others have founded, and have community support. Others have written about their work in books and articles. These three groups are easily studied. Countless unnamed others are engaged in the daily service, care, and work that relieves suffering and contributes to an enlightened society in the way that Chan Khong did in Vietnam in the 1960s.

Activism in the Political Sphere

Politically active Engaged Buddhists have focused on contemporary issues of ecology, consumerism and globalization, and peacework. These women are primarily members from North American communities of Zen and Theravada vipassana that have nourished an ethic of political activism; many are leaders of the Buddhist Peace Fellowship. All these women had been activists before they became Buddhist practitioners in civil rights, antiwar, feminism, environmentalism, and economic activism. For each, activism was deepened and strengthened by Buddhist practice. Several North American women have worked closely with Asian Buddhists to forge social visions that address contemporary issues. Others have begun new initiatives that express characteristically American values and priorities.

Joanna Macy, a peace movement pioneer, raised her family in the 1960s in Germany, Africa, and India, where she was introduced to Buddhism by Tibetan refugees. Later, studying for a Ph.D. at Syracuse University in the 1970s, her correlation of "systems theory," which traced systemic shift as the key to social change, with Buddhist teachings provided pivotal ground for her activist work. After her children entered college, Macy's antinuclear activism made her aware of a profound and crippling despair at the center of the peace movement.

> Because of social taboos against despair and because of fear of pain, it is rarely acknowledged or expressed directly. It is kept at bay. The suppression of despair . . . produces a partial numbing of the psyche. . . . [But] despair cannot be banished by injections of optimism or sermons on "positive thinking." Like grief, it must be acknowledged and worked through. (Macy, 15)

Drawing on Buddhist teaching of the "four limitless contemplations," Macy developed a series of meditation exercises for activists that allow them access to their own despair as a wellspring of caring for the earth and its inhabitants. Her work has taken her to areas in Russia devastated by Chernobyl, to development projects in Sri Lanka, and to antinuclear groups in Japan, the United Kingdom, and throughout the United States. Gradually Macy's work has broadened to include deep ecology, peacework, and community building. She was one of the first board members of the Buddhist Peace Fellowship and has been an adviser for two decades. Based in the Bay Area in California, she teaches at the California Institute of Integral Studies and the Graduate Theological Union. Her books *World as Lover, World as Self* (1991) and *Widening Circles* (2000) have helped shape the Engaged Buddhism movement worldwide.

Stephanie Kaza, a professor of environmental studies

at the University of Vermont, has been a longtime environmental educator and activist. In the 1980s Kaza became a Zen student of Kobun Chino, Roshi, and trained at Green Gulch and Jikogi Zen Centers in California. As her Buddhist practice and activism merged, she joined the board of the Buddhist Peace Fellowship during its vulnerable mid-1980s. She served as BPF board president for five years of her total of ten years of service, contributing organizational savvy, environmental leadership, and networking skills. Kaza found that her Buddhist practice brought her activism into a fuller understanding of the interdependence of mind, her own and others, and reinforced her commitment to nonviolence. "I deeply value a stable mind" in the midst of activist work, she observed (Personal communication). At the University of Vermont (UVM), she focused her activism in three areas: teaching courses on ecofeminism, environmental education, and consumerism; creating "green campuses" at UVM and elsewhere; and engaging in nonviolent mediation and conflict resolution. She has written *The Attentive Heart: Conversations with Trees* (1993) and edited, with Kenneth Kraft, *Dharma Rain: Sources for Buddhist Environmentalism* (2000).

As the longtime editor of the Buddhist Peace Fellowship's *Turning Wheel*, Susan Moon brought three passions with her to the journal: long-term activism, editing and writing, and Zen practice. The guiding principle of the journal is to "work for peace, reveal and address the causes of suffering in the world, and to that end, to publish writing that develops a theory and practice of engaged Buddhism" (Turning Wheel Mission Statement, 3). For example, an issue on hatred treated rage in the skinhead movement and in prisons as well as hatred in divorce, between siblings, and in domestic violence situations. These articles were interwoven with meditations on "composting hatred" and narrative accounts of how practitioners have broken open the heart of anger and drawn its intensity and richness into their care for the world. Moon is also a prolific writer, especially on women's issues. Numerous articles have been published in other journals, and she has coedited, with Lenore Friedman, *Being Bodies: Buddhist Women on the Paradox of Embodiment* (1997).

bell hooks, a visionary thinker and social critic, is concerned with the political implications of gender, race, and class inequities in America. An African American, hooks is a professor at City College of New York who practices Buddhism in the traditions of Thich Nhat Hanh and American nun and teacher Pema Chodron. A prolific author, she writes about feminism, racism, classism, and the importance of a spiritual perspective in social activist work. hooks observes that American culture has become so alienated and disillusioned with the possibility of love and genuine community that all its cultural aims have become acquisitional, and all suc-

cess is measured by money. The result is a cold consumerism that feeds directly into the globalization that has so impoverished the world. These patterns serve to deepen the alienation and suffering that spiritual traditions are dedicated to removing. From hooks's perspective, any spiritually based social activism must restore an ethic of love into the center of its vision. As a lecturer and a commentator as well as an author, hooks has become an influential example of Engaged Buddhism.

Paula Green, founder of the Karuna Center for Peacebuilding in Leverett, Massachusetts, began her Buddhist practice at Insight Meditation Society in Massachusetts in the 1970s. A longtime activist, she aided the Nipponzan Myohoji Japanese Buddhist peace order of monks and nuns to erect the Massachusetts Peace Pagoda and traveled widely in Asia in order to familiarize herself with international peace issues. Karuna Center is a consortium of peace consultants who offer training programs, both in the United States and abroad, in nonviolent social change based on Buddhist principles. Green noted, "For me, to commit to the spiritual realm and ignore the social realities is an incomplete spirituality. . . . As I understand it, spirituality brought to earth is justice" (Queen, 253). War-torn countries as diverse as Bosnia, Sri Lanka, Rwanda, and Israel/Palestine have invited Green and her associates to train leaders in nonviolent methods and peace building. In addition to her work at Karuna, Green is a teacher, mentor, and lecturer at the School for International Training in Vermont and at the International Fellowship Program in Coexistence at Brandeis University in Massachusetts.

Spiritual Care for the Infirm and Dying

Engaged Buddhist women have pioneered work in spiritual care for the chronically ill, the aged, and the dying. That this area is of special interest to Buddhists is no surprise, for contemplation on death has been important in all the Buddhist meditation traditions. According to Buddhist teachings, all suffering in life derives from an unrealistic expectation of permanence, pleasure, and inherent selfhood in human life. Yet humans universally face death and find these unrealistic expectations threatened. Contemplating the inevitability of old age, sickness, and death brought the Buddha to meditate under the Bodhi tree near the Ganges River and served as the basis of his awakening. In every Buddhist culture, contemplating these inevitabilities has brought awakening to countless Buddhists.

In North American Buddhism, women have served as the vanguard of this movement. Coming from a variety of Buddhist traditions, their approaches also vary, but all address the limitations of North American culture's spiritual support for the dying, the aged and infirm, the caregiver, and the living who face their own inevitable deaths. Many of these women have come to spiritual care because of grief and loss in their own lives; others have seen it as a natural extension of their understanding of central Buddhist teachings. This work has taken many women into jails and prisons, where they have taught meditation and worked with the dying. The AIDS epidemic provided many more opportunities for service, and many Buddhist women have brought compassionate relief to the suffering and have provided humane treatment of AIDS victims.

Joan Jiko Halifax, Roshi, trained as a medical anthropologist with a special focus on death and dying among the Dogon of Mali and the Huichols of Mexico. Since 1970 she has worked with individuals suffering from life-threatening diseases, beginning at the University of Miami School of Medicine, then with Stanislav Grof's pioneering work with dying cancer patients. Since the 1960s Halifax has practiced Zen in separate Korean, Vietnamese, and Japanese traditions. She was a founding teacher in the Zen Peacemaker Order and received Dharma Transmission (Inka) from Tetsugen Glassman, Roshi, in 1999. She developed an approach to the dying that cultivates an atmosphere of mindfulness in which both the patient and caregiver can open more fully to life. In 1990 she founded Upaya Zen Center, a Buddhist study and social action center in Santa Fe. Drawing from her eclectic background, at Upaya she practices, teaches, and works with individuals with catastrophic illnesses and with caregivers. Elements of her training health-care professionals are being introduced into medical and nursing school curricula in other U.S. institutions. She has also spread her teachings in such books as *The Human Encounter with Death*, with Stanislav Grof (1997), *A Buddhist Life in America: Simplicity in the Complex* (1998), and *Being with Dying* (1997).

After the 1977 death of her twenty-four-year-old husband of acute leukemia, Christine Longaker began her practice of Buddhism. She moved with her four-year-old son to northern California, where she studied with the Tibetan teacher Sogyal Rinpoche, author of *The Tibetan Book of Living and Dying* (1992), and cofounded one of California's early hospice programs. As she studied Tibetan Buddhism, Longaker was moved to bring their richness and wisdom to a wider audience, especially to caregivers, the dying, and those in bereavement. As she wrote, "Real hope comes as we begin discovering and nurturing a vast perspective on life—an outlook that views the whole cycle of life and death from the deeper dimension of our true nature" (Longaker, 232). With Sogyal Rinpoche, she developed a program called Spiritual Care for Living and Dying. They train caregivers in the art of spiritually guiding the dying and in preparing for their own certain death. She also introduces them to a deeper vision of life and death, central

to all spiritual traditions, and to meditations for developing compassion and authentic presence. Her book *Facing Death and Finding Hope* is a practical guide to emotional and spiritual care for the dying.

A founding teacher of the Zen Peacemaker Order, Pat Enkyo O'Hara, Sensei, is a Soto Zen priest and teacher in the White Plum Lineage of the Zen teacher Maezumi Roshi. Sensei manages the Buddhist AIDS Network, guides a meditation group for people with AIDS at the Gay Men's Health Crisis in Manhattan, and regularly leads zazen meditation retreats. As a Peacemaker, she is deeply involved in exploring a Zen Buddhist commitment to issues of difference around race, class, sexuality, and health. A resident teacher at the Village Zendo in Manhattan, Sensei leads street retreats that explore the experience of homelessness and urban poverty.

Acharya Judy Lief teaches and practices in the lineage of the Tibetan teacher Chogyam Trungpa, Rinpoche, who personally taught her the subtle teachings of the Tibetan Book of the Dead (*Bardo Thodrol*) from the early 1970s until his death in 1987. A president of Naropa University in Boulder, Colorado, in the 1980s Lief later moved into editorial work, dharma teaching, and care for the dying, always coming back to the foundational teachings she received from her lama. She works with AIDS patients at Greystone Foundation in Yonkers, New York, a project of the Peacemaker's Order, and with the terminally ill and dying in New York and Vermont. She has written *Making Friends with Death: A Buddhist Guide to Mortality* (2001), which is based on a vision of death as a present reality of every living moment rather than a future possibility about which we would rather not think.

Madeline Ko-i Bastis is an interfaith hospital chaplain and Buddhist priest in New York and the author of *Peaceful Dwelling: Meditations for Healing and Living* (2000). Ordained as a full Zen priest with Peter Matthiessen, Roshi, in 1997, Bastis has worked as a chaplain at Memorial Sloan-Kettering Cancer Center, at New York University Medical Center, and in the AIDS Unit at Nassau County Medical Center. She notes, "Zen meditation helped me be more present for patients during my chaplaincy training, but the chaplaincy experience influenced my Buddhist practice even more. I became interested in bringing the healing, empowering and transforming qualities of meditation to everyone" (Personal communication). In 1996, Bastis founded the Peaceful Dwelling Project to promote the use of meditation for spiritual, emotional, and physical healing by people with life-challenging illnesses, their caregivers, and health-care professionals.

Pioneering spiritual care has focused not only on the terminally ill but also on the elderly and infirm. Victoria Howard, a faculty member at Naropa University, trains

and supervises chaplains and caregivers in a contemplative approach to caregiving. Howard has been involved in caregiving since 1971, when she began her practice in the Tibetan tradition of Chogyam Trungpa, Rinpoche. She is best known for establishing, with Ann Cason, Dana Home Care, a nationally franchised managed-care agency based on Buddhist principles that provided an alternative to institutionalization for seniors. Cason, who wrote *Circles of Care: How to Set Up Quality Home Care for Our Elders* (2001), now lives in Vermont, where she continues private care management and training for caregivers. In 1984 Victoria Howard began to develop courses on aging that formed the foundation of Naropa University's Gerontology and Long-Term Care master's degree program, enlisting seniors in the design of care systems responsive to the personal tasks of aging. In 1998 she began training chaplains in the Clinical Pastoral Education internship program, which serves as a part of the Master of Divinity programs in Buddhist chaplaincy at the university. Numerous articles and tapes address the approach she developed. She continues to consult with support teams for the chronically ill and dying who provide an alternative to institutional care.

Enlightened Community Building

In the 1990s the Buddhist Peace Fellowship identified the shortcomings of a reactive approach to spiritually based social activism, citing the need to address the roots of violence in contemporary society. In an attempt to do more constructive work, BPF formed a kind of "think tank," which they called the Futures Process, to study the sources of consumerism, militarism, and glob-

alization that have so enveloped the planet. What they identified as the most important area for future endeavors was an understanding of "structural violence" and alternative forms of social organization. Community building is the cutting edge of the Engaged Buddhism movement, and women are providing key leadership in this area as well.

Diana Winston is the director of the Buddhist Alliance for Social Engagement (BASE) of the Buddhist Peace Fellowship. A "volunteer corps" type program, modeled on faith-based service communities like the Catholic Workers' movement, BASE is a training program to integrate Buddhist practice, social engagement, and community life into an organic whole. Winston trained in Vipassana meditation with Joseph Goldstein and U Pandita Sayadaw. Throughout her Vipassana training, she sustained an interest in social engagement. She was frustrated by her experience that Buddhist activists did not actually practice meditation and that fellow retreatants showed little interest in social engagement. Since 1995 BASE communities, under BPF staff supervision and local mentorship, spend six months in a social action or service volunteer job and meet weekly for meditation, study, training, and support. BASE workers have developed urban community gardens, mediated conflicts in high schools, cooked at homeless shelters, and cared for the dying in California, Massachusetts, and Tennessee. BASE is now billed as "North America's first Buddhist volunteer corps," serving needy populations in a variety of settings. The BASE paradigm is grounded in the principle that "social service and social change work is facilitated by an on-going community of like-minded people" (Winston and Rothberg, 4).

Two women of the Shambhala International, founded by Chogyam Trungpa Rinpoche, have provided special leadership in community building. Sara Levinson of Halifax, Nova Scotia, formerly the executive director of Shambhala International, and Susan Skjei serve on the board of directors while residing in Loveland, Colorado. In their respective roles, each leader nurtures a large international community, using models that reside between the extremes of hierarchy and the "grassroots." The Shambhala view suggests that a pure grassroots democratic model is limited in effectiveness, while an excessively hierarchical model divorced from its constituency may become despotic. Effective communities (and enlightened societies, for that matter) must combine these in order to manifest awakening. Both Levinson and Skjei were professionally trained in corporate organizational development and, after years of Buddhist practice, brought their skills from that world to their Buddhist community. Levinson worked in corporate Toronto, while Skjei trained in organizational development in California and worked at a software company. Separately, each has visited regional Shambhala Buddhist centers from California to Minnesota to Germany to assist burgeoning Shambhala communities with conflict resolution, mediation, and the development of enlightened principles of leadership and organization. Skjei also cofounded and teaches in a Buddhist management training certificate program, Authentic Leadership, at Naropa University. In their respective efforts with Shambhala International, they are developing community structures that are responsive to regional concerns, promote social harmony, and provide leadership models appropriate to the level of decision making.

This work has been focused on the development of a global community of peace, mixing peacework with community building. Virginia Straus is the director of the Boston Research Center for the 21st Century (BRC), an international peace institute founded in 1993 by the Japanese Soka Gakkai International organization, to engage scholars and activists in dialogue on common values across cultures and religions. BRC's mission is the promotion of world peace through the cultivation of a global ethic based on human rights, nonviolence, ecological harmony, and economic justice. A former urban policy aide in the Carter White House, Straus had become disillusioned by Washington's narrow political visions, convinced that genuine social change was unlikely, even impossible. But after practicing Buddhist meditation she was able to "break out of the box and see the global picture, feel the global picture with more empathy and possibility. Buddhism gives a more reliable guide for what people really need and want, and I could begin to work on the side of people rather than against them" (Personal communication). At the BRC, Straus has been able to build bridges of communication between people of different religions, nationalities, races, and ethnicities based on a common vision of peace and global community.

The emergent Buddhist communities of North America have yet to address issues of pluralism and inclusiveness effectively, but there are pioneers leading the examination of sexism, homophobia, and racism. Certainly these issues have been of concern from the inception of Buddhist communities in North America. What has been lacking is a truly integral Buddhist approach for tackling these endemic issues. And women are providing genuine leadership from within Buddhist communities, applying years of meditation practice to the removal of barriers to truly inclusive communities.

As outlined in her landmark book *Buddhism after*

Patriarchy (1993), Rita Gross's activism has focused primarily in her critique of the effects of patriarchy on Buddhism, both in its Asian heritage and in its manifestation in American culture. Gross, formerly professor of religion and philosophy at the University of Wisconsin, Eau Claire, has devoted much of her academic career to feminist theology and a study of women in religion in non-Western cultures. She began her Buddhist practice in the 1970s in the Tibetan tradition of Chogyam Trungpa, Rinpoche, and established a small meditation center in Wisconsin. In examining Buddhism, she found that patriarchy is not inherent to the tradition's foundational doctrines but was often a creation of institutional life and conservative commentary. She urged American Buddhists to join the liberative qualities of feminism with Buddhist practice in order to create a Buddhism more loyal to its fundamental heritage. She is especially concerned that the Engaged Buddhism movement in North America has yet to include the perspectives of feminism. As she remarked,

Engaged Buddhism often directs its comments and critiques outside, toward large systems of development, colonialism, and globalization. But internal critiques, such as those brought up by Buddhist feminists concerning patterns within Buddhism itself, are less likely to find a voice within the Engaged Buddhism movement. Such blindness to internal problems is often characteristic of movements of social protest and criticism. (Gross, xi)

Janice Dean Willis, an African American professor of religious studies at Wesleyan University and a renowned translator of Tibetan texts, has published numerous books and articles on Tibetan Buddhism, Buddhist philosophy, and women in Buddhism. In 1969 as a study-abroad student in India, when she met her Tibetan Buddhist teacher, Lama Thupten Yeshe, she recognized in him the unconditional love she had seen in Martin Luther King, Jr., during her days in the civil rights movement. Her recent work has moved to bridging her experience of the civil rights movement and American Buddhism, as can be seen in her book *Dreaming Me* (2001). She advocated opening American Buddhism to the participation and contribution of greater numbers of African Americans and other people of color. Most recently, she developed specific meditation practices for identifying personal bias in the areas of race, gender, and other perspectives of privilege as a way to integrate social consciousness into American Buddhist practice.

Lesbian women in North American Buddhist communities have been active in exploring the double bias of sexism and homophobia on their paths as Buddhist practitioners. Certainly, dharma practice offers spiritual liberation from fear, anger, and hesitation, but how can lesbian women fully inhabit Buddhist communities when they encounter resistance there? How can lesbian women challenge the bias of heterosexual communities, opening them to a more inclusive perspective? A student of the Vipassana teacher Ruth Denison, author Sandy Boucher has articulated this question in such books as *Turning the Wheel* (1994), *Opening the Lotus* (1997), and *Discovering Kwan Yin* (1999). Arinna Weisman, a Vipassana teacher in the Bay Area, offers retreats for lesbian and gay practitioners. However, there is much in this area, as in the areas of sexism and racism, that must be addressed by the Engaged Buddhism movement.

Engaged Buddhism in North America is an embryonic movement with few written records, little formalized structure, and few methods of communication. However, this lack has enabled women to provide leadership relatively unfettered by the patterns of patriarchy that have so dominated Buddhist communities in other parts of the world. Sociologists have observed that women often serve in charismatic or leadership roles in marginalized religions or in the first generation of religions being established in new cultural settings (Wessinger, 1–4). As these traditions enter the mainstream, they commonly copy the patterns of the cultures in which they reside, and these cultural settings are overwhelmingly patriarchal and androcentric. If the feminist influences of the late twentieth century are insufficient, North American Buddhism may return to a patriarchal pattern within the next several generations. If this is the case, the rich contributions of women in Engaged Buddhism will be forgotten, and a record of their accomplishments and insights may be expunged from the historical record. But the contributions of these Engaged Buddhist leaders are so significant in foundational North American Buddhism that women's vision and influence are likely to endure through the twenty-first century.

SOURCES: Records of Engaged Buddhism in North America in the late twentieth century are found now in collections of essays, as in Christopher Queen, ed., *Engaged Buddhism in the West* (2000), which documents specific movements and leaders; David Chappell, ed., *Buddhist Peacework: Creating Cultures of Peace* (2000), which describes specific peacemaking initiatives by Buddhist communities; and Arnold Kotler, ed., *Engaged Buddhist Reader* (1997), which samples the best writing from the movement for a period of ten years. The contributions of women to Buddhist communities are documented in part in Sandy Boucher's *Turning the Wheel: American Women Creating the New Buddhism* (1994). The most comprehensive study of sexism in Buddhist doctrine and institutions can be found in Rita M. Gross's constructive work *Buddhism after Patriarchy: A Feminist History, Analysis, and Reconstruction of Buddhism* (1993). Quoted sources in this essay include: Ngoc Phuong Cao, *Learning True Love: How I Learned and Practiced*

Social Change in Vietnam (1993); Joanna Macy, *World as Lover, World as Self* (2000); "Turning Wheel Mission Statement," Buddhist Peace Fellowship Report to the Board, January 1998; Christine Longaker, *Facing Death and Finding Hope: A Guide to the Emotional and Spiritual Care of the Dying* (1997); Diana Winston and Donald Rothberg, *A Handbook for the Creation of the Buddhist Alliance for Social Engagement* (1997); Rita Gross, *Soaring and Settling: Buddhist Perspectives on Contemporary Social and Religious Issues* (1998); and Catherine Wessinger, ed., *Women's Leadership in Marginal Religions: Explorations Outside the Mainstream* (1993).

WOMEN'S FREEDOM AND REPRODUCTIVE RIGHTS: THE CORE FEAR OF PATRIARCHY

Frances Kissling

NO SOCIAL MOVEMENT has threatened the power and authority of patriarchal religion more seriously than the movement for women's reproductive—and sexual—rights. For most of the twentieth century, and now into the twenty-first, advocates of a woman's right to control her life and fertility have challenged religious teachings and practices that consider sexuality evil, redeemed only when open to procreation and practiced in heterosexual, monogamous marriage. The need to control women and their ability to create new life is a strong element of most religious practice. To a considerable extent it is incredible that any progress has been made in changing the positions of religious bodies on reproduction, given the deeply entrenched sexism in religions.

But the mid-twentieth-century movement for birth control led by Margaret Sanger (1879–1966) did win considerable acceptance in the mainline Christian and Jewish communities, and she did because the early movement did not challenge religious beliefs about women's role in society or about sexuality, although Sanger had a strong commitment to women's freedom. Her mantra was: "No woman can call herself free until she can consciously control whether she will or will not be a mother."

In 1914 Sanger began to publish her work on contraception, and in 1916 she opened the first birth-control clinic in the United States. Sanger focused on contraception for married couples and especially for poor women. She emphasized the way in which too many pregnancies and too many children sapped women of their health and the strength to care for the family. She appealed to the compassion of church members, not to justice. The later movement for legal abortion was supported by the same denominations, again not out of an essential commitment to women's freedom but out of a fear of government intrusion into the religious sphere and a deep concern for the loss of life and health that resulted from botched, illegal abortions.

In spite of their support for legal access to birth control and abortion, most mainline Christian and Jewish denominations remain less than fully committed to the underlying values that motivate the secular reproductive rights movement. With few exceptions, even the liberal faith community continues to teach that sexuality is licit only within heterosexual marriage and that abortion is a measure of last resort, justifiable only in limited circumstances. The general sense is that abortion should be legal in a wide range of circumstances but is moral in far fewer cases. It is at best the lesser of two evils.

Thus, there is a practical and compassionate acceptance in the religious community of the need for reproductive health services rather than value-oriented acceptance of women's reproductive rights. This makes it possible for religious leaders to support sexuality education that advises abstinence for unmarried teens but also informs them about contraception if they cannot meet the ideal and might become pregnant outside of marriage. Abortion can be a moral choice when humans fall or severe health risks exist. Newer reproductive rights issues unrelated to health risks are causing even greater concern in the faith communities. These concerns include the legality of gay marriage and assisted reproduction and adoption for gay, lesbian, bisexual, and transgendered people.

In denominational statements on reproductive rights issues, it is rare to find simple unambiguous support for women as moral agents with bodily integrity who can be fully trusted to make good decisions about when, whether, and how to have children. The value of sexuality as an expression of love or a source of pleasure outside of heterosexual marriage has yet to be honored as healthy or holy. At best, sexual expression outside of marriage is seen as a minor transgression rather than serious sin. Such a weak ethical basis for supporting reproductive rights leads to weak advocacy. For the most part it has been left to individual leaders—theologians or ministers and rabbis—to defend reproductive rights rather than the institutions themselves.

On the other hand, those religions in which women are not viewed as equal to men and where the patriarchal view of family is dominant have been passionate in their opposition to the legal recognition of reproductive rights. Is it any accident that Roman Catholics, Mormons, and ultraorthodox branches of Judaism—none of whom ordain women to ministry—limit or ban contraception and oppose legal abortion? Is it a surprise that the Moral Majority and its successor organization, the Christian Coalition, have made opposition to legal abortion, sexuality education for adolescents, and gay rights the centerpieces of their policy agendas?

And, is it any surprise that the religious voice opposed to reproductive rights most often heard has been that of men, usually Roman Catholic men? After all, the official positions of the Roman Catholic Church on sexuality and reproduction are the most restrictive of any faith group. Abortion, contraception, sterilization, condoms to prevent the transmission of HIV/AIDS (human immunodeficiency virus/acquired immunodeficiency syndrome), most methods of assisted reproduction—all are forbidden, even to married couples, even to save a woman's life or health. No other religion prohibits abortion to save a woman's life; almost no other religion prohibits married couples from using contraception. So extreme is the mind-set of the institutional Church that it sees assisted reproduction using donor sperm as adultery. To even speak of or advocate the use of contraception is considered immoral. In the 1930s, it was New York's Catholic hierarchy that went so far as to demand the arrest of Margaret Sanger on indecency charges when she lectured publicly in the city. Shortly thereafter, Sanger found herself in court challenging the Comstock laws against mailing pornography that had been invoked to prevent the distribution of contraceptives through the mail. She won.

But by the time the birth-control pill was developed, the Catholic bishops had failed completely in their effort to convince Americans that contraception was morally wrong. When the Vatican subsequently issued the controversial 1968 encyclical *Humanae Vitae* forbidding the use of contraception, Catholics were first shocked and then rebellious. Some simply left the Church; most completely ignored the decision and proceeded to use contraception to the same extent as other U.S. women. The encyclical marked the moment of ecclesial adulthood for Catholic women. They lost confidence in the moral authority of priests and bishops and clearly took control over personal moral decision making that would be based on conscience and life experience. The political power of the bishops was also diminished. In spite of heavy lobbying in Washington, government funds for family planning were made available both for U.S. women and for women in developing countries. As the 1960s came to a close, one rarely heard Catholic leaders speak out in Church or in the legislature against contraception.

When the Supreme Court's 1973 *Roe v. Wade* decision affirmed the constitutionality of a woman's right to choose abortion, the Catholic bishops and most of the nation were shocked at its reach. The Court ruled that during the first trimester of pregnancy the state could pass no laws restricting a woman's right to choose abortion. In the second trimester, the state could pass laws, but only to protect women's health by making the abortion procedure safer. Wisely, the Court stated, "We need not resolve the difficult question of when life begins. When those trained in the respective disciplines of medicine, philosophy, and theology are unable to arrive at any consensus, the judiciary, at this point in the development of man's knowledge, is not in a position to speculate as to the answer" (*Roe v. Wade*, 410 U.S. 113 [1973], Article IX, Section B). This was the most woman-centered law in the world—and still is. Women needed no one's permission, not husbands', fathers', or physicians', and they need give no reason. It was a right, not a privilege. The federal government immediately included abortion services as part of the package provided to low-income women.

The bishops sprung into immediate action. They developed a national Pro-Life Action Plan that called for the formation of pro-life committees in every congressional district in the United States as well as a national secretariat in the Washington, D.C., headquarters of the U.S. Catholic Conference. Finding no real support among other religious groups and little public support for their position, the bishops took a quiet but decisive lead in founding the National Right to Life Committee to serve as a secular lobby with the goal of overturning *Roe v. Wade*. Evangelical and fundamentalist Christians had not yet entered the political fray, and for the next five years, the Catholic bishops were the major opponents to legal abortion. Ironically, their major achievement hurt poor women and their families most: the cutoff of federal funds for financing poor women's abortions, even in cases where women had been raped or were the victims of incest.

The advances of the women's movement as well as the legalization of abortion served to mobilize evangelical and fundamentalist Christians who traditionally had avoided politics as evil but now felt their patriarchal values were seriously threatened and required entry into the political arena. The Reagan presidency in 1980 was in part the result of the rise of political activity by religious conservatives. Groups such as the Moral Majority and Concerned Women of America organized at both the grassroots and national level to elect public officials who were committed to overturning *Roe v. Wade*. Both the Catholic bishops and the Moral Majority failed in their efforts, and the violent wing of the religious opposition to *Roe* emerged. Led by a fundamentalist preacher named Randall Terry, who urged his supporters with the charge, "If you believe abortion is murder, ACT like it is murder," massive demonstrations were organized at abortion clinics across the country. Women entering clinics were harassed; their pictures were taken; their license plates were used to track them down at home. The violence ultimately led to the bombing of clinics and murder of abortion providers.

In several instances the bombers and murderers were clergy. Michael Bray bombed seven abortion clinics in Maryland, D.C., and Virginia and was imprisoned from 1985 to 1989 for those crimes. He is cofounder and co-pastor of the Reformation Lutheran Church in Maryland. Paul Hill, a Presbyterian minister in both the Presbyterian Church of America (PCA) and the Orthodox Presbyterian Church (OPC), is in prison for the murders of a clinic doctor and his escort in Florida.

On an issue that is so critical to women—to their health, their identity, and their rights—what has been the role of women of faith?

During the early stages of the reproductive rights movement, religion was pretty much the province of men. It was male ministers Sanger and her colleagues sought out to lend religious credibility to the movement. As early as the 1950s Planned Parenthood had a clergy advisory group—all its members were men. One of the first organized clergy efforts in support of women with unintended pregnancies, the Clergy Consultation Service (CCS), started in 1967 and was composed of predominantly male, Protestant ministers. One early member told me that when the first woman minister came to a meeting, she received a standing ovation.

The Clergy Consultation Service operated in a climate where the social acceptance of contraception was increasing, a secular women's movement emerging, and more women began to discuss sexuality. Campus ministers in particular found themselves counseling college students who were able to acknowledge an unintended pregnancy and wanted help reaching the decision to have an illegal abortion and a referral to a safe service. They also saw women who had had illegal abortions under bad circumstances and wanted counseling. Married and single women in congregations also went to their ministers and rabbis seeking help when faced with pregnancies they could not support. The Clergy Consultation Service referred women to safe, compassionate providers of illegal services throughout the United States and in Canada and Mexico. The Reverend Howard Moody at Judson Memorial Church in New York was the founder, although the guiding force behind the CCS was Arlene Carmen, a lay worker at the church. In fact, Carmen and the Clergy Consultation Service were responsible for developing the first legal, nonprofit, free-standing clinic in New York when they opened what would become the Center for Reproductive and Sexual Health in 1970 when New York liberalized its abortion law.

But it was with the *Roe v. Wade* decision that women active in the religious world became active on the abortion issue. First, a critical mass of women in religion committed to women's rights had developed. Women rabbis and clergy were talking to each other. Women theologians were in senior teaching positions, and many more women were studying theology and ethics. The intense opposition of the Catholic Church galvanized many women to take on reproductive rights as a faith issue. Both Catholic and interfaith movements in favor of abortion rights began about the same time.

Within the Jewish community, where support for abortion rights was the highest in the nation, the National Council of Jewish Women and B'nai B'rith Women actively lobbied in Congress against early efforts by the Catholic Church to overturn *Roe v. Wade*. The National Council has continued to be an active advocate, bringing local members to Washington for regular briefings on the issue and for lobby days. The National Council has not only had its own program and publications, but it has been an active member of the Religious Coalition for Reproductive Choice (formerly, the Religious Coalition for Abortion Rights). Women rabbis played a key role as media spokespersons. One such rabbi was Shira Stern, who was a chaplain at Memorial-Sloan Kettering Cancer Center in New York. Rabbi Stern learned of serious developmental problems during her first pregnancy and together with her husband faced the difficult decision to have an abortion.

Within the Protestant churches, there was some reluctance by denominational leadership to take on the Roman Catholic Church. Ecumenism and the common interest in social justice meant that the churches were working together—against militarism and racism as well as for economic justice. The good old boys club did not want to rock the boat, and abortion rights were not important enough to shake that sense. For women in the denominations, however, abortion rights were an important component of women's rights in the church as well as society. Women working in the denominations began talking about forming a coalition that could act and speak in the absence of individual denominational voices.

The Women's Division of the United Methodist Church was the most powerful group within the Methodist Church. Half of the resources of the church were in the hands of the division that had a strong pro-choice position. The Methodist women took the lead in organizing a network that included denominational units in the Protestant churches, Jewish organizations, and free-standing faith-based organizations into the Religious Coalition for Abortion Rights (RCAR) in 1973. While full denominational membership in the coalition was rare, many powerful divisions within the churches were members, including the Women's Division of the United Methodist Church, Presbyterians, Lutherans, United Church of Christ, Unitarian Universalists, and Jewish groups.

The enthusiasm for RCAR came from women working within the denominations. Jessma Blockwick of the Methodists and Mary Jane Patterson from the Presby-

terians were early leaders and board members. The early boards were dominated by women, and the staff was predominantly comprised of women; RCAR was left to women because in many ways it was not important enough for male religious heads of denominations. Thus RCAR lacked sufficient high-level support to really challenge the Catholic bishops at the national level. It was rare for a denominational leader or for high-ranking clergy to actively and publicly speak out for abortion rights. On the other hand, RCAR had the freedom to lobby Congress, publish the pro-choice statements of the various members, and inform the national offices of the members of challenges to reproductive rights. It played a key role in mobilizing people of faith to speak out against congressional efforts to deny Medicaid funds for abortion to women who depended on the government for their health care and was one of the few racially diverse reproductive rights organizations in the country. These achievements were a direct result of the influence of black women from the mainline denominations within the coalition.

Within the mainline denominations attacks on pro-choice positions at the General Assemblies became commonplace. RCAR was instrumental in organizing delegates, especially women, to defeat these measures. And RCAR was successful. No denomination rolled back its pro-choice views.

In large part due to the efforts of women of color within the coalition, the agenda broadened to include a full range of reproductive health needs, and the coalition changed its name to the Religious Coalition for Reproductive Choice. The coalition hired its first male executive director, the Reverend Carlton Veazey, an African American Baptist minister who, in 1982, had ordained the first woman minister in the Baptist churches in the Washington area. Reverend Veazey began a program of outreach to the black churches, choosing teen pregnancy and sexuality as the centerpiece of the coalition's expanded agenda. An annual summit of black churches at Howard University draws pastors and church workers from all over the country to discuss these issues.

Perhaps as a result of RCRC's denominational history, the organization has never had the strong participation of feminist theologians and scholars. Part of its mission has been to serve as a witness to the support for reproductive rights that exists within what is commonly understood as the mainstream of Judeo-Christian bodies. A strong identification with those feminist scholars and theologians who are working to change religion might be counterproductive and perhaps not welcomed by the denominations who are members. The conflict regarding homosexual clergy in most denominations combined with the fact that both womanist and feminist theologians are deeply committed to denominational change on this issue probably leads to a reluctance on the part of RCRC to include this important group of feminists more actively in its leadership. This is true in spite of the fact that during the late 1990s RCRC's president, the Reverend Katherine Hancock Ragsdale, an Episcopal priest, was a prominent leader in feminist and lesbian rights struggles.

But individual women in religion have made profound contributions to the ethical framework that undergirds the whole movement. Religious leaders active in the reproductive rights movement brought a strong commitment to people of color and to low-income women, which has enriched the movement. Religionists who were opponents of abortion rights focused on fetuses and morality; secular proponents of abortion rights focused on women and rights. Secular feminists were highly suspicious of religion and moral discourse. An early bridge figure between secular and religious women was Beverly Harrison, now retired professor of Christian social ethics at Union Theological Seminary in New York. As Harrison pointed out in her groundbreaking book *Our Right to Choose: Toward a New Ethic of Abortion* (1993), moral arguments had been used for centuries to justify the oppression of women. But, she insisted, feminists must find a way to ground the right to abortion in a feminist, liberation ethic. Harrison was a tireless speaker on the pro-choice circuit and deserves substantial credit for the ability of the reproductive rights movement to embrace and develop an ethic based on conscience and moral agency.

Harrison also served as an adviser to the legal team working to overturn the Hyde Amendment, which prohibited federal funds from being spent to provide abortion for women on public assistance. Harrison provided information that demonstrated that opposition to abortion was rooted in sectarian religious views of the Catholic Church and not the common religious view of most faith groups. While the effort failed, it marked the first significant collaboration between secular and religious feminists advocating the reproductive rights of poor women.

The role of Roman Catholics also has been critical to reproductive rights. They have been the most successful challengers to the institutional Church's positions on reproductive rights and its misuse of political power. Many have paid a significant price as the institution has been vigorous and ruthless in protecting its control of the public discourse on abortion in the Catholic community. No one, the Church claims, can speak for it but the hierarchy. That most Catholics ignore these prohibitions and use contraception or have abortions when necessary has not deterred Church leaders from working to prohibit such services in Catholic health-care institutions or working in state and federal legislatures to ban or limit reproductive health services. And as the largest denomination in the United States (almost 25 percent of the U.S. population is Roman Catholic) and a significant provider of health care, serving one in five people in the United States, the Church has a lot of power.

Vatican officials as well as conservative bishops have consistently monitored Catholic hospitals and the women's religious orders that run them for compliance with Church prohibitions on reproductive health care. Prior to Vatican II, Church officials and women's religious orders could be counted on to act in concert on reproductive health. In the mid-1950s St. Francis Hospital in Poughkeepsie, New York, on what is widely believed to be instructions from the archdiocese, moved to revoke the hospital privileges of five non-Catholic doctors who were known to provide contraceptives. Wide publicity and the refusal of the doctors to resign resulted in a back-down by the hospital.

After Vatican II, women's religious orders modernized, and many sisters moved into the world, putting themselves in closer contact with other women and developing a feminist consciousness about their own rights as well as those of other women. This consciousness led to a showdown between the Sisters of Mercy and the Vatican regarding the provision of postpartum sterilization in their hospitals in 1978. At that time, the Sisters of Mercy ran the largest nonprofit hospital system in the United States. Only the Veteran's Administration hospital system was larger. As female sterilization was becoming more popular (sterilization is the most common form of contraception in the United States, with 28 percent of women of reproductive age using the method), the sisters noticed a rise in requests for sterilization from women.

In consultation with the medical staff as well as the system ethicist, Sister Margaret Farley, the sisters decided that medical ethics required that they offer this service when "determined by patient and physician to be essential to the overall good of the patient." In some instances, to deny it would mean that women would face increased medical risk because of the need to undergo two separate medical procedures—childbirth and, later, tubal ligation. The sisters believed that Church prohibition of sterilization did not justify that risk. As the sisters prepared to inform their hospitals in writing that they could offer sterilization, Vatican officials found out and notified the leaders of the Sisters of Mercy that if they sent the letter, the Vatican would dismiss their elected leaders and put in their place a Vatican-selected team with the full power to run the hospitals, schools, and other projects of the sisters. It was a difficult decision, but the sisters felt that the risk of a Vatican team's dismantling many of the progressive woman-centered policies they had instituted outweighed the benefit of offering sterilization. To this day, women's religious orders cite the Vatican's threat as a limiting factor in their caution regarding the provision of reproductive health services in their hospitals.

An important entry point for Catholic women is the right of poor and marginalized women to reproductive health care. Building on the Catholic theological concept of a preferential option for the poor, Catholic women found a theologically sound basis for speaking out for women. The National Coalition of American Nuns (NCAN) was the first organization to take a position in favor of public funding for poor women seeking abortions. While NCAN did not have a position on legal abortion itself, it was strongly committed to support for low-income women. Many of its members worked directly in impoverished communities and saw the effect that unintended pregnancy had on women's lives and that of their families. When Henry Hyde, a Catholic member of Congress representing Illinois, succeeded in 1976 in cutting off federal funding for abortion, NCAN issued a statement in solidarity with poor women, noting that as long as abortion was legal and available to women who could pay for it, women who relied on the government for their health care should also have access to funding for the procedure. While NCAN was criticized by the hierarchy for taking this position, no action was taken against the group.

Sister Theresa Glynn, a member of the Sisters of Mercy, added her voice to the debate in Florida about a proposed anti-choice amendment to the state constitution. Sister Glynn testified before the Florida state legislature in 1978 in favor of public funding for abortions and noted that the Catholic position on abortion is "not so cohesive, not so monolithic as is often presented." She stated her firm belief that "the Church will come to a more nuanced position in this area" (Testimony of Sr. Mary Theresa Glynn to the Florida State Senate Rules and Calendar Committee given in Tallahassee, FL, on Wednesday, May 24, 1978).

Other actions by Catholic women religious in favor of reproductive rights did not go unpunished. In December 1982, Agnes Mary Mansour, a Sister of Mercy, was appointed director of the state Department of Social Services in Michigan. As director, Mansour would preside over the state's health-care budget, which included funding for abortion for poor women. Vatican officials directed Mansour to refuse to release such funds or decline the post. Mansour decided that there was no moral conflict with serving as director of Social Services and releasing the money. Again noting the right of poor women to access to legal health services, Mansour refused to comply with the Vatican demand. Then Brooklyn Bishop Anthony Bevilacqua was sent by the Vatican to discuss the matter. Bevilacqua arrived with papers for the dismissal of Mansour from the Sisters of Mercy and demanded that she either resign her job or sign the pa-

pers. Mansour, in an effort to protect the sisters from Vatican action, agreed to resign from the order.

Arlene Violet joined the Sisters of Mercy when she was eighteen and remained with them for twenty-three years. During that time, she pursued an education in law and advocated for the poor. In 1982 she decided to run for Rhode Island state attorney general but had to leave the religious order in order to hold that office. She was elected and became the first woman attorney general in the state.

Elizabeth Candon was yet another religious sister whose efforts for women landed her in trouble with the Catholic hierarchy. In 1972 when the Vermont Supreme Court struck down the state's restrictive abortion statute, she allowed a group of women to meet at Trinity College in Burlington where she was president so they could organize the state's first outpatient abortion clinic. In 1976 she was appointed secretary of Vermont's Agency of Human Services and defended the state's policy of funding abortions for poor women. Her bishop John Marshall wrote an open letter in 1977 criticizing her public position that abortion is a decision that should be left to the woman. He threatened to excommunicate her and suggested she might have to leave her order.

The most public conflict between the Vatican and women religious occurred in the context of the 1984 presidential campaign. The first woman candidate for vice president, Geraldine Ferraro, a pro-choice Catholic Democrat, had been nominated by the party. New York's Cardinal O'Connor strongly criticized Ferraro for her pro-choice views on abortion, particularly for her introduction to a briefing book on Catholicism and abortion prepared for members of Congress by Catholics for a Free Choice, the leading voice for pro-choice Catholics in the public policy arena. In that introduction, Ferraro wrote, "As Catholics we deal each day, both personally and politically, with the wrenching abortion issue. . . . Some of us have taken strong pro-choice positions. Others are uncertain. That is what this briefing is all about. It will show that the Catholic position on abortion is not monolithic and that there can be a range of personal and political responses to the issue" (from the introduction to "The Abortion Issue in the Political Process— A Briefing for Catholic Legislators," September 30, 1982. Signed by members of Congress Geraldine A. Ferraro, Leon E. Panetta, and Thomas A. Daschle).

Catholics, especially Catholic women, were looking for a vehicle to express their disagreement with the attacks on Ferraro as well as to assert the right of Catholics to express views on abortion that were at odds with the official position without facing punitive measures from the Church. About two years earlier, Catholics for a Free Choice had drafted and begun to circulate among theologians a document called "A Catholic Statement on

Abortion." The statement asserted that there was more than one legitimate Catholic position on abortion, noted that the majority of U.S. Catholics supported legal abortion, and called on Church leaders to open a dialogue on abortion and to cease punishing Catholics who expressed views other than the official one. It had been signed by about eighty leading Catholic reformers, academics, and social activists, including some nuns and priests. In preparation for publication, it was circulated to members of the Women Church Convergence, a loose coalition of feminist organizations working for women's rights in the Church. A number of nuns signed the ad in the final days before its scheduled publication in the Sunday *New York Times* (October 7, 1984). Twenty-four women religious, two brothers, and two priests were included among the ninety-seven signers.

The ad was widely covered by the media, but there was little immediate reaction from Church authorities. Shortly after the presidential election the presidents of the communities of the nuns, priests, and brothers received letters from the Vatican agency responsible for governing religious life, demanding that the members of their communities who signed the ad publicly retract their signatures or face dismissal from their communities. Since the Vatican action was publicly announced, a hailstorm of international publicity ensued, probably more public attention on a single *New York Times* ad than in the history of advocacy advertising. In a demonstration of feminist collaboration, the women's communities began a process of meetings with the signers and with other community leaders. There was no evidence of similar collaboration among the men, and in fairly short order, the four men wrote to Catholics for a Free Choice and requested that their names be removed from the statement. The men's orders publicly announced that the men had complied with the Vatican demand.

A two-year debate between the women's communities and the Vatican ensued, with the Vatican softening its demands as the sisters refused to comply. Interestingly the Vatican refused to communicate directly with any individual signer. One sister, Mary Ann Cunningham, a Loretto sister, sent a letter with her picture to the Vatican, noting that she was a person, an adult woman, and requesting that the Vatican communicate directly with her if they had any demands or requests. She never received a response. Eventually, the Vatican reduced its demand to receiving written assurances from each order that the sisters accepted the teaching of the Church on abortion. There was considerable variation in how orders and the sisters themselves responded to this demand. No sister has ever removed her signature from the statement. In a few instances, the sister signers did accept Church teaching on abortion, their com-

munity informed the Vatican, and the cases were immediately settled. In at least one case, the order informed the Vatican that a sister accepted the teaching of the Church on abortion without the knowledge or consent of the sister. In other cases, the sisters and the order crafted a statement that said that the sister accepted the position of the Church on abortion, but the sister privately interpreted the teaching differently than the Vatican.

Two sisters, Barbara Ferraro (no relation to Geraldine) and Patricia Hussey, Sisters of Notre Dame de Namur, flatly refused to say they accepted Church teaching on abortion and publicly declared that they believed abortion could be a morally correct decision. The two had spent the last decade as directors of Covenant House, a homeless shelter in West Virginia, and seen close up what unintended pregnancy can do to women's and children's lives. Ultimately, the order refused to dismiss the two, and the Vatican backed down. The political victory was diminished by the personal fallout between the order and the sisters who resigned from the order about six months after their case was settled. Ferraro and Hussey have continued as codirectors of the shelter and activists for reproductive rights.

The Vatican's attack on the statement and on the sisters who signed it proved to be a major defeat for the Church's antiabortion agenda. First, in attacking the signers publicly, the Vatican exposed the fact that there was a diversity of opinion on abortion within the Church community—not only were some nuns and priests pro-choice; so were leading theologians and social activists. Signers included Marjorie Tuite, longtime activist for peace and democracy in Central America, and Donna Quinn and Margaret Traxler, Chicago-based activists for women's rights and economic justice. Six sisters of Loretto were signers—all well known in the progressive Catholic community. Second, the Vatican proved powerless to silence the nuns. None retracted, settlements were publicly acknowledged by the sisters as a sham, and some sisters went on the pro-choice speaking circuit, expressing more explicit pro-choice views over time than they had in the statement itself. Interestingly, the Vatican made no further attempt to silence any of these sisters following the "settlement" of their cases, nor have they moved to dismiss any sister worldwide who has expressed pro-choice views on abortion or on family planning. While the media focused on the sister signers, many lay signers also reported instances of retribution. Rosemary Radford Ruether, Daniel Maguire, Giles Milhaven, E. Jane Via, and other prominent Catholic scholars highly sought as speakers on the Catholic circuit had some engagements canceled as a result of signing the ad and noticed a decline in future engagements.

But as Margaret Traxler noted on national television: You cannot put the toothpaste back in the tube. The ad demonstrated what polls had long shown, and Church officials want to keep secret: The majority of Catholics are pro choice.

Much to the Church's chagrin, this included many Catholic public officials—male and female. High-profile male politicians were subject to some criticism, but never to the extent that women, more fragile politically, faced. Catholic men in political life were careful to distinguish their personal views from the political ones. Governor Mario Cuomo of New York consistently claimed to accept in his personal life the Church's judgment that both contraception and abortion were morally evil. However, he made an eloquent argument for the distinction between the personal and political. Governor Cuomo gave a major address on this distinction at Notre Dame University in 1984 that stands with John Kennedy's speech to the Greater Houston Ministerial Association in Texas in which he declared, "I do not speak for my Church on public matters, and the Church does not speak for me" ("Address to the Ministers of Houston," delivered on September 12, 1960, to the Greater Houston Ministerial Association, Houston, TX).

The more radical elements of the Catholic antiabortion movement, including one auxiliary bishop Austin Vaughn of New York, were highly critical of Cuomo. Vaughn told the New York *Daily News* that Cuomo was "going to hell." As a whole, however, the Catholic hierarchy treated Cuomo with kid gloves. And progressive Catholics who were at best ambivalent on abortion hailed Cuomo as their kind of guy. Catholic women in public life often believed that the personal was political and either openly disagreed with the Church position on abortion or did not emphasize their adherence to Church teaching enough. Moreover, they rarely had the same close personal relationship to clergy and bishops that male politicians had. The Church had less access to them as a result, and they were therefore more suspect.

The pride Catholic women felt when Geraldine Ferraro became the first woman to run for vice president on a major party ticket turned to shame when the hierarchy, most notably New York's Cardinal O'Connor, chose to attack her for her pro-choice views during the campaign. Catholic women turned out in droves at campaign stops with signs indicating their support for her and their own pro-choice Catholic views.

Attacks on pro-choice Catholic women in the legislatures increased as the anti-choice position was more threatened. In a 1989 special election for the California State Senate, pro-choice Catholic grandmother Lucy Killea ran on the Democratic ticket. If Killea won, the Senate would be pro-choice by one vote. Killea was an underdog, running as a Democrat in heavily Republican Orange County. But her victory was ensured when the archbishop of San Diego, Leo Maher, notified her by fax that she was under a Church interdict not to receive communion because of her pro-choice views. Maher also sent the fax along with a press release to local media, which ran with the story. Killea was elected and still serves in the state senate. The interdict still stands. Maher's successor declined to lift the interdict, and Killea, still a pro-choice Catholic, receives communion outside of the diocese whenever she can. (The interdict is only effective in the diocese in which it was declared.)

The frequent public clashes between Catholic women and the all-male Catholic hierarchy were a public relations problem for the bishops. Ironically, it was the bishops' failure to overturn *Roe v. Wade* that led to a key role for a woman within the bishops' conference. Recognizing in 1990 that their strategy to make abortion illegal was simply not working, the bishops retained the public relations giant Hill and Knowlton to advise them on how to repackage their message. Hill and Knowlton's first step was to advise the bishops to put a woman up front. Helen Alvare, a young, Hispanic lawyer working in the legal office at the U.S. Catholic Conference, became the bishops' spokesperson. Alvare, it was felt, would better reflect the general consensus that abortion was a woman's issue and would mute the frequently heard criticism of the bishops' antiabortion campaign: What do older celibate men know about women's lives and needs?

Other women were found to represent anti-choice Catholic views. Mary Ann Glendon, a respected Harvard law professor who had come full circle from liberal to conservative, frequently defended Church positions on both abortion and contraception. Glendon was the first woman appointed by the Vatican to head a Vatican delegation at the United Nations when she was appointed to head the Holy See delegation to the 1995 Fourth World Conference on Women in Beijing. Glendon frequently wrote and spoke about the "old feminism" in which Western women dominate and espouse a society in which hedonism and individualism dominate. This is contrasted with the "new feminism" articulated by the Vatican in which the communal values of developing world women are offered up as an antidote. "New feminists" are not interested in sexual or reproductive rights; they are rooted in concern for their children, family, and community. This type of feminism is what enabled Pope John Paul II to say at a Vatican meeting on reproductive health: "I am the feminist Pope."

While many of the high-profile flash points involving Catholic women in the struggle for reproductive rights have been the result of efforts by the Catholic hierarchy to retain control of the public presentation of the Catholic position on abortion, Catholic women have been an organized part of the reproductive rights movement since the early 1970s when three Roman Catholic laywomen, active in the National Organization for Women, organized first a local New York group called Catholics for a Free Choice (CFFC) and then a national organization with the same name in 1973. Like liberation theologians who first demanded social and political justice for the poor and marginalized from civil governments and eventually applied that same analysis to Church structures, the CFFC founders believed that just as women needed to lead the struggle for women's rights in the political sphere, so women needed to lead in demanding changes in the Church that would contribute to women's equality and well-being. Moreover, they believed that the Catholic bishops did not represent either the true position of the Church on abortion—a more nuanced and historically developed position than the hierarchy presented—nor the views of Catholic people.

CFFC was to serve as the voice of Catholics in the United States who believed abortion should be safe, legal, and available, especially to poor women.

The issues addressed by CFFC over the last thirty years provide insight into the development of pro-choice religious thought not only in the Catholic community but throughout the religious community. For example, in 1974, CFFC founder Patricia Fogarty McQuillan dramatically identified the link between Catholic opposition to abortion and male power in the Catholic Church by crowning herself pope on the steps of Saint Patrick's Cathedral. The act made an important ecclesial point—without women in leadership in the Roman Catholic Church, theological positions would always discriminate against women. It also made the point that the Catholic hierarchy was not to be taken too seriously. If there is

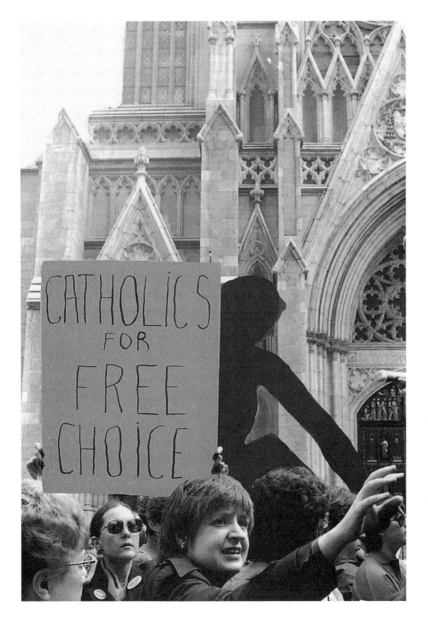

While many of the high-profile flash points involving Catholic women in the struggle for reproductive rights have been the result of efforts by the Catholic hierarchy to retain control of the public presentation of the Catholic position on abortion, Catholic women have been an organized part of the reproductive rights movement since the early 1970s, when three Roman Catholic laywomen, active in the National Organization for Women, organized first a local New York group called Catholics for a Free Choice and then a national organization with the same name in 1973.
Copyright © Bettye Lane Studio.

one thing that pomposity and arrogance takes offense at, it is being treated with humor. One cannot help but contrast the act of a woman crowning herself pope in 1974 to the June 2002 ordination orchestrated by seven Catholic women from Germany, Austria, and the United States who sought only priesthood and searched widely till they found a "bishop," Romulo Antonio Braschi, they believed to be in the correct line of succession to confer priesthood on them in a ceremony on the Danube River between Germany and Austria.

Perhaps the greatest strength of Catholics for a Free Choice has been its lay leadership. CFFC has had three presidents—Patricia Fogarty McQuillan, the founder who died of cancer in 1975; Patricia McMahon, president from 1977 through 1981, who had been active in the women's movement; and Frances Kissling, who came out of the secular women's and reproductive rights movements. None of us had a history in Catholic movements, and all of us had a healthy skepticism of an institutional Church. None of us were dependent on the Church for our livelihood or identity. This was also true of the CFFC board. Only one priest or religious ever served on the board; and it cost him his priesthood. Joseph O'Rourke, Jesuit antiwar, prison reformist was board president in 1975 when he went to Boston to baptize a baby who had been refused baptism because his mother was pro-choice. O'Rourke was dismissed by the Jesuits for this act. While the board has included well-known Catholic theologians such as Rosemary Radford Ruether, Mary Hunt, Daniel Maguire, Giles Milhaven, and Catholic intellectuals such as Mary Gordon, only one has worked for a Catholic institution, Daniel Maguire, and he is tenured. This absence of institutional control has helped CFFC challenge the Church fearlessly. As Mary Hunt once noted: "What are they going to do? Call our mothers and complain?"

Several CFFC projects have exposed it to virulent attacks by both the Catholic bishops and right-wing Catholic lay groups. Among these no effort has aroused more criticism within the institutional Church nor gained more public acceptance for CFFC than the See Change campaign that calls on the United Nations to review the unique membership status of the Vatican in that body. Under the name Holy See, the Vatican is the only religion to be considered a nonmember State Permanent Observer in the United Nations. This status enables the Vatican to maintain a mission and delegation at the United Nations; to sit on specialized bodies such as the International Labor Organization; to sign on to and to submit reservations to treaties, conventions, and other UN documents; and to vote and have a voice at UN conferences. Beginning in 1992, the Vatican increased its efforts to restrict family planning and access to safe legal abortion through the United Nations. First,

at the Rio Conference on Sustainable Development (1992) and then at the Cairo Conference on Population and Development, Vatican delegates launched strong attacks on feminists, claiming they wished only to impose hedonism and individualism on the women of the developing world. The Vatican's representatives also lashed out at governments that favored offering confidential access to sexuality education for teens, distribution of condoms to prevent the transmission of HIV/AIDS, and promotion of abortion policies that would reduce the maternal and morbidity rates currently plaguing women in the developing world.

The Vatican was often joined in opposing woman-centered reproductive health policies by countries where conservative Islam was strong; Libya and the Sudan were frequent allies. Surprisingly, though, the leadership of the Catholic countries of Latin America were notably absent from this coalition.

In these meetings, CFFC, which is accredited as a nongovernmental organization (NGO) in special consultation to the United Nations, provided governments and other NGOs with information about progressive Catholic views on reproductive health, separation of church and state, as well as polling information on worldwide Catholic attitudes and practices that would support reproductive health policies. CFFC was much aided in this work by its international colleagues. Beginning in 1987, CFFC had helped develop a Western Hemispheric coalition of CFFC groups from Canada to Chile. By 1992, groups calling themselves Católicas por el Derecho a Decidier (CDD) existed in Mexico, Uruguay, Brazil, Bolivia, Colombia, Chile, and Peru.

So effective was the CFFC/CDD counter to the Holy See that in 1995 the Vatican challenged the credentialing of CFFC and two CDDs for the Fourth World Conference on Women to be held in Beijing. The effort failed, and CFFC and CDD were present at the Beijing Conference. CFFC president Frances Kissling made a plenary presentation on challenging fundamentalism and received a standing ovation.

But the power of the Vatican in the United Nations continued unabated, and the See Change campaign grew. An open letter to Kofi Annan, UN secretary general, was launched. Almost 1,000 groups worldwide, including Catholic and other religious groups, human rights organizations, and women's and reproductive rights groups, signed on. Worldwide publicity from the BBC to the Botswana News ensued. The See Change campaign accomplished its first goal. The fact that the Vatican had a seat in the United Nations became public knowledge. And for once the Vatican was on the defense. Rather than lead an attack on reproductive rights, the Vatican had to defend its "rights."

While a change in the Vatican status at the United

Nations is not likely to occur during this papacy—or even over the next decade—the See Change campaign has put the United Nations and the Vatican on notice that caution in the mix of theology and policy needs to be observed. So challenged by the See Change campaign were the bishops that in remarks at a summer 2002 press conference on sexual abuse then president of the U.S. bishops conference Wilton Gregory noted that the Church was under attack from many directions. He claimed there are those who want to silence the Church in the United Nations and those who wish to destroy Catholic health care in the United States.

While both are mischaracterizations of CFFC campaigns, the fact is that they are both CFFC campaigns. Along with the See Change campaign, CFFC is a leader in research and monitoring the growth of the Catholic health-care system and its provision of reproductive health services. CFFC has reported that in over 171 mergers between Catholic and non-Catholic hospitals, reproductive health care from family planning and assisted reproduction to sterilization and abortion has been restricted in more than 50 percent of the non-Catholic hospitals.

CFFC's research on Catholic health care is the most extensive body of information available in the field and has been influential in legislative and regulatory efforts to prevent further erosions of reproductive health care throughout the United States of America.

Perhaps the most creative and important religiously based reproductive and sexual rights public awareness campaign was CFFC's 2001–2002 Condoms4Life campaign, launched on World AIDS Day, December 1, 2001. The campaign called on the Catholic bishops to support rather than oppose the use of condoms to prevent the spread of AIDS. CFFC was influenced in its decision to include condoms and AIDS as a women's reproductive health issue primarily because of the dramatic increase of AIDS among women and children. Another factor was the need to educate the Church regarding women's inability to say no to sex in situations where they are at risk and to educate women about their right to demand that men, including their husbands, use condoms to protect them.

The campaign began in Washington, D.C., with bus shelter billboards and advertisements in the Metro. Immediately the archdiocese of Washington reacted, calling on the Metro authority to remove the advertisements. The bishops claimed that the ads were untrue because they said the bishops banned condoms. They claimed they had no power to ban condoms. They pointed with pride to the fact that the Church was the primary health giver for 25 percent of the world's people with AIDS. CFFC retorted that that meant that over 10 million people with HIV/AIDS were not given the information they needed to protect their sexual partner from contracting the disease. This, CFFC said, was not the culture of life the bishops claimed to represent but a culture of death.

The ads also appeared in Toronto, Canada; Mexico City, Mexico; Nairobi, Kenya; Santiago, Chile; La Paz, Bolivia; Manila, the Philippines; Johannesburg, South Africa; and Managua, Nicaragua. In all cities, even a single billboard attracted wide public attention and media coverage.

As the scope of reproductive rights has increased—far beyond the single issue of abortion—the role for women of faith increases. The new reproductive technologies (and some old ones like surrogate motherhood) raise new questions. Is there a right to have children as well as not to have them? Do we own our genetic material and have a right not to allow it to enter the world against our will? Who owns frozen embryos? Should they be destroyed at any point? Is stem cell research a moral imperative or a moral tragedy? As these questions are debated over the next decade, the dramatic increase in women trained in theology and ethics will be of enormous benefit.

But some things will remain the same. The continued rise of conservative religious influence on U.S. politics will mean that women from faith communities will need to remain active. President Bush's courtship of the Religious Right includes his efforts to fund sectarian religious social services and health-care provision. It also includes efforts to further restrict access to family planning and abortion, both in the United States of America and in the developing world. The special commitments of women informed by progressive religious values—respect for the rights of the poor and marginalized, women's autonomy and bodily integrity—will be important tools in ensuring that reproductive and sexual rights are advanced.

SOURCES: Beverly Wildung Harrison explores the necessity of women's procreative choice to ensuring women's self-determination in *Our Right to Choose: Toward a New Ethic of Abortion* (1983). In *A Brief, Liberal, Catholic Defense of Abortion* (2000), authors Daniel A. Dombrowski and Robert Deltete analyze the Catholic Church's history of theological development and the development of science to show that a pro-choice position is defensibly Catholic. Looking at 150 years of birth control and debates over reproductive rights in the United States, Linda Gordon's *The Moral Property of Women* (2002) argues that control of reproduction is a topic central to promoting the status of women in society and that opposition to it has long been a tool of those opposed to gender equity. For a discussion of the history of the Clergy Consultation Service, see *Abortion Counseling and Social Change from Illegal Act to Medical Practice: The Story of the Clergy Consultation Service on Abortion* (1973) by Arlene Carmen and Howard Moody. Frances Kissling is the editor of *Conscience*, a quarterly news journal of Catholic opinion that investigates and contributes to discussions of sexual and reproductive ethics, social justice, gender equity, and the Catholic Church's influence on these issues.

ECOFEMINISM
Heather Eaton

ECOLOGICAL FEMINISM (ECOFEMINISM) emerged in the 1970s predominantly in North America, although the term was coined by French feminist Françoise d'Eaubonne in *Le Féminisme ou la Mort* (1974). Ecofeminism has matured over three decades and could be termed, loosely, as an evolving discourse created by the convergence of two important contemporary movements—ecology and feminism. Ecofeminism is considered by many to be a third wave of feminism.

The basic understanding is that connections exist between the oppression and domination of women and the oppression and domination of the earth or nature. In particular the mistrust or hatred of women (misogyny) and the fear of dependency on the natural world are interlocking. Ecofeminism opposes these negative connections, researches the historical and contemporary evidence, and works to improve life for women and nature.

History of Women and Nature

There are deep historical roots to this connection. To consider nature as feminine is a venerable tradition. In many cultures around the world, ancient and modern, the earth has been and still is associated with women. Terms such as *Mother Nature*, *Mother Earth*, or *Earth Goddess* are common. In North American indigenous traditions this language is familiar. In the past, the "feminine" earth or nature was revered. Women were seen to be closer to nature and at times highly respected. However, as Western societies developed, the ideas of connecting women to nature became negative. Over several centuries the beliefs that both women and nature were inferior and depraved became accepted as reality. Within most Western cultures, to be considered feminine or close to nature was of lesser value than to be masculine or to rise above nature.

Western cultures were heavily influenced by Christianity. Historically Christianity affiliated women and nature and considered them to be inherently corrupt. For example, some Christians taught that the earth is the devil's gateway, that the devil enters the world through women, and women are closer to the earth than men. For centuries Christian leaders taught that men were spiritual and women were bodily; that men, not women, were in the image of God; that women were born of nature and men were born of spirit; that women were intellectually like children and need to be controlled; that nature must be controlled. In the past, some male Christian theologians and philosophers decided that nature was chaotic and unruly, and because women were closer to nature, therefore educating women was unnatural. There are many such teachings connecting women to nature, then rejecting both as inferior to men and God. The worst of these teachings claimed that the earth was perceived to be irrelevant to God, and women and nature were to serve men and God.

Ideas about women and nature are entangled within a whole way of envisioning the world in pairs and opposites. This type of thinking uses hierarchical dualisms to understand the world. Examples of such dualisms are men/women, human/nonhuman, heaven/earth, supernatural/natural, culture/nature, spirit/matter, soul/body, thought/emotion, order/chaos, rational/irrational, light/dark, and divine/demonic. These are hierarchical because the first is given a priority value over the second. They are dualistic because they are understood to be opposites. There are also correlations among corresponding halves of the dualisms, such as among women, nonhuman, earth, matter, body, emotion, nature, chaos, irrational, dark, and demonic. Women have often been viewed to be more emotional, irrational, and bodily than men. Men are still considered in some cultures to be more intellectual and rational and possessing more spiritual qualities, such as strength or courage, than women. These hierarchical dualisms are not true about the world but are a way of understanding and ordering it. They are part of a patriarchal (literally, the rule of the father) worldview.

In *The Death of Nature* (1980), Carolyn Merchant studied the development of Western ideas and beliefs about the world during the period from 1500 to 1900. During this time science became important, and scientific discoveries about the world surpassed religious ideas. Merchant showed how hierarchical dualisms were embedded into science as well as religion and became foundational to Western thought, values, and attitudes. The negative connections between women and nature came to be seen as "natural." The consequences were that both women and the earth became exploited and dominated.

Deeply engrained within Western philosophy, science, law, and medicine are negative ideas about women and nature. They operate in subtle ways and indirectly influence thinking and actions within the world. Ecofeminism exposes and challenges these negative connections between women and nature and suggests that the earth or nature is exploited and dominated, in part, because it has been characterized as feminine. They show how these connected forms of domination are implicated in cultural worldviews, economic structures, and social patterns. It is not coincidence that still today most women do not share full equality with men, and nature is neither respected nor cared for. The women-nature identification has been used consistently to diminish the lives of women. Ecofeminists further claim that all oppressions (class, ethnicity, gender, orientation, ableism, and the natural world) are interconnected within a logic of domination. Interestingly, not all ecofeminists came to ecology and feminism by studying the history of Western culture.

Ecofeminist History and Development

Ecofeminism has been developing since the 1960s and is part of a rising consciousness about gender issues, ethnicity, class distinctions, and ecological health. Ecofeminism is comparable to an intersection of many paths, where one meets academics and activists, environmentalists and feminists, religious and nonreligious types, and local and international groups. While they share a basic concern for the connections between women and nature, there are different entry points on the path and distinct sets of concerns. All are part of ecofeminism.

Religion

One of the earliest North American ecofeminist voices was theologian Rosemary Radford Ruether, who in the early 1970s saw the layers of connections, at least in general terms, among ecology, feminism, and religion. In *New Woman, New Earth*, she called for a prophetic vision to shape a new world on earth, one that was not defined by domination. Out of her passionate concern for justice and a good life for all, Ruether saw that genuine social justice required a new vision and perhaps even a new religion.

> Women must see that there can be no liberation for them and no solution to the ecological crisis within a society whose fundamental model of relationships continues to be one of domination. They must unite the demands of the women's movement with those of the ecological movement to envision a radical reshaping of the basic socioeconomic relations and the underlying values of this society. (*New Woman, New Earth*, 204)

This new vision was compared to the negative women-nature associations. Both had to be examined carefully in terms of their connections to women's lives, the accelerating ecological crisis, and religious worldviews and values.

From the mid-1970s to the mid-1980s women from many religious traditions researched the women-nature, feminist-ecological questions. Some sifted through and reinterpreted Christianity, Judaism, indigenous spiritualities, and Buddhism, and others reclaimed Goddess traditions. Several Christian theologians were involved in the discussions such as Ruether, Anne Primavesi, and Sallie McFague. Judith Plaskow examined ecofeminism and Judaism. Of several North American indigenous women addressing ecological concerns, Paula Gunn Allen, a Laguna Pueblo-Sioux, explored practices connecting and ideas about nature, women, spirit, and creation. Joanna Macy and Stephanie Kaza, both socially engaged Buddhists, gleaned insights from Buddhism to reflect on the ecofeminist challenges. Delores Williams, from a womanist perspective, saw profound connections between the treatment of "black bodies" and the treatment of women and nature.

In response to the discovery of the negative history, the rise of feminist consciousness, and the growing ecological concerns, some women became attracted to alternative non-Western, nature-based, and/or ancient Goddess traditions. Women such as Charlene Spretnak (U.S. writer, speaker, and activist) explored Goddess and earth-based religions and revived the positive imagery between women and nature, or the earth. Carol Christ and Starhawk studied how human-nature relations were understood in Goddess, Wiccan, and earth-based spiritual traditions. Many other women joined this search for a living spirituality that honored both women and the earth. These efforts became a part of ecofeminist spiritualities and interreligious efforts.

During this time, women, coming from religious perspectives, were involved in ecofeminist projects, although not using the term. Canadian Ursula Franklin (feminist physicist and Quaker peace activist) examined the junction between women, technology, and ecological stress. Franklin exposed the attitude of domination within the ideas that technology will bring freedom and prosperity. She documented the systematic exclusion of women in technology as well as the resistence to examining the social and ecological consequences of technology. American and Canadian Rosalie Bertell (environmental epidemiologist, member of the Grey Nuns of the Sacred Heart) published her research findings on the controversial relationship between nuclear energy and human illness, such as leukemia. Both women have worked extensively since the 1970s, consistently motivated by justice, feminism, and a concern for the earth.

From another religious vantage point, several feminist-leaning orders of nuns in the United States and Canada dedicated their vision, mission, and property to ecological health and education. Miriam Therese McGillis, Dominican sister and founder of Genesis Farm, is one of these "green nuns." In both Canada and the United States there are dozens of religious orders of nuns dedicating themselves to the intersection of religion and ecofeminism.

Religion and spirituality have been well traveled ecofeminist pathways, although others came to ecofeminism from separate directions.

Activists and Social Movements

During the same time period of 1970 to the mid-1980s, but on different paths, women in the United States made ecofeminist connections within environmental and feminist movements as well as from antimilitarist, peace, antinuclear, and antiracist initiatives. For them ecofeminism represented types of social action where gender and environment intersected. For example, as toxic dumping turned into health problems, women organized to ban pesticides or other contaminants in soil, water, or air. In 1978 Lois Gibbs, of upstate New York, became one of the first environmental activists to bring the issue of environmental and health disasters to national and international attention. Her efforts led to the relocation of 833 households of Love Canal, New York. Noël Sturgeon, academic and activist, carefully documented the many roots of ecofeminism within activist and political movements in the United States (*Ecofeminist Natures: Race, Gender, Feminist Theory and Political Action*[1997]).

Conferences brought diverse people together and vitalized the connections between women and ecological concerns. Significant gatherings were: Women and the Environment, Berkeley, California, 1974; Women and Life on Earth, Amherst, Massachusetts, 1980; Ecofeminist Perspectives, University of Southern California, Los Angeles, 1987; and World Women's Congress for a Healthy Planet, Miami, Florida, 1991. These conferences united large numbers of people working on a range of issues and bought ecological-feminist associations into public places. For some, ecofeminism now represented women working in toxic waste, health, media, spirituality, art, theater, energy, urban ecology, or conservation and from the stance of theorist, activist, educator, dreamer, or social critic.

The activist groups, conferences, academics, and socially engaged citizens formed the base from which, over time, diverse perspectives emerged. During these years ecofeminist vitality and visions were evident. New developments occurred within publications on ecofeminism, ecofeminist theory(ies), and political philosophies. Ecofeminism began to shift to a different level, of historical critiques of the past and cultural and intellectual analysis of a viable and alternative future for women and the earth. Susan Griffin, writer and social thinker, exposed the historical evidence within Christianity, Western science, and philosophy of the depth of hostility toward women and the inseparable abhorrence of nature

(*Women and Nature: The Roaring Inside Her* [1978]). Mary Daly, educator and author, not only analyzed the historical identification of women with nature but supported women as being more rooted in nature than men (*Gyn/Ecology: The Metaethics of Radical Feminism* [1978]). Women such as social ecologist and political activist Ynestra King, then of the Social Ecology Institute in Vermont, developed theoretical connections to promote the holistic and political vision of ecofeminism. Ecofeminist anthologies appeared and created definitions of what ecofeminism meant. Edited books such as those by Judith Plant (*Healing the Wounds: The Promise of Ecofeminism* [1989]), Irene Diamond and Gloria Orenstein (*Reweaving the World: The Emergence of Ecofeminism* [1990]), and Carol Adams (*Ecofeminism and the Sacred* [1993]) further launched ecofeminism into academic conversations and popular movements. Ecofeminists, while sharing a basic understanding, were beginning to reflect differently on, if, and how to dismantle the women-nature link.

Academia

Concurrent with these developments was the advance of ecofeminist philosophy, principally by Karen J. Warren. Her edited collections *Ecological-Feminism* (1994), *Ecofeminist Philosophies* (1996), and *Ecofeminism: Women, Culture, Nature* (1997) and her book *Ecofeminist Philosophies* (2000) created a conceptual base for debates about ecofeminism. Academics engaged with historical and theoretical questions embedded in the women-nature and feminist-ecological linkages.

People in philosophy, sociology, political science, religion, ethics, economics, and environmental and women's studies shaped the basic ecofeminist connections. Ecofeminism was understood in four ways; as the history of the women-nature association, as a lens through which many disciplines (sociology, psychology, technology, etc.) could be refocused, as an alliance within political and social movements, and as a way of seeing how women's concerns (poverty, sexual assaults, health, etc.) are related to environmental degradation. As scholars developed their ecofeminist perspectives, university courses on ecofeminism became widespread.

Global Ecofeminism

During the 1980s and 1990s ecofeminism flowered. Academics and activists from diverse areas were intrigued by the term *ecofeminism* and what it could mean. Women engaged with ecofeminism from many angles and from different parts of the world. Ecofeminism was an interdisciplinary project. Some addressed the history of the association of women and nature; others examined particular topics. Carol Adams was the primary leader in bringing animal rights into the ecofeminist arena. The issues of meat-eating, the fur industry, experimentation on animals, and the sexualizing and feminizing of animals discussed in her book *The Sexual Politics of Meat* (1994) made an impact within the ecological-feminist conversations. Greta Gaard—activist, academic, and author—addressed a range of concerns for activists and animals. Justice concerns such as land claims, nuclear power, militarism, education, abortion, and cross-cultural issues were also appearing on ecofeminist pathways.

By the 1990s statistics accumulated on the relationship between ecological stress and several other factors; gender, health, militarism, and economics. Policies of economic globalization, the World Bank, and the World Trade Organization were criticized where they created, or demonstrated a lack of concern for, gender and ecological problems. Ecological disasters (Exxon oil spill, Bopal, Chernobyl, Gulf War, megadams, and rainforest destruction) were studied and exposed for the ecological and/or gender wreckage. These global issues became ecofeminist concerns. National organizations emerged that were ecofeminist in orientation, such as the Women's Environment and Development Organization (WEDO) in New York and Women, Environment, Education, and Development (WEED) in Toronto; and in conjunction with the UN Earth Summit in 1992, the theme of Women for a Healthy Planet became the impetus for countless local activist and education groups to appear around the world. Today there are hundreds of local communities in North America connecting women and ecological issues, as well as Web sites, newsletters, networks, and small organizations. Large institutions such as the United Nations Development Fund for Women (UNIFEM) and the World Council of Churches see the value, necessity, and wisdom of ecofeminism.

Ecofeminist Contributions

Ecofeminism was exciting! It was a connection that made sense to many and spread quickly in a short time period. People came together from many directions, learning from each other and collaborating. For some, it was a new idea, a fresh insight, and a helpful tool. For others it confirmed what they had been doing in political and social movements. Ecofeminism became a way of seeing aspects of the world, of analyzing certain problems, and of finding solutions. It also provided necessary resources from the past that helped the present and shaped the future. By 2000 ecofeminism was known in most universities and environmental and women's movements.

The history of ecofeminism is similar to people converging at a main crossroads. Ecofeminism is the totality of the various pathways to that point, the many conversations taking place on the way, and the exchanges at the crossroads. Each pathway requires its own discussion. The ecofeminist religious path has been well traveled, and although not central to all ecofeminists, some specific contributions are meaningful.

Religion and Spirituality: Old Problems and New Ideas

Ecofeminist perspectives are seeping into every aspect of religious understanding, including religious histories, systematic theologies, scriptural interpretations, images of the Sacred, spiritualities, and ethics. Some ecofeminists are studying and exposing the negative history and practices of their traditions. Others are examining texts and teachings for insights, redeeming what is helpful and negating what is not. In many cases, the mainline religious traditions have ignored the resources and teachings that foster a deep sensitivity toward the natural world. They have lost a reverence for the wonder of life, as well as an awareness of the immensity and magnificence of the earth.

Ecofeminists probe the Christian tradition for its part in developing and sustaining hierarchical dualisms. Other work involves the reinterpretation, expansion, or creation of particular doctrines, symbols, and metaphors that include and honor women and the natural world. For example, the classic division between heaven and earth has become an obstacle in motivating Christians to address ecological issues. By eliminating or reinterpreting the relationship between heaven and earth, ecofeminists open up the possibilities to encounter the Sacred on earth. Some address the broad horizons and foundations of Christian theology. Theologians Sallie McFague, Rosemary Radford Ruether, and Anne Primavesi, although differently, found ways to ground Christian theology in nonanthropocentric or earth-based frameworks. Catherine Keller's interest in eschatology and visions of the end of time led her to ponder these from ecofeminist perspectives. Conversations between religion and science intrigued Nancy Howell, and she brought ecofeminist ideas to this intersection. Experiences in Latin America and social ethics shaped Lois Ann Lorentzen's approach to ecofeminism and social justice. The divine "feminine" within Christianity, Judaism, Hinduism, and Buddhism inspired Eleanor Rae to develop images of the Sacred that are both feminine and earth-friendly.

Interreligious collaboration is growing. Feminists, ecofeminists, and those concerned with ecological problems often share resources and insights from multiple religious traditions. While expanding ecological and feminist awareness within each religion, interreligious cooperation assists people in finding common solutions.

Ecofeminism became a way of seeing aspects of the world, analyzing certain problems, and finding solutions. It also provided necessary resources from the past that helped the present and shaped the future. By 2000, ecofeminist theories were being published and discussed in most universities and throughout the environmental and women's movements.
Courtesy of Rowman & Littlefield Publishers, Inc.

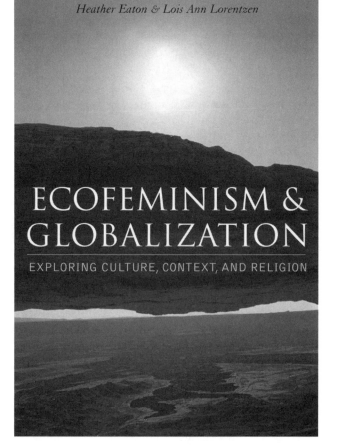

Heather Eaton & Lois Ann Lorentzen

ECOFEMINISM & GLOBALIZATION
EXPLORING CULTURE, CONTEXT, AND RELIGION

In an increasingly multireligious world, alliances among religions can greatly influence public policy on issues core to ecofeminism.

Ecofeminists, inspired by religion, often concentrate on areas such as ethics, biotechnology, agriculture, reproductive rights, economics, globalization, and social transformation. The intersection of ecofeminism and religion involves both transforming the religion and the social realities.

Many people engage ecofeminism with religious and spiritual traditions and while finding resources also show that there are limits to this intersection. Regardless of the religious tradition, challenging foundational presuppositions and reshaping religion(s) remain arduous tasks. A tension exists between how far a tradition can be stretched and reinterpreted and the need for new religious sensitivities. This tension mirrors the feminist ambivalence with patriarchal religions, among those who modify the existing system and those who create new traditions. There are limits to reworking some traditions that have accumulated misogynist notions and antiecological stances.

Some ecofeminists say we are in a time of a new spiritual awakening. What is most needed is a spiritual sensitivity toward the earth, wherein the earth is perceived of and experienced as Sacred. Such a religious or spiritual sensitivity is both a primeval and a contemporary awareness. *Interconnectedness, webs of relations, interdependence, mutually enhancing patterns of existence,* and the *subjectivity of life* itself are all terms commonly used to reach beyond the mechanistic, technical, and scientific-objective culture. The horizon of cosmology is also shaping ecofeminist spiritual efforts. The significance of knowing the earth as part of a living universe broadens consciousness and creates possibilities of new ways of perceiving the earth and resisting its destruction. Humans are understood to be one species among many, within a complex and magnificent unfolding of the universe and life on earth. There are countless ecofeminist spirituality efforts in creative earth-centered rituals, prayers, dances, art, workshops, cosmic walks, and spiritual retreats that foster a spiritual awakening. All of these efforts are directed toward awakening consciousness to the immense beauty and elegance of life in all its forms and reducing further ecological and social devastation.

Which Ecofeminism?

Ecofeminism was an insight that proved to be useful, illuminating, and instructive. Although it meant different things to different groups, the ecological-feminist connection was a valuable insight that sparked much interest and debate. Yet it was not reducible to any one easy definition. From the beginning, those who accepted that feminist theory and practice must include an ecological perspective and that solutions to ecological problems must include feminist analyses disagreed as to the nature of these connections. As ecofeminist philosopher Karen Warren writes:

[T]he varieties of ecofeminism reflect not only the differences in the analysis of the woman/nature connection, but also differences on such fundamental matters as the nature of and the solutions to women's oppression, the theory of human nature, and the conceptions of freedom, equality, epistemology on which various feminist theories depend. (Warren, "Feminism and Ecology: Making Connections," 4)

Those who committed themselves to ecofeminism wrestled with the range of issues and concepts that had gathered at the ecofeminist intersection. Many had used the term—and from distinct and differing vantage points. It was new and flexible, and no one controlled the definition. When there was enough material to do comparisons, it was evident that ecofeminism as a whole was inconsistent. For some, ecofeminism was so broad and carried so many issues that it became haphazard. Others were frustrated with the inner contradictions. The discomfort with ecofeminism became an explicit focus of conversation. Academics examined ecofeminist theories, assumptions, and particular interests. Although the original insights of the connections between the domination and exploitation of women and the earth constituted the basis of all ecofeminist research and practice, distinctions, disagreement, and contradictions were evident. Feminists and ecofeminists reflected differently on the relationships between women and the natural world, and misogyny and the ecological crisis. Some ecofeminists concentrated more on women's issues than environmental problems, and others the reverse. Spirituality was central to some ecofeminists; for others it was irrelevant or aroused suspicion. Ecofeminist differences became important.

Different Pathways and Interests

Several specific problems emerged. In-depth ecofeminist research revealed the extent to which Western cultures were rooted in ideologies of domination, a central one being the interconnected dominations of women and nature. While this work exposed the ideological substructure of the problem, it was not straightforward to know how to change it. A tension existed between those who developed ecofeminist theories and those working for political change in social movements. Some ecofeminists seemed to be more interested in the historical and symbolic connections between women and nature, or sophisticated theories of how the world should be, than in the actual suffering of women and ecosystems. Others perceived the greatest need to be in addressing economic and material realities and concrete issues of women's poverty and ecological stress. How was there to be a relationship between those providing historical and theoretical analysis and those resisting pollution, loss of agricultural land, or biodiversity decreases? As Rosemary Radford Ruether stated in *Women Healing Earth: Third World Women on Ecology, Feminism and Religion* (1996), activists and academics need to work together. She points out that the cultural-symbolic level of the relationship between sexism and ecological exploitation is the ideological superstructure that reflects and sanctions the social, economic, political, and religious order. At times correctives are needed for the my-

opias that plague ecofeminisms that emerge from white affluent or academic contexts. Ecofeminists who draw primarily from those whose frameworks do not recognize those at the bottom of the socioeconomic system perpetuate these myopias and contribute to an ecofeminism that is primarily cultural escapism rather than liberatory.

A second problem was around ethnicity. Most academic ecofeminists are white, yet in North America toxic waste is often dumped in Afro-American, Native American, or Hispanic neighborhoods. As with the development of feminism, concerns for ethnic, cultural, and contextual differences were required. Ecofeminists needed to address environmental racism.

Was ecofeminism as global as it seemed, or was it a North American discussion that did not consider the women-nature reality from other parts of the world? Environmental and feminist activist Vandana Shiva from India and German economist Maria Mies (*Ecofeminism* [1993]) challenged ecofeminists to understand that North American culture was only one culture, among many other and different cultures and viewpoints. The women-nature connection and the ecological and feminist movements are not the same everywhere, and ecofeminism will be unique, or perhaps irrelevant, in other places. Heather Eaton and Lois Lorentzen discovered that ecofeminism operates differently in Christianity than in Buddhism, and in Kenya than in Chiapas (*Ecofeminism and Globalization* [2003]).

Significant discussions also emerged around the question of early ecofeminist claims that there is a natural or essential affiliation between women and the earth. Some felt that women are closer to nature than men due to menstruation and child birthing. Others thought that it was "natural" for women to be caring, kind, communal, and relational, and thus their concern for the earth is a logical extension of a caring nature. These ecofeminists celebrated the connection between women and nature and, while opposing their mutual domination, kept the belief that women are more linked to nature than men. This "essentialism" was adamantly refuted by other ecofeminists. They want to dismantle the connection, saying there is no special women-nature link, and to maintain the link is to maintain the mutual domination. This topic was a debate, although by the mid-1990s essentialism had faded from most ecofeminist discussions.

Ecofeminism was thought by some to be hopelessly idealistic, claiming the beauty and dignity of women and the earth while seemingly ignorant of the social, political, and economic systems that perpetuated women's poverty and ecological ruin. It was seen as too spiritual, too theoretical or apolitical to be effective. A few ecofeminist analyses were challenged to be mistaken on particular historical data. There were some scathing critiques, such as that of social ecologist Janet Biehl in *Finding Our Way: Rethinking Ecofeminist Politics* (1991).

Some ecofeminist spiritualities were criticized for ignoring social, cultural, and historical contexts and conditioning and differences of class, culture, and ethnicity among women. They were challenged to move beyond beautiful ideas of how the world could be to examine the social structures of domination such as industrialism, militarism, and male consciousness. Ecofeminist spiritualities were feared to be ineffective if political transformation was primarily an internal and individual change of consciousness rather than collective action in social and political processes. While some of the new spiritualities claimed to be free from patriarchal constructs, they remained disconnected, disembodied, and escapist, although the gender of the Divine may be changed.

Theoretical Differences

People came to ecofeminism from a variety of directions and used it in many ways. This was largely due to theoretical differences within feminist and ecological schools of thought. Feminism is a challenge to patriarchy and androcentrism (male-centred values, beliefs, and practices). Both are embedded in Western worldviews and cultural practices and, prior to feminism, were accepted as normal, natural, and even God-given. Feminism confronts patriarchy and androcentrism, revealing the bias against women and bringing forth values and structures that support women's equality and autonomy. Feminists, while all wanting a better life for women, do not agree on the same analysis of patriarchy and androcentrism. Feminists also vary on what kind of world is desirable and how much, and what kind of, freedom is needed for women. They disagree on strategies of how to get there. Liberal feminists are content with women's equal access to the current cultural and economic system. Socialist feminists want more substantial changes in the economic system to eliminate differences in class and ethnicity. Postmodern feminists can tolerate great divergences among feminists, provided each group can self-define with full autonomy. Some feminists are essentialist, and others oppose specific characteristics to all women. Some feminists include or make pivotal concerns for specific cultural groups and ethnicity. Others consider spirituality as central. Still others are aware of the process of cultural and economic colonialization and stand for a radical cultural freedom. Some feminists see freedom predominantly in lesbian relations or women-oriented cultures. To further complicate this, many feminists are a combination of these tendencies, positions, and commitments. Feminists who embrace ecological issues bring these variations with them.

Ecological issues are also understood from many vantage points and with a range of ecological paradigms, from "light" to "dark" green. Light green means an anthropocentric paradigm, wherein humans are the most important species and where all life forms can be used for human well-being. Light green ecological responses are good stewardship and better management of the earth's resources. Dark green paradigms consider the whole earth as important, and all life forms need to flourish within sophisticated and complex interconnected ecosystems. Although ecosystems are made up of predator and prey relationships, a balance is maintained that allows most life forms to succeed. These nonanthropocentric paradigms are called *biocentric, bioregional, ecocentric, whole earth systems, Gaia, deep ecology*, or *cosmology*. In between light and dark green are viewpoints that connect ecological ruin to social tension and injustice, such as social ecology, ecojustice, or green socialism. Each viewpoint emphasizes or values particular aspects, and some are mixtures. In addition, all of these distinctions refer to differing political strategies for environmental changes. Ecofeminism is a combination of the distinct strands of feminism and different ecological viewpoints. The combinations are countless. This has led to a divergence of positions including liberal, cultural, social, socialist, radical, and postmodern ecofeminism.

Evaluation of the breadth of ecofeminism reveals many voices, theoretical positions, practices, and political leanings. Foundational assumptions differ, as did determining the pivotal issues. The goals and means to achieve them are divergent. Some found the diversity unmanageable and wanted ecofeminism to contain specific ideas and orientations. Some feared that ecofeminism was useless and ineffective because of these variations and inconsistencies. Others rejoiced in the multitude of voices, celebrating the differences and disagreements. They encourage such heterogeneity, including the contradictions, because diversity most reflects basic truths about the earth community. Some kept the ecology-feminist connection but changed the words, using phrases such as *feminist ecology, feminist social ecology, feminist green socialism, feminist environmentalism*, and *feminist analyses of the environmental crisis*.

Conclusion

Ecofeminism, like ecology and feminism, is heterogeneous and has distinguishable components and orientations. Many are drawn to ecofeminism as an analysis and movement that sees critical connections between the domination of nature and the exploitation of women. As observes Karen Warren, what makes ecological feminism *feminist* is the commitment to the recognition and elimination of male-gender bias and the development of practices, policies, and theories that do not reflect this bias. What makes it *ecological* is an understanding of and commitment to the valuing and preserving of ecosystems, broadly understood. "Any feminism which is not informed by ecological insights, especially women-nature insights, and any environmental philosophy which is not informed by ecofeminist insights is simply inadequate" (Warren, *Ecological Feminism*, 1).

Ecofeminism is an interdisciplinary discourse, a critique, and a vision, spawning myriad books, articles, workshops, conferences, retreats, rituals, art, activism, and politics. There are publications covering ecofeminist philosophy, spirituality and religion, science, psychology, sociology, political thought and activism, economics, and animal rights. The range of issues at the ecofeminist intersection point grows constantly, cutting across lesbian perspectives (Cris Cuomo), democracy (Catriona Sandilands), women's health (Sandra Steingraber), community building (Judith Plant), and economics (Marilyn Waring). Ecofeminists are engaging in agricultural issues including the use of pesticides, organic farming, genetically modified foods, and cancer-causing chlorides. Clean air, clear water, reproductive rights, environmentally safe schools, and a countless list of particular and global issues are being addressed within ecofeminist frameworks.

Although ecofeminism is not a mass movement, it is becoming a third wave of feminism and represents a new social theory and political movement. Charlene Spretnak claims that "ecofeminists address the crucial issues of our time, from reproductive technology to Third World development, from toxic poisoning to the vision of a new politics and economics—and much more" (Spretnak, 8–9). Ecofeminism is international in scope and connects women from around the world. As a meaningful cross-cultural analysis, ecofeminism is spreading, but it is not uniform and does not take shape in each context the same way.

Ecofeminism, while many things, is about social, political, spiritual, economic, and ecological transformation. It is analysis, critique, vision, and action. It is about transforming the forms and patterns of relationships between women and men, between races, peoples, and animals, and humans and the larger earth community. Given that ecofeminism embodies diversity and is evolving continuously, the implications of any ecofeminist theory or practice are impossible to describe. Lively debates continue around ecofeminism as transcultural or context specific, between theory and social transformation, in international conversations about democracy, globalization, dreams of a harmonious past or future, spiritualities, and essentialism. Many women and men, inspired by ecofeminism, are involved in projects to improve their part of the world. In general, ecofeminism is about a desire to heal the wounds caused by the splits between nature and culture, between mind and body, between women and men, between reason and emotion, between spirit and matter, between theory and action, and ultimately between humans and the earth.

SOURCES: There are over fifty books on ecofeminism and hundreds of articles. There are still more places where connections are made between ecology and feminism and may not use the term *ecofeminism*. Some key references by North American authors are Rosemary Radford Ruether, *New Woman, New Earth: Sexist Ideologies and Human Liberation* (1975); Susan Griffin, *Women and Nature: The Roaring Inside Her* (1978); Mary Daly, *Gyn-Ecology: the Metaethics of Radical Feminism* (1978); and Carolyn Merchant, *The Death of Nature: Women Ecology and the Scientific Revolution* (1980). A taste of the range of ecofeminism is presented in edited collections by Judith Plant, *Healing the Wounds: The Promise of Ecofeminism* (1989); Irene Diamond and Gloria Orenstein, *Reweaving the World: The Emergence of Ecofeminism* (1990); and Carol Adams, *Ecofeminism and the Sacred* (1993). Ecofeminist philosophy is explored in several books by Karen Warren. For ecofeminism and religion, some key references are Anne Primavesi, *From Apocalypse to Genesis: Ecology, Feminism and Christianity* (1991); Joanna Macy, *World as Lover, World as Self* (1991); Rosemary Radford Ruether's *Gaia & God: An Ecofeminist Theology of Earth Healing* (1992); and Ruether's edited book *Women Healing Earth: Third World Women on Ecology, Feminism and Religion* (1996). Noël Sturgeon with *Ecofeminist Natures: Race, Gender, Feminist Theory and Political Action* (1997), Greta Gaard with *Ecofeminist Politics: Ecofeminists and the Greens* (1998), and Catriona Sandilands with *The Good-Natured Feminist: Ecofeminism and the Quest for Democracy* (1999) all deal with ecofeminism and political transformation. For cross-cultural ecofeminism, see Heather Eaton and Lois Ann Lorentzen, ed., *Ecofeminism and Globalization: Exploring Culture, Context and Religion* (2003). Sources cited in this essay include Karen Warren, "Feminism and Ecology: Making Connections," *Environmental Ethics* 9.1 (1989): 3–20; Karen J. Warren, ed., *Ecological Feminism* (1994); and Charlene Spretnak, "Ecofeminism: Our Roots and Flowering," in *Reweaving the World: The Emergence of Ecofeminism*, eds. Irene Diamond and Gloria Feman Orenstein (1990). To get a good look at ecofeminist activities, search the Web!

JEWISH WOMEN'S SERVICE ORGANIZATIONS
Dianne Ashton

SINCE THE EARLY nineteenth century, women's organizations have proved vibrant and effective vehicles for Jewish women throughout the United States. Whatever the charitable, philanthropic, educational, or religious goals they wished to accomplish, the most successful groups also offered their members religious education and inspiration, secular knowledge, and the satisfaction of helping others in need. Moreover, upon joining, women found a network of supportive friends, assurance that they were proper American women, and an ability to affect the world beyond their homes. "I came in contact with bright women and was stimulated by interesting study groups and informative programs," explained one Hadassah member (Freund-Rosenthal, 78). Indeed, when women's groups occasionally were organized by male clergy or community leaders, these groups often were reshaped by the female members, and these bodies, too, became personally meaningful in their constituents' lives.

For some talented women, organizations offered a type of career. Before the late twentieth century, few American women obtained access to meaningful employment. Organizations provided them an arena in which to develop leadership skills and to exercise that leadership in effective ways. Women knowledgeable in Hebrew and in Jewish religious lore often selected religious organizations such as associations of synagogue sisterhoods. For many thousands of Jewish women, however, service organizations offered the opportunity to fulfill Judaism's ethical teachings that, for much of modern Jewish history, had played a central role in religious life. Members viewed these organizations as expressions of their Jewish identities, offering them a personal satisfaction that comparable Christian or secular organizations could not provide.

The Beginning of Jewish Women's Organizations in the United States

The first Jewish women's groups began in Philadelphia under the leadership of Rebecca Gratz (1781–1869), a middle child of twelve children in a wealthy family of merchants who also served as lay leaders of congregation Mikveh Israel. Gregarious by temperament and accustomed to the dense sociability of a large family, Gratz enjoyed a wide friendship circle, paid close attention to accepted standards of propriety and decorum, and always spoke her mind. She was an avid reader who feared that solitude unaccompanied by a good book led to depression. Her many friendships with witty men never led to marriage; it was in the title "sister" that Gratz looked "for such love as has been the most fertile source of comfort to me" (Ashe, 93). She outlived most of her immediate family and often reacted to the loss of loved ones by increasing her social obligations, sometimes establishing new communal institutions. Responding to the death of her sister Sarah in 1817 by deepening both her religious commitments and her ties to the women of her synagogue, Gratz established the Female Hebrew Benevolent Society. When her sister Rachel died in 1823, Gratz brought Rachel's six children home to raise. She "grew old together" with her three unmarried brothers with whom she lived throughout her life.

Service to the local community was a family tradition among the Gratzes and among the Philadelphians in their elite social and economic class. Like her mother, father, uncle, brothers, and the women, non-Jewish and Jewish, among her friends, Gratz helped to found and lead several service organizations. Unlike them, however, she made lifetime commitments to these groups, continuing her leadership until old age. Her work in five different organizations provided her a type of career. These were the Female Association (1801), the Philadelphia Orphan Asylum (1815), the Female Hebrew Benevolent Society (FHBS, 1819), the Hebrew Sunday School (HSS, 1838), and the Jewish Foster Home (JFH, 1855). The latter three, all Jewish groups, immediately found imitators in New York, Baltimore, Charleston, and later, Savannah, cities with the largest Jewish populations where women knew of Gratz and her work. By middle age, Gratz was well known among American Jews.

Begun during the rise in Protestant evangelical activity associated with the so-called Second Great Awakening, Gratz's Jewish organizations (the FHBS, HSS, and JFH) served three main purposes. They provided charity, shelter, and advice to poor Jews, mostly immigrants from central and western Europe. They offered English-language religious education to all the city's Jewish children, boys and girls, and adult Jewish education for the women faculty and administrators. Most important, they thwarted the efforts of Christian missionaries. Because many of the women workers knew each other, their work often overlapped in effective ways. A Hebrew Sunday School student without warm clothing would be helped by a woman from the Female Hebrew Benevolent Society. Similarly, an FHBS woman with a particular interest in religion and a talent for public speaking would be urged to join the HSS. Generations of women, especially those from Gratz's congregation, joined her groups and made them their own.

Each of Gratz's Jewish organizations set new precedents in American Jewish life. The benevolent society was the first nonsynagogal Jewish organization and the first independent Jewish women's organization in North America. In New York, women of the city's oldest Jewish congregation took the same name for their newly established group and invited Gratz to join as an honorary member. With increasing Jewish immigration from central Europe, by 1880 the Jewish population grew from 5,000 to 250,000. By late century, American Jews had established several avenues for charity to aid newcomers, and many different women's charities had formed based on Gratz's model of the Female Hebrew Benevolent Society. Although it was a charitable society, its women members conceived of charity broadly. In assessing each request for funds, the group strove to find ways to empower the woman petitioner to become free of her need

The first Jewish woman's group began in Philadelphia in 1819 under the leadership of Rebecca Gratz, a middle child of twelve children in a wealthy family of merchants who also served as lay leaders of congregation Mikveh Israel. Gregarious by temperament and accustomed to the dense sociability of a large family, Gratz enjoyed a wide friendship circle, paid close attention to accepted standards of propriety and decorum, and always spoke her mind. *Used by permission of the American Jewish Archives.*

for alms. In that process, it acted as employment bureau, medical referral system, health insurer, family counselor, and dispenser of financial and material aid.

From the outset, the members hoped to improve religious education for American Jewish children. Almost twenty years later, these women launched the Hebrew Sunday School, the first Sunday school in Jewish history and the first public arena where Jewish women could teach religion. Before its founding in 1838, Philadelphia's Jews depended on occasional private tutors and synagogue leaders who taught boys to read Hebrew. Gratz served the school as superintendent, while Simha Peixotto (1807–1892) and Rachel Peixotto Pyke, sisters who ran a school in their home, joined her to comprise its first faculty. The HSS soon enjoyed the support of most Jewish religious leaders, especially the important Isaac Leeser, leader of Gratz's synagogue and the most influential Jewish religious leader of the antebellum period. Gratz sent lesson plans to women in Baltimore and Charleston, where similar schools soon opened. By the time of the Civil War, Jewish Sunday schools operated in most sizable Jewish communities and relied on women faculty and administrative volunteers. By opening the schools, the benevolent society women forced

American Jews to attend to the educational needs of Jewish women and girls, to combat evangelical proselytizing, and to ensure religious continuity.

During the 1840s Gratz began garnering support for a Jewish Foster Home. Through her continuing activity with the Philadelphia Orphan Asylum (POA), she understood the needs of orphans and of families too poor to care for their children. Equally important, she knew that the asylum instructed its charges in Christianity; Jewish orphans would need to find care elsewhere. In 1855 the Jewish Foster Home opened in Philadelphia, the first such Jewish institutional home in the country. In other towns, foster families cared for Jewish orphans. When the Philadelphia home opened, its managers were deluged with requests for admission from around the country. By then seventy-four years old, Gratz at first advised younger women who held official duties. However, she soon took the post of vice president in order to reassure donors and parents that the home would be run responsibly.

A foster home was an expensive enterprise and faced repeated fiscal difficulties. Men served on an auxiliary fund-raising board until 1874. Then, during a fiscal crisis, the male board took over leadership and the women's board, overseeing the daily running of the home, became secondary. This latter pattern, men on the primary board, women on an auxiliary, emerged in both Jewish and non-Jewish institutions around the country in the decades after the Civil War as benevolent work was professionalized into social work.

Gratz never exercised her leadership through the presidency of her organizations. She served each organization as secretary, keeping minutes in great detail, producing and keeping track of correspondence, reporting on the state of her organizations, and publishing reports in the local and Jewish press. By settling other women into more prestigious positions, Gratz ensured their commitment. Her stature among antebellum Jewry is difficult to overestimate. She was widely believed to be the model for the character of Rebecca of York in *Ivanhoe*, published by Sir Walter Scott in 1819. A deeply pious woman who attended synagogue regularly, Gratz dedicated her life to furthering Judaism and Jewish life in America. She became a legendary figure and motivated Jewish women around the country to follow in her path.

All of Gratz's Jewish groups still survive in some form. The Female Hebrew Benevolent Society remained independent, though small, until the late twentieth century, refusing to join the United Hebrew Charities that emerged in Philadelphia under male leadership in 1869. Today it is a subsidiary of the Philadelphia's Federation of Jewish Charities but retains its distinctive philosophy and character as a women's organization. The Hebrew Sunday School, which also receives funding from the Federation, merged with another community school but retains its character as an independent Sunday school providing a Jewish religious education to many of Philadelphia's poorer Jewish children, especially its girls. Volunteers now assist and advise a paid staff. At the turn of the twentieth century, the Jewish Foster Home became part of Philadelphia's Association for Jewish Children as new models for child welfare emerged. These groups offered Jewish women of the Victorian era rewarding and effective associational experiences.

Immigrant and Refugee Aid in the Twentieth Century

Hannah Greenebaum Solomon (1858–1942), the founder of the National Council of Jewish Women (NCJW, Council), once remarked that she was "born a club woman just as [she] was born . . . a Jew" (Rogow, 1). Late-nineteenth-century club women distinguished themselves from other women, who might join a variety of volunteer associations, by the seriousness of their commitments. Women's clubs demanded systematic effort, usually combining educational programs, either literary or social, with communal service. A wealthy Chicagoan who already participated in the prestigious Chicago Woman's Club before she organized NCJW, Solomon and women like her felt the need of a club that would express their religious and gender identities and advance the role of Jewish women, while also serving the needs of poor Jews. The 1893 Chicago Columbian Exposition offered an opportunity to organize such a club. In conjunction with the World Parliament of Religions, a feature of the exposition, Solomon and sister Chicagoan Sadie American (1862–1944) organized the Jewish Women's Congress, a national gathering of leading Jewish women who delivered papers on the theme of women and Judaism, hoping that the event would culminate in the founding of a national Jewish women's organization. Established on the heels of the Congress, the Council took as its motto "faith and humanity" (Rogow, 32) and dedicated itself to furthering women's Jewish knowledge and launching social welfare programs serving Jewish women and children. Both Solomon and American were daughters of middle-class merchant families who practiced Reform Judaism, and both labored with other women's service organizations and settlement houses in Chicago in addition to their work in NCJW. Although their histories were similar, their personalities and leadership styles differed dramatically. Solomon drew on her previous experience in women's clubs and the administrative expertise gained there to lead the Council. She served as national president until 1905, when she declined reelection. Throughout her life, she remained a member, served on the boards of several other Chicago charities, and continued her commitments to women's suffrage and National Council of Jewish Women's goals. By contrast, American's drive and forceful personality brought her into early leadership and then forced her from it. Ultimately, although the NCJW claimed to be impartial regarding the various branches of Judaism, Sadie American's assimilationist philosophy and brusque manner thwarted her reelection to national office after 1914.

Historian Faith Rogow pointed out that NCJW's managers included both philanthropic women and female social workers, thus ensuring the Council's early effectiveness. Like most Jewish women's organizations, the idea of motherhood served as a guiding image justifying the group's activities. One woman admitted that she could not "detach Jewish motherhood from messiahship" (Rogow, 53). The Council aimed to strengthen Jewish families by increasing the religious knowledge and commitments of mothers, and its members participated in many study groups on Jewish texts and topics. The twin goals of social justice and advancing Judaism found energetic support among Jewish women across a broad spectrum of religious and political ideologies, and within five years of its founding, NCJW counted more than 5,000 members. By 1915 it had become America's largest Jewish women's organization. By 1920 NCJW initiated Council Sabbaths, yearly recognitions of the organization's work in which Council women led services in their home congregations. These occasions often provided the women with their first opportunities to lead religious services, but they sometimes triggered congregational disputes. Although the organization refused to officially endorse any single version of American Judaism, events like Council Sabbaths fit Reform Judaism more comfortably than other denominations. Some of the more traditionally religious women left the organization for other groups such as Hadassah, and NCJW grew ever more closely associated with Reform Judaism.

The National Council of Jewish Women began during the era of the immigration of nearly two million Jews from Eastern Europe, most of whom arrived with few possessions and little knowledge of English. There, anti-Semitic violence increased after the assassination of Czar Alexander II, when Russia entered a period of political, economic, and social turmoil. The Council aided more than 20,000 immigrant Jewish girls who arrived in America without guardians, serving as "friendly visitors" who assisted their beneficiaries in becoming self-sufficient. The Council built settlement houses, provided employment training, English-language classes, and tips on American manners. When their work was linked to a 40 percent decline in the number of Jewish women arraigned for prostitution in New York City, universities began teaching their methods. The Council also printed the first Jewish braille prayer book, provided for the ongoing religious, health, and educational needs of rural Jewish families in eight states, and monitored the public press for anti-Semitic newspaper articles, to which it responded vigorously.

As NCJW strove to answer new challenges it went through many changes. Because it hoped to prevent new problems while solving existing difficulties, the Council began taking political action and expanding its services. Early in the century, as its work with immigrants grew more important, its Midwestern center of power shifted to New York. Its early Victorian notions of motherhood prompted the Council to take political action to enact protective legislation for working women and to oppose the first Equal Rights Amendment, which it believed would leave working women unprotected under the law. At the same time, because it hoped to increase women's ability to protect themselves, it was the first organization to publicly demand legalization of birth control.

NCJW's work in immigrant aid diminished after the United States effectively closed immigration from Eastern Europe in 1924. At midcentury, Council women drew on their past experience with needy and displaced populations to help homeless Holocaust survivors after World War II. In 1945, the Council created the Ship-A-Box program to send educational materials to European children, built settlement houses in Paris and Athens, and provided college scholarships to Europeans studying social work in the United States. Although NCJW took no stand on Zionism before World War II, when the Holocaust of European Jewry proved the need for a Jewish homeland, it established a Department of Israel Affairs that built on its previous experience with immigrants. In the 1960s, the Council established a high school for the School of Education at Hebrew University, where it also supported the Center for Research in Education of the Disadvantaged and provided scholarships to Israeli schools of social work. Evolving to meet the changing needs and commitments of American Jewry, NCJW attracted 110,000 members by 1970.

Hoping to prevent social crises, Council women monitored government regulations and worked for political change. Although they rarely took radical positions, their political action eroded the traditional division between public and private arenas. As a body, the Council opposed nuclear weapons, McCarthyism, and the Vietnam War; advocated civil rights for all Americans; and supported the 1970s Equal Rights Amendment and Medicaid funding for abortions. NCJW has been perhaps the most flexible of all Jewish women's organizations, responding to the changing needs of various communities. A Canadian branch of the organization began in 1897 and its projects responded to the needs of Jews there. Several programs to aid disadvantaged children first developed in the United States were later utilized in Israel. For example, the organization's Home Instruction Program for Preschool Youngsters, developed in the 1970s, was implemented both in the United States and internationally. More directly, its Center for Research in Education for the disadvantaged at Hebrew University has worked to resettle Ethiopian and Russian immigrants in Israel and worked with at-risk youth. In the United States, the Council continues to assist women and their families as well as the elderly with meals and services to isolated older Americans.

But, like other volunteer organizations, the Council saw its numbers drop in the late twentieth century. Several factors contributed to this change. A great percentage of Jewish women engage in full-time employment. At the same time, major Jewish organizations that once were closed to women are welcoming them at higher ranks, offering many avenues for service to the Jewish community. In addition, the feminist movement of mid-century, which sharply criticized volunteer organizations for blunting women's power and ill rewarding their energy and effort, changed the climate of volunteerism. Hoping to attract new members, the Council has in the last twenty years supported leadership and advocacy differently from its early models. In 1987 a slide show designed to encourage women to exercise power directly, rather than work through influencing others, circulated among the Sections, as it calls its chapters. "Many of us have been loath to aspire to power because we see it in a negative context," one Council member explained. "But," she argued, "the ability to have and use power is essential if we are to act on our beliefs and use our influence to change minds and lives" (Rogow, 196).

Contemporary Jewish women are well educated. More than 25 percent of younger women have earned a graduate degree and only one in ten stopped her education with a high school diploma. To appeal to these women, the Council's educational efforts have grown more sophisticated. NCJW sponsors conferences on Jewish feminism, houses its papers at major archives, and supports scholarship about Jewish women. In these matters individual Sections set their own priorities. That "flexibility" is both the organization's strength and weakness, for it "has made it difficult for the Council to establish a clear national identity," according to Rogow. Nonetheless, the Council's 1987 stated goals seem to echo its 1893 commitments. The organization remains dedicated to unifying progressive Jews and integrating social justice activities with Jewish values. Most recently the organization established the NCJW Women and Gender Studies at Tel Aviv University, the first bachelor's degree–granting program of its kind in the Middle East. Supporting religious education for adult women and combating anti-Semitism through education, the organization still views social action as an expression of Jewish faith. The National Council of Jewish Women continues to attract women committed to its mix of social service, Judaism, and political action.

As early as the first decades of the twentieth century, American Jewish women cared deeply about education. As sociologist Sylvia Barak Fishman noted, in 1910, when Jews made up about 19 percent of the population of New York City, 40 percent of the women enrolled in night school were Jewish (Fishman, 70). Not surprisingly, then, a new organization that focused on providing vocational training and education to Jewish refugees found ready support. Women's American ORT (Organization for Rehabilitation and Training, WAO) has consistently focused on vocational training. While NCJW was organized by American women independently of any other organization, WAO began as a women's auxiliary of World ORT, an association founded in Russia in 1880 to promote vocational training among poor Jews there. By 1922, ORT branches had been organized in Berlin and the United States where they worked in concert with other Jewish charities. Women's American ORT began in New York in 1927 as an auxiliary to the men's organization in order to tap women's energies. Most WAO founders were wives of ORT officers and that link helped the organization in its early years. In the beginning, WAO supported trade schools in Eastern Europe to help Jews recover from World War I. A de-

cade later, as war loomed again, WAO worked in concert with ORT schools in Europe to assist refugees and intensified its involvement with Polish Jewish workers by expanding its trade schools. With the motto "A Trade Is a Refugee's Passport" (Moore and Hyman, 1491), WAO raised $50,000 for schools. As the Nazis conquered Europe, WAO funded refugee shelters in ORT facilities in France, vocational training in Switzerland, and even maintained workshops in Polish ghettos. After the war, it funded similar facilities in Displaced Persons camps in Israel, Holland, Belgium, and Greece.

Although it began as an auxiliary, by the 1950s Women's American Organization had grown to more than 12,000 members, becoming the "financial mainstay of World ORT" (Moore and Hyman, 1491). Turning its energy to providing vocational training in Israel, North Africa, Europe, India, and Iran, the organization joined larger Jewish fund-raising campaigns like the United Jewish Appeal, and contributed its own funds to the Joint Distribution Committee, which helped Jews in need worldwide. After adding social events to its list of activities, by 1970 the organization added more than 90,000 American Jewish women to its membership. Since then, it has hosted broad educational conferences around the country, opened schools in Los Angeles and Chicago in addition to New York, and provided vocational training to Jewish day schools in Miami. No longer limited to serving only Jews, Women's American ORT teaches English as a second language, computer skills, and robotics to refugees and newer American immigrants.

Zionist Groups

Henrietta Szold (1860–1945) was one of American Jewry's greatest leaders. Almost single-handedly, she transformed Hadassah from a humble reading group into the largest mass membership American Jewish organization, the world's largest Jewish women's organization, and the largest Zionist organization. While Gratz, Solomon, and American relied on family economic status and moral authority to guarantee their prestige, Szold was at first esteemed because of her intellectual heritage. She was the eldest of five daughters born to Sophie Schaar and Rabbi Benjamin Szold, emigrés from Hungary who arrived in Baltimore in 1859 to serve a congregation. In youth, Szold learned to translate and edit her father's manuscripts from German and Hebrew, and she served as his secretary as he aged. Although she had hoped to attend college after completing high school, her family required her small earnings as a teacher at a local girls school. Using the pen name "Shulamith," Szold began reporting on Jewish life in the press; by 1902 the Anglo-Jewish press called her the leading Jewish essayist in America. When anti-Jewish violence in Russia and Poland after 1881 brought two million Jews from Eastern Europe to the United States, both Henrietta and her father met the newcomers with advice and friendship. She began Baltimore's first night school, teaching English to the immigrants several nights each week; five years later the city took over the successful school. Through her friendship with the immigrants, Szold developed life-long Zionist convictions. Although she declined affiliation with any of several Zionist political parties that emerged in Europe after the publication of Leo Pinsker's *Auto-Emancipation* (1903), she agreed that Jews needed a safe homeland in order to thrive and grow both spiritually and culturally, to become a normal instead of a dispersed nation. With these ideas, Szold's understanding of the Jewish world broadened.

In 1893 the Jewish Publication Society of America (JPS) hired Szold to serve as secretary, a post she held until 1916. Her tasks included translator, annotator, proofreader, indexer, and editor. Though timid by nature, Szold delivered a speech called "What Judaism Has Done for Women" at the 1893 Jewish Women's Congress that launched the National Council of Jewish Women. Her lecture countered a common Protestant evangelical charge that Judaism neglected women. When the Baltimore NCJW chapter invited Szold as guest speaker soon after, she delivered her first public advocacy of Zionism.

After her father's death in 1901, Szold determined to prepare his papers for publication but lacked sufficient knowledge of Jewish rabbinic lore. The Jewish Theological Seminary (JTS) allowed her to attend classes (she was the only woman to do so), and Szold and her mother moved to New York City. At JTS she fell in love with Professor Louis Ginzberg, fourteen years her junior. For the next years Szold fulfilled her publishing duties, studied at the seminary, and provided English language instruction, translation, and editing services for the faculty, especially Ginzberg. When Ginzberg suddenly announced his engagement to a young woman he met in Germany, Szold suffered a severe emotional breakdown. Her quiet life devoted to scholarship ended. To recover, Szold and her mother traveled to Europe and Palestine. In Palestine they found that trachoma, malaria, typhoid, and cholera were common, drinking water was often contaminated, and poverty ruled most communities.

In response to that situation, Szold, along with other dedicated women, reorganized her zionistic reading group in 1912 as Hadassah, the Hebrew name of Queen Esther, famed for rescuing the Jews of Persia. Its biblical motto, "the healing of the daughter of my people," proved just as apt for Henrietta as for the individuals helped by Hadassah's medical assistance. She proved a brilliant organizer. Hadassah's central advisory commit-

tee, later named the National Board, handled administrative matters and advised new chapters around the country as they developed. Funds for administration were kept separate from the operating budget, rare among Jewish organizations of the day. Finally, Szold insisted that the organization "must have a project" (Freund-Rosenthal, 1), that people cannot be taught the importance of Zionism without a concrete way to express their commitment. Hadassah devoted itself to providing medical care and health education to Palestine's Jewish and Muslim residents. Szold viewed Hadassah's work as practical Zionism, creating living conditions able to support future communities. Szold believed that "women will work better when there are only women in the group" (Freund-Rosenthal, 1), and invited American Jewish women to attend parlor meetings featuring lantern pictures that displayed large, lighted images of life in Palestine. Like Gratz before her, Szold pointed out that Jewish relief efforts would save destitute Jews from conversion by Christian missionary nurses. She soon attracted Jewish women from all walks of life. In 1914, when it held its first national convention in Rochester, New York, Hadassah counted chapters in several cities, including a Philadelphia group named for Rebecca Gratz.

At first, Hadassah affiliated itself with the male-run political agency the Zionist Organization of America, but retained control of its funds. A distinctly American organization, Hadassah was influenced by the Progressive movement's social uplift agenda. Impressed by Lillian Wald's accomplishments in establishing the first Visiting Nurse system in New York City, and by Nathan Straus, who had funded the first free milk stations for infants in New York, Szold determined to provide similar service to Palestine. With Straus's financial backing, in 1913 two trained nurses sailed for Palestine to set up a Nurses' Settlement in Jerusalem. They began a midwives' service, checked the general health of schoolchildren, and provided nursing both at the settlement and around the city. With the outbreak of World War I, the area was further impoverished and health care worsened. When Britain announced its intention to allow Jews to settle there after 1917, Jewish immigration to the Middle East increased, adding to the local health needs. Also that year the first Hadassah chapters were established in Canada. When the World Zionist Organization asked that a medical force be sent to Palestine, Hadassah, with thirty-four chapters when America entered the war, was asked to supervise the effort. In 1918, forty-five doctors and nurses of varying specialties, along with five administrators, sailed to Palestine and set up the American Zionist Medical Unit in Jerusalem. Historian Deborah Dash Moore explained that although many groups offered emergency aid, Alice Seligsberg, Hadassah member and AZMU administrator, remembered that "we . . . were different . . . we wished to create something of lasting value to the land and the people . . . install[ing] a permanent system of examining and treating children at school . . . prevent[ing] disease . . . and . . . train[ing] . . . Palestinian girls according to American professional standards" (Moore and Hyman, 575–576). The medical unit set up three hospitals, sent dentists and nurses into schools and orphanages, made its laboratories available to local medical institutions and physicians, and just as importantly, supervised the organization of sanitation inspection teams. Hadassah won respect for its nurses and medical care because it answered the practical need to conquer disease more effectively than anyone else.

In the interwar period few American Jewish organizations officially supported Zionism. However, women were active in many relief projects and Hadassah's blueprint for eradicating disease in Palestine gave American Jewish women an ongoing purpose; its membership climbed to 44,000 by 1931. A 1925 newsletter explained that bringing news of Palestine to the non-Zionist public was "fully one-half of our task" (Waserman and Kottek, 137). Hadassah's medical work interested American women regardless of their Zionist feelings. Local fundraising ventures in communities throughout America explained the need for a Jewish homeland, Palestine's political history, and the history of the Zionist movement as well as Hadassah's work. Hadassah sought to convert the "old-time sense of responsibility in regard to Palestine" (Hadassah, 1917, 3) to modern Zionism. For Szold that meant "a movement of self-emancipation . . . for the Jewish people." "There is nothing but Zionism . . . to save us," she once remarked. Szold and her organization were invaluable to the larger goals of the Zionist effort.

By the 1930s, Szold had relocated to Jerusalem and regularly sent reports of Hadassah's projects to members at home. During that time Hadassah separated from the Zionist Organization of America. With steady growth, new projects were undertaken for which an expanded nursing school was the lynchpin: day care centers, school lunch programs, schools for girls, urban recreation programs, and the building of Hadassah Hospital in Jerusalem. The first of several children's villages for orphans from Hitler's Europe was established in 1934. As the first Zionist organization to mount a rescue operation, Hadassah galvanized public support. Directed by Szold, the program, called Youth Aliyah (Youth Settling in Palestine), transported, cared for, and educated 100,000 adolescents and teens from Europe, Iran, and Yemen. By 1967, a tenth of Israeli Jews under fifty years old were Youth Aliyah graduates. Under Szold's leadership, a Junior Hadassah, comprised largely of younger women, also thrived.

By the time of her death, an important volume on Szold's life had been published (1942) and she was widely recognized as one of the great leaders of world Jewry. She was inducted into Maryland's Women's Hall of Fame in 1986. Like Rebecca Gratz, Henrietta Szold's accomplishments were measured in part by her ability to mobilize other talented, dedicated, and energetic women. Tamar De Sola Pool, president during World War II, started *Hadassah News,* which developed into an informative monthly magazine. In 1951 when David Ben-Gurion, Prime Minister of Israel, determined to sell Israeli bonds to raise money for the new government, he asked Judith Epstein, former Hadassah National President, to oversee the effort's women's branch. "The women loved the idea!" Epstein said. "They understood that if you are a really successful mother, your child is independent of you" (Freund-Rosenthal, 27).

Beginning in the 1950s, many American Jews moved out of city neighborhoods into suburbs and new towns across the country. For many of these women, membership in Hadassah became a means to an instant community. Daughters of Hadassah members joined or created new chapters. Jennie Nachamson founded a chapter in North Carolina in 1919; her eight daughters each served as Hadassah presidents in towns across the South during the 1940s and 1950s. "We were all seeking a world beyond diapers and nursery" (Freund-Rosenthal, 78), one woman explained, and Hadassah offered them routes to both local community activities and international effectiveness. Members came from all backgrounds: refugees from Europe and native-born Americans, Orthodox and Reform Jews, college educated and unschooled. Hadassah's many projects offered its women variety in both meaningful activities and leadership positions. Young Judea, a teen group overseen by Junior Hadassah, formed during the 1930s and grew with the baby boom during the 1950s and 1960s. Most significantly in the post-war years, the Hadassah Medical Hospital in Jerusalem developed into a teaching and research hospital with over fifteen medical departments and schools of dentistry and pharmacy. Today it is the leading medical institution in the Middle East. Although Hadassah membership in general had suffered from attrition during the 1960s, after the Six Day War in 1967, when Israel regained all Jerusalem, membership increased to a new high of 360,000 by 1977. Today Hadassah sends delegates to the executive meetings of the Jewish Agency for Israel and is accredited with the United Nations as a nongovernmental organization.

Despite its earlier successes, in the 1980s Hadassah faced an aging and declining membership. The same general trends that affected National Council of Jewish Women also hampered Hadassah. First, the feminist movement criticized the pattern of female volunteerism that had dominated women's nondomestic activities throughout much of American history. With feminist successes, more women entered the work force; Jewish women were especially likely to obtain advanced degrees. As a result, the majority of Jewish women in every age group except for those over sixty-five were employed, leaving them little time for volunteer work. "Dual-career families dominate in every wing of American Judaism," reported sociologist Sylvia Barak Fishman (89). Jewish feminists also challenged Hadassah's tradition of avoiding direct political action and viewed the organization as weak. At the same time, Israel was seen as having less need for humanitarian aid. It was time to rethink Hadassah's mission.

To reach college-educated women, Hadassah determined to return to its roots as a study group. It soon published *Jewish Marital Status* and conducted seminars around the country on Jewish family issues. In 1991 it mounted a conference and university symposia aimed at promoting understanding between Israeli and American Jews. Most significantly, the Hadassah International Research Institute on Jewish Women was established in 1997 at Brandeis University under the direction of Professor Shulamit Reinharz. Building on research on the status of American Jewish women undertaken in 1994, the institute has supported five major conferences on issues important to Jewish women in the United States and Israel, academic research on women, exhibitions by women artists, archives, and *Nashim: A Journal of Jewish Women's Studies and Gender.* Today, Hadassah's 385,000 members enjoy a wider array of educational resources than any previous membership.

Despite its effectiveness, Hadassah did not appeal to every woman concerned for the Jewish homeland. Many Orthodox women felt more comfortable in Mizrachi Women, the women's affiliate of Mizrachi, the organization of religious Zionists launched in 1925 in New York by Bessie Goldstein Gotsfeld (1888–1962). Born in Poland, Bessie was the eldest of six children, and helped to raise her younger siblings after their mother's early death. Her father, a rabbinic scholar and hasid (pietist), welcomed travelers from Palestine into his home and sympathized with the early Zionist movement. Bessie received a religious education at home and a secular education at a local Catholic school, where she graduated as valedictorian. When she was seventeen, her family relocated to the United States, where she later married. Gotsfeld joined Mizrachi Women, but in 1925 led other Mizrachi women in forming a group of their own that would administer its own work. A year later she moved to Tel Aviv to oversee the group's projects in Palestine and for the next thirty years served as the Palestine (later Israeli) connection between Mizrachi women (later AMIT, or Americans for Israel and Torah), and their work overseas. Although she suffered from diabetes, Gotsfeld was a tireless worker known for her diplomatic and political skills.

Among the regular activities of AMIT were "tikvah (hope) teas" (Joselit, 114), where women would gather in each others' homes for informative talks on Israel, to plan fund-raising events, and to monitor the development of their various projects, along with bazaars and cultural events. Because these women followed Judaism's dietary laws, they were more likely to meet in homes than in public halls. They began by establishing vocational high schools for religious girls in Palestine, in Jerusalem in 1933 and Tel Aviv in 1938. Many other such schools followed. Girls were taught dressmaking, child care, education, farming, gardening, and dietetics. Their goal was to strengthen the future mothers of the *yishuv* (Palestine Jewish settlement community), because, as one member said, "home has always been the logical starting place for carrying out ideas" (Joselit, 114).

Membership grew to nearly fifty chapters in the United States by the mid-1930s. These chapters raised money for projects in Israel that the women oversaw. When refugee children brought by Hadassah's Youth Aliyah arrived in Palestine, AMIT established child-care facilities in order to tend the many children from religious households. During the 1950s, several students from Ethiopia attended the organization's newly established religious teacher-training schools, and its experience with those students helped it to serve the thousands of Ethiopian Jews who resettled in Israel between 1984 and 1991. By then AMIT had been designated the Israeli government's official network for religious technical education, giving the organization a prominent national voice on public education. Since the 1980s, it has cared for children from dysfunctional families, and in 1996 received Israel's Religious Education Prize for its efforts. Although AMIT sees itself as a religious Zionist organization, it is not a member of any political organization in Israel. Like Hadassah, AMIT has been declared a nongovernmental body by the United Nations. Indeed, since 1934, when it became completely independent from Mizrachi, AMIT has strived to heal divisions sometimes exacerbated by politics. Most recently, it developed a Curriculum on Tolerance and Unity, implemented in high schools after the assassination of Prime Minister Yitzhak Rabin, intended to foster understanding and good will between religious and secular Israelis. Its American activities similarly address topics such as religious education, psychology, and issues of interest to women. These themes appear regularly in its quarterly magazine, *AMIT*, along with Israel-related subjects. Its efforts reflect the imprint of Gotsfeld's diplomatic efforts to advance the lives of Jewish women and girls directly, while creating the social harmony that will benefit men, women, and children alike. For the women who joined, membership in AMIT, rather than Hadassah, affirmed their deep religious commitment and identity.

Religious women have always been a minority among Zionists. Particularly in the early decades of the twentieth century, Zionism was most popular among secular Jews who supported the labor movement and socialist causes. Indeed, Labor Zionism shaped the early government of the *yishuv* (Jewish settlement in Palestine) and laid the foundation for Israel's political and economic structure. While Bessie Gotsfeld organized Mizrachi women, Rahel Yanait (later Ben-Zvi) turned to a group of American Labor Zionist women, members of Poale Zion (Workers of Zion, PZ) to fund the digging of a well to supply her tree nursery near her agricultural school for girls in Jerusalem. In 1924, Yanait published an open letter in a New York Yiddish Jewish newspaper, *Der Tog* (The Day), explaining that her school had planted more than 130,000 saplings in seventeen areas in the Galilee and Judea. Evoking romantic images of women tending saplings to reclaim desolate, but exotic areas, Yanait's letter drew an enthusiastic response from working-class Jewish immigrant women. She obtained her goal of $500, and used the public support to campaign for an independent women's Labor Zionist organization which would span both the United States and the *yishuv*.

Because the Poale Zion relied on socialist principles and rhetoric, it believed that it had already liberated women, despite seldom including them in governing or administrative capacities. Because these women had no voice, in 1925, with the help of other women, including Golda Myerson, later Golda Meir, Prime Minister of Israel, Yanait formed an independent women's organization. To raise the visibility of women's efforts in the *yishuv*, they called themselves Pioneer Women (PW). During the interwar period the group's numbers grew to 28,000. Its early membership, Yiddish-speaking, working-class women who often also were members of trade unions, possessed a vision for social change unlike that of AMIT or Hadassah. Disdaining what they viewed as the bourgeois style of Hadassah, these women planned serious gatherings; only after many years did they allow themselves purely social events. Their core values were Yiddishkeit (Jewish identity), class-consciousness, and feminism. In the 1930s they published a Yiddish anthology featuring the personal reminiscences of women workers in the *yishuv*, along with photographs and essays about family life in agricultural collectives. The following year it appeared in English and was distributed in both the United States and Canada. The English translation tapped the folk culture of Zionism and provided a vision of fulfillment that contrasted sharply with the privation experienced by its readers among working-class American Jews during the Depression. PW soon began a youth organization, Habonim (builders), which supported clubs, summer camps, and co-educational activities for teens in both the United States and Palestine. By 1941 Pioneer Women counted 250 chapters in more than seventy cities. Then almost half of its members were Yiddish-speaking women. Younger members were served by English-speaking clubs, signaling that Yiddish culture was disappearing from America.

Beginning in the war years, Pioneer Women's style began to change under the influence of younger, acculturated members. Teas and luncheons were scheduled, and flowers appeared on tables. Sharper political rhetoric faded. But the group's social activism remained, and its volunteers participated in Red Cross and war bond drives, civil defense activities, blood drives, salvage work, and victory gardens. In the 1940s PW mounted emergency fund-raising campaigns to aid children rescued from Europe or born in displaced-person camps, living either in the *yishuv* or awaiting transfer there. After the establishment of the State of Israel in 1948, Pioneer Women turned to cultural education, revealing its concern for Jewish continuity in America. After the destruction of European Jewry, where American Jews had often turned for leadership in Jewish matters, the quality of Jewish life in America and Israel became vitally important. Pioneer Women promoted tourism to Israel and supported vocational and educational centers for Jewish and Arab women and girls, created a network of day care centers, and acted as a conduit to American Jewry for Israel's rising women's movement.

Since the 1970s, when membership peaked at 50,000, Pioneer Women's numbers have declined. Like many Zionist groups, it has seen many of its functions taken over by other, more mainstream Jewish organizations. In 1981, the organization changed its name to Na'amat (Women Working and Volunteering), the name of its sister organization in Israel. Its Yiddish character is gone, but it continues to provide a vehicle for women concerned with issues of feminism and egalitarian Zionism in both America and Israel. Together, the National Council of Jewish Women, Women's American ORT, Hadassah, Na'amat, AMIT, and the Hebrew Sunday School, provide arenas of public effectiveness, personal enrichment, and religious inspiration to thousands of American Jewish women.

SOURCES: For an analysis of American Jewish women in the early-nineteenth-century period, see Dianne Ashton's *Rebecca Gratz: Women and Judaism in Antebellum America* (1997). The best single work on the National Council of Jewish Women is Faith Rogow's *Gone to Another Meeting: The National Council of Jewish Women, 1893–1993* (1993). Hannah Greenebaum Solomon's autobiography *The Fabric of My Life: The Autobiography of Hannah Greenebaum Solomon* (1946) offers its own insights. For Orthodox women's groups, see Jenna Weissman Joselit's *New York's Jewish Jews: The Orthodox Community in the Interwar Years* (1990). Henrietta Szold has inspired several volumes that have explored facets of her life. Among the best are Baila Shargel's *Lost Love: The Letters of Henrietta Szold and Louis Ginzberg* (1997) and Joan Dash's *Summoned to Jerusalem: The Life of Henrietta Szold* (1979). Alexandra Levin's *Henrietta Szold and Youth Aliyah: Family Letters 1934–1944* (1986) and Marvin Levinthal's *Henrietta Szold: Life and Letters* (1942) look at Szold's Zionist work through her letters. Hadassah's history can be found in Marlin Levin's *Balm in Gilead: The Story of Hadassah* (1973). Miriam Freund-Rosenthal's edited volume *A Tapestry of Hadassah Memories* (1994) offers Hadassah members' accounts of their experience with that organization. Hadassah's pamphlet reports on its yearly accomplishments, including the 1917 report, can be found in the Hadassah Archives at the Center for Jewish History. Manfred Waserman's analyses of Hadassah's medical care in Palestine and Israel appears in a volume he edited with Samuel S. Kottek, *Health and Disease in the Holy Land: Studies in the History and Sociology of Medicine from Ancient Times to the Present* (1996). Sylvia Barak Fishman's *A Breath of Life: Feminism in the American Jewish Community* (1995) explains the impact of Jewish women's activities on contemporary Jewish life. Deborah Dash Moore and Paula E. Hyman edited the very valuable *Jewish Women in America: An Historical Encyclopedia* (1997). "Social Workers in the Muskeljudentum"; Jenna Weissman Joselit, *New York's Jewish Jews: The Orthodox Community in the Interwar Years* (1990). Mary McCune, "Social Workers in the *Muskeljudentum:* 'Hadassah Ladies,' 'Manly Men,' and the Significance of Gender in the American Zionist Movement, 1912–1928," *American Jewish History* 86.2 (1998): 135–165.

ABUNDANT LIFE FOR ALL: THE YOUNG WOMEN'S CHRISTIAN ASSOCIATION
Janine M. Denomme

THE EMERGENCE OF the Young Women's Christian Association in the United States and Canada took place within the context of increasing industrialization in the late nineteenth century. As industrial capitalism had begun to separate work from the home in the early nineteenth century, the household economy had started to shift to one based on family wages. Whereas once each person within a home, including servants and slaves, had been assigned specific responsibilities within the household in order for all to survive, with the rise of industrialization, some individuals began to go out for wage work. This pattern increased throughout the century. Each morning, more and more artisans left their homes, their original work sites, to ply their trades or new ones in factories. Many farmers and farmhands left

the land to earn their living building ships, laying railroad lines, and digging canals as the transportation revolution moved across the continent. In the United States, millions of immigrants poured into the country to work side-by-side with the new industrial workers. During the second half of the nineteenth century, the number of industrial workers in the United States increased from 385,000 to 3.2 million.

Industrialization also changed the nature of work for many women in both Canada and the United States during the nineteenth century. Especially during the latter half of the century, thousands of single young women began leaving their rural and small-town homes to find work in the cities among manufacturers. Whereas daughters had once played a vital role in the household economy, working alongside their mothers as they cleaned, cooked, tended gardens, sewed, and washed the laundry, they now began to play a different but equally as vital role as a wage earner. The late nineteenth and early twentieth centuries witnessed thousands of young women flood into the cities, each looking for work and a place to live. Between 1870 and 1900, the number of women working for wages in the United States nearly tripled. The needs of these young women, as well as the sudden opportunity they offered for evangelization, encouraged the emergence of the Young Women's Christian Association (YWCA) in both the United States and Canada.

The lives of many middle- and upper-class women also shifted with industrialization, especially in the North where industry first took hold. Following the U.S. Civil War, during which women had gained experience organizing on behalf of the war effort, these women discovered they had more leisure time, thanks to the many time-saving devices introduced into their homes such as sewing machines, stoves, and canned food (although some historians argue that such technologies actually increased women's workload). In addition, an evangelical revival among Protestant churches in the 1850s encouraged these same women to reach out to the unchurched, bring them the "good news," and provide services if necessary. The YWCA emerged within a context of increasing numbers of women's reform organizations, including the abolition, temperance, and women's movements during the antebellum period. Economically privileged women often joined reform-minded organizations like the YWCA as an attempt to combat the urban problems that had developed alongside industrialization. YWCA volunteers perceived the young women coming to the cities not only as evangelization opportunities but also as potential victims of the vices and temptations rampant in these places. Many middle- and upper-class women viewed themselves as the protectors of the less fortunate and therefore responsible for these young

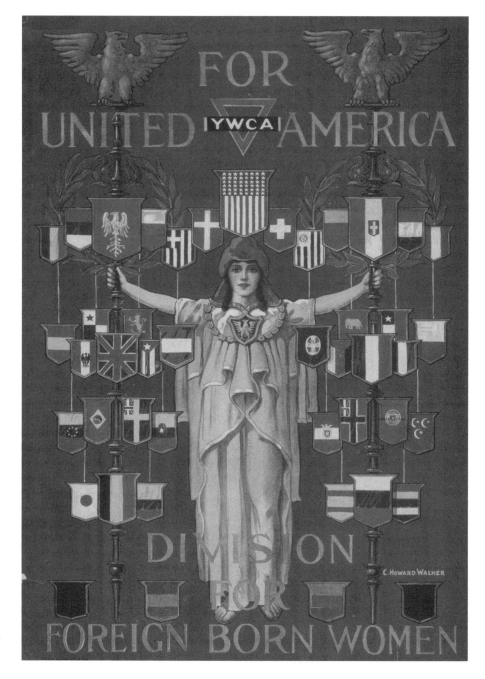

FOR UNITED ▽ YWCA ▽ AMERICA

DIVISION FOR FOREIGN BORN WOMEN

C. HOWARD WALKER

During the last two decades of the nineteenth century and the first two decades of the twentieth, 35 million immigrants came to the United States. The YWCA soon recognized that immigrant women had needs different than those of its white native-born clients. In 1910, therefore, the New York City YWCA sponsored the first International Institute to work with immigrant women. *Courtesy of the Library of Congress.*

women. As they moved into urban settings, the young women were most often alone, in need of work and a place to stay, and they certainly did not have a church to which they belonged. They presented the middle- and upper-class women with a splendid opportunity to combine their religious aspirations with meaningful work.

The YWCA of the U.S.A. considers Boston to be the site of its oldest local group, while also recognizing that both the YWCA and the YMCA (Young Men's Christian Association) developed in England before emerging in North America. A Ladies' Christian Association appeared in New York City in 1858. Boston, however, first

used the name Young Women's Christian Association in 1866 when thirty women met and adopted a constitution. These early groups first formed as prayer circles with no denominational affiliation and held religious meetings for young working women. The groups very quickly began providing residences for working women. Relying on Victorian notions of domesticity, the YWCA women believed they could best protect and influence female workers by providing them a Christian home. Within a few years, numerous associations appeared in other cities, seemingly independent of each other. These local groups first chose to come together in 1871 to discuss their programs and common problems. At that time there existed between twenty and twenty-five associations. After 1871, the YWCA local associations gathered for a conference every two years. The organizers for the conferences became known as the International Board, perhaps because the associations that had developed in Canada, beginning in 1870, were affiliated with those in the United States until 1895 when the first annual meeting of the YWCA of Canada was held in Ottawa.

From its beginnings, one of the strongest aspects of the YWCA was its college campus associations. The first student YWCA in the United States appeared in 1873 at Normal University in Normal, Illinois, forming for the joint purposes of studying the Bible and praying. Other student associations soon followed, mostly in the Midwest at coeducational institutions where the YMCA already existed. In 1886, the student associations united and formed the International Committee, eventually known as the American Committee. Informally associated with the Student Volunteer Movement, which emerged in 1888 to send lay volunteers to evangelize overseas, the college YWCA women became deeply interested in missionary work and, upon finishing school, often joined their churches' foreign missionary programs.

The YMCA also deeply influenced the YWCA college groups, thereby impacting the relationship that would form between the younger and older women's associations. The student YWCA groups inherited the YMCA's restrictive membership policy so that students could not join the YWCA unless they were members of an evangelical church. On the other hand, the International Board allowed local groups the autonomy to decide for themselves how they wanted to determine their membership. Some nonstudent associations asked that all voting members belong to evangelical churches; other local groups required only officers to be church members; and still others required no church affiliation for any of its members and even welcomed Roman Catholics. This difference in membership policy played a major factor in inhibiting the local and college YWCA associations in the United States from merging until the early twentieth century. Although the American Committee approached the International Board as early as 1885 to discuss uniting, the local associations refused to abide by the students' membership policy. In 1906, the two groups finally merged and became the YWCA of the U.S.A. At the time, they found a compromise that they could both live with: All current local YWCA groups and members were accepted whether or not they had a church affiliation; new local groups had to restrict their voting membership to those belonging to a Protestant evangelical church. This policy eventually changed and became more inclusive for both the student

associations and the community groups. Today, YWCA local organizations restrict voting membership to women and girls only. Auxiliary members may include men and boys. In 1906, the new national body had 608 local associations with a membership of 186,330 women and girls. Some 469 of those associations were student groups (high school and college), numbering over 41,000.

The YWCA of Canada also emerged in response to the needs of young single women moving to the cities in search of employment or education. The first, although short-lived, YWCA opened in St. John, New Brunswick. Others soon followed, including a boarding home in Toronto in 1873, the sight of the YWCA Canada headquarters by 1902. By 1900, fourteen branches had developed across the nation, and by 1930, that number had reached thirty-nine. YWCA women established programs to visit prisoners in jails, developed vocational training for women needing skills, built gymnasiums and swimming pools for recreation and physical education, and provided cafeterias, religious instruction, camping opportunities, and support to immigrants. The progress of YWCA Canada as an institution, as well as its programmatic focus, mirrored the YWCA of the U.S.A. The two shaped and deeply influenced the other. Similar to the middle-class women of the YWCA in the United States, Canadian YWCA women sought to protect young women from the potential dangers and temptations of the city. Sometimes, however, they failed to provide enough space for all those in need, as was reported in a 1917 letter written to the Edmonton YWCA by a local prostitute.

[I]t's too late for me; don't bother about any of us here, we're dead—but go back and tell the matron never to let a girl leave, even if she has to let her sleep in a chair; or sit on the steps or stand up all night. Tell her never, never, never to let a girl go; and tell the women to get bigger places, to shelter girls; they need it so badly. Surely if the women knew they would do something! (Pedersen, 230)

The YWCA of both countries continued to respond to the needs of young women and their families, changing in emphasis as the times dictated and expanding as its finances allowed.

Grace Hoadley Dodge (1856–1914) served as the first president of the YWCA of the U.S.A. and led the organization through its rocky beginnings as it strove to define itself and its mission. These early years in the YWCA reflected not only the Progressive Era of reform but also Dodge's personal and professional background. The daughter of an old and wealthy New York family, Grace Dodge combined her family's vast business experience with its leadership in civic and religious institutions when she agreed to the YWCA presidency. Not quite fifty when she took the helm, and an able businesswoman, Dodge oversaw the professionalization and bureaucratization of the institution. Under Dodge and the YWCA's first general secretary of the national staff, Mabel Cratty (1868–1928) of Ohio, the number of paid employees at the national level increased from 14 in 1906 to 101 in 1928. Likewise, the budget expanded over these same years from $136,000 to over $2 million. As a reflection of the era's emphasis on education as a means to understanding society's problems, especially in such fields as social work and sociology, the YWCA opened the National Training Institute in 1908 to educate its staff. A founder of the Teachers College at Columbia University, as well as a major funder and treasurer of this institute, Grace Dodge believed firmly in the need for educated workers. She also oversaw the construction of the YWCA headquarters in New York City, securing a gift of land at Lexington Avenue and 52nd Street from Mrs. Finley Shepard, daughter of Jay Gould. Helping to finance the building's erection herself, Dodge supervised its dedication in December 1912.

Dodge's peers remembered the YWCA president as personable and generous. One story reported that her mail carrier delivered thirty or forty letters to her each day and took away sixty or seventy, all of which Dodge had written herself. According to Dodge's personal records, during the years she served as the YWCA president, she wrote over 73,000 letters. With her blend of business capabilities, religious convictions, and congenial relationships, Dodge led the YWCA in both short- and long-term planning, ensuring that the organization would outlast her abbreviated life when she died at the age of fifty-eight.

The YWCA agenda shifted as the association extended its contact with clients. Although in its earliest years YWCA members initially sought to attend to working women's spiritual needs, eventually the association incorporated its clients' material need for housing as a means to provide a Christian influence. YWCA members soon discovered that their clients also needed jobs and job training. The association began to realize that the most crucial needs of the young women pouring into the cities were not necessarily spiritual in nature. In this way, young working women changed the YWCA agenda, refusing to have their goals dictated to them by more privileged women. Both groups were changed because of this interaction. YWCA activities and programs soon included not only housing but also classes in sewing, industrial work, typing, and domestic science. The YWCA provided recreation, literary and art programs, and hygiene information. By the end of World War I, in the climate of educational reform, the YWCA began to base their educational program designs on the needs

articulated by its clients. The association had moved far beyond its original motivation to bring young women to Christ while providing them a space for moral uplift.

Under Mabel Cratty, the YWCA became a harbinger on many social issues such as mental and physical health, labor reform, women's suffrage, temperance, international peace, and cultural pluralism. Known for her humor as well as her quiet leadership, Cratty once commented on a YWCA board member's resistance to changes in the organization by saying, "We might as well face it. Certain things will never be accomplished until certain people have gone to their reward!" (Robinson, 35). Born in Ohio soon after the Civil War, Cratty graduated from Ohio Wesleyan and taught for fourteen years before attending a YWCA training institute in 1902. First serving the state YWCA in Ohio for two years, Cratty then moved to Chicago as the American Committee's associate general secretary. When the American Committee merged with the International Board in 1906 to form the YWCA of the U.S.A., Cratty and her staff left their offices in Chicago and headed for New York City and Grace Dodge.

The community-based YWCA's first clients consisted mostly of native-born white young women who had come to the city to find work. However, in the early years of the twentieth century, partly in response to the new wave of immigrants, this focus widened to include other types of women, reflecting the YWCA's adage "An abundant life for all." During the last two decades of the nineteenth century and the first two decades of the twentieth, 35 million immigrants came to the United States. The YWCA soon recognized that immigrant women had their own particular needs, different than those of its white native-born clients. In 1910, therefore, the New York City YWCA sponsored the first International Institute to work with immigrant women.

Instead of creating programs for assimilation and Americanization, the International Institutes taught skills such as the English language for better adaptation while also encouraging immigrants to retain their own cultural identity, language, and history. The YWCA established International Institutes as separate YWCA centers in convenient locations for immigrant populations. Unlike so many other social welfare agencies working with immigrants, the Institutes hired foreign-born and second-generation women as case workers. Whereas most other agencies, including settlement houses, hired native-born white middle-class women only, the Institutes utilized women who knew the languages, traditions, history, and cultures of the people they served. Not only American history classes were taught, for citizenship purposes, but also classes in the history of the particular country and culture from which the immigrant community came. Cultural pluralism was celebrated at the Institutes, even during the most conservative interwar period in the United States when xenophobia was rampant and foreigners suspected of communism and other seemingly radical ideals. The International Institute movement, numbering fifty-five institutes by the mid-1920s, eventually grew into an independent institution during the 1930s.

Although progressive in its politics concerning immigrants, the YWCA did not do as well incorporating African American women's needs into the association. As early as 1870, independent black women's Christian Associations began to appear in various cities, including Philadelphia, Dayton, Ohio, New York City, Baltimore, and Washington, D.C. These groups experienced varying degrees of success in their attempts to gain recognition and support from either the white YWCA in the select cities or the International Board. Many African American associations remained independent well into the twentieth century when local and national white members, who controlled the YWCA, finally moved for inclusion. Although the National Board hired a few African American women to work with black community associations and student groups prior to World War I, the first African American National Board member was not in place until the mid-1920s, and the *Interracial Charter* was not adopted until 1946. The *Charter* endorsed a policy of integrated local associations, although many white local YWCAs resisted following through with this national resolution.

African American women, although greatly attracted to the mission and spirit of the YWCA, grew increasingly frustrated with the association's lack of resolve to ensure an "abundant life" for black women and their communities. The YWCA's foundation of Christian principles and fellowship, its focus on women, and its treatment of social ills all drew African American women to the association. The early spread of the YWCA on black college campuses especially contributed to a substantial African American membership in the national body. Most private black educational institutions had been founded and continued to be funded by various Protestant denominations, and so the schools' objectives included cultivating Christian young men and women. School administrators and faculty members, therefore, greatly encouraged the formation of YWCA (and YMCA) associations on their campuses. However, in 1908 only three of the fourteen black student associations were recommended for National Board affiliation. Likewise, only four black city associations were recommended. White women were, thus far, unwilling to contradict the prescribed racial mores in their country. W.E.B. DuBois's conviction that the major challenge for twentieth-century America would be the "color line" held true for the YWCA for most of the century.

The unwillingness of white YWCA members to admit African American women into the association contra-dicted its Christian mission. Many white women recognized this and worked to find some means to include their Christian sisters of color without upsetting their white members or their funders who were often the prominent businessmen in the city. In 1907, Grace Dodge, president of the national association, called a conference to discuss racial policy for the YWCA in the South. Dodge, however, did not invite any African American women to the meeting. The exclusion of black representation from this discussion, as well as the fear and prejudice among the white women, produced limited results benefiting African Americans. The YWCA apparently decided to not stop the work among African American students and communities that was already under way but also chose not to support the initiation of new "colored work" in the South. According to historian Adrienne Lash Jones, white southern YWCA members did not want to find themselves at a national conference with African American members from their city. The potential for their own embarrassment, if they were to run into the black women back home, was too great for the white women. That this stance contradicted the association's mission to serve *all* women and girls was the foundation of black women's challenge to the YWCA.

African American women would not let up and continued to demand that the YWCA recognize them. Organized extensively into clubs and associations among themselves, partly in response to their exclusion from white women's organizations, African American women looked to the YWCA for an avenue toward racial justice. Black women believed at the time that they needed white women as allies in order to advance their quest for equality and an end to the violence wrought on them by white America. In the years prior to World War I, the national YWCA hired a number of educated black women to oversee work among African American women and students. Addie Waite Hunton, Elizabeth Ross Haynes, and Eva Del Vakia Bowles all served as national YWCA representatives to the black associations. Their work, their presence among the staff, and eventually for Haynes in the 1920s, her participation on the National Board slowly moved the association toward a more honest discussion regarding race relations. By the 1920s, because of the ongoing challenge by African American women, the YWCA was at least including its black Christian sisters in that discussion.

Perhaps the one most intimately connected to the YWCA for the longest period of time, Eva Bowles (1875–1943), joined the association in 1905. Born in Albany, Ohio, she was brought to New York City at the age of thirty to oversee the Colored Young Women's Christian Association in New York (later the 137th Street YWCA in Harlem), becoming the national organization's first African American secretary. Always pushing the association toward true racial integration, Bowles oversaw the National Board Subcommittee for Colored Work and built it into a department with paid staff. She resisted, however, the Colored Department's permanency. She argued that the Central Association, made up entirely of white women, ought to include African American women as well. Black women, she contended, not only should oversee the work within black communities but also should influence the decisions and direction of the whole association. Following World War I, she increased her influence in the association by mediating between the YWCA and southern black women who had threatened to leave the organization, disgusted with its racist policies. She did so by getting more black women into important positions in the association and convincing the national organization to hold meetings only in places where all participants could be accommodated. Bowles stayed at the YWCA long enough to see the Colored Department and its staff consolidated into the other divisions of the association in 1931 with the goal of integrating the organization's administration. Unfortunately, she quit a year later when she realized that the consolidation had only served to diminish African American women's status and influence in the organization. Not until after her 1943 death did the association take more radical steps toward integration.

The history of the YWCA and race relations differs considerably when one compares the national policy with local efforts. As mentioned, it was not until 1946 that the YWCA convention passed the *Interracial Charter*. The *Charter* pledged to work on overcoming racial barriers at the local level, thereby eliminating segregated community associations. A glance at local associations, however, indicates that some cities did not wait for the national body to make this decision; other cities ignored the *Charter* altogether. Even as the national YWCA was moving toward recognizing black associations, it considered the white associations to be the central or main association in the city, while the African American groups were understood as branches. Although African American women controlled and managed their own associations, they were virtually overseen and supervised by the white local group. Different cities, some even prior to 1946, began experimenting with integrated meetings and services, but this happened primarily in the North where integrated meetings were not legally prohibited by state laws. After 1946, many cities were very slow to adopt the *Charter*, not moving forward until the National Board leaned on them. One such place, Charlotte, North Carolina, waited until the mid-1960s to open an integrated facility. However, the white members controlled the placement of the new YWCA building and thus located it in a white, suburban, middle-class suburb. The *Charter* did not resolve the race problem, nor did it adequately prepare white women on how to achieve racial integration within or beyond the association in ways that were just.

Since 1946, however, the YWCA has made great strides as a national organization to make the eradication of racial injustices one of its primary goals. The institution and many of its leaders and members participated in the civil rights movement of the 1950s and 1960s. It became one of the first organizations to hold interracial meetings in the South, including in Atlanta, Georgia. In 1972, the national office pledged to eliminate racism "by any means necessary." In 1992 the YWCA began an annual day of commitment to eliminate racism, a way for the national office to support local associations in their work for justice. Across the United States, the YWCA held discussions, walks and runs, Stop Racism Youth Challenges, and Racial Justice Award banquets to promote this aspect of its agenda. Throughout this time period, African American members and staff, including current national president Alexine Clement Jackson, have challenged white YWCA members and staff to make racial equality a priority.

The history of the YWCA in both the United States and Canada cannot be discussed without mentioning the association's work during both world wars. According to an early YWCA historian, Mary Sims, the organization did not become well known in the United States until its service during World War I. At that time, the federal government called on a number of organizations, including both the YWCA and the YMCA, to provide services for military personnel and their families. Receiving several million dollars from the U.S. government for its wartime programs, the YWCA established a War Work Council to oversee the money and work. With the enormous increase in funds and personnel, the YWCA in both countries set about establishing the main tenet of its wartime work: hostess houses in U.S. military camps at home and overseas where soldiers, their wives, and their children could find comfort and privacy to visit with each other. The associations also provided forms of recreation for men and women in military communities, hoping to steer soldiers away from what the YWCA and other progressive reformers considered to be immoral and unhygienic activities. In another facet of its war work, the U.S. association recruited and trained corps of Polish American women who traveled to Poland to assist their native country in its reconstruction efforts. As was true in the case of immigrant women and, eventually, in the case of racial equality, the YWCA adjusted its programs during World War I to serve the needs dictated by their clientele, albeit circumscribed by their own middle-class and religious values.

The federal government again approached the YWCA during World War II to fulfill the needs of military personnel. Similarly to World War I, the association again learned to cooperate with other existing organizations also being paid by the government to provide certain services. In addition, much of the YWCA's work during World War II was similar to its work in World War I. As a member of the United Service Organizations (USO) with the YMCA, the National Catholic Community Service, the National Jewish Welfare Board, the Salvation Army, and the National Travelers Aid Association, the YWCA again labored to create comfortable settings for soldiers and their families to relax away from the stressful wartime worries. In addition to serving military personnel, however, the YWCA and other organizations were also called on by the government to serve the needs of men and women workers in munitions plants and other wartime factories often built in remote areas. The services the association provided were often the very same ones they had been providing clients for over fifty years; the context had simply changed.

The example of the YWCA recruiting and training Polish American women for reconstruction efforts in Poland following World War I reflected the significant value the association placed on international work and relations. As mentioned in regard to the student associations, YWCA women often became missionaries overseas in their own churches' programs. However, the YWCA also funded the work and establishment of associations across the world. As a member of the World YWCA, the YWCA of the United States was fully engaged in creating good relations with women in other countries. Furthermore, the organization established a Foreign Department early on to lead in these efforts. By 1915, the U.S. YWCA supported thirty-two secretaries overseas. Depending on the specific context, these efforts can at times be understood through the lens of imperialism. U.S. middle- and upper-class women longed to bring Western, Christian civilization to "pagan" countries. On the other hand, under the direction of women like Grace Dodge, the association cultivated leadership in these countries and released control of local associations once they deemed the leadership to be prepared. Dodge preferred that American YWCA women, who had chosen to work in other countries, did so under the supervision of indigenous leaders. Furthermore, when U.S. foreign policy returned to isolationism following World War I, the YWCA Foreign Department increased its efforts so as to not abandon women's and their families' needs in foreign countries.

YWCA work during the wars, funded by the federal government, led to an immense increase in overseas workers. It was during World War I that the YWCA of the United States began to consider work in Mexico. However, it was not until 1921, after the Mexican Revolution had ended with nearly 2 million Mexicans dead, that the U.S. YWCA sent a representative to their neighboring country in the South to assess the potential for establishing a YWCA there. A year later in 1922, Caroline Duval Smith traveled south as the YWCA's first advisory secretary to Mexico with the intent of finding indigenous leadership. A former staff member at the San Antonio International Institute, Duval found a set of political, social, economic, and religious divisions that were impossible to ignore in her attempts to engender a homegrown YWCA. Further complicating matters, many Mexicans distrusted Smith as an American, reflecting the imperialist-based relationship the United States had established with Mexico dating back at least to the annexation of Texas in 1845 and the subsequent war and confiscation of Mexican lands in 1848. Although the relations between the two countries had improved following the U.S. Civil War, the recent intervention by the United States in the Mexican Revolution had deeply disturbed that relationship. This became clear when Mexican students accused Elena Landazuri, the first general secretary of the Mexican YWCA, of being "an apologist for the United States." Smith was also faced with the social and economic divisions between indigenous Mexicans and their more recently arrived European countrymen and women, the political instability following the Revolution, and a largely Catholic population, many of whom doubted the Protestant Christianity the YWCA grew out of. To make matters even more difficult, Caroline Smith's first summer in Mexico cast her into the middle of labor and international unrest. At the time, the United States was threatening to invade Mexico for economic purposes related to its oil interests. Smith, instead of focusing her energies completely on building a Mexican association, found herself meeting with other Protestant organizations to strategize on how to best prevent U.S. intervention in Mexico.

That which defined the YWCA, its application of Christian principles to social reform efforts and programs, also served as the major conflict between Catholics and Protestants in Mexico and therefore stood as an obstacle for Smith and Landazuri. Smith traveled south knowing she would have to convince Catholic women in Mexico of the importance of Christianity as a motivator in treating social ills. Furthermore, the Catholic Church had lost much of its support from the people, many of whom rebelled against the authoritarian and conservative hierarchy. The government had also removed its support of the Church, limiting its role in public education and taking back land and many of the Church's privileges. Smith and her YWCA associates hoped to gain the support of Catholic women who had moved away from the Church as well as those Protestants already interested in social service, especially services for the women in Mexico.

Despite the many obstacles, Smith and Landazuri soon had an association up and running. Early programs included health services, a vocational bureau, and girls' clubs. The poor and illiterate were the focus of such programs. On the other hand, middle-class women were also targets as YWCA leaders worked to open these women's eyes to the necessity of providing services for the poor. In November 1923, the Mexican YWCA founders sent a statement to the Foreign Division of the YWCA of the U.S.A. as well as the World's YWCA for approval of this newest national association. Their statement was accepted, and the new association was born. However, the divisions that Smith faced when she first entered Mexico continued to plague the association, including the conservatism of many Mexican women of European descent who refused to support the ideals and values at the base of the YWCA. Smith's major focus during her time in Mexico continued to be developing indigenous leadership. Therefore, when she left Mexico in 1925, the association still did not have a building of its own or a swimming pool. Such amenities were left for her successors to establish.

Today's YWCA organizations, across all of North America, reflect the current political and social agendas of progressive women in all three countries. Antiracism work, refugee programs, domestic violence initiatives, economic development, and the physical well-being of girls and women all comprise the YWCA of the early twenty-first century. In Ottawa, Canada, the National Capital Region YWCA served over 147,000 children, youth, and adults in 2000 with programs in over sixty schools, eight parks and beaches, numerous churches and community centers, and even two shopping centers. Ottawa's program priorities include expanding services to children, youth, and young adults with child care, camping, and outdoor education; encouraging a more culturally diverse clientele to participate in its programs; and expanding their programs for elders. In the United States, former National Organization for Women president Patricia Ireland was chosen as the new chief executive in May 2003. Such a choice, coupled with a move of the national office from New York City to Washington, D.C., seems to signify a desire on the part of the organization to have an increasing voice in national policy. According to Ireland, the U.S. YWCA's main two initiatives are economic empowerment and racial equality for women and girls. The YWCA in the United States includes 400 associations, including community and student associations. Together, these associations serve over 2 million women and their families each year. The national Mexican YWCA, located in Guadalajara, works with numerous organizations, including the Mexican government, to provide social, economic, and medical assistance. The association provides literacy classes for adults and handicraft classes for women who might be tied to their homes but able to manufacture objects for sale. According to the Mexican YWCA, their major objective is to make women increasingly aware of their rights in light of economic and gendered obstacles. Across North America, the YWCA continues to respond to women's needs—as women define them.

SOURCES: On the U.S. YWCA, see Nina Mjagki and Margaret Spratt, eds., *Men and Women Adrift: The YMCA and the YWCA in the City* (1997); Daphne Spain, *How Women Saved the City* (2001); Florence Radcliffe, *Simple Matter of Justice: The Phyllis Wheatley YWCA Story* (1985); Adrienne Lash Jones, "Struggle among the Saints: African American Women and the YWCA, 1870–1920," in Nina Mjagki and Margaret Spratt, eds., *Men and Women Adrift* (1997); Nancy Robertson, " 'Deeper Even Than Race?': White Women and the Politics of Christian Sisterhood in the Young Women's Christian Association" (Ph.D. diss., New York University, 1997); and Judith Weisenfeld, *African American Women and Christian Activism: New York's Black YWCA, 1905–1945* (1997). For institutional histories of the U.S. YWCA, see Mary Sims, *Natural History of a Social Institution: The YWCA* (1936); Mary Sims, *The YWCA—An Unfolding Purpose, 1935–1947* (1950); Mary Sims, *The Purpose Widens, 1947–1967* (1969); and Marion O. Robinson, *Eight of the YWCA Women* (1966). On the YWCA in Canada, see Diana Pedersen, " 'Building Today for the Womanhood of Tomorrow': Businessmen, Boosters, and the YWCA, 1890–1930," *Urban History Review/Revue d'histoire urbaine* 15.3 (February 1987): 225–242; Josephine Perfect Harshaw, *When Women Work Together: A History of the Young Women's Christian Association in Canada* (1966); Mary Quayle Innis, *Unfold the Years: A History of the Young Women's Christian Association in Canada* (1949); and Dawn Seibre, " 'To Shield from Temptation': The Business Girl and the City," *Urban History Review/Revue d'histoire urbaine* 17.3 (February 1989): 203–208. On the Mexican YWCA, see Nancy Boyd, *Emissaries: The Overseas Work of the American YWCA, 1895–1970* (1986).

WOMEN AND RELIGION IN THE BORDERLANDS
Daisy L. Machado

The Borderlands Defined

THE TERM *BORDERLANDS* can be used to simply refer to a place on a map, more specifically to the southwestern states of the United States that geographically run adjacent to the approximately 2,000 miles (3,200 kilometers) of what is today the Mexico-U.S. border. Indeed, the borderlands is all of this but also much more. The borderlands is also that place of intimate relations and territorial limitations where life has been shaped and continues to be shaped by the reality of conquest, race, gender, and hierarchies. Herbert Eugene Bolton, a twentieth-century U.S. historian, first used the term *borderlands* in 1921 and in his 1932 presidential address to the American Historical Association. Bolton argued that ignoring the nearly three centuries of Spanish presence in the southwestern half of the United States led to a history of the United States in "isolation, apart from its setting in the history of the entire Western Hemisphere, of which the United States are but a part" (Billington, 56).

Within the last two decades Latina/o historians as well as Latina/o writers from other disciplines have "rediscovered" the concept of borderlands and found it to be a useful metaphor. These writers have expanded the borderlands to mean and embrace more than what Bolton originally meant while keeping the basic idea that the history of one people can never be told in isolation from the history of those around them. As a result, the borderlands has come to be used to describe the Latina/o reality in the United States. As the term *borderlands* evolved and became more complex, it also included the reality of the changing demographics within the United States, in particular immigration from the Southern Hemisphere to *el norte*, north of the Rio Grande. The borderlands is that place where there is a confluence of life and experience, of language and culture, where those who conquered have in many ways defined and stereotyped those who were conquered. It is a place of encounters, where, historically speaking, Spain first met with people of central Mexico over five centuries ago; where North Americans first encountered the Tejanos (Mexican Texans) over two centuries ago; and where today the southern peoples of the Americas continue to meet the northern peoples of the Americas. Understood as having this depth of meanings, it becomes clear that the borderlands is more than a geographical location. The borderlands is a unique place where life is lived and understood to be on the margins.

Borderlands Life: Realities and Complexities

One reality life in the borderlands encompasses is that of a deep cultural, political, and economic chasm. On a very simple level, proof of this chasm or divide is found in the very fact that the river that separates both nations bears two names. It is called "Río Bravo" by the Mexicans due to the dangers involved in its crossing and "Rio Grande" on the U.S. side due to its vast longitude. One river, yet it is interpreted and understood by two peoples in very distinct ways. For the North Americans it is a natural boundary, a political landmark, and a national border. For the Mexican people it is an artificial creation born of the political machinations and violence of the Mexican-American War of 1848. As a result of this war, North American troops invaded and then annexed thousands of miles of Mexican land, incorporating many of the residents of that land into the U.S. reality. Then, between the years 1890 and 1930, more than an eighth of Mexico's population came to the

United States. The border, a political creation, did not and could not deter the movement of a people. Borderlands people had for centuries crossed a river that now, for the first time in the nineteenth century, separated two nations but could not sever ties of family, culture, religion, and language.

Therefore, one of the distinctive characteristics of the borderlands is that it is made up of land that has been historically conquered and colonized. And this happened not just once but twice. First, the inhabitants of the Americas experienced the Spanish *conquista* in the sixteenth century. This was followed by a second conquest and colonization in the nineteenth century when the national borders of the United States were expanded to include the northern territories of the newly formed Republic of the United States of Mexico, which were called Coahuila y Tejas. The key focus here should not be on the land, which was obviously the catalyst for the military action taken by the United States in its war against Mexico, but on the people who lived on the land. Overnight, as national boundaries were redrawn in the private chambers of political power, the Mexican people of Coahuila y Tejas were facing the choice of assuming a new citizenship or giving up their land and "moving" south of the Rio Grande to Mexico. However, beyond the land issue, which is very important, the fact remains that the Tejanos or Mejicanos were in many significant ways *different* from those who constituted the majority population of the new country that had annexed them. The people of Coahuila y Tejas were *mestizos*, a hybrid people, in whose veins flowed *la sangre india, negra, y española* (Indian, black, and Spanish blood). They were a people whose native language, which had already been forcibly changed to Spanish three centuries earlier, was being changed for a third time to English. They were a people who were culturally indigenous and Spanish. And they were also a people whose religion, which had been Roman Catholic since the sixteenth century, was being challenged by the Protestant missionary enterprise that began in the late nineteenth century.

The borderlands was a tumultuous zone where the Mexican and the indigenous were reconquered by the Euro-American, creating hybrid languages and home to often-violent clashes of ideologies and religions. In the borderlands there can be found a disparate economic system, a hierarchy of race, and a corridor of cultural interaction rich in ambiguities and contradictions. As a result of this history, the borderlands is that place of contrasts, difference, racism, tensions, poverty, and displacement. According to Chicana poet and activist Gloria Anzaldúa,

The U.S.-Mexico border *es una herida abierta* [an open wound] where the Third World grates against the first and bleeds. And before a scab forms it hemorrhages again, the lifeblood of two worlds merging to form a third country—a border culture. . . . A borderlands is a vague and undetermined place created by the emotional residue of an unnatural boundary. (Anzaldúa, 3)

This border culture that Anzaldúa refers to has at its core the unique characteristic of hybridization that is called *mestizaje* in Spanish. This *mestizaje* is a confluence of the disparities that converge in borderlands life and produce a third culture. It is a culture that encompasses struggle for identity, economic polarization, underlying racial politics, cultural adaptation, as well as cultural fusion such as intermarriages, holiday traditions, and religious observances. In the borderlands, life is lived in a social environment that is strongly configured by a very extensive system of mutual borrowing in both directions. The borderlands language, for example, is intermingled and replete with words that are constantly changing, thus creating a third language between Spanish and English, called by many "Span/glish." This language can juggle the many variables found in both Spanish and English but can at the same time also express the reality of life with a dual identity. Anzaldúa explains:

> For a people who are neither Spanish nor live in a country in which Spanish is the first language; for a people who live in a country in which English is the reigning tongue but who are not Anglo; for a people who cannot entirely identify with either standard (formal, Castillian) Spanish nor standard English, what recourse is left to them but to create their own language? A language which they can connect their identity to, one capable of communicating the realities and values true to themselves—a language with terms that are neither *español ni inglés*, but both. We speak a patois, a forked tongue, a variation of two languages. (Anzaldúa, 55)

The demographics and economics of the border region affect the entire country, as Bolton had argued decades ago. For example, a survey of the U.S.-Mexican border done by *Business Week* (May 12, 1997) concluded that this area "may be North America's fastest-growing region, with 11 million residents, 6.1 million in the United States and 5.1 million in Mexico and $150 billion in annual output." The population in the border region is increasing by 3 percent per year on the U.S. side and 4 percent per year on the Mexican side. Projections are that this border population will grow to 36 million persons by the year 2020 (30 million on the Mexican side and 6.3 million on the U.S. side). In 2002 the four fastest-growing cities in the state of Texas were the border cities of Laredo, Brownsville, McAllen, and El Paso.

The Texas portion of the U.S.-Mexico border area includes four states in Mexico: Chihuahua, Coahuila, Nuevo León, and Tamaulipas. Along this border there are eight "major sister city" pairs with a population of more than 4.5 million. These are certainly impressive and telling statistics, yet one important historical characteristic of borderlands life endures: a disparate economic reality intermingled with racism that plagues the people of the borderlands. What we find is an extreme poverty that continues to be part and parcel of borderlands life for many of its Tejano residents. This economic disparity is readily found in the 1,800 *colonias* that exist, a phenomenon found particularly in the state of Texas.

A *colonia* is an unincorporated community that lacks any city or county services such as water, sewers, streetlights, paved sidewalks, or garbage pickup. These communities have been compared to shantytowns found in any of the developing countries around the globe. The *colonias* began in the late 1960s and early 1970s when landowners offered to sell land on very easy terms to low-income Mexican Americans or Mexican immigrants who could not qualify for bank loans. Lacking any government supervision these lots were sold in areas that flooded easily or on land no longer useful for agriculture due to pesticide contamination. One of the oldest of these *colonias* is found in Brownsville, Texas, and is called Cameron Park. It ranks dead last in median per capita income, at $4,103 a year. About 6,000 people live in the unincorporated community near Brownsville, Texas, where their poverty has been worsened by economic trends that have hit the least skilled the hardest. The textile industry that employed many with working papers has disintegrated, while drought has meant fewer agricultural jobs in the region. In this reality of extreme poverty we again come face-to-face with the ambiguities and complexities of borderlands life. In a region of the nation that produces wealth for many multinational corporations, there is an underside of extreme poverty that continues to affect the lives of a great number of borderlands dwellers, the majority of them being Mexican American and U.S. citizens.

The residents of the borderlands that live south of the Rio Grande also share this underside of poverty. This region is growing with the expansion of the *maquiladora* industry, which represents 30 percent of Mexico's manufacturing employment. The first *maquiladoras* were established in 1966 in Baja California and Ciudad Juarez in the State of Chihuahua, Mexico, under what was then referred to as the Border Industrialization Program. Initially *maquiladoras* could only be established in the border areas of Mexico, a strip of land twenty kilometers (twelve and a half miles) wide along the U.S. border, and in the Baja California free trade zone. A *maquiladora* is a foreign-owned plant that assembles imported components to make products as diverse as television sets, computer mother boards, athletic shoes, women's underwear, automobile seat belts, and dialysis equipment, which are then exported from Mexico. Companies from the United States, Japan, Canada, Germany, Korea, and other countries have established *maquiladoras* to take advantage of the inexpensive Mexican labor and the close proximity to the U.S. market. Statistics from November 1998 show that there were 2,952 *maquiladoras* in Mexico, and 1,800 of those, or 61 percent, were located in major Mexican cities along the Texas portion of the U.S.-Mexico border. During this period, the *maquiladora* industry in general employed over 1 million workers, of whom 636,000 were associated with U.S.-Mexico border *maquiladoras*. Of those workers located along the border with the United States, 377,811 were employed by the 630 *maquiladoras* found in the Mexican cities such as Nuevo Laredo, Matamoros, and Reynosa, located along the Texas portion of the U.S.-Mexico border. *Maquiladora* workers earn an average of U.S.$5 to $7 a day plus benefits, despite the fact that $119 billion were generated in 1999 in gross production. The San Diego Dialogue, a binational citizen-business partnership, estimates that 40,000 people commute from the Tijuana area every day to work on the U.S. side of the border and that "thousands" of U.S. residents commute daily to jobs as managers of *maquiladoras*. To further compound the problems created by the *maquiladora* industry, many of the multinational companies also come for lax environmental enforcement, and that shows, too, in the widespread industrial pollution plaguing many border cities.

More than half of the over 1 million *maquiladora* workers are women ages fifteen to thirty-five. They live a life of economic hardship that is often accompanied by health risks due to exposure to the many chemicals used in the plants. Despite having to work in an unsafe environment with unhealthy conditions, these young women also have to provide for the daily needs of their children and other family members. A 2000 study showed that a *maquiladora* worker must work four hours to buy two pounds of beans; work eleven hours and thirty minutes to buy a box of diapers; work four hours and seventeen minutes to buy one gallon of milk. In addition, a female worker is never free from the fear of sexual harassment, a female worker must submit to mandatory pregnancy tests, and spontaneous abortions due to exposure to toxic chemicals are common. Gender and poverty come together to create great economic hardship for women in the borderlands. The organization Women on the Border actively monitors the *maquiladora* industry using what they call a "gendered lens" to critically examine the reality of women employed by the *maquiladoras*. They have found that Mexican woman's gender role is one where she is traditionally viewed as dependent on men and one who has little experience in the working world and thus with making demands for better pay or better working conditions. Many Mexican women interviewed who worked in the *maquiladoras* have internalized these attitudes, speaking of factory owners preferring women "because men created more problems for them" and of the women accepting they have "natural abilities" to perform delicate, fast, repetitive, and monotonous work. Interviews done in the *maquiladoras* have shown that factory owners prefer to hire young Mexican women in the plants because they are easier to manipulate and exploit. It can be said that in the last three decades the *maquiladoras* have overwhelmingly redefined the socioeconomic character of the borderlands life. The reality is that for some people life on the border is a constant skirting the edges of death. For many *maquiladora* workers exposure to life-threatening working conditions or inhaled production chemicals is a daily problem, which at the very least is an issue of human rights or environmental racism. The reality that the workforce in the *maquiladoras* is highly feminized, as well as the issue of women's treatment and their exploitation, should evoke the concerns of anyone who advocates for the rights of all women, regardless of economic class, race, or educational level.

Religion in the Borderlands

The borderlands, as we have already said, is also a place of religious encounters that often run parallel to the military, political, economic, and racial encounters that took place at the same time. In the religious history of the United States, the borderlands is the first region in which Protestantism was shared with Spanish-speaking people, in this case, Mexicans or more specifically Tejanos. While Protestantism was part of the great U.S. missionary enterprise of the late nineteenth to early twentieth centuries to the Spanish-speaking colonial islands of Cuba and Puerto Rico beginning in 1899, the Protestant expansion into the borderlands began at least sixty-five years earlier. This missionary enterprise in the borderlands also contained a variety of attitudes about the people being encountered that led to a coupling of missionary work with two main tasks: to "Christianize" and to "Americanize." These ideas of cultural imperialism, which were prevalent in the missionary efforts of Protestant missionaries in the borderlands, were to shape the work of just about all denominational groups for decades to come. We must note that North American Protestant missionaries often served as cultural agents who not only preached the gospel but also did so with regard to social customs such as dress and manners and with middle-class values. As a result, the Christian gospel was made indistinguishable from North American civilization. If one was to become a Protestant Christian

The organization Women on the Border actively monitors the *maquiladora* industry through a "gendered lens" to critically examine the reality of women employed by these factories. They have found that the Mexican woman's gender role is one where she is traditionally viewed as dependent on men, has little experience in the working world, and is inexperienced at making demands for better pay or better working conditions. *Courtesy of Denise Vergez, Women on the Border.*

in the borderlands, then the model to follow was that of the Euro-American missionary. Such cultural imperialism could not be free from racial stereotypes and gender expectations. In the borderlands, the ideas about race and gender brought by the missionaries not only created tensions but ultimately played a crucial role in the denominational work that was undertaken and the resources invested.

When Protestants first entered the borderlands they did so beginning in 1821. At this time the territory belonged to the newly formed Republic of the United States of Mexico, which had only a few years earlier gained its independence after centuries of Spanish domination. As these North American settlers entered this territory, they were bound by the Mexican Constitution, which clearly stipulated that Roman Catholicism was to be the only religion of the Republic. As the Mexican Constitution stated, in Article Three, "The religion of the Mexican Nation is, and will be perpetually, the Roman Catholic Apostolic." However, as more and more North American settlers began arriving in the northern Mexican territories of Coahuilas y Tejas, searching for land grants and economic prospects, the religious reality did not seem important. Even before the war with Mexico in 1836, which created the Republic of Texas, Protestant ministers were busy in the borderlands territories. The first sermon believed to have been preached in Coahuilas y Tejas was preached by a Baptist from Ohio,

Freeman Smawley, in 1822. In 1823, Joseph L. Bays held the first Methodist church service, and the first Sunday School was established by the Baptists in 1829. In that same year, Sumner Bacon, a Cumberland Presbyterian, began an itinerant ministry. In a mere seven-year period, from as early as 1822 to 1829, in the territories of Coahuilas y Tejas there could be found religious activities by Baptists, Methodists, and Cumberland Presbyterians. These denominational efforts were all directed at the newly arriving North American colonists who were moving south and west, a sea of immigrants that could not be easily contained at the border by the Mexican government. They were spilling into the northern Mexican territories, and like all immigrants, they brought their religion with them.

The earliest history of any effort made by Protestants to reach the Mexican population can be found in the Cumberland Presbyterians. Sumner Bacon, a controversial evangelist, began distributing Bibles in Spanish and English in 1834. He continued this work until his death in 1844. However, no one in the denomination continued his work. The first formal appointment of a Protestant missionary to work in Texas was made in 1839 when the Presbyterian's Foreign Board of Missions commissioned William C. Blair. Blair, who had worked with the Chickasaw Indians in 1822, moved with his family in June 1839 to Victoria, a town located between what is today Houston and San Antonio. His work with the

Spanish-speaking inhabitants was not very successful and reached few Mexicans. Work among Mexicans carried out by the major Protestant denominational groups was slow in getting started and checkered in its results. Groups like the Presbyterians or the Methodists or the Christian Church (Disciples of Christ) began their Spanish-speaking missionary efforts with the main goal of preparing Euro-American missionaries in Texas for the work to be done in Mexico and further south in Latin America. In many ways, these denominational groups saw the borderlands as a buffer zone against the Roman Catholic influence from South America. Again, history was being replayed in the borderlands, only this time with a very clearly defined Protestant agenda. The issue of racial prejudice played a great part in developing the missionaries' mentality. The Tejanos were seen as ignorant and superstitious, "deemed poor prospects for the conversion to Protestant Christianity" (Brackenridge and García-Treto, 13).

Melinda Rankin, a New England school mistress, was the first person to initiate a permanent Presbyterian mission to Mexicans in Texas. Locating first in Huntsville in 1852, Miss Rankin moved to Brownsville, directly across from Matamoros, Mexico, to start a school for young women. She halted her efforts and went back East to solicit funds for a more substantial school and returned to Texas to organize the Rio Grande Female Institute in May 1854, which she directed until 1861. Miss Rankin's continued and tireless efforts on behalf of the Tejanos marked what is known as the "first period" of Presbyterian involvement with Mexican Americans in Texas. Not until the 1880s was that denominational interest renewed. Presbyterians, Baptists, Methodists, and Disciples of Christ followed one another in their missionary efforts to the Tejanos of the borderlands throughout the late nineteenth century and into the early twentieth century. The missionary work done by these denominations was sporadic and underfunded, and as a result, there occurred a gradual change in the language used to describe the work. The old argument of antebellum missionaries that it was worthwhile to evangelize Mexican Texans because this would produce an influence upon Mexico was no longer effective. A new rationale had to be developed to produce interest in these borderlands missions. One that can be found in all denominations during this time is the idea of a "Mexican problem." This rationale, laden with racial stereotypes, racial hierarchies, and an abhorrence of Roman Catholicism, was very simple: If the Protestants do not do anything to convert the Tejanos to Christianity, the Roman Catholics will continue to dominate this group.

Missionary literature from the early 1900s abounds with references to the fact that Mexican Americans were indeed "ignorant, superstitious . . . most obedient sons of Rome," which made them "poor American citizens." Yet they were on U.S. soil and were U.S. citizens, which meant that the Protestant denominations were responsible for them. Giving evidence of very clear traits of cultural imperialism, the missionary literature of this period boasted "our work of evangelization has been promotive of the best good to the converts, hygienically, socially, civilly, morally, and spiritually" (Brackenridge and García-Treto, 15). To support such a missionary agenda meant to engage in the "uplifting" of a people who were not only influenced by a religion based on superstition but who were therefore morally inferior and unable to govern themselves and lacked education and even the basic skills of personal cleanliness and grooming. The Baptists stated their concern by saying, "It is our *duty* to save those born on Texas or Mexican soil who speak to us in an alien language" (Maldonado, 93). The Disciples of Christ made their plea: "The Christianization *and* Americanization of this large body of alien people is a task for the whole church" (93). What we see in these missionary reports and literature is a mentality that was doctrinally Protestant and patriotically American. God and Nation were to be served, and for the majority of those involved in this venture to become truly American, one must also become truly Protestant. To embrace Protestantism was to embrace the ideals of democracy, individualism, self-motivation, thrift, cleanliness, hard work—all those characteristics associated by the early-nineteenth-century North American culture with the pioneer spirit that had "conquered" the West.

The missionary work being done by mainline denominations was also gendered. Missionary work that focused on women, such as that done by Melinda Rankin for the Presbyterians in the 1850s, had been shaped by what historian Barbara Welter has identified as the "cult of true womanhood." This nineteenth-century ideal was pervasive and influential and assigned women four "cardinal virtues." The true woman was pious, pure, submissive, and domestic. Women were thought to be by nature religious and moral. The true woman was more interested than the male in religion and sought to develop spiritual qualities. She was also naturally pure and showed little, if any, sexuality. The true woman was also submissive, to her husband's authority in particular and to male authority in general. To want power, to be aggressive, was seen as unfeminine, not in keeping with the true woman ideal. And, of course, the true woman was domestic, drawn by nature to domestic concerns, to being a good wife and a good mother. This cult of true womanhood was part of the cultural imperialism that female missionaries carried with them into their work for the church.

In the borderlands the work of women such as Melinda Rankin was typical in that it focused on education and especially in training girls in North American ways. Critics say that the work done by female missionaries had limited success, and in many cases women missionaries reinforced class and racial structures as well as gender-defined roles. Because these women were themselves products of their own culture and class, they were often uncritical in what they offered the women of the borderlands. Mostly their message was one that elevated North American culture and its cult of true womanhood, maintained racial stereotypes, and saw the women of the borderlands as needing to be freed from an inferior religion and culture.

The Presbyterians, for example, developed what were initially called "houses of neighborliness." This evangelistic effort, officially called "The Home of Neighborly Service," was aimed at Mexican American women. The first such house was opened in 1920 in Azusa, California, quickly followed by other houses in Texas, Colorado, and Arizona. Sara J. Reed was the founder of the first house, or model home, in California, which was opened in the Mexican neighborhood. The goal of the home, "tastefully" decorated within the price range of neighborhood residents, was to "win the women and through them to develop Christian American homes" (Brackenridge and García-Treto, 142). Miss Reed was to teach her women personal hygiene, sanitation, baby care, cooking, sewing, and general homemaking. Even though she did not speak Spanish, this was not seen as a problem since it was expected that the Mexican American women would learn English. In this missionary effort to women we see the influence of the cult of true womanhood. The idea was to develop in these homes the domestic skills of the Mexican American women through the lens of North American culture. The woman missionary was offering a "better" way for the borderlands women. Such efforts clearly maintained the status quo between the genders, women remained passive and domestic, but their skills now reflected North American characteristics. They were becoming better homemakers, and what made them better was that they were becoming Protestant homemakers, American homemakers, and not Mexican homemakers.

The people of the borderlands were seen by the Protestant denominations as a people who needed uplifting through conversion to Protestantism, a turning away from Roman Catholicism, and an embracing of the North American culture. The issues of language, culture, religion, and identity were dismissed as unimportant. Religion, in this case Protestantism, came packaged in a cultural box that contained long-standing national beliefs that whatever was Mexican, Roman Catholic, Spanish, and non-Euro-American was inferior. This era of missionary work in many ways shows how the issues of race and religion became areas of tension and conflict for the people of the borderlands as they encountered their Euro-American neighbors. Life in the borderlands became complex and riddled with ambiguities. What did it mean for the women and men who left their Roman Catholic heritage and embraced North American Protestantism? Was it really to their benefit to become this new type of Christian and American? As the twentieth century progressed, history has shown that Latinas/os throughout the borderlands have remained marginal members and participants of the mainline Protestant denominations that sought them out decades earlier. They are still outsiders and still have to struggle to have their voices heard within denominational circles. Latina/o leaders have risen to national positions in some denominations, an achievement that can be traced to the 1980s. However, these national Latina/o leaders are in the minority and still struggle to make their influence felt within their denominations. As Gloria Anzaldúa has said of the continuous struggle of the Latinas/os in the borderlands to develop and flourish, "[W]e have never been allowed to develop unencumbered—we have never been allowed to be fully ourselves" (Anzaldúa, 86). As the forces of globalization continue to reshape the world, the borderlands will continue to evolve. Perhaps as we become more aware of how the borderlands was formed and learn to reflect critically on the forces that have shaped life in the borderlands, we will be able to find truth in these words:

> To survive in the Borderlands
>   you must live *sin fronteras* [without borders]
> be a crossroads. (195)

SOURCES: The historical writings that show the development of the ideas about the frontier and the Spanish borderlands can be found in John F. Bannon, ed., *Bolton and the Spanish Borderlands* (1964); Ray Allen Billington, ed., *Frontier and Section: Selected Essays of Frederick Jackson Turner* (1961); and Herbert Eugene Bolton, *Wider Horizons of American History* (1939). There are few denominational histories about work in the borderlands, but the following are available: R. Douglas Brackenridge and Francisco García-Treto, *Iglesia Presbiteriana: A History of Presbyterians and Mexican Americans in the Southwest* (1987) and Daisy L. Machado, *Of Borders and Margins: Hispanic Disciples in Texas, 1888–1945* (2003). An important anthology that focuses on Latina/o Protestantism is David Maldonado, ed., *Protestantes/Protestants, Hispanic Christianity within Mainline Traditions* (1999). A social/political examination of borderlands life/reality can be found in Gloria Anzaldúa, *Borderlands/La Frontera: The New Mestiza* (1987). Two very useful Web sites that give information about the economic realities found in the borderlands are http://www.tnrcc.state.tx.us/exec/oppr/border/border.html and http://www.womenontheborder.org/.

TURNING OFF THE TAPS: PUBLIC POLICY IN CANADA

Lois M. Wilson

"NEVER RETREAT, NEVER explain, never apologize. Get the thing done and let them howl" (*In Times Like These*, vii). Those oft-quoted words were spoken by Nellie McClung, a prominent Canadian Methodist campaigner for women's suffrage (1918), for appointment of women to the Senate (1929), and for women's ordination (1936). Born in 1873, she was a suffragist, temperance activist, politician, church worker, writer, public speaker, wife, and mother. She believed motherhood was the highest achievement for women but because of deep Christian conviction felt compelled to emerge from her home to redeem humankind with Methodist evangelical fervor. She cut her political teeth on the campaign for national prohibition conducted by the Women's Canadian Temperance Union (WCTU). In Canada, it was the temperance movement that first spurred women to seize opportunities for social and political action.

McClung knew the 1906 Election Act of the Dominion of Canada read, "No woman, idiot, lunatic, or criminal shall vote." Prior to winning women's suffrage in 1918, she was active in organizing a hilarious, satirical Women's Parliament in Winnipeg in 1914 where women and men reversed roles, and men became the sex without a vote. To the charge that women would not want to sit in Parliament, she said that "there are women who have stood before wash tubs so long that they would be glad to sit any place" (Hancock, 83).

She understood women's suffrage and women's ordination as two sides of the same coin. She worked for women's ordination in the United Church of Canada for twenty years before the first woman was finally ordained in 1936.

McClung became a public figure in church and society, her most lasting contribution to women and public policy being a thirteen-year struggle that came to be known as the Person's Case. An Albertan, Emily Murphy had been made the first ever police magistrate after suggesting that prostitutes should be tried by a special court presided over by women. Later she was to hear a case involving a breach of the Liquor Act when the counsel for the defense rose and objected to her jurisdiction as a magistrate. His argument was that she was "not a person" within the meaning of the Statutes and had no right to be holding court. This objection was based on the common law of England. "A woman is not a person in matters of rights and privileges, but she is a person in matters of pains and penalties" (McClung, *In Times Like These*, 29). In Canada, senators are not elected but appointed by the sole decision of the prime minister.

Historically, only men were appointed. In 1919 Murphy requested the Canadian government to appoint a woman to the Senate. The Minister of Justice responded that he could not appoint a woman because within the meaning of the British North American (BNA) Act women were not persons. Murphy's brother pointed out to her that Section 60 of the Supreme Court Act provided that any five persons could petition for an order-in-council directing the Supreme Court to rule on a constitutional point in the BNA Act. Murphy filed a petition and recruited four other women, including Louise McKinney (first woman to be elected to a legislature in the British Empire), Irene Parlby (elected to the provincial legislature in 1921), Henrietta Edwards (National Council of Women and an authority on laws that affected women), and Nellie McClung.

The pivotal question was posed, "Does the word 'persons' in Section 24 of the British North American Act, 1867, include female persons?" The case was finally heard in March 1928, and the ruling was that only men were fit for appointment. The five women appealed, and the question proceeded for decision to the Privy Council in London, England. On October 18, 1929, the decision was announced, and it reversed the decision of Canada's Supreme Court. Lord Chancellor of Great Britain stated that the "exclusion of women from all public office was a relic of more barbarous days and that an appeal to Roman law and to early British decisions was not in itself a secure foundation on which to build an interpretation of the BNA Act of 1867" (Hancock, 95). Women, it seems, were recognized legally as persons! The first woman senator, the Honorable Cairine Wilson, was appointed in 1930. Fifty years later, on October 18, 1999, Canada celebrated the recognition of women as persons when a statue of the Famous Five (as they are now called) was unveiled on Parliament Hill in Ottawa. Current women senators were the honored guests.

Turning Off the Taps—Structural Change at the Source

Nellie McClung wrote,

In a certain asylum the management have a unique test for sanity. When any of the inmates exhibit evidence of returning reason, they submit them to the following tests. Out in the courtyard there are a number of water taps for filling troughs, and to each of the candidates a small pail is given. They are told to drain the troughs. The taps still run full force. Some of them bail away, but of course the trough remains full in spite of them. The wise ones turn off the taps. (*In Times Like These*, 79)

Nellie McClung, a prominent Canadian Methodist campaigner for women's suffrage, for appointment of women to the Senate, and for women's ordination often said, "Never retreat, never explain, never apologize. Get the thing done and let them howl." Born in 1873, she was a suffragist, temperance activist, politician, church worker, writer, public speaker, wife, and mother. She believed motherhood was the highest achievement for women, but because of deep Christian conviction felt compelled to emerge from her home to redeem humankind with Methodist evangelical fervor. *Courtesy of the National Archives of Canada.*

Turning off the taps is what Canadian women do when they make public policy. It has to do with changing public policy on a structural level, rather than spending all one's energy on dealing with the casualties.

Turning Off the Taps—Amending the Indian Act, 1985

There was a strong move in the 1970s by Caroline Ennis, Sandra Lovelace, Glenna Perley, and other aboriginal women of the Tobique reserve in New Brunswick called "Indian Rights for Indian Women." Canada's Indian Act not only governs the lives of 350,000 Native Indians in Canada; it also defines who is and who is not an "Indian." From 1869 until 1985 Indian status was determined through a male person only. A number of aboriginal women who were either divorced or widowed from white husbands had been unaware of the far-reaching implications of "marrying out" and leaving the Tobique reserve for some years. When Ennis's and Lovelace's marriages with white men broke down and they moved back "home" to the reserve, they were shocked to discover that they had automatically lost their status as Indians, although the reverse situation did not apply to aboriginal men. This meant they lost their band membership and with it their property, inheritance, res-

idency, burial, medical, educational, and voting rights on the reserve where they had lived before marriage. Janet Silman, a United Church minister, lived with the women most affected by these policies and documented their conversations. She gave a voice to the voiceless.

As early as the 1950s Mary Two Axe Early from Caugnawaga, Quebec, had spoken out against the legislated sexual discrimination of the Indian Act. But in 1973 when the Supreme Court of Canada ruled that the Indian Act was exempt from the Canadian Bill of Rights, the women had no avenue left except the United Nations. It was decided that Sandra Lovelace would be a test case to appeal to the UN Human Rights Committee in Geneva.

On December 29, 1977, her complaint against the Canadian government was launched in Geneva. She appeared with the support of the Canadian churches through Project North, an interchurch coalition in support of Native people. It was agreed that the delegation would replace a white delegate of the United Church of Canada with an aboriginal woman.

The final verdict was not made until July 30, 1981. The UN Human Rights Committee ruled in Sandra Lovelace's favor, finding Canada in breach of the International Covenant on Civil and Political Rights, which covenant Canada had willingly signed some years previous.

There was in Canada wide publicity of the case, and embarrassed bureaucrats hastily announced that the Indian Act would be amended within a year. Lovelace traveled and spoke at the UN Copenhagen World Conference and to friends at home as well. "Some of the women I'd grown up with would say, 'Hey you don't belong here . . . you're non-status . . . a troublemaker.' But I wasn't about to stop for nobody" (Silman, 179).

Finally in June 1985 the Canadian Parliament passed a bill that ended over 100 years of legislated sexual discrimination against aboriginal women. The Sandra Lovelace case became celebrated as a major change in public policy for aboriginal women in Canada.

Turning Off the Taps—Taking Abortion Out of the Criminal Code, 1988

In 1988, the Supreme Court of Canada struck down the provisions in the Criminal Code that made abortion illegal, on the grounds that they offended basic freedoms entrenched in the Canadian Charter of Rights and Freedoms. The inclusion of the Charter in the Constitution Act, 1982, is widely regarded as the most important twentieth-century development in Canadian law. One woman in particular, Bertha Wilson, was pivotal to that legal decision and change in public policy, although she was not alone in her analysis. Wilson thought it was the most important decision to date dealing with woman's privacy rights as against the state.

Wilson had become a member of the United Church of Canada after emigrating from Scotland and served as a board member of the Toronto School of Theology and numerous other United Church committees. The Royal Commission on the Status of Women had been created in 1967 to ensure for women equal opportunities with men in all aspects of Canadian society. In 1971–1972 the commission successfully obtained the appointment of a government minister responsible for the Status of Women to review all policies and programs for their effect on women. The most controversial work for the United Church in which Wilson involved herself was a report on the church's position on abortion, an issue that her church had wrestled with since 1960. A commission initially chaired by her was appointed in 1974, and she worked in concert with United Church staff Ruth Evans, who was working with the Canadian Abortion Rights Action League (CARAL). In 1975 Wilson resigned from the commission, due to her appointment to the Court of Appeal.

The church's report was presented to the General Council of the United Church of Canada on August 18, 1980. It explored a full range of theological concerns and acknowledged that moral dilemmas cannot be neatly defined with inflexible rules. The report concluded that the taking of life is almost always wrong but that, in some instances, considering the quality of life as a whole and all alternatives in a given situation, abortion might be the lesser of two evils. Further, the church report recommended that the Criminal Code be amended to remove all sanctions against women and medical personnel performing abortions in licensed facilities within the first twenty weeks of pregnancy.

Although the Criminal Code made abortion illegal in Canada at that time, Dr. Henry Morgentaler, who had opened a number of abortion clinics in Canada, launched an appeal to the Supreme Court. While he faced a number of prosecutions, he had gained acquittals. The case came at a time when social consensus began to swing in his favor because of the newly minted Charter of Rights and Freedoms of 1982. Wilson was the only woman on the Supreme Court at that time. She received floods of anonymous and critical letters, written by fervent and dedicated antiabortionists. She (unlike her male colleagues) did not want to send this matter back to politicians. Rather, she wanted to establish "as a constitutional matter" that "it was highly unlikely any formulation could be found which would not substantially interfere with a woman's freedom of choice" (Anderson, 229). Where women's bodies were concerned, Wilson was convinced that state interference must necessarily infringe constitutional guarantees.

The 1988 Supreme Court decision struck down the provisions in the Criminal Code that made abortion illegal on the grounds that they offended against basic freedoms of the Charter of Rights and Freedoms, included in the Constitution Act of 1982. Feminists and pro-choice lobbies hailed Wilson's judgment as a victory. Attempts to bring in new legislation to control abortions came to nothing, and her judgment still stands in 2005. Yet there was no self-righteous certainty in her judgment and certainly no understanding that the decision about abortion had unambiguously been reached for all time as a victory for the rights of women. Her judgment stated a provisional and indeterminate truth, reflecting the intense ambivalence experienced by most women whose circumstances had led them to consider an abortion. While it is true that her judgment gave to women the right to decide for themselves about terminating a pregnancy, her judgment was tempered: because it also implicitly asserted women's responsibility to choose wisely. In the end, the decision reflected her strong beliefs in human dignity, female self-esteem, freedom of religion, and fundamental freedoms guaranteed in the Canadian Charter of Rights and Freedoms and dissolved the boundary between the private and the public. All this from a woman who, some years before, had been advised to take up crocheting!

Turning Off the Taps—Unpaid Work Recognized in Census, 1996

Another significant public policy change was the struggle of women, who perform the bulk of unpaid work, to count their work in the census. Census data is used to determine how much education funding should be granted to a region. Statistics Canada, a national statistical agency of the federal government, estimated that unpaid work is worth between $221.1 billion and $374.1 billion a year, equivalent to 32 to 54 percent of Canada's total economy. Spearheaded by Mothers Are Women (MAW), women from faith communities worked for recognition of their unpaid labor through one of the interchurch coalitions—the Ecumenical Coalition for Economic Justice (ECEJ).

In 1991, Carol Lees, a woman from Saskatoon, refused to fill out her census form because it ignored the unpaid work she did at home. The Working Group on poverty of the Women's Inter-Church Council of Canada (an ecumenical umbrella group for women of faith communities) picked up the idea. The Canadian Conference of Catholic Bishops, along with some Catholic religious orders, including the School Sisters of Notre Dame, Montreal, and other denominations, supported the action. Lorraine Michael, a Roman Catholic, wrote articles on women's unpaid work and brought her analysis of the impact of globalization and privatization on women's work to her writing. The 1996 Canadian census did finally include statistics on unpaid work.

Is Violence against Women a Public Policy Question?

Canadians were profoundly shocked on December 6, 1989, when news came that Mark Lepin, a male engineering student at L'Ecole Polytechnique in Montreal, had gunned down and massacred fourteen female engineering students. "They're just a bunch of feminists," he was reported to have shouted.

The Crucified Woman stands on the grounds of Emmanuel College, a theological college of the United Church of Canada, Toronto. Around this sculpture hundreds gather, year after year, to mourn the violence dealt to women and to express hope that such violence can be overcome through "social justice, honesty, and love" (Dyke, 71). Both the outrage and the hope prompted two women to propose changes in public policy, the Rape Shield Law of 1992 and the Firearms Act of 1995.

Violence against Women—The Rape Shield Law, 1992

The feminist movement began to deal openly with the need to address violations to women's bodies in the early 1990s. In 1992 the Rape Shield Act became law in Canada, mainly due to the collaboration and tireless persistence of women's groups. Anglican church warden Joy Kennedy was appalled by the Montreal massacre, and she was key to enactment of this new law. Through her the gathering of court-admissible forensic evidence of rape was established and the legal definition of rape changed.

Kennedy had noticed that the courts threw out the forensic evidence that was brought in rape cases and that a conviction rate of only 2 percent applied in these cases. Since the courts were asking for better evidence, she decided to provide it. Through Laura Sabia, a Roman Catholic woman who had campaigned politically for the establishment of women's regional action programs, Kennedy accessed government grants, and an incorporated body was created to prepare kits and train people to preserve evidence. Kennedy got the Justice Secretariat, medical personnel, hospital personnel, child psychologists, pediatricians, and coroners as well as provincial government departments to assist in training doctors and police personnel to deal with child abuse investigations more effectively.

A major obstacle was that rape was defined rather narrowly legally. A woman could be sexually assaulted, beaten, and abused, but the rape charge would not hold legally unless there had been penetration. Kennedy's women's group therefore decided that all rape cases should be defined as "sexual assault." So began the first study on rape in Canada conducted by a nonprofit incorporated group. The results of the study were published by the National Action Committee (NAC) on the Status of Women and critically assisted by legal experts, the Women's Legal, Education and Action Fund (LEAF). The police chief of St. Catherines, Ontario, called Kennedy names, but she persisted. Churches did not want to hear about rape—many volunteers working on this issue were volunteers drawn from congregations, but the official church bodies did not want to deal with it. Kennedy chaired the broad coalition of women's groups, which included NAC, LEAF, and several Marxist-Leninist groups. She and others had negotiated the dollars for the first rape crisis centers in the province of Ontario. They had cultivated a robust alternate vision for society that their religious tradition afforded them and resisted a culture that denied that vision.

Now they were faced with creating legislation. No one knew how to do it. So they identified and worked with allies within the government bureaucracy as well as national women's groups and female legal experts and rewrote the whole definition of rape. They needed to change Canada's Criminal Code, and they did. The new Rape Shield Act of 1992 legally defined "consent," put the onus on the defendant in all cases of sexual assault, and forbade using the past history of the victim as a proxy for consent.

Kennedy's critical work on rape then led her into a related area, namely, the sexual assault of children. The provision of evidence for the court in cases of sexual assault of children was extremely difficult to provide. So Kennedy gathered together an interdepartmental government committee and public educators who began to create a child abuse resource investigation kit. She let her imagination soar and devised strategies for change. She found male dolls with penises, and female dolls with fetuses and placentas, and created a doll that would allow children to reenact the rape. It had to be a family of four—an adult male and female, and a child male and female. When the victim played with the dolls and acted out the story of sexual abuse, identification of the perpetrator could easily be made by the child and was a useful initial indicator of abuse. She also began a School for Parents in connection with this "kit." In a group setting, for ten weeks the parents were helped to better understand the dynamics of family relationships and to develop skills in coping and communication.

Kennedy insists that "this is ministry." She remembers going into a church on a Maundy Thursday and praying that the victims of rape would some day savor victory. One line of scripture kept dancing through her head. "Religion pure and undefiled before God is this: to visit orphans and widows in their affliction" (James 1:27). Why were not rape victims also in that lineup, she wondered? Kennedy found that the churches could manage domestic violence but not rape because it opened up the questions, "Who is the rapist? A man I know? A priest?" She wondered if the churches would ever learn not to cast stones but to "cast out sin" and acknowledge the broken relationships that existed in the church community. She wondered if the church could ever come to terms with the need for justice and due process and its own need for healing. One of her most treasured possessions is a South African sculpture of a large black pregnant woman, sitting on the birthing stool, obviously straining to birth a child as she bears down hard and long. "This is the image for those in public ministry," she said in conversation with the author of this essay, "bringing new life to birth through pain, struggle and persistence."

VIOLENCE AGAINST WOMEN—THE FIREARMS ACT, 1995

Mark Lepin, who was responsible for the Montreal massacre in December 1989, had been able to acquire legally a semiautomatic military weapon with a large-capacity magazine capable of firing thirty rounds of ammunition without reloading. After committing suicide he was identified only after the police conducted a store-by-store search in Montreal to find who had recently sold the rifle, because at that time firearms were registered only at the point of sale. Shortly after the massacre,

Wendy Cukier, along with the families of victims and the engineering students in Montreal, initiated Bill C-68, calling for changes in gun-control legislation. It was crafted to register rifles and shotguns in the home that were frequently used to threaten or kill female spouses. On average, one in three women killed by their husbands are shot; 80 percent of them with legally owned guns. In a registration application, it was mandatory to list all former and current spouses, after which the Firearms Centre was notified that the applicant had registered a gun. Complaints by spouses who feared violence were screened, and a prohibition order against using the registered gun then could be issued. There was immediate support from the religious communities, both Christian and Jewish. As early as July 17, 1991, Bonnie Greene, a staff member of the United Church of Canada, had written Cukier that her church had long held the right of Canadians to security from violence and that right needed to take priority over the right of some individuals to bear arms. Support came from the police and a wide network of community organizations. There was fierce opposition from pro-gun groups. In 1994–1995 the Minister of Health unveiled a comprehensive package of gun-control proposals that included, among other things, licensing and registration of all firearms.

Although the pro-gun lobby sent Cukier bricks, manure, and men's underwear, postage-collect, the bill became law in December 1995. A few applied a feminist theological critique to public policy and brought a gender perspective to the bill. "If there were more women in the Senate this bill would have passed long ago," said Senator Janis Johnson. In response to constitutional challenges to the law, the Supreme Court of Canada upheld the Firearms Act (June 15, 2000). The purpose of the law was to register hand guns so that ownership could be traced in the event of spousal murder. But hunters, ranchers, and others practiced civil disobedience by refusing to register their guns, since they considered the law an intrusion on their right to own a gun. Scandalous costs for administration of the program escalated, and the government had to resist immense pressure to rescind the legislation.

Abolition of the Death Penalty, 1988

Until 1961 the penalty for all murders in Canada was death by hanging. After lengthy and emotional public debates over a fifteen-year period, Parliament passed legislation on a free vote abolishing capital punishment from the Canadian Criminal Code on July 14, 1976. Replacing it was a mandatory life sentence without possibility of parole for twenty-five years for all first-degree murders. For a time, Canada retained the death penalty for a number of military offenses, including treason and mutiny. But on December 10, 1998, new legislation removed all references to capital punishment from the Canadian National Defence Act. All the mainline churches opposed the death penalty, and religious leaders as well as ordinary members of congregations, both male and female, actively supported its abolition. They also resisted sporadic attempts to reinstate capital punishment, the latest being the 1987 attempt. Under the terms of the Canada/U.S. extradition treaty, Canada may choose to refuse an extradition request without assurances that prosecutors of the United States will not seek or impose the death penalty.

Non-Smokers Health Act, 1988

A private member's bill, introduced by Anglican Lynn McDonald, Member of Parliament, resulted in a ban on smoking in all federal government workplaces. The ban was valid for 10 percent of the labor force, including, for example, Air Canada, the Royal Canadian Mounted Police, the Armed Forces, banks, and Via Rail. It took six years of extraordinary effort to protect the health of nonsmokers, but Canada was the first country in the world to set such a standard. McDonald had listened to those whose health was being affected by secondhand smoke. Provinces and municipalities did not automatically follow the lead, and a number set aside "smoking areas" that persist to this day. The act turned public opinion around, and currently, one would be hard-pressed to find smoking allowed on buses, in hospitals, in schools, or in any public place.

Public Policy Issues across National Boundaries

The series of UN World Conferences for women, and especially the one in Beijing at which a significant delegation of women of faith was present, has highlighted the necessity of women linking in global solidarity for public policy changes. The World Council of Churches' programs on violence against women (Ecumenical Decade for Churches in Solidarity with Women), on human rights, and on corporate responsibility are cases in point.

Human Rights

Carmen Gloria Quintana was a Chilean student who was attacked by Chilean soldiers as she and her companion, Rodrigo Rojas, walked toward a student demonstration in her country in July 1986 during the dictatorial Pinochet regime. They were doused with gasoline and set alight by soldiers. Rodrigo subsequently died; Quintana survived despite burns to 62 percent of her body and fled with her family to Montreal, courtesy of the Canadian embassy, where members of the Inter-Church Committee on Human Rights in Latin America (ICCHRLA) began to care for her.

The committee was founded in 1977 with Roman Catholic Frances Arbour as its first cocoordinator working with a staff of five women and Bill Fairbairn, who succeeded Frances as coordinator. Believing that the stance of communities of faith should always be with the victims, Fairbairn suggested that the committee take Quintana to Geneva so she could tell her story firsthand to the United Nations Human Rights Commission (UNHRC).

Although the Canadian Council of Churches made plane tickets available, it took much more than that to get Quintana's story told. She would be allowed to speak only if she were sponsored by a nongovernment organization (NGO) with status at the United Nations Commission. Finally, the World Student Christian Federation, an accredited organization affiliated with the World Council of Churches, requested time on the agenda and appointed Quintana as their spokesperson on violations of human rights in Chile. "When she told her story to the delegates," wrote Father Tim Ryan, executive director of the committee who later documented the trip, "a dozen ambassadors rushed forward to embrace her. The Chilean delegation had asked for the right to respond, but thought better of it when they saw the reaction of the other delegates. The United States withdrew a resolution it had been circulating that had offered praise to the Chilean government for its progress toward democracy. Instead, a resolution condemning human rights abuses in Chile was adopted" (Greene, 134).

This was the first time women of faith and others had invested so much time and energy into public policy on this scale. Today there is an annual "human rights forum" in Ottawa between government delegates to the UN Commission, Canada's foreign minister, NGOs, and members of the churches' human rights coalition. Over the years this initiative has fostered mechanisms of accountability for public servants and parliamentarians responsible for implementing Canada's human rights obligations to which Canada agreed when it signed UN covenants. This is particularly relevant to Canada's foreign policy and the need to observe international human rights standards. In 2002, two female senators, Andreychuk and Wilson, founded the Canadian Senate's Standing Committee on Human Rights, charged with examining the machinery of government dealing with Canada's international and national human rights obligations. Probably Carmen Gloria Quintana never knew that her courageous testimony prompted new public policy.

Corporate Responsibility

One of the most remarkable stories about women, religion, and Canadian public policy is the story of the Task Force on Corporate Responsibility (TFCR). In the 1970s, Canadian churches began speaking up as minority shareholders of banks and corporations, following the lead of some churches in the United States. The purpose was to address decisions made in Canadian boardrooms about investments propping up oppressive regimes. Because "God so loved the world" it became mandatory for religious communities and people of faith to engage with the decision makers of their world. The Task Force critiqued a theology that divided the private from the public worlds, that confined religion to "churchly" or individualistic matters, or that addressed only gender-specific issues. In 1973 the publication of *Investment in Oppression*, authored by Renate Pratt, co-financed by a few Canadian churches, and published by the National YWCA, targeted South Africa as the emerging central theme for corporate responsibility. In two years' time, the TFCR was born, with Pratt as the first director, followed by Moira Hutchison and Bill Davis. Their method was to study existing public policy of churches, governments, and corporations on investments, then leverage some changes in accord with ethical principles.

International support and research on loans to South Africa came through the World Council of Churches' (WCC) Program to Combat Racism. Strong opposition came from the Canadian press as well as from within the institutional church with the establishment in 1977 of the Confederation of Church and Business People. Pratt responded by inviting key partners from South Africa (like Desmond Tutu, before he became famous) to come to Canada to advise the Task Force on strategy.

In 1985, collaboration and support came from a meeting in Harare sponsored by the World Council of Churches. That same year the Canadian government announced a "no new bank loans to South Africa policy," but without legislative backing.

Pratt fought losing battles for years against Ford Motor Company of Canada and Alcan Aluminum Limited for selling vans and materials to the South African military. Finally in 1986 she received word that Alcan was about to sell its South African interest. "Only the courage of the South African workers and the determination of the members of the Task Force brought to an end this Canadian complicity with the South African defence industry," she wrote (Greene, 117).

Renate Pratt's story as chief organizer of the Task Force over fifteen years constitutes one of the most sustained social actions for a change in public policy undertaken by the Canadian ecumenical community. Listening to partners who were victims of the oppression; collaborating with churches that held the same faith commitment in the public arena; basing its work on detailed knowledge acquired from church partners who were themselves deeply involved in the struggle; using international levers when possible; engaging in public education and advocacy; and ensuring that they carried the institutional churches with them—all contributed to their success.

Over the years the agenda of TFCR expanded to include the issues of Third World debt, accountability of financial institutions such as the International Monetary Fund, investment of pension funds in portfolios supporting oppressive regimes, Canadian bank loans to countries with gross violations of human rights, ethical performance of international financial institutions, corporate governance, shareholder action and secret ballots at annual meetings of corporations, environment and the economy, codes of conduct, and issues such as the management of nuclear waste disposal and forestry practices in Canada. Government policy concerning corporate responsibility of Canadian companies established overseas is now high on the government's agenda.

Setting the Agenda for Public Policy Changes

Local initiatives of Canadian women have helped set the agenda for changes in public policy. A peace initiative with national implications emerged through Dr. Jerilynn Prior, a Quaker. She consented to be the test case for 531 Canadians who had diverted roughly 10 percent of their income tax, which they considered war related, into a trust account known as Conscience Canada. They felt that any contribution to a war effort was a violation of their constitutional rights to freedom of conscience and religion. Prior herself felt that conscience was the essential link between faith and practice. "I have always felt that non-violent direct action by a humble but truth-filled person was stronger than any weapon" (Prior, 12).

Objecting to the use of part of one's income tax dollar grew out of strong resistance to compulsory military service rooted among the historic peace churches such as the Quakers, Mennonites, Hutterites, and Dukhobors. They had always opposed contributing manpower to any war effort and, to a lesser extent, opposed contributing money. But in the twentieth century the waging of war had changed. Now the stockpiling of weapons, not the mobilization of armies, posed the greatest threat to human life. For many, the priority had shifted from a concern about military service to one about military spending and their complicity in it. Prior did not say that she and others should not pay taxes. What she asked for was a means to enable her tax money to be applied to alternate service such as had been done in an earlier time for Quakers in lieu of military training

She pursued her case of conscientious objection to military taxation through the Canadian court system and twice appealed to the Supreme Court of Canada. Her case as a test case for the Canadian Charter of Rights was not allowed a hearing. In 1991 she appealed to the UN Human Rights Committee in Geneva, but in the end, she did not win. Whether or not Quakers and others will continue to withhold tax monies as a public witness to their faith is an unanswered question. Additional local peace initiatives are documented in *One Million for Peace* (2000).

Another example of "setting the agenda" was a program "Town Talk" mounted in 1967 in Thunder Bay, Ontario, by a dozen volunteers from the religious communities and directed by Lois Wilson. A community of 100,000 people was invited to focus in a coordinated way on issues affecting their community's future, and people of every stripe were invited to join in the conversation. Seventy-five percent of the population did—using existing community structures, public media, expert resource persons, school essays, university convocations, Pee Wee Hockey Leagues, regular board meetings of voluntary organizations, union meetings, church services, and every other local structure that enabled the whole community to set its own public policy agenda. It invited a coordinated month-long "blitz" by all community groups to what might now be characterized as an "online forum" where questions affecting the future of the city (especially their ethical dimensions) could be addressed. Wilson wrote,

The role of Christians in such an experiment is not difficult to find. The believing community must always be a source of permanent unrest and disturbance in society, allowing nothing to silence or dissolve it. Our experience of human community must continually be subjected to radical critique and reconstruction, for it is only in this way that we can make incarnate the hope of true community that God has promised us. (*Audenshaw Papers,* June 16, 1969)

Methodologies of Faith Communities for Changing Public Policy

The methods women use to effect change in public policy need scrutiny. Women continue to issue resolutions to government officials, write letters to their parliamentary representative, engage in public manifestations and marches, and submit well-researched briefs to government. They also need to ask how effective these strategies are. What alternate strategies need to be put in place? Is a feminist theological critique used?

Some of the history of women, Christian religion, and public policy in Canada, between the 1970s and early 1990s, is the history of small well-defined groups in English-speaking Canada who shared a commitment to change public policy at its source. There were over a dozen modest, ecumenical, made-in-Canada coalitions with specialized mandates, shoestring budgets, and small

staff, created by Catholics and Protestants in the early 1970s in which women were prominent. These coalitions were created to help the churches accomplish the research, analysis, and coordination that they needed to act effectively on any number of issues such as apartheid, world hunger, development, human rights, refugees, poverty, peace, and environment. They set out to keep alive in the church and the world the biblical vision of the healing of the nations.

These coalitions did not emerge out of mass movements but out of small, increasingly counterculture groupings within the Christian churches who worked in social partnerships with secular societal groups. They never exaggerated their power or authority to influence government or corporate policies. Their actions demonstrated their Christian convictions about the gospel bias for the poor, the oppressed, the widow, the orphan, and the marginalized without ever presuming that Canada is or ought to be a Christian country. They shared a compassionate vision of the future and exhibited fearless and strong leadership. Their stories are documented in *Canadian Churches and Foreign Policy* (1990), *In Good Faith* (1997), and *Coalitions for Justice* (1994). Currently, they are coordinated centrally through Kairos in Toronto.

Significant Milestones

There have been gains for women in public policy, and women of faith communities have been involved in either leadership or supportive roles in all these.

What Remains to Be Done?

The Canadian Women's March of 2000 identified thirteen public agenda items that needed attention (Women's Inter-Church Council of Canada, 30). The march (fully supported by the religious communities through the Women's Inter-Church Council) identified two prerequisites to those changes: a reform of the way Canadians elect parliamentarians and the need for education of women about the nature of the economic and political systems they seek to change. Currently in Canada, 20 percent of elected Members of Parliament and 33 percent of the appointed Senate are women.

Although the UN Development Index for 1995 ranked Canada first for quality of life, when women's equality was considered, Canada dropped to ninth. In 1981 Canada ratified the UN Convention to End Discrimination against Women (CEDAW) and the Optional Protocol in 2002, but no legislation has been passed for the express purpose of implementing it. The repeal of the Canada Assistance Plan (CAP) and cuts in social assistance and social services have had a

1918	The right to vote
1929	Women are persons; the right to sit in the Senate
1955	Married women could work for the federal government
1969	Birth-control information could be legally disseminated
1973	First women's shelters opened
1976	Abolition of the death penalty
1982	Abortion taken out of the Criminal Code
1985	Indian Act amended to give all Indian women full status
1992	Rape Shield Law, putting onus on defendant in sexual assault cases

particularly harsh impact on women, in particular single mothers, who are the majority of the poor, the majority of adults receiving social assistance, and the majority among the users of social programs. . . . [T]he unavailability of affordable and appropriate housing . . . create obstacles for women escaping domestic violence. . . . [T]here is inadequate legal protection of women's rights such as the absence of laws requiring employers to pay remuneration for work of equal value. . . . [R]estricted civil legal aid . . . conditions affecting immigrant, aboriginal and refugee women, women in prison and women with disabilities must be addressed." (McPhedran, 45)

Questions remain. Where, when, and how will women of faith equip themselves with tools for engagement with tough policy issues such as the implementation of the Kyoto protocol? Where can women find community that demonstrates a symbiotic relationship with the earth and all its creatures? Can women restore the focus of faith to the healing of divisions in human and nonhuman community? Where, in religious terms, can women be part of such resurrection, of such hope? And how can this be embodied in public policy?

SOURCES: Nellie McClung is a Canadian icon, and two primary sources are her *In Times Like These* (1972) and *Clearing in the West: My Own Story* (1935). Her linkage of faith with public policy is documented in Carol L. Hancock, *No Small Legacy: Canada's Nellie McClung* (1986). Janet Silman's *Enough Is Enough: Aboriginal Women Speak Out* (1987) has authentic, memorable quotes from aboriginal women themselves. Ellen Anderson's *Judging Bertha Wilson—Law as Large as Life* (2001)

details Wilson's legal opinion on abortion, as well as on a host of other controversial issues affecting women in Canadian society. After a national tragedy in Montreal in the 1989 shotgun murder of fourteen female engineering students, Doris Jean Dyke's *Crucified Woman* (1991) was published and tells the story of a sculpture raised to commemorate the women. For Canadian women's involvement worldwide on the issue of violence, refer to World Council of Churches, *Together with Energy—Towards the End of the Ecumenical Decade of Churches in Solidarity with Women, and Beyond* (1998). Violence against Chilean women, especially Carmen Gloria Quintana, is documented in Bonnie Greene, ed., *Canadian Churches and Foreign Policy* (1990). For information on the Canadian interchurch coalitions that are in the forefront of most social justice work of Canadian churches, read Renate Pratt, *In Good Faith* (1997); Chris Lind and Joe Mihevic, eds., *Coalitions for Justice* (1994); and Robert Matthews, ed., *Human Rights and Canadian Foreign Policy* (1988). Clarification on Canada's stance on its human rights obligations can be had from the Senate of Ottowa, *Promises to Keep: Implementing Canada's Human Rights Obligations* (2001). One woman's test case against paying taxes for her country's involvement in war is documented in Jerilynn Prior, *I Feel the Winds of God Today* (1992). An entire community's attempt to identify the ethical issues affecting their future is offered by Lois Wilson's *Town Talk Manual* (1969). Popular movements of women to create the climate for public policy change are written in Women's Inter-Church Council of Canada, *Report to Women across Canada from the Canadian Women's March Committee* (2001); Shirley Farlinger, *One Million for Peace* (2002); and Marilou McPhedran, *The First CEDAW Impact Study, Final Report* (2000). This short essay on women of faith and public policy had focused on only a very few Protestant and Roman Catholic women in English-speaking Canada.

THE PUBLIC LEADERSHIP OF WOMEN OF FAITH: ENTREPRENEURS, SOCIAL ALCHEMISTS, AND BEARERS OF RELIGION IN THE WORLD
Katharine R. Henderson

SOME WOULD SAY that putting together the words *public, leadership, women,* and *faith* is an oxymoron, that those words simply do not belong together. At the beginning of the new millennium, Americans remain ambivalent about the historic role of women in public life and uncertain about the role that religion should play in the public arena. During the course of the past decades, as American society has become more pluralistic and secular, and the potency of traditional religion has waned, the prevalent response in the public arena by progressive religion has been silence. Rather than risking the appearance of speaking from a narrow, sectarian platform or being associated with the Religious Right, many public servants, scholars, and religious professionals have avoided the topic altogether. The result is that there has been a moratorium on public discourse about issues of ultimate significance, even though an adequate response to the complexities of social issues begs for reflection and debate that draw upon the insights of religious traditions.

A recent research study conducted by the Center for the Study of Theological Education at Auburn Theological Seminary, *Missing Connections: Public Perceptions of Theological Education and Religious Leadership,* corroborates this trend toward quiescence and invisibility. Based on interviews of 250 persons—leaders in business and community affairs, local government, education, and media—in four cities across the country, the study concludes that religious leaders and institutions, across the theological spectrum, are largely invisible in the public realm. They are not seen as assets in their communities or as shapers of our common life but as inwardly focused, preoccupied with taking care of their own. Alarmingly, when those interviewed were asked whom they would invite to the table to launch a major public initiative in their community, in education and health care, for example, invariably religious professionals were not mentioned. The occasional exception was a Reform rabbi or African American pastor. Many respondents remembered with some nostalgia a time when clergy and religious people were involved in progressive transformative social causes—for example, during the civil rights movement—but felt that such transformative faith-based activism seemed largely a thing of the past. They had no clear image of what such leadership might look like in the current context.

A Phenomenon: The Caretakers of Our Common Life

Against this backdrop of invisibility and "missing connections," a phenomenon became evident that seemed to counter the trend: current women leaders who were in fact exercising progressive public leadership. Many seemed to be faith motivated. Their leadership echoed that of women reformers of the nineteenth century like Frances Willard and Elizabeth Cady Stanton or the Freedom Fighters of the 1960s. Yet the context in which these modern women offered leadership was distinctly different. While the nineteenth-century reformers worked within a predominantly Christian culture, the modern context is more secular, less influenced by organized religion, and religiously diverse.

This essay is based on a study of women leaders who seemed to defy the trend of quiescence and invisibility described in the *Missing Connections* study. The interviews were conducted from 1998 to 2000 with twenty women leaders whose faith traditions were Christian, Jewish, Muslim, Hindu, and broadly "spiritual." The purpose of the study was to see what role there might be for progressive religious leaders in the public arena to raise questions of value and meaning, lead debate, and help shape society by looking at a sample of those who were active in this area. The interviews were focused on such questions as: How do the women describe their work and the organizations many have founded? How do they understand themselves as leaders and as religious leaders? Do they use religious language/God-talk? If so, when? If not, why not? What formative factors in upbringing, education, and life experience shaped them for their current work? How do they understand the connection between their deepest religious convictions or values and their public commitments?

A definition of terms may be helpful. For the purposes of this essay *progressive* connotes commitment to the values of justice, equity, and pluralism, as well as to the transformation of society to achieve those ends. *Religious leader* is defined broadly to include both lay and ordained leaders. As will be shown, religion was a complex matter for these women. For example, although they may have come from a particular tradition, they were acutely aware and respectful of current multifaith realities. The respondents were also "entrepreneurs." This term, often limited to a business or corporate context, is used in a new way here. The leaders were socioethical entrepreneurs who were attempting to rebalance the climate of public debate through organizations based on feminine values of inclusivity, nurturing, compassion, and collaboration. Some had founded their own nonprofit organizations or international movements; others brought entrepreneurial energies to existing organizations.

These women's work addressed complex social issues like homelessness, hunger, poverty, the HIV/AIDS (human immunodeficiency virus/acquired immunodeficiency syndrome) crisis, crime, domestic violence, misogyny. The interviewees ranged in age from their thirties to their sixties. Many were veterans in the work, having been loyal to a particular cluster of social issues for twenty years. These were not mere dabblers in good works; many had in fact become public policy experts and savvy agents of systemic change. Of the eight who were ordained, only three practiced ministry in anything like a traditional parish setting. Yet all twenty women were offering religious leadership, broadly construed. They did so by dedicating themselves to the transformation of suffering and injustice, by being social alchemists. Because it is beyond the scope of this essay to describe all twenty stories in full, voices and organizations have been chosen that best represent the phenomena described. The first section will focus on an organization called the Rainbow Center as a representative example of the concept of a "holding environment." Then several distinctive patterns of leadership will be explored: the one-on-one/systemic dance, the dynamic of religion as a motivating factor, and the overarching theme of seamlessness, a feminist ethic of connection.

Social Alchemists Creating Holding Environments

Human suffering and need, as expressed through complex social issues like homelessness, hunger, poverty, crime, domestic violence, or misogyny, can evoke many human responses—avoidance, denial, despair, indifference, paralysis, or compassionate action. The women in this study acted creatively to alleviate suffering and injustice. They did so not out of a sense of duty or adherence to abstract principles but rather because they felt powerfully drawn to the work and, on balance, deeply sustained by their ongoing practice of it. They took the dross of society, the base metal—the people others would discard, the social issues that seemed intractable—and were able to see what others did not see—the human potential or gold within, the possibilities for transformation. They acted on the belief that those in need were children of God who were capable of thriving, or that these social needs and issues could be constructively addressed. Like the alchemists of old, they found that the work mysteriously carried them toward a greater sense of wholeness within themselves.

Whether within organizations of their own design or in established institutions, these progressive leaders sought to change individual lives, communities, points of view, and social systems. They did this by creating "holding environments"—spaces temporarily protected from the wider milieu in which new insights and behaviors could be modeled and incubated, or where systemic issues could be effectively addressed (Winnicott, 253). Both therapeutic and visionary, these were spaces that offered nurture, challenge, and lived experience of alternatives to mainstream social systems. Wherever mainstream solutions were not adequately addressing human needs and social issues, these holding environments attempted to fill the gap. In their particular area of concern, they tried to model "a better way." These women were not duplicating services; they were inventing the ones that society seemed unable or unwilling to provide. In many cases, this entailed upholding more fully the values that mainstream culture may have given lip service to but nevertheless did not fulfill.

For instance, the culture may *say* that "childhood is a terrible thing to waste" or that "every child deserves food, shelter, and a certain quality of care." Yet in New York City twenty years ago, Gretchen Buchenholz, then a day-care center director, came upon a holding pen in a municipal building in which hungry children were clawing at a metal door, begging for food. In response, she founded a nonprofit organization that she still directs, something as basic as ABC—the Association to Benefit Children—which provided all the things needed by children for optimal growth: food, shelter, safety, love, and education. ABC was simultaneously a critique and an alternative, embodying values that mainstream society had seemingly forgotten. Its very existence marked it as a vessel of resistance or opposition, functioning like a conscience within the body of mainstream society.

Like ABC, other organizations provided combinations of direct services, public policy advocacy, and education. Many served disenfranchised persons: people in broken environments, people with a history of homelessness, battered women and children, AIDS sufferers, women prisoners and ex-convicts, people on death row, people with disabilities, and those in health crises. As Laura Jervis, director of West Side Federation for Senior Housing in New York City, put it: "[W]e are there for these people in a way that only the best of families are" (Henderson, 259).

The Story of the Rainbow Center

The Rainbow Center is an example of an organization in which "the best of families" was given public form and a broader social reach. Like several organizations in this study, the Center was founded in response to the urgent needs of one particular person. The Rev. Henna Hahn, a Methodist minister, had been alerted to the plight of a Korean woman falsely accused of killing one of her children. Moved to help free the woman, Henna was drawn into the larger story of Asian women, often Korean and Vietnamese war brides, who had been victims of domestic abuse. In response, Henna founded the Rainbow Center, a nonprofit shelter shaped specifically for the needs of such women. In naming the organization, Henna deliberately invoked the sense of promise offered by the rainbow in the biblical story of Noah. She says of the women she serves, "[T]hey need the rainbow; no more punishment."

The Rainbow Center provides a full range of direct services: shelter, food, links with social services, English and citizenship classes, and legal assistance. The Center is also involved in advocacy campaigns on human rights issues related to immigration. But the Rainbow Center offers something beyond these important tangible services—something grounded in feminine sensibilities that proves essential to the women's healing. Henna modeled the Center around the Korean cultural concept of *Chin-Jeong Jip*, a phrase translated as "mother's house." In Korean tradition when a woman marries, she goes to her husband's home and family, where her role is to be of service. However, in prescribed circumstances, such as a family wedding or when she has morning sickness, she may return to her own mother's house for care. Having a living mother who welcomes her home gives a woman status in her husband's home.

The Rainbow Center is *Chin-Jeong Jip*, the mother's house to which these abused Korean women could "return" to find safety, shelter, renewal, and healing. This was a nurturing space for Henna as well, for she had lost her mother during the Korean war and for many years had felt herself to be a "poor, motherless child." This intertwining of the founder's personal story with the shape of her organization is a pattern reflected in other respondents' stories as well.

Although Rainbow Center is a secular nonprofit, there is a theological framework that shapes it. Henna said of its founding: "When I opened the Rainbow Center, everybody told me, 'You are the mother of the Center.' No! So, who is mother? God! God is mother. God is the mother and we are all sisters. So, I'm like a big sister" (Henderson, 264). Henna felt that the sisters' healing had a religious dimension, but she made it clear that by providing for this through worship, for example, she was not seeking religious conversions. Speaking of one sister, she said, "My intention is not to make her Christian; my only intention is to make her the whole human being God created originally" (265). Sharing Korean food around a table, though it echoed the Christian communion motif, was a healing ritual designed primarily for cultural and community support.

As the sisters gained a stronger sense of themselves, they were encouraged to become agents of healing by reaching out to other Asian women in distress. Calling themselves "The Dandelion Mission" because of the beauty and hardiness of dandelions in the face of adversity, these women began to find their way back into society.

In short, the Rainbow Center seeks to address needs and sponsor growth on many levels. Like other organizations founded by the women in the study, it responded to the basic human strivings of hearth, heart, grail, and soul. These women leaders were engaged in transforming dysfunctional public spaces and intransigent social issues with an innovative mix of feminine sensibilities and theological lenses. By reconstituting within public organizations the dynamics of the nurturing mother-child dyad and "the best families," they are helping to bring feminine wisdom to bear on challenging public issues. Further, they are doing so in a way that draws upon the transforming power of the best of religious image, story, and ritual. Their organizations may have an important therapeutic effect at the systemic level, "mothering" an ailing society toward greater wholeness and a more complete justice.

The One-on-One/Systemic Dance

One of the patterns of leadership that emerged in over sixty of the respondents is a dynamic called the one-on-one/systemic dance. As believers in transformation, many of these progressive women leaders worked on change at the micro- and macrolevels simultaneously, offering direct services to individual clients in a one-on-one mode while also trying to effect systemic change through policy initiatives, advocacy, and education. Moving back and forth between the micro and macro became a dance these leaders relied upon for insight, perspective, and a sense of agency. The fact that, unprompted, over half of the twenty women spoke of working in this way suggests that it may be a characteristically feminine way of exercising moral public leadership. The key dynamic appears to be the referencing back and forth between personal stories and systemic issues.

Sister Helen Prejean is a good example of operationalizing change in this way. Author of *Dead Man Walking* (1993), the book that became an award-winning film about her relationship with a man on death row, she also founded a national movement to abolish the death penalty in the United States. She is representative of several respondents for the study who founded national and international movements to work for societal change. Her work in this area began when she accompanied one convicted man to his death, serving as his spiritual adviser. Now over a decade later, she continues her spiritual work with individuals on death row as well as with families of murder victims. Yet she also moves in wider circles. Through public speaking, writing, and national and international networking, she attempts to transform the prevailing consciousness on criminal justice issues.

She felt that her one-on-one experiences with prisoners were essential to her work at the systemic level:

Well, it's like visiting with Dobie and people on death row, to me, is the anchor, that's the baseline. Being with murder victims' families and praying with them and being with people on death row, that's the personal. And every person's a universe. My speaking comes out of those experiences, and I think that's why the speaking thing has been so good. You know, solidarity with poor people and being in their company, being in their presence and being involved in the people who are suffering, is an essential spiritual dynamic. Without that, you begin to drift away. You put on gloves and you begin to do these commentaries on your experiences, once removed, twice removed, three

Sister Helen Prejean is a good example of operationalizing change. Author of *Dead Man Walking*, the book that became an award-winning film about her relationship with a man on death row, she also founded a national movement to abolish the death penalty in the United States. She is representative of women who have founded national and international movements to work for societal change. *Courtesy of Auburn Seminary.*

times removed. So, the experience of people suffering is just essential. (Henderson, 281)

While the "essential spiritual dynamic" of staying close to individual experience kept the work grounded, it was not sufficient.

> If I get in a personal ministry to people on Death Row and then I didn't engage in any of the efforts to change the system of it, abolish the death penalty, I would be doing something charitable—accompanying people to their deaths and comforting them—but I wouldn't be doing anything to resist the evil, and I couldn't do that. (282)

Like her, over half of the women interviewed repeatedly mentioned the one-on-one/systemic dance described by Sister Helen Prejean as an essential spiritual dynamic. They viewed the two modes not as separate from each other but as part of a continuum, where systemic issues became incarnate in the particular, and each individual seemed "a universe" or hologram of the systemic. Also, it seemed that particular people in need formed a community of accountability to directly resist the greater evils that they became aware of through the individuals who suffered.

Finally, working at both the macro- and microlevels seemed to create a sense of balance, agency, and enhanced satisfaction. Those women who did not have regular one-on-one encounters felt themselves to be more prone to fatigue and burnout. In fact, many of the women whose organizations had grown over time remembered with nostalgia when they knew the name of every client. Alisa Del Tufo, director of the Family Violence Project of the Urban Justice Center, a large program that effects public policy change around violence against women, said that in the next phase of her professional life she might consider going back to working one-on-one with the victims of domestic violence. The power experienced in the one-on-one encounters seemed to renew these women's sense of personal efficacy and, by extension, to lead to a trust in grassroots process as a means toward wider societal transformation. Believing that each individual is in fact a universe means knowing that changing individuals one at a time does indeed change the world.

Offering Critique and Hope as Radical Traditionalists

Religion proved to be a complicated dynamic for these public leaders. Those with a seminary education and ordination were no exception; in fact, they may have been even more intensely aware of the ambivalence they felt about religion, especially religious institutions. Many cited powerful positive religious messages at the root of their traditions that helped spawn and sustain their public work. At the same time, they acknowledged that a strong impetus for initiating their work was anger that religious and governmental institutions were inadequately addressing pressing social needs. Thus many expressed a kind of love/hate relationship with the church or synagogue, realizing that these institutions held potential and power that was imperfectly realized. Like the respondents for the *Missing Connections* study, these women leaders saw the church and other organized religious bodies as being absorbed with maintenance, survival, or the status quo rather than exercising their deeper vocation on behalf of justice and social change. Gretchen Buchenholz, who resisted the designation of a religious leader because of her anger toward religious institutions and leaders, offered a poignant and devastating critique:

There's a wonderful line in Archibald MacLeish's play, *J.B.*—do you know it? Someone says, "The candles in all the cathedrals are out, all the lights are out, there's nothing but darkness. Blow on the coals of my heart." You know, you think of that [*makes a blowing sound*] just that little bit of fire left in a coal and you blow on it, and I feel like I'm doing that. And, I don't mean to say that about the churches and synagogues and mosques, but that is how I feel. My own heart and their heart and the heart of it takes so much blowing, whereas here [in her agencies working with children], the light is clear, in every face. (Henderson, 342)

Despite their disappointment with religion-as-usual, most were not willing to give up on religious institu-

tions. These leaders were not iconoclasts but radical traditionalists, offering direction and hope for the role religious leaders and organizations might play in upholding substantial virtues. Lee Hancock, currently dean of Auburn Theological Seminary, expressed it this way:

I'm a bridge person; I'm a person that believes that the church exists to serve the world, but I'm not a person who's willing to give up the church and just go out into the world and be an activist on health care issues because I think whatever religion is about, and that is to say about healing and wisdom and education and activism and justice. . . . I mean, I think all of those more substantial virtues and goals, for the lack of a better word, aren't really valued or raised up any other place. . . . So, that's to say, I will continue to be rooted in religion, although the church is far too small and self-involved, as far as I'm concerned. (Henderson, 344)

For some of the women, like Gretchen Buchenholz, disappointment with religious institutions and leaders carried over into a reluctance to identify themselves as a religious leader. Some did not want to be associated with the conservative agendas that their denominations were pursuing, for example, regarding the ordination of homosexuals and lesbians. All were aware of the complexity of taking a religious stance in contexts that were secular or pluralistic and where they would need to deal with assumptions and suspicions about their politics and agendas.

Despite these caveats about being a religious leader, almost all the respondents perceived their work as being faith based or spiritually rooted. Still, they were finding it necessary to redefine the terms and reframe images, carving out a new role for themselves as public religious leaders in a pluralistic society. Consciously avoiding sectarian dogma or doctrine, they sought images and understandings that honored and more adequately held the diversity and complexity of the modern multifaith context. Often, they found valuable orientation in basic tenets shared by many traditions—tenets that emphasize love and compassion and offer images of justice and community. Many felt there was a "natural link" between these tenets and public activism. As Constance Baugh, founder of Citizens Advocates for Justice and Justice Works, organizations serving women in the criminal justice systemic, put it:

I think of "Love one another as I have loved you," which is the mandate from Jesus and which is to do good—not simply avoid evil, but resist evil. It's just part of the religious mandate. The wounded person on the other side of the road. You know, to me, the impetus for compassion, comes out of religion. And that is finding God in the face of the other, especially those who are hurting the most. There's a long tradition that says that's where God's found. To me that's the natural link. (Henderson, 351)

This mandate for public action is present in other faith traditions as well. Riffat Hassan, a Muslim, expressed the undeniable connection between worship and social activism.

You know, it's almost like a form of worship for me, because striving for justice, for the rights of the disadvantaged, is fundamental to our traditions. All of our traditions talk about the care of the widow, the orphan, the disadvantaged person, the person discriminated against. For me personally, this is religious work, although there are people who are joining this effort who are not religious, who are doing it because they are human rights activists. And that's fine, but I think that many people who are religious are also beginning to see the importance . . . beginning to see that there is much more to being religious than simply leading a good life within your own sphere of activities, but that you have to go out into the world and do something to change it. (Henderson, 352)

Today, Riffat Hassan is leader of an international movement, organized largely through the Internet, to stop honor killings of women in Muslim countries. For decades, both as a personal quest and in support of her teaching, she has studied gender references in the Koran. Convinced that the Koran itself supports the equality of men and women, she is dedicated to making better religious arguments against those who hold to a patriarchal interpretive tradition that leads to the oppression of women.

In addition to referring to basic religious tenets, the leaders spoke of specific images of God that had taken root in their psyches. They felt these sustained their own faith and provided a rationale for shaping a particular kind of nurturing organization. Often these images involved fresh interpretations that supported particularly feminine forms of public activism. For instance, Mychal Springer, a rabbi in the Conservative movement, formerly director of Pastoral Care at Beth Israel Hospital in New York, said:

One of the images that has really guided me is, you know, in the Ten Commandments, God says that God is an *el kanah*, which is often translated as "a jealous God," but actually means "an im-

passioned God, God of all feelings." So, I understand myself as being created in God's image, as being a woman of passion, an impassioned person. And, it's through those passions that I connect with people and have access to what's sacred in them. (Henderson, 352)

Understanding herself as a person whose passions were encompassed by God seemed to give her freedom to use all her feelings to help patients, staff, and chaplaincy students be meaningfully engaged with the inevitable pain and suffering that comes with human life.

Sister Helen Prejean also held an image of God which linked passion and action:
What motivates me, what moves me, is my faith, at the core of action. I mean, my prayer is a whole way of alignment, of aligning myself with the energy of God. And to me the big image is energy, movement, a stream, and so you put your little boat in the stream. And, when you're in the stream, and God's love is flowing through you, you can be bold. You just say, for example, the death penalty is wrong, people are suffering, there's great injustice. I will take it on; I will work for its abolition. And, if you don't know your own desires, then you're easily prey to anybody coming along and saying, "you ought to do this" and you haven't even touched base with your own soul. . . . At the heart of it is to get in touch with your own deepest desires. (Henderson, 353)

Henna Hahn, executive director of the Rainbow Center, found special meaning reenvisioning God's mightiness as an extraordinary ability to bend low.

What is the almightiness of God? Now, I can realize God's almightiness is lowness, not highness. Before this ministry, I thought that God is big and strong and powerful and highness, authority, something like that. I cannot bend much lower, but God can bend because God is almighty. That's what I want to try to do myself, not to be strong and powerful—the leader—I'm not that person. I want to be more powerless, bending. (Henderson, 354)

Combined with her image of God as a compassionate mother, this view shaped the nonhierarchical structure of her organization, where God was the mother of the house, and she and the clients were sisters.

Some respondents still found great value in powerful images they had been given in childhood. Ginny Thornburgh, executive director of the Religion Project of the National Organization on Disability, remembered going down to the docks in New York City with her father to watch cargo from ships being unloaded in huge, bulging nets. She said that her faith and even her image of God had always been like "this net holding me, and holding me even if I was straining, even if the load was heavy or awkward" (Henderson, 355). In general, the interviews were replete with compassionate, nurturing images of God that emphasized relationship, connection, and impassioned resistance to injustice.

There was also evidence that these women found meaning in the practices and images of faith traditions other than their own. Lee Hancock, a Presbyterian minister who has spent twenty years involved in ministries of healing and health care, is sustained by feminist understandings of God as well as exposure to other spiritual practices like Vodou. Mychal Springer, a Jewish rabbi of the Conservative movement, organized and regularly sang in a gospel choir with fundamentalist Christian staff members as a way of building community in the hospital where she worked as director of Pastoral Care. Helen Hunt, founder of the New York Women's Foundation and the Sister Fund, and a Christian feminist, is influenced by Native American traditions and thought. Laura Jervis, executive director of West Side Federation for Senior Housing in New York City and a Christian minister, regularly attends Catholic Mass as well as Sabbath services at a synagogue with whom she has close ties. Jan Orr-Harter, formerly pastor of West-Park Presbyterian Church in New York City, feels her interpretation of faith is more Jewish than Christian because she is profoundly affected by *tikkun olam*, the Jewish conviction about each person's responsibility to take part in the "repair of the world."

Many realized the importance of diversities of all kinds—religious, race, class, and ethnicity—in forming their organizations. The boards of directors and decision-making bodies often reflected these concerns. When Constance Baugh, executive director of Justice Works, became the founding pastor of the Church of Gethsemane in Brooklyn, New York, ex-convicts were among the ordained elders of the church. The board of directors of Justice Works, the church's partner non-profit organization, is intentionally multifaith. The ways in which these modern religious leaders value and take into consideration religious pluralism is decidedly different from either more conservative contemporary religious leaders or women reformers of the last century, who worked in an acknowledged Christian milieu.

Practitioners of a Revitalized *Religio*

These modern women, then, were leaders who took the core religious mandates of their own and other traditions deeply to heart—to clothe the naked, feed the hungry, visit the imprisoned. In this, they were radical traditionalists, for within their pluralistic contexts, their response was to draw upon radical (root) religious teachings. In the truest sense, they practiced *religio* (to bind up), for they constantly forged connections between their beliefs and actions in the world, between themselves and others, between people and the services they needed, between disparate groups, between God and human beings.

Within a pluralistic and secular society, they were bearers of a revitalized religion, standing for alternative values, offering resistance, exhibiting uncommon integrity, being inclusive of all God's children, and believing in transformation. As systemic strategists, they were wise as serpents; as compassionate caretakers, gentle as doves. Combining a robust sense of agency, an entrepreneurial spirit, and a preference for collaborative work, they accomplished in the public realm what others thought could not be done. In so doing they have given us a new measure of what constitutes effective faith-based leadership.

Seamlessness: A Feminist Ethic of Connection

One of the overarching themes that surfaced in the study is the seamless quality of the women's lives and leadership. The characteristic of seamlessness differs sharply from the compartmentalization that is a common feature of the modern milieu. Compartmentalization is the degree to which people separate out the different parts of their lives—public/private, religious/professional—tolerating behaviors in one sphere that they would not condone in another. The women leaders in this study differed markedly from this trend. All wanted to draw the disparate parts of their lives—personal, professional, and spiritual—into a whole. Laura Jervis put it this way:

My life on the West Side is really life in community, and there is a sense of seamlessness to my life . . . which I sometimes resent a little bit because sometimes you feel you can't escape . . . but most of the time I think it's the right way to live. But it is a kind of public life . . . it's the community board, it's the churches and several of the synagogues; it is the West Side Federation for Senior Housing community . . . and it's all really one. (Henderson, 413)

One way or another, all the women in this study held the conviction that acting in the world in harmony with their deepest convictions was the way life should be lived. But the content of those convictions was critical to them. Hitler was acting in harmony with his convictions, yet, unprompted, a quarter of the women cited the Holocaust as a vivid reminder of a society's capacity for evil. For them, it was natural to enact their religious beliefs in the form of their public commitments, but only because their beliefs were mandates to honor diversity and complexity, strive for inclusivity, and alleviate suffering in all its forms. In short, though many of these women were of deep faith, they thought critically about faith traditions and religious institutions. They remained wary of religion's potential to alienate and divide or to maintain an unjust status quo. Yet they acted upon the belief that religion's true vocation is to sponsor an ongoing transformation toward "society at its best." "Best," they said when asked, meant "an interdependently connected, complex, differentiated whole." As two of them put it:

Well, a phrase that first comes to mind is unity within diversity—that society does not become homogenized, far from it. People are free to be extremely individual, but in addition to becoming individual, they learn the art of interconnectivity and connection. And we would be a society of dialogue, mutual respect, of willingness to trust an enlarged perspective.

. . .

And, I think society works best when people live in community, and that community is life-giving and nurturing and values each person for who they are, and loves them all equally. . . . I think it's very hard work, it doesn't happen by itself. . . . [W]e need each other. . . . [N]o one can do it by themselves and have a whole life. And that wholeness does not depend on achievement or ability, but on acceptance. It needs to go beyond tolerance to real acceptance and understanding. (Henderson, 422)

For the women in this study, being faithful to such visions primarily took the form of making connections between realms that are often kept separate—too separate, they felt, for our common good. They sought to remove or make permeable the boundaries between marginal and mainstream, public and private, suffering and success, sacred and secular, and even in some cases church and state. Justice, they said, was the larger good to which these classic dichotomies must give way. As Sister Helen Prejean said:

I see the connection between religion and a public domain as being through the common good and this respect for human life across the board, all of us. Religion is the thing that's going to get you into who's hurting in the family, who's left out in the family. We've got to go to those people, we've

got to be there for them—and that gets you involved in justice. (Henderson, 419)

This emphasis on sponsoring a just wholeness—within their organizations and communities, as well as within themselves and their clients—is what I have termed an "ethic of seamlessness." Cultivating relationship and dialogue is essential to it. In fact it is central to how these women practice their faith. Constance Baugh elaborated on this point:

God is a God of relation. . . . I think that the most authentic spirit is God among us and between us. That's why I believe so strongly in bridging, in making bridges and community. Once upon a time I believed that you work with the poor and the hell with the rest. Now I believe that you must work not with the rich about the poor, not with the poor alone, but with the communities . . . and bring those communities into dialogue with one another. (Henderson, 417)

As this quote reveals, these women leaders had their own dichotomies and compartmentalizing tendencies to overcome. For instance, when Laura Jervis first founded West Side Federation for Senior Housing (WSFSH) twenty years ago, she was reticent about letting people know she was a Presbyterian minister because she did not want to alienate secularists or people from other faith traditions who sat on her board or were her clients. Over the years, as her faith and leadership matured, she found that it served a larger good if she blended her minister's sensibilities with those of a chief executive officer. Now she views West Side Federation for Senior Housing "more and more as my parish." Her work includes not only running 1,200 units of housing in Manhattan but performing traditional religious rituals like marrying and burying or "setting the tone" for ethical decision making about end-of-life matters.

For Jervis, living a seamless life also meant that formative experiences from her past were closely linked with her present public work. She had grown up in a community of mentally disabled adults where her father was a doctor. She and her siblings were often taken care of by these adults, and for many years she did not distinguish that they were different from her in any significant way. What she did learn was what respectful, interdependent, well-functioning community felt like, and it was this image that stood behind her creation of WSFSH with its emphasis on housing, the best of family caring, and appropriate work and learning opportunities that offered clients a sense of agency.

Whether their pasts were graced like Jervis's or challenged with adversities like Hahn's, the important thing to these women was that these vivid memories were gathered up and held within their current work. Just as they wanted the world to be whole, they wanted their lives to be of a piece, to have integrity. For many, integrity was a quality they admired in role models and mentors and sought to incarnate themselves.

In fact, it appeared that practicing an ethic of seamlessness had carried most of these women to a particularly cherished point of personal, professional, and spiritual integration. Though not all were comfortable using religious language to speak of it, most indicated that they had found their calling. When Jervis said the seamless life was "the right way to live," she quickly added:

> I should say, this is the way life is to be lived for me. I don't have a feeling of disrespect for people who don't live this way. But this is really the only way I can live. It's not really a choice for me, in the ultimate sense. I'm one of the lucky ones. It's my vocation. I found it. I love it. It's the work that is meaningful and that I can do. Is it a sacrifice? No, not at all. (Henderson, 417)

She and the other women leaders continually confirmed that no matter how difficult and heartbreaking it could be to stay close to suffering and the world's brokenness, the practice of gathering all of life into a seamless whole was finally joyous, meaningful work. Because it tapped their entire beings and made them a vital part of society, living the seamless life seemed to them a privilege. As Joan Campbell, former general secretary of the National Council of Churches, put it:

> I think this is a job that I probably spent my life training for. Every day that I do this job I need everything that I know and all the experience that I've had. The greatest satisfaction is feeling part of my age, part of history, part of the society in which I live. I'm a participator. I'm not a watcher, I'm a player. Not everyone has that privilege. (Henderson, 403)

Effective Religious Language

But with the privilege of participating comes the responsibility of using faith-based language effectively to offer challenge, vision, and inspiration. In a multifaith and increasingly secular context, this is a complex task. These women leaders were acutely aware of the hazards of using explicit religious language, or even language with a spiritual/ethical valence, for fear of alienating those with whom they wished to communicate. Yet much was at stake if they failed to do so. As Helen Hunt put it:

To shy away from religious language gives all the religious language to the political right to shape and define very ancient terminology from one political perspective. Those of us in the progressive social movement have a real onus on us right now to use those terms and shape them in a way that matches our value system. We've got to get in there and complete the picture. We've got to craft fuller and more relevant definitions. (Henderson, 378)

These women who had founded organizations to meet unaddressed needs had discovered that they were called to be entrepreneurs with language as well. The metaphor of bilingualism describes how people of faith must be fluent in a public language for negotiation "at the wall" (i.e., in the marketplace or secular public arena) as well as a communal language for processing "behind the gate," within a given community of faith (Little, 178).

I would suggest that the women leaders for this study are also experimenting with a third realm. They are beginning to give voice to a potentially universal language of meaning appropriate for a complex milieu that is at once multicultural, religiously plural, and conventionally secular. By whatever means they can devise, they are trying to appeal to a deeper faith shared by many. This characteristic distinguishes these women leaders from those of the last century, like Frances Willard or Elizabeth Cady Stanton, who were exercising leadership in a predominantly Christian context.

Laura Jervis, for instance, who had initially found it strategic to refrain from using explicitly religious language in her multifaith organization, now finds herself increasingly using those words that have a broader resonance. Explaining the transition, she says:

> [It has to do with] my own sense of comfort with the language and my own understanding and goal for an integrated life. . . . So I don't censor the language anymore, but I use it in terms of *transformation, redemption, incarnation,* those sorts of words, which I believe are not just the product of Christianity, but a really more universal kind of language. Certainly, my initial understanding is Christian, but I think they're greater, they're beyond Christianity. (Henderson, 375)

These leaders, then, are not just bilingual, but multilingual, because they are experimenting with language and images that convey the deeper, broader convictions shared by all faith traditions and people concerned for the common good.

It was clear that language usage was very much a work in progress. Some women were more comfortable as nascent multilinguists than others, but none felt she had fully mastered the art. They agreed that it required them to be especially sensitive to the assumptions and capacities of various audiences and contexts. First and foremost they were pragmatists, trying to find language that would be most effective. As Linda Tarry-Chard, founder of Project People Foundation, a program focused on women's economic empowerment in South Africa, put it:

> Do I use faith language in my conversations? Carefully. I assess the person. I'm not ashamed to be known as a woman of faith. But I also am smart, and I usually have an agenda, and the point is, how are you going to get across what you want to say, and that depends on the person. (Henderson, 369)

They also agreed that the most effective "language of meaning" for the modern milieu had the power to "straddle" different realms. Lee Hancock noted:

> One of the reasons why I like activism in the public square is that you can talk about issues of justice more. *Justice* is a word that straddles. *Suffering*—that's a word that straddles. And *healing* is increasingly a word that straddles, which is good, so there will be some way to think about those words with a certain bifocality. (Henderson, 378)

Connie Baugh said she much preferred to use the language of her faith because she felt more connected when she did so. Yet she was particularly articulate about the necessity of framing things for different contexts. She used "straddling" terms in secular contexts as well as within her congregation:

> In a religious community, you could talk about every human being is a child of God. In the secular community, you had to talk about every human being having value, and no one being expendable. And, although most people in the secular world recognized that the passion with which I spoke was religiously motivated, I never spoke with terms that weren't acceptable. So *empowerment, advocacy, legislative change, progressive left, the common good*—all those were terms I could use.
>
> To me, faith is the commitment to participate. That's what it is—it's the commitment to participate in life, with God, in the ongoing creation and liberation of the world. When I talk with progressives about that, I try to talk about the struggle for justice being the commitment not to leave anyone behind. . . . [To express my feelings] about

each person being in the image of God, I talk about our common bonding—that the more we recognize our connectedness, the better our public life would be. [I translate in the other direction too.] During Communion, I say, "communion means 'common union.' We are first united under humanity, and then we're united in our faith." (Henderson, 386)

Other strategies that the women found effective were using the moral language of right and wrong; appealing to broader principles like responsibility, fundamental human rights, or the common good; focusing on questions of worth and meaning; and offering images of transformation, redemption, forgiveness, and renewal. Some respondents relied on the power of storytelling to convey a religious or moral perspective in a nonsectarian manner. Gretchen Buchenholz, for instance, said she often used stories of the children her agency serves. One was of a ten-year-old boy, living in a single-room occupancy hotel, who said that every day he had to put his head down on his desk in school because it hurt to be hungry. Then he declared: "When I'm president, no ten-year-old will go to school hungry." Such images have the power to translate across cultures, religions, and boundaries of all kinds.

Though many of the women had stories to tell of how using religious language continues to be problematic, they felt that the effort to use it well was worth it on two counts. First, there is an underlying hunger for it in these times. Mychal Springer, a rabbi in a Jewish hospital, said that it was partly her interactions with the fundamentalist Christian hospital staff that had convinced her of the need to be more forthright with her own religious language:

> Every month I get 200 copies of the *Daily Word*. I put them out and they go like hotcakes. People are thirsty. So what they've taught me is that if I can speak a more solidly religious language, that the hidden religiosity in many people will be nourished. . . . Because I'm a rabbi, and it's a Jewish hospital, you know, you've got to be respectful that people may or may not be believers. . . . But if I risk putting in the more mysterious aspects, I always receive the feedback that people are really with me. (Henderson, 375)

When speaking in other settings, she has found that people in our "sunshine culture" really respond when she makes space for

> pain and suffering and all the things that really matter but no one talks about because it's this polite society that insists we're all shining. The min-

ute you say, "hey, I live in the realm of the shadow and that's o.k.," people come crawling out and say, "touch me, be with me." It just makes everything different. (Henderson, 360)

These women leaders know that right images and words, appropriately offered, indeed have the power to make everything different on a much broader stage. As Joan Campbell put it:

I'm just convinced that the church can make a huge difference. I mean, I've seen it, I've experienced it, I've seen when the church decided that there shouldn't be a war in Vietnam, that the civil rights laws needed to be passed, that apartheid was evil and had to end. . . . I mean, you can just go through the litany of times in which the church came together and said, "this we are going to stop." Now, an interfaith coalition is beginning to be extremely effective in the environmental movement. They have come together to say this is a moral issue. (Henderson, 344)

To remain silent, invisible, and at the periphery is itself an act. Gretchen Buchenholz, who ironically does not consider herself a religious leader, spoke with eloquence and passion on this point.

When people allow atrocities to occur and they are silent, just as during the Holocaust, the silence is an act. It means you go along with it. Silence is complicity. And I think the community of faith has been silent. And so I think that's left room for other viewpoints that fly in the face of what we all know, including those people, is the right thing to do. . . . And their job is to open their mouths and do something, speak. I mean, say, "this is a sin." Everyone should be saying that. There has to be a groundswell of protest. . . . This is everyone's responsibility. . . . The public argument has squeezed out the voices of faith. They have to get their place back, the moral dimension has to be put back in, or what are we? We're not a civilized people. (Henderson, 230)

These women leaders followed Gretchen's mandate above through actions and through experimentation with particular kinds of religious or moral language and usage to awaken a world more attuned to issues of justice. Through sensitive experimentation with language and images that carried religious or ethical insight, these women were all actively working on putting a progressive moral dimension back into the public sphere.

Directions for the Future

The public progressive women leaders of faith represent both hope and challenge to religious institutions and the wider culture. Taking the core tenets of their religious traditions to heart has put their lives close to those in the most acute need. In a society where campaign rhetoric adheres strictly to the code language of "working families," these leaders by contrast acknowledge the "invisible" poor still with us who may never be neatly categorized by the pundits. While religious institutions are turned inward, taking care of their own, these women have moved out into public spheres as social entrepreneurs inviting themselves to the decision-making "table," or convening conversations at tables of their own. In a culture where the creation of wealth is the great national pastime, these women leaders embody the satisfaction and meaning that can come from spending one's intelligence, energies, and imagination on behalf of others. At a moment in time when the separation of church and state is variously interpreted, these leaders do not hesitate to let progressive religious values shape their actions in the public arena, while being simultaneously attuned to the emerging multifaith reality. In all these ways the women leaders are countercultural; their very lives pose the question: Who will be the caretakers of our common life?

At the same time, these women leaders are shapers of postmodern culture, living at the leading edge of it, insisting that it open itself to the unique perspectives that come from those who are excluded, including those whose vision of the whole is shaped by a passionate, personal faith. In a "sunny culture" that often seems to be dominated by the voices of the most successful, they urge a readiness to listen to a diversity of voices. This commitment goes deeper than rhetoric. The governing structures of their organizations and the people involved in them represent this diversity. Typically, their faith practices and beliefs are influenced by a broad exposure beyond their own identifying religious traditions. And their experimentation with language embodies a desire to communicate in a robust way life's deeper meanings under a God whose care knows no boundaries.

For churches and other religious institutions, this leadership paradigm posed the challenge of how to live faithfully—to move beyond parochial concerns in the public sphere—to become "players" again on matters of ultimate significance in how we live our lives together. These women leaders reminded us that you do not wait to be invited to areas of decision making: You invite yourself. How do you raise up leaders, and when you have such leaders in your midst, how do you nurture them instead of pushing them to the periphery?

For seminaries, theological institutions, and other

arenas of formation, professional and otherwise, these leaders posed the question of how to educate and nurture such leadership. Although the study found that there are many other equally important factors of formation such as early family/parental messages, exposures to mentors, and historical influences, educational experiences are not particularly important unless there is a definite experiential component. A major focus on the experiential dimension, especially when there is direct involvement with persons of diverse backgrounds and life situations, will be essential if professional schools are to play a role in nurturing a new generation of progressive public leaders.

For those in the liberal religious mainstream, these women leaders challenge the quietude and assumption that the only style of public religious leadership that can have an impact in this culture is the style that has been shaped by televangelists or persons from the Religious Right. For those who assume that the waning influence of mainline religious institutions means that progressive religion must remain in the private realm, these women represent powerful examples to the contrary—and a source of genuine hope for the future.

SOURCES: All of the quotes from the respondents interviewed for this study are taken from interviews conducted by Katharine Henderson during 1998–2000. They can be found in her unpublished dissertation, titled "The Public Leadership of Women of Faith" (2000). The use of the term *holding environment* in this essay blends and extends the work of child psychiatrist Donald Winnicott, *The Maturational Process* (1965), and leadership theorist Ronald Heifetz, Leadership without Easy Answers (1994). Winnicott uses the term to describe the relationship between therapist and client, mirroring the mother-child bond. Heifetz applies the insights of the therapeutic dyad to social groups confronted with complex social issues. For both, "holding" involves creating a hospitable environment where there is both challenge and support. The use of religious language has been explored by Christan educator Sara Little in "Experiments with Truth: Education for Leadership," in *Caring for the Commonweal: Education for Religious and Public Life*, ed. Parker J. Palmer, Barbara G. Wheeler, and James W. Fowler (1990). She suggests that religious people must be bilingual, using a public language for secular circumstances and a communal language within the community of faith. Also see Center for the Study of Theological Education, *Missing Connections: Public Perceptions of Theological Education and Religious Leadership* (2004), and Katherine Henderson, "The Public Leadership of Women of Faith" (Teachers College Columbia University, 2000).

Part XII

❦

Women-Centered Theology

WOMANIST THEOLOGY
Emilie M. Townes

WOMANIST THEOLOGY IS a form of reflection that places the religious and moral perspectives of black women at the center of its method. Issues of class, gender (including sex, sexism, sexuality, and sexual exploitation), and race are seen as *theological* problems. Womanist theology takes old (traditional) religious language and symbols and gives them new (more diverse and complex) meaning. This form of theological reflection cannot be termed *womanist* simply because the subject is black women's religious experiences. The key for womanist theology is the use of an interstructured analysis employing class, gender, and race. This kind of analysis is both descriptive (an analysis and sociohistorical perspective of black life and black religious worldviews) and prescriptive (offering suggestions for the eradication of oppression in the lives of African Americans and by extension the rest of humanity and creation).

A key feature of womanist theology is its evolving character. From its formal beginning in 1985 with the publication of Katie Geneva Cannon's article "The Emergence of Black Feminist Consciousness" (*Katie's Canon*, 47–56), it has developed in the following ways: an orientation to black women's survival in an oppressive social order that is classist, racist, and sexist; a framework for interpreting and critiquing the role of the Black Church; an interrogation of and critique of the Black Churches' appropriation of scripture in oppressive ways; a model for black women's organizational strength; a critique of the black social stratification; advocacy for justice-based spirituality; the inclusion of ecological concerns; a concern for health care; a consideration of black sexuality; and the issue of work. Within this evolving character, womanist theology often melds theological and social scientific analysis with cultural studies, literary studies, and political economy and often addresses public policy issues affecting African American communities. To date, most womanist theology has been Protestant Christian, although Roman Catholic voices have been strong from its inception. This is changing as the influence of Santería, Yoruba, Vodou, and other African, Afro-Carribean, and Afro-Brazilian religions begin to make an impact on womanist theological discourse.

As an intellectual movement, womanist theology addresses the shortcomings of black theology and feminist theology. Black theology early demonstrated an unwillingness to deal with sexism and classism. Feminist theology often reduced the variety of women's experiences to those of white middle-class women, which, womanist theologians point out, does not address racism or class-

ism. Womanist theology also addresses conscious and unconscious homophobia in theological discourse.

Foundations

Far from being a strictly theoretical enterprise, womanist theology evolved from the life and witness of black women. The roots of womanist theology span the 256-year period of chattel slavery in the West and the survival and support commitments of black women during this period including the new racism of the 1980s, 1990s, and early 2000s. Womanist theology is not like the character Topsy in Harriet Beecher Stowe's *Uncle Tom's Cabin*—who, when asked by her white mistress Miss Ophelia, "Who are your parents?" responded with, "I just growed"—but is born in the womb of black women's experiences and has been cultivated throughout history.

Womanist theology employs materials by and about black foremothers as resources for contemporary reflection that provide a conscious background for God-talk. Rather than assume the universal claims of traditional theologies, womanist theology acknowledges that all theological reflection is limited by human cultural, social, and historical contexts. These limits are not negative but merely representative of our humanity. Rather than restrict, these limits can serve as a challenge to explore the particular ways in which any group having similar characteristics (e.g., age, denomination, ethnicity, sexuality) experiences divine activity in life. These differing perspectives need not ultimately separate but can enrich us as we acknowledge the limits of what we know in listening to the voices of others. Ultimately, womanist theology points us to the largeness of God and the various ways in which human beings often seek to confine God.

Many African American women theologians gravitated to the use of Alice Walker's term *womanist* as both a challenge to and a confessional statement for their own work. Walker first used the term in a 1978 short story, "Advancing Luna and Ida B. Wells," eventually published in the 1980 anthology *Take Back the Night: Women and Pornography*, edited by Laura Lederer, and in Walker's 1982 collection of short stories *You Can't Keep a Good Woman Down*. In this story, a black couple struggles with the husband's addiction to pornography. As the wife becomes more radicalized by the black feminist movement, she gives her husband articles to read that challenge his justifications for his love of pornography. She also signals her unwillingness to ignore his sexual addiction. Walker offers one simple illustrative line that she does not elaborate, "A womanist is a feminist, only more common" (*You Can't Keep a Good Woman Down*, 41).

Later, Walker reviews Jean Humez's publication of Rebecca Cox Jackson's (1795–1871) writings in *Gifts of*

Many African American women theologians gravitated to the use of Alice Walker's term "womanist" as both a challenge to and a confessional statement for their own work. Walker first used the term in a 1978 short story, "Advancing Luna and Ida B. Wells," which was eventually published in the 1980 anthology *Take Back the Night: Women and Pornography*, edited by Laura Lederer, and in Walker's 1982 collection of short stories, *You Can't Keep a Good Woman Down.* Copyright © Bettmann/CORBIS.

Power: The Writings of Rebecca Jackson. Jackson was a black female Shaker eldress who founded a Shaker community with Rebecca Perot, also a black Shaker. Walker appreciates Humez's editing but challenges Humez's assessment that Jackson and Perot were a lesbian couple by contemporary standards, although Jackson described herself as dead to sexuality or "lust." Walker challenges a white scholar's decision to assign a label that the black woman has not chosen for herself and argues that *if* Jackson and Perot were erotically bound, they would have had their own word for it. Walker then uses the word *womanist* to define the diverse ways in which black women have bonded sexually and nonsexually. She also questions the wisdom, or the appropriateness, of tying black women's sexuality and culture to the Isle of Lesbos, given that black women's bonding is more ancient

that Greek culture and is not separatist but seeks liberation for the entire community in an overarching oppressive social order.

Walker has a four-part definition of *womanist* in her book *In Search of Our Mothers' Gardens: Womanist Prose* (1983), which contains the organic and concrete elements of tradition, community, spirituality and the self, and critique of white feminist thought. Her definitions provide a fertile ground for religious reflection and practical application.

Womanist 1. From womanish. (Opp. of "girlish," i.e., frivolous, irresponsible, not serious) A black feminist or feminist of color. From the black folk expression of mothers to female children, "you acting womanish," i.e., like a woman. Usually referring to outrageous, audacious, courageous or willful behavior. Wanting to know more and in greater depth than is considered "good" for one. Interested in grown up doings. Acting grown up. Being grown up. Interchangeable with another black folk expression: "You trying to be grown." Responsible. In charge. Serious.

2. Also: A woman who loves other women, sexually and/or nonsexually. Appreciates and prefers women's culture, women's emotional flexibility (values tears as natural counterbalance of laughter) and women's strength. Sometimes loves individual men, sexually and/or nonsexually. Committed to survival and wholeness of entire people, male and female. Not a separatist, except periodically, for health. Traditionally universalist, as in: "Mama, why are we brown, pink, and yellow, and our cousins are white, beige, and black?" Ans.: "Well, you know the colored race is just like a flower garden, with every color flower represented." Traditionally capable, as in: "Mama, I'm walking to Canada and I'm taking you and a bunch of other slaves with me." Reply: "It wouldn't be the first time."

3. Loves music. Loves dance. Loves the moon. *Loves* the Spirit. Loves love and food and roundness. Loves struggle. *Loves* the Folk. Loves herself. *Regardless.*

4. Womanist is to feminist as purple to lavender. (*In Search of Our Mothers' Gardens: Womanist Prose*, xi–xii)

Because Walker's definitions are rich in historical allusions to black history and black women's commitment to freedom, womanist theology often begins with an exploration of some key figures and movements found in black women's experiences. For instance, an allusion to Harriet Tubman (1820–1913), who led more than 300 slaves out of slavery on the Underground Railroad, is found in the second part of Walker's definition. Tubman's life is a model of Christian faith, commitment to freedom, wisdom, and humanity during a period when whites questioned black people's full humanity. Other exemplars and guides for womanist theology of the late eighteenth and nineteenth centuries include Jarena Lee (1783–?), Sojourner Truth (1797–1883), Maria Stewart (1803–1879), Julia Foote (1823–1900), and Amanda Berry Smith (1837–1915). Using the genre of spiritual autobiography, Lee challenges women's exclusion from the ordained ministry in the early African Methodist Episcopal Church. Foote discusses the significance of sanctification (process of achieving salvation), and as the first woman ordained in the African Methodist Episcopal Zion Church, she offers insights into Methodist women's concepts of salvation and righteousness. Maria

Stewart wrote prayers, meditations, and political essays in which she challenged black northerners to be active abolitionists and take their political, economic, and educational situations into their own hands in obedience to God's justice.

Another resource for womanist theology is found in the countless numbers of black women's clubs formed in the 1800s. The women of the club movement yoked their religious and social perspectives to address the racial, economic, and sexual exploitations of their day. Most club members were active church workers or at least attended church regularly. Groups and programs evolved out of the needs of the immediate communities, with common themes being education and care for the aged. Sharecroppers, housewives, students, salesgirls, dressmakers, artists, teachers, and school principals came together to form women's clubs for community uplift and support. This activism included establishing night schools, working with prisoners, caring for aged former slaves, creating insurance-type funds for illness benefits, educating black girls and women, and agitating for the rights of black womanhood. Members included women such as Josephine St. Pierre Ruffin (1842–1924, the organizer of the first convention for the women's clubs that led to the creation of the National Association of Colored Women [NACW]). A few of the prominent women who were members and leaders of the NACW were Gertrude Mossell (1855–1948, journalist and author), Anna Julia Cooper (1858–1964, who was an educator, a "race woman," and a feminist), Ida B. Wells-Barnett (1862–1931, journalist and leader of the antilynching crusade), and Mary Church Terrell (1863–1954, lecturer and "race woman" who served as a president of the NACW). As exemplars, these women were not perfect. Club women often displayed a measure of elitism concerning class, color, and geographic origin. This same elitism is found in some great black male figures of their day such as W.E.B. DuBois and Frederick Douglass. Nevertheless, these shortcomings are instructive warnings for contemporary womanist theology, and their strengths are solid foundations for womanist work.

Novels and short stories also serve as resources for womanist theology. Stretching from Frances Ellen Watkins Harper's *Iola LeRoy: or Shadows Uplifted* (1892) to contemporary novelists such as Toni Morrison (*Beloved* [1987] and *Paradise* [1998]), Alice Walker (*The Color Purple* [1982]), Tina McElroy Ansa (*Baby of the Family* [1989]), Gloria Naylor (*Mama Day* [1988]), and Edwidge Danticat (*Krik? Krak!* [1995]), black women novelists have written about the religious meaning found in everyday black lives. For example, the works of Zora Neale Hurston (*Their Eyes Were Watching God* [1937], *Mules and Men* [1935], *Moses Man of the Mountain* [1939], and *The Sanctified Church: The Folklore Writings of Zora Neale Hurston* [1981]) blend literary and cultural anthropological insights from black lives and in the particular worlds of black women. Authors such as Harriet Jacobs (*Incidents in the Life of a Slave Girl* [1861]), Pauline Hopkins (*Contending Forces* [1900]), Nella Larson (*Quicksand* [1928]), and Marita Bonner (*The Purple Flower* [1928]) explore themes of slavery, colorism, sexism, and racism.

Representative Contemporary Voices

The term *womanist* is confessional. This means it is a term that cannot be imposed but must be claimed. This provides an organic undertaking of constant self-reflection in the context of the "doing" of one's theological reflection. Also, the womanist is not free to name others as womanist if this is not a term they claim for themselves. For example, it is inaccurate to describe black women from the nineteenth century as womanists. Although many, like Ida B. Wells-Barnett and Anna Julia Cooper, employed an interstructured social analysis in their activism, none of these women claimed the term *womanist* for herself. At best, these women embody a nascent womanism that provides a rich framework for womanists of this era to flesh out in their theologies.

Katie Geneva Cannon was the first woman of African descent ordained by the United Presbyterian Church in the U.S.A. (PCUSA) in 1974 and the first black woman to earn a doctorate from Union Theological Seminary in New York (1983). Cannon was the first to use the term *womanist* in the religious disciplines in her 1985 article "The Emergence of Black Feminist Consciousness." Cannon's article, included in the 1991 anthology edited by Letty M. Russell, *Feminist Interpretations of the Bible*, and later in Cannon's 1996 collection of essays, *Katie's Canon: Womanism and the Soul of the Black Community*, shifts from the use of black feminist consciousness to black womanist consciousness as an interpretative principle that addresses oppression, identifies texts that empower—specifically biblical texts—to "dispel the threat of death in order to seize the present life" (*Katie's Canon*, 56).

Delores S. Williams was the first to use the term *womanist theology* in her 1987 *Christianity and Crisis* article "Womanist Theology: Black Women's Voices." Williams, who earned her doctorate from Union Theological Seminary in New York and is a Presbyterian laywoman, uses Walker's definition of *womanism* as a theoretical outline for womanist theology that consists of four elements. The first is a multidialogical intent. This values conversations with people from various religious, political, and social communities. Womanists enter these conversations with the reality of the slow genocide of black people as their primary focus to maintain their integrity and accountability to black communities as they engage in these multiple conversations with many dialogue partners. The second element is a liturgical intent in which black female clergy and scholars develop a theology relevant to the Black Church in its action, thought, and worship. Womanist theology challenges the Black Church to examine the oppressive messages it gives both consciously and unconsciously to black peoples. These messages include ageism, classism, colorism, homophobia, racism, sexism, and others. For Williams, the liturgy itself must be infused with and proclaim justice. The third element is a didactic intent. This considers teaching and how the Black Church deals with the moral life through a concern for justice, quality of life, and survival. Finally, the fourth element is a commitment to reason and female imagery and metaphorical language when constructing theological statements. An example of this is Williams's term "demonarchy," which she sees as a more relevant concept than *patriarchy* when looking at the source of black women's oppression in that it involves both white males' *and* females' complicity in systems of domination and social control. This last element clearly distinguishes womanist theology from other forms of theological thought. Traditionally, theological language has valued reason over image and metaphor. Williams rejects this hierarchy for a more dynamic and accurate articulation of theological ideas.

Cannon's *Black Womanist Ethics* (1988) establishes the overarching framework for womanist liberation ethics. She draws on the work of writer and anthropologist Zora Neale Hurston to argue that black women's literary tradition is the best literary source for understanding black women's social and religious experiences. Cannon uses an interdisciplinary approach that includes ethics, history, literary studies, and political economy in a systematic analysis of class, race, and sex. Her aim is to show that black women's moral agency is different than the white male norm (dominant ethics) due to the existence of the triple oppressions of class, race, and sex. In dominant ethics, the freedom of choice is assumed. Cannon argues that no such assumption can be made for those in situations of oppression. By its very nature and dynamic, oppression limits the options of the oppressed so that a desirable norm in dominant ethics such as frugality is a necessary reality for poor black women. In making this argument, Cannon clearly distinguishes womanist ethics from dominant ethics.

Also in 1988, Hebrew Bible scholar Renita J. Weems, a doctoral graduate of Princeton Theological Seminary and an ordained African Methodist Episcopal Church minister, published *Just A Sister Away: A Womanist Vision of Women's Relationships in the Bible*. Weems looks at several well-known biblical stories that feature women (Hagar and Sarai, Ruth and Naomi, Vashti and Esther, Miriam and her Ethiopian sister-in-law, Jephthah's daughter and the mourning women, Lot's wife and her daughters, Martha and Mary, the women who followed Jesus, and Elizabeth and Mary) to explore black women's relationships with themselves and with each other while moving toward a vision of humanity for all. Weems combines womanist biblical criticism with its passion for reclaiming and reconstructing the stories of biblical women and the black oral tradition, with its gift for dramatic storytelling. Weems's creative reconstructions are not designed to mirror "fact" but to suggest realistic scriptural testimonies to produce womanist midrashes (stories that explain and/or amplify the text). These stories enable Weems to explore contemporary reflections on grief, friendship, loyalty, love, obedience, independence, and jealousy.

Systematic theologian Jacquelyn Grant published *White Women's Christ and Black Women's Jesus: Feminist Christology and Womanist Response* in 1989 where she explores Jesus as a key figure in black Christian theological reflection. Grant, a doctoral graduate of Union Theological Seminary in New York and an ordained minister in the African Methodist Episcopal Church, echoed the common theme among all Christian womanist theologians when she pointed to the tridimensional oppressions of classism, racism, and sexism and the need to use a holistic approach in theological reflection. Grant argues that God and humanity meet through God's direct communication with poor black women through Jesus and through God's revelation in the Bible. She notes that black women must receive and interpret God in their own context. Hence, the significance of Christ is his humanity, not his maleness. For Grant, when theology uses Jesus as a symbol and a sanctioner of male or white or economic supremacy, this imprisons Jesus in an elitist, racist, and sexist symbol system that often results in a notion of servanthood that devalues the humanity of black women and oppressed others. This understanding of servanthood has been used to reinforce obedience and docility in those who are oppressed socioeconomically, thus allowing the privileged to deny the existence of Jesus' real servanthood by changing his poor status into a royal one.

Womanist theology has not emerged without its critics. In 1989, the *Journal for Feminist Studies in Religion* published a round table discussion that was prompted by Cheryl J. Sanders's essay "Christian Ethics and Theology in Womanist Perspective." Sanders, who earned her Th.D. from Harvard Divinity School and is a Church of God pastor, suggests that using Walker's definitions as a foundation for normative discourse in theology and ethics may be a gross conceptual error. Responding to Sanders were Katie Cannon, M. Shawn Copeland, Cheryl Townsend Gilkes, bell hooks, and Emilie M. Townes. This lively exchange explored the issues of defining a womanist perspective in theology and ethics. Also at stake, particularly for each of the respon-

dents, were the dangers of developing too narrow a view of womanist theology so that it ceases to embrace the great diversity of African American life and religious experiences.

A key event of 1989 was the first academic gathering of womanist scholars at the American Academy of Religion (AAR) as the Womanist Approaches to Religion and Society Consultation. This was a one-year project that moved to a Group status in 1990. The Womanist Approaches Group exemplifies the interdisciplinary nature of womanist religious thought. The women (and men) who participate in the Group represent the traditional theological disciplines: theology, ethics, pastoral care, biblical studies, pastoral theology, church history, liturgics, Christian religious education. Sociologists, anthropologists, psychologists, historians, and artists are also discussion partners. The sessions focus on theoretical issues and the practical questions that inform them.

In 1993, four works by Delores Williams, Renita Weems, and Emilie Townes were published. In *Sisters in the Wilderness: The Challenge of Womanist God-Talk*, Williams rejects the exodus model of black theology and turns to wilderness imagery as a better representation of black women's reality. For her, survival and productive quality of life represent the core of womanist theology rather than black theology's focus on liberation. Using Hagar and wilderness concepts gives Williams a biblically based Christian model that deemphasizes male authority and empowers women. In Hagar's story (Genesis 16:1–16; 21:9–21), Williams finds that God acts as a supreme being who offers survival and hope for a productive quality of life for the African slave Hagar and her son Ishmael rather than as a liberating divinity. She broaches the theme of atonement (salvation), which she returns to at the 1993 Reimagining Conference when she was asked, "What is to be our theory of the atonement?" Williams's reply was,

I don't think we need folks hanging on crosses and blood dripping and weird stuff. I think we really need to see the sustaining, the sustenance images, the faith that we are to have. The fish and loaves, the candles we are to light, that our light will so shine before people so that we can remember that this message that Jesus brought, I think, is about life, and it's about the only two commandments that Jesus gave; about love. (Williams speech)

In *Sisters in the Wilderness*, Williams argues that the passion of Jesus represents human defilement and an attack on the divine. Accordingly, she argues that black women should avoid surrogacy and turn to the ministerial vision God gave Jesus when he was alive that includes right relations through words, touch, and the destruction of evil. Prayer, compassion, faith, and love replace manifestations of evil. For Williams, this new model of God's activity and revelation in the world allows her to see the Hagar passage as a resource for social, personal, and religious issues such as motherhood, surrogacy (in both pre– and post–Civil War periods), ethnicity (particularly a focus on skin color), and wilderness (as it parallels Hagar's life in the wild) in contemporary black women's lives.

Christian ethicist Emilie M. Townes published two books in 1993. Townes is a graduate of the University of Chicago Divinity School (D.Mn.) and Northwestern University (Ph.D.). She is also an American Baptist clergywoman. The first book, *Womanist Justice, Womanist Hope*, combined the spirituality and activism of the black women's club movement with the social and moral views of Ida B. Wells-Barnett as a role model for the recovery of black women's tradition because of Wells-Barnett's strong commitments to both the church and justice. Townes names five aspects of a womanist Christian ethic in Wells-Barnett's social and moral perspectives: authority, obedience, suffering, liberation, and reconciliation. Townes sees that there are two possible moral responses to authority: one that thrives on subjugation and domination or one that reflects community, partnership, and justice.

Also published in 1993 was the first of two anthologies of womanist thought edited by Townes that bring together fourteen scholars, clergy, and lay professionals, *A Troubling in My Soul: Womanist Perspectives on Evil and Suffering*. Writers in this anthology use various disciplines (New Testament studies, sociology, theology, Christian ethics, pastoral care, musicology, and sociology) and Christian denominations to address the question of persistent evil and suffering through an integrated analysis of class, gender, and race. The most distinctive feature of this book is that the authors do not construct the question of theodicy (why is there evil in the world) from the traditional theological framework that puts God at the center of the question. Rather, the authors center the question on human activity and our inability to live as full partners with God through more just human relationships. The seventeen contributors to the companion volume *Embracing the Spirit: Womanist Perspectives on Hope, Salvation, and Transformation* (1997) refuse to allow evil and suffering to have the last word about the nature of humanity and the ways in which the divine works in lives. Applying the same ecumenical and interdisciplinary model as the first volume, the authors of this second anthology use literature, gospel music and spirituals, health care, sexuality, and spirituality to explore hope as it is yoked to salvation and transformation.

Kelly Brown Douglas and Marcia Riggs published books in womanist theology in 1994. Theologian Kelly Brown Douglas, a doctoral graduate of Union Theolog-ical Seminary in New York and an Episcopal priest, believes that womanist theology must be accountable to poor and working-class black women. In *The Black Christ*, Douglas expands Grant's earlier work and argues that Christ is black because he does have black skin and black features, given his religious and social location in the biblical world. She also sees that Christ is black because we meet God as sustainer, liberator, and prophet who challenges and engages black communities. Further, womanists must teach in churches and community-based organizations as well as in seminaries and other institutions of higher education. In addition, Douglas notes that womanist theology must engage in conversations beyond the academy if it is to stay in touch and remain accountable to church- and community-based women. In doing so, womanist theology must work with churchwomen to affirm their power, to help empower those who need it, and to encourage the articulation of black women's voices and theological perspectives in the leadership of the Black Church in order to help the church grow and change into a more inclusive and responsive community. Douglas points to a key feature found in the majority of womanist theologians—a commitment to and participation in the church and community by working with women in these groups, both large and small.

Christian ethicist Marcia Y. Riggs earned her doctorate from Vanderbilt University and is from the African Methodist Episcopal Zion tradition. Her first book, *Awake, Arise, and Act: A Womanist Call for Black Liberation*, considers the social stratification in black communities as a moral dilemma. Riggs uses the black women's club movement of the late nineteenth and early twentieth centuries as instructive for developing distinct socioreligious models for a contemporary womanist ethical response to the moral dilemma of black social stratification. She then provides an ethical praxis to address this dilemma by exploring the development of competitive individualism versus intragroup social responsibility in black communities. Tracing the rise of the contemporary black middle class sparked by integration in the 1960s, Riggs argues that integration has not had a universally positive effect on black communities but has also ushered in black class division based on a kind of individualism and competitivism that is destructive rather than creative and unifying. Riggs argues for both a functional separatism (making time and space to sort through one's history and options away from other possible dialogue partners) and a mediating ethic that is not based on certainty or assuming solidarity with all parties who seek more just relationships. Riggs argues for a more realistic assessment of human abilities to stand in solidarity and mutuality with one another and offers a three-part moral vision to achieve this: renunciation, inclusivity, and responsibility. *Renunciation* is the virtue of giving up one's privilege of difference—be it class, gender, or race. *Inclusivity* is both a value and obligation in which we cross the lines of difference to struggle for justice. *Responsibility* is the virtue of linking racial uplift with God's justice.

Several works in womanist theology appeared in 1995, among them were works by Katie Cannon, Diana Hayes, Cheryl Sanders, and Emilie Townes. As a Christian ethicist, Cannon has provided an important ethical model for womanist thought in *Katie's Canon: Womanism and the Soul of the Black Community*. Cannon adapted feminist ethicist Beverly Wildung Harrison's "dance of redemption." This model describes the process of recognizing oppression and forming ethical decisions and moral stances in relation to it. It, like the preceding model, does not have a predetermined entry point and is also nonlinear:

- Conscientization: When reality does not fit into what is normative, "Cognitive Dissonance."

- Emancipatory Historiography: What are the systems/logos which hold the structures of oppression in place?

- Theological Resources: How do the theological disciplines as well as your spiritual community uphold or liberate the structures of oppression?

- Norms Clarification: How are your values clearer? To whom are you accountable? "Where do you come down?"

- Strategic Options: Brainstorming; How can I use my conscientization, what have I learned? What are the possible consequences of the option I consider?

- Annunciation and Celebration: "I can't do this . . . by myself." "Together remember, name and celebrate the presence and power that sustains our struggle."

- Re-reflection/Strategic Action: the process begins again from the insights and knowledge of the previous struggle, but at a deeper level. (*Katie's Canon*, 140)

Cannon has also proposed a womanist model for analysis of narratives or literature. A survey of her thought reveals the following elements of this model and its flexibility—one can enter this model at any point to engage in womanist analytical reflection. Cannon poses questions and gives directions in this highly dialogical enterprise.

- How does this source portray blackness, darkness, economic justice for non–ruling class people?

- What are women doing in this text? Are women infantalized, pedestalized, idealized, or allowed to be free and independent?

- Identify and define the mode of oppression.

- Locate causal dynamics of pervasive cultural racism and manufactured patriarchalism, especially ecclesial clericalization and hierarchalization.

- Explore intellectual breadth, conceptual depth and structural linkage of domination and oppression in their domestic and international manifestations.

- Test passage as to whether or not it aids the victims in their struggle to overcome victimization.

- Critique the presuppositions, intellectual concepts, politics and prejudice of the writer.

- Critically evaluate the primary motives, politics, allegiance of interpreters/reviewers.

- Talk about the revelation of God in this text.

- Identify "spirit helpers," indigenous people who create opportunities of transformation.

- In what ways does this text help African American women clean ourselves of hatred and contempt that surrounds & permeates our identity as women in this society?

- Refuse to trim the contours of your "hermeneutics of suspicion."

- Give particular care not to generate monolithic assumptions.

- Examine the living laboratories that expose the actual historical events and contradictions in which people are engaged as moral agents.

Roman Catholic theologian Diana Hayes earned her doctoral degrees at the Catholic University of Louvain in Leuven, Belgium. Her *Hagar's Daughters: Womanist Ways of Being in the World* features the text of the 1995 Madeleva Lecture in Spirituality sponsored by the Center for Spirituality at Saint Mary's College in Notre Dame, Indiana. Hayes uses the lives and stories of Harriet Tubman, Zora Neale Hurston, and Hagar to call upon black women to avoid defining themselves by societal stereotypes. She challenges African American women to listen to the Spirit within themselves and utilize their creativity, intellects, and talents to find their own voice. Hayes explains that "mothering" African American women are those who maintain nurturing traditions that reveal how their culture evolved; those grandmothers, aunts, mothers, and older sisters form a community of women that sustains the spirit within it.

Ethicist Cheryl Sanders edited *Living the Intersection: Womanism and Afrocentrism in Theology*. Arguably, womanism and Afrocentrism are the two most influential currents in contemporary African American culture. Both heighten black cultural self-awareness while deepening knowledge of cultural historical sources. As womanism probes the religious wisdom of African American women for Christian theology, Afrocentricity excavates an African past to liberate the oppressed from Eurocentric worldviews through a predominantly male lens. The authors in this important interdisciplinary volume investigate the compatibility of womanist theology and Afrocentricity, given the latter's mostly male voice. The authors consider the Afrocentric idea and explore the intricate relationship between Afrocentric and womanist perspectives in their lives and commitments.

In *In a Blaze of Glory: Womanist Spirituality as Social Witness*, Townes asserts that womanist spirituality grows out of individual and communal reflection on African American faith and life. In this book, she argues for a distinction between spiritual practices and spiritual disciplines (e.g., prayer, meditation, fasting) and spirituality. For her, womanist spirituality "is not grounded in the notion that spirituality is a force, a practice separate from whom we are moment by moment. It is the deep kneading of humanity and divinity in one breath, one hope, one vision" (11). Using Toni Morrison's *Beloved*, Alice Walker's *The Color Purple*, and Paule Marshall's *Praisesong for the Widow*, Townes explores issues of environmental racism, gender and sexuality, and identity and colorism (the color caste system). In doing so, she argues that womanist spirituality is both a style of living and a style of witness that seeks to cross the yawning chasm of hatred and prejudice and oppression into a deeper and richer love of God as we experience Jesus in life. Further, as an embodied, personal, and communal spirituality, it is a social witness that speaks to issues of survival, social activism, self-worth, and self-esteem.

Breaking the Fine Rain of Death: African American Health Issues and a Womanist Ethic of Care by Townes appeared in 1998. This is a contextual look at black health and health care through the framework of a biblical lament modeled after the book of Joel and the traditional womanist concern for class, gender, and race. Townes integrates the debate on health and health care from the perspective of social ethics (a focus on structures and systems and how the individual and groups respond and shape them) with an ethic of care (a focus on relationships between individuals and groups) concerned about health and health care, lament, and hope. Based on her understanding that health is more than the absence of disease (it involves our biological, emotional, and spiritual well-being), Townes sees health as a cultural production—that health and illness are social constructs dependent on social networks, biology, and environment and individual choice. Health is embedded in our social realties and is the integration of spiritual, mental, and physical aspects of our lives. This interdisciplinary work draws on Christian social ethics, biblical hermeneutics, philosophical ethics, social history, public health, and sociology.

Karen Baker-Fletcher's *Sisters of Dust, Sisters of Spirit: Womanist Wordings on God and Creation* also appeared in 1998. Baker-Fletcher has a doctorate in theology from Harvard University and is an American Baptist clergywoman. Building on the theme of voice she explored in her first book, *A Singing Something: Womanist Reflections on Anna Julia Cooper* (1994), this is the first book-length examination of ecofeminism in womanist theology. Baker-Fletcher yokes reflection on her own journey with keen insights into environmental racism to develop a constructive religious vision that recovers and renews the strong historic tie of black and Native peoples to the land. Baker-Fletcher's book explores a justice-oriented spirituality of creation that evokes a strong sense of God in nature. Using the concept of "wordings" (writings or talk that comes from the heart, the spirit, the bodily experience of daily life), Baker-Fletcher evokes the lyrical nature of spirituality as she works with both biblical and literary metaphors of dust and spirit to address the embodiment of God, Spirit, Christ, creation, and humans.

An important essay by Linda E. Thomas also appeared in 1998. Thomas earned her Doctor of Philosophy degree from American University in cultural and social anthropology and is also a United Methodist clergywoman. In her 1998 article "Womanist Theology, Epistemology, and a New Anthropological Paradigm" in *Cross Currents*, Thomas notes that the method of womanist theology "validates the past lives of enslaved African women by remembering, affirming, and glorifying their contributions." Thomas argues for the inclusion of ethnography in womanist theology in echoing Douglas's call to place the lives of ordinary black women at the center of womanist work. For Thomas, ethnographic approaches allow womanist theologians to enter the actual communities of poor black women to "discover pieces to create a narrative for the present and the future."

In 1999, Kelly Brown Douglas published *Sexuality and the Black Church: A Womanist Perspective*. This is the first book-length investigation of black sexuality in both the Black Church and the black community. Douglas argues that treating sexuality as taboo has interfered with constructive responses to HIV/AIDS (human immunodeficiency virus/acquired immunodeficiency syndrome), teenage pregnancy, homophobia, and unhealthy male and female relationships and rendered black and womanist theologians largely mute on sexual issues. Douglas has three purposes in this work: (1) to understand why sexuality has been a taboo subject for the Black Church and community; (2) to advance a discourse on black sexuality; and (3) to promote theological discourse and analyses that will nurture healthier attitudes and behaviors toward sexuality within the Black Church and community context. Of particular concern for her are homophobia and heterosexism. She seeks to provoke black men and women to enjoy the fullness of their humanity. She also returns to a theme found in *The Black Christ* in that she wants womanist theology to be "accountable to 'ordinary' Black people as they struggle through life to 'make do and do better' " (*Sexuality and the Black Church*, 8).

Future Trajectories

Other important contributors to the development of womanist theology include theologian Cheryl A. Kirk-Duggan (*Exorcizing Evil: A Womanist Perspective on the Spirituals* [1997]), theologian Joanne M. Terrell (*Power in the Blood?: The Cross in the African-American Experience* [1998]), Christian ethicist Joan M. Martin (*More Than Chains and Toil: A Christian Work Ethic of Enslaved Women* [2000]), and sociologist Cheryl Townsend Gilkes (*If It Wasn't for the Women . . . : Black Women's Experience and Womanist Culture in Church and Community* [2001]). There is no one voice in womanist theology but a symphony that at times may move to a creative cacophony. There is ongoing discussion about how womanist scholars engage the four-part definition of womanist proposed by Alice Walker. Some womanist theologians challenge Walker's inclusion of homosexuality in the second definition of womanist as a desirable norm in the African American community. Others resonate with her theme of the mother-daughter dialogue in the first of Walker's definitions and see this as pivotal for their work. Still others are drawn to explore the dimensions of self-care and self-love and affirmation given by Walker. Some focus on the need for a piercing critique of white feminism (academic and practical). Finally, there are those who believe all four of the parts of Walker's definition must determine one's theoretical and analytical framework.

As womanist theology moves from its largely Protestant and Christian base, it ushers in conversations with African-based religions from African countries, from the Caribbean, and within the United States. It is also sparking discussions with other women of the African diaspora from Brazil, the Caribbean, and the Netherlands. These conversations are in their initial stages and bode well for future womanist theological reflection. If womanist theology is to continue its evolving yet contextual nature, it must continue to question and push beyond its present boundaries to engage in these wider conversations and also maintain its ongoing conversation with black Christian churches and communities in the United States. This conversation includes advocacy for full partnership between men and women, the care and nurture of children and respect for the dignity and wisdom for the elderly, a prophetic witness within Christianity, and a relentless insistence that the church universal and its theological principles reflect a spirit of justice and love for all humanity and the rest of creation.

SOURCES: Womanist theology has its beginnings in the four-part definition of *womanist* by Alice Walker in *In Search of Our Mothers' Gardens: Womanist Prose* (1983). Four foundational texts for womanist theology are Katie Geneva Cannon's *Black Womanist Ethics* (1988) and *Katie's Canon: Womanism and the Soul of the Black Community* (1996); Jacquelyn Grant's *White Women's Christ, Black Women's Jesus: Feminist Christology and Womanist Response* (1989); and Delores S. William's *Sisters in the Wilderness: The Challenge of Womanist God-Talk* (1993). Books by Marcia Y. Riggs, *Awake, Arise, and Act: A Womanist Call for Black Liberation* (1994), and Kelly Brown Douglas, *Sexuality and the Black Church: A Womanist Perspective* (1999), address Walker's appeal to the diversity of black life in the United States. Renita J. Weems, *I Asked for Intimacy: Stories of Blessings, Betrayals, and Birthings* (1993), and Karen Baker-Fletcher, *Sisters of Dust, Sisters of Spirit: Womanist Wordings on God and Creation* (1998), explore the themes of self-love and self-respect found in Walker's definition of womanist. The authors in the two anthologies edited by Emilie M. Townes, *A Troubling in My Soul: Womanist Perspectives on Evil and Suffering* (1993) and *Embracing the Spirit: Womanist Perspectives on Hope, Salvation, and Transformation* (1997), breathe new life into the traditional theological concepts of theodicy, salvation, and hope. See also Alice Walker, *You Can't Keep a Good Woman Down* (1981); Emilie M. Townes, *Womanist Justice, Womanist Hope* (1993); Kelly Brown Douglas, *The Black Christ* (1994); Diana Hayes, *Hagar's Daughters: Womanist Ways of Being in the World* (1995); Cheryl Sanders, *Living the Intersection: Womanism and Afrocentrism in Theology* (1995); Kelly Brown Douglas, *The Black Christ* (1994); Emily Townes, *In a Blaze of Glory: Womanist Spirituality as Social Witness* (1995); Emily Townes, *Breaking the Fine Rain of Death: African American Health Issues and a Womanist Ethic of Care* (1998); Linda E. Thomas, "Womanist Theology, Epistemology, and a New Anthropological Paradigm," *Cross Currents* 48 (Winter 1998–1999): 488–499; and Delores Williams, speech given at 1993 Re-Imagining Conference, November 4–7, 1993, Minneapolis, Minnesota.

EURO-AMERICAN FEMINIST THEOLOGY
Lucy Tatman

THERE ARE THREE small but immediate issues with the topic "Euro-American Feminist Theology." What does *Euro-American* mean? What does *feminist* mean? And what does, or could, *theology* mean when combined with the first two terms? To begin with, *Euro-American* is an odd catchall term that refers broadly to white, educationally, and usually economically privileged individuals who were born and live in North America but whose ancestors (or grandparents or parents) came from somewhere in Europe. It also implies "with a Christian background," unless explicitly stated otherwise. An unwieldy term indeed. For the purposes of this essay, *Euro-American* means that sort of feminist theology written by white, North American Christian women. And what of *feminist*? It too is a rather odd term, with as many definitions as there are people who name themselves, or others, feminist. As a rough guide, here it stands as an acknowledgment and affirmation of the full and unqualified humanity of every woman, man, and child without exception. It is a value judgment—in other words, a statement of the utter worth and dignity of each and all, without qualification.

What happens when white, North American Christian women engage in theology, or God-talk, from a feminist perspective? Now things begin to get interesting. Rather, let us back up, for contemporary Euro-American feminist theology began to be written in the 1960s; and in order to understand this theology, it is crucial to have a sense of the conditions and influences that made it possible. At that time in the United States the civil rights movement, massive demonstrations against the U.S. involvement in the war in Vietnam, and by the end of the decade, the increasingly visible women's liberation movement collectively called into question the structure of society. Who had the power to decide that one race was superior to another? Who had the power to send troops from the United States to kill and be killed in a small Asian country? Who was excluded from the country's (white male) economic and political and military strongholds? The 1960s were a time of cultural and political upheaval. Long-held values and underlying assumptions about "the way things are" and how they ought to be were being radically questioned.

It was in this context that a growing number of theologians were of the opinion that, given the Nazi Holocaust, Hiroshima, Nagasaki, and napalm, to speak or write of an immutable (unchanging), omniscient (all-knowing), omnipotent (all-powerful), and all good God was rationally untenable and morally unconscionable. According to them, God literally was dead. With Dietrich Bonhoeffer's words as a rallying cry, the death-of-God theologians proclaimed it was time for "man to come of age," to live in the absence of God. Concretely, what this meant, at least in part, was for "man" to live knowing that "he" is responsible for what does and does not happen in the world. For the death-of-God theologians there simply was no longer an all-powerful God prepared to come to the rescue of "man." The focus of their theological attention was on this world as it is here and now. A similar "this-worldly" focus was also prominent in the work of a number of theologians concerned with secular society, in particular Harvey Cox.

Meanwhile, in the Roman Catholic Church there were two momentous developments: In the early 1960s Pope John XXIII, cardinals, bishops, and laypeople were preparing for Vatican Council II, during the course of which the active participation of the laity in the affairs of the Church was encouraged, while in Peru (1968) Gustavo Gutiérrez, among others, was insisting that all theology is shaped by the context in which it is developed and that theology developed by economically privileged Europeans or North Americans was not appropriate to the context of the poor in Latin America. The God of the gospels is a God with a preferential option for the poor, said Gutiérrez, and liberation theology began to be voiced most strongly.

At the same time as white, middle-class men were burying God or turning to the "secular city" and liberation theology was beginning to take shape in Latin America, in the United States a number of black churchmen (and they were primarily men) were meeting and beginning to relate Black Power to theology. In the summer of 1966 the underlying foundation of black theology was established with the publication of a full-page advertisement in the *New York Times*, titled "Black Power: Statement by the National Committee of Negro Churchmen, July 31, 1966." Signed by forty-seven black churchmen and one woman, it was clear that from where they stood God was fully alive and sustaining the struggle of black communities to liberate themselves from the racist, violent, and oppressive conditions imposed upon them by white America(ns). In marked contrast to most theology written by white male authors, the emphasis on black churches and the black *community* was coupled with the absence of any reference to individual lives; thus whatever was/is "redemptive" about black theology is redemptive in a collective, corporate sense. In other words, black theology is, like Latin American liberation theology, a theological paradigm unto itself.

These distinct theological paradigms (or sets of ideas) multiplied during and following the 1960s, and rather than attempt to deny the validity of all other paradigms, they each sought instead to bear witness to the lived truths and faith claims of particular, *theretofore marginalized* communities. This is a critical point. What happened in the 1960s was that *groups* of people who had previously been denied entrance into the academic discipline of Christian theology came together and created the spaces in which they could speak and write and piece together their own theological ideas. Those who had previously been ignored or made the objects of theological reflection became active theological subjects, including white, North American Christian women. Among those Euro-American women who began to do Christian theology from a feminist perspective at that time were Mary Daly and Rosemary Radford Ruether, two tremendously important thinkers. However, while Ruether has continued to write as a feminist Christian theologian, it is important to note that Daly stopped writing as a theologian after her book, *Beyond God the Father: Toward a Philosophy of Women's Liberation*, published in 1973. Accordingly, when identifying Daly's thoughts here, reference is made exclusively to those texts she wrote while still writing as a feminist Christian theolo-

Contemporary Euro-American feminist theology began to be written in the 1960s. In order to understand this theology, it is crucial to have a sense of the conditions and influences that made it possible. At that time in the United States, the civil rights movement, massive demonstrations against the United States' involvement in the war in Vietnam, and, by the end of the decade, the increasingly visible women's liberation movement collectively called into question the structure of society. *Copyright © Bettye Lane Studio.*

gian. Equally important, while Daly's contributions to Euro-American feminist theology will be discussed first, followed by the thought of Rosemary Radford Ruether, the choice of order is based on the alphabet. They were both writing, publishing, and speaking in this new theological language at the same time, both well aware that the subjects of theological reflection (God, humanity, and the world) had been defined for thousands of years primarily by a small, elite group of privileged men. Although humans known as women make up half the hu-

man race, it was from the perspective of the male half that women had been defined.

And it was this issue that Mary Daly first examined: How, exactly, had "woman" been defined throughout the history of the Christian church and what was the effect of this definition of "woman" on the lives of women? In *The Church and the Second Sex*, first published in 1968, she presented a historical overview of traditional Christian theological pronouncements concerning woman, covering everything from the characterization (in the New Testament) of Eve as both secondary to Adam and responsible for the advent of sin and evil in the world through various Church Fathers' representations of women as fickle, shallow, too talkative, weak, incapable of much rational thought, and of no real use to men apart from childbearing. On she went, calmly dredging up quotes that posited women's "natural" inferiority to men, women's "naturally" subordinate role in relation to men, women's "natural" susceptibility to sin, and women's "natural" destiny—that of motherhood, and nothing else. After noting that the church, especially the Roman Catholic Church, was now rather out of step with modern Western society regarding its views on women, she suggested that perhaps the time had come for "a more prophetic vision of the Church as a movement in the world, concerned primarily with betterment of the human condition, and seeking to cooperate with all those who are striving for this goal" (184–185). Using the strongest language she used anywhere in the book, Daly noted as well that as long as "the demonic myth of the eternal feminine" is affirmed in theological texts, there will be no chance that Christian theology can support the betterment of the human condition (193). Daly established that if in fact women are included in "humanity," then by defining "woman" as inherently, "naturally" subordinate to men and in suggesting that women obediently wait until they get to heaven to be rewarded for their earthly suffering, most traditional Christian theology works against the betterment, here and now, of women's lives and thus against the betterment of humanity as a whole.

After describing the theological history that denied women the status of full personhood, and denied as well women's capacity for fully rational thought (thereby making it impossible for women's thoughts and words to be taken seriously when they disagreed with this characterization of themselves), Daly turned her attention to providing a theological alternative. While more fully developed in *Beyond God the Father*, her basic theological innovations are present in an earlier essay, "After the Death of God the Father," first published in *Commonweal* in March 1971. Here she begins from the assumption of the full, *unqualified* humanity of all women, men, and children, blasting the concepts of "eternal masculinity" and "eternal femininity" (and the rigid identification of male with masculine, female with feminine) that have shaped Western culture. Such concepts have acted as cultural straightjackets, producing "caricatures" of human beings, qualifying and limiting the ways in which male and female persons are supposed to be and act. Daly affirmed that feminine and masculine stereotypes have functioned to restrain people from developing into their full personhood, *whatever* that might be. Moreover, she noted that as long as "God in 'his' heaven is a father ruling 'his' people, then it is in the 'nature'

of things and according to divine plan and the order of the universe that society be male dominated" (54). In other words, the symbolic universe conveyed through much traditional Christian theology functioned as both a *model and the justification for* unequal relations between men and women on the earth, relations of dominance and subordination, respectively.

Accordingly, Daly embraced a different understanding of God, turning to Paul Tillich's image of God as the ground and power of being. Such a conception of God could not be used, she believed, to support or sanction domination of any sort, for *all* that exists is both grounded in and empowered by God. By implication, no part of creation is inherently any more valuable or worthy or God-like than any other part. From this perspective, Daly was able to name as sinful all social, political, and theological structures or ideologies that support the subordination or oppression of any sort of human being, any aspect of creation. In particular, she was able to name sexism as a sin. While perhaps not such a revolutionary thought now, at the time it was radical indeed. Further, she was able to show how deeply a change in one fundamental theological presupposition (the conception of God, in her case) affected assumptions about the nature of human beings and the nature of sin. Rather, she demonstrated how conceptions of God, humanity, and sin are all interwoven, inextricable from each other. Change one, and one's "whole vision of reality" can change.

Like Daly, Rosemary Radford Ruether was and remains interested in changing the vision of reality conveyed through Christian theology. She, too, has traced a history of misogynism through the history of the Christian church and has shown how these woman-hating tendencies are closely associated with the world-negating influence of apocalyptic and Platonic thought—two strands of thought taken up by early Christian writers. In other words, according to Ruether, in Christianity the (never particularly strong) Jewish apocalyptic belief that this world and everything in it would soon be destroyed, only to be replaced by God with something much better, was combined with the Platonic belief that bodies and souls were absolutely separable and that souls were of much higher value than bodies. Furthermore, some bodies in particular, like all female bodies and all enslaved bodies, were particularly susceptible to their own bodiliness, their own materiality and corruptibility. The consequence of this apocalyptic-Platonic merger in Christian thought was "a set of dualities that still profoundly condition the modern worldview" (Ruether, *Liberation Theology*, 115). Heaven, the future, spirit, mind, light, good, man, the eternal—all these are ranged against, and valued more than, the earth, the present, bodies, emotions, darkness, woman, temporality, and change. Given that these dualities were and to a large extent are still believed to be reflective of the way things naturally "are" in the universe, it is no surprise, for Ruether, that Western culture literally has been constructed in this dualistic image.

Everything from the way cities have been built to allow privileged men to enter exclusive business districts during the day while keeping their wives and children away and out of sight to the location of ghettos, industrial factories, and sweat shops crammed among each other, Ruether reads all these as indications of what and whom a culture values and does not value. The destruction of so much of the environment, of so many species of earth creatures, points to a devaluation of the earth itself, which again is not surprising if an all-powerful God is expected to replace the current world with a new one in the future.

Accordingly, Ruether has perceived her task as a theologian to be to challenge this mind-set: to propose another way of understanding the nature of the universe and God and to construct a theology that promotes equally the embodied lives of all, as well as the well-being of the earth itself. For Ruether it is vital that no one form of oppression be elevated above others, for she perceives them all to be interlinked. Concretely, what this means is that she is clear that sexism should not be analyzed apart from a consideration of racism, classism, and the ways in which these oppressions are associated with one another, combining to have different effects on different living bodies. Like Daly, Ruether, too, is excruciatingly clear that the Western cultural understanding of "the feminine" as passive, weak, dependent, must be challenged but only in connection with an equally strong challenge to the concept of "the masculine." In Ruether's words, "What is called 'masculine' is the egoistic attitudes of the powerful, and what is derogated as 'feminine' is the defeated traits of the powerless, both of which have little to do with the full potential of men and women as they might exist in an equalitarian society" (New Woman, New Earth, 142). Importantly, while stressing that neither women nor men have had the opportunity to become fully who they might become in this culture, Ruether does not affirm that human beings have any core, fixed essence. She emphasizes that what has been lacking is any sustained opportunity to grow and change in unexpected ways, stuck as we all have been in a culture that insists that certain body types and skin colors behave in specific manners.

According to Ruether, what links the stereotypical Western conception of "femininity" and "masculinity" to oppressions such as racism, classism, and environmental destruction is the understanding that all women, all men of the nondominant race, all laborers, and the earth itself are identified primarily with the (passive) body, with matter to be acted upon, shaped, and used by those who are (mentally) active. Paradoxically, such mentally passive bodies are also seen as being emotionally uncontrollable, liable to behave in disruptive ways if they are not closely monitored. In the end, what links all oppressions is the question of power: Who has it? How are they using it to define and often deform the lives and bodies of others?

Theologically, how does Ruether address this issue? Like Daly, she turns away from an understanding of God as an omnipotent (father) figure abiding in heaven above. Such a God has too often been used by other father figures to justify their own use and abuse of power. Instead of a personal God above, Ruether writes of an everlasting "divine matrix," the source and resource of all that is, that "subsists underneath the coming to be and passing away of individuated beings and even planetary worlds" (Sexism and God-Talk, 257). Such a conception of the divine carries with it a number of important implications. On the one hand, in characterizing the divine as "the source of being that underlies creation," Ruether asserts that all creation is dependent upon God, for without the source of all that is nothing would exist. On the other hand, no aspect of creation is in any way privileged over any other, for all that is comes from and returns to the divine matrix. Further, everything that is, is in an interdependent relationship with everything else, related from their source, and unable to exist apart from the whole of creation. In other words, no isolated, independent entity can exist, for existence itself is relational, or interdependent, and constantly changing.

When God and creation (meaning the whole universe) are conceived in this way, it becomes clear that to misuse or abuse any aspect of creation is to damage the fabric of the whole. It also becomes clear that finitude or death itself is valuable, necessary. Life cannot sustain itself on nothing; growth cannot happen in the absence of decay; Ruether's divine matrix is not an infinite supply of the stuff of life but is able, perhaps, to recycle from the stuff of the universe unto infinity. But this is the business of the divine. For Ruether, it is not humans' business at all. Rather, she strongly affirms that "it is not our calling to be concerned about the eternal meaning of our lives, and religion should not make this the focus of its message. Our responsibility is to use our temporal span to create a just and good community for our generation and for our children" (258). Like the death-of-God theologians, Ruether adopts a profoundly "this-worldly" focus in her theology.

What matters to her is that this earth, this garden, be cared for now, while it can still sustain life. What is redemptive and salvific in her theology is any act of care for one another and for other earth creatures, here and now. While every struggle against injustice, abuse, or oppression may well result in perceived failure, or "crucifixion," such crucifixions are not demanded by any

God. Rather, they are the result of human greed and abuse of power. Strongly pragmatic, Ruether asserts that time may well be running out; currently certain humans are using up far too much of the earth's resources, damaging the environment in ways that may not be able to be repaired. (Think of the growing hole in the ozone layer, the devastation of the Amazon rain forests, the growing desertification of portions of China, Africa, Egypt.) Unfortunately, such rampant consumption threatens the lives of all, not just those who are feeding their gluttonous habits.

Lastly, Ruether is exceedingly clear that salvation is both context specific and never a once and for all occurrence. Actions that may help to sustain life and lives in one location may well not be appropriate in another, and (given that change seems to be the fundamental characteristic of all that is) no single action can ever fix anything for all time. Further, because all of us are bound to the mind-set of our era, there will come, inevitably, other ways of perceiving things, different visions of reality that will expose different sins and injustices that our descendants will have to address in their time and place.

For over thirty years Ruether has contributed to establishing the foundations of Euro-American feminist theology, to the creation of a new theological paradigm. She has done so from her perspective as a Roman Catholic historical theologian and is certainly the most prolific writer on the subject. However, she has not been alone in this endeavor. Two Protestant feminist theologians, Carter Heyward and Sallie McFague, have also made significant contributions.

Carter Heyward, one of the eleven Episcopalian women first (albeit "irregularly") ordained to the priesthood in 1974, has been challenging theological boundaries ever since. With the 1982 publication of her doctoral thesis, *The Redemption of God: A Theology of Mutual Relation*, Heyward changed the feminist Christian theological landscape. Taking seriously the idea that lived experience matters, that the particularities of one's life help to shape how one thinks about and interprets the world around one, Heyward writes with a searing honesty about her own life, refusing to abstract theological reflection from the ordinary and extraordinary messiness of everyday existence. She writes as a lesbian feminist, as a lover and friend, as a priest and teacher, as a southerner, as a daughter and sister and aunt, and as a beloved companion to many furry critters. She writes as well to redeem both God and humanity from the centuries of theological pronouncements that have stressed the omnipotence and self-sufficiency of God while insisting on the powerlessness and dependency of humankind.

For Heyward (who takes with utmost seriousness the horror of the Holocaust) this understanding of God and humanity completely obscures the fact that humans have a great deal of power that we use for both good and evil. The human capacity for sin is enormous, but so too is our capacity to "god" with one another, to make love and justice incarnate in the world around us. Like Ruether and Daly, she rejects an all-powerful God, positing instead the notion that God is "our power in mutual relation," the "resource and power of relation" (Heyward, *Touching Our Strength*, 188–189). Put differently, Heyward stresses the fact that if *we* do not do justice and love one another, it is not going to happen. But when in those rare instances we do engage in acts of justice and love, at those moments we are together doing the sacred work of God. Of equal importance in her thought is her insistence that it is with and through our *bodies* that we relate to one another. When we are in mutual relation with another, which means a relationship of justice and love, it is our bodies, our fleshy, feeling bodies that are filled with the sacred, erotic yearning to connect with one another, and it is through our bodies that the power of relation, love, God flows. Likewise, where there is injustice there are *broken, suffering bodies*, whether human or not.

And for Heyward, the point is that injustice is rampant, that in this world "relation is broken violently" and often, and that the very structures of society (in Western culture) sustain such brokenness (*The Redemption of God*, 35). To comprehend what Heyward means by this it is vital to understand the distinction in her thought between relationality and interdependence. Like Ruether (and following process theology, but that is another story), Heyward understands the fundamental nature of the universe to be that of interdependence and change, ceaseless change. This is neither a positive nor negative thing; it simply is. However, the sort of relations that we form with one another in our interdependent state, these (always changing) relations can be either justice-enhancing or destructive, mutually empowering or nonmutually disempowering. Accordingly, when we live in a society that systematically discriminates against entire categories of people because of age or ability or religion or sexual practice or skin color or educational level or perceived sex/gender, then we are *all* entangled in the threads of nonmutual, violent relations.

It is impossible not to sin, not to participate in such unjust relations, no matter how well intentioned one is. It is impossible not to sin because it is into a world of broken relations that each one of us is born; however, it is in this world (that we know only through our often bruised bodies) that we can, occasionally, cocreate with one another instances of radical love and justice, quite literally adding God's presence to the world. (And, yes, Heyward's thought is of a piece, difficult to separate into distinct elements.) Is Heyward saying that there is no such thing as "God" apart from human actions? No. She affirms an understanding of God as the source, power, and resource of all that is, God as "more than" the power that flows between humans participating in mutual relations. But she is saying that God, too, is in a relationship of interdependence with creation. She is saying that the power that sustains all of creation needs human assistance to be made (differently) incarnate again and again in human lives in various times and places.

On the subject of human lives, in a theological move that has sometimes been misinterpreted as an "essentialist" one, Heyward, like Ruether, is insistent that "liberation from injustice in the world is dependent upon the theological value we give to our shared humanity" (*The Redemption of God*, 16). Put differently, she is adamant that unless *every* particular, specific, unique, and uniquely embodied individual is accorded the same measure of respect and value as *every* other human being, then relations between different individuals will inevitably reflect the devaluation and perceived unworthiness of certain people(s). With this deceptively simple move, which is indeed at the heart of Euro-American feminist theology, what is at stake is not the *sameness* of all but the equal value and worth of all.

Differences among, between, and even within individuals can be recognized, honored, and celebrated from this perspective. It is not that all humans or "all women" or "all men" are lumped together as being "all the same on the inside"—far from it. Rather, the always somehow elusive and mysterious differences between people (even between people who seem to be quite alike) can be appreciated instead of feared or denied. What we share, as human beings, is the fact of difference from all others. It is precisely because people are not all the same, and because some perceived differences are interpreted as being signs of inferiority rather than, simply, difference, that this theological move is so important. But this sounds as though this is but a version of the "different but equal" approach to human rights. No. Again, the radical differences between people who appear to be similar are stressed, as are the differences that occur within an individual over the course of a lifetime. Change happens to everyone; no one lives in isolation from a changing world, changing relations with others, and changing self-understanding. In Heyward's words, "[W]e are unchanging, or constant, in our changing" (*The Redemption of God*, 65). Regardless of such change at the level of being, however, Euro-American feminist theology posits the unchanging value and worth of every human life. Further, because such theologians tend not to perceive humankind as being the reason for the existence of the universe, there is a strong tendency to affirm the difference and intrinsic value of all nonhuman creation as well.

Perhaps more than any other Euro-American feminist theologian, Sallie McFague has stressed the inherent value and worth of all creation. Relentlessly acknowledging the complete dependence of humankind on the earth, the soil and air and water, and other earth creatures whose destruction will result in our own extinction, nonetheless McFague affirms the value and goodness of the "other" apart from such human dependence. She believes that the wonder and blessing of creation, of the fact that anything *IS* at all, needs to be honored apart from the value humans place on resources that can be used to sustain human life.

In other words, McFague seeks to decenter humanity, to distract our attention from (an overblown image of) ourselves and to encourage us all to pay attention to the intricate profusion of improbable life forms and entities of which we are but a small part. On the other hand, she seeks as well to make human beings face the fact that as a species we now have the power and tools to destroy all life on earth. (She is quite clear that only a few enormously privileged and powerful individuals, primarily men, hold such power at any one time, but her point remains.) At this time human beings can uncreate what has taken millions and millions of years to come into being. Humans, through our actions, can and are destroying entire species of plants and animals at a horrifying rate. Unless we can learn to value "earth others" for their own sakes rather than as a means to our own ends, we will continue destroying them. And as long as we continue to destroy the "others," we are contributing to the destruction of our own species. It is this vicious circle that McFague is trying to break by her model of the world, actually, the entire universe, as God's body. Her point is simple: "[T]he world is not *ours* to manipulate for *our* purposes. If we see it as God's body, the way God is present to us, we will indeed know we tread on sacred ground" (*McFague*, 185). She believes that if we can learn to perceive all matter, all bodies as being in some way the embodiment of God, then we may be inclined to treat all that is in a much more respectful and caring way.

Through her presentation of various models of God (including God as Mother, Lover, Friend, and Spirit), McFague is attempting to provide alternative stories, other ways to understand humans' relationships to each other, to the earth, and to the divine. Stories matter in her thought, for she is adamant that we tend to live our lives according to the stories that we hear and tell. According to McFague, "[T]he moral issue of our day—and the vocation to which we are called—is whether we and other species will live and how well we will live" (*The Body of God*, 9). The stories that which we in the West are most familiar, stories of human domination and God swooping down from on high to destroy, then replace this small planet, these stories are no longer stories on which we ought to model our behavior. Instead, McFague asks humankind to take responsibility for our actions, to grow up. Like Ruether and Heyward, she is deeply pragmatic and more than a little sceptical of our ability to do so. We cannot bring to life that which has already been destroyed, and there is abundant evidence that humans, particularly enormously wealthy ones, are reluctant to alter either their lifestyles or their factories' smoke stacks. Yet the future hangs in the balance.

This is a thread that runs strongly through most Euro-American feminist theology: the uncertainty of the present. It is obvious we no longer live in a world recognizable to our grandparents, yet it is not clear what sort of world we do live in. In addressing this issue from drastically different perspectives, Catherine Keller and Melanie May reach surprisingly compatible conclusions. In *A Body Knows: A Theopoetics of Death and Resurrection*, May considers what it means to live each day as if it were Holy Saturday, the day in between crucifixion and resurrection. While it "is a day about which the Gospels are silent," it is a day about which the time has come to speak, for it feels strangely like our day (19). It is a day of "precarious presence" and unutterable absence, a day in which the strength to "not let go" ebbs and flows through each of our bodies. A day of risk, a day of "threshold activity," a day in which May affirms, with every fiber of her being, the yearning for life abundant. It is a day, a month, a year, a lifetime, in which May calls for the practice, *but not the celebration*, of resurrection. Quite simply, "the resurrection of the body—which, in turn, transfigures the mind—happens whenever and wherever we participate in a new solidarity with and presence to our own bodies and the bodies of others" (104). To practice the resurrection of the body is to affirm life in the midst of death; it is to witness to the living presence of the body, all bodies. Despair is also present, and deeply felt pain, for the crucifixion has indeed occurred, but even so there is still life. We can choose not to run, not to deny, but to remain nakedly present to one another in the face of an always unknown future.

To offer words adequate to the time in which we seem to be living is what Catherine Keller strives to do in *Apocalypse Now and Then: A Feminist Guide to the End of the World*. Keller suggests that we ("we" in the culturally Christian West, at least) do not need to go to the end of the world, for we are already there, "in apocalypse—in its narrative, its aftermath, its compulsion, its hope" (xi). The *apocalypse*, a term that originally meant revelation or unveiling, has come to mean dramatic end (and new beginning), and stories of dramatic endings are culturally pervasive, unavoidable. Keller makes the case that we live in their midst, no matter what our individual relationship to such apocalyptic stories may be, no matter what assumptions about the end of the world we may hold. The apocalypse is thus an unavoidable presence here and now; "we live, arguably, among its effects" (2). What Keller does is to negotiate her way through an assortment of apocalyptic effects, naming but trying to avoid the extremes of infantile optimism and indifferent despair.

It is to other elements of the apocalypse that she directs her attention, the more contradictory and inexplicable, the better. Apocalyptic times, for all their focus on the future, are times of extraordinary attention to the present. Signs and portents (real and imagined) are read and interpreted, judgments are made and remade, there is a stirring in the air, movements begin and do not end, carrying those caught up in them to some very odd places. Keller's point (one of them, at least) is that these are not stable times, yet their very uncertainty is cause for hope *in the present*. We humans have proven ourselves to be remarkably bad at foretelling the future; happily, we are also remarkably bad at living according to any prewritten scripts, though we do seem to love them. The fact that all sorts of women have spoken up in large numbers across much of the world signals an end to the enforced silence of women as a category, yet the words different women are speaking could hardly have been predicted. There are those who want the chance, for the first time, to stay at home with their children, those who desire the chance to work full-time; those who wish for other women to stop criticizing them for wearing a veil, those who wish to abolish all signs of femininity. The end of silence gives way to a cacophony of sound.

And this, perhaps, is the message of Euro-American feminist theology. What has been—or traditional ways of perceiving and interpreting God, humanity, and the world—is no longer adequate. No longer ought any one sort of human define what it is to be another, and no longer is there a monopoly on descriptions of God. What there is, is the difficult, uncertain effort to put momentarily into words a sense of what is appropriate here and now. Euro-American feminist theologians tend to believe that it is appropriate, here in North America and now, at the start of the twenty-first century, to affirm the full and unqualified humanity, or value and worth, of every human being without exception. We tend to believe that God needs to be reimagined as the source and resource of all that is, neither omnipotent nor omniscient but necessary all the same. We affirm strongly the dependence of all life upon the earth and the earth's natural resources, the products of millions of years of evolutionary development. We are highly critical of the abuse of power, power used to benefit a few at the expense of many, and we realize that we too are utterly entangled in power-riddled dynamics and relations, benefiting from our skin color and educational privilege at the same time as we white, North American women are structurally barred from access to most of the power in the continent. What to do?

In this uncertain place, into these uncertain times, slip thoughts and words difficult to pin down. "To do justice is to make love." "What is redemptive in one place will not be redemptive in another." "Our bodies' sacred yearning . . ." "The end is at hand, and so too are any number of beginnings." If Hope is no longer clad in radiant garb, she is still grinning, still to be found wherever there are odd-looking human bodies gathered. Of course, it is entirely possible that she is laughing *at* us. There is a definite edge to Euro-American feminist theology, an edge that may provoke much discomfort. It may also keep Euro-American feminist theology from becoming too complacent with itself.

SOURCES: Sources cited in this essay are Mary Daly, *The Church and the Second Sex* (1968) and "After the Death of God the Father," *Commonweal* (March 1971): 7–11; Rosemary Radford Ruether, *Liberation Theology: Human Hope Confronts Christian History and American Power* (1972), *New Woman, New Earth: Sexist Ideologies and Human Liberation* (1975), and *Sexism and God-Talk: Toward a Feminist Theology* (1983); Carter Heyward, *Touching Our Strength: The Erotic as Power and the Love of God* (1989) and *The Redemption of God: A Theology of Mutual Relation* (1982); Sallie McFague, *Models of God: Theology for an Ecological, Nuclear Age* (1987) and *The Body of God* (1993); Melanie A. May, *A Body Knows: A Theopoetics of Death and Resurrection* (1995); and Catherine Keller, *Apocalypse Now and Then: A Feminist Guide to the End of the World* (1996). In addition to the texts named in the essay, the following works provide a basic overview of the range of Euro-American feminist theology. Unfortunately, this list is of necessity quite partial; however, readers interested in pursuing the subject will find the bibliographies in these books most helpful: Nelle Morton, *The Journey Is Home* (1985); Catherine Keller, *From a Broken Web* (1986) and *Face of the Deep* (2003); Joanne Carlson Brown and Carole R. Bohn, eds., *Christianity, Patriarchy, and Abuse* (1989); Rebecca Chopp, *The Power to Speak* (1989); Mary Hunt, *Fierce Tenderness* (1991); Elizabeth Johnson, *She Who Is* (1993) and *Friends of God and Prophets* (1999); Rosemary Radford Ruether, *Women and Redemption* (1998); Serene Jones, *Feminist Theory and Christian Theology* (2000); and Lucy Tatman, *Knowledge That Matters* (2001).

LAS HERMANAS: LATINAS AND RELIGIOUS/POLITICAL ACTIVISM
Lara Medina

LAS HERMANAS, A national organization of Latina Catholics, exemplifies the determination of Latinas to recreate church based on equality, justice, and the empowerment of grassroots women and the poor. The organization emerged during a time of intense social upheaval in the Roman Catholic Church, U.S. society,

and the world. Ethnic movements for civil rights and self-determination, modern feminism, anti–Vietnam War protests, civil wars in Latin America, international student protests, and Vatican Council II contributed to a milieu of social unrest and radical transformation. On April 2–5, 1971, fifty primarily Chicana religious sisters met in Houston, Texas, in response to the efforts of Gregoria Ortega, a Victorynoll sister from El Paso, and Gloria Gallardo, of the Sisters of the Holy Ghost in Houston. Their intent was to organize Chicana sisters "who have tried to become more relevant to our people and, because of this, find themselves in 'trouble' with either our own congregation or other members of the hierarchy" (Circular letter, 1970, 1). Sister Ortega had been transferred from her teaching position in the diocese of San Angelo, Texas, where she had supported student walkouts and opposed the severe physical abuse of Chicano/a students by their teachers. Sister Gallardo worked as a community organizer and catechist in Houston among Chicanos living with chronic unemployment, inadequate health care, and malnutrition.

The fifty Chicanas present at the first meeting had joined religious life prior to Vatican Council II or shortly thereafter. They represented varying levels of political and ethnic consciousness. The majority shared the common experience of having to suppress their ethnicity and language once they entered religious life. Many expressed frustration and anger at not being permitted to minister in their own ethnic communities. Yolanda Tarango of Texas reflects on her experience: "At that time you were supposed to leave behind your past as it was not desirable to work with one's people. I experienced much racism. We were forbidden to speak Spanish even in hospitals, schools, not even to the janitors. It was a violent tearing away from our pasts" (Interview, 1990). The call to unite in Houston and the opportunity to tell their stories enabled the women to recognize similarities, identify the elements of oppression, and, as Tarango states, "realize it was not just my order or my life, but that we were in a widespread situation. In the coming together we raised each other's consciousness" (Interview, 1990).

As a fifth-generation Chicana whose family helped settle Ysleta near El Paso, Texas, Tarango joined the Sisters of Charity of the Incarnate Word in 1966 "because her first choice to become a priest was impossible." Sister Tarango resides in San Antonio, where she directs the Visitation House of Ministries, a transitional housing program for homeless women and children that she cofounded in 1985. As a doctoral candidate of ministry at Austin Presbyterian Theological Seminary, Tarango also teaches religious studies at the University of Incarnate Word. She recently completed a six-year term as general councilor of her international religious order, the first Latina to fill that position, and she served as national coordinator of Las Hermanas for three consecutive terms (1985–1991).

Experiencing discrimination comprised only a portion of the women's concerns. A lack of representation in the Church hierarchy exacerbated their grievances. Latinas, for example, represented less than 1 percent of women religious, while Latinos represented 28 percent of the U.S. Catholic population. Latinos represented only 3 percent of the priesthood. In 1970, only one Mexican American, in the history of the U.S. Roman Catholic Church, Father Patricio Flores, had been named bishop. In contrast, Irish Americans, who comprised 17 percent of the U.S. Catholic population, had a representation of 56 percent among Catholic bishops and 36 percent among all priests, both diocesan and in religious orders. This historical underrepresentation of Latinos in positions of ecclesial authority created a severe absence of culturally relevant ministries, leading to overt discrimination in many parishes. Documented stories abound of Latino Catholics prohibited from worshipping at the same time as their Euro-American peers, or of being required to sit in the back of the church and be the last ones to receive communion. Oftentimes separate and unequal churches were built to prevent the integration of a parish, or Latinos would be restricted to worshipping in the basement of church buildings.

At the first conference of Chicana/Latina religious, four goals received unanimous support. These women desired to activate leadership among themselves and the laity; effect social change; contribute to the cultural renaissance of La Raza; and educate Anglo-dominant congregations on the needs of Spanish-speaking communities. The decision to form a national organization took root quickly, and those present chose "Las Hermanas" as the official name as well as the motto, "Unidas en acción y oración" (United in action and prayer). In reflecting on their choice of name, representatives wrote in 1975:

Our title signifies the common vision and purpose of the first members. In our native language, the term "sisters" means much more than a blood relationship. Its more profound meaning is a relationship of sisterhood which demands a certain identity with and sharing of the total self with the whole of humanity. (Espinoza and Ybarra)

The need to express "a certain identity" led to the decision to limit full membership with voting rights to native Spanish-speaking sisters and others of Latin American ancestry. The few Euro-American sisters present, who had been ministering in Spanish-speaking communities, either chose not to return or remained as associate members with limited privileges. Teresa Basso of California, a former Catholic sister, recalls:

There were some Anglo sisters who were very hurt by this decision and never came back, but we felt that this organization was going to allow us to develop our own leadership abilities. That would not happen if the Anglo sisters had a vote. (Interview, 1997)

A follow-up letter soon after the conference further clarified the need to be exclusionary: "[A]t this particular time there is a greater need to help ourselves with our own self identity problem and to better establish ourselves among La Raza" (Circular letter, 1971, 1). These women needed to reclaim their identities on their own terms and in their own spaces.

Teresa or "Teresita" Basso, whose family helped settle Baja California, spent her first five years growing up in Tijuana, Mexico. After relocating to East Los Angeles, Basso attended Bishop Conaty High and joined the Sisters of the Presentation of the Blessed Virgin Mary in 1962 at the age of eighteen. The experience of leaving East Los Angeles for the novitiate in wealthy Los Gatos, California, "seemed like going to another world, a real culture shock" (Interview with Theresa Basso, March 7, 1997, Moreno Valley, California). Basso taught elementary schools in East Los Angeles during the height of the Chicano movement. She would later earn a master's degree in Mexican American Studies at San Jose State College. Working part-time for the United Farm Workers while designing and teaching some of the first Chicano Studies courses at Bay Area community colleges placed Basso at major sites of the Chicano movement. Growing up in *el movimiento* gave her a strong sense of her identity and a level of self-acceptance not found in religious life. Basso also worked as a pastoral associate at parishes in the Los Angeles area and served as a Las Hermanas national coordinator between 1976 and 1978. Teaching, however, remains her chosen profession even after leaving religious life after twenty-eight years. The Southern California Latino/Native American Hall of Fame honored her as a "model educator" for her bilingual teaching at Stallings Elementary School in Corona, California.

The concerns of Las Hermanas expanded beyond the boundaries of the institutional church. In secular society, underemployment, poor education, little political representation, overt discrimination, and the Vietnam War compelled a generation of Chicanos nationwide to respond to injustices with a "politics of mass protest." Chicano/a activists challenged the Catholic Church for institutional support. Las Hermanas and Padres Asociados para Derechos Religiosos, Educativos y Sociales (PADRES), an organization of Chicano clergy mobilizing in 1970, responded with the desire to serve their people. They defined their ministerial role to include both religious needs and political activism. Members of

Las Hermanas, a national organization of Latina Catholics, exemplifies the determination of Latinas to re-create church based on equality, justice, and the empowerment of grassroots women and the poor. At this 1999 national convention in Denver, Colorado, an intergenerational blessing was given as part of the liturgy. *Courtesy of Cecilia Flores.*

Las Hermanas and PADRES participated in central arenas of the Chicano movement including student protests for educational rights, community organizing, and the farm labor struggle under César Chávez and Dolores Huerta. Through their direct involvement in *el movimiento Chicano*, both organizations brought the ethnic struggles for self-determination into the religious realm. They expanded the ministerial role of the Roman Catholic Church by bridging spiritual needs and civil rights. This activism represents the first time a critical mass of Chicana/o and Latina/o religious leaders and laity integrated religion and politics. In the process, Las Hermanas expressed and articulated a spirituality and a theology rooted in the Mexican/Cuban/Puerto Rican Roman Catholic faith but shaped by their experiences as feminists fused with their politically informed ethnic identities.

Within six months of the first Las Hermanas meeting, membership grew from 50 to 900 women representing twenty-one states. Sisters of Puerto Rican and Cuban descent soon joined the organization, and by 1975 Latina laity joined. Highly educated religious women and working-class laity created an ethnic and class diversity that led to their recognition as "the most creative and successful effort for solidarity in a diverse U.S. Latino

reality" (Díaz-Stevens, "Latinas and the Church," 268). Over the years membership has fluctuated due to a vacuum in leadership and scarce financial resources during the late 1980s and early 1990s. However, a restructured leadership team and a renewed sense of purpose in the twenty-first century have invigorated the organization. Approximately 200 members now attend the biennial conferences, and laity comprise the majority of approximately 600 registered members.

Acknowledging their "unique resources as Spanish-speaking religious women," the members of Las Hermanas dedicated themselves, individually and collectively, "to enable each other to work more effectively among and with the Spanish Speaking People of God in bringing about social justice and a truly Christian peace" (Letter to Leadership Conference of Women Religious, 1971, 1). Teresa Basso elaborates: "It was the beginning of Hispanic [religious] women coming together to respond to the voice of the people and to work as agents of change within the Church because we knew that we did have some power there" (Interview, 1997). Seeing themselves as agents of change and committed to social justice transformed their use of power within the institutional Church. As Yolanda Tarango states, "Our identity developed with the people. This is related to how we saw power. For Las Hermanas power was participating in the liberative action of the folks" (Interview, 1996).

The leadership structure chosen by Las Hermanas exemplified their understanding of power as enablement. Early on the membership voted to transform the traditional structure of hierarchical leadership with a president, vice president, and secretary to a team government. Three national coordinators held equal status and authority to represent the organization. Sister Carmelita Espinoza of Colorado explained, "In this way, we would show the community in general, and the Hispanic community in particular, a new model, one that promotes creativity and co-responsibility in leadership" (*Reporte sobre la Organizacíon Las Hermanas de 1972/1974*, 1974). Shared leadership, "one of the basic themes of Chicana feminism," continues to enhance the feminist model promoted by Las Hermanas (Ruiz, 100).

The organization received minimal financial resources from the institutional Church and none from the Bishop's Campaign for Human Development despite their avowed commitment to grassroots communities. Funding came primarily from donations and nominal membership dues. Women religious congregations have provided the bulk of financial support from the beginning. Not until 1979 did the organization begin to establish a more solid funding base with the purchase of certificates of deposit (CDs) under the leadership of Sylvia Sedillo of New Mexico during her term as national coordinator. Interest from the CDs supported organizational activities into the late 1990s.

Sylvia Sedillo joined the Sisters of Loretto at the age of twenty-one. She realized during her college years in Albuquerque, New Mexico, in the late 1950s that she had a calling for ministry. Seeing few options for women other than marriage or clerical work convinced Sylvia that religious life would allow her to devote her life to helping others. After forty years of religious life, she has no regrets. Sedillo earned a Masters in Romance Languages/Spanish from the University of Missouri at Kansas City in 1973 that led her to teach at a Loretto high school in El Paso and later in Kansas City. Meeting Las Hermanas representatives in 1973, however, convinced Sedillo to serve as the first director of the language institute at the then-nascent Mexican American Cultural Center in San Antonio, Texas. From 1979 to 1981, Sylvia served on the national coordinating team of Las Hermanas and significantly increased the financial stability of the organization. Between 1986 and 1993, Sedillo founded and directed the Women's Spiritual Center in Santa Fe, an interfaith and multicultural retreat center, "a place where women of all paths can explore and discover their spirituality together—outside the confines of traditional religious institutions" ("City's Sister Spirits,"

Santa Fe Reporter, 1992, 1). Sedillo recently returned to teaching Spanish in the Santa Fe Public School District.

As annual expenditures consumed limited revenues, the projects envisioned by Las Hermanas in the early 1970s faced serious constraints. Members, however, chose autonomy for the sake of direct service to their people. According to María Iglesias of New York, "We did a lot of the work on our vacations and at our own discretion, we never asked for money. We operated on a shoestring. We didn't want to put our money into trappings like a national office with fancy furniture. We wanted to go directly to the people" (Interview, 1997). Despite limited financial resources, members pooled their skills and "kept going on the impetus, the dedication and the faith of the women" (Interview, 1997). Optimism and courage overcame the limited resources.

María Iglesias of Cuban and Puerto Rican ancestry was born and raised in New York City, where she grew up in a predominantly Jewish neighborhood. Attending Catholic schools with Irish American peers provided Iglesias with a cultural experience helpful to her when she entered the Sisters of Charity of St. Vincent de Paul at the age of eighteen. Forty years later her commitment to religious life remains strong. Iglesias's work over the years with Las Hermanas and Latino communities has sustained her and has challenged her religious community to broaden their perspective. Iglesias served as a national coordinator of Las Hermanas from 1975 to 1977 and represented the organization at the Women's Ordination Conference in 1975. Iglesias has broadened the Church's understanding of Latinos as she has represented the concerns of Puerto Ricans in the Northeast at numerous diocesan and national assemblies. She now works at RENEW, a national organization based in New Jersey, focusing on revitalizing parish communities in their Christian faith.

In its first decade Las Hermanas influenced the policies of major ecclesial bodies including the U.S. Catholic Conference/National Conference of Catholic Bishops (USCC/NCCB), the Leadership Conference of Women Religious (LCWR), and the Secretariat for Hispanic Affairs of the U.S. Catholic Conference regarding institutional representation and culturally sensitive ministries. Together with PADRES, Las Hermanas lobbied to increase the number of Chicano and Latino bishops in the United States, which totaled twenty-one by 2000. Las Hermanas also developed national and international alliances with the National Association of Women Religious (NAWR), Sisters Uniting, Women's Ordination Council (WOC), and the Latin American Conference of Religious Congregations (CLAR). Las Hermanas played an integral role in the three national Hispanic pastoral *encuentros*, or conventions, held in 1972, 1977, and 1985. They lobbied consistently for the full recognition of Latinas in the leadership of the Church, including ordination. They also played a pivotal role in the founding of the Mexican American Cultural Center in San Antonio, the first pastoral center in the United States to train ministers for Spanish-speaking communities.

Despite their willingness to collaborate with Chicano and Latino clergy, significant efforts were made to marginalize their voices as politically conscious Latinas. As feminists they experienced great tension in working in a sanctified patriarchy. Even though they received support from PADRES as an organization, individual clergy found it impossible to accept women as mutual partners in leadership. After nearly a decade of collaborative work, Las Hermanas found it necessary to focus explicitly on the empowerment of women.

In reflecting on their early consciousness, Yolanda Tarango recalls:

When we first started it was more of a dormant feminist consciousness. Through our involvement in the Chicano movement we began to translate that analysis to the Church and name the racism and sexism that we saw there. We wanted to create an organizational basis to challenge the Church. It was not specifically a women's agenda but the women's version of advocating for rights of Latinos in the Church. (Interview, 1996)

This "dormant feminist consciousness" transformed into a clear agenda focused on grassroots women by 1976. While some members would never claim a "feminist" identity, others proudly used the term. According to Margarita Castañeda of Texas, a feminist herself, "This is the reality in Las Hermanas and the Catholic Church. You have those who believe in feminist issues and those who don't" (Interview, 1997). Over the years, as in the broader Chicano movement, Las Hermanas has made room for the spectrum of Chicanas and Latinas. As sociologist Mary Pardo argues, it is the implicit values, goals, and outcomes that determine whether an organization can be called feminist. Feminist outcomes include women's transformation, i.e., improved self-esteem, a sense of autonomy or agency, and political awareness. Las Hermanas qualifies as a feminist organization as it challenges not only sex-based inequality but also race/ethnic and class oppressions. In national conferences and its newsletter *Informes*, Las Hermanas continues to focus on issues affecting the empowerment of women including moral agency, reproductive rights, sexuality, domestic abuse, labor exploitation, and the global economy.

Their second decade marked a significant shift from a primarily community-based focus to that of women's empowerment as members recognized "the indifference of the Church towards women" ("Informes y Análisis de la Reunión de NAC," *Informes*, 1987). For Las Hermanas, however, the two concerns, community and women, are not exclusive as they understand that the empowerment of women is directly tied to the empowerment of the Latino community. According to historian Vicki Ruiz, "a community-centered consciousness" characterizes much of Chicana activism (100).

By 1980 the spirituality and theology of Las Hermanas were clearly grounded in a struggle to transform personal, social, and political constraints. Las Hermanas became a source of inspiration for the Latina Catholic theological understandings first published in Ada María Isasi-Díaz and Yolanda Tarango's *Hispanic Women: Prophetic Voice in the Church* (1988). Drawing on several small group retreats organized by members of Las Hermanas, the two theologians synthesized the religious understandings of grassroots Latinas. Financial support from numerous women's religious congregations, individuals, and organizations including the Center of Concern, Quixote Center, National Assembly of Religious Women, and the National Coalition of American Nuns enabled the authors to converse with and listen to Latinas in various parts of the country. According to Tarango and Isasi-Díaz, Las Hermanas provided "a real link" and "the seedbed" for the production of *mujerista* theology, the name chosen for a Latina feminist theological perspective.

Influenced by Latin American liberation theology, these Latina theologians emphasize "doing theology" as a liberative praxis or critical reflective action, rather than a solely intellectual exercise. As feminist theologians, they challenge traditional theology that ignores the experiences and perceptions of women, particularly women of color. Tarango and Isasi-Díaz place theological authority in the hands of grassroots Latinas whose faith and lived experience inform their beliefs and actions. The goal of this theology is to maintain Latino/a cultural values with a commitment to the struggle against sexism in all its manifestations and to reach "not equality but liberation ... [from] socio-political-economic oppression" (Isasi-Díaz and Tarango, *Hispanic Women: Prophetic Voice in the Church*, xii).

Many members of Las Hermanas named themselves *mujeristas* and their beliefs and praxis *mujerista* theology in order to distinguish their concerns from a form of white feminism mainly concerned with gender oppression. *Mujeristas* understand their challenge to be the interlocking dynamics of gender, class, and racial/ethnic oppressions. Influenced by the song "Cántico de Mujer," by Rosa Martha Zárate, a *mujerista* is defined as a Latina "who struggles to liberate herself not as an individual but as a member of a Hispanic community." *Mujeristas* are called to be faithful to the task of making justice and peace flourish. The definition of *mujerista* is nonstatic or open to change so that new understandings of other types of oppression can be addressed when necessary. *Mujerista* theology reflects a commitment to the self-determination of Latinas held by Las Hermanas. Although not all members utilize the term *mujerista* for self-identity, many were instrumental in its formulations. As Rosa Martha Zárate stated, "I do not use the term feminist or *mujerista*, but I refer to myself as a woman who has assumed her historical and social responsibility" (Interview, 2000).

Zárate emigrated from Mexico in 1966 as a member of the Sisters of the Blessed Sacrament, which she describes as a "very conventional community." Meeting Las Hermanas representatives in 1970 while she helped develop a convent and school in San Ysidro, California, taught her about the exploitation of Mexican sisters like her self. "We were teaching children for less pay than the Irish sisters and the priest was always reprimanding us" (Interview, 2000). Initially she believed that "Las Hermanas was too radical. But little by little I began to see they had something to say. Then I saw them as very free, *mujeres muy libres*, very free women." Involvement with Las Hermanas led Zárate to become the first Mexicana in Latino ministry for the diocese of San Diego in 1973. Her religious community, however, disapproved of her position. Zárate's work in organizing *comunidades eclesiales de base*, or small base communities, youth choirs, and schools of ministries for the laity, took her to the San Bernardino diocese in 1978 where she eventually was forced to leave. Her teachings on liberation theology proved too radical for her superiors and even many of her clerical peers. Losing her suit for wrongful termination against her bishop and the Roman Catholic diocese in 1994 has not prevented Zárate from direct involvement in Chicano/Mexicano communities. She continues to organize poor communities through CAL-PULLI, a network of cooperatives in San Bernardino County, emphasizing economic self-empowerment and cultural knowledge. Zárate and Father Patricio Guillen work closely with a team of laity in successfully applying the tenets of liberation theology in southern California. Zárate is also an internationally recognized composer and singer of liberation music, or *la nueva canción*. Lyrics speaking of justice and self-determination for oppressed peoples articulate Zárate's spirituality. Zárate is involved in international indigenous struggles for liberation, and she participated in the Zapatista struggle as a civil rights observer. Her revolutionary vision of the role of the Church in society has not faded despite the tremendous obstacles placed in her path by the institutional Church.

For members of Las Hermanas, what is vital to embracing a commitment to social responsibility is a deep faith in a transcendent presence desiring justice for *el pueblo*, the Latino community, and for women. It is this "sense of the divine" that illuminates the manner in which members of Las Hermanas respond to the challenges of life. As Ada María Isasi-Díaz pointed out, it is this "sense of the divine in their lives that gives them strength for the struggle—a struggle that is not part of life but life itself" (Isasi-Díaz and Tarango, *Hispanic Women: Prophetic Voice in the Church*, 103). And for Yolanda Tarango,

> The challenge is in transforming that struggle so that it has, not only a redeeming but an energizing effect. The transformation [of struggle] is critical for the liberation of Hispanic women for assuming control over one's life. *La Vida es la lucha*, implies the struggle we must embrace and learn to love in order to survive in the present and envision life with dignity in the future. ("La Vida Es la Lucha," *Informes*, 1990, 1)

Furthermore, faith in women's creativity, inherent power, and nurturing relationships witnessed over generations of women enables Las Hermanas to express a spirituality of transformation beyond the boundaries of the institutional Church.

This "transformative spirituality" finds expression most clearly at Las Hermanas' annual conferences, women-centered rituals, and in newsletters, public speeches, songs, and *mujerista* theological writings. These venues create the space to articulate issues integral to the daily lives of Latinas and to devise strategies for change and empowerment. These physical, artistic, and literary spaces stand in sharp contrast to the silence of the ecclesial hierarchy on matters of gender, race, class, and sexuality.

At the 1989 national conference in San Antonio, Texas, the issue of power and the need to redefine power held primary attention. Defining power as the ability to create, to act reflectively, rather than control or dominate, set the framework for the participants to examine their own concepts of power; how they use power in their daily lives; and what social forces, including religion, attempt to keep women powerless. Utilizing the women's own experiences as a starting point validated Latinas "who have never been taken seriously, [who have] not been taken into account" (*Informes*, 1989, 4). A portrayal of power emanating from within the individual, existing between companions in the struggle for liberation, and emerging from the desire to make a difference in one's life gave the women a deep sense of their own personal power. Conference participant Teresa Barajas describes the impact that redefining power had on her life:

For me and I believe for many of us, the conference opened up a wider perspective of the meaning of the word *poder*. I saw in many of us that the word awakened a fear because we have always associated it with oppression, violence, and absolute control that many of us have experienced since we were little. We learned that power is something very good in us if we know how to use it. We also saw that we often use our power without even knowing it. ("Reflexiones Desde San Antonio," *Informes*, 1989, 2)

Many of the women attending the conference shared stories of abusive power by priests, bosses, husbands, their children, and the government. But as Rosa Martha Zárate pointed out, "[T]hese women also shared experiences of resistance, of struggle, of contestation, of liberation. This was an assembly of hope!" ("Encuentro Nacional de Las Hermanas," *Informes*, 1989, 3). Discussing issues of power and the limitations of traditional gender roles imbued many of the women with the knowledge that they were not alone in the struggle for liberation. As María Inez Martínez remarked, " 'Together we have the ability to plan and act—therefore *we have power*' " ("Empowerment, Enablement, Hope," *Informes*, 1989, 1).

Las Hermanas convened their nineteenth and twentieth national conferences at Ft. Meyers, Florida, in 1993 and at McAllen, Texas, in 1995. Discussions around moral agency and sexuality held primary focus at both conferences. Information on domestic violence and sexual abuse targeted Latinas who are vulnerable to sexual violation. Professionals including psychologists, doctors, and social workers enabled the women to examine the different forms of violence present in their own lives. The safe environment created by and for the women empowered victims of violence to share their painful stories. Rituals, designed by members, provided healing. According to Ada María Isasi-Díaz, "[F]or over forty-five minutes the women named their hurts and asked for healing. They could say aloud what some of them had not dared to verbalize even to themselves. These women empowered each other, nudged each other into articulating their pain" (Isasi-Díaz, 196–197). Claiming space, claiming one's voice previously rendered silent, remains central to the Latina struggle for self-determination.

Despite a precarious financial situation, members express "sheer will" and "an unwillingness to let go" of the organization. The conferences held in New York City in 1997 and in Denver, Colorado, in 1999 reflected enthusiasm and a determination to continue. Board member Linda Chávez of New Mexico raised substantial funding from religious communities to sponsor the 1999 conference and the 2001 conference in El Paso, Texas. Deliberations at the 2001 conference resulted in a restructuring of the national leadership team. Revitalization now comes from the action and prayer emanating from regional Las Hermanas groups. A National Coordinating Team made up of one representative from each local group has replaced the existing three-member team. The level of action and the size of the new team depends on the vitality of local groups rather than on the effort of national leadership. Additional fund-raising has made the hiring of a part-time executive secretary possible for the year ahead. The biennial conferences continue to take place and provide the opportunity for all members to gather, to make policy decisions, "to share and celebrate being '*unidas en acción y oración*' " (*Informes*, 2002, 1). A revised Mission Statement and Goals declare:

Las Hermanas–USA is a network of women's groups united to empower themselves and others to participate actively in prophetic, loving transformation of Church and society through sharing riches of Hispanic culture, language, spirituality, and traditions.

Goals: To promote continual growth in self-respect, dignity, healing, and mutual support among Hispanic women.

To promote activities that educate and develop leadership and participatory skills directed toward justice, peace, and the integrity of creation. (*Informes*, 2002, 4)

Women, culture, empowerment, shared leadership, solidarity, education, justice, and spirituality remain as hallmarks of Las Hermanas for the twenty-first century.

The role that Las Hermanas takes in providing Chicanas and Latinas a space to raise critical issues regarding women in the Church *and* in society has not been mirrored by any other national organization of Latinas in the United States. Creating a space for education and critical dialogue among Latina Catholics remains one of its most significant contributions. Under an increasing conservative papacy and growing social disparity for Latino communities, the need for Las Hermanas as a critical voice of dissension remains high. The ongoing need for leadership development, political education, and moral authority among Latinas in the United States continues to present Las Hermanas with a clear agenda for the twenty-first century. The mixture of spirituality and political activism for which Las Hermanas is known is its distinctive contribution to the strategies utilized in ethnic/racial, gender, and class struggles. The decision to remain an autonomous organization with decentralized power provides the freedom to create a new form of being church for numerous Latinas needing more than what the "official" Church allows or offers. In the words of Yolanda Tarango, "All of our experiences with the official church and social institutions create the urgency to say, 'No, we have a difference perspective and we are going to give it a public voice'" (Interview, 1996). At the center of this perspective, at the center of the legacy of Las Hermanas, lies the critical, creative, and prophetic voices of Chicanas and Latinas. The struggle continues, and the transformation of injustices remains the ongoing challenge.

SOURCES: Las Hermanas papers and privately printed texts are archived in the Center for Mexican American Studies and Research, Our Lady of the Lake University, San Antonio, Texas, including Carmelita Espinoza and María de Jesús Ybarra, "La Historia de Las Hermanas." All interviews were conducted by the author and can be found in *Las Hermanas: Chicana/Latina Religious-Political Activism in the U.S. Catholic Church* (2004). The *Journal of Feminist Studies in Religion* 17.2 (Fall 2001) includes a significant article on the spirituality of Las Hermanas, also written by Medina, "Transformative Struggle: The Spirituality of Las Hermanas." Timothy M. Matovina provides a lengthy exploration of Las Hermanas and PADRES in his essay "Representation and the Reconstruction of Power: The Rise of *PADRES* and *Las Hermanas*," in *What's Left? Liberal American Catholics*, ed. Mary Jo Weaver (1999). Ada María Isasi-Díaz discusses *mujerista* rituals at Las Hermanas conferences in *Mujerista Theology* (1996). Ada María Díaz-Stevens includes Las Hermanas in her lengthy essay on Latina Catholics, "Latinas and the Church," in *Hispanic Catholic Culture in the U.S.: Issues and Concerns*, ed. Jay P. Dolan and Allan Figueroa Deck (1994). In this same text, Edmundo Rodríguez also discusses Las Hermanas in his essay "The Hispanic Community and Church Movements: Schools of Leadership." The reference works *Contemporary American Religion,* ed. Wade Clark Roof (1999), *Latinas in the United States: An Historical Encyclopedia*, ed. Virginia Sánchez Korrol and Vicki L. Ruiz (2003), and *In Our Own Voices: Four Centuries of American Women's Religious Writing*, ed. Rosemary Radford Ruether and Rosemary Skinner Keller (1995) also include entries on Las Hermanas. See also Vicki L. Ruiz, *From out of the Shadows: Mexican Women in Twentieth-Century America* (1998); and Ada María Isasi-Díaz and Yolanda Tarango, *Hispanic Women: Prophetic Voices in the Church* (1988).

MUJERISTA THEOLOGY
Ada María Isasi-Díaz

MUJERISTA THEOLOGY IS an enterprise that a group of Latinas—Cubans, Mexican Americans, Puerto Ricans, Dominicans—who live in the United States have been elaborating for the last twenty years. It is a theology that has as its source the lived experience of Latinas who are discriminated against by the dominant group and culture in the United States and who, for the most part, are poor. The goal of *mujerista* theology is the holistic liberation of these Latinas.

To name oneself is one of the most powerful acts a person can do. A name is not just a word by which one is identified, but it also provides the conceptual framework, the point of reference, the mental constructs that are used in thinking, understanding, and relating to a person, an idea, a movement. This is why a group of Latinas, keenly aware of how sexism, ethnic prejudice, and economic oppression subjugate Latinas, started to use the term *mujerista* to refer to themselves and to use *mujerista theology* to refer to the explanations of their faith and its role in their struggle for liberation. The need to have a name of their own, for inventing the term *mujerista* and investing it with a particular meaning, became more and more obvious over the years as Latinas attempted to participate in the feminist Euro-American theological enterprise and movement in the United States. Latinas became suspicious of this movement because of its inability to deal with differences, to share power equally among all those committed to it, to make it possible for Latinas to contribute to the core meanings and understandings of the movement, to pay attention to the intersection of racism/ethnic prejudice, classism, and sexism, and because of the seeming replacement of liberation as its goal with the attainment of limited benefits for some women within present structures, benefits that necessitate some groups of women and men to be oppressed in order for some others to flourish. These serious flaws in the Euro-American feminist movement have led grassroots Latinas to understand *feminism* as having to do with the rights of Euro-American middle-class women, rights many times attained at the expense of Latinas and other minority women. The need to find another word that would indicate the understandings about women's liberation of Latinas is what has led to use of the word *mujerista*, an invented word derived from the Spanish word for woman, *mujer. Mujerista*, therefore, is the word chosen to name devotion to Latinas' liberation.

A *mujerista* is someone who makes a preferential option for Latinas, for their struggle for liberation. *Mujeristas* struggle to liberate themselves not as separate individuals but as members of a Latina community. They work to build bridges among themselves while denouncing sectarianism and divisive tactics. *Mujeristas* understand that their task is to gather their people's hopes and expectations about justice and peace. Because Christianity is an intrinsic part of Latino culture, *mujeristas* believe that central to their struggle is the claim that Latinas are made in the image and likeness of God. Turning to theology specifically, *mujerista* theology, which includes both ethics and systematic theology, is a liberative praxis: reflective action that has as its goal liberation. As a liberation praxis, *mujerista* theology is a process that enables Latina women by insisting on the development of a strong sense of moral agency and clarifies the importance and value of who Latinas are, what they think, and what they do. Second, as a liberative praxis, *mujerista* theology seeks to impact mainline theologies that support what is normative in church and, to a large degree, in society—what is normative having been set by non-Latinas and often to the exclusion of Latinas.

Vital to *mujerista* theology is enabling Latinas to understand that the goal of liberation is not to participate in and to benefit from these structures but to change them radically. In theological and religious language this means that *mujerista* theology helps Latinas discover and affirm the presence of God in the midst of their communities and the revelation of God in their daily lives. It helps them to understand the reality of structural sin and find ways of combating it because such sin effectively hides God's ongoing revelation from them and from society at large.

This leads to *mujerista* theology's insistence on defining Latinas' preferred future: What would a radically different society look like? What will be its values and norms? In theological and religious language this means that *mujerista* theology enables Latinas to understand the centrality of eschatology—the realization of the vision of fullness of life embodied in the gospels—in the Christian life. Latinas' preferred future breaks into their present oppression in many different ways. Latinas recognize those eschatological glimpses, rejoice in them, and struggle to make them become their whole horizon.

Another task of *mujerista* theology is to enable Latinas to understand how they have already bought into the prevailing systems in society—including the religious systems—and thus have internalized their own oppression. *Mujerista* theology helps Latinas to see that radical structural change cannot happen unless radical change takes place in each and every one of them. In theological and religious language this means that *mujerista* theology assists Latinas in the process of conversion, helping them to see the reality of sin in their lives. Further, it enables them to understand that to resign themselves to what others tell them is their lot, and to accept suffering and self-effacement, is not a virtue.

The *locus theologicus*, the place from which Latinas do *mujerista* theology, is their *mestizaje* and *mulatez*: the condition of people from other cultures living within the United States, a reality applicable to Mexican Americans, Cubans, Puerto Ricans, Dominicans, and Latinas from many other countries of origin. *Mestizaje* refers to the mixture of white people and native people living in what are now Latin America and the Caribbean. *Mulatez* refers to the mixture of black people and white people.

Mujeristas' usage of these words goes beyond their original meaning to include the mixing of Latinas with those of others races—cultures who live in the United States, as well as the mixing among themselves, among Latinas coming from different countries of Latin America and the Caribbean. *Mestizaje* and *mulatez*, which refer both to the mixing of cultures and to the mixing of races, first of all proclaims a reality. Even before the new *mestizaje* and *mulatez* that is being created at present in the United States, Latinas come from *mestizo* and *mulato* cultures, from cultures where the white, red, and black races have intermingled, from cultures where Spanish, Amerindian, and African cultural elements have come together and new cultures have emerged. *Mestizaje* and *mulatez* are important to Latinas because they vindicate what the dominant culture with its pervading racism and ethnic prejudice condemns and degrades: Latinas' racial and cultural mixture. Finally, *mestizaje* and *mulatez* are Latinas' contribution to a new understanding of pluralism, a new way of valuing and embracing diversity and difference. This kind of pluralism is about distributing opportunities, resources, and benefits in an inclusive way. It is, first and foremost, about making sure that

> institutional and economic elites are subjected to effective controls by the constituencies whose welfare they affect, that neither the enjoyment of dominance nor the suffering of deprivation is the constant condition of any group, and that political and administrative officers operate as guardians of popular needs rather than as servants of wealthy interests. (Parenti, 28)

Theologically, *mestizaje* and *mulatez* are what "socially situates" Latinas in the United States. *Mestizaje* and *mulatez* as the theological *locus* of Latinas delineate the finite alternatives there are for thinking, conceiving, and expressing their theology. For example, because *mestizaje* and *mulatez* socially situate Latinas, *mujerista* theology cannot but understand all racism and ethnic prejudice as sin, and the embracing of diversity as virtue. This means that the coming of the kin-dom of God has to do with a coming together of peoples, with no one being excluded or at the expense of no one. Furthermore, *mestizaje* and *mulatez* mean that the unfolding of the kin-dom of God happens when instead of working to become part of structures of exclusion, Latinas struggle to do away with such structures. Precisely because of the way mainline society thinks about *mestizas* and *mulatas*, *mujerista* theology cannot but talk about the divine in nonelitist, in nonhierarchical ways.

Mestizaje and *mulatez* for Latinas and Latinos are not gives. In many ways they are something they choose repeatedly; they are something they have to embrace in order to preserve their cultures, in order to be faithful to their people, and from a theological-religious perspective, in order to remain faithful to the struggle for justice and peace. In choosing *mestizaje* and *mulatez* as their theological *locus, mujerista* theology claims that this is the structure in which Latinas operate, from which they reach out to explain who they are and to contribute to what is normative in theology and religion in the society in which they live. *Mestizaje* and *mulatez* and the contributions they make to society's understanding of pluralism, therefore, are building blocks of *mujerista* theology.

From the very beginning *mujerista* theology has insisted that its source is the lived experience of Latinas. *Mujerista* theology has insisted on the capacity of Latinas to reflect on their everyday lives and their struggle to survive against very difficult obstacles. When *mujerista* theology refers to liberative daily experience, to Latinas' everyday struggles, it is referring to *lo cotidiano. Lo cotidiano* has to do with

> particular forms of speech, the experience of class and gender distinctions, the impact of work and poverty on routines and expectations, relations within families and among friends and neighbors in a community, the experience of authority, and central expressions of faith such as prayer, religious celebrations, and conceptions of key religious figures. (Levine, 317)

These key religious figures are not only those of Christianity, Jesus and Mary his mother, but also those more exclusively Catholic like the saints, those of popular religion, such as the orishas of African religions, and the deities of Amerindian religions.

However, in *mujerista* theology, *lo cotidiano* is more than a descriptive category. *Lo cotidiano* also includes the way Latinas consider actions, discourse, norms, established social roles, and their own selves. Recognizing that it is inscribed with subjectivity, that one looks at and understands what happens from a given perspective, *lo cotidiano* has hermeneutical importance; that is, it provides the lens through which Latinas look at reality. This means that *lo cotidiano* has to do with the daily lived experiences that provide the "stuff" of their reality.

Mujerista theology uses *lo cotidiano* neither as a metaphysical category that has to do with reality beyond the historical context nor as an attempt to see Latinas' daily lived experience as fixed and universal. Rather, it is a way of referring to the "stuff" and the processes of Latinas' lives. *Lo cotidiano* is not a category into which one fits the daily lived experience of Latinas. *Lo cotidiano* of Latinas is a matter of who they are, of who they become; and, therefore, it is far from being something objective,

something they observe, relate to, and talk about in a disinterested way. Finding ways to earn money to feed and clothe their children and to keep a roof over their heads is part of *lo cotidiano* for Latinas. Finding ways to survive corporal abuse is part of *lo cotidiano*. Finding ways to struggle effectively against oppression is part of *lo cotidiano*.

Besides its descriptive and hermeneutical task, *mujerista* theology appropriates *lo cotidiano* as the epistemological framework of its theological enterprise; that is, *lo cotidiano*, the daily experience of Latinas, not only points to their capacity to know but also highlights the features of their knowing. *Lo cotidiano* is a way of referring to Latinas' efforts to understand and express how and why their lives are the way they are, how and why they function as they do. Of course, there are other ways of coming to know what is real; there are many forms and types of knowledge. The emphasis on *lo cotidiano* as an epistemological category, as a way of knowing, has to do, in part, with the need to rescue Latinas' daily experience from the category of the unimportant. *Lo cotidiano* has been belittled and scorned precisely because it is often related to the private sphere, to that sphere of life assigned to women precisely because it is considered unimportant.

The valuing of *lo cotidiano* means that *mujerista* theology appreciates the fact that Latinas see reality in a different way from the way it is seen by non-Latinas. It means also that it privileges Latinas' way of seeing reality insofar as the goal of their daily struggle is liberation. This is very important, for although *lo cotidiano* carries so much weight, it is not the criterion used for judging right and wrong, good and bad. It is only insofar as *lo cotidiano* is a liberative praxis, a daily living that contributes to liberation, that *lo cotidiano* is considered good, valuable, right, redemptive. To claim *lo cotidiano* as an ethical/theological criterion, norm, or principle would be to romanticize *lo cotidiano*. There is much that is good and life giving in *lo cotidiano*, but there also is much that "obstructs understanding and tenderness, allowing to appear an abundance of postures of self-defense that are full of falsehoods, of lies, that turn *lo cotidiano* into a behavior that is not open to life" (Gebara, 24). As a category of knowing, *lo cotidiano* goes well beyond adding another perspective and points to the need to change the social order by taking into consideration the way Latinas see and understand reality. *Lo cotidiano* points to the fact that how Latinas, women who struggle from the underside of history, constitute themselves and their world is an ongoing process. *Lo cotidiano* takes into consideration many different elements that are used to define Latinas within the United States at the beginning of the twenty-first century.

In *mujerista* theology, *lo cotidiano* has made it possible to appeal to the daily lived experience of Latinas as an authentic source without ignoring social location. On the contrary, *lo cotidiano* makes social location explicit, for it is the context of the person in relation to physical space, ethnic space, and social space. *Lo cotidiano* constitutes the arena where their own communities confront Latinas. This makes it possible for them to judge their own personal understandings, aspirations, ambitions, projects, and goals in their lives. Therefore, *lo cotidiano* is where morality begins to play a role for Latinas. *Lo cotidiano* becomes the lived text in which and through which Latinas understand and decide what is right and good, what is wrong and evil. As such, *lo cotidiano* is not a private, individual category but rather a social category. *Lo cotidiano* refers to the way Latinas know and what they know to be. *Lo cotidiano* is literally the cloth out of which their lives as a struggling community within the United States is fabricated.

Using *lo cotidiano* is for Latinas a way of understanding, explaining, and articulating what they know about the divine. This is in contrast this to the academic and churchly attempts to see theology as being about God instead of about what humans know about God. *Lo cotidiano* makes it possible for Latinas to see their theological knowledge as well as all their knowledge as fragmentary, partisan, conjectural, and provisional (Maduro, 136). It is fragmentary because what they will know tomorrow will not be the same as what they know today, though it will stand in relation to today's knowledge. What they know is what they have found through their experiences, through the experiences of their communities of struggle. What they know is always partisan; it is always influenced by their own values, prejudices, loyalties, emotions, traditions, dreams, and future projects. Their knowledge is conjectural because to know is not to copy or reflect reality but rather to interpret in a creative way those relations, structures, and processes that are elements of what is called reality. And finally, *lo cotidiano* makes it clear that, for *mujerista* theology, knowledge is provisional, for it indicates in and of itself how transitory the world of Latinas and they themselves are.

Using *lo cotidiano* of Latinas as the source of *mujerista* theology is an act of subversion. *Mujerista* theology challenges the absolutizing of mainline theology as normative, as exhaustively explaining the gospels or Christian beliefs. Using *lo cotidiano* as the source of *mujerista* theology means that Latinas are not the object of this theology. Instead, Latinas are the subjects, the agents of *mujerista* theology.

Being a liberative praxis, *mujerista* theology seeks to be effective; it seeks to contribute to eliminating injustice. This means that the understanding of justice that *mujerista* theology proposes is precise enough to force

an option. Following are some elements of justice that embrace and reveal Latinas' expectations regarding a just world order.

The first element of a *mujerista* account of justice has to do with its goal: establishing justice rather than building a systematic theory. The liberative praxis of Latinas to establish justice starts by claiming an intrinsic union between practice and reflection. Praxis is not to be understood as action apart from reflection but rather refers to reflective action. However, a *mujerista* account of justice does not avoid rational thinking. Latinas' liberative praxis is not a doing without a thinking. The thinking and reflecting, the analysis and arguments that are part of Latinas' liberative praxis, clarify the meaning of ideas and issues, describe the relations among Latinas and between Latinas and society at large, and make clear Latinas' ideals and principles. Because the aim of a *mujerista* account of justice is not correct articulation (thought it does not exclude it) but effective justice-seeking praxis, a *mujerista* account of justice is a process that reflects the ever-changing reality of Latinas.

The second element of a *mujerista* account of justice refers to its concreteness: Because justice has to be concrete, it has to be historical. This is why a *mujerista* account of justice begins with injustice: That is the reality of the vast majority of Latinas' lives today. A *mujerista* account of justice does not depend on philosophical reasoning but on the stories of oppression Latinas tell. The role these stories play in elaborating a *mujerista* account of justice builds on and supports the contention that justice must be constructed from within the struggle for justice, from the perspective of injustice. This means that good social, political, and economic descriptions and analyses of Latinas' reality are needed, always keeping in mind that the descriptions and explanations have to be critical; they have to evaluate and point to liberation.

The third element of a *mujerista* account of justice is the other side of the previous one: A *mujerista* account of justice points to a discontinuity—some discontinuity, not total discontinuity—with the past and present reality. This means that justice does not depend exclusively on possibilities known in the past. This discontinuity is based on the role that the realization of the kin-dom of God plays in Latinas' *proyecto histórico*—historical project. In *mujerista* theology, history is one; there are not two histories, a secular one and a sacred one. The history of salvation—the realization of the kin-dom of God—does not happen apart from the daily struggles of Latinas to survive. "Without liberating historical events, there would be no growth of the Kingdom [*sic*]. But the process of liberation will not have conquered the very roots of human oppression and exploitation without the coming of the Kingdom, which is above all a gift" (Gutiérrez, 104). This claim to a discontinuity between what is and what justice will be is also based on the epistemological privilege of the poor and the oppressed that *mujerista* theology claims for Latinas as oppressed people.

The fourth element of a *mujerista* account of justice has to do with recognizing and dealing with differences rather than just acknowledging the "problem" of differences. To recognize and deal with differences, to embrace differences, is to reject assimilation, to reject an essentialist meaning of difference that places groups and persons in categorical opposition, in mutual exclusion. To embrace differences means to insist that what is specific about Latinas is a relational matter rather constituting categorical attributes. Furthermore, justice has to move beyond acceptance that there are different ways of being to real interaction. Interaction between those who are different is not possible unless one recognizes how cultural imperialism, racism, and ethnic prejudice function, how those who do not belong to the dominant group are conceptualized as other, as inferior and deviant. Interaction among Latinas and non-Latinas must lead to participation and inclusion in a way that does not require Latinas to renounce who they are. Interaction leads to opportunities for Latinas to make their own contribution to what is normative in society, to be protagonists in society.

The fifth element of a *mujerista* account of justice has to do with power. A *mujerista* understanding of power, like its account of justice, starts from the underside of history, from those who are powerless. Power, therefore, has to be understood both as a personal and as a structural process that can be used for oppression or liberation. Oppressive power uses force, coercion, and/or influence to control, to limit, the self-determination and decision making of individual persons or groups of persons. Liberative power uses power to transform oppressive situations, situations of domination. In a liberative use of power, there is still a person with power and a person without it. However, the focus is on the person without power; the focus is on empowering her to take power, to become self-defining and self-actualizing.

The sixth element of a *mujerista* account of justice is the insistence at all times that Latinas' rights are both socioeconomic—having to do with redistribution of goods—as well as civic—political rights. Justice has to do with the right one has to food, to adequate housing, to health care, to access to the fertility of the earth, to the productivity of industrialized society, and to the benefits provided by social security. *Mujerista* theology's understanding of justice also has to do with freedom of religion, expression, assembly, and due process of the law, participation in the creation of social and political structures, and participation in the leadership and government of such structures.

This proposal regarding rights is quite different from the classical, liberal agenda of justice if the following points are taken into account. First, what is proposed here is not the goal but a place to start the *mujerista* considerations regarding rights. Second, this insistence on socioeconomic and civic-political rights might not seem very radical by itself, but in *mujerista* theology this is just one element of a much broader proposal regarding justice. Third, this call for recognition and granting of rights to Latinas is coupled in this account with a radically different understanding about differences than the prevalent one of equality. This means that claiming these rights is done not so Latinas can become just like the rest of society but rather so Latinas and their communities can be intrinsic elements of the U.S. society without losing their specificity. For that to happen a radical change as to how this society understands itself has to take place. Finally, in emphasizing both socioeconomic as well as civic-political rights, this *mujerista* account of justice makes it clear that considerations of social justice, what are considered by some to be macroissues, cannot be articulated apart from personal justice, usually classified as microissues and considered by many as unimportant.

The seventh element of a *mujerista* account of justice is solidarity. Solidarity has to do with understanding the interconnection that exists between oppression and privilege, between the rich and the poor, the oppressed and the oppressors. It also refers to the cohesiveness that needs to exist among communities of struggle. Solidarity is the union of kindred persons who recognize their common responsibilities and interests. Solidarity moves away from the false notions of disinterest, of doing for others in an altruistic fashion. Instead, grounded in common responsibilities and interests, shared feelings are aroused that lead to joint action.

The starting point of solidarity is not a generalized conception of oppression that easily becomes an abstraction. The starting point is the oppression of specific people, oppression caused or maintained, directly or indirectly, by the privileges of the oppressors. Solidarity is a worldview, a theory, about the commonality of interests that links humanity. Solidarity is also a strategy to bring about recognition of common interests, recognition that cannot be obtained without true dialogue born of a deep sense of mutuality. Mutuality between the oppressor who embraces conversion and the oppressed struggling to be liberated—that is solidarity.

The eighth and final element of justice, reconciliation, follows on the heels of solidarity and is linked to the understanding of how to deal with the differences embodied in *mestizaje* and *mulatez*. Reconciliation has to do with healing the rifts that separate oppressor and oppressed; it is a key process in the struggle to create communities of solidarity committed to building a future together.

Reconciliation sees moral responsibility focusing on responding to others and establishing and maintaining mutuality. This redefines the concepts of autonomy, self-reliance, and self-definition. The work of reconciliation focuses on responsibility as

> participation in a communal work, laying the groundwork for the creative response of people in the present and the future. Responsible action means changing what can be altered in the present even though a problem is not completely resolved. Responsible action focuses on and respects partial resolutions and the inspiration and conditions for further partial resolutions . . . [by themselves] and by others. (Welch, 68)

The work of reconciliation has to recognize that those who have been apart and opposed to each other need to move together, one step at a time, willing to accept that risk, ambiguity, and uncertainty are part of the process. The work of reconciliation asks above all for a commitment to mutuality, to opening possibilities together even if one might never see them become a reality—this over and above a desire for tangible changes. Reconciliation is not a matter of making known preconceived answers to a given situation. Instead, the work of reconciliation projects itself into the future, opening up and concentrating on possibilities. Reconciliation understands that there is a plurality of truths, and this plurality is precisely what is at the heart of possibilities; that is what makes choices possible, what roots human freedom.

Reconciliation is a moral choice. Good intentions are not enough, and moral actions require the risk of taking steps together, of being accountable to each other, of participating in a process that concentrates on the future precisely by working to alter the present. Reconciliation as moral action makes it clear that healing the rifts that divide people cannot be incidental to the work of justice; it is essential to being a responsible person, a person fully alive.

The elaboration of *mujerista* theology has just begun. Its success will depend on the contribution it makes to the struggles for the liberation of the Latinas who live in the United States and to women's struggles everywhere. The success of *mujerista* theology has to do with its contributions to the struggle for survival, self-definition, and self-determination of Latinas and of all women.

SOURCES: Yvone Gebara, *Conhece-te a ti misma* (1991). Gustavo Gutiérrez, *A Theology of Liberation*, 2nd ed. (1988). David Hollenbach, *Justice, Peace and Human Rights* (1990). Ada María Isasi-Díaz, *En la Lucha—In the Struggle* (2003). Ada María Isasi-Díaz and Yolanda Tarango, *Hispanic Women: Prophetic Voice in the Church* (1993). Karen Lebacqz, *Justice in an Unjust World* (1987). Daniel H. Levine, *Popular Voices in Latin American Catholicism* (1992). Maria Lugones, "On the Logic of Pluralist Feminism," in *Feminist Ethics*, ed. Claudia Card (1991). Otto Maduro, *Mapas para la Fiesta* (1992). Cecilia Mino G., "Algunas reflexiones sobre pedagogía de género y cotidianidad," *Tejiendo Nuestra Red* 1.1 (October 1988). Michael Parenti, *Power and the Powerless* (1978). Thomas Wartenberg, *The Forms of Power* (1990). Sharon Welch, *A Feminist Ethics of Risk* (1990).

LATINA ROMAN CATHOLIC THEOLOGIES
Nancy Pineda-Madrid

THE CATEGORY "LATINA Roman Catholic theologies" represents a loosely gathered body of theological writings rather than a particular, self-designated theological movement. It is intended to be an umbrella category for the entire body of Latina Roman Catholic theologians' writings. All these thinkers take as their point of departure the Latina/o experience, although each thinker approaches and interprets that experience differently. Still in nascent form, Latina Roman Catholic theologies do not necessarily fit easily into clear subgroups. Even so, within this broader category, two distinguishable theological commitments have begun to emerge. First, a number of Latina theologians self-identify as "feminist"; hence their assertion that gender, as well as culture and ethnicity, must constitute a primary category in the development of theology. A second group identifies their work as primarily "pastoral." This group endeavors to interpret contemporary Latina/o experience through the lens of history in order to respond more effectively to the immediate concerns of the Latina/o community.

Before discussing the distinctions between the two groups, it is necessary to clarify the meaning of certain terms. For example, a number of different terms are used to designate Latin American ancestry. The majority of theologians represented in this essay prefer the term *Latina* because it highlights the communities' Latin American roots. It recognizes the Spanish, Amerindian, African, and Portuguese origins of contemporary Latina/o communities, and it is a self-selected term. Other terms frequently used are *Hispanic*, *Chicana*, *mestiza*, and *mulata*. Many Latina/o theologians have rejected the term *Hispanic* because the U.S. government designated this term for Spanish-speaking and Spanish surnamed people and intended by its use to elevate the Spanish ancestral roots and to dismiss the Amerindian and African roots. *Hispanic* is not a self-selected identifier. *Chi-*

cana designates not only a woman born in the United States of Mexican or Mexican American heritage but also a woman who critically assumes a class/race/gender political consciousness as framing the way she views the world. *Mestiza* means a woman whose identity emerges from the biological, cultural, and religious mixing of the Spanish and the Amerindian; and *mulata* from the mixing of the Spanish and the African. Neither term is inclusive of all women of Latin American heritage.

As Roman Catholic theologians, these Latinas relate their knowledge of the Latina/o experience to their knowledge of scripture, the history of theology, and church teachings. Out of this dynamic process, these theologians strive to develop an interpretation of the faith for this particular moment in history.

For Latina theologians who identify as Christian "feminists," their theologies emerge out of the recognition of the disparity between the Christian ideal of cherishing the full humanity of women as well as men and the omnipresent subordination of women to men. The domination of men over women is sinful, and patriarchy is a sinful social system. Far from reflecting the true will of God and the nature of women, such theological constructions subvert God's creation and distort human nature. Feminist theology is about the deconstruction of these ideological justifications of male domination and the vindication of women's equality as the true will of God, human nature, and Christ's redemptive intention (Ruether, 8).

Thus, Latina "feminist" theologians share with white feminist theologians a rejection of the patriarchal social system. But for Latinas the distortion of human nature concerns not only gender but also race and class. Race and class function as preeminent organizing principles within society, which means that a Latina becomes a woman not only in contrast to men but also in contrast to women of other classes and races. With Latino theologians, Latina "feminist" theologians share a critique of the subordination of Latinas/os to whites and the subordination of economically poor people to those of the middle and upper economic strata.

The term *feminist* appears in quotes throughout this essay to signify that it remains a contested term among Latina Roman Catholic theologians. For example, there are Latina theologians who point out that feminism has been a vital concept in multiple Latin American women's movements for more than a century. Thus, since the term *feminist* bears significant historical weight within the context of Latin America and among U.S. Latinas, they argue that the term must not be viewed as a concept transplanted from white, First World feminist and women's movements. Therefore, to name this body of writing "Latina feminist theology" is entirely tenable. The majority of Latina theologians with a feminist commitment subscribe to this view. Yet there are other La-tina theologians for whom the term *feminist* invariably means that sexism plays *the* primary role in every woman's experience of oppression and invariably is defined by its association with white, middle- and upper-class women of the First World. This association, these Latinas claim, renders racism and classism secondary. Hence, these Latinas distrust the term and name their experience of oppression using terms that for them signify the interrelated character of race/class/gender oppression. *Mujerista* (in support of women) theology exemplifies this position. Still other Latina theologians believe that *feminism*, as it is interpreted by much of feminist theology, focuses too narrowly on women and women's concerns. Among these Latinas, some claim that their work focuses not only on women but also on men and the community as a whole. In other words, because they interpret *feminism* to be a narrow issue, an explicitly "feminist" theology does not bear priority for them. Many of the Latina pastoral theologians manifest this viewpoint. However, the perception that *feminist* is narrowly interpreted moves yet other Latina theologians to a different position. These Latinas distance themselves from *feminism* the term but not the idea. Because they are deeply conscious of, and strongly renounce, the subordination of women, these Latinas strive to create a critical gender consciousness through their publications. The term *feminism* may sparingly, if ever, appear in their publications, but they consistently attend to the ways that gender influences all forms of thought. This position characterizes the publications of a couple of Latina "feminist" theologians.

Mujerista theology, originated in the mid-1980s by Cuban-born Ada María Isasi-Díaz, is one notable and well-developed example of a self-named Latina Roman Catholic feminist theology. *Mujerista* theology distinguishes itself from the theologies discussed in this essay through its use of ethnography, a method that is based on the reflective knowing processes of Latinas. Unlike *mujerista* theology, the Latina feminist theologies discussed in this essay draw on other social science disciplines, the literary arts, and philosophy.

For Latinas whose theology may be described as pastoral, their driving concern is how the faith is witnessed to and communicated to Latinas/os at this moment in history. Hence they discuss, among other ministerial foci, questions of religious education, spiritual growth, liturgical practice, and the practice of the Church. While these Latina theologies do express interest in how faith has been expressed throughout history (historical theology) and do express interest in how the coherency and significance of revelation are interrelated (systematic theology), their overriding concern remains how to respond to the pastoral needs of individual Latinas/os and their communities.

Sociohistorical Origins

Latina Roman Catholic theologies must be understood as an outgrowth and expression of the long history of a particular Latinas' consciousness. That consciousness or critical recognition arises from the lived experience of gender, culture, race, and class inequities, coupled with the lived experience of enduring faith. Short of this understanding, Latina Roman Catholic theologies can be too easily misinterpreted as emergent exclusively in reaction to the white women's movement, thought, and theology, and in reaction to Latin American liberation theology. While these have undeniably made their contributions, Latinas' own particular history of struggle has played as prominent a role in the development of these theologies. At times throughout the course of history, Latinas have spoken out against the socially restricted role of women, and Latinas have confronted and resisted the forces that have attempted to render their humanity somehow lesser. Latina Roman Catholic theologies represent an attempt to interpret this history of Latina critical recognition and struggle. A few examples from history will illustrate this sojourn.

In the period before the arrival of the Spanish into what is now Mexico, the Nahuas (often called Aztecs) elevated and glorified the myth of Coyolxauhqui, which may have been intended to teach a lesson to all Nahua women and men who resisted the dictates of Nahua patriarchal social norms. Coyolxauhqui is the daughter of Coatlicue and sister to 400 (male) gods of the South, including Huitzilopochtli, the God of War. Upon learning of their mother's pregnancy with Huitzilopochtli, Coyolxauhqui and her 400 brothers decide that Coatlicue's pregnancy has dishonored them. Huitzilopochtli represents a patriarchal worldview where periodic ritual violence is sacred. Coyolxauhqui incites her brothers and leads them in a plot to kill their mother. But, while still in the womb, Huitzilopochtli learns of the plot. At the moment of the attack, Coatlicue gives birth to Huitzilopochtli, a full-grown warrior, dressed for battle and enraged at his sister. Huitzilopochtli takes a serpent made of fire; he strikes Coyolxauhqui, cutting off her head. Her decapitated body rolls down the hill, and in the process her limbs break off. Her arms and hands fell in one place, her legs in another, and her body in yet another. After decapitating and dismembering his sister, Huitzilopochtli proceeds to ravenously pursue and annihilate every one of his 400 brothers. For the Nahuas the city of Tenochtitlan was the center of the world, and the Templo Mayor served as the religious center. Here, the Nahuas dramatized the myth of Huitzilopochtli and Coyolxauhqui. At the top of one of the two huge pyramids that comprised the Templo Mayor sat an exalted image and temple honoring Huitzilopochtli, and at the base of this pyramid's long majestic stairway rested a twenty-two-ton circular stone image of the dismembered Coyolxauhqui, certainly an ominous warning. While we do not have explicit accounts of Nahua women who confronted Nahua social norms, it can be surmised that at least some Nahua women did so and thereby posed a serious threat. For if not, why would the Nahua patriarchal power structure so dramatically elevate this myth above all others and regularly reenact this story through ritual? Presumably some force was deemed threatening enough that it warranted this brutally violent response, and undeniably that threatening force was imaged as female, as Coyolxauhqui.

In the centuries after the conquest, the Spanish viceroys and their officials supplanted the Nahua worldview with a Spanish one. In the midst of this violent transition the life and work of Sor Juana Inés de la Cruz (1648–1695) serves as example of an extraordinary woman who was painfully aware of how the traditional expectations for a woman (marriage and family) rendered other possibilities all but impossible. Sor Juana made the difficult choice not to follow tradition. Fulfilling traditional expectations would have severely limited her time for reflection and intellectual pursuits. The writings of this Mexican intellectual genius reveal an amazing command of the most important works in the fields of literature, science, philosophy, and theology, among others. She entered a convent of the religious order of St. Jerome (the Hieronymites) seeking, in the Virginia Woolfian sense, "a room of her own." Even though male scholars of her day could not help but acknowledge her brilliant, creative mind, eventually Church authorities judged Sor Juana's brilliance repugnant for a woman. She resisted, claiming in her famous *Respuesta a Sor Filotea de la Cruz* that to suppress her intellectual work would be to defy God, who gave her intelligence for a purpose. In this same *Respuesta*, Sor Juana cogently argued for the rights of all women to do scholarly work.

For many Latinas/os the U.S. American experience begins in 1848, the year that Mexico and the United States signed the Treaty of Guadalupe Hidalgo. This treaty ended the Mexican-American War and resulted in Mexico ceding to the United States what are today the states of California, New Mexico, Nevada, and parts of Colorado, Arizona, and Utah. Mexico also acknowledged the southern border of Texas as the Rio Grande. All the Latinas/os living in these lands automatically became citizens of the United States by the terms of the treaty. As such, however, their status and standing in fact were diminished. The treaty was one manifestation of a particular worldview, which became pervasive throughout the nineteenth century and following, namely, the political doctrine of Manifest Destiny. This doctrine "justified" the racist system of belief that those of the white race were inherently superior human beings chosen and destined by God to dominate and control all land from the Atlantic ocean to the Pacific. Accordingly, only white males deserved rights before the law (e.g., land rights, language rights). This provoked a stinging awareness of the social restrictions faced not only by women but also by Latinas/os.

For several decades after 1848, few Latinas living within the United States had an opportunity to learn to read or write, and for the more fortunate, "education" focused primarily on enhancing domestic skills. Thus, the great majority of young Latinas ended up assisting their mothers in earning a living for their families through various domestic jobs. From a study of the oral histories of Latinas living in California and the Southwest, one can discern a scant but unmistakable critical recognition of the social limitation placed on women. For example, in her 1878 memoirs, California resident Doña María Inocencia Pico criticizes the operative social norm for marriage. Whenever very young girls were sought for matrimony, they were customarily married off. Also, María Cristina Mena, born in Mexico in 1893, wrote short stories that included female characters who resisted their socially subordinate position and through whom Mena revealed the absurdity of reducing women to objects of beauty.

In the early decades of the twentieth century, New Mexico writers like Nina Otero-Warren (1881–1965), Cleofas Jaramillo (1878–1956), and Fabiola Cabeza de Baca (1884–1991) each chronicled the staggering loss of culture, language, land, and livelihood that resulted from the Treaty of Guadalupe Hidalgo (1848). Their work reflects a cultural and ethnic critical recognition, specifically, a painful awareness of the physical and institutionalized violence against the Spanish, the Mexican, and the Indio precipitated by zealous Anglo-Americans determined to profit from the racist socioeconomic systems concerned only with the advancement of whiteness.

In her effort to resist this racist, sexist system, Nina Otero-Warren became active in public life and worked tirelessly on behalf of women. Otero-Warren played an instrumental role in ensuring that the women of New Mexico secured the right to vote in 1920. And in 1922 she called into question New Mexico's strictly male, largely white political establishment by running for Congress.

The 1960s was another period during which Latina critical recognition intensified. This period saw a wave of social protest movements, among them the Chicano/a movement, or El Movimiento. El Movimiento, triggered by a 1968 high school student strike in Los Angeles, fueled a new wave of critical awareness relative to race, gender, and class, thereby providing the seeds of contemporary Chicana and Latina thought. Within El Movimiento, however, a division among the Chicana leaders emerged. For some Chicanas, if the movement was to be true to the vision of the liberation of la raza (the Chicano people), it also needed to be utterly committed to the liberation of Chicanas as women. Another group of Chicanas, dubbed "loyalists," opposed this commitment.

Many loyalists felt that these complaints from women ("feminists") were potentially destructive and could only divide the Chicano movement. If sexual inequities existed, they were an "in-house" problem that could be dealt with later. However, right then and there, there were more important priorities to attend to, for example, Vietnam, La Huelga (the farmworkers strike), police brutality (García, 89). Liberation for the "loyalists" meant liberation of la raza as defined by the male leadership of El Movimiento.

Many practicing Roman Catholic Chicanas and Latinas supportive of El Movimiento confronted yet another layer of conflicts. During the late 1960s, the institutional Roman Catholic Church positioned itself as opposed to all El Movimiento represented. Latina/o sisters, priests, and other Church leaders were typically and explicitly instructed by Anglo church leadership not to celebrate Mass or offer any ministry in Spanish. Yet El Movimiento stirred the pride and ethnic consciousness around being Mexican American and around being Latina/o by directly challenging the overt racism not only of society at large but also that within the institutional Church. Latinas, particularly women religious, found themselves caught in the middle. Would they remain within the Church, challenging its blatant racist practices, or would they leave? In 1971 some fifty women religious gathered and formed Las Hermanas, whose mission was to promote effective ministry among Latinas/os. From its inception the projects of Las Hermanas focused on the injustices experienced by Latinas, particularly at the hands of the Church. A few years passed before Latinas began writing theology.

At the end of the 1970s and the beginning of the 1980s, Latina Roman Catholic theologians Marina Herrera, Ada María Isasi-Díaz, and María Pilar Aquino published their first articles. These Latina theologians began publishing roughly a decade after their male colleague who had long been recognized as the originator of U.S. Latino theology, namely, Virgilio Elizondo. With the desire to support and foster theological, intellectual expertise, a group of Latina/o theologians came together in January 1988 to discuss the formation of a new theological academy—the Academy of Catholic Hispanic Theologians of the United States (ACHTUS). Of the eight founding members, one was a woman, María Pilar Aquino. Soon after, many other Latinas joined: Marina Herrera, Ada María Isasi-Díaz, Ana María Pineda, Jeanette Rodríguez, Gloria Inés Loya, Carmen Cervantes, and Zoila Díaz.

Mexican and Mexican American history forms the core of the historical snapshots included herein. Obviously missing are the histories of U.S. Puerto Rican and Cuban Latinas and U.S. Latinas from other Latin American countries. Research into these histories is still in embryonic form.

All Latina Roman Catholic theologies grow out of some understanding of Latina/o consciousness. Some Latina theologians place greater emphasis on gender, others on culture, and still others attempt to interrelate gender, race, and class. Some are concerned with developing a coherent interpretation that addresses several theological questions; others are concerned with theological responses to the immediate needs of the community. An examination of the field surfaces these differences.

"Feminist"/Gender-Conscious Theologies

These Latina theologies each reflect a strong liberationist orientation revealing the imprint of Latin American liberation theologies, feminist theologies, and U.S. Latino theologies. Yet each also offers a significant critique of these contributing theological movements. First, Latin American liberation theologies and U.S. Latino theologies remain largely androcentric, resisting a recognition of the way gender influences all thought. Second, Latin American liberation theologies and feminist theologies for the most part do not seriously engage the significance of race and ethnicity. Finally, for distinct reasons, each of these contributing theologies tends to ignore the connections between sexism and classism, more specifically, the benefits enjoyed by First World women at the expense of Third World women. The impulse for Latina feminist and gender-conscious theologies comes from a desire to honor the singular contributions of the Latina faith experience that none of these contributing theological movements amply represent.

María Pilar Aquino, born in the state of Nayarit in Mexico, has been publishing, teaching, and lecturing not only in the United States but also throughout Latin America and western Europe since 1980. Her work is more widely known than that of any other U.S. Latina/o theologian with the possible exception of Virgilio Elizondo. Aquino distinguishes her publications through her extensive use of Latin American feminist theologians and theorists and her growing attention to the connections between Latin American feminist theology and U.S. Latina feminist theology. Aquino has a long history of active participation in the Ecumenical Association of Third World Theologians (EATWOT).

For Aquino, theology fulfills its primary purpose when it contributes to the liberation of oppressed peoples. Therefore, theology must be judged by how well it furthers the work of women and men who search for ever new and increasingly mutual, increasingly human "ways of living together." However, Aquino interprets this purpose as stretching beyond the challenge of human relations. Theology, because it must serve to further the transformation of all unjust realities, must include the whole nature world within its purpose. Aquino claims that the point of departure for theology must be human experience:

> Theology . . . refers to an experience of living rather than to a speculative exposition of abstract truths. It starts from experience and reflects on God's self-communication in the history of the world. The understanding of faith is a never-ending effort to reach the ultimate meaning of life, history and the fate of the world and humanity. (Aquino, 49)

Actual human experience as the point of departure has enormous implications for Latinas both in the United States and throughout Latin America, whose daily experience tends to be an experience of immense suffering and, until recently, an experience of invisibility. The near absence of women's experience in Latin American liberation theology and U.S. Hispanic theologies is a glaring omission. If, as has happened in these theologies, women's voices are collapsed into the voice or the experience of the community as a whole, then women's liberation becomes overlooked and subsumed, hence negated. But Aquino interprets this historical moment as the moment of the irruption of the poor, particularly women, onto the stage of history. The poor are no longer objects of concern but are subjects and agents who shape their own history.

Aquino draws on the work of feminist theologians Rosemary Radford Ruether and Elisabeth Schüssler Fiorenza and synthesizes their insights with those of Latin American theologians Gustavo Gutierrez, Leonardo Boff, Ignacio Ellacuria, and Jon Sobrino. The effective blending of these sources develops through Aquino's extensive use of Latin American and Third World feminist theologians and theorists as her prime interlocutors: Elsa Tamez, María Clara Bingemer, Ivone Gebara, Virginia Fabella, Tereza Cavalcanti, Nelly Ritchie, Carmen Lora, and Ana María Tepedino.

Throughout her work, Aquino not only identifies and examines Latinas' particular ways of knowing but also makes clear the resulting contribution to Latina feminist theology. When women's "vision and speech" stretch the otherwise more narrow outlook of liberation theology, Latinas inevitably not only criticize this theology's androcentric predisposition but also offer a corrective by transfiguring the meaning and force of liberation. Thus, the inclusion of Latinas' "vision and speech" must not be interpreted as exclusively a matter of language. Fundamentally, the inclusion of Latinas' "vision and speech" concerns the expansion of "liberation theology's *epistemological horizon*" (Aquino, 109). How we come to know, and what can be known, changes.

A second significant theme in Aquino's writings is the sacramental character of theology. Theology must conceive human reality (and all reality) as a single bodily and spiritual whole, which as a whole bears the capacity for revealing the Divine. Aquino uses this holistic conception of reality to argue that Latin American feminist theology must honor the human affect, desire, embodiment, and creativity. With this claim, she challenges the affect-intellect split so prevalent in much of modern theological discourse.

Finally, throughout her writings, Aquino builds a case for the reinterpretation of traditional themes of systematic theology informed by the experience of Latinas. This experience refashions how we think about God as triune, about our gendered humanity, about Jesus Christ, about Mary, and other traditional themes. The norm guiding such a reinterpretation is the claim that in a thorough and uncompromising manner God is the God who frees the oppressed, a God who liberates.

The publications of Jeanette Rodríguez, a native New Yorker of Ecuadorian parentage, evidence her interdisciplinary approach. Specifically, she draws on a number of social science disciplines, especially psychological theory, to lay bare human experience, and then she forms a theological interpretation of that experience. She defines theology as faith seeking expression, expanding Anselm's age-old "faith seeking understanding." She claims that theology must include ritual, myths, song, visual art, story—in other words, many expressions of faith—and that theology, when faithful to a liberating orientation, must develop from a self-conscious awareness of its context. She poses the following three questions: "1) Under what conditions is this theology being done? 2) For whom is theology done? 3) To whom is it addressed?" (*Stories We Live*, 3–4).

Rodríguez uses social science, particularly psychology, to frame human experience. The resulting interpretation of human experience serves as the starting point for her theology. Given her approach, Rodríguez's theological contribution tends to be more descriptive than prescriptive. Among her most prominent interlocutors are social scientists James Fowler, George DeVos, and Jerome Frank; theologians Virgilio Elizondo, Clodomiro Siller-Acuña, and Elizabeth Johnson; and Chicana scholar Gloria Anzaldúa.

The greater part of Rodríguez's research has been devoted to an examination of the influence and significance of the symbol of Our Lady of Guadalupe in the lives of Mexican American women. As a result of her research, Rodríguez maintains that this symbol plays a crucial role in fostering the identity and reinforcing the strength of Mexican American women.

Cultural memory constitutes a complex theme in Rodríguez's theology. It includes elements of tradition, worldview, historical memory, and myth, each in their own way responding to the human need for "identity, salvation, hope and resistance to annihilation" (*Stories We Live*, 13). The importance of cultural memory resides in its ability to link an historical event with humanity's drive toward transformation and growth and to link the indelible, collective experience of a people with a radical shift in their religiocultural world of meaning. Our Lady of Guadalupe serves as an ideal example in that this symbol arouses an affection that connects individuals both to each other and to their hopes and aspirations, as they connect to her.

For Gloria Inés Loya, a Mexican American Bay Area resident, theology is born out of the dynamic interrelationship of a keen and attentive listening to the lived experiences of Latinas and the serious study of the scriptures, the tradition, and the authoritative teachings of the Catholic bishops. Loya uses this dynamic exchange to create a theological interpretation toward liberative action. Loya observes that attentive listening to the experience of Latinas, her chosen point of departure for Latina feminist theology, needs to take many forms (e.g., social science, literature, oral tradition). However, in her writings, Loya's interests patently rest with female models and images, particularly Dolores Huerta, Malintzín (La Malinche), Our Lady of Guadalupe, and Sor Juana Inés de la Cruz.

Loya's guiding vision for Latina feminist theology consists of Latinas as *pasionaria* (passionate commitment) and *pastora* (pastoral leadership). Together these terms refer to "a high level of leadership, commitment to justice and love for [the] people" and a commitment to prayer (Loya, 124). Yet both of these terms refer to different aspects of Latinas' public role, namely, the relationship of Latinas to the community. *Pasionaria* calls attention to the character of public leadership exemplified by Dolores Huerta, the vice president of the United Farm Workers union. *Pastora* underscores the varied ways, often unnoticed, in which Latinas feed the spirit and soul of the community.

Cuban American Michelle Gonzalez has devoted her work to an examination of the theological contribution of Sor Juana Inés de la Cruz as a vital resource for the discourses of U.S. Latina/o theology and feminist theologies. Drawing on the work of literary scholars, historians, feminist theorists, and contemporary theologians, Gonzalez argues that Sor Juana's theological contribution provides an exceptional point of departure for the development of a Latina interpretation of the Divine as Beauty itself, in other words, a Latina theological aesthetics.

Pasionaria calls attention to the character of public leadership exemplified by Dolores Huerta, the vice president of the United Farmworkers Union. *Pastora* underscores the varied ways, often unnoticed, in which Latinas feed the spirit and soul of the community. *Copyright © David Bacon.*

In her writing, Mexican American Nancy Pineda-Madrid explores the potential liberative character of U.S. Latina theology in terms of two theological problems—first, the relationship between epistemology and liberation and, second, the challenge of liberation in the face of the experience of evil, or suffering. Pineda-Madrid employs the work of feminist theorists, contemporary theologians, Chicana theorists, and North American pragmatist philosopher Josiah Royce both to reveal the particularity of "Latina experience" and to clarify the questions confronting U.S. Latina theologians.

Pastoral Theologies

Latina pastoral theologians recognize that to effectively communicate the faith experience of Latinas/os means retrieving historical sources, evaluating their relevance, and proposing a compelling interpretation that responds to contemporary pastoral needs. Some of these theologians publish in the context of academic settings; others publish out of a desire to make sense of various ministerial needs of the Latina/o community.

Ana María Pineda, born in El Salvador and publishing since the late 1980s, maintains that U.S. Latina/o theology grows out of the U.S. Latina/o communal context, and in turn, theology must strive to support and enliven the faith experience of the community. For Pineda, the contemporary character and concerns of U.S. Latinas/os can only be understood in light of their historical experience. Therefore, a significant portion of her research involves a retrieval of the Mesoamerican oral tradition, the sixteenth-century Spanish *conquista* (conquest), and the *segunda conquista* brought about by the 1848 Treaty of Guadalupe Hidalgo. Not only does she uncover this largely buried history, but she also advances an original interpretation of how these decisive and formative events are revelatory of the sacred for contemporary U.S. Latina/o experience. Hence, culture is an "explicit source of theology" and not simply "a vehicle for the Gospel." As a theological source, culture has the potential to transform and reshape theology. Pineda's interlocutors include historians of the Mexican and U.S. Latina/o experience, key ecclesial documents, contemporary anthropologists, and contemporary theologians.

Pineda uses various strategies to explore the relationship between theology and ministry. Some of her writing focuses on how wisdom was passed down from one generation to the next and who was responsible for this transmission within the Nahua community of the sixteenth century. A form of these cultural patterns, she claims, endures to this day within the Latina/o community. She proposes that the distinctiveness of the Latina/o community can be attributed, in part, to this legacy. In other publications, Pineda concentrates on the importance of *pastoral de conjunto* (a process based on a group's common goals and method) as characteristic of the way many Latinas/os approach ministry and theology. Related to this topic, Pineda has also written on the contemporary challenge confronting both universities and seminaries as they strive to educate and form the next generation of Latina/o theologians and pastoral ministers.

Anita de Luna, a Mexican American Tejana (Texan), has developed the first Tejano spirituality, which she bases on several Mexican and Mexican American catechisms dating from the mid-sixteenth, the nineteenth, and the twentieth centuries. She centers her work on both these primary sources and scholarship from the fields of history (Mexico and Texas), anthropology, theology, spirituality, and rhetoric to interpret these sources. In addition to taking the historical and contemporary Mexican American experience as her point of departure, she also engages the experience of Roman Catholic women's religious communities as a starting point for her development of a contemporary spirituality.

As a group, Latina pastoral theologians have a long and rich history of publications dating from Dominican-born Marina Herrera's first article, "La Teología en el Mundo de Hoy" (*Theology in Today's World*), published in 1974. Since then Herrera has authored numerous articles primarily in the field of multicultural catechesis and ministry. However, her work also reflects an ongoing interest in the role of women in the Church. From the 1980s forward many other Latina pastoral theologians have been making important contributions: Rosa María Icaza (Mexican born) in spirituality and liturgy; María de la Cruz Aymes (Mexican born) in catechesis; Carmen Nanko (Spanish Czech) in Catholic social teaching and campus ministry; Dominga Zapata (Puerto Rican) in pastoral ministry. Additionally, the writings of sociologist of religion Ana María Díaz-Stevens (Puerto Rican) make a notable contribution to the study of Catholic Latinas and religion. She offers detailed historical and social portraits of Latina leaders and of the Puerto Rican Catholic experience.

At the dawn of the twenty first century, Latina Roman Catholic theologians have begun to address an expanding horizon of questions and interests. What might be the relationship between Latina feminist theologies and womanist theologies? And Asian women's theologies? How is the work of Latina Roman Catholic theologians in the United States similar yet distinct from the work of women writing theology in Latin America? How might Latina Roman Catholic theologians collaborate with their Prostestant colleagues? Not only do their questions reflect wider interests, but today Latina Roman Catholic theologians turn with greater frequency to the literary arts, philosophy, feminist theory, and other fields to enrich their work.

SOURCES: María Pilar Aquino's monograph *Our Cry for Life: Feminist Theology from Latin America* (1993) is an important initial work in the field of Latina theologies. With a couple of colleagues, she edited a volume of writings of Latina theologians: María Pilar Aquino, Daisy L. Machado, and Jeanette Rodríguez, eds., *A Reader in Latina Feminist Theology: Religion and Justice* (2002). Jeanette Rodríguez's works include *Stories We Live, Cuentos Que Vivimos: Hispanic Women's Spirituality* (1996) and *Our Lady of Guadalupe: Faith and Empowerment among Mexican-American Women* (1994). Gloria Inés Loya has published a worthy article in this field. See "The Hispanic Woman: Pasionaria and Pastora of the Hispanic Community," in *Frontiers of Hispanic Theology in the United States*, ed. Allan Figueroa Deck (1992). In the field of pastoral theology, Anita de Luna has written an important monograph, *Faith Formation and Popular Religion: Lessons from the Tejano Experience* (2002). The work of Ana María Pineda is also noteworthy. See her article "The Oral Tradition of a People: Forjadora de Rostro y Corazón," in *Hispanic/Latino Theology: Challenge and Promise*, ed. Ada María Isasi-Díaz and Fernando F. Segovia (1996). Rosemary Radford Ruether's writings have been influential for Latina theologians. See *Women and Redemption: A Theological History* (1998). Alma M. García's edited volume *Chicana Feminist Thought: The Basic Historical Writings* (1997) is an essential collection.

REBIRTH OF THE RELIGION OF THE GODDESS
Carol P. Christ

WHEN THE FEMINIST movement was reborn in the late 1960s in the United States, the rebirth of the religion of Goddess was not far behind. Some of the activists in the nineteenth-century women's rights movement, including Elizabeth Cady Stanton and Matilda Joslyn Gage, recognized the importance of religion in the shaping of women's secondary status in society. Cady Stanton in *The Woman's Bible* (1895, 1898) focused her attention on deconstructing the Christian Bible. *In Woman, Church, and State* (1893) Joslyn Gage, drawing on theories of prehistoric matriarchies, which were well accepted in her time, penned a wide-ranging feminist reinterpretation of religion and culture in which the worship of Goddesses and the roles of priestesses in ancient societies played a prominent role. Both of these women were castigated for daring to suggest that Protestant Christianity was not the highest development of humankind's religious consciousness.

Another factor that prepared the way for the rebirth of the religion of the Goddess was the widespread interest in theories that the earliest cultures of humankind were "matriarchal" and "Goddess-worshipping." The German J. J. Bachofen in *Das Mutterrecht* (The Mother Right) first proposed the idea that matriarchy preceded patriarchy in 1861. Bachofen's views had a wide influence, informing the work of diverse scholars, theorists, and popular writers, including economic theorists Karl Marx and Friedrich Engels, psychologist Carl Jung, classicist Jane Ellen Harrison, and historian of religion Mircea Eliade. Indeed, up until the 1960s, the notion that the Paleolithic and Neolithic cultures of Europe worshipped the Great Goddess was taken for granted, especially in Britain. Most of the thinkers who wrote about the Goddess and matriarchy took an evolutionary view of human culture, assuming that it was natural that a more "primitive" matriarchy would be superceded by a more "advanced" patriarchy. Still, it is evident that many of these thinkers appreciated the earlier stage of culture. Carl Jung, for example, stated that his culture suffered from domination by the "masculine" and needed a new infusion of "feminine" values. When feminists started questioning the hegemony of God the Father, a large body of literature about the Goddess was available.

The rebirth of the Goddess also tapped into a long current of disillusion with industrialism, which had sparked a desire for closer connection to the natural world and nostalgia for pre-Christian paganism. These were major motifs in German and English romanticism. A new pagan religion that worshipped the Goddess and the God and gave important roles to priestesses had taken up and developed these themes. Known as pagan witchcraft or Wicca, it was created in the 1940s and 1950s by an Englishman with a keen interest in religion, folklore, and the occult. His name was Gerald Gardner, and he claimed that a witch from the New Forest in England who had inherited traditions through her family had initiated him.

In the 1970s, the feminist critique of religion came into its own. In the United States, the severing of the study of religion from religious institutions that occurred in the 1960s attracted increasing numbers of undergraduate and graduate women to the study of religion, which formerly had been a domain largely restricted to men who were studying for or had studied for the ministry. At the same time, priests, ministers, rabbis, and professors of religion initiated a free-floating discussion of religious values through their linking of religion with the civil rights movement and the antiwar movement that followed. Led by figures like Allen Ginsberg and Alan Watts, the countercultural and humanistic psychology movements had begun to question traditional Western religious views of the body, sexuality, and nature. A sense of oneness with all of nature experienced while on drugs kindled interest in non-Western religions and practices, including yoga and meditation. When the women's liberation movement surfaced out of this radical political and cultural questioning, discussion about religion and its role in the shaping of culture was very much in the air.

In 1971 in "After the Death of God the Father" (then) liberal Roman Catholic theologian Mary Daly made a connection between the image of God as Father ruling the universe and the domination of men in the hierarchies of power in religion and culture. That year Elizabeth Gould Davis published the widely read *The First Sex*, which argued that women were once the dominant sex and rekindled interest in Goddesses and matriarchies. At about the same time, Z (Zsuzsanna) Budapest in Los Angeles was forming the Susan B. Anthony Coven #1 and writing the first version of her Goddess manifesto, which she titled *The Feminist Book of Lights and Shadows*. Budapest, a self-taught Hungarian refugee, called upon women to worship the ancient Goddess and provided a sourcebook of rituals and spells describing the practice of "Dianic" witchcraft (for women only). Simultaneously women around the country were beginning to name and question the patriarchal aspects of Judaism and Christianity. Others were reading books about the Goddess by Esther Harding, Erich Neumann, Helen Diner, and Robert Graves that argued that Goddess worship had once been widespread. In 1971 at the first gathering of women theologians held at Alverno College in Milwaukee, (then) graduate student Carol P. Christ was inspired to issue the call that led to the founding of the Women's Caucus in the academic field of religion. In 1974, the first issue of *WomanSpirit* magazine described a gathering of feminist spiritual women who had created a ritual celebrating women's menstrual blood as sacred. That same year an (then) obscure academic archaeologist named Marija Gimbutas, whose previous work had focused on the Indo-Europeans, published *The Gods and Goddesses of Old Europe*, arguing that the religion of "Old Europe" centered on the Goddess. This was followed in 1976 by the widely read

In the 1970s, the feminist critique of religion came into its own. In the United States, the severing of the study of religion from religious institutions which occurred in the 1960s attracted increasing numbers of undergraduate and graduate women to the study of religion, which formerly had been a domain largely restricted to men studying for the ministry. *Copyright © Joan Biren.*

When God Was a Woman by Merlin Stone and *Of Woman Born* by poet Adrienne Rich, both of which synthesized previous research on Goddesses from feminist perspectives. Susan Griffin's prophetic *Woman and Nature* (1978) articulated many women's feelings that their sense of connection to nature could become a source of empowerment and inspired the later ecofeminist movement.

By the late 1970s "the feminist spirituality movement" had been born. This was a burgeoning grassroots movement of women who experienced the spirit in nature and who were increasingly attracted to prepatriarchal cultures and images of Goddesses. In 1979 in the *The Spiral Dance* Starhawk (Miriam Simos) synthesized earth-based spirituality, feminism, humanistic psychology, and radical politics in her theory of "feminist witchcraft" as the "rebirth of the ancient religion of the Great Goddess." Naomi Goldenberg's *Changing of the Gods*, published in the same year, gave academic legitimacy to the new movement.

At the turn of the millennium, the impact of what was by then being called the Goddess movement was widespread in North American culture (as well as in Great Britain, Australia, and New Zealand). Starhawk's first book alone had sold well over 100,000 copies, and Carol P. Christ's essay "Why Women Need the Goddess," originally delivered as the keynote address at "The Great Goddess Re-emerging" conference held in Santa Cruz, California, in 1978, had been reprinted in scores of books, including one used to train undergraduate students in critical thinking. In the 1980s and 1990s hundreds of books and essays on the Goddess were published. Goddess circles, womanspirit groups, and covens, many, but not all of them, for women only, had been established all around the country. In 1994 in *Priestess, Mother, Sacred Sister*, anthropologist Susan Starr Sered would name the feminist spirituality and Goddess movements as among the few living religions worldwide created and led by women.

Participants in the movement speak of image of the Goddess as healing for women, echoing Ntozake Shange's cry, "I found god in myself, and I loved her fiercely" (63). Others would agree with Adrienne Rich that "she is beautiful in ways we have almost forgotten" (93). Most have created altars using reproductions of ancient images of the Goddesses, many of which are full-figured or, by the standards of contemporary culture, "fat." Women find it affirming and liberating to live with ancient images that suggest understandings of female power quite different from those evoked by childlike anorexic models served up by capitalist advertising. In addition to images and pictures of Goddesses, a typical altar might include stones, feathers, a chalice or bowl holding water, family photographs, and flowers or a living plant. Participants say that the symbols of Goddess religion connect them to "the web of life," the whole human and nonhuman world, and to the cycles of light and darkness, birth, death, and renewal that are found within it.

Starhawk's and Z Budapest's books (and many others that have followed) have been used as "cookbooks" by those experimenting with the creation of Goddess rituals. They suggest that rituals be held on the new and full moons and on the eight "seasonal holidays," which are February 2, Beltane or Brigid's Day; March 21, Spring Equinox; May 1, May Day; June 21, Summer Solstice; August 1, Lamas; September 21, Fall Equinox; October 31, Halloween; and December 21, Winter Solstice. Though seasonal festivals are age old, this specific holiday cycle was created by Gerald Gardner, who got the idea from Margaret Murray's *The Witch Cult of Western Europe* (1921).

Starhawk and Z Budapest explained how to raise what they called a "cone of energy" or "power" by nonverbal chanting, and they suggested themes appropriate to each season. Starhawk and Z also proposed creating rituals for special occasions including menstruation, birth, abortion, menopause, and healing. They encouraged women to experiment, rather than slavishly following rules, to do what seemed right. Thus, although the direct influence of Z and Starhawk can be found in many Goddess circles, others are quite eclectic. Celebrations of the seasonal holidays and full moon rituals are practiced by most groups.

A typical spring ritual might be held during daylight hours in a backyard or at a local park. Participants might be asked to wear festive clothing, bright colors, or flower crowns symbolizing the rebirth and abundance of life typical of the season. The ritual might include creating a circle, singing or chanting, dancing, and a meditation in which each participant thinks about something in her life or the world that is about to come to fruition. A winter ritual more likely would be held at night with a meditation for entering into the darkness, the unknown, the feared in order to receive a gift of healing or insight. Passing through the ritual cycle of the year, one affirms darkness as well as light, death as well as life and rebirth.

The Goddess movement is one of the major threads within the feminist spirituality movement, which also includes some who resist the notion of a personal Goddess, preferring to invoke nature or the spirits of all living things. Within the Goddess movement, there are many who identify with feminist "Wicca" or witchcraft as defined by Starhawk, Z Budapest, or others. The Old English *wicca* and *wicce* mean "wizard" and "witch." The name "Wicca," which can be traced to Gardner, has been variously explained, for example, as referring to the craft of the wise or to the practice of those who bend or shape reality. Wiccans or witches trace their practice to the "Old Religion" of Europe. They allege that those persecuted as witches in the late Middle Ages and early modern period refused to renounce the "Old Religion" for Christianity.

Recent research (especially that of Ronald Hutton in *The Triumph of the Moon* [1999]) suggests that Gerald Gardner (probably in conjunction with a woman known as "Dafo" and with the later help of Doreen Valiente) created the contemporary Wiccan or pagan witchcraft tradition. He was indebted to Margaret Murray's (then) widely accepted theory that the witches of western Europe practiced a pre-Christian pagan religion. He drew on his extensive knowledge of folklore and tribal religions, as well as on the ritual and magical traditions of Western occult and secret societies including Freemasonry (the Masons), Rosicrucianism, and the Golden Dawn. Gardener's original contribution was in giving the Goddess and the priestess equal (if not superior) status to the priest and the God. This made the Wiccan tradition attractive to women in general and to feminists in particular.

Starhawk and Z Budapest learned of the Gardnerian witchcraft through reading and contact with those influenced by Gardner. Z Budapest had also learned from her mother about remnants of paganism found in peasant traditions of her native Hungary. These included telling fortunes, speaking to the dead, reverence for nature, and herbalism. (Gimbutas studied the survivals of Goddess worship in folk traditions in her native Lithuania.) However, because Starhawk and Budapest apparently believed that Gardner and his followers were transmitting genuinely ancient traditions, and perhaps also because Gardner was a male, both tended to speak generally about the "Old Religion" without attributing its reformulation as the Wiccan or witchcraft tradition to Gardner. American feminists gave the Goddess clear pride of place and asserted that women could worship the Goddess apart from men. (Gardner had insisted that "energy" must be passed from female to male, and vice versa. His covens required an equal number of males and females worshipping nude, though it appears that they did not engage in ritual sex.) Early on, many feminist followers of the Goddess rejected the hierarchy involved in the (Gardnerian) notion of a high priestess and high priest. Some designated the position of priestess as a status all could aspire to, while others dispensed with it all together. Moreover, though Gardner's politics were conservative, Starhawk and Z are radical feminists. Starhawk and her followers have been active in the antinuclear and antiglobalization direct resistance movements.

There are many in the Goddess movement who do not identify as Wiccans or witches. They believe their traditions are related to ancient Goddess religion and to pre-Christian paganism but not to the alleged traditions of the witches. In general, they are not attracted to the "high ceremony" of Wiccan traditions, including set ways of doing rituals, secrecy, initiation, and hierarchy (much of this was derived by Gardner from the Masons in any case). Some feel that the name *witch* carries too many negative connotations; others that the Goddess religion they practice derives from sources other than the religion allegedly practiced by the historic "witches."

Most in the Goddess movement agree with Merlin Stone, who wrote: "At the very dawn of religion, God was a woman" (Stone, 1). Some trace their religion to "Old Europe" (a term coined by Marija Gimbutas) in the Upper Paleolithic (up to 25,000 years ago) and to the Neolithic (c. 6500–3500 B.C.E. in Europe). Others suggest that prepatriarchal Goddess religion existed in many other parts of the world as well. The idea that Goddess religion is far older than Christianity is a great source of attraction. However, this view has become a subject of academic controversy.

The view that the earliest cultures of Europe were "matriarchal" and worshipped the Great Goddess was uncontroversial for much of the nineteenth and twentieth centuries. The term *matriarchy* was often imprecisely defined, yet it was never understood (as it often is by contemporary critics of the Goddess movement) to be "the opposite of patriarchy." This would mean not only that women had great influence family and community but also that they beat their husbands, held men as slaves and concubines, ruled over large empires, and waged wars of domination and conquest. In this sense of the word, there is no evidence that "matriarchy" ever existed, and few feminists would wish that it had! To avoid misunderstanding, careful scholars who write sympathetically about Goddess history use words like "prepatriarchal" or "matrifocal" to refer to cultures that are not male dominant and hierarchical.

Anthropologist Peggy Reeves Sanday in *Female Power and Male Dominance* (1981) analyzed data from a large number of societies studied by anthropologists. She found many societies that revered women and nature, sometimes symbolizing these powers as Goddess. In such cultures, which were mostly small scale, women held a great deal of power in the family and in the community. However, these societies were not female dominant or matriarchies, because women shared their power with men, and the societies were egalitarian.

Archaeologist Marija Gimbutas excavated five Neolithic cultures in southeast Europe and examined and classified thousands of artifacts and figurines, using a theory of interpretation she called "archaeomythology." She concluded that the cultures of Old Europe worshipped the Goddess as the Giver, Taker, and Renewer of Life. Unlike her predecessors who viewed Goddess cultures as "primitive," Gimbutas argued that "Old Europe," the name she gave to prehistoric and pre-Indo-European cultures of the Paleolithic and Neolithic, was a highly artistic and peaceful "civilization." She said that the later Indo-Europeans were in many ways "primitive" or less civilized. Combining her analysis of the symbolism with the different burial customs of the Old Europeans and the later Indo-Europeans (who spoke a series of related languages that include Greek, Latin, Sanskrit, German, French, English), Gimbutas described Old European culture as "matrifocal" and "egalitarian." Grave goods were relatively evenly distributed in Old European society, and there was no evidence of the chieftain or big man graves that are characteristic of later Indo-European burials. Though she worked with new data and proposed fresh analyses, and though her theories differ significantly from earlier ones, Gimbutas is often accused of simply repeating outdated theories of "primitive matriarchy." In fact, she was challenging widespread theories that assume cultural "progress" and claim classical Greece as the birthplace of civilization.

Contemporary archaeologists (including some feminist archaeologists) and their followers in the field of religion (Rosemary Radford Ruether and Cynthia Eller, among them) dispute the claims of Gimbutas and the Goddess movement, questioning whether prepatriarchal societies ever existed and challenging the view that humanity once worshipped a "Great" Goddess. Contemporary archaeology is "materialist," which means that archaeologists are more interested in carefully recording excavated materials than in developing grand theories about the religion and culture of earlier societies. Materialist archaeologists (who are often themselves atheists) say that it is nearly impossible to understand the religions of ancient peoples. They view Gimbutas's theories about the religion and culture of Old Europe as speculative and unproved. Gimbutas's detractors refer to Peter Ucko's *Anthropomorphic Figurines of Predynastic Egypt and Neolithic Crete with Comparative Material from the Prehistoric Near East and Greece* (published in 1968, before Gimbutas's work on Old Europe). In it, Ucko alleged that the theory that female figurines represent a Great Goddess cannot be proved. He suggested that the figurines might be children's toys or symbolic concubines. Ronald Hutton expressed puzzlement that

Ucko's theories so quickly unraveled several generations of scholarly consensus, given that Ucko did not "disprove" earlier interpretations of the figurines but only showed that other interpretations were possible.

A common criticism of the Goddess movement's vision of history states that in classical Greece and in classical and contemporary India, worship of Goddesses coincides with patriarchy and the suppression of women. Yet Gimbutas specifically argued that when Indo-European warrior groups entered Greece and India, they transformed preexisting cultures while maintaining aspects of earlier religious symbolism. Gimbutas's focus was on the Neolithic. Others contend that there is no evidence for the worship of a single Great Goddess, but rather there were many local Goddesses. Gimbutas was well aware that "the Goddess" had many names and a variety of local traditions. Yet she sensed a unity of vision behind a plurality of images and traditions. The fact that there were many images and names of Goddesses does not automatically imply that those who worshiped them did not also intuit a Great Goddess. (After all, Christians worship a Father, Son, and Holy Ghost, yet few accuse them of not being monotheists.) It is unlikely that Gimbutas imagined that she would be read as asserting that Old Europe practiced exclusive monotheism of the biblical variety.

Because the stakes in the debate are religious and political as well as academic, and because the two sides have vastly different methodological assumptions, it is unlikely that their disputes about the history of the Goddess will soon be resolved. Many academics are uncomfortable with the idea of a "religion" or "culture" of the Goddess, viewing it as a threat to long-standing theories of cultural progress and to traditions of Christian and male dominance. Many academic feminists are uncomfortable with religious feminism, arguing that women should seek to achieve their goals through political and economic means. Some religious feminists believe that feminist effort is better spent transforming traditional religions.

The issue of relation of the Goddess and Wiccan movements to European witchcraft or to practices associated with survivals of European paganism is even more complicated. Gardner's claim to have received his information from a woman whose ancestors secretly preserved the traditions of the witches from the burning times is apparently false. What about the more general claim of Margaret Murray that the witches were persecuted for practicing the "Old Religion"? Murray's views were widely accepted for some fifty years. However, Ronald Hutton in *The Triumph of the Moon* (1999) states that recent scholarship has totally discredited them. He contends that Europeans understood themselves as Christian even when their traditions included elements derived from non-Christian sources. He questions the view that folk traditions carry elements unchanged from the distant past, arguing that folk traditions interact with dominant cultures and change over time. He has proved that elements of contemporary Wiccan tradition commonly attributed to "Old Religion" in fact have their sources in the Masonic movement. These include, among many others, the pentagram (five-pointed star), calling the directions and the "guardians of the watchtowers," and the closing words "happy meet and happy part," which have been received into the Goddess movement as "merry meet and merry part." The theory of a direct and unbroken transmission of the "Old Religion" from the early Christian period to those burned as witches to contemporary Wiccans is no longer tenable. However, the Masons inherited many of their ideas from Western occult traditions, which may have transmitted some elements of ancient paganism. Moreover, folk traditions and Christianity itself contain elements that derive from pre-Christian religions. There is no reason that these elements cannot be reclaimed by contemporary pagans, witches, and Goddess worshippers.

Before leaving the subject of the witchcraft and the witch persecutions in western Europe (there were no such persecutions in the Byzantine or Ottoman empires), it is important to address one final subject. Nineteenth-century American feminist and self-taught scholar Matilda Joslyn Gage has now been recognized as having first proclaimed the widely repeated figure of 9 million women having been killed as witches in western Europe. While it is now agreed that up to 80 percent of the victims of the witch persecutions were women, it is likely that the actual numbers killed were closer to 40,000 to 100,000. Given that the burning or hanging of even one innocent woman might have been enough to terrorize an entire community, this is a significant number.

As is well known to historians of religion, the power of a religion is not dependent on the literal truth of its history. Many Christians and Jews question the historicity of the foundational stories of their religions, yet continue to accept them as mythically, if not literally, true. Contemporary Goddess religion will probably continue to assert that Goddesses and a Great Goddess were worshiped at "the dawn of time," as long as this interpretation of the evidence cannot conclusively be disproved. Nor has it been disproved that some of those killed as witches were wise women and healers whose knowledge threatened the authority of the all-male Christian hierarchy.

Let us turn now from the history of Goddess religion to a consideration of its contemporary theology and ethics. Starhawk once defined Goddess worship as a religion of poetry, not theology. However, as the movement developed, theological questions inevitably arose.

Is the Goddess one or many? Kind or cruel? How should we live? What happens when we die? In 1997, Carol P. Christ published the first Goddess "thea-logy," *Rebirth of the Goddess*. Melissa Raphael's *Introducing Thealogy* followed in 1999. *Thealogy* is a word coined (probably by Naomi Goldenberg) from *thea,* "Goddess," and *logos,* "meaning." Thealogy is reflection on the meaning of the Goddess.

In "Why Women Need the Goddess" (1979), Carol P. Christ asserted that the image of the Goddess overturns all of the images of religion and culture that portray the female, the feminine, and women as weak and powerless, or devious and evil. The symbol of Goddess affirms the legitimacy and goodness of female power, the female body, and women's bonds with each other. This essay had a wide impact because it struck a chord of knowing in many. Some have said that images of the Goddess reinforce stereotypes by identifying women with the body and nature but not mind and culture. Some Jungian and New Age depictions of "the Divine feminine" fall into this category. Yet many others state that Goddess religion, properly understood, views both women and men as embodied and embedded in nature. Carol Christ (*Rebirth of the Goddess* [1997]) argues that the "metaphoric power" of the Goddess calls into question all the dualisms (or dualities) of conventional thought, leading to a new valuing of female and male, darkness and light, nonrational and rational, body and soul, nature and spirit.

In the popular imagination, God is an old white man sitting on a throne in heaven, meting out rewards and punishments to his servants on earth. Traditional theologies construct God as utterly "transcendent" of the world. In contrast, Goddess thealogies imagine Goddess as "immanent" in the processes of birth, death, and renewal in the natural world. "She" is known in the world and in the human body-soul. The earth is the body of the Goddess. Carol Christ defines Goddess as "the intelligent, embodied love that is the ground of all being" (*Rebirth of the Goddess,* 107). This means that intelligence, embodiment, relationship, and love are the "stuff" of life. Insofar as human beings (and all beings) are "in the image of Goddess," their goal is to embody intelligence and love in all relationships. She also suggests that process philosophy's "panentheism" (the view that the divine is in the world) provides an alternative to traditional theism and pantheism and to traditional understandings of immanence and transcendence.

In traditional Christianity, Eve brought sin and death into the world. All are caught in the web of this Original Sin. The wages of sin is death. Jesus as the Christ came to save human beings from sin and death. In Goddess thealogy there is no Original Sin. Human beings and all beings have a degree of freedom consistent with finitude and participation in the processes of birth, death, and renewal. Human (and to some extent other) beings are the creators of good and evil in the world. Humans can work with Goddess to bring about greater healing and harmony in the universe. Death is not a punishment for sin. Birth, death, and renewal are the structures of the body of the Goddess. In Goddess religion death is accepted as the natural ending of human life. Some believe that "renewal" after death will take the form of reincarnation (in the Hindu sense). Others are satisfied to imagine that human bodies will be composted and recycled and become part of other lives in the body of the Goddess.

Goddess religion's valuing of darkness as well as light stands in contrast to biblical notions of divine power as "light" in the "darkness" of sin and evil and to Eastern conceptions of salvation as en-"light"-enment. Because racist cultures value "white" and "light" over "black" and "dark," it is important to call attention to Goddess religion's challenge to this "habit" of thought. In Goddess religion the "dark" earth, as well as the starry heavens, is the body of Goddess; the mystical darkness of caves is often understood as her womb; and in the cycles of the day and the year, "darkness" is associated with gestation and transformation (not sin or frightful monsters). This positive valuing of the dark is helpful in the struggle to overcome racism.

The image of the Goddess connects all beings in "the web of life." Plants and animals and so-called inanimate objects as well as human beings are her "children," or more exactly, part of "her body." For many Goddess feminists this is an important corrective to what they view as the biblical God's primary focus on human beings. Goddess religion validates experiences of the sacred in nature (sometimes called "nature mysticism") that do not easily "fit in" to Jewish or Christian notions of spirituality.

Critics have caricatured Goddess worshippers as narcissistic navel gazers, interested "only" in helping women to heal from the damage done to them in male-dominant cultures. Yet in a world where many women have been abused physically, sexually, and psychologically, and when religious and cultural symbols consign women to secondary status and sometimes implicitly or explicitly condone abuse, the effort to help women to heal and to find images of female wholeness is valid and important. Moreover, critics often ignore the ecosocial dimensions of the Goddess movement. Knowledge that the earth is the body of Goddess and a sense of connection to all beings, human and nonhuman, evokes ecological and social concern. Goddess feminists have been active in the ecofeminist movement. Z Budapest advocates radical feminist activism, and Starhawk has been jailed while protesting ecological destruction and global social injustice. Carol Christ proposed "Nine Touchstones" of the ethics of Goddess religion. "Nurture life. Walk in love and beauty. Trust the knowledge that comes through the body. Speak the truth about conflict, pain, and suffering. Take only what you need. Think about the consequences of your actions for seven generations. Approach the taking of life with great restraint. Practice great generosity. Repair the web" (*Rebirth of the Goddess*, 167). For many women and men Goddess religion provides a vision of ethics rooted in deep feelings of connection, rather than in fear of judgment or hope for reward.

SOURCES: Margot Adler gives a sympathetic account of the rise of neopaganism in the United States in *Drawing Down the Moon: Witches, Druids, Goddess-Worshippers, and Other Pagans in America Today* (1979); Cynthia Eller does the same for the Goddess movement (though her conclusions trivialize the movement) in *Living in the Lap of the Goddess: The Feminist Spirituality Movement in America* (1993); Ronald Hutton places the Goddess and neopagan movements in historical perspective *in The Triumph of the Moon: A History of Modern Pagan Witchcraft* (1999); while in *Priestess, Mother, Sacred Sister: Religions Dominated by Women* (1994), Susan Starr Sered considers the feminist Goddess movement as a religion created and led by women. The American feminist Goddess movement was inspired by Z (Zsuzsanna) Budapest's *The Holy Book of Women's Mysteries, Part 1* (1989), originally published as *The Feminist Book of Lights and Shadows* (1974); by Starhawk's *The Spiral Dance: A Rebirth of the Ancient Religion of the Great Goddess* (1979) and *Dreaming the Dark: Magic, Sex, and Politics* (1982); by Naomi Goldenberg's *The Changing of the Gods: Feminism and the End of Traditional Religions* (1979); and by Carol P. Christ's "Why Women Need the Goddess"—see Carol P. Christ and Judith Plaskow, eds., *Womanspirit Rising: A Feminist Reader on Religion* (1979), 279–299. *WomanSpirit* magazine published from 1974 to 1984 (back issues available from 2000 King Mountain Trail, Sunny Valley, OR 97647) provided a place for women to name the sacred. Susan Griffin's *Woman and Nature: The Roaring Inside Her* (1978) gave voice to women's feelings of connection to the natural world. Mary Daly's influential works, including "After the Death of God the Father," in *Womanspirit Rising*, 53–62, and *Beyond God the Father: Toward a Philosophy of Women's Liberation* (1973), created a climate in which leaving Christianity seemed reasonable. Merlin Stone's *When God Was a Woman* (1976) sparked feminist interest in Goddess history, while archaeologist Marija Gimbutas's *The Gods and Goddesses of Old Europe 6500–3500 BCE* (1974), *The Language of the Goddess* (1988), and *The Civilization of the Goddess* (1991) brought forth new evidence and theory that gained wide popular following. Cynthia Eller's critique of matriarchy in *The Myth of Matriarchal Prehistory* (2000) is marred by imprecise definition of the term and antipathy to the whole idea of a Goddess movement, according to Kristy Coleman in "Matriarchy and Myth (Review Article)" in *Religion* 3 (2001): 247–263; feminist archaeologists consider the controversy surrounding Goddess history and prehistory from more balanced perspectives in *Ancient Goddesses* (1998), ed. Lucy Goodison and Christine Morris. Luisah Teish considers the Goddess from a black woman's perspective in *Jambalaya: The Natural Woman's Book of Personal Charms and Prac-* *tical Rituals* (1985); see also Ntozake Shange, *for colored girls who have considered suicide when the rainbow is enuf* (1990). Christine Downing's *The Goddess: Mythological Representations of the Feminine* (1981) is one of many influential Jungian feminist musings on the Goddess. Carol P. Christ in *Rebirth of the Goddess* (1997) and Melissa Raphael in *Introducing Thealogy: Discourse on the Goddess* (1999) reflect thealogically on the meanings of the rebirth of the religion of the Goddess from feminist perspectives.

WOMEN'S ISSUES IN CONTEMPORARY NORTH AMERICAN BUDDHISM
Rita M. Gross

THE SHEER DIVERSITY and variety of forms of Buddhism practiced in North America make it very difficult to generalize about Buddhist women's issues. Every denomination of Buddhism practiced in the contemporary world is represented in North America. Asian forms of Buddhism that had little contact with each other for centuries are now being practiced in the same North American city—Theravada Buddhisms from Southeast Asia, Vietnamese, Tibetan, Korean, Chinese, and Japanese varieties of Buddhism—are all present. Some Asian Buddhisms, especially Japanese and Chinese, have been practiced in North America for four or five generations. Many other Buddhists have arrived only recently, after changes in immigration policy in the 1960s facilitated immigration from Asia. In addition, a significant number of North Americans with no Buddhist antecedents have converted to Buddhism since about 1970. Initially, in the 1960s, these converts expressed countercultural dissatisfaction with Euro-American religion and culture and responded to the many Asian teachers who began to reach out to non-Asian audiences. At the beginning of the twenty-first century, convert Buddhists from ethnic groups not traditionally Buddhist have become part of the North American religious landscape. This development adds even more complexity to North American Buddhism, for their concerns, as Buddhists, are often quite different from those of traditionally Buddhist populations.

Making it even harder to generalize is the paucity of contact between the various groups to date. Not only is this the case for interactions between so-called immigrant Buddhists and so-called convert Buddhists; even within these two broad groups, the various subgroups often have little interaction. Generally, members of any North American Buddhist community are more interested in communication with their Asian forbears than with other types of Buddhists in North America. This is not because of hostility among the groups; rather, it is so difficult and time-consuming to be a Buddhist in

North America, of whatever kind, that little energy seems to be available for ecumenical Buddhist activities.

At the beginning of the twenty-first century, no one is sure how many Buddhists there are in North America. The best available estimate suggests between 4 and 5 million, about half of whom are women. All observers agree that Buddhists from traditionally Buddhist cultures far outnumber convert Buddhists, although converts have captured the spotlight in terms of public attention. Usually well educated, somewhat well off, and used to being part of an elite, converts have commented copiously on Buddhist topics themselves and also have been written about more frequently. For example, in a typical bookstore, many books about Buddhism are written by convert Buddhists or Western scholars of Buddhism; the remainder are written by Asian teachers such as the Dalai Lama. Only recently have a few Asian American Buddhists written books about their forms of Buddhism intended for those outside their communities. Likewise, the various conferences about American Buddhism or women and Buddhism have been attended largely by convert Buddhists, and most of the speakers have been converts or Asian Buddhists. Thus, the majority of North American Buddhists, men as well as women, are somewhat invisible to the North American public.

In fact, convert Buddhists *have* been far more innovative, both in their thinking and practice. Many observe that for immigrant Buddhists, no matter how many generations they have lived in North America, Buddhism is a conserving force promoting links to and memories of their Asian cultures and ancestors. Usually, they express little dissatisfaction with Buddhism as they have received it and have little interest in "Americanizing" Buddhism. For converts becoming Buddhist was part of a protest against conventional North American values. But converts have no loyalty to Asian cultural forms either and often find the traditional Asian forms that encase Buddhism awkward at best. Those curious and radical enough to leave behind an inherited religion often will not hesitate to bring a similar spirit of exploration to their new religious identity, and convert Buddhists have done just that. Aspects of Buddhist thought and practice that are distinctive to North America are usually found in convert communities. For this reason, rather than because of the ethnicity of its practitioners, "American Buddhism" often refers to convert Buddhism.

Throughout its long history, Buddhism has crossed many cultural frontiers and taken on forms distinctive to each different culture. These new Buddhist cultural forms were developed by indigenous people who became Buddhists, not the travelers and missionaries who brought Buddhist teachings into a new home. In the same way, one would expect that eventually an "American Buddhism" would evolve, and convert Buddhists will certainly play a massive role in this development. At the beginning of the twenty-first century, the "Americanization" of Buddhism is a very controversial topic. But all observers agree that the Americanization of Buddhism will include different roles for women than were traditional and that convert women will play a large part in those developments. In fact, many observers claim that the challenges of democracy, psychology, and women's equal participation in Buddhism are *the* three issues that American Buddhism must successfully negotiate if it is to be adopted widely in North American society.

To understand what is at stake for women in North American Buddhism, it is necessary to understand some important typical features of traditional Buddhism. First, like all major world religions, Buddhism has been historically male dominated. The meditations and philosophical explorations that many would consider the heart of Buddhism were practiced almost exclusively by men. Although according to traditional texts, the Buddha had reluctantly initiated parallel women's monastic institutions in which meditation and philosophy could be studied intensely, they were poorly supported, without prestige, and have died out in much of the Buddhist world. Therefore, those with respect and honor in the Buddhist communities were almost always men. Second, with the exception of Japan, all traditional Buddhist societies are marked by a strong lay-monastic dichotomy. Buddhism began as a religion of world renouncers, and it has never lost that flavor or the demands and values that accompany the choice to leave career, family, and worldly society behind. Female world renouncers, often called "nuns" in Western literature, are found in most forms of Buddhism, but, as already stated, they are not nearly so well supported, nor do they have the prestige of male world renouncers, usually called "monks" in Western literature. For a son to renounce the world brought great honor to the family, while a girl who renounced the world to become a nun brought little prestige to the family and could even be embarrassing. Additionally, the meditative and philosophical disciplines associated with Buddhism were practiced almost exclusively in the monasteries, which is why they were practiced almost exclusively by men. By and large, lay practitioners, men as well as women, had neither the time nor the inclination to pursue meditation and philosophy to any great extent. Different disciplines, especially merit-making practices that would accumulate fortunate karma for the next rebirth, and various devotional practices were developed by and for lay practitioners.

Convert Buddhists have seriously questioned all three of these practices that dominate traditional Asian Buddhism and in many cases significantly modified them. Though convert Buddhist communities still experience some male dominance, women are much more visible in all aspects of public Buddhist life and teaching, and gender equity is a high priority for many of these communities. Second, among convert Buddhists, monastics are rare. The symbiotic relationship in which lay practitioners engaged in merit-making by supporting monastics is simply not in place among converts, and so monastics have difficulty surviving economically. However, convert monastics are about evenly divided between men and women, and some Western nuns are influential Buddhist teachers who have been active in improving conditions for nuns all over the Buddhist world, including efforts to revive the full ordination for nuns in those parts of the Buddhist world in which it has been lost. Additionally, some nuns, for example, Pema Chodron who practices in a Tibetan tradition, have become widely known popular authors. Third, lay convert Buddhists regard meditation and study as the heart of *their* Buddhist practice, so much so that many express surprise and scorn for more traditional lay Buddhist practices. They often dismiss Asian American Buddhist communities as less serious about being Buddhist because meditation and study are not at the heart of their lifestyles. Women converts simply assumed that meditation and philosophy were disciplines relevant to them, with the result that the dichotomy between male expert meditators and female economic supporters, so typical of Asian Buddhism, simply is not found in convert communities. A higher percentage of women function as Buddhist teachers among convert Buddhists than in any other Buddhist community in history.

Few studies of Asian American Buddhist communities have been done, either of those in North America for several generations or those recently arrived, and even fewer specifically about women's perspectives and issues. Most observers surmise that patterns similar to those found in other immigrant communities will emerge. Prominent among these patterns are conflict and accommodation between the generations, as the second generation breaks sharply with its parents, while the third generation is more curious about its grandparents' heritage. But there is little data with which to speculate about how much, for Buddhist immigrants, these breaks and reconciliations will have to do with either Buddhism as a religion or women's roles in Buddhism.

Several stereotypes common among convert Buddhists about immigrant and Asian American Buddhists should be addressed. The first is that while women have not played the roles in Buddhism that feminist convert women seek for themselves, women have not been irrelevant either. Women's most important traditional role is that of donor or patron, a role that was central to the Buddhist understanding of how things work for all of its Asian history. Women usually have more authority over family donations to the monastics than men in tra-

ditional Buddhist societies. Furthermore, women participate freely and eagerly in the activities sponsored by temples and monasteries for lay Buddhists. Women may have little influence or prestige in the monastic community, but they are not second-class participants in the lay community. And the role and importance of traditional lay communities has seldom been understood by convert Buddhists. Finally, as in all traditional societies, women are considered primary religious educators of the next generation in their role as caregivers to young children. In North America, this role is compromised by the competition of secular culture for young people's attention.

Another stereotype about immigrant and Asian American Buddhists common among converts is that they are "only" interested in Buddhism to maintain community and identity. This point is often made as a scornful contrast with convert Buddhists, who claim that because they meditate and study so much, they are better Buddhists. The problem with this stereotype is not so much that it is untrue—converts usually do study and meditate more than Asian American or immigrant Buddhists—as that viable community is not something whose religious significance, for women or for men, should be belittled. "Community," understood by some Buddhists to include both lay and monastic Buddhists and only as the monastic community by others, is the third of Buddhism's "Three Refuges." No confession of faith in Buddhism is more basic or frequent than "taking refuge in the three jewels," one of which is "community." Thus, to regard belonging to a viable community as an insufficient reason to be a Buddhist is to misunderstand Buddhism seriously. Ironically, a great problem for convert Buddhists is lack of strong sustaining communities. This weakness has been the topic of many discussions and experiments, few of which have been overwhelmingly successful to date.

Convert Buddhists, with few exceptions, are white, well educated, and economically comfortable. These facts cause concern among many, who would like their community to be more diverse and suggest that for Buddhism to be successful in North America in the long run it must appeal to a wider spectrum of the North American population. At the beginning of the twenty-first century, only Soka Gakkai, among the various forms of convert Buddhism in North America, was racially and culturally diverse. Organizations for Buddhists of color are developing among converts, and these will help address why Buddhism is underrepresented among ethnic and racial minorities, both women and men.

Aside from the difficulties of communicating across racial and cultural lines, Buddhism, as it is defined by converts, presents economic challenges that make it difficult for many people to participate. Traditionally, meditation and study were carried on largely by monastics who were supported economically by a lay community. But, as indicated, converts reject this division of labor for many reasons, and very few are monastics. Instead, lay Buddhists try to take on disciplines of study and practice that are more typical of monastics in traditional Buddhism. These disciplines take a great deal of time and money to pursue properly. Serious lay practitioners are expected to travel to meditation and study programs that are often far from their homes and that can last for months at a time. Not only do the costs involve travel and time lost from employment; such programs themselves often have relatively high program fees because, given the absence of donors, those who wish to attend must pay for the programs themselves. Most meditation centers do have scholarships, work-study programs, and sliding fees based on income, and many centers state publicly that no one will be turned away due to lack of money. Nevertheless, one still must have leisure time and some money to practice Buddhism as converts desire to practice it. Given the economic realities of North America, leisure time and money are more available to white professionals than to any other group. The ironic result is that a religion known for its economic moderation and its teachings about the inability of materialism to bring satisfaction ends up being available mainly to middle-class professionals! These factors, more than anything else, explain the lack of racial and cultural diversity in convert Buddhism.

These factors also affect women disproportionately; women earn less money than men on average and have more child-care responsibilities. If they are single mothers with much work and little money, Buddhist study and practice will be even less available to them, even if communities or meditation centers give them significant financial aid. On the one hand, convert Buddhism makes the central Buddhist disciplines of meditation and study more available to women because it makes these traditionally monastic practices available to laypeople. On the other hand, only the minority of women who are somewhat well off economically will be able to take advantage of this innovation. This contradiction has not been resolved, or even addressed, by most converts to date.

This troubling trend is not unprecedented. In its previous migrations, Buddhism has always been adopted by the well educated and well off before it became widespread in a culture. Core Buddhist teachings about suffering and the causes of suffering may be more appealing to those who are well off but still suffer than to those who believe that sufficient material wealth would alleviate their suffering. Eventually, as Buddhism spreads more widely through a society, other forms of Buddhist practice develop or are adopted when it becomes clear that many people are not able to devote so much time and energy to study and practice or may not even care

very much for such pursuits. Thus, convert Buddhists may find themselves needing to learn more about how a viable community sustains immigrant Buddhists and provides a fulfilling and meaningful way for them to practice Buddhism.

Though many members of racial and ethnic minorities face structural problems with convert Buddhism's availability, lesbian women fare better, on average. Though the monastic code is very strict, Buddhist attitudes toward sexuality for laypeople are not rigid. Typically, the dominant cultural attitudes toward sexuality are simply adopted by Buddhists. The educated liberals most likely to be convert Buddhists are also relatively accepting of homosexuality; thus, Buddhist lesbian women usually do not face the homophobia they may encounter in other religions. In cities in which large numbers of convert Buddhists are found, organizations and meditation groups for lesbian and gay Buddhists are relatively common.

All these developments are part of an emerging "American Buddhism," a Buddhism that would share family resemblance with all other forms of Buddhism but that would also be distinctive and distinctively "American," as Chinese forms of Buddhism are distinctively Chinese, and so on. To date, the way in which American lay practitioners, who also have jobs and families, attempt to pursue the time-consuming disciplines of study and practice is its most radical departure from Asian models. For converts, Buddhism *is* study and practice; they have largely ignored many other aspects of Buddhism developed in Asia. Perhaps even more striking is the way in which women participate in American Buddhism. Some Buddhist commentators claim that providing models of more equitable participation of women is the special karmic task of Western Buddhism. Western Buddhist women and men have taken up this task; already Western Buddhist groups look quite different from their Asian counterparts regarding the visible, active presence of women in meditation centers and other public Buddhism forums. Some observers claim that the most noticeable difference between Asian and American Buddhist meditation centers is the presence of women in the latter. This claim is meant to draw attention not only to the presence of women but also to the faithfulness with which Westerners have reproduced most other aspects of a meditation center. The iconography is the same; the meditation practices are the same; often the liturgies are chanted in Asian languages, and in many cases, people wear Asian robes during meditation. But women practice side by side with men rather than being isolated in an underfunded women's practice center that has no prestige.

Undoubtedly, the strong presence of women in convert Buddhism owes something to the timing of Buddhism's arrival in North America. Though Buddhists had been present in North America before the 1960s and 1970s, these decades saw the influx of many Asian Buddhist teachers and large numbers of Euro-American converts to Buddhism. These years also marked the emergence of the second wave of feminism. The women most likely to be attracted to Buddhism were not about to play a secondary, supportive role to enable men to study and practice while they provided domestic services. These women insisted that if study and practice were good for men, they would also be good for women, and they took up these disciplines as enthusiastically. This coincidence, this lucky timing, may forever change the face of American Buddhism and may well impact Buddhism worldwide.

The Buddhism they encountered seemed paradoxical to these women. On the one hand, the basic teachings were gender free and gender neutral, and many found the practice of meditation not only gender free but intensely liberating. To many feminist women of the 1960s and 1970s, Buddhism and feminism seemed to be allies, for good reason. On the other hand, the forms through which these teachings and practices were delivered were as male dominant as those of any other religion. The teachers and other leaders were, for the most part, men. Male language abounded in the liturgies, at least those that were translated into English. And though the basic teachings were gender free and gender neutral, deeper explorations into the traditional texts revealed misogynistic passages as well as a strong overall tendency to favor men over women in matters of study and practice. Many women also encountered criticism and were ostracized for pointing out these facts. They were told that the dharma (Buddhist teachings) is beyond gender and that women were being overly sensitive and divisive when they were bothered by misogynistic stories or institutional male dominance.

The issues faced by convert women can be divided into two major areas of concern. The women faced the problem of finding their way in a tradition that, by and large, had not been especially concerned with women's participation in its most valued institutions—the worlds of study and practice. And convert women faced the problem of trying to integrate their more traditionally feminine pursuits with their desire to participate fully in the worlds of study and practice.

Most convert women who began to practice Buddhist meditation and to study Buddhist teachings in the 1960s and 1970s probably were not immediately aware either of the historical significance of their activities or of common traditional attitudes toward women. Though gender practices were very different in their Asian homelands, the Buddhist teachers who came to teach in North America did not treat women students differently from men students. That these teachers worked with women students largely without prejudice is one of the more

remarkable facets of this story. Asked later why they did not apply the more familiar Asian Buddhist norms and expectations regarding gender in North America, two reasons were given. First, the women students asked for teachings, and that a student ask to be taught is the most important requirement. Second, given that women participated with men in Buddhist gatherings, they assumed that North American gender norms were different from Asian norms. The lucky coincidence of feminism and the arrival of Buddhist teachers must be noted again, for if these teachers had arrived ten or twenty years earlier, in the 1950s, the situation would have been very different.

Nevertheless, women noticed the prevalence of men as teachers and other Buddhist authorities and the androcentric (male-centered) language of most liturgies. Those who knew more about Buddhist history and traditional teachings were troubled by teachings concerning the spiritual inferiority of women and their inability to attain liberation until they were reborn in a man's body. However, until they had received sufficient training in the various Buddhist disciplines, women were in a poor position to challenge these views or to suggest alternatives.

Convert women employed many of the same strategies for dealing with Buddhist male dominance as Christian and Jewish women had used in their struggles. The main tasks were to work toward gender-inclusive and gender-neutral liturgies, to advance women into positions of leadership, and ultimately, for women to become fully qualified Buddhist teachers. The two former tasks were accomplished earlier and more easily in many communities, but at the beginning of the twenty-first century, many convert women had become Buddhist teachers as well.

Though meditation is the main religious discipline practiced by convert Buddhists, chanted liturgies are an important part of many meditations. This is especially the case for Tibetan Vajrayana *sadhana* practice and, to a lesser extent, for Zen Buddhism. (*Sadhanas* are long chanted texts that describe the visualizations upon which one meditates.) Many convert *sanghas* (groups or communities) chant their liturgies in an Asian language, which means that gender references are less clear to them, but other groups use English. The early translations were made before the demise of the generic masculine as acceptable English usage, and often the English translations were more androcentric than the Asian originals. Words that carry no specific gender in an Asian language were translated as "son," rather than "child," or "man" rather than "human," and the pronoun "he" was always used to refer to the meditator. Once in place, these translations took on an almost canonical status among some groups. Those who objected were ridiculed and told that, as Buddhists, they should

Roshi Pat Enkyo O'Hara is a Zen Priest at the Village Zendo in New York City. Women teachers like O'Hara are becoming more common among convert Buddhists, but especially among practitioners of Zen and Vipassana Buddhisms, where women were authorized to teach relatively soon after men. *Used by permission of Sensei Pat Enkyo O'Hara.*

be "above such silly, worldly, unimportant issues, since everyone knows that these terms refer to and include women." Gradually, most liturgies have been or are being changed at the beginning of the twenty-first century.

A deeper problem emerged. Chanting the names of the lineage ancestors, from one's own generation back to the Buddha or some other central teacher, is an important part of many Buddhist services. Such chants verify the authenticity of one's lineage and one's own place in the transmission of teachings that go back to the foundations of Buddhism. The lineage ancestors, with very few exceptions, are men. Many women experienced great sorrow at the lack of female ancestors and role models and searched the Buddhist records for such figures. There have been great women practitioners in the history of Buddhism, but they are rarely as prominent in Buddhist memory as their male counterparts. One of the most popular sources for convert women became the *Therigata, The Songs of the Female Elders.* These stories and poems record the accomplishments of the first generation of Buddhist women, direct disciples of the Buddha who attained the same level of realization as his male disciples. At least one Zen Buddhist community, the San Francisco Zen Center, began the practice of chanting the names of female elders recorded in the *Therigata*, ending with an acknowledgment of "all the forgotten women ancestors," on alternating days. However, some male members of the community objected that these female elders were not in the direct line from the Buddha to the teachers of this community and, though they were considered fully realized disciples of the Buddha, a crucial transmission had been given only to one male disciple who became the direct ancestor of all Zen teachers. Most members of the community, nevertheless, continue to regard the lack of known and named female ancestors as a problem. As research is continued, previously unknown highly accomplished women emerge from historical records.

More central still is what some feminist convert Buddhists began to call "the problem of the male teacher." This "problem" has two aspects, one of them limited to a specific time and set of circumstances, the other more fundamental. The first concerned a series of sexual scandals that devastated many convert *sanghas* in the 1980s. A number of Asian teachers participated freely in the sexual license that characterized the 1960s and 1970s, conducting frequent sexual affairs with their students. In some cases, this behavior was open and known by everyone in the community, but it other cases, these affairs were secret. Though teachers who conducted secret affairs usually had many fewer partners, the secrecy proved extremely problematic in the long run. By the 1980s, mores had changed considerably, and many women expressed outrage at male teachers they felt had taken advantage of them. There was also considerable discussion about the ethical propriety of sexual intimacy between partners so unequal in power. The eventual result of this turmoil is that almost all convert *sanghas* now have explicit guidelines discouraging sexual activity between teachers and students, and the sexual safety of female (and male) students is a high priority.

The more basic "problem of the male teacher" concerns Buddhism's long-standing practice of limiting the teaching role almost exclusively to men. Some commentators identified the lack of female teachers, historically and in the present, as *the* single most important issue for women in Buddhism. Historically, this lack results in the problems that occur with the absence of women in the lineage chants as well as the lack of role models and the wisdom of women practitioners that is missing from the tradition's teachings. The practice of having only male teachers sends a strongly discouraging message to women students. To take seriously Buddhist claims that the dharma is beyond gender is difficult if all those who embody and teach it have male bodies.

Fortunately, women teachers are becoming more common among convert Buddhists. It takes many years for a student of Buddhist meditation and philosophy to become qualified to teach, and the first students to be authorized by their Asian teachers to teach the dharma were men. But especially among practitioners of Zen Buddhism and Vipassana meditation, women were authorized to teach relatively soon after men. Only among practitioners of Tibetan Vajrayana Buddhism are almost no women teachers found, but almost no convert men have been fully authorized as teachers either. Many observers comment that convert practitioners of Tibetan

Buddhism were about a generation behind practitioners of Zen and Vipassana in becoming fully trained as teachers. In recent gatherings of Western Buddhist teachers, nearly half the teachers present were women, ample indication that American Buddhism may indeed be fulfilling its potential to address some of Buddhism's long-standing difficulties.

Much as study, practice, and teaching are at the forefront of many Buddhist women's concerns, nevertheless many convert lay practitioners also became involved in family life. This activity presented different challenges to women practitioners: How can one combine child care with the demands of practice and study? Traditionally, this question did not arise because most practice was done by men; the women who practiced seriously were almost always nuns—childless by definition. By and large, convert Buddhist communities have responded that the problem of integrating child care and practice should not be left to mothers alone. Commonly, Buddhist fathers take on significant child-care responsibilities. Dharma centers often provide some child care during programs so that parents can participate more fully. Many parents find the arrangements inadequate and wish for more help and support, but parents are encouraged to continue to practice and study in a serious way while they are raising children, rather than waiting for the children to grow up before resuming their own practice. This attempt is a major Buddhist experiment. At the beginning of the twenty-first century, it remained to be seen how well that experiment proceeded and whether it will persist from generation to generation.

Another problem encountered by converts who became involved in family life is how to raise Buddhist children in a non-Buddhist culture. Asian American Buddhists also encounter this problem, but their situation is different. At least their children have many Buddhist relatives and a more cohesive Buddhist community used to sponsoring family events and activities for teenagers, and they may live in an ethnic neighborhood surrounded by other Buddhists. Converts usually live among non-Buddhists, and most or all of their relatives are non-Buddhists. Furthermore, not having grown up as Buddhists, converts have little idea how to present their Buddhist practice, which is not especially child-friendly, to their children. This is truly uncharted territory for them. Larger Buddhist communities have sometimes sponsored day school intended primarily for their children, and many centers try to combine some Buddhist education with child care during meditation periods for adults. At the beginning of the twenty-first century, the first generation of non-Asians to have grown up as Buddhists are reaching maturity. Many of them have left the Buddhist community, at least temporarily; many would consider themselves Buddhists but do not participate actively in Buddhist life; and others are following their parents into committed Buddhist practice. Many of them are in their teens or early twenties, much younger than their parents often were when they became Buddhists.

SOURCES: Sandy Boucher, *Turning the Wheel: American Women Creating the New Buddhism* (1993). Marianne Dresser, ed., *Buddhist Women on the Edge: Contemporary Perspectives from the Western Frontier* (1996). Lenore Friedman and Susan Moon, eds., *Being Bodies: Buddhist Women on the Paradox of Embodiment* (1997). Rita M. Gross, *Buddhism after Patriarchy: A Feminist History, Analysis, and Reconstruction of Buddhism* (1993). Rita M. Gross, *Soaring and Settling: Buddhist Perspectives on Contemporary Social and Religious Issues* (1998). Charles Prebish, *Luminous Passage: The Practice and Study of Buddhism in America* (1999). Charles Prebish and Kenneth K. Tanaka, *The Faces of American Buddhism* (1998). Mrs. C. A. F. Rhys-Davids and K. R. Norman, trans., *Poems of Early Buddhist Nuns (Therigatha)* (1989). Richard Hughes Seager, *Buddhism in America* (1999).

LESBIAN AND BISEXUAL ISSUES IN RELIGION
Mary E. Hunt

LESBIAN, BISEXUAL, AND women-identified women have been involved in the development of theology in the United States for as long as heterosexual women. However, because of heterosexism and homophobia, especially in religiously related institutions, "coming out," that is, being explicit about their sexual orientation, has been difficult and costly.

The sexism that kept all women from having access to theological education and public ministry played a role in silencing lesbian and bisexual women. The individualizing, privatizing dynamics of patriarchal graduate education contributed to keeping women apart. For women of racial/ethnic groups that are discriminated against, racism added yet another barrier to full disclosure. Thus, it is quite remarkable that so many lesbian, bisexual, and women-identified women in theological studies contributed so productively in the late twentieth century.

Terminology in Flux

The terms *lesbian*, *bisexual*, and *women-identified* illustrate the complexity of the problem in that they are inadequate to convey the fullness of women's lives. Moreover, they can be used in patriarchal ways to divide and conquer women. Positive contemporary definitions, and the courage to use them, are products of feminist struggles.

In patriarchal terms, *lesbian* is defined as a woman whose affective preference is for women over men, a shameful and sinful way of living according to many religions. In feminist terms, *lesbian* is a way to describe a deep personal and political commitment to women, including, but by no means limited to, an openness to sexual relations with women. This evolution of the term *lesbian* is part of the theoretical and theological work at hand. While the work is by no means finished and prejudice is still rampant, there is a clear change in progressive religious circles from *lesbian* being a negative term to one that is now simply descriptive.

Religious studies professor Christine Downing articulated the situation well in 1989 when she wrote that "because there is no other word that communicates the depth of our commitment to each other and our bond to other women who have defined their lives by their love for women, we continue to rediscover the importance of claiming this name" (*Myths and Mysteries of Same-Sex Love*, xxx).

Likewise with *bisexual*, a patriarchal definition would stress that such a woman is open to sexual relationships with people of both genders. But now that gender categories are in flux—it is not clear what a woman is or what a man is—the meaning of the term is less obvious. It is used by people who understand themselves to be sexually attracted to both men and women and is taken seriously as such. But even bisexual activists agree that *bi* is a dynamic term whose meaning is changing. *Transgender persons*, that is, those whose gender preference conflicts with their given gender identity, raise fundamental questions about sexuality in general. These terms when used without nuance end up reinforcing gender categories that are no longer useful. Admittedly, this is complicated, but to pretend otherwise is to contradict the discoveries of feminist thinkers, including religious scholars.

In the 1970s, the feminist terms *women-identified* and *women-connected* arose in an effort to build links between and among women. Feminist religious educator and theologian Nelle Morton favored this approach. Such usage prevented women from being divided on the basis of male-defined categories or on the basis of the gender of their intimate partners. The first, *women-identified*, was a way of speaking of women who, in a culture that pressured them to be male-identified, gave women, including themselves, their primary focus. The second, *women-connected*, was an antidote to the privatizing, essentializing tendencies of "identity." It stressed the importance of being accountable to a community of women, not simply known on the basis of one's individual identity. The term never really caught on, but it represents an important feminist theological intuition that life is relational.

Both of these terms were sometimes used as coded

ways of describing so-called lesbian women without using the term *lesbian*, especially in cases where women were in great danger if their sexuality were made public. But use of the terms was also a way for women whose affective preferences were for men, and women who were unsure or confused about their sexuality, to be part of a movement that rejected male-identity for women. The constructive point was to move beyond being male-defined women to a deeper sense of gynergetic power. In so doing, women linked to women instead of being divided from them regardless of their intimate partners. Some feminist/womanist theologians saw this and called it good.

The pernicious power of patriarchy is such that these more inclusive labels lost currency as the gay/lesbian, later bisexual and transgender work in the field trumped the feminist work. Much of the later "queer" theology gives evidence of this loss of feminist insight as the particularity of lesbian experience is subsumed under the rubric "queer," as it had been under the term "gay" until feminist women insisted on their own Sapphic language.

Thus it is legitimate to look at "lesbian" and "bisexual" women's theological perspectives, but only bearing in mind that the categories must be understood carefully. A similar exploration of heterosexual women's theological perspectives begs to be written, pointing to the limits and dangers of the categories. After all, even separating out the work can be taken as a tacit acknowledgment of the normativity of heterosexuality.

There is a corps of women who self-define as lesbian or bisexual. There are still more women who problematize issues of sexual identity in their work whose contribution is useful regardless of their personal proclivities. And, of course, there are many lesbian and bisexual women who simply do not consider their sexuality relevant to their work or are fearful of the consequences of making it so. Nonetheless, the body of work that deals with explicitly lesbian/bisexual issues bears examination.

Who's Who?

A historiographic problem attends this topic. Naming women "lesbian" or "bisexual" is a delicate matter. Historians do not agree about what constitutes a lesbian or bisexual woman, especially in cases where women did not use these words about themselves. Does it mean a woman who has sexual relations with another woman? Does it include women whose primary affection is for women regardless of sexual behavior?

For example, one well-known pioneer in feminist theology from the mid-twentieth century was known to live for decades with a woman friend, probably a lover. They never acknowledged the nature of their relationship, undoubtedly because they did not have categories in their time that explained it positively. Honesty would

have cost them their livelihood. Were they lesbians? Another prominent late-twentieth-century churchwoman who wrote extensively and worked on the ordination of women in her denomination was known to fall in love with women. Again, circumstances, including racism in her case, simply made the cost of candor too high. Was she a lesbian? How about nuns who vow celibacy? Surely their sexual preference need not be expressed physically for them to claim themselves lesbian or bisexual. How are they to be understood?

Such cases show that the question "Is she or isn't she?" is wrong since a "yes" or "no" answer does not explain much. Rather, one can say, "I hope so," trusting that a patriarchal culture makes women's love for one another so difficult that its triumph is something to be encouraged. In the historical cases, one can say that these women paved the way, even in secret, for those who followed them. A generation of scholars beginning in the 1970s assumed the theopolitical task of reflecting on their lesbian/bisexual experiences, producing what is now a growing body of literature.

Christian and Jewish lesbian and bisexual women number among the most well respected and influential feminist/womanist theologians: Rebecca Alpert, Mary Daly, Carter Heyward, Virginia Ramey Mollenkott, Irene Monroe, Judith Plaskow, Emilie Townes, among them. My own work has focused on this area as well. Pagan and Wiccan women have added to the body of knowledge but not with systematic claims. Muslim, Buddhist, and Hindu women are less visible, but they are beginning to make inroads in their respective traditions. A look at the history and development of lesbian/bisexual theological work makes clear that intercultural and interreligious conversation pushes it well beyond its U.S., predominantly white, North American history, though the cost of being out rises for women who are already oppressed because of race and class.

History of Lesbian/Bisexual Theological Perspectives

Feminist theologians from the Christian tradition provided the foundation for lesbian/bisexual work in the field of religious studies. Early work by Mary Daly, Rosemary Radford Ruether, and Elisabeth Schüssler Fiorenza, among others, laid the groundwork for dealing with sexuality by looking critically at race, class, and sex as dimensions of oppression that shaped theological discourse and social structures. The early stirrings of the gay and lesbian liberation movement in the late 1960s and early 1970s made theological reflection necessary. Gay theological and pastoral work was initiated among men by John McNeill and Troy Perry. As the name *gay* implies, they included only the most cursory, if any, remarks about and attention to women.

Reconstructionist Rabbi Rebecca Alpert, professor of women's studies at Temple University, offered a programmatic approach to Judaism and lesbianism. She proposed new interpretations of Torah that can be helpful in finding common ground between lesbians and Jewish tradition. She offered liturgical suggestions, for example, spilling some of the wine from the cup used at heterosexual weddings, to signify the incompleteness of a community in which same-sex love is not honored. Alpert observed that Judaism, far from being a welcoming place for Jewish lesbians, can be a locus of exclusion for its own people. *Used by permission of Rabbi Rebecca Alpert.*

In the early 1970s scholar-activist Sally Miller Gearhart wrote a pioneering piece, "A Lesbian Looks at God-the-Father or All the Church Needs Is a Good Lay—On Its Side," the first contemporary lesbian theological reflection of which I am aware. She originally delivered it as a lecture in February 1972 at a pastors' conference at Pacific School of Religion in Berkeley, California. When she tried to publish it, the Program Agency of the United Presbyterian Church turned down the article for obvious reasons of prejudice. Happily, the Philadelphia Task Force on Women in Religion published it as a pink supplement to *Genesis III*, their feminist newsletter edited by Nancy Krody, a longtime lesbian activist.

Sally Gearhart's piece was passed hand to hand in mimeographed form, amazing readers who simply had not dealt with such issues in a religious context. She claimed, "I cannot separate the lesbian from the woman," a clear affirmation of the need to leave aside male definitions and an invitation to all women to identify themselves on their own terms (1). She went on to affirm that "being a lesbian involves for me some growing political consciousness. That means I am committed to assessing institutions like the church, which, as far as most women are concerned, takes the prize as the most influential and in itself the most insidiously oppressive institution in Western society" (2). Gearhart, a Methodist turned Lutheran who eventually left Christianity altogether, set the pace for lesbian and later bisexual women to reject privatized, individualized analysis. All did not, of course. But she encouraged women to embrace an explicitly theopolitical agenda.

She coedited with William R. Johnson an early book in the field that included her essay "The Miracle of Lesbianism." Indeed it was against great odds that she and her friends came out, even in the seeming safety of feminist circles. Lesbian women were encouraged to keep their sexual identity quiet, lest all feminists be labeled "lesbian." Sally Gearhart was not to be silenced. "The love that dares not speak its name" until then had been associated with men in religions settings. Thanks to Sally Gearhart, it now had a beautiful female face.

Around the same time, feminist philosopher Mary Daly critiqued what she called "Heterosexuality-Homosexuality: The Destructive Dichotomy," arguing that these patriarchal classifications privilege men whose experiences are considered normative even when transgressive. She later distinguished between "Lesbian," when meaning a woman-identified woman, and "lesbian," meaning women who, though they may relate sexually to women, are really allied with men. It was her way of saying that while feminism was clearly about women, the so-called gay liberation movement was really about men as its name conveyed. It did not encompass women on their own terms. While this distinction never caught on in the literature, it was a helpful reminder that not all lesbians are feminists and not all feminists are lesbians.

Mary Daly's approach paralleled the lesbian separatist sector of the larger women's movement. She was not separatist in a simplistic way, rather more like the womanist writer Alice Walker who urged periodic separatism for reasons of women's health. Mary Daly insisted on women's control of their own bodies, including their sexuality, and discouraged any imitation of heterosexual coupling by persons in same-sex relationships.

Carter Heyward, an Episcopal priest and professor at Episcopal Divinity School, is a Christian lesbian feminist theologian. She was ordained in 1974 in the first group of Episcopal women who broke their church's laws by becoming ordained "irregularly," that is, before the church body had approved women's ordination. She came out as a lesbian in 1979. Ellen Barrett was the first openly lesbian woman to be ordained in the Episcopal Church in 1977.

Carter Heyward's work on relational theology is based on her lesbian-rooted insight, "To speak of the erotic or of God is to speak of *power in right relation*" (3). She couples that with a constant concern for social change in its myriad forms, beginning with economic, racial, and imperialistic injustices that shape an increasingly violent world.

She insists that justice for the people of Nicaragua and for lesbian/gay/bisexual and transgender people are of a piece. Antiracism efforts are central to lesbian women's well-being. Concern with professional boundaries and attention to animal rights round out Carter Heyward's theological program and demonstrate her wide scope. Her prayers, sermons, and essays are cited frequently as examples of lesbian theological insight made accessible to a broad, appreciative audience.

Virginia Ramey Mollenkott, an evangelical feminist professor of English at William Paterson College, in New Jersey, wrote the groundbreaking volume *Is the Homosexual My Neighbor? Another Christian View* with sociologist and sex researcher Letha Scanzoni in 1978. Both were heterosexually identified Christian women. Their clear "yes" to the question troubled conservative Christians who could not easily refute their scripturally based case. Some years later Mollenkott came out, explaining that her lesbian voice preceded her feminist voice by decades even though it had not been heard in this book.

Her work on god-language and her collaboration on inclusive language translations for Christian scripture demonstrated her talent for making complex concepts accessible to wide audiences. She wrote of "sensuous spirituality," linking, as Carter Heyward did, the struggles of people who are poor and oppressed with the struggles of persons who love those of their own gender. She saw in women's bodies and in previously forbidden relationships between women a reflection of the divine.

In her later work, Mollenkott had the courage to take on the binary categories of male and female, heterosexual and homosexual, arguing that these are not adequate to capture the many ways people live and love in the world. She offered careful analysis of the lives of transgender people and proposed "omnigender" as an alternative paradigm. This approach challenges all the categories and demands a rethinking of even the most basic arguments in favor of, and for that matter against, same-sex love. It is risky work at a time when backlash is virulent. But Mollenkott's intellectual and theopolitical integrity led her to ask questions others preferred to postpone asking.

As a Catholic lesbian feminist theologian, I wrote on women's friendships. My approach to "fierce tenderness" is another example of lesbian-based analysis that seeks to redefine foundational terms. Far from seeing "friendship" as primarily a personal, intimate relationship, I claim that friendship is a deeply political activity. In patriarchal culture women are prevented from taking other women seriously as friends, so the very act of loving women, whether sexually or not, including loving oneself as a woman, is an act of resistance. Alison Webster and Elizabeth Stuart's feminist theological work on friendship in England and Janice Raymond's philosophical work on friendship in the United States enriched these insights as part of the global lesbian religious conversation.

Collaborating with an international, interreligious group of scholar-activists, I proposed the human right to "good sex," that is, sex that is safe, pleasurable, community building, and conducive of justice. Thus friendship based on lesbian experience became a useful theological category for understanding the nexus between personal and social commitment, an antidote to normative, privatized heterosexuality.

Bernadette J. Brooten, Catholic lesbian professor of Christian Studies at Brandeis University, explored homoerotic relationships between women in early Christian writings. She concluded that such love was well known in ancient times. She argued that female homosexuality in the early Christian community was condemned not so much on sexual grounds per se, but because it was seen as a transgression of the gender paradigm that gave a man and not a woman power. In a relationship involving two women, the power structure was not at all obvious. The notion of shared power simply did not exist.

Mary Rose D'Angelo of the University of Notre Dame wrote about "Women Partners in the New Testament," arguing that such love relationships are there for the finding. E. Ann Matter, historian at the University of Pennsylvania, focused on the lives of lesbians in medieval Europe. She concluded, consistent with Brooten's findings, that women were condemned for conducting themselves like men, not necessarily for what is today considered lesbian sexual activity.

This resonates with the contemporary critique from theological conservatives that feminism would lead to lesbianism in that men would no longer hold power. This is true if power is shared. While the intention of lesbian religious scholars was not that all women would choose women lovers, the option for a woman to be sexually involved with a woman was another step toward changing the patriarchal power equation.

Womanist theological scholars handle these questions from an African American perspective. Renee Hill, an Episcopal priest, was among the first to come out. She invited African American churchpeople to look seriously at the intersection of racism and homophobia. Irene Monroe, a doctoral student at Harvard Divinity School, writes regularly in the secular gay/lesbian press about religious issues. Womanist theologian Emilie Townes, professor of ethics at Union Theological Seminary, addresses lesbian/gay concerns in her wide-ranging ethical work, insisting on an end to homo-hatred as part of a larger justice agenda.

Interestingly, a provocative womanist voice on these issues is from a heterosexual ally, Kelly Brown Douglas, professor of religion at Goucher College. She describes the loss of many friends to HIV/AIDS (human immunodeficiency virus/acquired immunodeficiency syndrome) as the catalyst for her insistence that the African American community, and especially womanist theologians, deal with issues of same-sex love. She outlines how white racism functions to vilify black sexuality such that it is far too dangerous for African Americans to broach the matter of homosexuality. While there is no evidence to suggest that black churches are any more sexist than other religious institutions, Douglas argues that the history of racism ought to be enough to dissuade African Americans from discriminating against anyone, including gay, lesbian, bisexual, and transgender people.

Several groups of Christian lesbians were formed so that women were able to share their experiences and develop strategies for changing heterosexist churches. The Conference for Catholic Lesbians (CCL) formed in 1982, bringing nuns and other Catholic women together for prayer, sisterhood, and strategizing. Christian Lesbians Out Together (CLOUT) started in 1990 when lay and ordained Protestant women, with a few Catholic friends, formed an organization to strengthen their efforts to bring about sexual justice. Their agenda is explicitly antiracist as well as concerned with the needs of bisexual, transgender, and other marginalized persons.

Unlike the denominationally connected groups like Dignity (Catholic) and Affirmations (Methodist) that were primarily male, these all-female groups are energizing networks of women who seek to hold together their lesbian identity with their Christian faith. This is not an easy task in religious groups like the Catholic Church that condemn homosexual acts as "objectively evil" and homosexual orientation as "intrinsically morally disordered," and in those Protestant churches that ban the ordination of people who are out about their same-sex love.

Such overblown language and blatant oppression only solidified lesbian women's resolve to proclaim that their lives and loves were healthy and good. For example, *A Faith of One's Own* (1986), edited by Barbara Zanotti, is the record of some Catholic women's responses to such oppression. Lesbian nuns shared their stories in a widely read collection that opened the cloister closet door. Some Protestant women detailed their experiences in *Called Out* (1995), edited by Jane Adams Spahr, Kathryn Poethig, Selisse Berry, and Melinda V. McLain (strong stories, photos, and prayers by Presbyterian lesbians who have defied that denomination's ethos by being visible in their churches).

Jewish lesbians were equally active in the development of religious insights. Evelyn Torton Beck's pioneering work *Nice Jewish Girls: A Lesbian Anthology* (1982) started a rich conversation with myriad voices. The fundamental contradictions between Judaism and same-sex love were explored, as were the links between anti-Semitism and homo-hatred. Poems, photos, even letters make clear that religious experience is not simply what theologians write but more profoundly what believers experience.

This discussion was followed by Christie Balka and Andy Rose's anthology *Twice Blessed: On Being Lesbian, Gay and Jewish* (1989), which features writers who consciously choose to hold together the previously unthinkable, namely, being Jewish and being homosexual. Lesbian writers deal with issues of children and family as well as the theological contradictions that make life so complicated for Jewish lesbians.

Judith Plaskow, professor of religion at Manhattan College and founding coeditor of the *Journal of Feminist Studies in Religion*, addressed some of the central theological issues in her landmark reimagining of Judaism, *Standing Again at Sinai* (1990), from a lesbian feminist perspective. Her writing, both scholarly and popular, helped to shape a theological context in which being Jewish and lesbian is increasingly compatible. While obviously easier to reconcile for Reformed than for Orthodox Jews, the fundamental issues of sexuality and religion are recast through Plaskow's learned and creative approach. Like many other lesbian theologians, Plaskow connects the goodness of embodied love with other struggles for social well-being. She sees communities of resistance within religious communities as necessary to overcome the recalcitrance of the various traditions and to provide support for members in the meantime.

Reconstructionist Rabbi Rebecca Alpert, professor of women's studies at Temple University, offered a programmatic approach to Judaism and lesbians. She proposed new interpretations of Torah that can be helpful in finding common ground. She offered liturgical suggestions, for example, spilling some of the wine from the cup used at heterosexual weddings to signify the incompleteness of a community in which same-sex love is not honored. Alpert observed that Judaism, far from being a welcoming place for Jewish lesbians, can be a locus of exclusion for its own people. She called for renewed religious education, lesbian-friendly readings of texts like the Book of Ruth, and *asot mishpat*, or doing justice, as ways to bring about a vision of inclusive community.

Rabbi Alpert coedited *Lesbian Rabbis* (2001), a volume on the first generation of lesbian rabbis. The eighteen women whose stories are included describe their struggles in a 5,000-year-old religious tradition that has heretofore rejected both women's leadership and same-sex love. It is not easy to embody this enormous change, much less to create new forms of family in the process. Interestingly, the majority of early lesbian rabbis have partners and/or children. These brave, creative women tell painful stories of Jewish institutions rejecting their own best and brightest because they are lesbians. They also tell stories of fulfillment and acceptance as the theo-political climate melts a bit through their efforts.

Bisexual Theology

Bisexuality presents its own complexity. For a long time bisexual voices were virtually missing in theology. The word *bisexual* was added eventually to the litany of *gay and lesbian* with *transgender* added later. In fact, until quite recently, it has been hard to find many explicit references to bisexual theological work. Some women who later identified as lesbian may have used it occasionally while they were reassessing their heterosexual identity.

In the twenty-first century the term is taken much more seriously as a description not of some transitional stage but of a bona fide sexual self-understanding. Indeed, much of what has been written has been in denominational newsletters and not given widespread attention. But as the word gradually crept into the strategic lingo, the reality of bisexual people needed to be explored critically.

Debra R. Kolodny, a bisexual activist, edited the first anthology by bisexual people of faith, *Blessed Bi Spirit* (2000), including Jewish and Christian writers as well as many New Age, Hindu, Buddhist, pagan, and other spiritual approaches. The spectrum is broad in terms of what people understand to be bisexuality at a time when gender terms are so fluid. But the consensus is that loving across the gender spectrum is an authentic way to express the divine-human relationship despite the many obstacles to its practice. Susan Halcomb Craig is an out bisexual pastor in the Presbyterian Church whose doctorate in ministry work is focused on this topic. But bi work is very much in its initial stages.

Transgender challenges remain to be heard in the theological arena. To date there is no theological work done by a male to constructed female nor female to constructed male that has reached publication. But this will undoubtedly change soon.

Achievements and Future Directions

Theological work on lesbian, bisexual, and women-identified themes is useful insofar as it is based on and enhances the experience of its subjects. In the thirty years since Sally Gearhart's initial reflections, remarkable changes are evident both in religion and in society at large.

Virtually every mainline religious tradition is dealing with the matter of same-sex love. Most of these discussions are polarized between those who approve and those who disapprove, resulting often in stalemates but sometimes in increased openness. In almost every instance, substantive debate helps to demonstrate the startling ordinariness of most same-sex love. Human beings seek and find love, then live with illness, aging, children, work, neighbors, and the like, that are part of daily life. So, too, with lesbian and bisexual lovers. The unique aspects have to do with oppression caused by homo-hatred, not difference by homosexuality.

That ordinariness is why there are few claims to lesbian superiority or special insights about the divine that come from same-sex experience. Of course, insight about oppression in a heterosexist society is heightened for lesbian/bisexual and women-identified women. Much of the first thirty years of this theological work has been focused on overcoming that oppression so that more people can live ordinary lives. The cost—economic, emotional, social, and political—remains high for same-sex lovers.

Scholars have formed the Lesbian Feminist Issues and Religion Group at the American Academy of Religion, a professional association for people in religion where some of the latest research is shared at its annual meeting. The National Religious Leadership Roundtable, a project of the National Gay and Lesbian Task Force, includes a number of activist scholars who work across denominations and traditions to bring progressive religious voices to the wider conversations.

Moves toward same-sex marriages and the increase in same-sex families with children push the boundaries of theological anthropology and legal definitions. Since religious institutions are often the gatekeepers of social morals, these issues come under scrutiny as lesbian, bi, and women-identified religious leaders engage in the critical analytic work within their traditions of dealing with such changes and communicating those insights in the larger public conversation. Same-sex commitment services, blessings for women's homes, and other liturgical offerings have helped to promote religious support where none existed.

There is not agreement on the marriage question. Some women-identified scholars favor granting full marital rights to same-sex couples. Others argue that to do so is to buy into and reinforce the heterosexual model that privileges couples over single people and confers benefits accordingly. On the matter of children, there is consensus that families can be formed in a range of gender constellations. What provokes more discussion are the ethical matters of multiple partners and the pastoral matters of helping people deal with the pressures of coming out and coping with unwelcoming families.

Theologians help to name and clarify issues, in this case, articulating women's love for one another as blessed despite contrary social messages. Much remains to be done to convince a culture firmly based on heterosexual couples that love comes in a variety of packages. But lesbian, bisexual, and women-identified scholars have laid a strong foundation in the theological world for love that dares speak its holy name.

SOURCES: The extensive bibliography in the field includes early Christian work by Sally Miller Gearhart, "A Lesbian Looks at God-the-Father or All the Church Needs Is a Good Lay—On Its Side," Philadelphia Task Force on Women in Religion, *Genesis III* 3.1 (May–June 1973), insert; and her volume edited with William R. Johnson, *Loving Women/Loving Men: Gay Liberation and the Church* (1974). Women's love for women in Christian scripture is analyzed by Bernadette J. Brooten, *Love between Women: Early Christian Responses to Female Homoeroticism* (1996). Carter Heyward looked at ethical issues in *Touching Our Strength: The Erotic as Power and the Love of God* (1989), as did Mary E. Hunt in *Fierce Tenderness: A Feminist Theology of Friendship* (1991). Kelly Brown Douglas articulated a womanist perspective on sexuality in "Daring to Speak: Womanist Theology and Black Sexuality," in *Embracing the Spirit: Womanist Perspectives on Hope, Salvation and Transformation*, ed. Emilie M. Townes (1997), 234–246. Jewish sources include Evelyn Torton Beck's anthology *Nice Jewish Girls: A Lesbian Anthology* (1982) and *Lesbian Rabbis: The First Generation*, ed. Rebecca T. Alpert, Sue Levi Elwell, and Shirley Idelson (2001). Judith Plaskow's groundbreaking *Standing Again at Sinai: Judaism from a Feminist Perspective* (1990) laid out the contours for renewed Jewish understanding of sexuality. Debra Kolodny paved the way on bisexuality in her anthology *Blessed Bi Spirit: Bisexual People of Faith* (2000), while Virginia Ramey Mollenkott opened the transgender discussion with *Omnigender: A Trans-religious Approach* (2001).

JEWISH FEMINISM
Judith Plaskow

BECAUSE JEWISHNESS IS more than a religious identity, Jewish feminism is more than a religious movement. A glance through the two Jewish feminist periodicals *Lilith* and *Bridges*, or through major anthologies on Jewish feminism, makes clear that the transformation of women's status and roles within the Jewish religious tradition is just one of the issues on the Jewish feminist agenda. Some of the subjects of major concern to different groups of Jewish feminists are the absence of women's leadership in Jewish communal institutions, anti-Semitism and homophobia in the culture and the women's movement, the place of Jews in multiculturalism and the relationship of Jewish feminism to broader struggles for social justice, the roles of women in Israeli society, and the stance of feminists toward the Israeli Occupation. The first two national Jewish women's conferences, held at the McAlpin Hotel in New York City in 1973 and 1974, each had several sessions on religious issues, but they also looked at such topics as growing up Jewish, women in Jewish education, Jewish women and aging, and being Jewish and poor. In other words, Jewish feminism is a loose, complex, and diverse religious, social, and political movement, as diverse and complex as Jewish identity itself.

Beginnings and Beyond

That said, however, it is certainly the case that the critique and transformation of Judaism are central to the Jewish feminist project and that religious feminism is a rich and heterogeneous movement in its own right. Although individual women voiced their dissatisfactions with women's secondary status within Judaism from the beginnings of the modern era, the *movement* dedicated to protesting and remedying women's subordination in public Jewish religious life emerged in the early 1970s. It was at that historical moment that some Jewish women involved in the second wave of American feminism applied the insights they had gained in the broader movement to their status and roles within Judaism and began to agitate and organize for change. Two early articles helped to articulate and focus a growing discontent among American Jewish women. In the fall of 1970, Trude Weiss-Rosmarin wrote an article in *The Jewish Spectator*, a journal she edited, titled "The Unfreedom of the Jewish Woman," in which she criticized the disabilities of women under Jewish law. Several months later, in the spring of 1971, Rachel Adler published "The Jew Who Wasn't There," a piece that has since become a classic, in the countercultural journal *Davka*. Adler's article was a clarion call to Jewish women to confront their peripheral status in halakah (Jewish law) and to demand or create legal decisions that would "permit Jewish women to develop roles and role-models in which righteousness springs from self-actualization," rather than masochism and self-annihilation (in Heschel, 17).

Also in 1971, a group of eight young feminists associated with the New York Havurah (an intimate fellowship group focused on prayer, study, and social action) founded a study group to reflect on their roles within Judaism and called themselves Ezrat Nashim (a pun on the name of the women's section of the synagogue also meaning "help for women"). In 1972, the group, many of whose members had been educated in the Conservative movement, decided to take the leap from study to activism by bringing the issue of women's equality to the annual convention of Conservative rabbis. In separate meetings with rabbis and their wives, they issued a "Call for Change," in which they demanded equal access for women to Jewish religious leadership and roles within the synagogue and called for the equalization of women's rights in marriage and divorce. Although Ezrat Nashim remained a small group, its importance was magnified by two factors: First, the story of its trip to the Rabbinical Assembly was picked up by the New York press, an event that helped to publicize the name of the group and bring Jewish feminist issues to a broad audience. And second, four of the founding members of Ezrat Nashim—Martha Ackelsberg, Arlene Agus, Paula Hyman, and Elizabeth Koltun—continued to make important contributions to the development of Jewish feminism.

By the time the North American Jewish Students' Network sponsored a first national Jewish women's conference in 1973, dissatisfaction with women's roles was growing in many segments of the Jewish community, and 500 women gathered to discuss the need for change. Three days of programming, including plenary sessions, small group discussions, workshops, and worship services, brought together scholars, communal leaders, congresswomen, and activists to discuss everything from liturgy to education to politics. After a second large conference on "Changing Sex Roles" in 1974, some participants tried to establish a national umbrella Jewish Feminist Organization, organized in regional sections. Although the effort quickly foundered, the conferences were successful in spurring the creation of numerous Jewish feminist groups at the grassroots level and in inspiring the creation of an early feminist literature.

Jewish feminist organizing has taken many forms. Activists in Ezrat Nashim and the North American Jewish Students' Network published a special issue of *Response* magazine, titled *The Jewish Woman*, in 1973. Three years later, a revised and expanded version, edited by Elizabeth Koltun, appeared in book form under the title *The Jewish Woman: New Perspectives*. This was to be the first of numerous anthologies on Jewish feminism, including Susannah Heschel's *On Being a Jewish Feminist*, published in 1983, which reflected the developments of the next decade. In 1976, Susan Weidman Schneider and Aviva Cantor launched *Lilith*, a Jewish feminist magazine Schneider continues to edit. At the same time that a new literature was being developed, Jewish feminists were also working to establish spaces in which the contours of a feminist Judaism could emerge.

In the absence of a national organization, some activists managed to establish Jewish feminist centers in local communities. In 1977 Irene Fine created the Women's Institute for Continuing Jewish Education in San Diego, California, which has not only brought speakers and artists to southern California but published collections of feminist midrash and ritual that have been distributed nationally. In 1991 a gift from the Nathan Cummings Foundation made it possible for Rabbis Laura Geller and Sue Levi Elwell to establish the Jewish Feminist Center in Los Angeles (now defunct), with Elwell as founding director. In 1994, Ma'yan, the Jewish Women's Project in New York City, was founded by philanthropist Barbara Dobkin; Dobkin serves as executive director, and Elwell was invited to serve as the initial rabbinic director. In addition to these more formal organizations, Jewish feminists created a range of women's groups, retreats, conferences, and collectives that could provide space and uninterrupted time to explore and create a feminist Judaism. In 1981 a group of Jewish feminists founded B'not Esh (daughters of fire), a feminist spirituality collective that has continued to meet annually and that seeded spin-offs Achiyot Or (sisters of light) and the short-lived Bat Kol (daughter of the voice/the divine voice). While differing in tone and emphasis, each of the groups has tried to imagine and create a Judaism that thoroughly integrates women's experiences. Such collectives—as well as ongoing local groups and onetime conferences and retreats—offer participants a particularly intense experience of Jewish feminism that generates ideas and resources that then can be shared with a much larger Jewish feminist community.

As Jewish feminism grew and developed, its agenda also expanded and changed. The initial demands of religious Jewish feminists were fairly clear: They wanted an end to the "unfreedom of the Jewish woman" (to use Trude Weiss-Rosmarin's phrase). They wanted equal access for women to public Jewish religious life; the right to take on leadership roles in the synagogue; for Conservative Jews, ordination of women; and the end to women's disabilities in Jewish family law. The issues that first dominated feminist discussion were not so much ones that feminists chose as ones that chose them: the exclusion of women from a minyan (the quorum of ten [men] necessary for communal prayer); the fact that, even in some Reform congregations, women were not called up to bless and read from the Torah; in the Orthodox community, the exclusion of women from serious Jewish study; and the inability of women to initiate divorce under Jewish law. The early Jewish feminist movement was an equal rights movement, trying to redress these grievances and seeking justice for women in the synagogue and the family.

At least within the non-Orthodox Jewish denominations, to which 80 percent of all affiliated Jews in the

United States belong, this equal rights movement has been highly successful—in some ways beyond the wildest dreams of those who issued early calls for change. Within twenty years of Ezrat Nashim's first public feminist action, women were counted in minyanim (plural of quorum) in synagogues across the country; they were regularly conducting services and chanting from the Torah, and they were serving in a variety of other religious leadership roles. The Reform and Reconstructionist movements, which began ordaining women in 1972 and 1974, respectively, had graduated significant numbers of female rabbis by the 1990s, and the Conservative movement, which ordained its first woman in 1985, was also developing a cohort of women in the rabbinate. With considerably less fanfare, the non-Orthodox movements also all found different ways to address the inequality of Jewish divorce. Although serious battles over egalitarianism rage on in individual Conservative congregations, and many women rabbis have come up against a "glass ceiling" blocking their advancement, the overall direction of change seems clear. The struggle for equality has now shifted to Orthodox Judaism. There, women's inability to initiate divorce remains a serious problem, and women still seek access to expanded ritual roles, as well as space in the synagogue that does not shunt them to the periphery and block their access to public ritual. The Orthodox community has also undergone major changes in the last thirty years, however, especially in the area of education. Many girls receive far more comprehensive Jewish schooling than was available a generation ago.

Equal access to all the rights and responsibilities of public religious life (for Orthodox feminists, within the framework of halakah) initially seemed the be all and end all of religious Jewish feminism and for many feminists remains the ultimate accomplishment and goal of the movement. For others, women's ordination and growing participation in the synagogue had the ironic effect of highlighting the contradictions between these new involvements and the *content* of tradition. As more women led services, for example, it became increasingly clear that the *language* of all Jewish prayer books was profoundly male—both in terms of images of God and in terms of references to the covenantal community. Women rabbinical students and other women newly exploring Mishnah and Talmud (the central texts of rabbinic Judaism) found themselves delving into sources that women had no hand in framing and that seemed to exclude their questions and perspectives. Women seeking a Jewish way to celebrate the birth of a baby, or to mark the moment of weaning or the onset of menstruation, discovered that in a tradition rich with blessings for dozens of occasions, there were almost none to mark the significant moments associated with female biology. Early feminist groups such as Ezrat Nashim were

aware that equal access might be just the first of many necessary steps to women's full inclusion in Jewish life, but at a time when the concrete forms of women's exclusion were so visible and painful, often it was hard to see beyond them to envision the outlines of more far-reaching change. The success of equal access opened the way to a more thorough-going critique and transformation of Jewish tradition and created a cohort of women able to bring new questions and perspectives to many areas of Jewish practice and thought.

Deeper Questions

Although theology is not a central mode of Jewish religious discourse, the small group of Jewish feminists interested in theology have often taken the lead in articulating the deeper questions at stake in moving beyond equal access to a systemic critique and reconstruction of Jewish life. In "The Right Question Is Theological," an article published in 1983, Judith Plaskow argued that attempts to remedy the halakic (legal) disabilities of Jewish women failed to address the deeper assumptions concerning women's otherness that underlie specific halakic problems. Feminism demands a new understanding of the central categories of Jewish religious thought, she contended, "an understanding of Torah that begins with acknowledgement of the profound injustice of Torah itself," an "understanding of God that reflects and supports the redefinition of Jewish humanity," and an "understanding of the community of Israel which includes the whole of Israel and which allows women to speak and name our experience for ourselves" (in Heschel, 231–232). The implications of trying to reconceptualize and transform Jewish thought and practice were spelled out by Plaskow in *Standing Again at Sinai* (1990); by Rachel Adler, in numerous articles and her book *Engendering Judaism* (1998); and by Ellen Umansky, Lynn Gottlieb, Drorah Setel, Rebecca Alpert, and others in a host of articles and books published in the 1980s and 1990s.

Rachel Adler's shift from a straightforward call for more sensitive legal decision making to an examination of the presuppositions of the halakic system clearly illustrates the ways in which, for some feminists, the contradictions generated by demands for equal access led to a transformational agenda. In an article published twelve years after "The Jew Who Wasn't There," Adler pointed out that if Jewish religious life rests on the continued interpretation of a received body of knowledge that excludes the perceptions and concerns of women, then many questions raised by women about how to function as autonomous religious agents lie completely outside the realm and imagination of halakah. This problem cannot be resolved by a more woman-friendly application of the rules of the legal system, she said, because questions that do not fit the categories of the system will always be discarded as nondata. By the 1990s, Adler was arguing that the project of feminist Jews is not simply to revise halakah but to transform the normative universe Jews inhabit by telling new stories and embodying those stories in the practices of a community committed to a covenant that includes both women and men.

Such fundamental criticisms of the halakic system point to an overarching issue for Jewish feminists: the need to rethink the authority of Torah, a term denoting both the five books of Moses and the entire continuing history of oral interpretation. While no Jewish feminist has simply turned her back on Jewish sources, non-Orthodox feminists have often characterized Torah as partial and incomplete. Only a truncated record of Jewish encounter with God has been passed down through the generations, and Jewish feminists must lift up women's voices within the tradition and discover and recover the contours of what is missing. Reclaiming women's religious experiences is partly a historiographical task but also presupposes a process of continuing revelation through which women, in interaction both with traditional sources and one another, come to new understandings of themselves and of Jewish stories, practices, and beliefs. What is crucial is that Jewish feminists are characterizing and accepting as Torah the insights emerging from diverse avenues of exploration. Thus, the stories of Genesis are Torah, but so is *Deborah, Golda, and Me* (1991), Letty Cottin Pogrebin's narrative of coming to a Jewish feminist identity; so are the stories of Jewish lesbians recorded in Evelyn Torton Beck's groundbreaking *Nice Jewish Girls* (1982); and so is the work of Jewish feminist historians, artists, dancers, novelists, and poets struggling to find and define themselves within and against the context of Jewish tradition. Torah in its traditional sense is thus decentered and placed in a context in which the experience of the whole Jewish people becomes a basis for legal decision making and spiritual and theological reflection.

This expansion of the meaning of Torah poses a challenge to its content in a number of different areas. A major Jewish feminist issue has been the transformation of God-language, for, as Rita Gross argued in the mid-1970s, Jewish failure to develop female imagery for God is the ultimate symbol of the degradation of Jewish women. In order to dethrone the King robed in majesty, and relativize the powerful image of a mighty male hand leading the Jewish people out of Egypt, feminists have tried both to expand the gender of God and to reconceptualize God's nature and power. Some changed Hebrew and English prayers from the masculine to the feminine, systematically replacing "God-He" with "God-She." Others drew on the image of the Shekhinah, the female aspect of God in the mystical tradition, or looked for Hebrew names for God—like *rakhmana*, mother of

wombs—with feminine resonances. Still others looked for imagery that would convey God's immanence, rather than transcendence, and communicate a sense of empowerment, rather than majestic and distant power. In insisting on the metaphorical character of God-language and calling for the freeing of the Jewish symbolic imagination, feminists also signaled a new understanding of monotheism. Rejecting the dominant Jewish conception of God that has generally identified God's oneness with the worship of a single image of God, feminists embraced a view best articulated by Marcia Falk, that an "authentic" monotheism is not "a singularity of image but an embracing *unity* of a *multiplicity of images*" ("Notes on Composing New Blessings," 41). Monotheism is not the worship of a single male being projected as infinite and above the world but the capacity to find the One in and through the changing forms of the many.

The Centrality of Ritual and Liturgy

Although feminist theologians helped to articulate the theoretical questions involved in a feminist transformation of tradition, it is not in the theological realm that experiments with God language, or many other issues, have been worked out most fully. Both because Judaism is a religion in which *practice* plays a more significant role than theology, and because ceremony and liturgy are central forms in which Jewish beliefs and attitudes are transmitted and embodied, Jewish feminist understandings of God, history, and tradition often have found richest expression in the creation of new liturgies and rituals. At the same historical moment (1976) that Gross first addressed the theoretical importance of female imagery, for example, Maggie Wenig and Naomi Janowitz created a prayerbook for Jewish women undergraduates at Brown University, in which they used female pronouns to refer to God and reimagined God as giving birth and protecting the earth with her womb. Similarly, while Marcia Falk has been an important participant in Jewish feminist theological discussions of God-language, her richest contribution has come through giving liturgical voice to new conceptions of God. Her book *The Book of Blessings: New Jewish Prayers for Daily Life, the Sabbath, and the New Moon Festival* (1996) reworks large portions of the traditional liturgy, evoking a God not outside of and other than the self but present within ordinary experience. "Let us bless the source of life," she writes, "that brings forth bread from the earth," and "Washing the hands, we call to mind the holiness of body" (11). Lynn Gottlieb's *She Who Dwells Within* (1995) brings together theoretical reflection on the feminist renewal of Judaism with the rituals and performance pieces for which she is best known. Drawing boldly on Ancient Near Eastern Goddess imagery and Native American sources, Gottlieb invokes the Shekhinah using dozens of female and natural metaphors—from Birdwoman and Dragonlady to Queen of Heaven to Silvery Moon and invisible web. These, and other feminists liturgies and experiments with God-language under way in communities throughout the country, have influenced a number of synagogue, community, and denominational prayer books.

Just as important as feminist liturgies has been the creation of new rituals, some of which incorporate new God language, others of which highlight women's voices and experiences within Judaism in alternative ways. Since 1976, when Arlene Agus first wrote about *rosh hodesh* (the new moon) as a woman's holiday, *rosh hodesh* groups have sprung up in many communities and have proved popular and enduring contexts for the creation of feminist ritual. Using the association of women with the moon in midrash and folk tradition as a jumping-off point for many kinds of activities, *rosh hodesh* groups have explored feminist spirituality through discussion, ritual, and prayer. A Boston *rosh hodesh* group developed the popular ritual of *Kos Miriam* (the cup of Miriam), in which a goblet filled with spring water is linked with living waters from Miriam's well and with strength and healing in women's lives. Although many *rosh hodesh* ceremonies circulate privately or are spontaneous inventions, some appear in collections such as Penina Adelman's *Miriam's Well* and the newsletter *Rosh Hodesh Exchange*. Orthodox women's *tefillah* (prayer) groups, in which, in the absence of men, women lead services and read from the Torah and haftarah (additional reading for the Sabbath), also often meet in conjunction with *rosh hodesh* and have produced new liturgy of particular relevance to women. A prayer for *agunot* (women whose marriages have ended but who can never remarry because they cannot obtain a Jewish divorce) asks God to "free the captive wives of Israel" and to "infuse our rabbis with the courage to use their power for good alone" (on the Jewish Orthodox Feminist Alliance Web site, www.jofa.org/).

Passover Seders (liturgical meals) have been another central locus of feminist organizing and ritual inventiveness. As the most widely celebrated Jewish holiday, and one that is a primary vehicle for passing on to children the story of Jewish enslavement and liberation from Egypt, the Seder is a particularly appropriate context for discussing both women's roles in the central events of Jewish history and women's unfinished liberation. Aviva Cantor's "Jewish Women's Haggadah" was just the first of many attempts to use the structure and themes of the Haggadah (Passover liturgy) to reflect on the situation of women within Judaism. Many college campuses and feminist community groups around the country have established a tradition of third Seders, at which women remember their foremothers and share their visions of liberation. E. M. Broner's *The Telling*

(1993) records the history and Haggadah of one group of prominent Jewish feminists that has been creating an annual Seder since 1976. Ma'yan, the Jewish Women's Resource Center in New York City, started a Seder in 1994 that, under the leadership of Tamara Cohen and singer and songwriter Debbie Friedman, has proved so popular that it is offered on four evenings, with over 500 participants attending each night.

The importance of Debbie Friedman's presence to the Ma'yan Seders—and earlier, to the Seders of the Jewish Feminist Center in Los Angeles, which she also led—points to the great significance of music as a form of Jewish feminist expression and also to the widespread incorporation of music into feminist liturgy and ritual. Singer/composers such as Friedman, Linda Hirschhorn, Penina Adelman, Faith Rogow, and the group Miraj (Margot Stein, Geela Rayzel Raphael, and Juliet Spitzer) have created a wealth of music for a range of religious and other occasions. In writing new songs in Hebrew and English, putting some of Marcia Falk's blessings to music, celebrating women, and trying on new God-language, they have helped to unify an often scattered movement. Because of the popularity of their CDs and performances, a feminist from the East Coast visiting a *rosh hodesh* group in San Francisco might well find herself singing the same Linda Hirschhorn or Debbie Friedman song familiar from home.

While communal ritual and song are central elements of Jewish feminism, not all feminist rituals are communal in inception and focus. Birth ceremonies for girls were the earliest feminist ritual innovation and the one that has been most widely accepted by all branches of Judaism. The differential welcome accorded male and female infants seemed emblematic to feminists of the unequal roles and status of Jewish women throughout their lives. From the early 1970s, many individual couples tried to create ceremonies for the birth of a daughter that would provide occasions for celebration as important as *B'rit Milah* (the covenant of circumcision that a boy enters at eight days). In 1976, Toby Fishbein Reifman, with the help of Ezrat Nashim, edited and distributed a pamphlet that brought together seven new naming rituals. The challenge in creating such ceremonies has been to find an act or series of acts that might have the power and significance of circumcision. Feminists have tried or suggested a variety of symbolic gestures from washing a girl's feet as a sign of welcome to breaking her hymen (a ceremony that may never have been enacted outside the first chapter of E. M. Broner's novel *A Weave of Women* [1978]) to offering her a ritual object (such as a kiddish cup or prayer shawl) that expresses her parents' hopes for her future participation in the Jewish community.

Once feminists experienced the effectiveness of liturgy and ritual as vehicles for developing new skills, sanctifying important moments in women's lives, and taking the power to shape the future of Judaism, new ceremonies multiplied to mark a wide range of occasions. Jewish feminists have created rituals for—among other things—menarche, childbirth, weaning, miscarriage, rape, and hysterectomy. A number of women, including Savina Teubal and Marcia Cohn Spiegel, have held "croning" ceremonies, in which, on reaching sixty, they celebrate gaining wisdom and entering into a new phase of life. Other rituals have sought to sanctify important nonbiological turning points in women's lives, such as rabbinic ordination, moving across the country, becoming a vegetarian, or coming out as a lesbian. Given the absence of a national Jewish feminist organization that might collect and order such ceremonies, many ceremonies spent years circulating hand to hand, so that women looking for new rituals were often forced to invent them from scratch. In the 1990s, however, two collections brought some of these resources together, making them available to a wide audience. The Women's Institute for Continuing Jewish Education in San Diego published *A Ceremonies Sampler* (1991), a selection of rituals for diverse occasions, and Debra Orenstein's *Lifecycles* (volume 1) provided a more systematic approach to the female life cycle by combining rituals and ceremonies with essays and personal narratives.

The creation of new rituals poses special challenges to Jewish lesbians, who are doubly excluded from the Jewish ceremonial cycle. Rebecca Alpert, a leader in this area, points out that lesbians must both reconstruct those rituals they hold in common with all other Jews and create new rituals that speak to their difference. While commitment ceremonies have been the most visible area of lesbian ritual creativity, lesbians must also transform mourning rituals that do not recognize a lesbian partner as a mourner, find ways to celebrate the birth or adoption of a child in the context of a lesbian relationship, and make connections between the cycle of the Jewish year and lesbian experiences of oppression and liberation. The fact that some feminist Seders, for example, incorporate references to Jewish lesbians or highlight lesbian experiences indicates that Jewish lesbians have been active and involved in all areas of Jewish feminist experimentation, even as they have had to remain alert to the continuing heterosexual bias present in some feminist events and ceremonies.

Midrash and Commentary

Liturgy and ritual are not the only traditional forms into which Jewish feminists have poured new content and meaning. Textual interpretation is a central mode of Jewish religious creativity and expression, and feminists have written midrash and begun to produce commentaries that bring new perspectives and questions to traditional texts. As a classic Jewish technique for explicating and expanding on biblical stories, midrash has been a favorite tool for feminist reinterpretation of tradition. Just as the rabbis brought their own questions to the Bible and resolved contradictions or filled in silences in biblical texts, so feminists have approached the Bible with new questions, often, though not always, centering on the lives and experiences of women. Where was Sarah when Abraham took the child of her old age to offer him as a sacrifice on top of Mount Moriah? Why did Lot's wife look back as the family fled from Sodom? How did Miriam feel as she stood at the shores of the Red Sea about to lead the women across, or when she and Aaron both challenged the authority of Moses, but only she was punished with leprosy? In classes, workshops, and women's groups, feminists have been using midrash as a way of connecting biblical texts with their own experiences and, in doing so, infusing tradition with new life and meaning.

While much of the exploratory work done in informal settings remains in drawers or circulates privately, the San Diego Women's Institute for Continuing Jewish Education has collected a small sample of feminist midrash in two editions of *Taking the Fruit*. Midrash, moreover, is becoming an increasingly popular form for Jewish feminist poets and novelists, so that it is making its way into a broader feminist culture. Alicia Ostriker's midrashic poetry, for example, includes a lament for the death of Jephthah's daughter that can be read or performed as a solemn ceremony, allowing participants to grieve and ponder the meaning of her sacrifice. Ostriker is also author of *The Nakedness of the Fathers* (1994), a book that is somewhat unusual for feminist midrash in that it explores the thoughts and feelings of male figures such as Cain, Abraham, and Joshua, in addition to biblical women. Anita Diamant's novel *The Red Tent* (1997) is an extended midrash on the narratives of Genesis with a particular focus on the story of Dinah, daughter of Jacob. According to Genesis 34, Dinah's brothers murder Shechem, his father, and townsmen to avenge the rape of Dinah, but Diamant sees Dinah as deeply in love with Shechem and the brothers' brutality as causing her profound anguish and sending her into exile in Egypt.

Sometimes feminist midrash shades into, or is part of, sustained commentary on the Torah and other Jewish texts. Jews read the entire Torah (first five books of the Bible) on an annual or three-year cycle, and just as the *d'var Torah* (words about the Torah) is an important part of the Sabbath service, commentaries on the Torah are important resources for those seeking deeper understanding of the weekly Torah reading. Several explicitly feminist biblical commentaries began to appear in the 1990s. *The Five Books of Miriam* (1996), by Ellen Frankel, combines scholarly and midrashic commentary on the Torah in the form of conversation among a number of "dramatis personae." "Our daughters," "our mothers," "our bubbes" (grandmothers), "Lilith the rebel," "Sarah the ancient one," and many other voices discuss and comment on sections of each book of the Torah. *The Women's Torah Commentary* (2000), edited by Rabbi Elyse Goldstein, offers commentaries on the fifty-four weekly Torah portions, each by an ordained woman. Varying considerably in tone and perspective, they nonetheless all seek to bring some piece of "women's wisdom" to the Torah texts, including those dealing with topics seemingly very far from women's lives. Debra Orenstein and Jane Litman's *Lifecycles* (volume 2) brings together personal narratives organized around the themes of the Torah in order to explore the impact of biblical texts on contemporary women's experience. Torah study and commentary are also important activities among Orthodox women. Both informally organized classes, and those offered by programs such as the Drisha Institute in New York City, the premier center for adult Jewish women's study, attract large numbers of women interested in acquiring more facility with Jewish texts. While not all such study is feminist in orientation, feminism has helped fuel the desire and expand the opportunities for women's study.

A rather different kind of commentary is found in *Beginning Anew: A Woman's Companion to the High Holy Days* (1997), edited by Gail Twersky Reimer and Judith Kates. The contributors to this volume, who span the full range of Jewish affiliation from secular to Orthodox, each comment on one of the Torah or Haftorah readings for Rosh Hashanah or Yom Kippur. Reimer and Kates's intention is to bring "women's voices, women's perspectives into the quintessential mode of Jewish spirituality, the study of Torah" (19), which for centuries has been the province of men. *Beginning Anew* is a follow-up to another book edited by Kates and Reimer, *Reading Ruth* (1994). That volume brings together thirty novelists, essayists, psychologists, rabbis, and scholars to reflect on one of the few biblical books that places women at its center, and thus to illuminate the connection between women and traditional Jewish texts. All these new commentaries take their place on what British Jewish feminists have called "the half-empty bookcase," or perhaps better, in the half-empty library of Jewish commentaries on the Torah and other normative texts that, until recently, had been written entirely by men.

Feminist Scholarship

Several of these areas of feminist endeavor shade into another important arena of Jewish feminist creativity, namely scholarship. Jewish feminists have both drawn on and participated in the development of new methodologies in feminist studies in a wide range of disciplines. They have offered important critiques of normative texts and used the tools of archeology and other fields to illuminate the social worlds surrounding these texts; they have developed a body of theory, made significant contributions to feminist historiography, and begun to investigate the religious lives that women created within the context of patriarchal Judaism. By no means does all this new scholarship focus on Judaism as a religion. Historians Paula Hyman and Marion Kaplan, for example, have done very important work on gender, immigration, and assimilation, and on German Jewish women, respectively, and a number of the contributors to Judith Baskin's *Jewish Women in Historical Perspective* (1991) are interested primarily in social history. A large body of writing, however, has addressed the significance of gender in the construction of Jewish texts and practices and expanded knowledge about women's participation and exclusion in different periods of Jewish history, so much so that the lineaments of the more holistic understanding of Judaism called for by feminists are beginning to come into view. Although feminist scholars stand in different relationships to Jewish feminism as a movement (and not all are Jewish), the existence of their work helps to provide historical grounding for feminist arguments for a more inclusive Jewish community. Some of the information and texts discussed by scholars, moreover, have contributed to other forms of Jewish feminist expression, such as midrash, liturgy, and textual commentary.

One significant and huge area of feminist research has involved analyzing, critiquing, and illuminating the historical and social contexts of normative Jewish texts. In biblical studies, for example, Carol Meyers has used archeological materials and cross-cultural studies of tribally organized societies to try to shed light on the lives of ordinary women in the biblical period, while Tikva Frymer-Kensky has located the emergence of biblical monotheism in the context of the Goddess-worshiping societies of the ancient Near East. Ross Kraemer and Bernadette Brooten, among others, have focused on Judaism in the Greco-Roman period, using archeological and literary evidence to reconstruct women's religious lives and comparing extracanonical evidence with rabbinic sources. Many feminist scholars are interested in the complex relationship between normative texts and the social and religious contexts out of which they emerge. They have pointed to the ways these texts ignore or erase information about women's social, religious, or economic roles available from other sources. One would never know from reading the Mishnah (the second-century code of Jewish law that forms the basis of the Talmud), for instance, that some elite women exercised leadership roles in the ancient synagogue; yet archeological evidence testifies to that reality.

Other scholars have done close work on canonical

texts themselves, approaching these texts with a variety of methods and agendas. Rachel Biale's *Women and Jewish Law*, a straightforward presentation of rabbinic teachings on a range of topics relevant to women, has served as an important resource for those lacking the tools to handle primary sources. Judith Romney Wegner and Judith Hauptman, both scholars of rabbinics, have focused on particular questions concerning women's status in rabbinic texts. Wegner asks in what situations the authors of the Mishnah defined women as legal persons and where as legal chattel, and Hauptman is interested in the ways in which the rabbis modified certain laws over time to ameliorate the situation of women. Miriam Peskowitz, rather than beginning with the assumption of gender difference, explores the ways in which the rabbis of the Mishnah *create* gender through what they take for granted about work, marriage, and property relations. Daniel Boyarin and Howard Eilberg-Schwartz have focused on the construction of Jewish masculinity in rabbinic and (in Eilberg-Schwartz's case) biblical sources. Boyarin explores the ideal of the "feminized" [*sic*] male in Jewish culture as an alternative to European ideals of manliness, and Eilberg-Schwartz looks at the problems and contradictions generated for human masculinity by the idea of a disembodied God. The work of Peskowitz and Boyarin is also representative of the postmodern turn that some Jewish feminist scholarship began to take in the 1990s. The growing body of literature that falls under this rubric is characterized by an expansion of the notion of text, an investigation of the contradictions and fractures in Jewish sources, a denaturalizing of gender, and an exploration of the role of texts in creating gender, rather than simply reflecting gender categories already built into the body.

At the same time that many scholars have mined ancient canonical and noncanonical materials for what they reveal about women's roles and/or the construction of gender, others have turned to modern and contemporary sources that potentially shed direct light on women's religious practices and their relationship to the larger tradition. Chava Weissler, for instance, in her book *Voices of the Matriarchs* (1998), uses a genre of Yiddish devotional prayers called *tekhines* as a window into early modern Ashkenazic (central and eastern European) women's lives, customs, and concerns. Written for women, some of them by women, the *tekhines* endow women's private sphere with religious value, lending dignity and holiness to women's lives by providing prayers for numerous ordinary tasks and occasions. In valorizing women's sphere, however, the *tekhines* also accept and reinforce it, so that while they provide access to women's culture, they also show how that culture accommodated to male domination and male constructions of gender. A similarly ambiguous picture of women's culture emerges from Susan Sered's work with elderly Kurdish Jewish women living in Jerusalem. Exploring the religious lives of uneducated, illiterate women in a male-centered and text-based tradition, Sered also notes that the women find ways to sacralize their own experiences. But as she describes how her informants ritualize literacy or view food preparation as a religious activity, she, like Weissler, uncovers contradictory layers of resistance and accommodation in the Judaism these women created.

While feminist scholars who study normative texts often hope that their work will contribute to the creation of alternative constructions of gender, work on women's culture has seemed, at least on the surface, more directly "usable" by feminists today. Thus, in addition to the fact that some feminists may recite a traditional *tekhine* as they light candles on Friday night, the *tekhine* form is echoed in the poetry of Merle Feld and the poems and prayers collected by Nina Beth Cardin that find spiritual meaning in the everyday experiences of contemporary women's lives. Ellen Umansky and Dianne Ashton's collection *Four Centuries of Jewish Women's Spirituality* includes *tekhines* and poetry from the sixteenth century that might be used in present-day rituals. But it also contains a number of contemporary rituals as examples of twentieth-century women's religious expression. In this text, therefore, there is clearly a direct relationship between the documentation and creation of a women's spirituality.

The Jewish Orthodox Feminist Alliance

While the many forms of Jewish feminist expression discussed here have emerged from a loose and often-fragmented grassroots movement, the late 1990s saw an important development within Jewish feminism: the emergence of an umbrella Orthodox organization, the Jewish Orthodox Feminist Alliance (JOFA). Orthodox feminism is certainly not a creation of the 1990s. Blu Greenberg, president of JOFA, was the keynote speaker at the first Jewish women's conference in 1973, and her book *On Women and Judaism*, which laid the foundations for a halakic Jewish feminism, was published in 1981. The establishment of JOFA can be seen as the result of decades of steady and often quiet change within the Orthodox community: the creation of a network of women's prayer groups that have flourished despite a certain amount of rabbinic opposition; expanding opportunities for girls to celebrate a bat mitzvah and for women to say kaddish (the mourner's prayer traditionally recited by close male relatives); the development of institutions for women's study and increasing possibilities for study in mainstream yeshivot (traditional schools of Jewish study); and activism around the issue of divorce.

In February 1997, a coalition of Orthodox women's

groups, including the Drisha Institute and the Women's Tefillah Network, sponsored the first International Conference on Women and Orthodoxy at the Grand Hyatt Hotel in New York City. Characterized by much the same level of excitement and energy as the first Jewish women's conference in 1973, the two-day event drew 1,300 participants interested in discussing the achievements of and challenges facing Orthodox feminism. Prominent North American Orthodox feminists such as Greenberg, Susan Aranoff, Rivka Haut, and Norma Baumel Joseph, as well as feminists from abroad, discussed a wide range of topics from the general state of Orthodox feminism to the plight of *agunot* to new visions of learning to women and self-empowerment. Workshops on Torah study, on the personal realm, and on spiritual expression focused on such subjects as *mikvah* (the ritual bath), infertility, life-cycle ceremonies, and tallith

and tefillin (prayer shawl and phylacteries). One of the outgrowths of the conference was the establishment of the Jewish Orthodox Feminist Alliance, which then cosponsored a second, equally large Feminism and Orthodoxy Conference in 1998 and put on a third entirely on its own in 2000. The conferences have provided opportunities both for strategizing around particular issues of concern to Orthodox feminists and for reporting on new opportunities and developments in the Orthodox community, such as women taking on new mitzvah (commandments) like kiddush (the blessing over wine) and reading the *Megillah* (book of Esther), the hiring of female rabbinic interns in a few modern Orthodox synagogues, and even the beginnings of rabbinic study for women.

JOFA locates itself at the intersection of these developments and is dedicated to expanding the "spiritual,

In February 1997, a coalition of Orthodox women's groups, including the Drisha Institute and the Women's Tefillah Network, sponsored the first International Conference on Women and Orthodoxy at the Grand Hyatt Hotel in New York City. Characterized by much the same level of excitement and energy as the first Jewish women's conference in 1973, the two-day event drew 1,300 participants interested in discussing the achievements of and challenges facing Orthodox feminism. *Copyright © Linda Eber.*

ritual, intellectual and political opportunities for women within the framework of halakha," in the firm conviction that this will "enrich and uplift individual and communal life for all Jews." Because the inability of women to initiate divorce within Judaism has the power to destroy women's lives in concrete and immediate ways, advocacy for *agunot* is a central Orthodox feminist issue. JOFA, in conjunction with a number of other organizations specifically concerned with the plight of *agunot*, is involved in a multipronged program to ameliorate their situation. JOFA also publishes a journal and a series of booklets on women and ritual that keep members informed of issues and developments of interest to Orthodox feminists and that make available resources for women interested in bat mitzvah or wanting to participate more fully in mourning rituals, birthing ceremonies, and observance of the Sabbath. It is also working with schools and other communal institutions to advocate for the inclusion of girls and women to the full extent possible within the framework of halakah, and it is planning "a study on innovative synagogue architecture that provides equal and inclusive space for women" (on the JOFA Web site, http://www.jofa.org/).

The fact that JOFA was established in 1997, almost twenty-five years after the first women's conference, points to the evolution and liveliness of Jewish feminism as well as the divisions within it. From a liberal Jewish perspective, many of the issues central to Orthodox feminism could easily be resolved by stepping outside a halakic framework; yet the fact that Orthodox feminists seek to expand opportunities for women within the boundaries of halakah involves them in serious Torah study and careful analyses of particular legal issues that add depth and breadth to the overall Jewish feminist project. Whether, as Orthodox women gain fuller access to the public religious arena, they will then follow non-Orthodox women in creating new scholarship, new theology, and new religious forms remains to be seen. It also remains to be seen what the next steps are for non-Orthodox feminists in creating a Judaism fully inclusive of women.

SOURCES: It is very difficult to select a small number of texts from the extensive bibliography of Jewish feminist work. Of the works quoted here, Rachel Adler's frequently reprinted "The Jew Who Wasn't There" is most readily available in Susannah Heschel's *On Being a Jewish Feminist: A Reader* (1983). Judith Plaskow's "The Right Question Is Theological" is published in the same volume. Marcia Falk's "Notes on Composing New Blessings: Toward a Feminist-Jewish Reconstruction of Prayer," *Journal of Feminist Studies in Religion* 3 (1987): 39–53, anticipates issues taken up fully in her volume *The Book of Blessings: New Jewish Prayers for Daily Life, the Sabbath, and the New Moon Festival* (1996). The prayer for *agunot* and information about JOFA are available on the JOFA Web site at www.jofa.org. Gail Twersky Reimer and Judith Kates discuss

women's Torah study in *Beginning Anew: A Woman's Companion to the High Holy Days* (1997). Of the many other works mentioned, some of the more basic follow: Rachel Adler, *Engendering Judaism: An Inclusive Theology and Ethics* (1998). Rebecca Alpert, *Like Bread on the Seder Plate: Jewish Lesbians and the Transformation of Tradition* (1997). Rachel Biale, *Women and Jewish Law: An Exploration of Women's Issues in Halakhic Sources* (1984). Aviva Cantor, "Jewish Women's Haggadah," in *Sistercelebrations,* ed. Arlene Swidler (1974). Blu Greenberg, *On Women and Judaism: A View from Tradition* (1981). Elizabeth Koltun, ed., *The Jewish Woman: New Perspectives* (1976). Elizabeth Resnick Levine, *A Ceremonies Sampler: New Rites, Celebrations and Observances of Jewish Women* (1991). Debra Orenstein, *Lifecycles: Jewish Women on Life Passages and Personal Milestones,* vol. 1 (1994). Debra Orenstein and Jane Rachel Litman, *Lifecycles: Jewish Women on Biblical Themes in Contemporary Life,* vol. 2 (1997). Judith Plaskow, *Standing Again at Sinai: Judaism from a Feminist Perspective* (1990). Ellen M. Umansky and Dianne Ashton, *Four Centuries of Jewish Women's Spirituality* (1992).

THE CASE FOR NATIVE LIBERATION THEOLOGY
Andrea Smith

WHILE THERE HAS been a proliferation of liberation theologies rooted in diverse communities of color, the development of Native liberation theology, particularly Native women's theology, has been a slow process. Nonetheless, Native women's perspectives on spirituality and social justice have much to contribute to the field of theology, particularly liberation theology.

There are a number of reasons for the reluctance of many Native religious scholars to embrace theology. First, theology's often traditional emphasis on proscribing proper doctrines and beliefs often runs counter to indigenous spiritual practices. Jace Weaver similarly argues that theology is inconsonant with indigenous worldviews that hold that the systematic study of God is both presumptuous and impossible. "Traditional Native religions are integrated totally into daily activity," Weaver argues. "They are ways of life and not sets of principles or creedal formulation.... Native 'religion' does not concern itself—does not try to know or explain—'what happens in the other world' " (*That the People Might Live,* vii).

Prominent scholar Vine Deloria, Jr., argues that even liberation theology is grounded on a western European epistemological framework that is no less oppressive to Native communities than is mainstream theology. "Liberation theology," Deloria cynically argues, "was an absolute necessity if the establishment was going to continue to control the minds of minorities. If a person of a minority group had not invented it, the liberal establishment most certainly would have created it" (*For This Land*, 100). According to Deloria, Native liberation must be grounded in indigenous epistemologies—epistemologies that are inconsistent with Western epistemologies—of which liberation theology is a part. "If we are then to talk seriously about the necessity of liberation, we are talking about the destruction of the whole complex of western theories of knowledge and the construction of a new and more comprehensive synthesis of human knowledge and experience" (106). The challenge brought forth by Native scholars/activists to other liberation theologians would be—even if we distinguish the "liberation" church from mainstream churches—Can the black church, or any church for that matter, escape complicity in Christian imperialism? Deloria in particular raises the challenge that Christianity, because it is a temporally rather than a spatially based tradition (that is, it is not tied to a particular land base but can seek converts from any land base), is necessarily a religion tied to imperialism because it will never be content to remain within a particular place or community. "Once religion becomes specific to a group, its nature also appears to change, being directed to the internal mechanics of the group, not to grandiose schemes of world conquest" (*God Is Red*, 296–297). Hence, all Christian theology, even liberation theology, remains complicit in the missionization and genocide of Native peoples in the Americas.

These arguments are compelling. However, these critiques often presuppose a comparative religious studies approach as an alternative to theology for addressing Native religiosity and hence insufficiently fail to acknowledge religious studies as a colonizing discourse, particularly within Native communities. This colonizing discourse is evident in Emile Durkheim's classic *Elementary Forms* (1915), in which Durkheim argues that the individuals best prepared to study a religious tradition are those who do not actually practice it. Only the Western scientific mind has the necessary power of analysis to correctly ascertain the nature of indigenous religion; indigenous people lack the appropriate intellectual cultivation and reflection. Durkheim's maxim continues to inform the discipline of comparative religions today. A 1997 exchange between Sam Gill and Christopher Jocks in the *Journal of the American Academy of Religion* shows the influence. Gill, a prominent non-Native scholar in the study of religion, provoked controversy when he argued that Native communities had no notions of earth as mother, that Native religions actually derived the concept from white people. Native peoples in the field of religion challenged this argument because, they argued, Sam Gill did not know Native languages, nor did he have an in-depth understanding of Native religions and hence was ill-informed. In response, Gill wrote an essay in which he contended that because Native religious

scholars subscribe to the religious beliefs they study, they were ill equipped for this type of scholarship. Like Durkheim, he contended that only those who stood outside Native religious worldviews were in a position to understand them properly.

In addition, rejecting theology (or any discipline, for that matter) as inherently white presumes that Native cultures have somehow managed to remain untainted by white culture or that Native communities can completely untangle themselves from the larger colonial society. Roberto Mendoza notes that this kind of separatism does "not really address the question of power. How can small communities tied in a thousand ways to the capitalist market system break out without a thorough social, economic and political revolution within the whole country?" (Mendoza, 8). If a revolution is necessary, then it would seem wise for Native scholars and activists to use any tool that might be helpful in changing society "by any means necessary."

Furthermore, the anthropological focus of comparative religious studies lacks an explicit concern about ethics that is integral to the discipline of theology, particularly liberation theology. It is not enough to understand or describe Native religious experience; it is necessary to advocate for the survival of Native spiritual practices and an end to colonialism. Liberation theology brings to Native studies an explicit concern for the victims of colonialism and highlights the importance of struggle against oppression in its framework. Recently, George Tinker, Clara Sue Kidwell, and Homer Noley published the first book-length book on Native theology, *A Native American Theology*, which attempts to articulate theology from an indigenous cultural and spiritual framework. While helpful in furthering the conversation on how Native peoples can develop theologies that are accountable to Native communities, it does lack a strong gender analysis as well as a strong political focus on liberation. Thus, for a Native feminist theology, it is important to look toward other sources.

The methodologies of both womanist and *mujerista* theologians offer possibilities for uncovering Native women's perspectives on spirituality/liberation praxis. As a matter of principle, feminists theologians focus on the experiences of women as a starting point for theology, but here a host of methodological questions arise: Whose experiences are being represented, and by whom? What counts as "accurate" representation? How does the theologian claim to "know" the experience of the collectivity, and what authorizes her to be its voice? *Mujerista* theologian Ada María Isasi-Díaz calls upon theologians to account for their methods: Are they rooted in the day-to-day experiences of the people they write about?

To get at the voices of women in their communities, many womanist and *mujerista* theologians use stories to represent black and Latina women's voices. Because slaves were not allowed to read the Bible and learned it by word-of-mouth, black communities have tended to experience the Bible through the flexibility of an aural culture. According to Renita Weems, the protean nature of oral tradition has given black communities the freedom to modify and retell stories from the Bible to suit their changing needs. Delores Williams, for example, uses this freedom to tell the story of Hagar in a manner she thinks will speak to African American women today. But storytelling is not limited to biblical stories. M. Shawn Copeland uses slave narratives to analyze black women's experiences of suffering. Katie Cannon claims that black women's literature is a crucial link to the oral traditions of the past as a mode of ethical instruction and cultural dissemination.

Like African American culture, Native cultures are orally based. Consequently, storytelling is a critical resource for uncovering Native women's experiences. The burgeoning literary tradition of Native women provides a window into how story maintains community. Such literature is generally more accessible and more likely to be written with Native people in mind, unlike theological texts, which are written for a non-Indian audience. Consequently, Native women's literature as well as the more academic writings of Native women, even by women who are not professional theologians, can be a helpful theological resource.

However, while feminist/womanist/*mujerista* theologians often utilize a variety of resources to give voice to the communities they represent, they often do not emphasize the perspectives of activists and organizers in their work. The problem that this approach presents for a theology *of liberation* is that most people, even most women, are not activists or organizers for social change. Therefore, to identify Native women's liberation theology, it is also important to highlight the spiritual and political perspectives of Native women activists specifically. Based on these sources, one can detect some central themes emergent in Native women's theology. These themes may not be based on standard Christian theological terms. In order to address Vine Deloria's charge that Christianity is implicated in genocide against Native peoples, it would be important to center on indigenous beliefs and practices rather than Christian doctrines in theological formations. In addition, because Native religions, like Native cultures in general, are orally based, they are quite flexible. Indians give less weight to an orthodoxy of religious belief than to spiritual centeredness and ethical behavior—what Native people call "walking in balance." Second, as mentioned previously, Indian spiritualities tend to be more practice than belief centered; that is, what makes one Indian is not simply holding the proper set of core beliefs but behaving like an Indian. Of course, this should not be taken to mean

either that Indian religions have no content or that anyone gets to be an Indian who "decides" to "behave like one." These points suggest that in looking at Native women's activism as a source for liberation theology, standard theological categories may have less relevance than they do for other communities.

Relationship to Tradition

The spiritual practice of Native women generally stands in a mixed relation to Christianity, on the one hand, and to the indigenous traditions of Native women, on the other. Of course, there are Native women who choose to embrace a variety of other foreign traditions, from Judaism to Zen Buddhism, but Christianity has long been the colonizing religion of Native women, as it has been for African American women.

Many Native women engaged in liberation struggles reject Christianity in its entirety. Haunani-Kay Trask (Hawaiian), for example, calls Christianity "the most vicious religion in the world." Unlike African Americans, Native Americans have not developed separate Christian institutions that have fought at the vanguard of our liberation struggles. (A possible exception is the Native American church, which has never achieved the prominence among Indians as the black church has among African Americans.) In addition, the most recent effects of Christian colonization are not very far off in history for many Native Americans, as they may be for African Americans. Many indigenous people can trace the dysfunctionality within their families within a generation or two to Christian mission boarding schools where physical, emotional, and sexual abuse was rampant. The complete rejection of Christianity is most prominent among urban Indians who were raised as Christian but who now view it as a hindrance to liberation for Native people.

In some respects, however, the neotraditional rejection of Christianity is a legacy of Christian dualistic thinking. Vine Deloria notes that neotraditionalist attempts to reclaim Native spirituality draw upon an either/or logic system foreign to Native cultures. Belief systems that seem mutually inconsistent to European and Euro-American culture, like Christianity and indigenous religions, can coexist in indigenous cultures. To illustrate with a real-life example: At a conference several years ago, this author heard a story about an Indian man who gave a speech in which he claimed that the next speaker was going to say things that were completely wrong. When his turn came, the next speaker, also Indian, began not by attacking the preceding speaker but by announcing that everything he had said was completely true, then went on with his talk. The event is notable because it struck no one present—not the speakers, not the Indian audience—as odd.

Consequently, even Natives raised with a more traditional worldview do not always feel the need to reject Christianity outright, even as they criticize its abuses. Indians tend to relate to both Christianity and their Native traditions along a continuum. Some define themselves as wholly Christian, others as wholly traditional, but probably most relate to both in some fashion: All but the most European-identified Native Christians will occasionally take part in a traditional ceremony, while others who are primarily traditional will still go to church now and then. This flexibility lessens the need for Native Christians to "reinterpret" Christian concepts that they find oppressive: They simply ignore what they find inadequate or offensive in Christianity and look elsewhere, usually to Native traditions, for what they need. For example, in contrast to white Christian feminists who focus on reenvisioning scripture, many Indian women do not try to "reenvision" scripture because they do not read it in the first place. For instance, at one sermon, the pastor noted, "Obviously reading the Bible is not necessary for salvation, because otherwise no Indians would be saved." For those that do read the scripture, the capacious, flexible, and essentially pragmatic worldviews of indigenous peoples can allow them to embrace contradiction without necessarily dispensing with Christianity. Until recently, this radical decentering of foundational truth-claims, especially of Christian truth-claims, has had no counterpart in European thought. According to the European positivist grammar of truth, if proposition *p* is true, then not-*p* must be false. Indigenous peoples have never thought this way; even their creation stories take no epistemological precedence over those of other cultures. Europeans have always found this thinking maddening. Charles Eastman (Sioux) illustrates with the following story:

> A missionary once undertook to instruct a group of Indians in the truths of his holy religion. He told them of the creation of the earth in six days, and of the fall of our first parents by eating an apple. The courteous savages listened attentively, and after thanking him, one related in his turn a very ancient tradition concerning the origin of maize. But the missionary plainly showed his disgust and disbelief, indignantly saying: "What I delivered to you were sacred truths, but this that you tell me is mere fable and falsehood!" "My Brother," gravely replied the offended Indian, "it seems that you have not been well grounded in the rules of civility. You saw that we, who practice these rules, believed your stories; why, then, do you refuse to credit ours?" (Deloria, *God Is Red*, 86)

Of course, while Indian liberation may not necessitate the wholesale rejection of Christianity, the revitalization of indigenous traditions will probably be at the heart of Indian liberation, with Christianity playing, at best, a supporting role. Those with a vested interest in white Christian hegemony find such decentering even more threatening than absolute rejection because it changes Christianity from an ontological foundation to an appropriable resource. That means, among other things, that Christianity and white culture in general no longer have to be at the center of every conversation. As Menominee poet/activist/maid Chrystos says in her poem "Rude as 2:20 am," "I don't have time/ to hate white folks/ which offends you because it means you aren't/ the center of the world as your whole life/ has conspired to teach you" (*Dream On*, 49).

While Native people may feel comfortable moving within a number of spiritual traditions, their approach is not necessarily "syncretistic," or synthesizing, in the fashion of Latina/Chicana theologies that emphasize *mestizaje* (or the blending of races and cultures together, particularly European, African, and indigenous cultures).

While Native women, in contrast, often describe themselves as living in more than one world, they do not necessarily try to synthesize these worlds. As a spiritual leader once said, when you are with Indians, be completely Indian; when you are with whites, be completely white; do not try to mix the two. Because indigenous people have more access than Latinos do to their specific traditions, they are better able to maintain the integrity of each. Of course, it is not realistic to suggest that indigenous religions continue to exist in a "pure" form. Besides being affected by the colonizing culture, the pan-Indian movement and urbanization have led to the mingling of different Native traditions. Some Native people celebrate this mixing and affirm it as a positive cultural response to the modern world. As Leslie Marmon Silko writes in her novel *Ceremony*:

> At one time, the ceremonies as they had been performed were enough for the way the world was then. But after the white people came, elements in this world began to shift; and it became necessary to create new ceremonies. I have made changes in the rituals. The people mistrust this greatly, but only this growth keeps the ceremonies strong. (126)

Others, however, describe the changes brought about by contact with European and other indigenous cultures as a loss to each individual Native tradition. Moreover, to keep Indians within the church, some denominations have begun grafting aspects of indigenous culture onto Christian liturgy in their services.

While Indians may debate the significance of the mixing of indigenous traditions with each other and with outside traditions, only the most assimilationist would deny the need for Native people to know as much as possible about their specific traditions. Integral to the indigenous spiritual and cultural revitalization movement is the recovery and preservation of Indian language.

The controversial notion in Indian communities of blending traditions, as opposed to moving "discretely" through several, naturally comes to a head in the vexed relationship between Native and *mestizo* women. In fact, Native scholars like Ines Hernandez-Avila (Chicana–Nez Percé) refer to *mestizaje* as a "colonizing" discourse directed against indigenous women. Hernandez-Avila is suspicious of claims that *mestizaje* equally validates all cultures: If so, why do so few *mestizos* know anything about indigenous cultures other than Aztec, Mayan, or Incan? Why is the language of *mestizaje* Spanish or Portuguese, rather than an indigenous or African language? Why do *mestizos* seldom make more than a perfunctory effort to recover their indigenous or African languages and cultures? They argue that much discourse on *mestizaje* is based on primitivist notions of indigeneity that is imaged simply as a tributary to *mestizo* identity that elides contemporary indigenous struggles for land and culture.

Unlike many other feminist theologians, Native women have generally not felt a need to grapple with the oppressive features of their own traditions. They generally tend to argue that, prior to colonization, Indian societies for the most part were not male dominated. Women served as spiritual, political, and military leaders. Many societies were matrilineal and matrilocal. Violence against women and children was infrequent, unheard of in many tribes. Native people did not use corporal punishment against their children. And although there existed a division of labor between women and men, women's and men's labor were accorded similar status. As Winona LaDuke (Anishinabe) states:

Traditionally, American Indian women were never subordinate to men. Or vice versa, for that matter. What native societies have always been about is achieving balance in all things, gender relations no less than any other. Nobody needs to tell us how to do it. We've had that all worked out for thousands for years. And, left to our own devices, that's exactly how we'd be living right now. (In Jaimes, 118)

Concerned with "balance in all things," Native societies were far less authoritarian than their European counterparts. Seventy percent of tribes did not practice war at all. When societies did practice war, their intent was not to annihilate the enemy but to accrue honor through the bravery of their warriors. A warrior accrued more honor by getting close enough to an enemy to touch him, then leaving him alive, than by killing him. Consequently, most Native women regard sexism within indigenous communities today as the result of colonialism.

Nonetheless, Native women must struggle with issues of cultural change. In times of genocidal danger, the idea of transforming traditions to meet current needs can seem especially threatening. Particularly among Native cultures like the southeastern tribes that have been subjected the longest to colonization, patriarchy is firmly entrenched. Consequently, women like former principal chief of the Cherokee Nation Wilma Mankiller, who strive for political leadership, are accused, ironically, of not being traditional. Another example of change is the women's Sun Dance. (The Sun Dance is probably the most sacred ceremony of the Plains tribes.) First, women decided to hold a women-only Sun Dance. Then Native lesbians who were forced out of their tribe's Sun Dance—which, prior to colonization, would never have happened—began their own Sun Dance. Then, this Sun Dance began to admit white women and women who were menstruating. Mary Crow Dog discusses some of the ensuing controversy:

While Leonard [Crow Dog, her husband] stressed the importance of women in Indian religion, he was careful never to blur the role of men and women in traditional Indian life.... When [women] put on their own Sun Dance, excluding men from participating, he was angry. Neither men nor women should be prevented from taking part.... The only exception was that menstruating women should not take part in ceremonies because a woman's period is considered so powerful that it wipes out any other power and renders rituals ineffective. When, recently, a small group of women wanted to put on a lesbian Sun Dance, Leonard just freaked out.... A lot of changes in thinking had occurred during his absence [in jail] and he had to deal with that. (Crow Dog, 249)

How much change can a community, Indian or otherwise, accommodate and still be traditional? And who decides what "tradition" is, anyway? Native cultures have always changed to meet contemporary needs. One attribute of oral cultures is the ability to adapt rather than to try to maintain itself against a written fixed set of principles. Of course, the only cultures that *never* change are the dead and petrified kind; however, after the mostly damaging transitions forced upon Native cultures by colonization, now virtually all change is regarded with suspicion. The challenge, then, is to find a way of welcoming change that may be helpful, but to root it firmly within tradition. As Silko writes:

"There are some things I have to tell you," Betonie began softly. "The people nowadays have an idea about the ceremonies. They think the ceremonies must be performed exactly as they have always, maybe because one slip or mistake and the whole ceremony must be stopped. . . . That much is true. . . . But long ago when the people were given these ceremonies, the changing began . . . if only in the different voices from generation to generation. . . . You see, in many ways, the ceremonies have always been changing. . . .

. . . Things which don't shift and grow are dead things. . . . That's what the witchery is counting on: that we will cling to the ceremonies the way they were, and then their power will triumph, and the people will be no more." (Silko, 129)

Spiritual/Cultural Appropriation

In feminist theology, cultural appropriation is becoming a hot topic. The article "Appropriation and Reciprocity in Womanist/Mujerista/Feminist Work" in the *Journal of Feminist Studies in Religion (JFSR)*, based on a special session at the 1991 American Academy of Religion, highlights many of the issues at stake. Contributing writers describe cultural appropriation as an important problem but not a survival issue. Delores Williams has also remarked that appropriation, while annoying, is perhaps not the most pressing topic on the discussion agenda of feminists, womanists, and *mujeristas*. Among Native women, however, appropriation is widely regarded as a matter of *survival*. Most Indian activist groups have written position statements condemning the use of their cultural traditions by outsiders, describing it as a form of genocide. Indian nations are even using the legal apparatus of intellectual property rights to file lawsuits against those who make a profit by stealing Indian culture.

Non-Indians tend to downplay appropriation as a political and spiritual concern, but if appropriation is really as trivial as non-Indians suggest, why are Native people subjected to such violence when they condemn it? For example, when a mere handful of Native students began a peaceful campaign to eradicate Chief Illiniwik as the mascot of the University of Illinois/Champaign-Urbana, they and their children received death threats, dead animals were left at their doors, they were beaten by the police, a white student union formed at the university, the Ku Klux Klan organized a chapter nearby, and the FBI began recruiting Indian students on campus. Most Indian students found the situation intolerable and were forced to leave. Then the Illinois state legislature passed a resolution, the first of its kind, in support of the mascot. Antimascot campaigns have led

to similar violent and reactionary displays across the country.

Most of the authors cited in this essay have stressed the value of cross-cultural education. They have not questioned intercultural "borrowing" per se; rather, they have attempted to formulate guidelines to ensure that this borrowing remains respectful. Native people question the value of this kind of "education" for Native liberation. Certainly Native women want others to be informed about our scholarly analyses, political struggles, and intellectual work; however, the contributors to the *JFSR* article do not distinguish between these forms of sharing and cultural or spiritual sharing. It is these latter kinds that Native women find most suspect. Noted theologian Fumitaka Matsuoka sheds some light onto the problem. He notes that the important struggle for Indians these days is not cultural validation. The dominant culture is prepared to accommodate a little bit of "multiculturalism"—a pow wow here, a pipe ceremony there—as long as the structures of power are not fundamentally altered. Native activists contend that true sharing cannot happen as long as the structures of colonization remain unchallenged.

Responding to the prevalence of Native spiritual and cultural appropriation, the traditional elders' circle has issued a communiqué on what is appropriate to share with non-Indians. The simple message is that all of creation is connected. People must live in balance with each other and with the earth to ensure our collective survival. Abuse, repression, and exploitation of the earth's resources are not a part of "the natural law"—values that are probably common to all indigenous cultures. Spirituality is not something to be purchased by way of a bogus $300 pipe ceremony. Instead, it is a way of living in "right relation" with the awareness that everything one does affects everything else. As Chrystos writes in her poem "Shame On," "We've been polite for five hundred years/ & you still don't get it/ Take nothing you cannot return/ Give to others, give more/ Walk quietly/ Do what needs to be done/ Give thanks for your life/ Respect all beings/ simple/ and it doesn't cost a penny" (*Dream On*, 101).

Land Nationalism

Unlike other feminist/womanist/*mujerista* theologies of the United States, Native women's spirituality/liberation praxis is centered in a national land-based struggle. Native women activists have often been reluctant to call themselves feminists because they generally experience colonialism, rather than sexism, as their primary mode of oppression. As mentioned previously, Native women remember precontact Native societies as generally egalitarian. It was colonization that introduced the structures of homophobia, racism, capitalism, and sexism into most Native nations. Because Native women regard themselves as members of autonomous indigenous nations, the struggles they face are not civil rights struggles, either in terms of racial or sexual equality. Rather, Native women tend to argue that the real struggle is a land-based, national struggle.

Mary Crow Dog articulates the difference between Native women and most racial and "ethnic" minorities in the United States. "They want *in.* We want *out!*" (Crow Dog, 77). This is somewhat of an oversimplification, of course. Other feminist theologians also stress the importance of community self-determination and question the limits of civil rights struggles. However, the eventual self-determination of the community in question is often envisioned as taking place within a larger, diverse society. Native nationalists, in contrast, are often not interested in interacting with "a wider society," especially if that society is Canada or the United States. "Never forget," admonishes Chrystos, "america is our hitler" (*Dream On*, 13). Many indigenous people do not consider themselves citizens of the United States or Canada and refuse to vote in nontribal elections or to be counted in the census. Some reservations have their own license plates and passports. Often, Indians do not even identify with the umbrella term "person of color": Either you are Native or you are not. In fact, not all Indians even identify primarily as Indians; some identify primarily by nation.

Spirituality is integral to this anticolonial struggle because Native spiritualities depend upon the land base that gave rise to them; they cannot easily be transplanted to another geographical area. Many ceremonies must be performed at specific locations. This close relationship with the land makes environmental issues central to indigenous liberation struggles. Like Rosemary Radford Ruether, Sallie McFague, and other ecofeminist theologians, Native women center concerns about restoring the relationship between humans and the rest of the creation in its proper balance. However, non-Native feminist theologians often fail to emphasize the relationship between environmental degradation and colonization, imperialism, and capitalism and often talk about environmental destruction as a future possibility rather than a current reality. Meanwhile, the environmental practice of Native people comes from a context of immense environmental concern because uranium mining and nuclear testing takes place on or near Indian land. Consequently, Native communities face 60 percent birth defect rates in some areas, 80 percent cancer rates in others. Native activists precisely locate the environmental crisis in the question "Who controls the land?" The majority of the energy resources in the United States are on Indian land, and thus Indian people are generally the first to be affected by the destructive nature of resource extraction. Indian lands are also targeted for toxic waste dumping. Indian activists believe that treaty rights are the best protection against environmental destruction wrought by rampant capitalism. Multinationals believe it, too, which is why they fund anti-Indian hate groups to fight treaty enforcement. Native women activists recognize that the struggle to protect the earth entails a long, hard battle against the U.S. government and multinational corporations. As Mililani Trask argues:

> We cannot stand by the stream and say our chants and beat the drum and pray that the river people will survive. . . . Natural resource management is a tool, a skill, and a weapon that the women warriors of today need to attire themselves with if they are going to be prepared for battle. Prayers are the foundation, but . . . [we need] to seize control and political power. We cannot go out and fight America with the spear and a prayer; we need to do more. (Trask, 17)

Native women are prominent in these struggles through such organizations as the Indigenous Environmental Network and Native Americans for a Clean Environment (NACE). Through the leadership of Pame Kingfisher, NACE shut down Kerr McGee's Sequoyah Fuels (responsible for the death of Karen Silkwood) in Oklahoma, which had supplied 20 percent of the world's uranium hexafluoride.

Healing

While in the past indigenous women's struggles were almost entirely land based, it has become increasingly clear that Native people, and particularly Native women, must also heal from the psychological effects of colonization. Sexual abuse, domestic violence, alcohol abuse, and teen suicide—the legacies of colonization and particularly of Christian boarding schools—have devastated Indian families. In response, there is a growing "wellness" movement, largely spearheaded by women, that stresses healing from abuse, both on the individual and on the community level. The University of Oklahoma sponsors national wellness and women conferences each year, which over 2,000 Indian women attend. These conferences help women begin their healing journeys from various forms of abuse and teach them to become enablers for community healing. The Indigenous Women's Network also sponsors gatherings that tie together the healing of individuals and communities from the trauma of this nation's history. At the 1994 conference, conference speaker Cecelia Firethunder stated:

> We also have to recognize and understand that we carry the pain of our grandmothers, mothers, and

the generation that came before us. We carry in our heart the pain of all our ancestors and we carry in our hearts the unresolved grief [and] the loss of our way of life.... There is no way we can move forward and be stronger nations without recognizing the trauma and pain that took place within our nations, our families, and within ourselves.

Spirituality is an integral part of this movement because mainstream paradigms for dealing with abuse—for example, the "twelve-step" model of Alcoholics Anonymous—tend to be less effective for Native communities than traditional spiritual practices. As Vine Deloria notes, healing is a central motif of Indian spiritualities. Because indigenous spiritual traditions are land based, healing necessarily involves restoration to a proper relationship with the land. Beth Brant's collection of short stories *Food and Spirits* illustrates this connection. Her characters come to terms with abuse while reestablishing their relationship to the earth and its creation. In "Swimming Upstream," Anna May overcomes her desire to commit suicide by watching a salmon with a torn fin struggle to swim upstream. As the wounded fish completes its journey, Anna May throws away her bottle of alcohol and begins life again.

While liberation theologians have properly stressed the political structure of evil, Native activists have found that it is impossible to maintain the fight for liberation without a simultaneous movement to heal from the damage done by colonization. Much of the American Indian movement's drug and alcohol abuse and its mistreatment of women are due to the fact that its male leadership did not deal with the impact of colonization on their psyches. The growing recognition of sexual and domestic violence in Indian communities has probably been one of the primary factors in the increasing number of Native women who either identify as feminists or at least more fully address issues of sexism. Whereas Native women activists once tended to view the struggle against sexism as standing at odds with anticolonial struggles, increasing numbers now see the fight against sexism as consonant with, even necessary to, sovereignty movements.

Anthropological Poverty

In *For My People* (1984), black liberation theologian James Cone has argued that one of the fundamental distinctions between liberation theology and more mainstream theologies is that mainstream theologies concern themselves with the "nonbeliever," whereas liberation theology concerns itself with the "nonperson." That is, liberation theology strives to concern itself with the anthropological concern of doing theology within a capitalist, racist, and sexist society in which some peoples (particularly poor people and people of color) have been deemed nonpersons undeserving of basic human rights. Rather than focus on "true propositions about God," Cone argues liberation theology must focus on concrete, oppressed human beings.

African theologian Englebert Mveng further develops this framework with his concept "anthropological poverty," which signifies the "despoiling of human beings not only of what they have, but of everything that constitutes their being and essence—their identity, history, ethnic roots, language, culture, faith, creativity, dignity, pride ambitions, right to speak" (Mveng, 220). Mveng's anthropological poverty includes racial, economic, and cultural analyses of poverty. Not only has the West ravaged the economic resources of Africa, but it has ravaged its cultures as well. Furthermore, by identifying black Africans as subhuman, the West has robbed them of their dignity and self-respect. This anthropological poverty is inclusive of political, racial, and economic pauperization but also includes religiocultural poverty.

Native Americans, like other colonized peoples, have cultures that are severely "impoverished" by colonialism through the process of anthropological poverty. About sixty-five Indian languages are expected to disappear by the end of the decade, and with them will go the cultures of which they are a part. Consequently, many Native Christian theologians, such as Steve Charleston, William Baldridge, George Tinker, and other, have attempted to reinterpret the Bible and other Christian doctrines within indigenous frameworks.

Although more indigenous people today are trying to reclaim their traditions, it is a very difficult process, given the extent to which Indians have been colonized by Western education and Christianity. Native activist Lakota Harden speaks to the difficulties of remembering tradition within the context of colonization. She states:

And so, in trying to piece together our history, and our stories, and our legends ... because we're so Americanized now, we're so colonized now ... it goes through the colonized filter and comes out changed. So how much of the tradition was really originally ours; how much of it was already Christian-influenced, already cavalry influenced, already dominant culture influenced. . . . Because in my own process and learning about being a traditional woman—women didn't carry the pipe. ... I really look at a lot of this, and questioning how much of that was really our culture, how much of it was because Christianity influenced us to say women shouldn't do this, or shouldn't do that. . . . Knowing the way women are now, how could we accept less? How could we let ourselves be ignored or degraded, or whatever . . .

And I remember at our school, all us kids and everybody were preparing and we had a sweat lodge in our backyard. Our backyard was huge, the plains. And I remember . . . one of the boys [who said] women can never carry the pipe. And now I realize that all comes from Christianity. Women never used to do this or that. And I remember feeling very devastated because I was very young then. I was trying to learn this. I was quite the drama queen and going to the trailer and my aunt was making bread or something. Auntie, this is what they're saying. She said, well you know, tradition, we talk about being traditional. What we're doing now is different. When we talk about trying to follow the traditions of say, our ancestors from 100 years ago, it's probably different from 300 years ago. If when the horses came and we had said, oh we don't ride the four-legged, they are our brother. We respect them; we don't ride them. Where would we be? Hey man, we found those horses and we became the best horse riders there ever were, and we were having good winters. So tradition is keeping those principles, the original principles about honoring life all around you. Walk in beauty is another interpretation. Respecting everything around you. Leave the place better than you found it. Those were the kind of traditions that we followed. But they change as we go along, as long as they stay in tune with that. So that's all, she told me that story.

And in a few minutes, then I went back to a roomful of guys, and at that time part of picking up that pipe, you don't drink alcohol, you don't smoke marijuana, you don't take drugs, you don't fight with people, you don't abuse anyone. And I was really was trying to follow that because that's what my uncle taught me. So I went to the middle and I said I want everybody here who is following the tradition, who has given up the things I just named to stand here in the circle with me? I said until this circle is filled with men, I'll do something else. I'll learn how to make fry bread, but until then, there has to be someone standing here doing this, and if you're not going to do it, I will. (Smith, 322)

Her words speak to how the sexism of Christianity influences how Native traditions are remembered. In addition, the notion that one can be a spiritual leader without changing one's behavior (by continuing to drink, do drugs, etc.) is similarly Christian influenced. This attitude reflects a Christian view of spirituality in which belief is more important than practice. Indigenous traditions, however, actually place a higher value on practice—and on practice throughout all of one's life. Thus living one's life in a good way is central to Native spiritual traditions; it is not something one does only in ceremony.

In addition, another important contribution Native theology makes to the project of theological anthropology is questioning the centering of humanity in theology. This is because indigenous worldviews do not privilege human (or "anthro") experience over the experience of other beings in creation. Terms that privilege humans—*anthropology*, *humanism*, and so on—often tend not have much currency in indigenous circles. Consequently, Native theological anthropology questions its very conceptual framework. States Kidwell and colleagues in *A Native American Theology*:

> Theological anthropology is concerned with defining the human person as a religious being. For Native Americans, the intimate relationship with the natural environment blurs the distinctions between human and non-human. Human beings are not the only people in the world. . . . We must move beyond the Christian tradition of humans as unique creations of God to the idea that the world of persons is embracing. (86)

In addition, liberation theologians have extended concern for theological nonpersons to those marginalized *within* communities of color. Elias Farajaje-Jones, Kelly Brown-Douglas, and Renee Hill point to the importance of theologizing around the nonpersons within black communities and, by extension, other communities of color, such as peoples with AIDS (acquired immunodeficiency syndrome), lesbians, gay, bisexual, and transgendered peoples, and prisoners. As Farajaje-Jones and Brown-Douglas argue, one of the techniques of white supremacy has been to image black peoples as sexually perverse and hence deserving of subjugation. This reality has led Frances Wood to question a common precept in liberation theology: that God sides with the oppressed. Such an approach, she argues, does not address the reality that there is not a simple dichotomy between oppressors and oppressed peoples. Rather, there are multiple axes of oppression; those that are oppressed on one axis may well be oppressive on another axes. Consequently, she argues, it is more appropriate to say that God stands against oppression, rather than sides for the oppressed.

In this regard, the writing of Native women activists also critiques the marginalization that occurs within Native communities. Similarly, Elizabeth Cook-Lynn describes in "The Big Pipe Case" that at the same time

Native peoples were rallying around prominent Native political prisoner Leonard Peltier, no one stood beside Marie Big Pipe when she was incarcerated on a felony charge of "assault with intent to commit serious bodily harm" because she breast-fed her child while under the influence of alcohol. She was denied services to treat her substance abuse problem and access to abortion services when she became pregnant. Not only did her community not support her, but they also supported her incarceration. In doing so, Cook-Lynn argues the community supported the encroachment of U.S. federal jurisdiction on tribal lands for an issue that would normally be under tribal jurisdiction. Meanwhile, the federal government, which is supposed to prosecute "major crimes" on Indian land, prosecutes virtually no cases of rape committed against Indian women. Cook-Lynn recounts how this demonization of Native women was assisted by the publication of Michael Dorris's *The Broken Cord*, which narrates his adoption of a Native child who suffered from fetal alcohol syndrome. While this book has been crucial in sensitizing many communities to the realities of fetal alcohol syndrome, it also portrays the mother of the child unsympathetically and advocates repressive legislative solutions targeted against women substance abusers. As Cook-Lynn notes:

> Dorris directs his frustrated wrath toward some of the least powerful among us: young childbearing Indian women. He says they must pay the price for the health crisis and family disintegration that can be observed not only on Indian reservations but in cities and rural areas throughout the country. Forcing these young women, as much the victims as their martyred children, into detention centers is presented as a solution to failed health care systems, inadequate education, poverty, and neglect. (Cook-Lynn, 14)

Within Native communities, the growing demonization of Native women substance abusers has prompted tribes to collude with the federal government in whittling away their own sovereignty. Similarly, Lee Maracle makes a trenchant critique of internalized oppression within Native communities, the creation of theological nonpersons:

> If the State won't kill us
> we will have to kill ourselves.
>
> It is no longer good etiquette to head hunt savages.
> We'll just have to do it ourselves.
>
> It's not polite to violate "squaws"
> We'll have to find an Indian to oblige us.

> It's poor form to starve an Indian
> We'll have to deprive our young ourselves.
>
> Blinded by niceties and polite liberality
> We can't see our enemy,
> So, we'll just have to kill each other. (12–13)

By centering the experiences and analyses of communities rather than abstract propositions of God in the theological enterprise, liberation theologies hope to counter anthropological poverty. In addition, these approaches have the further effect of potentially transforming the theological project from an individual project to a collective project. This focus recognizes that theology, most particularly a theology of liberation, cannot be done by one person but must be done in community in order to inspire collective action. In addition, the contribution of Native women challenges the parameters of theology beyond the confines of Christianity. Consequently, the future of Native feminist theology lies in the collective struggle of Native women activists for sovereignty and self-determination.

SOURCES: The most sustained work on Native theology is *A Native American Theology* (2001) by Clara Sue Kidwell, Homer Noley, and George Tinker. Vine Deloria's *God Is Red* (1973) is the foundational work from which most subsequent books on Native theology are based. His key religious writings can also be found in *For This Land* (1999). Jace Weaver's *Native American Religious Identity* and *That the People Might Live* (1998) are also helpful starting points on this topic. In addition, Robert Warrior's *Tribal Secrets* provides an intellectual grounding for the development of Native theologies. For sources of Native theology from a gender perspective, Lee Maracle's *I Am Woman* (1996) is one of the most incisive articulations of Native feminism. In addition, the works of Elizabeth Cook-Lynn, such as *Why I Can't Read Wallace Stegner* (1996), are foundational writing. Haunani-Kay Trask's *From a Native Daughter* (1993) articulates the relationship between patriarchy and colonization from the point of view of indigenous peoples in Hawaii. Annette Jaimes's *State of Native America* (1992) also contains essays that are commonly cited. In the fields of poetry and fiction, the poetry of Chrystos in works such as *Not Vanishing* (1989) and *Dream On* (1991), Beth Brant's *Food and Spirits* (1991), and Leslie Marmon Silko's *Ceremony* (1977) also provide important feminist analysis from a spiritually grounded perspective. Mary Crow Dog's controversial *Lakota Woman* (1990) also provides a narrative of the American Indian Movement from a woman's perspective. Native women's perspectives can also be found in the periodical *Indigenous Woman* published by the Indigenous Women's Network. In addition, a larger discussion on Native American feminism can be found in Andrea Smith's "Bible, Gender, and Nationalism in American Indian and Christian Right Activism" (Ph.D. diss., University of Santa Cruz, 2002). See also Robert Mendoza, *Look! A Nation Is Coming: Native Americans* and the Second American Revolution (1984); "American Indian Religious Traditions and the Academic Study of Religion: A Response to Sam Gill," and "Rejoinder to Christopher Jocks," both in *Journal of the American Academy of Religion* 65.1 (1997): 169–182; Mililani Trask, "Indigenous Women Are the Mothers of Their Nations," *Indigenous Women* II (1995): 26; Englebert Mveng, "Third World Theology—What Theology? What Third World?: Evaluation by an African Delegate," in *Irruption of the Third World: Challenge to Theology*, ed. Virginia M. M. Fabella and Sergio Torres (1983).

Part XIII

෭

Contemporary Women's Issues in Religion

WOMEN-CHURCH
Mary E. Hunt

WOMEN-CHURCH IS a global ecumenical feminist religious movement with roots in the Roman Catholic tradition. It consists of groups, individuals, and organizations that seek to be church without the trappings of patriarchal theology and practice. Women-church holds together the twin aspects of sacrament and solidarity, engaging in worship as well as social justice work.

The movement began in the United States in the 1970s as a consequence of feminism, the Vatican's refusal to ordain women, and the growing consensus among progressive Catholics that new models of church were necessary. Women-church groups are also active in Australia, Germany, Iceland, Korea, and Switzerland, among other countries. They are characterized by a desire to create communities with both religious and secular foci that approximate a "discipleship of equals," a term coined by feminist theologian Elisabeth Schüssler Fiorenza. This biblical notion signals a move away from hierarchical governance toward democratic practices, away from a corporate model toward small base communities. It involves a concern with political as well as theological issues.

Decades after its inception, women-church remains a small but powerful movement that attempts to live out new ways of "being church," a phrase that comes to English from Spanish and means functioning in the fashion of, while not necessarily being connected to, an ecclesiastical organization. At the same time, the movement pressures Christian denominations, especially Catholicism, to become more egalitarian. Women-church cooperates with church reform groups such as the Catholic Organizations for Renewal but differs from them in seeking to create concrete alternatives now, new models for contemporary communities. It does not seek to tweak the existing model by adding women to its clerical, hierarchical mold but to "be church" on women's terms.

Women-church arose out of the Catholic feminist movement's exploring the ordination of Roman Catholic women. In 1975, following the ordination of Episcopal Church women in the United States, a group of Catholic women led by Mary B. Lynch, a social worker and feminist, convened a gathering in Detroit, Michigan, under the rubric "Women in Future Priesthood Now—A Call for Action." This was an explicit public call for the ordination of Roman Catholic women to the priesthood and an implicit challenge to renew the institutional Church so that it might reflect the growing consensus that Vatican II's call for lay leadership needed to be taken seriously. Part of this vision included fundamental changes in the priesthood, beginning with the abolition of mandatory celibacy. Clearly, Catholic women were in no danger of being ordained!

The ensuing discussion served both to empower women as theological protagonists capable of making important contributions to the Church at large and to alert the Catholic hierarchy that the days of male-only ministry and decision making were numbered. This context formed part of the framework for the emergence of women-church.

In 1978 a second meeting on ordination was held in Baltimore, Maryland, after the Vatican had made clear in its "Declaration on the Question of the Admission of Women to the Ministerial Priesthood" that women did not "bear a natural resemblance" to Jesus, thus were not fit to be ordained. This recalcitrance on the part of the hierarchical Church was a source of deep disappointment but not surprise. It raised the question whether priesthood would ever be open to women and, if so, whether that priesthood would be sufficiently egalitarian and democratic that progressive women would ever aspire to be ordained. This formed another part of the foundation of women-church, which as a movement has avoided a clergy of its own and relies on a "priesthood of all believers" approach to ministry.

A number of Catholic women in the United States received theological degrees in the 1970s with the hope of being ordained. Moreover, those women predominantly were members of religious congregations, engaged in innovative ministerial work. They served as pastoral ministers in parishes, prisons, hospitals, and university campuses, settings that heretofore had been off-limits to women. They went on to create whole new areas of ministry, for example, with battered women, persons with disabilities, and others who had been ignored by the male clergy. Women theologians produced original, insightful work in virtually every theological discipline—church history, systematic theology, ethics, and biblical studies. Their writings showed how women and women's insights had been systematically ignored, dismissed, or rejected in the formation of contemporary Christian theology. More important, women scholars went on to constructive work, recovering hidden history, proposing new ways of shaping ethical problems, and envisioning a postpatriarchal future. All this resulted in a strong group of Catholic women prepared for ministerial leadership but without an institution to receive them.

The scandal occasioned by the Vatican's resistance, combined with strong feminist principles of inclusivity and equality, led many Catholic women to form small base communities in which to celebrate Eucharist and other liturgies. At a conference sponsored by the Center of Concern in 1981 titled "Women Moving Church," feminist theologian and biblical scholar Elisabeth Schüs-

The Metropolitan Church in Baltimore, Maryland, is an example of the intent behind women-church, which originated with the idea of including females, children, slaves, even animals who had been left out of the power paradigm. Only by adding "women" to "church" could one speak meaningfully of a complete community in which all are welcome and decision making is shared. *Copyright © Joan Biren.*

sler Fiorenza introduced the term *ekklesia gynaikon,* the ecclesia of women. Liturgist Diann Neu translated this into English as *women-church.*

Women-church was never meant to be a church of women only. Rather, as *ekklesia* it had its roots in what theologian Edward Schillebeeckx described as the regularly convoked assembly of free male citizens who made decisions for the whole community. Accordingly, *woman* signified females, children, slaves, even animals who had been left out of that power paradigm. Only by adding *women* to *church* could one speak meaningfully of a complete community in which all are welcome and decision making is shared—a far cry from the contemporary Roman Catholic Church.

By the early 1980s, increased racism and sexism, economic inequality, and militarism made clear to theologically progressive people that they could no longer focus simply on in-house issues like ordination. Rather, they had to act as church, offering a witness against injustice even if Catholicism in its official guise contributed to some of the problems. Catholic-connected women's groups, including the National Assembly of Women Religious, Chicago Catholic Women, National Coalition of American Nuns, Las Hermanas, and the Women's Alliance for Theology, Ethics and Ritual (WATER), constituted the Women of the Church Coalition. They sought to be a feminist Catholic voice at a time when alternatives to the institutional Church simply did not exist.

The Coalition convened a landmark conference in 1983 in Chicago, "From Generation to Generation: Woman-Church Speaks." Thousands of attendees went home inspired to start their own base communities. Speakers exhorted people to deepen and broaden a movement whose agenda was not driven in response to the patriarchal Church but was proactive. For example, instead of asking for admission to the priesthood, these women imagined new forms of ministry that did not rely on ordination as a sacrament conferred on an in-

dividual. Rather, ministry was understood as the common vocation of all adults who are baptized into the faith community.

The growing diversity of the movement was signaled by the change from singular to plural, from "woman-church" to "women-church," as it has been known since. The hyphen was a deliberate effort to link women and church, a sign that without women, as current Roman Catholic structures stand, "church" is incomplete. Following the 1983 conference, the Coalition officially changed its name to the Women-Church Convergence.

In 1987, another conference, "Women-Church: Claiming Our Power," was held in Cincinnati, Ohio, with over 3,000 participants. This time emphasis was clearly on the melding of religious and political concerns, a sense that the movement was now maturing to the point of being a social force based on feminist religious ideas. Speakers included prominent "secular" feminists as well as religious feminists, scholars, and activists. While pressure was still on for the ordination of women and the revamping of the institutional Church, the major energy of the women-church movement focused on how to be responsible citizens in an unjust world.

A third such gathering in 1993 in Albuquerque, New Mexico, "Women-Church: Weavers of Change," showed just how difficult the task of being women-church can be. The multiracial, multiethnic, multicultural reality of common life in the United States made for difficult dynamics in this mostly white, Anglo, middle-class Christian movement. However, the conflicts helped to force a more conscious self-awareness and opened the way for women-church to become more diverse.

In subsequent years, the movement has continued to take root in local communities. Though not always called "women-church," when women's groups gather and feminist liturgies are celebrated, the inspiration is clear. Many such groups belong to the Women-Church

Convergence. Other groups simply meet and act as church without reference to a larger reality. Still other groups are influenced in their practice by women-church, though quite separate from it.

Women-Church Convergence

The Women-Church Convergence is "a coalition of autonomous Catholic-rooted organizations/groups raising a feminist voice and committed to an ekklesia of women which is participative, egalitarian and self-governing" (Women-Church Convergence brochure). More than thirty member groups belong to the Convergence, ranging from local base communities such as San Antonio Women-Church and Chicago Women-Church to national groups like the Grail Women Task Force and Catholics for a Free Choice. The stated goal of the Convergence is to gather groups that work "to eradicate patriarchy, especially sexism and racism, in order to transform church and society . . . from a paradigm of domination to one of mutuality" (Women-Church Convergence brochure).

This is no simple task. The Convergence has had problems making it happen. But such a lofty goal is concretized in the action alerts, liturgies, theological reflection, public education projects, and coalition building that are the work of Women-Church Convergence. For Catholic women who believe, as the Convergence affirmations read, that "women are free moral agents with authority to take full responsibility for their lives," who believe that "spirituality and social justice are essential to being church," and who affirm that "women are, and of right ought to be, the primary decision makers in matters of reproduction, sexuality and women's health" (Women-Church Convergence brochure), women-church is a concrete way to live out one's values.

Representatives of those groups meet twice a year to network, to develop educational work, and to engage in common public actions. For example, the Convergence has spoken in one voice against labor injustices and in favor of Catholic women theologians who have been marginalized by the institutional Church. Various Convergence groups have formed alliances to organize local protests, for example, at the male-only ordinations in their dioceses or at the U.S. Catholic Bishops' annual fall meeting. The Convergence is a locus for sharing resources for worship and education, for encouraging groups to take a public stance in their own communities, and for networking people who seek to be church on egalitarian, democratic terms.

The Convergence is structured accordingly with two coordinators who function as an executive committee between meetings, and various standing and ad hoc committees. Meetings are open to all who wish to attend, though only member groups have a vote. A Web site (http://www.womenchurchconvergence.org/) keeps members and the general public informed about the group's activities.

The work of the Women-Church Convergence focuses both on secular and religious fronts. Equal distribution of economic resources and an end to profit as the primary motor for development are common commitments. Eradicating racism, sexism, and heterosexism in personal and structural ways is another shared goal. Efforts to eliminate violence, especially that directed toward women and children, forms a third common bond. While far from achieving these goals, the very articulation of them gives women-church groups a common ground for action.

The Practice of Women-Church Groups

Women-church groups vary considerably in their practice. There is no set formula or pattern—indeed, seemingly infinite variety and creativity in the groups both large and small. Some groups are house churches, like Sisters against Sexism (SAS), a group in the Washington, D.C., area, which began in 1979 shortly after the pope's first visit to the United States. Like the early Christian communities, these groups share a meal and celebrate a liturgy.

For example, Catholic women in the greater Washington, D.C., area, mostly members of canonical religious congregations, had been gathering regularly for prayer, calling in a priest to preside when they wanted to celebrate the Eucharist. Some of them were among the nuns who stood in silence in the Shrine of the Immaculate Conception in 1979 when Mercy Sister Theresa Kane welcomed the pope on behalf of all religious women. She reminded him gently that women were still not able to engage in the fullness of ordained ministry. Her benign words occasioned a virulent backlash from the pope and his advisers, who realized the power of U.S. women's commitment to equality.

Scandalized by the pope's reaction, the SAS group never called a male priest again but continued to celebrate Eucharist. They formed what is considered to be the first women-church community and still meets more than twenty years later. SAS gathers in the homes of its members for a liturgy and a potluck supper every three weeks. The group spends a weekend on retreat twice a year and has celebrated feminist liturgies from naming or baptism to croning (a woman entering her later years) and retirement.

Other Convergence groups are larger, often a subset of an even larger group, for example, the Loretto Women's Network. This is the group within the Loretto Community (i.e., the vowed Sisters of Loretto and their comembers) that focuses on women's issues. The BVM

(Sisters of Charity of the Blessed Virgin Mary) Network for Women's Issues and the Sinsinawa Dominican Women's Network are similar in form. At first glance they seem unusual, a women's committee inside a women's organization. But on closer examination their strategic wisdom is apparent. This approach allows feminist members of canonical religious orders to function in relation to, but not in the name of, their entire congregations. This is especially important as the difficult issues of homosexuality and abortion come to the fore, both in the Convergence and beyond. Otherwise, religious congregations would jeopardize their canonical standing, that is, their authorization as official Catholic groups, by taking public positions at odds with the hierarchical Church, a risk few congregations have taken. This creative model has helped feminist nuns find their voices on their own terms in their own groups, as well as in conjunction with other Catholic women.

Some member groups, such as Catholics for a Free Choice (CFFC), the Intercommunity Justice and Peace Center, the Women's Alliance for Theology, Ethics and Ritual, and the Women's Ordination Conference (WOC) are national/international organizations in their own rights with staffs, offices, and programs. They add a certain stability and some resources to the mix but in fact have no more say than any other member group. These differences in size and structure present certain challenges to the Convergence when it comes to the division of tasks. Obviously those groups with staffs and budgets have an easier time taking on responsibilities. But on balance, it is remarkable how well the Convergence has worked through such differences and how carefully the women have tried to live up to high goals against great odds.

One active local group is Massachusetts Women-Church, a small band of committed women who exemplify the women-church movement's rich commitment to a new model of being church. With a core group of a dozen or so women whose median age is close to seventy, without an office or headquarters other than their living rooms and kitchen tables, these women manage to be a model of church while upsetting the conservative Catholic theological apple cart in Boston. They have been banned by the local ordinary, Bernard Cardinal Law, from meeting on any church property because of their public support of women's ordination and other justice issues. Their long and fruitful dialogue with the local Jesuits was stopped when those men capitulated to the cardinals' wishes despite their order's strong words on paper about solidarity with women. This effectively ended their relationship with Massachusetts Women-Church.

Massachusetts Women-Church members and friends are found on the steps of the Cathedral in Boston each year on ordination day, protesting the exclusion of women. They led a local campaign when Sister Jeannette Normandin was fired from her job at Boston's Jesuit Urban Center because she allegedly participated in a baptismal ceremony with gestures reserved for ordained hands. One year they rented advertisement space on top of local taxicabs calling for women priests. Through it all, they function as a community that meets for prayer and education, sharing a good cup of tea and nicely baked pastries, a real feminist base community that is strong in its rejection of injustice. Their actions embolden and enrich the entire movement.

Theological Dimensions of Women-Church

There is no orthodox theology of women-church, but there are several important contributing strands of thought that have helped to shape the movement. Feminist philosopher Mary Daly provided fundamental insights in *The Church and the Second Sex* (1968) and *Beyond God the Father* (1973), though she no longer considers herself Catholic. She correctly identified the structural inequalities in Catholicism and went on to propose concrete conceptual as well as strategic alternatives that laid the groundwork for this movement. She exhorted women to leave places where they are not welcome as full members and create other opportunities where they are in charge. This insight is in the deep background of the women-church movement.

Elisabeth Schüssler Fiorenza not only named women-church but also summarized its early theological grounding in the epilogue of her landmark book *In Memory of Her*. She describes the *ekklesia of women* as the place where women "in the angry power of the Spirit, are sent forth to feed, heal, and liberate" (346). A longtime participant in a women-church base community and an enthusiastic supporter of several Women-Church Convergence member organizations, Schüssler Fiorenza provided major intellectual shape to the movement through her writings and lectures.

She spelled out the parameters of a movement that would be equal parts political and religious, a force for social as well as ecclesial change. To those who argued that women-church was not "fully" church, she responded that neither was any patriarchal expression of church that excluded women. To charges that she envisioned a separatist community, she answered to the contrary: "Because the spiritual colonialization of women by men has entailed our internalization of the male as divine, men have to relinquish their spiritual and religious control over women as well as over the church as the people of God, if mutuality should become a reality" (*In Memory of Her*, 347).

Obviously feminist men can be part of women-church. However, some local base groups consider it too early in the process of healing and reshaping to invite men to join their worship on a regular basis. Conferences and other public gatherings, for example, a Pentecost gathering of small base communities in Washington, D.C., sponsored by WATER, have long been open to feminist men. Children are encouraged to be part of women-church.

Elisabeth Schüssler Fiorenza also coined the term *kyriarchy*, to describe the interlocking structures of oppression that result in the literal "lording over" by those with power, whether racial, economic, gender, or other forms of power. This has advanced an important dimension of women-church's theory and praxis, namely, the move away from gender-focused work toward critical concern for the broad and deep web of oppression that prevents a "discipleship of equals" from being possible. This helpful concept underscores the political dimension of women-church, its work in the culture at large to be a feminist religious presence working for justice on a range of fronts.

Kyriarchy also helps to explain the success of the "nonordination of women," the fact that Catholic women are not coopted by the kyriarchal church into clerical, celibate, hierarchical priests. Rather, as women-church they are free to exercise feminist ministry, along with men, in egalitarian communities. This has been a source of debate, with some Catholic feminists favoring ordination to the present model of priesthood in the hope that women's presence will bring about fundamental change. But a critical analysis of kyriarchy makes clear that gender exclusion is but one dimension of a deeply flawed system. Kyriarchy is based on the essential distinction of clergy and laypeople with clergy having decision making as well as sacramental power, and laypeople, even the most well educated and involved, banned from even the most minimal sacramental tasks.

Rosemary Radford Ruether, a Church historian and theologian, took another approach to women-church, focusing her attention on the need for women to leave patriarchal Catholicism and create new options. In her view, women-church is a feminist exodus community that uses the same dynamics of leaving behind and creating the new that other liberation communities have used. She is always careful to maintain a link with the institutional Church so as to be effective in critiquing and transforming it.

Ruether's emphasis on the ecclesiology of women-church showed parallels with other groups that left patriarchal Catholicism, including mainline Protestant groups, for a more horizontal, less hierarchical form of community. She gathered a very useful collection of early liturgies that served as models for groups fashioning their own rituals. Among the occasions were healing from divorce or miscarriage, rape or battering. Her practical suggestions on how groups form and sustain themselves complemented her historical contribution.

She even made architectural suggestions for what such physical spaces would look like when groups moved beyond their homes to common spaces that would function in the larger community as places of welcome and celebration.

As a theological ethicist who cofounded WATER, the Women's Alliance for Theology, Ethics and Ritual, this author has defined women-church as a global, ecumenical movement made up of local feminist base communities of justice-seeking friends who engage in sacrament and solidarity. This author emphasizes and encourages the international and interreligious dimensions as women-church groups and publications spring up around the world. As a longtime member of the Women-Church Convergence, this author helped to shape the theological issues of ministry, ethics, and praxis as they unfolded.

After its initial years, the women-church movement was not confined to Catholicism but found expression in a range of denominations and cultural settings. Feminist resources from Judaism, Goddess religions, pagan traditions, as well as reconstructed Christian materials are all part of the data on which women-church is based.

Liturgies of Women-Church

For many participants, women-church is primarily a liturgical community, one in which to pray, act in solidarity, and find like-minded colleagues. While each group is structured and operates differently, a common element is some form of liturgy or ritual. But that expression can vary widely, from those who use the rubrics of the Roman Catholic mass without an ordained male presider to those who imagine and invent rich varieties of rituals. Diann Neu, a liturgist and therapist at WATER, wrote and directed many of the creative celebrations through which the theology of women-church finds its expression. Groups like Chicago Women-Church offer monthly worship.

Some groups follow a seasonal rotation, moving through the natural and liturgical seasons with attention to the specific images and symbols of the time. Other groups let occasions and world events shape their prayer. Still others pick a theme for the year—like justice or women's life cycles—as a way to organize their programs.

The sacramental dimension varies as well. There are groups that share Eucharist in some form each time they meet, much like the Roman Catholic mass. Sheila Dierks wrote extensively on this matter. Others celebrate Eucharist occasionally, more on the Protestant model. Some groups have named and welcomed children or adult converts to Christianity through a form of baptism. More common are liturgies that lift to public expression the ordinary life events of women that heretofore had no expression in church life. For example, the onset of menstruation for a young woman or reaching the age of a crone (usually fifty-six or older) for a mature woman are occasions for festivity. These celebrations include reflection on the moment of passage and sharing of wisdom by other women. There are often special foods and prayers, perhaps special clothing or flowers that signify this is an unusual time that the community marks with reverence and rejoicing.

Other women-church liturgies celebrate ecological connections and political views, such as those that focus on peacemaking. For example, A Critical Mass is a creative group that meets monthly under a freeway in Oakland, California, near the site of the former cathedral there. These women celebrate Eucharist for all who gather, including street people, and provide a meal at the adjacent soup kitchen. Still other celebrations are relationally oriented, whether marriage or covenant, religious commitment, or a ritual recognizing divorce. In short, the creativity is endless. The common thread is the effort to link religious faith with everyday life on terms that take women's well-being seriously.

International/Ecumenical Expressions of Women-Church

Women-church began as a U.S. movement and is best known as such. The movement is found in many parts of the world with global expressions influencing the American groups, and vice versa. For example, in Seoul, Korea, the Reverend Sook-Ja Chung leads Women-Church, a small but influential group. She is ordained as a Presbyterian minister who describes her process of unlearning the meaning of her ordination. Instead of being set apart from her lay colleagues, she now sees herself as called to women's ministry that "must promote the ideology and practice of equality in all relationships" (73).

This insight lived out in Korea helps to bridge the gap between a women-church approach and that of ordained women in other traditions and, eventually, inevitably, in Catholicism. On the one hand, this model shows that being ordained and being part of women-church are not mutually exclusive. On the other hand, the model shows how ordained women need to rethink the meaning of their ordination if they have accepted the concept on patriarchal terms. This is globalization of feminist theology at its best, sharing insights and appropriating them according to different contexts.

Another expression of women-church is found in Iceland where the Reverend Audur Eir Vilhjalmsdottir, the first woman ordained in the Lutheran church there, presides over Kvenna Kirkjan, or The Women's Church. She and six other women founded the group in 1993 on feminist principles of inclusivity and participation.

Kvenna Kirkjan functions officially as part of the National Church but acts on its own. The group holds monthly services in churches around the country. Because the local church is part of the official body, it is able to use that church's resources. These religious feminists in Iceland have creatively translated some biblical texts into their gendered language, for instance, rendering the masculine word "disciple" as "male and female friends of Jesus."

In Germany and Switzerland, some Frauen Kirchen groups use institutional settings for their meetings. Others function out of the house church model. Likewise, some ordained clergywomen participate. But much like their counterparts in the United States, women-church is often as an added dimension of their ministry, part of their personal spirituality and not necessarily part of their regular job. In the Netherlands the term *women-church* has been questioned given its stereotypic feminine connotation in Dutch. But the movement of women and faith there and the historical women's synod held in 1987 are instructive for women-church groups around the world.

Women in Argentina and Uruguay have used the term *Mujer Iglesia* to describe their efforts to form feminist base communities. Many of them have developed associations with international groups like WATER and Catholics for a Free Choice, which collaborate in educational and political work. The rich exchange of information, music, dance, and art for liturgy, and the deep ties that bind these groups, are evidence of the degree to which this global movement, while still small, is effective.

Women-church as a movement can learn a lot from these women, beginning with how to think about being part of but in some sense autonomous from the institutional Church. Obviously having access to the larger pool of resources is only just. But how to do so without being coopted is something that women-church groups struggle to accomplish. Indeed, in many settings in the United States where women-church is not welcome in certain dioceses, this would be hard to achieve.

The importance of having access to the resources gathered by previous generations is another way to signify that women-church is *church* in the fullest sense of the term. Likewise, using a term like *synod*, which is so obviously linked with the patriarchal tradition, can function in an iconoclastic way, as in the Dutch case, proving that women can create churches that function effectively for their members. This pushes reform of the entire tradition.

Future of Women-Church

The future of the women-church movement lies principally in two areas: networking and children. The movement will grow and have influence only if the groups connect with one another through concrete actions for justice. Women-church groups will also need to link with other reform groups that seek similar goals. Otherwise, the movement runs the danger of being small communities that function quite independently without any collective identity or power. Periodic larger gatherings provide a sense of the whole, an experience of connection to the global and historical Jesus movement as well as to other communities of resistance against patriarchal religious values.

Women-church will also need to pay increased attention to the children whose normative experience in a faith community is in such groups. Their religious education remains to be developed. Their celebrations of welcome and coming of age are important times for taking seriously the future of a movement still in its youth after just two decades. Children's impact on the larger religious context will be the measure of success of the women-church movement in creating inclusive, justice-seeking communities.

SOURCES: The Women-Church Convergence materials are housed at the Women and Leadership Archives, Ann Ida Gannon, BVM, Center for Women and Leadership, Loyola University, Chicago, Ill., http://www.luc.edu/orgs/gannon/archives/gcollection.html#w. Major theological work was done by Elisabeth Schüssler Fiorenza and Rosemary Radford Ruether. Schüssler Fiorenza's classic volume *In Memory of Her: Feminist Theological Reconstruction of Christian Origins* (1983) lays the foundation. Her *But She Said: Feminist Practices of Biblical Interpretation* (1992) and *Discipleship of Equals: A Critical Feminist Ekklesia-logy of Liberation* (1993) flesh out the theoretical and practical issues. Ruether's important contributions include *Women-Church: Theology and Practice* (1985), a solid introduction to the movement, and a later overview essay, "Women-Church: An American Catholic Feminist Movement," in *What's Left: Liberal American Catholics*, ed. Mary Jo Weaver (1999), 46–64. Mary E. Hunt provides an insider view in "We Women Are Church," in *The Non-Ordination of Women and the Politics of Power*, ed. Elisabeth Schüssler Fiorenza and Hermann Häring, *Concilium*, 1999.3: 102–114 and "Sophia's Sisters in Struggle: Kyriarchal Backlash, Feminist Vision," *In the Power of Wisdom*, ed. Maria Pilar Aquino and Elisabeth Schüssler Fiorenza, *Concilium*, 2000.5: 23–32. Mary E. Hunt and Diann Neu collaborated on a *Women-Church Sourcebook* (1993). Liturgical materials include Diann L. Neu's *Women-Church Celebrations* (1985) and Sheila D. Dierks's *WomenEucharist* (1997). International expressions of women-church include Sook-Ja Chung's "Women-Church in Korea: Visions and Voices," *The Ecumenical Review* 53.1 (January 2001): 73; and *Women-Church: An Australian Journal of Feminist Studies in Religion*.

NEW FEMINIST RITUAL
Janet Walton

IN THE EARLY 1970s when women began to speak about how they felt after worshipping in churches or synagogues, something new happened. While these feelings certainly were not new, the moment was. Struggles for justice, long overdue changes to acknowledge the rights of people of color and women, and organized protests against the U.S. participation in the Vietnam War marked the 1960s and early 1970s in North America. Active protests and civil disobedience were a critical part of these movements. In the 1960s also, the Roman Catholic Church, an institution that kept its rituals fixed for 1,500 years, also acknowledged the need for change. The civil rights movement, the women's movement, the protest against the war in Vietnam, the demonstrations for lesbian and gay rights, and Vatican Council II provided a fertile context for women to act on what they felt in churches and synagogues. These models of struggles for justice urged action. In the midst of this momentum, New Feminist Rituals began to emerge.

What was wrong in traditional religious rituals was the dominance of everything male: male leadership, male decision making, male language. Public religious rituals were constructed on what men knew, ways in which men expressed who God is and who human beings are, as if what were true for men were true for everyone. Women were invisible except as passive receivers of what men thought. In most denominations women could not assume ordained leadership. Practically no one imagined God through any words or images that reflected women's experiences. In fact, though the foundation of biblically based religions asserted that all humans are created in the image of God, that truth would be difficult to argue, given the language, symbols, ritual forms, visual environment, and leadership of religious rituals. While there were earlier instances in religious history when this imbalance was pointed to and sometimes acted upon, for example, the publishing of the women's bible, in general, traditional public religious rituals continued to be dominated by a male lens.

As more and more people began to recognize the limits and implications of this exclusion, women began to do something about it. In many places across the United States and beyond these borders as well, groups of women, and sometimes men, started to plan rituals based on principles of inclusion rather than exclusion. What they knew, without doubt, was that something was wrong. In fact, they came to understand that what was being done in our churches and synagogues was neither true nor good. What they did not know, at the beginning, was how to correct it. The process of discovering another way of worshiping is what has come to be named New Feminist Ritual. Small groups of people, and eventually, larger ones, came together in various places to express what they were learning together about God, themselves, and their world. They did not rely only on talk but rather experimented. They wanted to know what rituals would feel like if they prayed with a variety of stories and metaphors, if women assumed leadership. So they practiced through many ways of knowing, of emerging visions of power and beauty and justice. What happened is that they educated themselves through study and action. They put themselves in the way of change, deliberately and consciously trying something new and discovering alternatives to what they had inherited. New Feminist Ritual pointed to another way of encountering God, one another, and this world, thus another way to pray and live.

As in any movement to correct injustice, one stone unturned led to more and more awareness. Soon feminists realized that male dominance was not the only problem. Everyone of color, males and females, everyone whose body was challenged by sense impairment, anyone deemed too young, too old, too poor, or anyone different in any way from able-bodied white males—all were marginalized. Their human experiences, too, were considered inferior and even, in some cases, signs of God's displeasure. While New Feminist Ritual takes its name and its initial awareness from women's experiences, the movement quickly broadened to include everyone who had been systematically excluded from the texts and textures of public religious rituals. The path to correct this exclusion has not been easy. Institutional authorities have been slow to hear and see what needs to be changed. Some congregations still consider the issues trivial. Even some women resist these shifts in perception. Women of color and those marked by sense impairment regularly point to the dominance of white women and able-bodied people in leading the New Feminist Ritual movement, thus repeating the pattern established by white males. The work of New Feminist Ritual challenges everyone. While much of the experimentation occurs primarily in groups of women who meet outside traditional institutional structures, some also happens in congregational settings. There is a constantly unfolding process of experimentation and correction. With thirty years of trial and error and many publications that record its development, there is ample information to describe its history.

General Characteristics

Fundamental to understanding feminist rituals are two convictions: God is more that any one historical age or tradition can express, and the variety in all creation offers glimpses of God's ongoing revelation among human beings. Though these facts may seem obvious, a simple examination of our religious rituals makes clear how difficult it is to embody these truths. Since ritual expressions rely on a variety of languages, words, space, gestures, and sounds, some brief comments on each of these areas are included to demonstrate the magnitude of the problem.

WORDS

Words offered one of the first clues to religious feminists that something was wrong in liturgies. The language in traditional religious rituals referred to God as if God were male and referred to humans as if they were all men.

To name God primarily through male words is not only inaccurate but also idolatrous. No description of God can exhaust the revelation of God. To try to contain the mystery of God in any particular words is an attempt to control human understanding of God; it defies the essence of God. Every image is incomplete. The most common example is naming God as father, primarily because Jesus, according to ancient traditions, prayed to God as father. Throughout Christian history there have been many other names for God, including those that use female experiences and the whole created world as metaphors. While it is more common in these days to hear names for God such as Consuming Fire, Light of the World, Sun of Justice, Sublime Fruit of the Earth, female names for God are rarely used in official texts. Indeed, to call upon God as mother using metaphors about birthing, breast feeding, or any other aspects of mothering, even though these words clearly express distinctive aspects of divine/human relationships, can be counted on to cause immediate consternation. Some would go so far as to say that a baptism where the traditional Trinitarian formula Father, Son, and Spirit is not used would be invalid.

As the naming of God is critical to our religious identities, so, too, is our naming of ourselves. To describe all human beings using the words *man* or *men* is inaccurate. Women have very different human experiences from men. The dominance of male terminology suggests these differences are not significant, that they are not important clues about how human communities express faith, that they are not critical for knowing how to live differently in an unjust world. When female experiences are invisible, aspects of truth are missing for everyone. To subsume female experiences within male words has been devastating for women. Invisibility leads to inferiority; inferiority leads to self-doubt, even self-hatred, and to a history of men treating women as objects of their control.

There are examples, too, of verbal inaccuracies that lead to distorted human/divine relationships. The use of the color black to imply what is bad or evil promotes

In feminist rituals—in homes, churches, or synagogues—feminists want to practice mindfulness, using their bodies to encourage accountability and solidarity. They reject any posture that harms them or inhibits growth. Though some may be awkward and self-conscious, they dance, move their bodies in concert with each other, and touch each other with a sense of playfulness, solidarity, and respect. *Copyright © Joan Biren.*

fear of black people and underlines the suspicion that black people are more prone to violence and evil than white people. This color-coded language perpetuates racism; it denies attitudinal change. In a similar way, language that connects able-bodied people to goodness and disabled people to sin—"I am blind, but now I see"—perpetuates discrimination. Any language that dehumanizes groups of people, whether in adjectives to describe them as out of step (such as the poor, the homeless) or language that perpetuates stereotypical images (such as older people, gays or lesbians, teenagers), defies one of the main premises of worship, namely, that this time is one when each person, no matter what the human condition, is a part of the revelation of God in our midst.

New Feminist Ritual focuses on action: correction, imagination, and experimentation. There is a dynamic process of naming God not through paucity but through abundance including distinctively female metaphors, for example, *midwife, crone, bakerwoman, Goddess,* and *mother.* Feminists correct demeaning interpretations, like *gossip* and *witch,* or like *white,* which wrongly enables some to claim purity and goodness. They reject words that dishonor God and do violence to them. The word *father* for God is one example for women or men who have known a physically violent human father, a distant, uninterested father, or an unusually dominant father. To call on God as father raises very disturbing feelings about who God is. Feminists use female pronouns as well as male to refer to God and themselves. With such a long history of male-only descriptions, using gender-neutral language is not enough. Feminists may refer to God as Lover, as Sophia; they call upon a multicolored God and a God who is known beyond any of our limitations. Feminist ritualizing includes an unrelenting process to discover words that layer and stretch

and press our glimpses of God and each other. This process of naming changes our understanding of power, God's and our own. God is known in all of creation, weak and dying, dry and full of milk, people who use their toes to eat or boxes for shelter. What marks God and us, too, is potential.

TEXTS

As with words, so, too, of course, with texts, especially sacred texts. The stories men and women read in institutional settings generally focus on men, for example, Moses, Abraham, Isaac, Jesus, Peter, and Paul. The interpretations of the few women included, such as Eve, the woman who anointed Jesus, Mary the mother of Jesus, and Hagar, are often distorted and misreported. One of the most egregious examples is the woman who anointed Jesus, so often pictured as a whore and a sinner rather than a faithful friend of Jesus, who had the courage to anoint her. With the help of historical, biblical, and theological scholarship, New Feminist Ritual searches relentlessly for what has been left out, what has been overlooked, and for multiple lenses through which all of us can understand the lives of historical and biblical women.

SPACE AND OBJECTS

What feminists see, feel, and touch in their rituals also profoundly affect what they know and who they are. Since New Feminist Ritual began in small groups in participants' homes, much learning about space has evolved from what they recognized and tried in these settings. Of primary importance is the arrangement of the space. Even before a word is said, the space suggests what people expect of each other. Feminists are coming to know the importance of embodying their interdependence, of using their bodies to unfold truths, to layer their convictions and to correct their misdirections. Ritual space ought not embody a hierarchy of holiness. No one presides as if at the head of a table; no one sits or stands high above all others. Space can remind each person that each is an agent of the other's freedom and development, that each one is an expression of God's revelation. Feminists want to reinforce the belief that each person has special knowing, but no one has a claim on holiness more important than another.

In these spaces, feminists use objects that remind them of their desires as well as their heartaches. Pictures of ancestors, women, children and men, saints and sinners, connect people with their own possibilities and limits. Ample and particular symbols connect them with wonder and healing. They may be natural elements such as water, oil, food, or objects created for a particular time. For example, a wreath decorated differently at various rituals can express layered experiences, some pleasant, some not. Or a cord to represent the bathrobe belt a father used to quiet a child while raping her reminds all of the terror and prevalence of sexual abuse (Walton, 62).

GESTURES

As feminist liturgical scholar Marjorie Proctor-Smith has stated, posture matters. People gather with eyes open, heads up, kneeling only when it expresses their relationship to God, and not a subservient relationship to other human beings. They acknowledge God's authority best through body language that expresses the possibilities inherent in an encounter with God through the actions of one another. Feminists do not invite each other to assume any position that hinders reciprocity or that harms or demeans. Closing one's eyes, bowing one's head, and kneeling before a man, in particular, have been dangerous for women. In feminist rituals, in our homes or in our churches or synagogues feminists want to practice mindfulness, using their bodies to encourage accountability and solidarity. They reject any posture that harms them or inhibits growth. Though some may be awkward and self-conscious, they dance, they move their bodies in concert with each other, and they touch each other with a sense of playfulness and solidarity and respect.

SOUNDS

In New Feminist Ritual, all sounds that express aspects of human experiences are welcomed. Feminists particularly attend to what has been left out. They wail as well as chant, listen to sounds of terror as well as comfort, use rhythms with drums and other percussion instruments that connect us to their bodies. Whether recorded or newly made sounds, hymns or popular melodies, edited or newly written texts, the choices about what to include follow similar guidelines mentioned above with other elements. Most of all, feminists expect their sounds to enhance our emotional engagement. They want sounds to explore the whole spectrum of experiences, from the most intimate to the most transcendent. Feminists expect sounds to help them feel the power of their relationships in rituals, that is, to know the meanings of what they are doing, under their skin and beyond their heads.

Examples of New Feminist Ritual

The choice of examples that follows is not exhaustive but rather illustrates some of the possibilities of New Feminist Ritual, whether in large congregational settings or more intimate domestic gatherings. They include three different responses to varied challenges. The first example focuses on an exploration of the meanings of a particular biblical text; the second demonstrates a new way of experiencing an inherited liturgical form; and the third centers on remembering death. The rituals are described in some detail and in the present tense in order to offer a sense of immediacy for the reader.

The first example centers on the story of Judges 19: 1–30, a particularly distressing reading in the Hebrew Bible, a gang rape of a concubine, the dismembering of her body into twelve pieces, and the sending of these pieces to the twelve tribes of Israel. The text is a horrible, shameful, and terrifying record of male violence. To no one's surprise, this story is not read often in congregational settings. However, in a misogynist world where every woman fears rape and all too many women are raped, it is incumbent to hear this text. The story calls men and women to face the realities of violence, to examine the implications of using women as objects of men's pleasure, to encounter the truth that there are times when no one, not God, nor any human being, comes to the rescue, and to reflect on one's life and commitments in light of what a persons sees and feels and hears.

An object focuses our attention. Elizabeth Schell, one of the planners of the ritual at Union Theological Seminary, created a twelve-foot soft sculpture of a woman's body in twelve pieces (big woman). She covered the pieces with names of women and men whose bodies had been violently abused and also with natural images that extend the interpretation of torture to the raping of the earth. The texture of the object is soft and resilient. To touch it feels like a contact with a human body. The colors are bold, passionate, and dynamic. The "big woman," as she is called, is beautiful to look at and to touch. To see her in twelve parts poignantly expresses the destruction of daring, strength, imagination, and potential. She makes tangible the awful truth of rape and dismemberment. The ritual begins with an announcement: This experience might bring up deep-seated, terrifying memories in some people. There are people present who are prepared to help where and whenever necessary.

The retelling of the story from Judges 19 begins at the entry of the main space. The story is complicated; there are many layers of interpretation. The focus for this day is on a man and his concubine. The host welcomes the strangers for dinner and the night as a respite on their journey back to their own home. After eating, in response to the request of the men of the city, the host hands over the concubine for their pleasure. The men spend the night raping her. The next morning the owner takes her body to his home and dismembers it, sending a piece of it to each of the twelve tribes of Israel.

After hearing the text the congregation goes into the main space, singing, "My God, my God, why have you abandoned me?" As they walk inside they see the pieces of this big woman strewn over the floor. People gather around, pick a piece to examine, look carefully, and feel it in silence. One of the leaders for the day then speaks about some meanings of this text. Another invites members of the community to express their responses in prayer and then invites them to tie together the twelve parts of this big woman's body and carry it to the foot of a large cross. This action does not suggest resacrifice but rather an expression of solidarity at this place of suffering. The singing of "Be Not Afraid" accompanies the participants' walking to the cross. At the cross people add names and images to the sculpture. They claim this big woman and all that such a claiming implies. The big woman has become a container of sorrow, rage, healing, and perhaps for some, complicity. People linger with her for a long time after the formal ritual is over.

The big woman is an example of a ritual object created for an occasion. It functioned as a symbol, a sensual focus for our encounter with God (in this text, an absent God), humanity, and the world. The object invites disclosure and engagement. No one interpreted the object for the congregation. There is no definitive interpretation. The big woman is a symbol of relationships gone awry. The worshippers see, touch, and write on her in order to find their own stories, whatever they might be. It is given to them as an incentive to act. This occasion was for participants a time of personal healing, for others a moment for repentance, for others a time of commitment, for all an experience of anger. We live in a world where women are still murdered and raped and the earth disregarded. We cannot stand by and watch.

A second example is of an ancient ritual form reclaimed: Eucharist in a Roman Catholic community of women. Sharing food and telling stories are common activities in any gathering. They are the primary actions that communicate who people are, where they have come from, and where they are going as human beings. These same actions convey the heart of persons' identities as Christians. In Eucharistic celebrations women and men remember how God has been known and continues to be present, and they respond to that presence using words and food. However, in the evolution of forms for celebrating the Eucharist, the storytelling and eating have become so formalized that only a few people's stories are heard, and eating is limited to a sip of wine or juice and a hint of bread, hardly the stuff of nourishment and pleasure. The following example of New Feminist Ritual illustrates a model for reclaiming this Eucharistic tradition.

The women who are gathering for Eucharist have known each other for many years, in some cases, more than thirty or forty years. They live interdependently; that is, they share an understanding of their commitment to God and one another, and they hold in common all their human and material resources. This commitment affects their decisions, their work, their living, and their praying. As Roman Catholic women who have gathered for Eucharist all their lives, sometimes daily, they know the traditional form well. It is a part of their deepest embodied memory. The problem they confront is that according to the law of the Roman Catholic Church a single presider leads their Eucharistic praying and offers most of the interpretations of biblical and other stories. This presider is always male and not a part of their community.

For many women, over many years, this situation has felt odd, even wrong. How can someone who is a casual acquaintance, at best, drop in to lead the public prayer of this community? Though the institutional Church does not recognize or condone any change in this situation, a group of women decided to reclaim the leadership of this ancient ritual for themselves. Using what can be imagined of ritual meal traditions and the most natural experiences of storytelling, they improvise a Eucharistic celebration.

The women gather in a large space with chairs arranged in small groupings of five or six. On the walls of the space are pictures of all kinds of people, living and dead, who serve as reminders of how and why they are here in this world. The pictures, projected on the walls, reflect their commitments, their relationships to family and friends as well as their dreams about justice for all people. Today, there are pictures of a family reunion, a polluted environment, Mexican guest workers, children dying from AIDS (acquired immunodeficiency syndrome), women who have just passed their high school equivalency exams, women celebrating their fiftieth year of commitment in a religious community, and the baptism of a new child.

There is singing, too, songs anyone suggests from the songbook, rewritten texts to familiar tunes. After a while the pictures fade out and the women sing: "We gather together to offer thanksgiving, for friends and for dear ones, both living and dead. . . . Give us the courage to live our lives boldly and courage to speak what we know to be right" (Ware, *New Words for Old Hymns and Songs*, 14). Storytelling follows: One of the planners tells the group the story from the Hebrew Bible of the widow of Zarephath (1 Kings 17:8–24), a widow with a child, both of them about to die, who nevertheless share their last morsels of food with the prophet Elijah. At the conclusion of the story, one of the planners talks briefly about the text and invites the women to talk to one another about it. When did they take a risk that cost something? What gives them the courage to move beyond comfort and security? After some time for their reflection, she invites anyone who desires to speak to share what she felt, heard, or said with the group.

Then the people walk to the dining room. As they sing, they call out names of ancestors and present companions to accompany them. They respond to each name, singing or shouting, "walk with us." Once settled at the tables the women bless God through words, eating, promises. A member of the group coaches the community to recall how God has been present among them, to remember actions of God in human history and in the present time that shape their lives, and layer an emerging tradition among them. Then she asks those present to focus on memories of meals, particularly in the context of our storytelling today, meals when Jesus took risks, and when they or others have acted knowing a reputation, a job, or a life was threatened. In the midst of these stories, someone includes the story of the Last Supper. Finally, she invites someone to call upon the spirit of God beyond and in and around to bless this food and their lives.

Then everyone eats bread, drinks grape juice or wine, and consumes the food they have brought to share with one another. At the end of the meal all take the time to tell one another about some upcoming moments, difficult ones or those full of pleasure. They draw upon the strength and hope of one another to act boldly to change the injustice in the world. They pass around a basket, not for the scraps of bread left but, in this case, for some money to extend this meal to others who are also hungry. This liturgy concludes with the singing of another song, also rewritten. An excerpt:

> There is a balm in Gilead
>   for those whose hopes are dead;
> There is a balm for neighborhoods
>   where racial hates are fed.
> In spite of lamentation, destruction, burning,
>   strife,
> The sacred day of Sabbath can move from death
>   to life. (9)

The people send each other forth to act in light of the faith and history they share and their potential yet unfolding.

What happened in this celebration was new. Each person was responsible for all others. Everyone's story mattered. Using traditional stories mixed with their own, the women claimed their lives at the heart of telling of the Christian story. Rather than listening from the margins, that is, hearing someone interpret the sacred texts for them and pray in their name, they urged each other to speak and in so doing claimed their place as a part of a larger church. The community ate and drank to remind itself that all are accountable for each other's hungers and many others' as well. They left prepared to resist injustice where it reigns, to advocate where another is vulnerable, to hope, regardless of the circumstances, to live with delight and thanks.

The third example illustrates the challenges of a life cycle event when a mother of a member of a feminist ritual community dies. The relationship of mother and daughter is tender yet fraught with frustration. How shall the community share her daughter's sorrow, support her grieving, help her to move forward? How shall they remember her mother? How do they engage each other so that in their remembering and imagining they urge each other to live differently?

The ritual begins with a recounting of the life of Doris. A son-in-law tells her story. The daughter talks about some artifacts, photographs, and books she has brought and placed on a table in the center of the room. They illustrate Doris's particular dreams and realities. The daughter plays a piece of music that expresses some aspects of her relationship to her mother.

Then a series of three poems, interspersed by reflections among the members, follow. The first poem, from the perspective of a mother, reminds us of limits. Mothers cannot meet all the needs their children have. The mothers in the group offer concrete examples from their own experiences with daughters. Next, the members listen to a poem from the perspective of a daughter that then invites them to imagine the choices a mother makes for the life of a daughter and the costs of those decisions. One of the leaders invites the community members to remember concretely some of what their mothers gave them as well as what they did not. Each person draws an image that comes to mind or writes words that express what she recalls. The third poem expresses qualities of mother/daughter connections, at times precious, irreplaceable, and at other times burdensome, irritating, and limiting. What, they are asked, have they dared in our lives that their mothers could not dare in theirs? What have they dared because of mothers or in spite of them? There is time for silence and then for speaking about a time of daring in our own lives.

As each person speaks, she plants some crocus seeds in a pot of earth. With their fingers they feel the potential of dirt to nourish these seeds; they remember that seeds begin in darkness and emerge with both predictable and surprising characteristics. The plant is a gift for the daughter. As it blooms, the women want her to remember their collective bonding and care, the daring of her mother and her own willingness to dare. The members end by singing a chant about change, the change wrought in them by their divine mother, by the exigencies of life and death, and by their own actions.

Future Directions

New Feminist Ritual is a young movement. Like every struggle for justice, it requires persistence and imagination. Its future depends on sharing the burden of its rigors: listening carefully to one another, speaking honestly about what happens, paying attention to details, trying what is not comfortable, pushing beyond boundaries, regular evaluation, correction of what does not help, studying what scholars are writing, developing new leaders, and time, lots of time needed to plan and lead new ritual forms. Already some changes are institutionalized in some churches and synagogues, such as language to describe human beings, ordained women, and corrections and additions to sacred texts where the interpretations are blatantly inaccurate, such as expanding a genealogy to include the names of the mothers (*Remembering the Women*). However, words for God are still overwhelmingly male; female metaphors are still verboten, and the eagerness or even willingness to learn from the daily stuff of life experiences of each person in any community, large or small, which leads to all these changes, is minimal.

The vision of New Feminist Ritual requires changing fiercely protected truths and traditions. As illustrated in the above examples, New Feminist Ritual is not about a wholesale disregard of traditions but rather is a careful critique of them, keeping what is good and true, letting go what is not. As with other deeply ingrained attitudes that perpetuate injustice, such as racism, homophobia, and classism, this kind of change is not easy. It is about transforming a way of life. New Feminist Ritual embodies practices where power is shared rather than centralized, where claims of truth evolve rather than remain static, and where all our experiences, of pain and pleasure, are acknowledged as essential components of our ritual expressions.

SOURCES: From the beginning of the New Feminist Ritual movement, Ann Pat Ware and Marjorie Procter-Smith have been pivotal in its development. Ware's publication *New Words for Old Hymns and Songs* (2000) and her research to add the names of the mothers in the genealogy in the book of Matthew,

as published in J. Frank Henderson's *Remembering the Women* (1999), are examples of some of her work. Procter-Smith's books *In Her Own Rite* (2000) and *Praying With Our Eyes Open* (1995) have offered both critique and imagination to provide concrete directions for change. Ritual examples help as well. Those cited in this essay can be found in full in Janet Walton's *Feminist Liturgy* (2000), or in the case of *Big Woman*, from artist Elizabeth Schell.

WOMEN AND HEALING IN NORTH AMERICA
Susan M. Setta

IN NORTH AMERICAN history and throughout the world, healing has been predominantly a woman's art. Nevertheless, historical studies undervalue and underrepresent women's healing arts.

Regardless of the time or place, women's healing systems share common characteristics. First, women develop faith systems that support believers in times of sickness and in times of health; physical illness is never their only concern. Second, women's healing arts distinguish themselves from scientific medicine by focusing on the totality of a person's experience of a particular illness rather than solely on the disease. Because they see a connection between the ailments of the body, the ills of the soul, and disruption of community bonds, women combine palliative treatments for the body, spiritual comfort for the soul, and community rituals to empower the patient. Many women's systems favor natural remedies, but others comfortably combine science and natural healing.

Women healers view the spiritual cause of disease as more important than its physical symptoms; the first step toward a cure is spiritual diagnosis. Illness arises from any combination of sin, spirit or demon possession, or bad thought. Most religious healing systems see breach of their law as the main cause of disease—some go so far as to name this as the only cause. To treat infraction-based illness, the healer talks with the person seeking treatment to discover the offense, prescribes penance and sometimes restitution, and performs rituals that range from purging baths to prayer. If a person is possessed, the healer prays, performs rituals to placate angry spirits, and exorcises demons. When a patient is ill because of bad thought, the healer restores health by making an effigy, neutralizing a curse, or creating a ritual. The patient, family, and community actively participate in all types of treatments.

Care of the sick begins as a private enterprise; women nurture their families by providing potions, balms, and special food, lending a healing touch and offering words of comfort and prayer. The potions may vary from culture to culture and from one historical period to another, but women continue to be the first line in the defense against illness. When a patient does not respond to private treatment, public healers with additional knowledge and skill enter the healing enterprise. Whether they are the "wise women" of colonial times or the medicine women of Native American tradition, public healers typically share an important characteristic: They are wounded healers whose firsthand experience with illness preceded their call to heal.

Native American Healing Practices

There are few records of Native American healing practices in the period of American exploration and colonization. A glimpse of women and healing comes to us from the journals of Jacques Cartier's 1535–1536 Canadian expedition. Native American women treated seventy-five crew members who were dying from scurvy. Using bark preparations, sweat lodges, and "magical incantations," they saved every life. We do not know who these women were or the specific treatments they proffered, but the magical incantations the women used were undoubtedly prayers and rituals.

In general, the role of women in Native American cultures varies among tribes. In the past, shamanistic traditions have usually restricted themselves to men. This ancient way of life, which continues into the present, centers around individual shamans who harness the spiritual power of plants, animals, and objects for cultural harmony and healing and who travel between the physical and spiritual worlds to heal disruptions and rectify injustices. Aside from acting as shamans, however, women play key roles in healing, especially after menopause. Among the Iroquois there are separate medicine mask societies for men and women. Men carve and wear basswood "faces" representing spirit beings; women don braided cornhusk masks that stand for forest or vegetative spirits. All masks embody a spirit that can bring healing. Only after an individual is healed by a mask can he or she join the society. Among the Mohegan, Algonquin, Shasta, and Oneida, the primary healers have been women who aim to cure both the individual and societal imbalance that caused sickness. Whether they use a mask or a dance, all healers begin by invoking and appeasing the appropriate spirits. Then they provide herbal remedies. The stories of two twentieth-century women, Comanche medicine woman

Mohegan Gladys Tantaquidgeon illustrates Native American healing practices and points to the broad definitions of sickness and medicine in Native American culture. Tantaquidgeon came to healing from an unbroken line of medicine women who were herbalists. As medicine woman, Gladys turned her efforts toward recovering, classifying, and restoring healing practices in North American tribes. *Courtesy of the Mohegan Tribe.*

Sanapia and Mohegan Gladys Tantaquidgeon, illustrate Native American healing practices and point to the broad definitions of sickness and medicine in Native American culture. Sanapia attended to the direct healing of individual illnesses; Gladys Tantaquidgeon worked to restore healing spirits and traditions to the entire Native American community.

Like her counterparts throughout Native American history, Sanapia (1895–1968) became a healer through heredity and conquering her own illness. Sanapia specialized in treating a type of recurring paralysis she calls ghost sickness. Though she was not entirely opposed to scientific medicine, Sanapia believed that only her cures offer complete and permanent relief because they address the cause. Sanapia believed a ghost throws a feather into the patient's body. Unless the feather is removed, the patient will die.

Treatment began when an intermediary contacted Sanapia. The patient lived with Sanapia and her family until healing occured. Through lengthy conversations, Sanapia elicited the patient's explanation of the offending actions and diagnoses the spiritual problem. She gave the patient a semipublic purifying bath to reduce the power of the harmful spirits. Then Sanapia summoned her spirit helper, the eagle, to find appropriate herbs and suitable locations for the prayers she used to enter a trancelike state. When Sanapia felt she had sufficient healing power, she began chanting while massaging the patient with appropriate herbs. Once she was confident that the offending ghost could be extracted, she sucked it out. Because she thought patients benefited from tangible evidence of healing, Sanapia showed the patient an actual feather. If her initial attempts did not work, Sanapia performed a public ritual involving the patient's extended family and community. When healing was complete, Sanapia covered the patient with red paint to give thanks for the blessing and intervention of Mother Earth. In her treatment, Sanapia blended palliative and spiritual treatment, admission of fault, right thinking, and community involvement.

Mohegan medicine woman Gladys Tantaquidgeon came to healing from an unbroken line of medicine women. From her aunt, she learned the plant lore that was all that remained of the original Mohegan healing arts. Later, Gladys expanded her role as medicine woman in efforts to recover, classify, and restore healing practices in North American tribes. She noted that plants were only one tool of medicine and that art, especially healing beadwork, song, and dance, were key aspects of any practice. Moreover, in traditional Mohegan healing, herbs or rituals only became efficacious when the healing spirits, Granny Squanit and the Little People, blessed them. Gladys felt called to return these spirits and their power to the community.

Curanderas in the Southwest

Curanderismo, a healing tradition with roots in Spanish colonialism, made its way to North America in the 1500s. It blends healing practices of the colonized people with Roman Catholicism. Although contemporary forms vary according to geography, male (curandero) and female (curandera) healers subscribe to the same basic principles.

When the healing attempts of a family fail, they consult a curandera, a healer whose powers are hereditary. Tradition has it that a potential curandera cries while she is still in her mother's womb. All curanderas believe they heal through God's power. Healing only occurs if God desires it; plants or techniques work because God put them on earth to be used in healing. A curandera combines specific healing techniques with repetitive Christian prayer, such as, "In the name of God, I will heal you," and supplications to saints known for their ability to treat specific illnesses. Most curanderas specialize in one type of healing such as midwifery or herbalism. A few, like Josephita Ortiz y Davis of New Mexico, become curandera total, a term reserved for women with powerful healing gifts. Davis used ritual, symbol, and herbs, moved in and out of the spiritual dimension, and consulted specialists when necessary. She had an eclectic array of healing tools, including a crystal globe, a bear's head, replicas of Jesus and Mary, and a broad assortment of herbs.

Although curanderismo is still found throughout North America, it is gradually disappearing. Families who want to assimilate into American culture often look with disfavor on traditional forms of healing.

Healing among Euro-American Colonists

Like healers everywhere, Euro-American colonial women had to adapt to their changing situation and new land. Early records show their willingness to incorporate Native people's knowledge of healing plants into their own treatment methods. This trust of "Indian Potions" has persisted throughout American history despite the fact that North Americans were often grossly intolerant of other aspects of Native healing arts and set out to reform what they disparagingly called heathen ways.

Despite the apparent cultural differences, the colonists' healing practices shared the idea that illness had a moral, spiritual cause with the Native American people. Because the colonists were Christian, they saw sin, God, and possession by the devil as the most likely sources of disease. They combined confession, herbs, and prayers by and for the patient in attempts to bring about a cure.

When care at home failed, the community consulted "wise women" or midwives. Through apprenticeships these public healers gained knowledge of herbal treatments and became exceptionally skilled at prayer and spiritual diagnosis.

In the early 1600s, public healers were typically female. There were only a few male physicians in the colonies; generally the community did not trust them. By the late 1600s, the number of male physicians increased, but unlike their European counterparts, American doctors had no specific medical training; the same course of study led a young man to either the ministry or to the practice of medicine; often a man did both. For the entire community, care of the soul was paramount.

The actual practices of wise women and physicians differed very little. They provided palliative cures and usually located the cause of illness in sinful activity or bad thought. A patient, parent, or even the whole community could sin. Because illness was God's punishment for sin, no palliative cure would work until the spiritual issue was rectified. When some people survived the small pox epidemics of the sixteenth and seventeenth centuries while others perished, the community's belief in the spiritual origin of disease was legitimated. During the witch trials of the last decades of the 1600s, colonists blamed the devil for some illness but also claimed that most possession occurred because someone had broken God's law.

The few surviving records of female public healers show that colonial pharmacopoeia included early forms of digitalis, aspirin, ibuprofen, and belladonna. Colonial healing practices were not stagnant; women continually developed and borrowed treatments to combat whatever illnesses arrived on the scene. One late-seventeenth-century medical treatise notes, for example, that an African woman created a vaccine to ward off smallpox, a disease that had reached epidemic proportions in the colonies. Typically, the male writer does not name her.

Male, Scientific Medicine

A blend of wise women, midwives, and male physicians practiced in rural areas until well into the nineteenth century. But in urban areas by the 1750s, male physicians replaced female healers, and scientific explanations displaced spiritual diagnosis. Scientific medicine embraced the views of Enlightenment philosophy that separated the body and soul and viewed any form of religious healing as merely superstition or magic.

The rise of male, scientific medicine led to setbacks in community and women's health. Scientific medicine abandoned traditional healing practices. Claiming to rely on empirical evidence, the new physicians substituted toxic substances like calomel, arsenic, and mercury potions for botanical remedies that female healers carefully used. Male physicians advocated what came to be known as "heroic medicine," which included dangerous treatments like bloodletting and ridiculed using water even to hydrate a fever or bathe a wound.

Accompanying the rise of male medicine was the arrival of a new creature on the American scene, the ailing woman. This woman was constantly ill with painful but non-life-threatening problems. Where women's health had formerly rested in the hands of female practitioners, by the nineteenth century the female body became the special domain of male medicine. Scientific male medicine developed a new and highly problematic view of women that determined the treatments it prescribed. Scientific practitioners understood women as physically inferior creatures, controlled completely by their reproductive organs—as one physician put it, "[T]he Almighty, in creating the female sex, had taken the uterus and then built the woman up around it" (Holbrook, 15). For ailments including the common cold, headaches, and nervousness, one branch of physicians treated the uterus. They filled it with concoctions ranging from honey and milk to leeches and caustic chemicals. Toward the end of the nineteenth century, J. Marion Sims (1813–1883), the celebrated father of gynecological surgery, went so far as to treat nervousness with hysterectomy—a technique he perfected by practicing on slaves.

Another group of physicians named unfeminine activity as the primary cause of female illness. When women thought too much or became educated, they lost some of their submissive nature and invited illness. Passivity, these physicians contended, would restore women's health. They advocated rest cure, which treated women as if they were infants by hand-feeding them, forcing them to remain in bed for months, allowing them to speak only to their doctors, and prohibiting all intellectual activity including reading.

Not surprisingly, uterine manipulation and rest cure resulted in increased female illness. Despite the overwhelming evidence that their methods were dangerous, scientific medicine proceeded with their "cures."

Because these new practices were at best ineffective and at worst hazardous, many Americans abandoned scientific medicine for alternative treatments such as water cure, nutrition science, and mind cure. Women organized Ladies' Physiological Societies, founded health-oriented journals, and authored hundreds of articles on the latest treatments. Although popular medicine offered safer and relatively more effective methods than the scientific variety did, cures were often short-lived. The basic ineffectiveness of popular medicine stemmed from two facts. First, popular medicine accepted the notion that physical inferiority caused women's illnesses, differing from medical science only in treatments. Second, like its scientific counterpart, popular medicine focused on treating the body and not on caring for the spirit.

New Religious Movements of the Nineteenth Century

In the middle of the nineteenth century, a variety of new religions appeared on the American scene. Many reincorporated healing into their religious systems. Although they differed significantly from one another, Spiritualism, Christian Science, and Seventh-day Adventism all proclaimed that care of the soul was primary and that religion and healing should no longer be separated.

Spiritualism

The belief that the spirits of the dead can interact with the living is found in most cultures. In 1848, it appeared in full force in Rochester, New York, when Margaret and Katherine Fox became mediums and communicated with the spirits of the dead. From its start, Spiritualism attracted people from a wide range of economic, ethnic, and racial groups. It appealed to women and men, white and black, Jew and Christian. African Americans saw a natural affinity between their African-influenced religions and Spiritualist practices. Women were far more likely to serve as mediums than were men, but men were very active in the movement.

Many Spiritualists voiced strong dissatisfaction with medical orthodoxy. They turned to Spiritualism, called on the dead to heal the living, and used popular health remedies. Spiritualists advocated living within the laws of nature and working with the spirit world to enhance life on earth. Its proponents had a social agenda as well; they opposed slavery and supported women's rights. Many public mediums specialized in healing. One, Mrs. J. C. Dutton, entered a trance to consult the spirits on the treatment that would best restore balance. For one patient, the spirits might advise her to use homeopathy, for another botanical treatments or electromagnetism. African American Madam Julian advertised her healing powers in the main publication of the American Methodist Episcopal Church.

Spiritualism flourished throughout the latter half of the nineteenth century, but its numbers decreased as its followers turned to Christian Science and Theosophy.

Mary Baker Eddy and Christian Science

Until her discovery of Christian Science in 1866, Mary Baker Eddy's life (1821–1910) typified ailing womanhood. Her father, Mark Baker, attributed her frequent illnesses to the fact that her head was too big for her body, a common assessment of the underlying reasons for poor female health.

In seeking relief Eddy tried most every cure offered in the nineteenth century, including scientific medicine, water cure, and mind cure. Eddy did receive brief symptomatic relief from some of these treatments, especially Phineas Parkhurst Quimby's mind cure, but her ailments always returned. In 1866 Eddy sustained injuries from a fall that she and her physician believed to be life-threatening. That same night, God revealed the principles of Christian Science to her, and she recovered completely. Christian Science focused on wrong or erroneous thinking as the cause of disease.

In her attempts to understand the principles of what she also called Divine Science, Eddy made one of the most significant medical discoveries of the nineteenth century. People, especially women, she claimed, were ill because the culture considered them sickly, frail, and inferior creatures.

Central to Eddy's understanding of disease was her belief that God could create neither evil nor sickness. She reasoned that illness is only illusion. People, she wrote, are created in the image of the Father-Mother God. Since God is not matter, neither are people. Using the term *Man* to refer to all humanity, she claimed that Man, like God, is perfect and incapable of having disease. An individual with the illusion that she or he is a material being will feel sick, but the truth was, in Eddy's estimation, that every individual is entirely healthy.

Christian Science offered nineteenth-century women a new view of themselves and gave them responsibility for their own health. Countering the medical practices of both uterine manipulation and rest cure, Eddy stated simply but firmly that women had no physical body. Even the idea of the uterus was a product of the erroneous material thought. To those who claimed that women were ill because they were thinking too much, Eddy stated that women were a reflection of God's intelligence, just as males were. Society, not God, produced the idea of gender. Christian Science attracted many men and women. It has persisted over time, when its self-help counterparts did not because it offered both spiritual and physical health to its adherents.

Some of Eddy's followers branched out on their own, often because of disagreements with Eddy. Augusta Stetson (1842–1928) organized a New York branch of Christian Science. Emma Curtis Hopkins (1853–1925) opened a Chicago-based Christian Science Seminary that trained more than 350 women. In the 1880s, two of Hopkins's students, Myrtle Fillmore (1845–1931) and her husband Charles (1854–1948), founded their own branch of New Thought called The Unity School. Other groups developed through the indirect influence of Eddy, most notably Jewish Science founded by Rabbi Morris Lichtenstein (1889–1938) and headed by his wife Tehilla (1893–1973) for more than thirty years after his death. Because all these religious systems share the idea that the mind plays a key role in sickness and in health, they are categorized as part of the New Thought movement.

ELLEN WHITE'S MEDICAL MINISTRY

Ellen G. White (1827–1915), like Mary Baker Eddy, was an ailing woman for much of her life. Like Eddy, she left school because of poor health. In adolescence she became convinced that she was entirely sinful, which contributed to her bouts with illness.

Raised a Methodist, she became intrigued by William Miller's claim that the Second Coming was imminent. An ordained Baptist minister, Miller announced that Jesus would return on October 22, 1844. When his prediction proved false, White, like other Millerites, turned to other religious expressions. In 1860 she and her husband James founded Seventh-day Adventism. Ellen gave the new movement its distinctive theology through revelations she regularly received from God. Belief in both the immanence of the Second Coming and the divine inspiration of White's visions form the core of Seventh-day Adventism. The healing component developed over time.

In 1863, White turned to water cure, and she recovered from an illness scientific medicine had failed to cure. In that same year, her health-related visions started when God told her that water cure was divinely ordained. Attributing most illness to sin, White claimed sickness entered the world when Adam and Eve disobeyed God and persists because of sinful activity. Although White believed that Satan could cause disease, she did not think this was the origin of most illness. Sinful activity such as breaking the dietary commandments of the Bible, improper sexual activity, especially masturbation, all resulted in illness.

White believed individuals to be fully capable of following all the laws of God. When an individual acted in accordance with the will of God, she reasoned, he or she would enjoy perfect health. Since bad practices or bad habits led directly to disease, good practices such as prayer, proper diet, and moral goodness paved the road to health.

In nineteenth-century America, illness and frailty defined what it meant to be a good woman. White undercut this idea by believing that actions, not intrinsic nature, caused illness. Rather than legitimating the idea of ailing womanhood, White claimed sickness was itself a sin. She provided a system for women to heal themselves and a community of faith to support the believer in sickness and in health.

White's revelations regarding health included instructions for the establishment of Seventh-day Adventist hospitals and medical schools. Today, the followers of Ellen White have the longest life span and the lowest incidence of cancer and heart disease of any group of Americans.

Female Acceptance of Scientific Medicine

Though many nineteenth-century women abandoned scientific medicine, others embraced it. In the early nineteenth century Catholic women's religious orders began founding hospitals that incorporated scientific medical practice into a religious milieu. Toward the end of that same century Protestant women followed their lead.

Roman Catholicism never severed the connection between religion and medicine to the extent that Protestantism had. Miraculous healing remained a criteria for sainthood; prayers for healing and undertaking healing pilgrimages were commonplace. European orders had established themselves as caretakers of the sick; their American counterparts led the way in establishing and administering hospitals devoted to both physical and spiritual care.

The Sisters of Charity, an order founded by Elizabeth Seton (1774–1821) in 1809, opened the first Catholic hospital in the United States. By the beginning of the twentieth century, sisters had established more than 265 hospitals, all of which embraced scientific medicinal practices. The sisters administered their own hospitals, although the bishop was their superior. The sisters provided nursing care and spiritual counsel and operated the pharmacy.

Physicians preferred Catholic sisters to Protestant nurses, claiming that the sisters were more obedient and less likely to question authority than their Protestant counterparts. It is true that the sisters acquiesced to the will of the physicians, whereas the Protestant nurses were more likely to voice opposition, but the sisters had good reason. First, anti-Catholic sentiment made it extremely difficult for all Catholics. Violence against Catholics, in general, and nuns in particular, was an unfortunate part of the American landscape. For the sisters to protest scientific medicine was virtually impossible. Opening hospitals endorsed by the new medical establishment was a way to gain acceptance by American society. Second, women religious had considerable experience with male organizations. The sisters knew that initial submission eventually led to autonomy. When the bishop believed the sisters were following his rules, he would often withdraw his scrutiny, leaving the sisters with complete control. The sisters used this same technique with physicians. One sister reported that when the doctors saw everything done according to their orders, the physicians withdrew and rarely visited the hospital again (Ewens, 289). Thus, the sisters retained control of their hospitals.

The sisters' hospitals and their nursing skill on the battlefields of the Civil and Spanish American Wars helped change the attitudes of the nation toward both Catholicism and female nurses. In war and in the face of mass contagion, the sisters offered significant spiritual and physical care to Protestant and Catholic alike.

During the second half of the nineteenth century, Protestant laywomen took up the idea of founding hospitals based on Christian principles. Lutheran and Methodist deaconesses and the Women's Missionary Society, for example, established hospitals in every major city. Unlike founders of new religions who brought healing into religion, the women who established hospitals attempted to take religion into the scientific arena. For some hospitals the women raised funds to include chapels complete with pews, organs, and stained-glass windows. Some of the first female physicians, including Unitarian Elizabeth Blackwell (1821–1910), spoke eloquently of the necessity of bringing spiritual values into scientific medicine.

Although both Catholic and Protestant women participated in administering the hospitals when they opened, physicians soon wrested control from Protestant women. Although Catholic bishops attempted to reassign leadership of the sisters' hospitals to men, the sisters were usually able to thwart attempts to oust them from leadership positions. Many of the hospitals founded by women religious remain under their control in the twenty-first century.

When Jewish groups began founding hospitals in the early twentieth century, men and women worked together. Jewish women, like Protestant women in mainline denominations, established organizations devoted to public health and to rectifying social conditions that led to disease.

African American Healing in the Nineteenth Century

Brutally separated from their homelands through slavery, African Americans were prevented from recreating their cultures in North America. The West and central African ancestors of American slaves inhabited a world alive with spirits. They viewed life as basically good but threatened by evil forces that surrounded them. To find security in the world, they looked to gods and their ancestors for protection. African religions turned to priests and priestesses, mediums, and healers who used ritual, magic, divination, sacrifice, and charms to control the evil around them and to maintain harmony with spiritual forces.

Christianity became appealing to slaves in the late 1700s when the Methodist Church and individual Baptist churches took stands against slavery and began allowing black men to preach and sponsor revivals. Attracted by the spirit-filled, "physical exercises" of the revivals, the slaves found a connection to the spirit possession that was central to African religion. The new converts grafted African ideas and practices onto American Protestantism.

Both physical and spiritual transformation characterizes individual conversion experiences. In their conversion narratives, former slaves describe feeling depressed and lethargic before entering a trance. During the trance they feel Jesus first destroying and then recreating their bodies. This experience, which they called "new birth," provided a profound sense of spiritual well-being and freedom from preexisting physical ailments.

New converts expressed their faith in various ways. "Shouting," considered possession by the Holy Spirit, could happen anywhere, in the fields, at home, or in church. More women than men became Shouters. Shouting churches were more organized expressions of this ecstatic behavior. The services used musical instruments, singing, and a ring dance called a Shout to bring on the Spirit. After the service, Shouters felt revitalized and noted that "sin-sickness" had vanished through the power of the Spirit. Healing took place in one of two ways: Either the Spirit healed directly or provided instructions about the proper remedies to use to cure the ailment. Many Shouters were recognized as skilled herbalists.

Conjuring, another popular healing technique, probably began among southern slave populations soon after they arrived on American shores, but records of conjure practice do not appear until the mid-nineteenth century. Conjure translated African sacred charms into African American life and attributed all illness to the enmity of others. Conjure doctors, also called hoodoo doctors, were mysterious people feared by the community because of their power to hurt or to heal. To treat their patients, who included white southerners, conjurers first determined whether or not the patient was hexed. If the illness was due to conjure, the conjurer had to locate and neutralize the hexing charm. Conjurers tricked, trapped, and banished the evil spirits that caused illness while providing herbal treatments for symptomatic relief.

Early-Twentieth-Century Immigrants and Healing

Catholic, and to a lesser extent Protestant and Jewish, women brought their traditional healing practices with them when they relocated to North America. They erected statutes, built shrines, recreated rituals, and used prayers that reminded them of their homes. In their drive to assimilate the immigrants into American culture, many clergy tried to suppress Old World healing, but a few practices survived. Devotion to the Madonna in Italian Harlem, pilgrimage to the Canadian shrine of St. Anne de Beaupré, and the powwowing practices of some Pennsylvania Germans linked religion and medicine and connected women to their ethnic roots.

Judaism has never had a strong tradition of women public healers apart from midwives. Women's healing prayers, such as those found in Yiddish prayers called *tkhines*, focus exclusively on menstruation and childbirth and do not extend to illness and health in general. When American Jews began embracing Christian forms of healing in the 1920s, Tehilla Lichtenstein and her husband founded the Society of Jewish Science to provide an alternative for American Jews.

Ethnic healing practices remained almost exclusively in their original communities. American culture as a whole viewed immigrant healing practices as superstitious ways of unenlightened individuals. The 1929 American creation of a society dedicated to St. Jude attracted American Catholic women in large numbers and found support among American Protestants to a lesser extent. It would not be until the last three decades of the twentieth century that American interest in immigrant healing practices would blossom.

THEOSOPHY

Rooted in Spiritualism's belief in the existence of a world where the souls of the dead resided, Theosophy began in 1875 when Russian-born Helena Blavatsky journeyed to the United States to explore the claims of Spiritualism. Blavatsky added several features to distinguish her brand of Spiritualism from the rest of the American scene. She blended occult and Hindu ideas into the core of Spiritualism. Blavatsky advanced the idea of the Great White Brotherhood of the Ascended Masters and focused on contacting the Masters to capture their wisdom and power for healing and advice.

Variations on Theosophy appeared in the late nineteenth and early twentieth century. Alice Bailey (1880–1949) added belief in the Second Coming of Christ to Theosophy. Katherine Tingley (1847–1933) built a luxurious, ocean-front commune at Point Loma in San Diego where members integrated popular health methods and theosophical principles. Edna Ballard (1886–1971) and her husband Guy (1878–1939) founded the I AM movement in 1930 and provided their audiences with dramatic healings. In all these forms of Theosophy, one key individual served as the vehicle through which the Ascended Master made his presence known.

Faith Healing

Christian faith healers personally facilitate healing by acting as a "vessel" for the Spirit of God. Isolated cases of individual healers, like Shaker founder Ann Lee, crop up in American religious history before the nineteenth century. But faith healing as a national movement developed first within factions of the Holiness movement and later as an integral part of the Pentecostal movement. Most nationally known faith healers were men,

but a few women captured national attention. The first of these, Marie Woodworth Etter (1844–1924), began her healing career as part of the Churches of God founded by German Reformed minister John Winerbrenner. Etter held large healing services throughout the Midwest in the 1880s. Etter joined the ranks of Pentecostalism in 1916.

Like other healers of the day, Etter believed that healing was one of the "gifts of the spirit" that had become available because the Second Coming of Christ was imminent. By all accounts she produced spectacular healings and "spirit filled" services. Those who came in contact with her during her services were "slain in the Spirit," a term used to describe the ecstatic practice of falling to the floor and becoming unconscious for a brief period of time.

Aimee Semple McPherson (1890–1946) is perhaps the best known female faith healer. At age eighteen, she joined a Pentecostal church near her home in Ingersoll, Ontario. She was baptized in the Holy Spirit and began speaking in tongues. She married Robert Semple, the young minister who converted her, and joined him on a missionary venture to China, where Robert soon died.

After she was miraculously healed from a serious illness, she began her own ministerial career. Reluctant at first, she finally accepted the call to ministry and left her second husband, Harold McPherson. Like other Pentecostals, she preached that healing was possible, but she did not, as she tells it, actually believe it. When a young woman was healed at one of her services, McPherson became a believer and launched her healing ministry. McPherson attributed the faith of the young woman with demonstrating the truth of Divine Healing. McPherson began to focus on a healing ministry. She drew huge crowds as she traveled from Boston to Los Angeles, holding stretcher days in sporting arenas and civic auditoriums.

McPherson's ideas were in line with most of Pentecostalism. She accepted scientific medicine as a gift from God, believed Adam and Eve's sin caused sickness, and saw the death of Jesus as both redeeming all sin and becoming the source of healing. To be healed, an individual needed faith and rebirth. Once the believer was reborn, he or she had only to "claim" the healing.

McPherson had several unique ideas. She personified healing as the Divine Handmaiden, the bride of Jesus. Together Jesus and the Divine Handmaiden provided complete health. To spread her message, McPherson used whatever means would attract followers. She staged church services that were more like musical or dramatic performances; she used radio before any other evangelist; and she created a prayer tower staffed by volunteers who prayed around the clock in response to specific prayer requests sent in by McPherson's radio listeners.

Although scandals occasionally rocked her life and

threatened her ministry, McPherson was able to institutionalize healing. By establishing the International Church of the Four Square Gospel and a theological seminary that prepared many women and a few men for ministry, McPherson created an enduring community of faith. Unlike most faith healers, her ministry survived her death.

Although Kathryn Kuhlman (1906–1980) never took personal credit for healings, her role was central. She repeatedly said that Jesus and the Holy Spirit did the healing. But in fact, many who were cured at her services believed in God's healing power long before they encountered Kuhlman but were healed only when they actually heard Kuhlman speak.

Unlike other Christian healers, Kuhlman claimed theology was completely unnecessary. Her methods were unusual as well. During her services, she announced healings that were taking place in the room by saying, for example, "Someone is being healed of asthma. Come forward, claim your healing." Those who believed they had been healed came forward to discuss both their illnesses and their cures and were invariably "slain in the Spirit" when they touched Kuhlman during this confession of faith. At one point, Kuhlman's gesture toward her audience resulted in more than 400 people simultaneously collapsing to the floor.

Kuhlman created what anthropologist Victor Turner called *liminality*, a term derived from the Latin for "threshold." Liminality may occur during a ritual, pilgrimage, or healing; the individuals are separated from the everyday world and are on the threshold of possibility. Kuhlman, more than any other faith healer, created the atmosphere in which the possibility of spiritual healing was maximized. Because the power to heal resided in Kuhlman alone, she was unable to transfer her healing power to any of her followers. Although a handful of people tried to perpetuate her work through the Kathryn Kuhlman Foundation, Kuhlman's ministry died with her.

Charismatic Healing

One important development in the history of women and healing is the rise and rapid growth of charismatic healing groups in the 1960s and 1970s. As a group, charismatic Christians speak and sing in tongues, hold healing services, and subscribe to many of the same principles as Pentecostalism does. Charismatic Christians, however, are often found within Roman Catholic and mainline Protestant churches. Women's Aglow Fellowship, or Aglow International as it is sometimes called, is a rapidly growing, interdenominational, charismatic Christian group that began in 1967 as an offshoot of the Full Gospel Business Men's Fellowship International. Typically, Aglow women are white, conservative, middle and upper-middle class who find themselves in one of the approximately 2,000 local fellowships. On the national level, Aglow sponsors a prison ministry and stresses bringing the world to Christ. On the local level, healing is central. While Aglow women think that sin can sometimes lead to illness, they contend that the cause of most illness is part of the mystery of God. Because they see God as all good and all powerful, they do not make the claim that God causes sickness. As in many other groups, there is ambiguity in Aglow's view of the origin of disease.

Aglow preaches that women should be submissive to the men in their lives but paradoxically claims that women are morally and spiritually superior to men. This superiority, in their view, accounts for the special effectiveness of women's prayers. They see one of the main roles of Christian women is to provide intercessory prayer for physical and spiritual healing.

Aglow believes scientific medicine is a gift from God and that spiritual tools can ensure medical success. Ecstatic prayer is their primary healing method. Members set up prayer chains that are immediately set into motion when they find out about an illness or when someone requests their intercession. They pray in tongues while doing their housework or when speaking to another Aglow member on the telephone. They employ laying on of hands and anointing with oil for situations where a person's faith is weak and turn to a form of exorcism, called binding and loosing the devil, whenever they discern the presence of a demonic power. In all cases, Aglow claims, it is God who provides the cures. In every case, healing is a community enterprise.

Healing and Recent Immigrants

For the most part, the practices immigrant women bring to North American stay within their communities. As the new arrivals assimilate into American culture, their connection to the old healing traditions fade. Until the end of the twentieth century, Americans as a whole ignored these practices; medical practitioners continue to work to eradicate them.

In the closing decades of the twentieth century, Americans took increasing interest in alternative forms of healing. As a result, mainstream American culture adopted techniques extracted from a variety of traditions but did not embrace the underlying system. Acupuncture and assorted Chinese herbs, for example, are sometimes incorporated into a Western scientific approach. Oncologists might suggest acupuncture and herbal teas as an antidote to the side effects of chemotherapy, but they do not, generally, subscribe to the beliefs that gave rise to the techniques.

Many late-twentieth-century Asian and Pacific Island immigrants arrived from countries such as Korea and

Taiwan, which have traditions of women healers. It is not yet clear whether these traditions have survived in America.

SANTERÍA AND VODOU

Two recent additions to the American religious scene, Santería and Vodou attract converts who do embrace the entire religious system. Of Cuban origin, Santería became more visible in the United States with the increased immigration that followed the Cuban Revolution of 1959. Similarly, Haitian Vodou became more prominent when Haitians headed for North America after the 1986 fall of the Duvalier regime. Both traditions originate in contiguous parts of West Africa. Santería traces its roots to the Yoruba people and Vodou to the neighboring Fons people of what is today Benin. Both came to North America through the slave trade in the sixteenth century. Unlike their North American counterparts, Haitian and Cuban slaves were allowed to reconstruct African traditions. As a result, they preserved the African spirits in what they called spirit houses. Although both groups borrow ideas and saints from Roman Catholicism, the structure and focus of Santería and Vodou are more akin to the original African traditions. In both religions, priests and priestesses provide leadership and communicate with the spirit world. Through divination and sacrifice, for example, Brooklyn Vodou priestess Mama Lola learns what the spirits desire, directs their power for healing, and becomes a vehicle for the manifestation of the divine.

Both traditions are flourishing in urban areas and are attracting increasing numbers of black nonimmigrants and a few whites as well. Santería and Vodou provide services for their followers to a degree that American society does not. They offer priests and priestesses to heal, guide, and counsel and a supportive community in times of crises.

Healing and the New Age

At the end of the nineteenth century, Theosophists coined the term *New Age* to describe the approaching era when all the forces of the universe would be harmonious. The term regained its popularity in the 1980s and now refers to movements that believe they are reclaiming and restoring ancient wisdom.

NEOPAGANISM

Gerald B. Gardner (1884–1964) is credited with reawakening interest in the ancient rites of witchcraft he called Wicca, from the Anglo-Saxon word *Wicce*, meaning "to bend" or "to shape." His ideas quickly took hold. Adaptations of Gardner's ideas resulted in many variations on this tradition. By and large, neopagans are white, well educated, and female. They can practice a solitary form of Wicca or gather in larger groups, called covens. Z Budapest, a hereditary witch whose ancestresses practiced in Hungary, and Starhawk, for example, combine neopaganism and feminism. Understanding illness as one of many possible signs of disharmony, Starhawk and Budapest offer magic, rituals, and spells to refocus the believer on their primary deity, the Goddess. Proper thought will restore health and balance to the individual and the global community.

NEW AGE ECLECTICISM

New Age movements have rekindled interest in a variety of traditions such as Spiritualism, Theosophy, and other alternative healing methods that either began or were popularized in the nineteenth century. They are also fascinated with Native American practices and Eastern religions and borrow from some immigrant traditions.

When her husband Mark L. Prophet (1918–1973) died, Elizabeth Clare Prophet took over leadership of the Washington, D.C.–based organization, The Summit Lighthouse, her husband had founded as a platform for publishing his teachings. In 1974, she expanded the influence of The Summit Lighthouse by incorporating the Church Universal and Triumphant. Prophet believes she channels (a new term for medium) for both male and female Ascended Masters, including Saint Germaine, a prominent figure in the Theosophy-based I AM movement of the 1930s, Chinese Buddha Kuan Yin, St. Teresa of Avila, and Mary the Mother of Jesus. Unlike the original I AM movement, however, all Church Universal and Triumphant members can intercede on behalf of the sick. Prayer requests can be electronically mailed to volunteers who stand ready to pray and use the forces of the Ascended Masters for healing. In 1986, believing in the imminent destruction of the world, Prophet moved her group to Corwin Springs, Montana; adopted a survivalist strategy; blended Christian, Eastern, and Theosophical ideas; and awaited the coming cataclysm. In 1998 she provided a date for the final showdown. When the events failed to occur as she predicted, many of her followers abandoned her movement and her commune. Poor health forced her retirement from leadership of the group in 1999.

NEO-SHAMANISM AND ECLECTIC WITCHCRAFT

Both neo-shamanism and eclectic witchcraft extract their practices from a wide variety of sources. Neo-shamanism draws primarily on Native American traditions but also uses ideas from Eastern religions and Wicca as well. The political activist group the American Indian Movement (AIM) condemns neo-shamanism, which it sees as religious imperialism devoted to stealing Native American practices.

Silver Raven Fox, a self-proclaimed hereditary witch, typifies New Age eclecticism. Her popular books contain Wiccan chants and spells, Pennsylvania German pow-wow incantations, Native American healing rituals, and even charms to empower household cleaning supplies and cosmetics.

Conclusion

The late-twentieth-century women's movement made visible the hidden history of women and challenged medical orthodoxy's assumptions about sickness, health, and traditional healing. Americans, especially women, began reclaiming the stories and practices of a variety of healing traditions. The twenty-first-century spiritual healing marketplace offers healing crystals, curing stones, services in mainline denominations, Native American chants, Wiccan spells, visualization, and meditation techniques. The people most likely to use unorthodox healing are white, middle- and upper-middle-class, well-educated women.

Although the National Institutes for Health now sponsors an office for Alternative Medicine, many physicians remain skeptical of alternative and spiritual healing claims. Scientific and spiritual healing do not use the same criteria to define a cure. Science requires clear laboratory results; proponents of spiritual healing count any symptomatic relief as a success. An individual whose pain eases but whose test results do not change will count herself healed, though her physician will not. For scientific medicine, there are hopeless cases. In religious healing systems, there are none. The ultimate goal, spiritual health, can be reached even when a condition is physically terminal.

Women's interest in the art of healing has been constant throughout North American history. By the end of the 1700s the dominant medical culture marginalized and belittled women's healing practices, calling them old wives' tales or superstitions from a less-enlightened age. Though cultural forces conspired against them, women remembered that illness affects body and soul. They preserved the art of healing and its fundamental understanding that physical, spiritual, and social health cannot be separated.

SOURCES: For general information on the history of health-care practices, see Ronald Numbers and Darrel Amundsen, *Caring and Curing: Health and Medicine in the Western Religious Traditions* (1986). For a general view of scientific thought in North America, see Charles E. Rosenberg, *No Other Gods: On Science and American Social Thought* (1976). For historical information on Native American practices, see Virgin J. Vogel, *American Indian Medicine* (1970). For an example of early co-lonial understanding of the interrelationship of spiritual and physical health, see Cotton Mather's *The Angel of Bethesda* (1692). For an overview of women and religion in America, see the three-volume work by Rosemary Ruether and Rosemary Keller, eds., *Women and Religion in America* (1981–1986). A number of books document women's plight in the care of North American medicine. See Barbara Ehrenreich and Deirdre English, *For Her Own Good: 150 Years of the Experts' Advice to Women* (1979), and Deborah Kuhn McGregor, *Sexual Surgery and the Origins of Gynecology: J. Marion Sims, His Hospital and His Patients* (1989). For a sense of the nineteenth-century male physician's view of women, see M. L. Holbrook's *Parturition without Pain: A Code of Directions for Escaping the Primal Curse* (1875). Norman Gevitz's anthology *Other Healers: Unorthodox Medicine in America* (1988) provides a good look at a number of alternatives to orthodox medical practice. For an overview of women and healing, see Jeanne Achterberg, *Woman as Healer* (1991). For detailed histories and analyses of particular types of traditions in which women played important healing roles, see Ann Braude, *Radical Spirits: Spiritualism and Women's Rights in Nineteenth-Century America* (1989); Mary Ewens, *The Role of the Nun in Nineteenth-Century America* (1971); Karen McCarthy Brown, *Mama Lola: A Vodou Priestess in Brooklyn* (1991); Melissa Jayne Fawcett, *Medicine Trail: The Life and Lessons of Gladys Tantaquidgeon* (2000); Bobette H. Perrone, Henrieeta Stockel, and Victoria Krueger, *Medicine Women*, Curanderas, *and Women Doctors* (1989); Susan Setta, "Healing in Suburbia: The Women's Aglow Fellowship," *Journal of Religious Studies* 12, no. 2 (1986): 46–56; Betty Snellenberg, "Four Interviews with Pow-wowers," *Pennsylvania Life* 18, no. 4 (1961): 40–45; and the chapter on Elizabeth Clare Prophet in Timothy Miller's *America's Alternative Religions* (2001). For materials written by the healers themselves, see Mary Baker Eddy, *Science and Health with Key to the Scriptures* (1875); Clifton Johnson's anthology *God Struck Me Dead: Religious Conversion Experiences and Autobiographies of Ex-Slaves* (1969); Kathryn Kuhlman, *I Believe in Miracles* (1976); Aimee Semple McPherson, *Healing in His Wings* (1924); Laurel Thatcher Ulrich, *A Midwife's Tale: The Life of Martha Ballard, Based on Her Diary 1785–1812* (1991); Ellen G. White, *Ministry of Healing* (1905); and Starhawk, *The Spiral Dance* (1979).

WOMEN IN PROTESTANT CHURCH SOCIETIES AND BUREAUCRACIES
Susan M. Hartmann

WOMEN'S PARTICIPATION IN Protestant ecumenical and denominational organizations has taken three forms: Women often outnumbered men in congregations and provided a majority of the volunteer labor for the work of the church, while men occupied paid and unpaid leadership roles. Second, women formed their own local and national societies where they exercised considerable power and autonomy. And, in recent decades, they moved into both salaried and voluntary leadership positions in the national bodies of their religious institutions. A recurring issue for women seeking an equitable place in religious bodies has been whether to organize separately or to focus their energies on integration. While separatism reached its apogee in the late nineteenth and early twentieth centuries, it continues to exist side by side with integration and to serve as a spur to women's acquisition of greater power in religious institutions.

Obstacles to religious leadership and authority for women in many ways ran parallel to the obstacles blocking women's full participation in secular society. At least three elements of Christianity, while simultaneously nourishing secular discrimination against women, gave specific strength to the exclusion of women from decision-making positions in the churches: a masculine image of God with the assumption that his earthly priests and ministers would be male; the traditional view of women as second in Creation and responsible for the Fall; and scriptural interpretations that defined women's role in the church as silent and subordinate. In a very practical way women's historical exclusion from the ministry limited their presence in church governance since ordination was frequently required for holders of denominational positions.

Women partially dodged these obstacles in the latter decades of the nineteenth century by forming their own national organizations separate from the regular church bodies dominated by men. Moved to save both bodies and souls and especially to minister to groups that men could not or would not reach, women organized local benevolent societies to help the poor and spread the gospel as early as the 1790s. After the Civil War, they increasingly formed regional and national organizations to coordinate their mission work at home and abroad. In 1861, Christian women founded the first interdenominational organization, the Women's Union Missionary Society, and in 1868 Congregational women established the Women's Board of Missions, followed rapidly by similar bodies in the Methodist, Presbyterian, Episcopal, Baptist, and other churches.

These societies operated hospitals, schools, and orphanages at home and abroad; supported women missionaries, created training schools for female church workers; and moved ahead of male-led organizations in the creation of publicity for and literature about missions. They collected and administered vast amounts of money, sometimes raising more than the main mission boards of their denomination. The sixteen women's organizations that had sprung up in the two decades after the founding of the Women's Union Missionary Society, for example, raised nearly $6 million by 1882, even though the women's boards were not allowed to solicit funds in general church meetings. Northern Presbyterian women alone raised more than $13 million in the fifty years after founding of the Women's Foreign Missionary Societies of the Presbyterian Church, U.S.A. in 1870; by the 1920s, they were dispensing about $3 million a year for various mission projects.

In 1900, twenty-one-year-old Nannie Helen Burroughs expressed both the obstacles to women's participation in religious work and a solution, when she appealed to the National Baptist Convention to authorize a Woman's Convention. Entitling her speech "How the Sisters Are Hindered from Helping," she referred to the "righteous discontent" of African American Baptist women and their "burning zeal" to do Christ's work (Higgenbotham, 150). In addition to founding and heading the National Training School for Women and Girls, Burroughs led the Woman's Convention until her death in 1961. Like the white women's organizations, it raised and disbursed funds for educational and mission projects, but with the added imperative of meeting the social welfare needs created by a racist society.

Despite their fund-raising prowess and the experience in leadership and management gained through mission work, however, women failed to shake the male monopoly of decision making in their denominations. When the Methodist governing body, the General Conference, refused to allow female delegates in 1891, Mary Lathrap responded with some bitterness that the men "would not have enough church to be buried in if it were not for the efforts of the women" (Bendroth, 39). Women in the African Methodist Episcopal (AME) Church did not even enjoy autonomy over their own missionary efforts. In 1915, when southern women asked the AME Church's missionary department for the right to receive the money they had raised, they were rebuffed. Among the very few exceptions to the continuing male dominance in church governance was Helen Barrett Montgomery, a Wellesley graduate married to a successful businessman, teacher, writer, social reformer, and associate of Susan B. Anthony. After serving as president of the Women's American Baptist Foreign Mission Society and of the National Federation of Women's Boards of Foreign Missions, Montgomery was elected as president of the Northern Baptist Convention in 1921.

In the early decades of the twentieth century, when denominations did move to grant women fuller participation on governing boards, it often came at the expense of women's leadership in their own mission societies. For example, the Southern Methodist General Conference gave virtual autonomy to its Woman's Board of Home Missions in 1898 but in 1910 placed it under control of the denomination's general mission board. In 1923, the Presbyterians approved a restructuring plan that dissolved the women's home and foreign mission boards and reorganized their work within general boards of home and foreign missions.

Obstacles to religious leadership and authority for women ran parallel in many ways to the obstacles blocking women's full participation in secular society. Women partially dodged these obstacles in the latter decades of the nineteenth century by forming their own national organizations separate from the regular church bodies dominated by men. In 1907, the Baptist Woman's Convention took up the work of Jesus Christ and elected its first set of officers.
Courtesy of the Smithsonian Institution, National Museum of American History.

These and similar rearrangements in other denominations—notable exceptions included the Methodist and Episcopal churches—were presented as progressive moves to integrate women more fully into the churches' structures. And they reflected broader, secular trends of centralization and bureaucratization as corporations and other institutions sought efficiency and elimination of waste. But integration also resulted from male leaders' desire to control these successful operations and their belief that women were creating a parallel church and deflecting resources from the "main" operations of the churches.

Many women saw integration as a positive move, but they also worried about retaining influence, and a number of leaders did not welcome losing control over the money they raised. One woman expressed "shock that after so many years of faithful cooperation" their organizations should be "swallowed whole" (Bendroth, 56). Moreover, when the Presbyterian General Council commissioned a study after women's contributions to missions declined in the wake of integration, it found considerable discontent. The report, "Causes of Unrest among the Women of the Church," coauthored by Katharine Jones Bennett, who had headed the woman's board, noted that the merger was "taken by the men of the church with but the slightest consultation with the

women." And the report warned that women were questioning their place in the church "when a great organization which they had built could be autocratically destroyed by vote of male members of the church" (Lindley, 304). Losing the autonomy they enjoyed in their all-female organizations prompted some women to push for a larger role in the general governance structures of their denominations.

Church leaders usually allocated women seats in the newly merged structures but in quite limited numbers. An exception occurred in the Disciples of Christ, which created a new and integrated United Christian Missionary Society in 1919 and allocated half of the seats on the governing board to women. More typically, women failed to gain much ground in the overall governance bodies of the churches. At the 1943 meeting of the Presbyterian General Assembly, for example, 8 women were among the 464 participants. Episcopal women kept their separate mission organizations but were limited to just four of the more than thirty seats on the denomination's executive council, the decision-making body for the church between meetings of its General Convention. Moreover, until 1967 male delegates to the General Convention defeated resolutions to permit women to serve as delegates.

Women were better represented in some denominations. For example, the Congregational church required that one-third of the national board members and General Council delegates to biennial meetings be women. In 1948 Congregationalists elected a woman as moderator of the General Council. And in 1946 a second woman served as president of the American Baptist Convention. Yet these were exceptions. As late as 1969, a study of governing bodies of seventeen churches undertaken by the National Council of Churches reported that the data collected demonstrated a sharp contradiction between verbal assumptions of equal opportunity and actual widespread discrimination against women.

The movement to achieve more substantial female participation in the churches' leadership and policymaking originated in international ecumenism and preceded by two decades the resurgence of the secular women's movement in the United States. Stimulated in part by European women's assumption of ministerial duties during World War II and in reaction to Hitler's exploitation of women's traditional roles to serve Nazi ends, the first assembly of the World Council of Churches in 1948 considered the topic of women's roles in the church. In 1950, it established a Commission on the Life and Work of Women in the Church. The U.S. National Council of Churches of Christ (NCCC) and several denominations followed suit. No dramatic changes occurred, but several churches, including the Northern Presbyterians and the Methodists, did begin to ordain women.

Church Women United (CWU) played a central role in challenging the male monopoly of ecclesiastical power. Founded as the United Council of Church Women in 1941 by several denominational women's groups, the organization attached itself to the National Council of Churches, the largest ecumenical body in the United States, representing Christians in thirty-three Orthodox and Protestant denominations. Its decision to become a department of the National Council was not made lightly, and Church Women United leaders negotiated very deliberately to ensure that their organization would not suffer the fate of the independent women's mission societies decades earlier.

From its beginning, Church Women United leaders recognized the enormous disparity between women's contributions to church work and their presence in decision-making positions. In the 1950s and 1960s they promoted investigations of women's status in the denominations and urged more adequate representation. The organization also addressed issues concerning women in the secular world. By 1965, emboldened in part by the social activism of the 1960s, the CWU committee on the changing role of women issued "a radical challenge to the Church," rebuking male leaders for "minimiz[ing] the personhood of women" (Hartmann, 93).

Church Women United also came to grips with the limitations of integration into the National Council. Its executive director complained in 1968 that the women resented how little influence their substantial financial contributions bought. Another CWU leader, Claire Randall, was even more direct, declaring that women's role in the church was "to be used. We are used to dispense the ideas men have decided upon, to feed the money to support the projects that men have decided on and are running" (Hartmann, 99). She noted that the CWU was being asked to contribute to the NCCC's peace budget, but the council refused to include a woman in pacifist delegations to Vietnam unless CWU paid her expenses.

In March 1970, CWU decided to go its own way, its president warning that "Church Women United must not be the substitute for the fuller participation of women as individuals and church representatives in the NCCC" (Hartmann, 101). The women's organization had already taken steps to prevent this outcome, when in 1969 it gave birth to a women's caucus at the National Council's general assembly meeting. There all the women delegates and observers rose as Peggy Billings, an executive in the United Methodist Church, read a statement citing statistics showing that women were just 12 percent of the delegates in the assembly of an organization dominated by "white-skinned male clergy over 40" and calling for "women's liberation in the life of the Church" (Hartmann, 102). The caucus remained active through the 1970s and beyond.

The National Council of Churches' 1969 assembly also marked a turning point by electing the Council's first female president. Her nomination preceded the emergence of the women's caucus, but Cynthia Wedel's election gave a lift to women's aspirations. She was a former CWU president and committed to advancing women's leadership in the churches. Even more important to women's cause was the election of feminist Claire Randall in 1974 to the post of general secretary, the highest staff position in the NCCC, an event the *New York Times* called "a break with 2,000 years of tradition." Four years earlier, Randall, who came to the office from Church Women United and had played a key role in creation of the women's caucus, had complained that churchmen had no idea "how long and how much women [had] talked among themselves with deep concern and frustration about their inability to have a real part in shaping the church" (Hartmann, 93). Not only did Randall win the opportunity to help shape the church for ten years, but she brought other women with her. By 1979 women claimed nearly one-fourth of the seats on the Council's governing board, and their presence on the professional staff had grown from 10 to 35 percent. In the last decade of the twentieth century, another woman, the Rev. Dr. Joan Brown Campbell, once again served as general secretary of the Council.

The history of the NCCC in the 1970s and 1980s demonstrated what a difference women's newfound influence made on its policy and practice. The governing board adopted resolutions, and Randall often testified in support of key aims of the secular women's movement, including ratification of the Equal Rights Amendment, affirmative action, and federal funding of day-care facilities. This support helped to counter religious arguments made by antifeminists, and it kept the Religious Right from monopolizing the church's voice on feminist issues.

Even more significant were the projects initiated by women staff within the NCCC divisions that aimed at transforming women's position in the churches. Central to these efforts was the Division of Education and Ministry (DEM), headed by Emily V. Gibbes, the first African American woman to serve as an associate general secretary. As did most women who pushed for greater opportunities for women, Gibbes came out of the separatist tradition, having worked as an executive for United Presbyterian Women and served as president of Pennsylvania's Church Women United. Upon suggestions from Claire Randall and others for a body to encourage women's employment in the churches, Gibbes launched a Commission on Women in Ministry (COWIM) in 1974. Its semiannual meetings attracted about fifty individuals who were sent by their denominations or ecumenical organizations and who regularly engaged in consciousness-raising sessions about various forms of prejudice, a practice that one participant characterized as a "chaotic and creative process of giving birth to a feminist model of ministry in our midst" (Hartmann, 120–121). Although it fell short of its goal, the commission strove for 50 percent minority representation at its meetings, created a Task Force on Ethnic Women in Ministry, and sponsored the first ever conference of minority women in ministry. It also launched a Task Force on Gay Women in Ministry, published a resource packet on gay issues and ministry, and cosponsored a conference in 1979, "Journey to Freedom, Lesbian-Feminist-Christian."

A second endeavor within the Division of Education and Ministry that demonstrated women's ascending influence was its challenge to male-exclusive language in scripture and religious practice. Members of the National Council's women's caucus and women in member denominations expressed their discomfort with sexist language; a few denominations had already begun to examine language in religious materials. In 1974, the Division, which held copyright to the Revised Standard Version (RSV) of the Bible and under whose charge the RSV Bible Committee periodically issued new editions of scripture, established a Task Force on Sexism in the Bible, composed of women with strong credentials as biblical scholars. One of them, Phyllis Trible, a professor

at Andover Newton Theological Seminary, described herself as "a feminist who loves the Bible" and wanted to "redeem the past (an ancient document) and the present (its continuing use) from the confines of patriarchy" (Hartmann, 125).

Professional, practical, and spiritual impediments stood in the way of these women's desire to eliminate male language from the Bible. Their project challenged both the professional standards and masculine authority of members of the RSV Bible Committee, scholars who were deeply invested in the scripture as they and men like them had translated it. Biblical revision also could affect the division's budget, which depended in part on royalties from the RSV Bible. Finally, as much as the Bible Committee respected those alienated by masculine imagery, they were concerned about Christians who would be upset by alterations of biblical language.

While they struggled to influence the RSV Bible Committee, in 1976 the Task Force on Sexism in the Bible published a study guide for church members, *The Liberating Word: A Guide to Nonsexist Interpretation of the Bible*. The task force members who wrote the guide explained the power of language and why it was important "to liberate the interpretation of God's Word from male bias"; showed how biblical texts reflected the time and environment in which they were written; provided alternative readings of certain texts; and suggested specific changes, such as avoiding patriarchal terms like *Master* and *Father* to refer to God. The 120-page paperback attracted attention in national newspapers and magazines as well as in religious media.

The Division of Education and Ministry took an even more controversial step in 1983, when it published an *Inclusive Language Lectionary*, a series of primary Bible passages read aloud at services throughout the church year. The new texts referred to God as "Father and Mother," substituted "the Human One" for "the Son of Man," and adopted a number of other changes. Although most ministers refused to use the new lectionary, worshipers in a sizable minority of churches became accustomed to hearing the scripture in woman-affirming language. And the still overwhelmingly male RSV Bible Committee eliminated many of the masculine pronouns referring to human in its new 1989 edition of the Bible. The struggle over religious language revealed the limitations of women's enlarged presence in the NCC, but the project was, in the words of Virginia Mollenkott, one of the lectionary authors who was raised in the fundamentalist tradition, "immensely important to me because as an evangelical woman, I know first-hand the oppression of women who are linguistically and structurally excluded" (Hartmann, 129).

Along with the changes taking place in the National Council of Churches, women in specific Protestant denominations achieved greater representation in their church bureaucracies. The United Methodist Church, for example, adopted a plan in 1972 that allocated women one-third of the seats on most of the church's national bodies, along with one-third laymen and one-third clergy. Pursuing simultaneously the strategies of separatism and inclusion, leaders of the Women's Division opposed a plan to limit the division to twenty-five representatives on the Board of Global Ministries and obtained fifty-eight seats. The church's permanent General Commission on the Status and Role of Women, begun in 1976 and composed of forty-two women and men, carefully monitors the position of women and vigorously advocates for issues of particular relevance to women, such as gender-inclusive language.

Although tremendous variations in organizational behavior existed among men and among women, women's ascension into powerful positions encouraged the exercise of new styles of leadership in churches, as they did in the secular world. Female leaders seemed more prone to an inclusive decision-making process and to participatory management, and they often took greater care to examine the impact of decisions and actions on individuals and on human relationships. The Reverend Joan M. Martin, for example, employed a "collective feminist style" in her leadership of the Justice for Women program that the National Council of Churches' Division of Church and Society established in 1975.

The rise of the Christian Right in the 1970s and 1980s posed a countermovement to women's expanding power in church government. In 1963 and 1976, the Southern Baptist Convention elected women as vice presidents. But as fundamentalists gained the upper hand, the percentage of women serving in leadership positions as clergy or laity declined. In 1984, the Southern Baptist Convention condemned female ordination, a matter that church policy left to local congregations. The resolution approved "the service of women in all aspects of church life and work other than pastoral functions and leadership roles entailing ordination." Its rationale echoed historic reasons for the exclusion of women from church leadership: "to preserve a submission God requires because the man was first in creation and the woman was first in the Edenic fall" (Lindley, 350). In addition to the fundamentalist churches, the Lutheran Church–Missouri Synod and Eastern Orthodox churches similarly continued to restrict female leadership.

In the mainstream Protestant bodies, however, women continued to inch their way into positions of leadership. African American women gained leadership roles more readily in white denominations, but in 2000, the African Methodist Episcopal Church elected its first female bishop, the Rev. Vashti McKenzie, a graduate of Howard University's School of Divinity and pastor of a large Baltimore congregation. Of the fifty-one bishops in the United Methodist Church in 2000, eleven were women, including three women of color; and women constituted 36 percent of the delegates at the 2000 General Conference. In 1999, the Presbyterian Church elected a woman, Freda A. Gardner, moderator of the 211th General Assembly and thus principal ambassador for the denomination for the ensuing year.

At the beginning of the twenty-first century women were no longer marginalized in most of the traditional Protestant denominations. In no church did they enjoy equal power with men, but there were few national offices that women had not held. How far women's movement toward equality would go remained in question. Methodist women had retained their separate organization as a vital force within the church, even as they saw their numbers increase in general governance bodies. Yet women's organizations found it increasingly difficult to attract younger members, a basic imperative if they were to continue to pursue the separatism-within-integration strategy that had moved them toward equality in the past. Moreover, women's gains in mainstream Protestant church governing bodies occurred as these churches declined in membership and in influence in the larger society while the thoroughly male-dominated fundamentalist churches flourished.

SOURCES: The following provide historical overviews of women's status in the churches: Margaret Lamberts Bendroth, *Fundamentalism and Gender, 1875 to the Present* (1993); Susan Hill Lindley, *"You Have Stept Out of Your Place": A History of Women and Religion in America* (1996); and Catherine Wessinger, ed., *Religious Institutions and Women's Leadership* (1996). For studies of women in particular Protestant denominations, see Nancy Tatom Ammerman, *Baptist Battles: Social Change and Religious Conflict in the Southern Baptist Convention* (1990); Lois A. Boyd and R. Douglas Brackenridge, *Presbyterian Women in America: Two Centuries of a Quest for Status* (1996); Evelyn Brooks Higgenbotham, *Righteous Discontent: The Women's Movement in the Black Baptist Church* (1993); and Catherine M. Prelinger, *Episcopal Women: Gender, Spirituality, and Commitment in an American Mainline Denomination* (1992). Chapter 4 of Susan M. Hartmann's *The Other Feminists: Activists in the Liberal Establishment* (1998) examines the women's movement in the National Council of Churches and Church Women United.

PLURAL RELIGIOUS IDENTITIES AND HOUSEHOLDS
Rita DasGupta Sherma

PLURAL RELIGIOUS IDENTITIES arise from various factors. Among them are interreligious marriages, interest and participation in religions and spiritual practices outside one's birth faith, or attempts to reconcile the majority religious culture with one's own faith heritage. All these factors have increased as a result of a proliferation in communications due to new technologies; breakdown in rigid social and religious restrictions; the liberation of women, leading to increased intergender socialization at educational and work institutions; the greater availability of religious options; and the increasing acceptance of pluralistic and multicultural ways of life.

In North America the past three decades have seen a steady rise in the number of households that can be defined as "dual faith." There are various reasons for the continued growth of interfaith marriages and partnerships. In *The Social Sources of Denominationalism* (1929), H. Richard Niebuhr noted that American religious life was characterized by denominationalism, which was grounded in the distinctions of race, social and economic class, and ethnic origin. A 1956 study of Southern Baptist clergy showed that 96 percent were against sharing communion with other Christians; similarly, 80 percent of Episcopalians opposed holding joint worship with others. In the last several decades, however, increasing pluralism has resulted in a widespread support for ecumenism, suggesting a significant erosion of denominationalism. The pluralistic trajectory is visible in the growing popularity of nondenominational community churches, alternative faith groups, and the increase in the number of individuals who have changed or altered their religious affiliations.

In North America the past three decades have seen a steady rise in the number of households that can be defined as "dual faith." Many couples find compromise solutions for the contentious issues that often involve an implicit acceptance of a plural religious identity. Such compromise may be achieved through alternating attendance of each other's house of worship, creating blended ceremonies to follow at home, or celebrating joint festivals and integrating perspectives of both faiths into the family's lifestyles. *Courtesy of Rabbi Barry Tuchman.*

A Gallup poll conducted in 1955 showed that only 4 percent of the adult population belonged to a different denomination or faith than one into which they were born. Thirty years later, in 1985, a similar Gallup poll showed that 33 percent no longer considered themselves members of denominations in which they were raised. Certain denominations have been more heavily affected by this new mobility than others. Approximately 45 percent of persons who were raised Presbyterian now belong to other denominations or to none at all; for Methodists, the figure is 40 percent; Episcopalians had a defection rate of 38 percent, Baptists and Lutherans had 25 percent, and Catholics had 15 percent.

A survey conducted in the 1980s found that 60 percent of Americans had attended a religious service of a denomination other than their own at least on three different occasions, and 33 percent had explored five. These figures clearly indicate a weakening of denominational loyalty. Education ranks as one of the most important factors for denominational mobility. As the level of education rises, so does the frequency and variety of denominations explored. Those with a college education are three times as likely to have attended six or more denominations and are more likely to change from their own. This exploration often results in individual religious syncretism and hence a plural religious identity.

Exploration of traditions significantly different from the birth faith seems to be more pronounced among women than men. The predominance of women in loosely structured, nontraditional "spirituality circles" and the neopagan movement may, in part, explain this lack of numerical parity. A major poll on neopagans, conducted between 1999 and 2000, found that 71 percent of Wiccans are female. The American Religious Identification Survey (ARIS), conducted in 1990 and again in 2001, reports that the number of Wiccans rose by 17 percent during this period. Such a rise is the highest of any faith group monitored by the survey. The significant growth of neopaganism and its dominance by women may be an important indicator of the future leadership of pluralistic, alternative religious movements.

The ARIS is the first American survey to examine the religious composition of marriages and domestic partnerships: It shows a substantial movement toward secularism among American adults. ARIS also found 22 percent reported being part of a mixed-faith household. The lowest levels were among Mormons (12 percent), followed by Baptists and Evangelicals (both about 18 percent). The highest incidence of interfaith households was among Episcopalians (42 percent) and Buddhists (39 percent). The survey also found that 16 percent of adults had "switched" from their natal faith for a variety of reasons.

Interfaith Marriage

Intermarriage is a major cause of denominational change. Among Jews, marriage outside the Jewish community is commonly believed to be about 50 percent. It is estimated that 18 million (25 percent) of the Roman Catholics in the United States marry outside their faith; estimates for Canada is 40 percent; for Britain it is close to 75 percent. The total of Church-sanctioned marriages has decreased (382,861 in 1970 versus 293,434 in 1995) despite the increase in the Catholic population in the United States during the same period. The Greek Orthodox Archdiocese of America acknowledges that 67 percent of marriages conducted in the archdiocese are interfaith or intrafaith.

Civil ceremonies are increasingly favored by interfaith couples. In view of the fact that more interfaith weddings currently take place outside the church than within, the Interchurch and Interfaith Committee at the 1996. Clergy-Laity Congress warned that a failure to reach out to interfaith couples may threaten the future of the church. Intermarriage for Jews rose steadily from 3 percent in 1965 to nearly 50 percent in the 1990s. Similar trends are visible within Christian denominations.

In about two-thirds of interfaith unions, the couples eventually achieve some degree of religious unity. Either one spouse joins the religion of the other (40 percent), or both switch to another denomination or faith (30 percent). In keeping with rising denominational mobility, a specific denominational identity currently seems to have less significance for many interfaith households.

A survey was conducted for this essay in order to glean new information about interfaith couples in the North American context, especially for groups that are underrepresented in most statistical tracking such as individuals born into Asian religious traditions. Marriages with one spouse claiming a denomination of Christianity as the birth faith were in the majority (66 percent), followed by couples with one Jewish partner (18 percent); mixed marriages with one Muslim, Hindu, or Buddhist partner comprised 16 percent. Couples in both Canadian and American cities were involved in answering informal survey questions regarding the impact of their heterogeneous natal traditions on their relation-

ships and on familial religious affiliation. There were no overwhelming differences between the genders regarding loyalty to, or longing for, one's birth community, but the impact of gender was discernible in cases where a decision had been made to follow one tradition exclusively. Of the couples surveyed, close to 40 percent had decided to affiliate with one partner's natal faith. In these cases, the woman's closeness to her birth family often determined the outcome: Where the woman claimed a close allegiance to her birth family, there was a high incidence of the couple's affiliation with her tradition. However, there did not seem to be a similar high correspondence between familial closeness and religious affiliation for males.

For women, religion itself was also more important than for their spouses. In response to questions about the significance of religion for family life, 35 percent of women answered in the affirmative versus 24 percent of men. This finding is supported by related data from the ARIS general survey: When asked whether the respondent regarded herself or himself as religious, 42 percent of women, as opposed to 31 percent of males, answered affirmatively.

There are a number of factors that influence the rate of interfaith marriages. These include increasing enrollments at four-year colleges and universities where young people from a variety of religious backgrounds socialize away from their home and faith context; movement from ethnic neighborhoods into more heterogeneous areas, which lowers barriers to interfaith dating; the increase in the influence of secular culture as church attendance falls; and the fact that young people are being increasingly raised in homes that no longer revolve around religious commitment.

The children of interreligious marriages are more likely to have interfaith marriages themselves. It is, therefore, expected that interfaith unions will continue to proliferate, adding to the likelihood of households with plural religious identities. As North American secular society increasingly encourages cultural, lifestyle, ethnic, and religious diversity, resistance to interfaith unions continues to erode.

There are no reliable studies on the difference in survival rates of mixed-faith unions versus single-faith marriages. It is commonly believed that, in general, single-faith marriages have a higher survival rate. However, rates vary depending on the religious composition of the marriage. For example, data maintained for over three decades by Canadian Hindu Pandit Madhu Sahasrabudhe, for several hundred interfaith marriages performed by him after formal counseling, present a very high survival rate (only two divorces).

Life-cycle rites, including the wedding itself, as well as ceremonies of initiation at puberty, death rites, and other such occasions that are points of contact between the two sides of the family, often bring underlying conflicts into focus. Dealing with multiple faiths can create difficulties such as the issues of whether to attend church, sacred circle, mosque, synagogue, or temple; which religious festivals to observe; or the choice of tradition in which to bring up the children. Apart from theological distinctions, different religious traditions have vastly dissimilar rules and practices relating to concerns such as appropriate family size, abortion, birth control, diet, food preparation, worship styles, sexual abstinence, power and status structures, and kinship relations that impact the rearing of children.

Many couples find compromise solutions for these contentious issues that often involve an implicit acceptance of a plural religious identity. Such compromise may be achieved through alternating attendance of each other's house of worship; creating blended ceremonies to follow at home; or celebrating joint festivals and integrating perspectives of both faiths into the lifestyles of the family.

The attitude of a religious community toward non-observant adherents and their partners is greatly influenced by their beliefs about other religious traditions. Faith groups that are, for the most part, exclusivist oppose interfaith alliances; inclusivist groups such as Unitarian Universalists encourage pluralism. Many conservative Christian churches actively discourage interfaith marriages. This aversion is based on biblical warnings about being "unequally yoked," which applies to unions between church members and persons who are not baptized Christians. Liberal Christian ministers are, at times, willing to perform ceremonies for such couples.

Hindu priests, generally, have no problem with marrying interfaith couples. Islam has numerous rules restricting them. A Muslim man is only permitted to have an interfaith marriage with a woman who is either Christian or Jewish. Women of other faiths must first convert to Islam. If any of the offspring of an interfaith union are raised as non-Muslims, the father will no longer be considered a Muslim. A marriage between a Muslim woman and a non-Muslim man is regarded as invalid.

Many contemporary Jewish rabbis fear that the future of the Jewish tradition is at risk due to the increase in rates of intermarriage and, therefore, actively discourage marriage with non-Jews. This concern is based on the general assumption that 50 percent of all Jews currently marry non-Jews. This is an issue of grave concern to many leaders. Rabbi David Fellman of the Jewish Center of Teaneck, New Jersey, argues against interfaith marriage for Jews, stating, "The future of the Jewish people is realized through in-marriage and not through out-marriage. This does indeed ask individuals to place Judaism's survival and viability above one's own romantic or personal consideration" (Beliefnet.com, September

2000). Judaism is not limited to doctrines; it is a way of life and involves observances at home as well as the synagogue. Some Jewish leaders believe that important practices and rites meant to be carried out at home cannot be adequately observed in an interfaith household.

Before the Vatican Council II, the Catholic Church enforced strict regulations for interreligious marriages. If the couple wed outside the Church, the marriage was not recognized. Currently, however, dispensation may be obtained to have the wedding performed in another house of worship.

The degree of conflict and depth of religious difference in plural religious households cover a wide spectrum. The underlying potential for disagreement often becomes acute after the arrival of children. The field research conducted for this essay showed the following methods for resolving conflicts:

Tolerance. For those with a strong commitment to their birth faith, especially women, compromise is often unacceptable. In such situations, it becomes necessary for each partner to observe their respective faiths separately. At times, formal agreements are drawn that clearly define how the children are to be raised in terms of religion.

Alternative faith traditions. In many cases the household adopts a new, compromise religion, such as Unitarian Universalism, Baha'i, or a Yoga community. About 30 percent of interfaith couples follow this path with significant success. The new community is, in turn, enriched by the continuous integration of new perspectives.

Conversion. Often, as a condition of marriage, or due to the desire to have a common faith, one partner adopts the religion of the other. Estimates are that this option is chosen by about 40 percent of interfaith households. The avoidance of friction in such situations is only achieved if the conversion is undertaken without duress. Difficulties arise from the disapproval of family members of the spouse who has converted; from exposure to unfamiliar doctrines; and the longing for the festivals and fellowship of the birth community.

Pluralism. With cooperation from both faith communities, the family affiliates with both traditions. This may involve alternating attendance at functions and worship services of each faith and the development of a lifestyle that honors both religions. The aim is not syncretism as much as the celebration of diversity.

Creative syncretism. As an extension of the above approach, an interfaith couple may explore both religious traditions and combine what they perceive as the "best" of each faith according to the specific needs of their household. Such an ecumenical perspective results in what is, virtually, a new, syncretic faith—one that can be sustained and strengthened by joining with similar couples to form a house church, an informal Buddhist *sangha, satsang*, or sacred circle. Often, it is women who initiate and maintain these associations.

Cessation of formal religious activity. One or both partners may desist from participation in organized religious activity and from religious discussions within the family. This, undoubtedly, decreases conflict but is rarely sustainable. Desires for religious community and a faith tradition in which to raise children often emerge later in life.

While there are many circumstances that compel interfaith families to become integrated-faith households, there are also a variety of circumstances that lead to the decision to remain a plural-faith family. For many, a strong familiarity with worship contexts, doctrines, and ceremonies is foundational to their ability to stay spiritually connected. These individuals find it difficult to worship with the same level of feeling in a new and unfamiliar tradition. In addition, they may believe that it is a form of betrayal to convert to another faith.

Apart from devotion to one's birth religion, there is the issue of loyalty to family culture, ethnic heritage, and ancestry. Abandonment of these anchors can lead to a sense of isolation or alienation. In our survey, respondents with profound attachment to their ethnic culture considered the act of conversion to another religious tradition as tantamount to losing their identity.

On the other hand, when both spouses have relatively low levels of religious and cultural involvement and interest, there are no compelling reasons to become an integrate-faith family since religion is marginal to family life anyway. If only one of the partners is nonreligious, the relatively more observant partner sets the trend for the religious culture of the family. This tendency is more pronounced if the observant spouse is female. The household, in these cases, essentially becomes a single-faith family.

Individuals who have themselves been raised in interfaith homes can maintain distinctly plural-faith households without tension. Their childhood experience tends to imbue them with an inclusivist perspective and respect for diversity. As a demographic group, these offspring of interfaith unions are increasing as the rate of such unions continues to rise.

The birth of children raises many concerns. Positions regarding religious education and participation in faith community activities tend to harden. Some agree to teach their children about both religions. Others educate children differently—for example, sons in the religion of the father, daughters in the religion of the mother.

Still others, while continuing some degree of participation in their respective faiths, bring up their children in a compromise tradition. Significant numbers of such children, however, receive little or no exposure to any religion due to parental concerns about the potential for family conflict. Many adults who have been raised in such families tend to avoid religion altogether or have a plural religious identity and are more likely to explore new faith groups. Such exploration is, by no means, limited to interfaith couples or their offspring and has become a significant trend in the religious life of North Americans.

Plural Religious Identities

The latter years of the twentieth century have seen a renewed interest in religion, as evidenced by the significant impact of religion on politics; the growth of spirituality as a popular literary genre; the large number of Internet sites dedicated to new and mainstream faiths; and perhaps most important, the proliferations of alternative religions in North America. The reasons for this phenomenal growth in interest include the ubiquity of new communications systems, rendering heretofore unavailable information accessible, and the preeminence of secular culture, which has eroded the influence of traditional mainstream religious institutions. As a result of these technological and social changes, plural religious identities have emerged as an important cultural phenomenon. Individuals develop plural religious identities because of birth in an interfaith household; marrying a spouse of a different faith; or encountering and embracing one or more religious traditions outside one's original belief system. While there are a vast number of alternative religion movements, the interface between the major world faiths that has occurred in the North American context, in the lives of individual seekers, has been more widely documented.

In the survey undertaken for this essay, certain themes have emerged. The majority of individuals exploring alternative religious traditions are of Christian or Jewish backgrounds. Among the more prominent movements that integrate or highlight religious plurality are neopaganism (including Wicca), Western Buddhism, North American Yoga schools and Hinduism-based systems, and Western Sufism.

Neopaganism

Most neopagan movements define themselves in contradistinction to traditional, mainstream religion. Christian pagans, however, seek to maintain and reinterpret aspects of Christian belief from a pagan perspective, thus acquiring a plural religious identity. For example, Christmas and Easter are celebrated in conjunction with the winter solstice and the spring equinox, respectively.

The aim is not to relinquish Christian identity completely but to transform the meaning of that identity by citing evidence for textual and ritual mimesis on the part of the early Christians. Pagan Christians believe that major Christian doctrines, festivals, legends, and ceremonies have evolved from, and are related to, preceding nature religions and ancient Mediterranean and Near Eastern pagan traditions. Christmas, for instance, is correlated to the festival of the birth of the Persian deity Mithras, which was believed to have been observed on, or about, December 25 and associated with gift-giving.

While European pre-Christian paganism is much better known among earth-based alternative religions, there is also a movement that can be identified as Judeopaganism, or Semitic paganism. Jewish paganism is distinct from Jewish mysticism. Jewish pagans seek to reclaim what they perceive as the polytheistic sources of Judaism and to recover the relationship between other ancient pagan Near Eastern religions and early Judaism. The aim is to reintegrate what is believed to be lost pagan roots back into Jewish practice. Women seem to be more active than men in this effort to include ancient goddesses, and gods such as Baal, as well as emphasize feminine images of the divine from normative Judaic history including Astarte, Lilith, and Shekinah. Difficulties arise in synthesizing Judaic theology with pagan magical practices and in forming relationships with non-Jewish pagans. Judeopagans consider it important to educate those in the broader pagan and magical communities about Jewish-pagan beliefs in order to combat and prevent anti-Semitic attitudes. While the pagan and magical communities are relatively tolerant, there are pockets of anti-Semitism within the communities, such as the neo-Nazi faction of the Germanic pagans.

EASTERN FAITHS

Buddhist centers, monasteries, temples, and retreat facilities can now be found all over North America. In the United States, there are about a million Buddhists, with up to 100,000 non-Asian, American-born practitioners. There are many others who practice Buddhist meditation techniques, while still adhering to their Christian or Jewish identities. Sylvia Boorstein, a voice representing the pluralistic religious experience of many Jewish Buddhists, and author of the book *That's Funny, You Don't Look Buddhist* (1997), suggests that viewing Judaism through Buddhist insights allows for the preservation of mystical and spiritual elements of Jewish practice and imbues Jewish rituals and scriptures with new meaning.

Western women of Judeo-Christian origins, who have adopted Buddhism, have often integrated into their spiritual practices the social justice ideals of the prophetic traditions; the insights of feminist theory; the ecological consciousness of Native American religions; and deep ecology. Writers such as Rita Gross have sought to transform male-dominated religious hierarchies in many Buddhist denominations into more egalitarian leadership vehicles. Helen Tworkov, the editor of *Tricycle*, the quarterly Buddhist journal, has written about the need to integrate the principles of equality, democracy, horizontal rather than vertical structures, the insights of psychotherapy, and social activism into Buddhist practice. In 1993, nearly twenty-two members of the Network of Western Buddhist Teachers went to Dharamsala, India, to meet with the Dalai Lama. The agenda included tradition versus cultural contextualization; monasticism and the adaptation of teachings; issues of sectarianism; sex in the "forbidden zone" of teacher-student relations; alcohol and drug use; the role of the master/teacher; and the place of psychotherapy in Buddhist practice, sexism, and ethics.

Hinduism-based movements including yoga traditions have established an identifiable, institutional presence in North American since 1893 when the Vedanta Society was established by Swami Vivekananda. From the outset, Hindu religious leaders in the West responded to the overwhelmingly Christian context by espousing a religious universalism and theological pluralism. Vivekananda, whose Vedanta Society enjoyed significant financial support and organizational assistance from Christian, American women, often preached that one could remain faithfully Christian and still engage in the meditational and worship practices of Vedanta. The presence of North American women alongside men in the movement raised the issue of the authority, status, and leadership of the women religious in the organization as a whole, since, traditionally, it has been considered inappropriate for men and women religious to have membership in the same Hindu order. As early as 1947, however, the Sarada Convent in Santa Barbara, California, was established by the Vedanta Society for the administration of full *brahmacharya* status (preliminary novice vows) for women religious.

The Self-Realization Fellowship (SRF), founded by Paramahansa Yogananda in 1935, has, along with the Vedanta Society, the oldest Hindu institutional presence in North America. Yogananda stressed the common features of the religious experiences of Hindu yogis and Christian mystics. The SRF continues to encourage plural religious affinities, in addition to the practice of the spiritual discipline of kriya yoga. An American woman of Christian birth, Sri Daya Mata has been the president of SRF's worldwide organization since 1955.

The pluralistic tone initiated by Vivekananda and Paramahansa Yogananda has been continued in the teachings of many Hindu gurus and yogis. These teachers, who have come to the West in the latter part of the twentieth century, have established spiritual movements and centers that, while imparting Hinduism-based meditation practices, theological concepts, and healing systems, maintain a strongly pluralistic stance.

THE SUFI ORDER IN THE WEST

Of the several Sufi orders represented in North America, the one that is best known among ecumenical spiritual seekers for its universalism and pluralistic approach is the Sufi Order in the West, founded in 1910 by Hazrat Pir Inayat Kahn. Hazrat, trained by the Sufi dervishes of India, came to America believing that it was his mission to interpret and transmit Sufism for the new century. His message was a synthesis of Hindu Advaita Vedanta and Islamic *wahdatal-wujud*—"unity of being" philosophy. According to this perspective, Sufism was not limited by historical Islam but, rather, embodied transcultural, universal truths regarding harmonious co-existence and the fundamental unity of all being.

Hazrat Khan's teachings were informed by the doctrines and imagery of classical Sufism, as well as the unconventional belief that it is essential to design new, universalist forms of piety and practice that affirm what he perceived as the integrity and common ground of all faiths. The renewed interest in Eastern religion during the 1960s and 1970s saw a revival of Hazrat Inayat Khan's teachings under the leadership of Hazrat's European-educated son, Pir Vilayat Kan. During the 1970s facilities were established to facilitate the Order's "Universal Worship" services, as well as to host activities as varied as Sufi sacred music and dance, consciousness raising, and holistic healing, with influences by systems as diverse as Chi-Kung, Buddhist meditation, and psychotherapy.

Because of its pluralistic attitude, many Islamic communities do not regard the Sufi Order in the West as an authentic model of Sufism. The group's influence in the New Age movement, however, has been greater than its membership numbers indicate.

Conclusion

As the population of North America becomes increasingly diverse, and racial and ethnic barriers more fluid, the parameters of religious identity become ever more permeable. The trend toward a loosening of denominational ties is reflected in households and individuals with plural religious affinities and in the emergence of new faith groups that have a clearly pluralistic trajectory. Further, the boundary between religious and secular activity continues to erode as practices from alternative traditions make inroads into areas outside the purview of mainstream religion, such as health and healing. This is visible in the growing acceptance of the medical uses of yoga, the use of Buddhist psychology in Western psychotherapy, or the application of meditation techniques for the treatment of stress disorders.

The leaders in these new directions are from both genders, but women tend to dominate the ranks of the practitioners at the many centers that offer integrated, pluralistic practices and teachings. While no reliable data are available on the gender ratios in New Age and other multireligious venues, the anecdotal evidence seems to suggest a plurality of women. The possibility that women may be at the vanguard of this movement toward religious pluralism is significant because the exposure to concepts and perspectives that have, as their source, other faith traditions can lead to a critical appraisal and radical transformation of the worldview in which an individual was raised and, corporately, the cultural ethos in which we all function.

SOURCES: A survey was conducted for this essay to gather data on the effects of interfaith marriage on a family's faith affiliation(s) and general attitude toward religion. Taking into account the experiences of minority religious adherents—often unrepresented in most studies on interfaith marriage—the survey was based in four U.S. and three Canadian cities and was conducted by means of a questionnaire that focused on the impact of familial loyalties on the religious association of both genders. Data gleaned from the survey were limited to questionnaires that were properly completed; this yielded 757 couples categorized according to type of interfaith marriage. This essay was partly based on data from the Gallup Organization, North American Operations Center, Lincoln, Nebr.; the American Religious Identification Survey 2001 (City University of New York), Barry A. Kosmen and Egon Mayer, principal investigators; the Dovetail Institute for Interfaith Family Resources, Boston; The Interfaith Families Project, Takoma Park, Md.; "Church and Church Membership in the U.S., 1990," Glenmary Research Center, Mars Hill, N.C.; National Council of Churches, Office of Information, Riverside, N.Y.; James Davidson, "Intermarriage in America," *Commonweal Magazine* (September 10, 1999); Rabbi David Feldman of The Jewish Center of Teaneck, as quoted by Vera Lawlor, in "The Religion Roundtable" (March 1, 1999), The Bergen Record Corp., Hackensack, N.J.; and *Hearts and Wings* (Spring 1992), the Western Sufi Order's quarterly journal. For perspectives on intermarriage from the Jewish American standpoint, see E. J. McClain, *Embracing the Stranger: Intermarriage and the Future of the American Jewish Community* (1995).

WOMEN'S CONTRIBUTIONS TO JEWISH-CHRISTIAN RELATIONS
Mary C. Boys

THE PAST HALF-CENTURY has witnessed a revolution in relations between Christians and Jews. Scholarly studies in Bible, theology, and history proliferate, unsettling conventional conclusions and revealing the complex interactions between the traditions in their nearly 2,000-year encounter. An array of agencies, institutes, and organizations sponsors conferences, workshops, and symposia in which Jews and Christians meet each other in ways their ancestors in faith could scarcely have imagined. Dialogue groups abound, churches and synagogues offer joint study sessions, and Internet sites provide rich resources. An extensive body of statements, beginning with the "Ten Points of Seelisberg" by the International Council of Christians and Jews in 1947, heightened in the declaration from the Vatican in 1965, *Nostra aetate* (In Our Time) and continued across the range of most major Christian denominations, reflects a determination to confront anti-Jewish teaching embedded in church life. In September 2000, a group of Jewish scholars issued *Dabru Emet* (Speak Truth): *A Jewish Statement on Christians and Christianity,* an eight-point declaration responding to Christian initiatives. Tikva Frymer-Kensky of the University of Chicago was one of four authors, and numerous women were among the signatories. In June 2002, the Christian Scholars Group on Christian-Jewish Relations issued *A Sacred Obligation: Rethinking Christian Faith in Relation to Judaism and the Jewish People.* Authored collectively by the twenty-two-member group of Protestant and Catholic scholars, seven women participated in the writing process and signed the document. In short, Jewish-Christian relations, with its burgeoning literature and network of organizations, had become a field.

A Field Emerges

It was not always the case. Judith Hershcopf Banki tells of her interview in 1955 with Rabbi Arthur Gilbert for a position in the newly established department of Interreligious Cooperation at the Anti-Defamation League. When she inquired about the nature of the job, Rabbi Gilbert explained that it focused on building bridges of understanding to confront stereotypes and prejudices. Banki replied that though the job sounded wonderful, it was not for her. He pressed her, "Why not?" "I have no experience in this field," she replied. Gilbert retorted, "My dear young lady, there is no field."

If today there is a field, it is in no small measure because of women. Yet few have noted women's role; in most cases, men holding office in the churches and synagogues have overshadowed their achievements. Nonetheless, whether as scholars, activists, clergy, or professionals in Christian or Jewish agencies—or in some combination thereof—women have been involved since the earliest days of Jewish-Christian dialogue. Over the years, many more women have become involved, though men continue to have the most visible roles.

While the pioneering generation seldom garnered much publicity, its commitment to the work of reconciliation was lived in creative ways. This is evident in the work of Rose Thering, a member of the Order of Preachers (Dominican), who analyzed the content of Catholic religion textbooks in her 1961 dissertation at St. Louis University. Aware that her study illumined areas of prejudice in a Church unaccustomed to public self-criticism, Thering felt that the Catholic populace would regard her findings as credible only if a priest published them. She suggested John Pawlikowski, a priest of the Servite Order and ethicist, be commissioned to write a book on her dissertation and that of her colleagues Linus Gleason of the Sisters of Charity of Providence and Rita Mudd of the Sisters of St. Joseph, whose dissertations had analyzed literature and social studies textbooks. Pawlikowski agreed; his *Catechetics and Prejudice: How Catholic Teaching Materials View Jews, Protestants and Racial Minorities* appeared in 1973. Thering had not anticipated the larger impact her study would make when Judith Banki, now working in the Interreligious Affairs office of the American Jewish Committee, drew upon Thering's dissertation and the work of Claire Huchet Bishop, who had initiated similar studies in Europe. Banki drafted a memorandum that the American Jewish Committee submitted on July 13, 1961, to Augustin Cardinal Bea, a biblical scholar and head of the Secretariat for the Promotion of Christian Unity. Titled "The Image of the Jew in Catholic Teaching," the thirty-two-page memorandum detailed the caricatures and distortions of Judaism that the Thering and Bishop studies had uncovered. While no single factor suffices to account for the promulgation of *Nostra aetate* on October 28, 1965, the textbook studies seem to have exercised a major influence on Cardinal Bea, the driving force behind Vatican II's declaration.

On the scholarly front, two historians stand out for pioneering work that has extended over four decades. Alice L. Eckardt, now professor emerita of religious studies at Lehigh University, had her historian's interests heightened by her marriage to A. Roy Eckardt. His 1947 dissertation at Columbia University and Union Theological Seminary, "Christianity and the Children of Israel," launched his own long and distinguished career as a scholar of Jewish-Christian relations. Although she did not publish her own article, "The Holocaust: Christian and Jewish Responses," until 1974, Eckardt coauthored several articles and a book with her spouse in the late 1960s and early 1970s. While the prolific Eckardts continued to collaborate for some thirty years (until Roy's death in 1998), her probing essays, books, and indefatigable efforts made a distinctive mark.

The trajectory of Eckardt's research reveals the expanse of the "field" of Jewish-Christian relations as well as her own historical and theological predilections. While her preoccupation with the Shoah (a Hebrew term meaning "whirlwind," which she and many others argue is preferable to Holocaust, a whole burnt offering specified as part of worship in the Temple) never receded, it led into an exploration of related issues. The questions she pursued about the theological meaning of suffering, as well as about power and powerlessness, framed her exploration of repentance, forgiveness, and the State of Israel. The Shoah has been the backdrop of her study on the Reformation and the Jews and of her analysis of Protestant documents on the church's relation with the Jewish people.

If the ineradicable problem of the Shoah impels Alice Eckardt, a similar conviction characterizes her contemporary Eva Fleischner. During her doctoral studies in historical theology at Marquette University in the late 1960s, the Viennese-born Fleischner became conscious of anti-Judaism in Christian theology and experienced her first encounter with the Shoah through Jean-François Steiner's 1967 book *Treblinka*. This opened a door that Fleischner never closed, leading her to Germany in 1970 to research attitudes of Christian theologians on the conversion of Jews (published in 1975 as *The View of Judaism in German Christian Theology since 1945: Christianity and Israel Considered in Terms of Mission*). It motivated her return to the classroom, where she began teaching a course on the Shoah at Montclair State College in New Jersey (later Montclair State University) in 1973. Fleischner was an organizer of the 1974 international symposium "Auschwitz: Beginning of a New Era?" at New York City's Cathedral of St. John the Divine. She gave a paper (a response to Emil Fackenheim's presentation on "The Holocaust and the State of Israel: Their Relation") and edited the book that bears the same title as the symposium. Published in 1977, it has become a significant text for Holocaust studies.

More recently, Fleischner has approached the Shoah from the perspective of rescuers, seeking to discover goodness amidst so much evil (*Cries in the Night: Women Who Challenged the Holocaust*, with Michael Phayer, 1997). Among those Fleischner interviewed was French rescuer Germaine Bocquet, who provided refuge for historian Jules Isaac from the Nazis. During his two years with Bocquet, Isaac worked on the manuscript published in 1948 as *Jésus et Israël* (and in English in 1959 as *Jesus and Israel*, translated by Claire Huchet Bishop). Bocquet assisted him by traveling to various libraries to gather research materials. Isaac's identification of the "teaching of contempt"—the Church's legacy of anti-Jewish teaching—eventually led to a meeting with Pope John XXIII on June 13, 1960. In turn, Pope John sent Isaac to Cardinal Bea to tell him to put the Church's relationship with the Jewish people on the agenda of the Council he had announced in January 1959. Isaac's influence on John XXIII and the formative role of *Jesus and Israel* in the Council's watershed declaration *Nostra aetate* have long been recognized. What Fleischner revealed was Germain Bocquet's role in pre-

serving Isaac's life and enabling him to work even during Europe's bleakest years.

Historian of theology Rosemary Radford Ruether startled the Christian world with her 1974 assertion in *Faith and Fratricide* that anti-Judaism was the "left hand" of Christology. Ruether claimed that the church had conflated the historical world and the messianic age, thereby setting the Christian historical era over against Judaism and making Judaism a type of unredeemed humanity. A Patristics scholar, she examined the ways in which early church writings continued and developed the anti-Jewish polemic of the New Testament by portraying Jews as reprobates for having rejected Christ. She then traced that trajectory through the centuries, arguing that anti-Judaism was a psychopathology of Christianity. Ruether asserts this was Christianity's projection upon Judaism of its own unredeemed side; that is, Jews represent what Christianity repressed: the unfinished character of redemption.

If *Faith and Fratricide* proved something of a lightning rod, so too did Ruether's 1989 book *The Wrath of Jonah: The Crisis of Religious Nationalism in the Israeli-Palestinian Conflict*. Coauthored with her husband Herman Ruether, a political scientist and Islamic scholar, their ardent argument for the Palestinian cause criticized Israeli "occupation" of Palestine. According to Ruether, Western Christians and Israeli Jews who embraced the arguments of *Faith and Fratricide* viewed *The Wrath of Jonah* as a renunciation of her commitments. To the contrary, she believes. Ruether sees the two books as complements, grounded in the same fundamental principles. Since both criticize the misuse of religion to justify domination, she pairs them in the same course.

Ruether's views on the Israeli-Palestinian conflict stand in tension with those of Alice Eckardt and Rose Thering, both longtime members of the Study Group on Jewish-Christian Relations, founded in 1969 by the Faith and Order Commission of the National Council of Churches and the Secretariat for Catholic-Jewish Relations (now the Christian Scholars Group on Jewish-Christian Relations). Thering also served for three years as the executive director of the National Christian Leadership Conference for Israel and remains as secretary.

Solidarity with Israel is evident as well in the work of Gemma Del Duca, a Sister of Charity from Seton Hill, Pennsylvania. Her fellow Pennsylvanian and Benedictine priest Isaac Jacobs invited Del Duca to collaborate in building a Christian community that would be a witness of respect for Judaism and the State of Israel. Moving to this Christian kibbutz, Tel Gamaliel (midway between Tel Aviv and Jerusalem, near Bet Shemesh) in 1977, Del Duca lived a pioneer's life: no electricity, water, indoor plumbing, or telephones. Those who visited Tel Gamaliel found its members devoted to both Torah and Gospel. This meant intense study of Hebrew, including praying in Hebrew. Del Duca and two others translated the Rule of St. Benedict into modern Hebrew as a means of providing a Christian framework (e.g., the Rule's emphasis on stability and on the importance of physical labor in the spiritual life) for settlement in Israel. They observed Shabbat as well as the Sunday Eucharistic liturgy. Eventually, Del Duca's presence in Israel led to the founding of the National Catholic Center for Holocaust Education at Seton Hill College (now Seton Hill University) in Greensburg, Pennsylvania, where she had been a professor of history. Following Jacob's death, Del Duca moved Tel Gamaliel to Jerusalem, where she continues her work for the Seton Hill program at Yad Vashem, Israel's memorial to Holocaust victims and international study center.

Among Jewish women active in dialogue on the Middle East, Inge Lederer Gibel stands out. Named director of women's interreligious programming in 1972 by the American Jewish Committee, Gibel organized a group of Jewish, Christian, and (one) Muslim women, sharing leadership with Presbyterian Sarah Cunningham and Roman Catholic Ann Patrick Ware of the Sisters of Loretto. After two years of meetings, this group, the Women's Interreligious Dialogue on the Middle East, embarked in 1975 on an all-women's trip to Egypt, Jordan, Syria, and Israel. Gibel also organized a task force, Women of Faith, convening two national conferences in 1975 and 1980.

During this period, Annette Daum, director of Interreligious Affairs for the Union of American Hebrew Congregations (the umbrella organization of Reform Ju-

daism in the United States), did similar work. She coordinated a group, "Feminists of Faith," sponsoring a conference by the same title. Among the first to detect anti-Judaism in Christian feminist thinking, Daum published two important articles in the late 1970s and early 1980s, "Blaming the Jews for the Death of the Goddess" and (with Christian scholar Deborah McCauley) "Jewish-Christian Feminist Dialogue: A Wholistic Vision."

Author and lecturer Blu Greenberg has likewise been active in interreligious matters in her commitments to bridge feminism and Orthodox Judaism. Although her work is principally within the Orthodox world, including a 1984 essay in *Judaism* speculating that the Orthodox movement would eventually join the Conservative, Reform, and Reconstructionist movements in ordaining women, Greenberg is a frequent lecturer at Jewish-Christian events. She chaired two conferences on Feminism and Orthodoxy in 1997 and 1998 and cofounded the Jewish Orthodox Feminist Alliance. In 1990, she traveled with a small Jewish delegation to Dharamsala, India, at the request of the Dalai Lama. As the leader of 115,000 Tibetan refugees living in India in exile, he hoped to learn from them how his people might survive in exile, as had Jews. Greenberg's interreligious involvements also included participation in Bill Moyers's "Genesis" special on PBS (October 1996) and membership on the Board of Advisers to the PBS *Religion and Ethics Newsweekly*.

Fleischner and Eckardt have continued their historical work in retirement. In 1999, the Vatican appointed Fleischner as one of six scholars (and only woman) on

The past half-century has witnessed a revolution in relations between Christians and Jews. As an example, the National Catholic Center for Holocaust Education, established on the campus of Seton Hill College in Greensberg, Pennsylvania, in 1987, initiated a national Catholic movement of Holocaust studies. Gemma Del Duca, a Sister of Charity, and Rabbi Sara Perman work together to build a Christian community that witnesses respect for Judaism and the State of Israel. *Courtesy of Seton Hill University, National Catholic Center for Holocaust Education.*

the International Catholic-Jewish Historical Commission. Mandated to review the eleven volumes of archival material from the Vatican, *Actes et Documents du Saint Siège relatifs à la seconde guerre mondiale*, this commission was assigned to study important questions about the Catholic Church's role in the Shoah. (The commission later disbanded, in part over disagreement about access to the Vatican archives.) Eckardt maintained a rigorous research agenda in Holocaust studies and collaborated with a Catholic and Lutheran colleague in editing a volume on Church statements promulgated since Helga Croner's 1977 collection *Stepping Stones to Further Jewish-Christian Relations.* Banki now serves as director of special programs with the Marc Tanenbaum Center for Interreligious Understanding, and Thering engages in a range of volunteer commitments (including involvement with the Sister Rose Thering Endowment for Jewish-Christian Studies at Seton Hall University in South Orange, New Jersey). Ruether carries on her advocacy for Palestinians in various publications, occasionally collaborating with Jewish activist Marc Ellis. On her retirement in 2002 from Garrett Evangelical Theological Seminary in Evanston, Illinois, Garrett sponsored a conference in honor of her contributions to interreligious dialogue, ecofeminist theology, and women's history. Ruether has been appointed to a professorship at the Graduate Theological Union in Berkeley, California.

Leaders in the Field: The Sisters of Sion

Throughout the entire period in which relations between Jews and Christians have come of age, the Sisters of Our Lady of Sion have forged new pathways. The change they initiated within their community, with its distinctive history, has exercised a profound effect on a much wider circle.

A congregation of Roman Catholic women founded in France in the 1840s to work for the conversion of Jews, Sion's energies were largely absorbed in the labor-intensive mission of running boarding schools, including several in the United States and Canada. Nevertheless, Jews remained prominent in their prayers; their Constitutions of 1874 mandated that the sisters recite "special invocations for the salvation of Israel every day." In the 1950s, Sion began to reassess its mission. Some of their communities in Europe had hidden children or worked with refugees during the Shoah, leading them to rethink Christian views on Judaism. Sisters living in the newly formed State of Israel (1948) had come to know Jews as neighbors—as real people, not simply as a religious abstraction. New theological ideas, such as those summarized in the "Ten Points of Seelisberg," circulated, particularly in European circles. Consequently, the Sion leadership issued a letter in September 1962, mandating that members renounce work and prayer for the conversion of Jews, requesting instead their involvement in countering anti-Semitism, and recommending serious study of Judaism.

In subsequent years, Sion established Jewish-Christian relations as a priority, as its Constitutions of 1984 reflected: "Our vocation gives us a particular responsibility to promote understanding and justice for the Jewish community, and to keep alive in the Church the consciousness that in some mysterious way Christianity is linked to Judaism from its origin to its final destiny." Members of the congregation engaged in study of Judaism—including a number sponsored for graduate work in Judaica—and established various institutional structures to support their new vision. For example, they founded an international journal in 1968 that appears three times a year, *SIDIC (Service International de Documentation Judéo-Chrétienne)*, with editions in English and in French. They also began a documentation and study center in Rome and founded another study center in Jerusalem, the Christian Center for Jewish Studies, Ratisbonne (named after the founders of the congregation, Theodore and Alphonse Ratisbonne, priests and blood brothers).

Among the pioneers living Sion's new vision in North America was Marie-Noëlle de Baillehâche, who arrived in Montreal from France in 1959. Collaborating with several priests, Roman Catholic and Anglican, she launched a permanent dialogue program in the mid-1960s at Montreal's Ratisbonne Centre, which she renamed "Centre MI-CA-EL." The Centre sponsored lectures and discussion groups and became an important site for candid discussions between Jews and Christians. Her 1964 speech on developments in Catholic-Jewish relations at an Orthodox synagogue occasioned a major interview with the Montreal *Star.*

As the Sisters of Sion in North America reevaluated their ministry under the leadership of Mary Jo Leddy, who had written her dissertation on Hannah Arendt (and who later left the congregation), they decided in 1986 to extend the Centre's work beyond Montreal by transforming it into a network for North American initiatives, the Christian-Jewish Relation and Encounter (CJRE). Led by a team of three members living in geographically dispersed regions of North America, the CJRE is intended to foster mutual understanding among Christians and Jews through education, to promote dialogue, and to combat injustices, especially those related to religion, race, and ethnicity. As of 2005, a three-member team of the Sisters of Sion leads Christian-Jewish relation and encounter. In addition to CJRE, Sion has entered into a partnership with the American Jewish Committee in Chicago to advance dialogue in that metropolitan area; they continue their interreligious efforts in Montreal under the leadership of Diane Willey, co-director of the Center for Ecumenism and head of the

Interfaith Office. Celia Deutsch, a professor at Barnard College and New Testament scholar, is a longtime member of the Christian Scholars Group on Jewish-Christian Relations.

Saskatchewan native Kay MacDonald has exercised critical leadership in Sion's history. As the first North American to head the international congregation (1974–1986), MacDonald successfully guided Sion's revised Constitutions of 1984 through the process of Vatican approval. This proved a delicate work of diplomacy in view of Vatican reluctance to endorse Sion's claim "that in some mysterious way Christianity is linked to Judaism from its origin to its final destiny" (*Constitutions of the Sisters of Our Lady of Sion*, Rome 1984, #4). Later (1990–1996), as head of the Mediterranean province, centered in Jerusalem, she led Sion during times of great tension in the Middle East, including both Intifada I and the Gulf War of 1991. MacDonald, subject of the 2000 documentary film *Sister Kay*, returned in 1997 to Saskatoon, where she works with Sion's Christian-Jewish Relation and Encounter.

Another Saskatchewan native, Maureen Fritz, founded the Bat Kol Institute (Daughter of the Voice) in Toronto in 1984 to promote Torah study among Christians. Now incorporated in the State of Israel in 1992 and centered in Jerusalem, Bat Kol offers study sessions on Torah as transmitted through Jewish traditions, on Jewish prayer and festivals, and on ways for Christians to integrate knowledge of Judaism into their self-understanding. It also provides Torah commentary online through its Web site. Fritz, professor emerita from St. Michael's College in Toronto, serves as Bat Kol's president.

The Field Expands

A considerable continuity exists between pioneers in Jewish-Christian relations and a later generation of scholars and activists. Yet differences are apparent as well. As more women have entered academe, they have contributed significantly to nearly every dimension of scholarship touching on the relationship between the two traditions. They have swelled the ranks of Holocaust historians, made major strides in biblical studies, advanced new theological perspectives, and moved educational considerations beyond textbook analysis into the construction of conceptual frameworks for teaching more adequately about the other tradition. Unlike the previous generation, many of these scholars restrict their contribution to their academic specialization and are less active in circles of dialogue organized by churches, synagogues, or agencies.

Jewish and Christian women scholars often share a feminist perspective. As that scholarship has been refined, Jewish and Christian biblical scholars and theologians have addressed the contentious point of anti-Judaism apparent in much early feminist writing in the West that also influenced works emanating from Third Word liberation theologians. In many instances, Jewish and Christian feminist scholars collaborate, such as in the decade-long partnership of Judith Plaskow and Elisabeth Schüssler Fiorenza as founding editors of the *Journal of Feminist Studies in Religion*. A new phenomenon is the appointment of Jewish New Testament scholars to faculty positions at Christian divinity schools: Pamela Eisenbaum (Iliff School of Theology), Paula Fredriksen at (Boston University School of Theology), Amy-Jill Levine (Vanderbilt Divinity School), and Sara Tanzer (McCormick Theological Seminary). All work from a feminist perspective, as does Claudia Setzer, who holds a position in New Testament at (Roman Catholic) Manhattan College (where theologian Judith Plaskow also teaches). A number of Christian biblical scholars, all working through feminist lenses as well, have made study of Judaism a critical element of their work. Eileen Schuller of McMaster University in Hamilton, Ontario, and a member of the Ursuline community, is among the preeminent scholars of the Dead Sea Scrolls and an active participant in dialogue groups. New Testament scholar Barbara Bowe of Catholic Theological Union in Chicago and a member of the Society of the Sacred Heart has collaborated with Tanzer in teaching a course on the Gospel of John. She reported she hopes to always have this kind of relationship in teaching the Fourth Gospel to Christian divinity students. Deirdre Good, a New Testament scholar at General Theological Seminary in New York City, serves as the interim director of its Center for Jewish-Christian Studies.

Such partnerships have helped to dispel the tensions between Jewish and Christian feminists. These began in the early 1970s with the sweeping claim that Jesus, a feminist, liberated women from the patriarchy and misogyny of Judaism. A series of associated claims typically followed. Jesus freed his followers from the oppressive purity laws, made the primitive sacrificial offerings of the Temple meaningless, and showed what real intimacy with God was like in the way he related to his "Abba," a God of compassion and mercy. Thus, the corrective to sexism in the contemporary church—the result of the failure of Jesus' male followers to grasp his message—was to be found in Jesus' critique of Jewish patriarchy.

Another layer of problem developed over claims that matriarchal cultures, in which Goddesses were worshiped, held sway over the ancient Near East until monotheism—that is, patriarchal Judaism—arose. A more virulent form of this viewpoint accorded the rise of violence and war to monotheistic religions, alleging that devotion to the "jealous" god of the Old Testament fostered intolerance.

Such views represent the "old" anti-Judaism in feminist dress. Theologian Katharina von Kellerbach argued in *Anti-Judaism in Feminist Religious Writings* (1994) that three rules of formation govern Christianity's distorted representation of Judaism and account for the continuity of the anti-Jewish myth throughout different eras, cultures, nations, and worldviews. Judaism is, first, the antithesis of Christian beliefs and values. Second, Christian theology casts Israel into the role of scapegoat, whether blaming Judaism for the death of Jesus or of the Goddess. Third, Christianity reduces Judaism to the status of prologue: Judaism is merely prehistory, a relic of the ancient world. Susannah Heschel's entry "Anti-Judaism/Anti-Semitism" in *Dictionary of Feminist Theologies* (1996) complements von Kellenbach's analysis. Heschel, a historian of thought, has written extensively on anti-Judaism in German Liberal Protestantism, most notably in *Abraham Geiger and the Jewish Jesus* (1998); she has also edited an anthology of the writings of her father, the eminent rabbi, scholar, and ecumenist Abraham Joshua Heschel.

Biblical scholars have provided ample critique of feminist naïveté. By means of painstaking historical reconstruction and close textual analysis, they have situated women's experience in historical context. For example, Tikva Frymer-Kensky has shown the continuation of Goddess worship beyond antiquity (*In the Wake of the Goddesses* [1992]). Bernadette Brooten has documented women's leadership in the synagogue (*Women Leaders in the Ancient Synagogue* [1982]). Ross Shepard Kraemer and Mary Rose D'Angelo have collaborated on a volume situating Second Temple Judaism (from which both Christianity and Rabbinic Judaism came) in the context of Greco-Roman culture (*Women and Christian Origins* [1999]). Amy-Jill Levine, editor of a twelve-volume series, *Feminist Companion to the New Testament and Early Christian Writings*, has analyzed how anti-Judaism often blights postcolonial and liberationist approaches to biblical scholarship.

Holocaust studies, a field in itself, bears obvious connection to Jewish-Christian relations, even if not all scholars participate in activities explicitly linked to the latter. Women's contributions as historians, memoirists, psychologists, and sociologists to the study of the Shoah constitute a major bibliography exceeding the genre of an encyclopedia entry. Of note is the feminist scholarship pioneered in the early 1980s by historian and philosopher Joan Miriam Ringelheim. Ringelheim argues that sexism put women at an extreme disadvantage during the Holocaust by depriving them of skills that might have enabled more of them to survive. Carol Rittner, who has collaborated with John Roth in editing a number of Holocaust-related volumes, includes an important essay by Ringelheim in their 1993 anthology *Different Voices: Women and the Holocaust*. Rittner and Roth's volume also includes memoirs from survivors—a genre in

which women speak with poignancy and clarity. Notable among this genre are Nechama Tec's *Dry Tears: The Story of a Lost Childhood* (1984), Lucy Dawidowicz's *From That Place and Time: A Memoir 1938–1947* (1989), and Eva Hoffman's *Lost in Translation: A Life in a New Language* (1989). Helen Epstein studies the impact upon survivors' children in her 1979 *Children of the Holocaust*. In her moving memoir, Helen Fremont (*After Long Silence* [1999]) uncovers the Jewish identity kept secret by her survivor parents. Pearl Oliner (with Samuel Oliner [*The Altruistic Personality* [1988]), Vera Laska (editor, *Women in the Resistance and in the Holocaust* [1983]), and Nechama Tec (*When Light Pierced the Darkness* [1986]) are among those who have studied rescuers and participants in resistance movements. Yaffa Eliach's *Hasidic Tales of the Holocaust* (1982), the first collection of Holocaust stories about these Jewish pietists originating in eighteenth-century eastern Europe, also gave voice to the experience of Hasidic women. In 1984 Carol Rittner organized an international conference, "Faith in Humankind: Rescuers of Jews during the Holocaust," from which the book and documentary film *The Courage to Care* emerged.

Susan Zucotti has authored three books: *The Italians and the Holocaust: Persecution, Rescue, and Survival* (1996), *The Holocaust, the French, and the Jews* (1999), and *Under His Very Windows: The Vatican and the Holocaust in Italy* (2001). Deborah Lipstadt, who criticized those who deny the historicity of the Shoah (*Denying the Holocaust* [1993]), was catapulted into a highly public role when David Irving sued her for libel in the British courts, *David Irving v. Penguin Books Ltd. and Deborah Lipstadt*. Irving, whom Lipstadt had called "one of the most dangerous spokespersons for Holocaust denial," lost his suit in a decisive 2000 ruling. Margot Stern Strom, founder, executive director, and president since 1979 of the highly regarded educational project Facing History and Ourselves National Foundation, led efforts to engage teachers and students in analyzing racism, prejudice, and anti-Semitism as a means of promoting a more humane and informed public. Facing History and Ourselves prepares teachers to include the Holocaust and other examples of collective violence in the curriculum and trains them to teach history in ways that invite students to connect it with the moral choices they confront in their own lives.

Other women have taken up historical studies in ways that involve them actively in Jewish-Christian relations. Mary Christine Athans of the University of St. Thomas in St. Paul, Minnesota, and a member of the Sisters of Charity of the Blessed Virgin Mary, exposed the sources of the anti-Semitic rhetoric of Fr. Charles Coughlin in her 1991 book *The Coughlin-Fahey Connection*. Athans participates in dialogue, collaborating in that university's Jay Phillips Center for Jewish-Christian

Learning. Independent scholar Victoria Barnett, who analyzed the complex situation of the Confessing Church in Nazi Germany in her *For the Soul of the People: Protestant Protest against Hitler* (1992) and authored *Bystanders: Conscience and Complicity during the Holocaust* (1999), works as a consultant for the United States Holocaust Memorial Museum. Susan Nowak of Nazareth College of Rochester, New York, a Sister of St. Joseph whose work focuses largely on women's issues in Holocaust studies, is involved in a wide range of that city's interreligious activities. Margaret Obrecht, staff director of Church Relations at the United States Holocaust Memorial Museum, has been an active supporter of local dialogue and is a member ex corde of the Christian Scholars Group on Jewish-Christian Relations.

In the liturgical realm, Gail Ramshaw has argued for a way of interpreting the relationship of Old and New Testaments in the lectionary that does not reduce the former to mere preparation. Marcia Sachs Littell and Sharon Weissman Gutman have collaborated in editing an interfaith anthology of *Liturgies on the Holocaust* (1986). Jewish liturgical scholar Ruth Langer serves as the Judaica scholar at Boston College's Center for Christian-Jewish Learning.

On the educational front, much has transpired since the textbook studies of the early 1960s directed at eliminating anti-Judaism from Christian texts. A more complex undertaking has succeeded that task: establishing a deeper understanding of both traditions in relation to each other. Many Christians with educational responsibilities in the churches have engaged in continuing education programs, such as the "I Am Joseph Your Brother" program at Villanova University directed by Fayette Veverka in which experienced Catholic educators studied Judaism under the tutelage of faculty from Gratz College (a Jewish institution) and then designed curricula for their respective institutions. From 1993 through 1995, Mary C. Boys of Union Theological Seminary and a member of the Sisters of the Holy Names of Jesus and Mary, and Sara S. Lee of Hebrew Union College, Los Angeles, directed a "Catholic-Jewish Colloquium." This involved twenty-two educational leaders from the two traditions interacting in six intensive live-in sessions. This project in "interreligious learning" led to continuing collaboration between Lee and Boys, as they explored ways Catholics and Jews might make a deep and learned commitment to their own faith traditions while also building a religiously pluralistic society. Boys built upon these educational endeavors in her two books on Jewish-Christian relations (*Jewish-Christian Dialogue: One Woman's Experience* [1997] and *Has God Only One Blessing? Judaism as a Source of Christian Self-Understanding* [2000]).

If in 1955 it was hard to imagine a "field" of Jewish-Christian relations, today it is equally difficult to envisage this field without the involvement of women.

CANADIAN WOMEN'S RELIGIOUS ISSUES
Tracy J. Trothen

TO IDENTIFY CANADIAN women's religious issues, one must first have some understanding of the Canadian context. Canada is both a colonized and an imperialist nation. The mere fact of including an entry with this title is indicative of a way of perceiving and defining Canadian women's religious issues; there is no corresponding U.S. entry. As a sociocultural and economic satellite of the powerful United States, Canada follows many of its trends and lives, in part, as a colony of the United States. However, Canada also has significant power. We have asserted this power, at times, in oppressive ways including our treatment of First Nations peoples. At other times, Canada has stood firm in its inclusive social commitments, as in the case of universal health care.

A survival theme has characterized much of Canadian history and emergent identity. Part of this theme has been the concept of a cultural mosaic rather than the American melting pot. In 1867, Confederation brought together the disparate cultures of French-speaking and English-speaking Roman Catholic and Protestant Christians and effectively laid the groundwork for the marginalization and exploitation of "Indians," especially women. Canada's commitment to peace, order, and good government, as set down by the British North America Act in 1867, was designed to promote harmonious coexistence in a heretofore tumultuous context; the "Lone Ranger was no hero here" (Legge, 36). However, simply because we claim these ideals does not mean that we are always harmonious and hospitable. Regionalism, replete with histories of abused power and damaged relationships between francophones and anglophones, First Nations peoples and white European peoples, prairie folk and easterners, farmers and urbanites, forms a patchwork quilt of difference and often imperialism across Canada. However, these differences have also added to our richness. As a country with a long-standing, if not troubled, commitment to community and mutual survival, Canada's founding ethos created fertile ground for coalitions, ecumenical movements, and other modes of honoring difference.

Religion has been a significant part of this difference, and religious commitments have been woven throughout our cultural and political fabrics. Although there is no formal relationship between church and state, there is no formal separation either. Canada's political history demonstrates some of the ways that faith values and worldviews have been connected with the country's governance. A three-party system with a clear place for conservative, liberal, and leftist politics has characterized Canada's political identity. Notably, the Social Gospel movement known as "Radical Christianity" gave rise to the Cooperative Commonwealth Federation (CCF) in the 1930s. The CCF eventually became the leftist New Democratic Party that continues today, albeit with significantly less support, at least on a national basis. Currently, it appears that we are in a place of political transition in which both the Right and Left are changing. This history of alliance between politics and faith commitments manifests a belief that the personal is political.

Women and women's movements, in a particular sense, have been linked to religious and political issues. As women gained public voice through, for example, more paid work during the world wars and with the second wave of feminism in the late 1960s and 1970s, so too did many women gain voice in religion. This connection continues; for example, as violence against women has gained more recognition as a social issue, religious communities have begun to respond to women's voices, in particular, by creating policies and procedures for addressing abuse.

Although women have indeed gained significant voice, research and writing dedicated to Canadian women's religious issues is quite sparse and more is needed, particularly regarding the relevance of a Canadian context to these issues. As a result, in writing this essay the author draws on conversations with many women as well as written reflections and some scholarly writings. Themes have emerged from these varied sources which the author will identify and begin to explore. Some, such as the widespread value placed on religion's relevance to women's lived experiences, a critique of systemic power imbalances, including sexism and racism, and abuse thereof, as well as a critique of extreme individualism in the midst of a celebration of community, will be woven throughout the following themes: multicultural and multifaith issues, ecumenical issues, First Nations issues, soul hunger, new rituals, women in leadership, embodiment, sexual orientation, reproductive technologies, violence against women, poverty, and finally, vision and hope. There are many more issues that are not identified; this is but one page, written from one perspective, from the Canadian album.

Multicultural and Multifaith Issues

A major religious issue for Canadian women, and men, concerns how we talk with one another across and about our differences. Interwoven in the multifaith fabric of Canada is culture; culture shapes how we experience life, including our social interactions and faiths. Our cultures cannot be clearly differentiated from our ways of being religious or not. Canada's earliest spiritual ways were those of indigenous peoples. European explorers and settlers began to bring Christianity, particularly Roman Catholicism, and other European cultural preferences with John Cabot's 1497 exploration of the now St. Lawrence Seaway and coastal region. Much later, the first synagogue was constructed in 1760 in Montreal. Later still, in 1938, the first mosque was built in Edmonton. Other world religions have trickled in and continue to grow. According to the 1991 census—the most recent tabulated census to include a question about religious affiliation—3.85 percent of our populace identify themselves as belonging to religious groups other than Christian. The largest increase between 1981 and 1991, in the religious groups identified by the census, occurred in the "Eastern Non-Christian" religions, which increased by 144 percent. As the number of those belonging to religious groups other than Christian increases, multifaith awareness and sometimes struggle with that awareness, both within and outside of these faith communities, increase in Canada.

Of the over 100,000 Muslims in Canada, approximately three-quarters are foreign born. Creating home in a country that values diversity in principle, but often not in reality, can be challenging. For instance, Canadian laws often contradict the *shari'ah*, the Islamic holy law. Unlike the *shari'ah*, Canadian law does not prohibit mixed marriages or premarital sex. A concern for some is that Canadian-born Islamic children will lose their traditional values because of this inconsistency. In this instance, how does one embrace community without negating one's particularity?

We must become aware of our own particularities, including our biases, if we are to move beyond mere tolerance of difference towards celebration of difference. Sharon Todd, a professor at York University in Toronto, examined the case of twelve-year-old Émilie Ouimet who was expelled from a Montreal high school, in 1994, for wearing the *hijab* (veil). Todd shows that the respective cultural experiences of the French- and English-language media, not the actual religious meanings of the *hijab*, determined how the issue was defined and subsequently acted upon. The Muslim practice of wearing the *hijab* is motivated by many claims; some understand it as liberating and empowering for women, while others see it as oppressive. Part of learning how to talk with one another is becoming aware of our respective concerns and differences. Certainly there are several ongoing religious school debates in Canada that require such learning.

In 1977, with the passage of Bill 101 by Quebec's first Separatist provincial government, all immigrant children had to attend French-language schools, unless exempted. As a result, the Quebec separate school system was introduced quickly to multiculturalism. Previously, these separate schools (i.e., schools with Roman Catholic confessional content) were largely homogenous. When the Ouimet incident occurred, the French-language press were most interested in the confessional significance of the *hijab*, whereas the English-language press saw the issue in terms of individual rights and freedom of religious expression. The debate became framed in us/them terms, fueled by the long-standing question of whether or not Quebec should become a sovereign nation, apart from Canada.

This example illustrates the volatility of religious issues as well as their intertwining with cultural issues in the Canadian context. Religious school debates continue to flourish as Canadians celebrate and struggle with increasing diversity. Clearly, francophone/anglophone issues have caused much tension, and the related religious issues have not remained strictly between Roman Catholics and Protestants. Even the basic issue of communication between those who speak different languages has religious implications, as the women of the St. Columba House collective, an outreach ministry of the United Church located in Montreal, experienced: "In Point St. Charles, 60 per cent of the residents are francophones and 35 per cent anglophones. . . . It's hard to function together on committees because you might understand the other language, but not enough to express yourself and really participate" (Chamberlain et al., 19).

Ecumenical Issues

Dialogue between and within faith groups is, indeed, no easy task, but in Canada many women invest much time and energy creating space for this to happen. This is evidenced by a unique Canadian commitment to the fostering of interchurch coalitions. Such coalitions include the Réseau oecuménique des femmes du Québec/ Women's Ecumenical Network (ROF/WEN), a feminist collective that began in 1988 through the efforts of two women who wanted to plan something to celebrate International Women's Day in light of two upcoming events—the fiftieth anniversary of Quebec women's right to vote and the Decade of Churches in Solidarity with Women. This network of women from the United, Presbyterian, Anglican, and Roman Catholic Churches is dedicated to bringing together feminists of all Christian churches. As Carolyn Sharp, feminist theologian, notes, the "late 1970s and the 1980s saw the emergence of francophone feminist theology" (401).

Other interchurch women's coalitions include the Women's Inter-Church Council of Canada (WICC) and its newly created Ecumenical Network for Women's Jus-

tice (April 2000). As expressed on their Web site (http://www.wicc.org/):

> The WICC traces its beginnings to 1918 when representatives of the Women's Missionary Boards of several churches came together to dialogue and find ways of promoting "the spread of Christ's kingdom by united prayer, united action and a stronger voice in national questions." The WICC "invites Christian women to experience working ecumenically; to share spirituality; to organize around concerns as women [and]; to take action together for social justice and human rights."

The Ecumenical Network for Women's Justice was created in response to the close of the Ecumenical Decade of the Churches in Solidarity with Women in Church and Society (1988–1998) with the goal to continue this work.

Other interdenominational ecumenical coalitions have emerged from grassroots needs such as the Ecumenical Network of Women of African Heritage. This is a Christian interdenominational group committed to supporting and deepening connections among women of African heritage in Canada; racism, and our responses to it, continues to be an important issue for many religious Canadian women.

There are also several women's ecumenical groups within religions other than Christianity. For example, the National Council of Jewish Women of Canada was established in 1897 as the first Jewish women's organization in Canada. The main mandate of this women's group has been to advocate for children, the elderly, families, the disabled, new Canadians, and the disadvantaged in both the general and Jewish communities.

There are fewer interfaith Canadian women's coalitions. Most interfaith networks are not specifically created by or for women. For example, the Canadian Christian-Jewish Consultation (CCJC) does much work in facilitating understanding and dialogue between Jews and Christians. While there has been opportunity for the women involved in this consultation group to have dialogue, the main focus of the group has not been on women's concerns. Also, most interfaith women's groups tend to meet around issue-specific concerns such as poverty or violence and, as such, are often more informal or temporary and task oriented.

Aboriginal Issues

Aboriginal peoples have long suffered in Canada. One of the most significant issues at this time in our history concerns attempts at justice in response to the harms caused by the imposition of residential schools

The Women's Inter-Church Council of Canada traces its beginnings to 1918, when representatives of the Women's Missionary Boards of several churches came together to find ways of promoting "the spread of Christ's kingdom by united prayer, united action and a stronger voice in national questions." The WICC's 2000 World March of Women covered a broad social justice agenda, including poverty and violence against women, economics, and formed an ecumenical network for women's justice. *Courtesy of Women's Inter-Church Council of Canada.*

on aboriginal peoples. In particular, the Canadian federal government and the Roman Catholic, Anglican, and United Churches are struggling to respond to lawsuits and, more important, to the call for healing. The abuses that occurred in residential schools continue to have devastating effects on families, communities, and individuals. Intertwined with this are issues including land rights, the protection and fostering of aboriginal spirituality, and the many manifestations of systemic racial oppression such as addictions, poverty, and high suicide rates.

It was not until 1985 with the passage of An Act to Amend the Indian Act that the government of Canada reinstated women and their descendants to their native communities; previously men had the sole authority to decide if families would retain aboriginal membership. A woman's band membership and community status previously had been removed if she married a "non-Indian" man. She could no longer vote in the elections of Indian Act chiefs and councillors. Though Bill C-31 was a significant step, aboriginal women continue to experience discrimination relative to aboriginal men regarding civil and property rights. Aboriginal women's recovery of membership and status is essential to the

strengthening of community, which, in turn, fosters spiritual growth, particularly in traditional ways.

The recovery of aboriginal spirituality has taken many forms, ranging from the retelling of stories and the repracticing of rituals and traditional spiritual medicine to the creation of new spiritualities that are being birthed through the creative gathering of a variety of faith traditions. For example, Marilyn Johnson, of Ojibway ancestry, has combined aboriginal spirituality with pagan practices and beliefs. She has discovered life-giving similarities between an aboriginal women's healing gathering, which is a cedar ceremony for women only, and certain pagan celebrations.

Some aboriginal women have become leaders and inspirational role models in their religious communities. One such prominent women is Dr. Jessie Prettyshield Saulteaux. Born in 1912, Jessie was the granddaughter of Ocapeoda, an Assiniboine medicine woman, who taught her that all life is sacred and we are to only take what we need, always with thanks. Jessie grew up learning to combine her Assiniboine spirituality with Christianity. The first woman to become a chief in Saskatchewan (on Carry the Kettle reserve), she also served as a United Church lay minister. A church elder, she nevertheless experienced ridicule throughout her service as a female aboriginal United Church lay minister. "People saw me as a sinner and thought I shouldn't do the service. They thought of the white ordained minister as a perfect person and they looked up to him" (Carlson and Dumont, 64). The Dr. Jessie Saulteaux Resource Centre for training aboriginal leaders in ministry was opened in 1984 at Fort Qu'Appelle, Saskatchewan. At the center, aboriginal people are taught ministry in a way that affirms and strengthens their culture. This unique center continues today in Beausejour, Manitoba.

One of the first graduates of the Dr. Jessie Saulteaux Resource Centre was her granddaughter, Bernice Saulteaux. A year before her 1987 ordination in the United Church, Bernice's niece died due to an overdose of pills. Bernice feared that her introduction of traditional aboriginal culture in the burial ceremonies would cause much upset and anger in the church, since the expression of traditional rites had not been allowed by residential schools:

> My mother had not yet returned home from a meeting in Saskatoon. Shortly after she arrived, two aunts came over to her place. I knew I was in trouble. . . . They told my mother, "You missed a beautiful service. We had the drummers singing those old death and honour songs that our grandparents and elders used to sing: the smell of sweetgrass, the men smoking the pipe, the feast of food to celebrate her life. All this was done in the church." The conversation ended with these words: "It's sad we had to lose our granddaughter to find our old ways again." (Lebans, 62–63)

The work of reclaiming the old ways continues to be important and challenging. The residential schools and other Canadian legislation have left a legacy of forgotten ritual, language, culture, and spirituality. Some aboriginal women want to draw on aboriginal spiritualities as well as parts of Christianity and, sometimes, other religions. Others are recreating and remembering aboriginal spiritualities. Racism and sexism continue to be experienced by Canada's indigenous peoples. These are very significant issues for the culpable institutional church. Aboriginal women have played, and continue to play, an important role in the recovery and re-creation of native spirituality.

Soul Hunger

Canadians are searching with renewed vigor for meaning and purpose in a society that is advancing faster technologically than we are able to keep pace with ethically, spiritually, and relationally. The Canadian weekly magazine *Maclean's* not long ago published a cover story regarding this search: "Canadians are increasingly checking into a wide array of retreats. They go to monasteries, temples, ashrams and sweat lodges, which offer everything from spartan rooms to spa-like luxury. When they leave, visitors . . . profess to a profound peace of mind, and even a restored feeling of faith" (Driedger, 3). For many Canadians, organized religion, in its conventional forms, is not adequate to feed their "soul hunger."

While many women remain involved, the institutional church is facing a loss of members due, in some measure, to a sense that it lacks relevance and is weak as a source of spiritual nourishment. In a recently published collection of stories of Canadian women's lives, the editor observed "the diminishing importance of organized religion in regulating the lives of women in Canada" (Hofmann Nemiroff, 14). Similarly, the women of St. Columba House write, "There are many churches in the Point, but for the majority of residents, organized religion doesn't have a very profound effect on their lives now" (Chamberlain et al., 19, 20–21). For these women, their collective as a place of meaningful social action has become their church.

In an attempt to address women's religious issues, the World Council of Churches declared the decade from 1988 to 1998 to be the Decade of the Churches in Solidarity with Women. At "Daring Hope"—the Canadian conference to mark the official end of this decade—June Anderson, a conference organizer, was not alone in her contention that the church still has a lot of work to do if more women are to be truly welcomed.

> "We have not felt that our calls to empowerment and encouragement were fully received by the church. . . . [Some women] have said they can no longer stay in a place where they don't feel welcome, where they don't feel appreciated and where they don't find God." These women are finding other outlets through study groups or "house churches" to pray and read Scriptures at home. "We restrict spirituality or religion to buildings, and church really is a gathering of people. It's not just in a church structure that wonderful, spiritual things happen." (Kilpatrick, L16)

Many such women's groups are meeting across Canada. For example, Tapestry, a Jewish feminist group in Calgary, meets monthly to "gain an understanding of women in the Torah, to discuss their roles, highlight their contribution to Judaism, and enhance their own spirituality through an understanding of their legacy" (*Canadian Woman Studies/Les Cahiers de la Femme*, 9).

New Rituals

Women from many religions are seeking ways of breathing life into their faith traditions to keep these traditions relevant today. An issue of the *Women's Studies Journal/Les cahiers de la femme* (York University in Toronto) on "Female Spirituality" provided a picture of women's experiences of spirituality. For example, Saroj Chawla, professor of sociology and social science at York University in Toronto, has, through the recovery of an ancient women's ritual, found it life-giving to return to Hinduism and its worship of goddesses and gods (*Canadian Woman Studies/Les Cahiers de la Femme*, 40–43). Similarly, Susan Berrin has reclaimed Judaism by participating in the creation of women's rituals being observed on Rosh Chodesh, a Jewish holiday that, according to Jewish midrash, "was given to women as a reward for their refusal to relinquish their jewelry to the building of the golden calf" (63). These rituals mark many stages of women's life including birth, onset of menarche, marriage, divorce, fertility, infertility, menopause, and aging. As Berrin points out, "Rosh Chodesh serves as a welcoming, open door to women long estranged from Jewish life as well as a focal point for women steeped in tradition. The range and variety of Rosh Chodesh observances—from the gatherings of women in an Orthodox *tefillah* (prayer) group in Montreal to diverse groups in Winnipeg, Vancouver, and Victoria—attests to its wide appeal" (63–64).

Other women are leaving institutional religion entirely or creating new variations on established religions by weaving together strands that offer meaning. Wicca and other Goddess-centered religious movements are increasing in Canada. These movements generally attend very closely to the creation of new rituals that arise out of and in response to women's experiences.

Women in Leadership

The role of women in organized religion continues to be an issue for Canadian women. Who, for example, has the right to be a religious leader? Who are the rabbis, shamans, deacons, priests, ministers, pastors? What is the place and role of laypeople? What are our theologies of lay and ordered ministries? The way we worship and function as faith communities takes in many other issues including inclusive language, interpretation of holy text, physical worship space, ritual, outreach, administration, and education, to name only a few. These issues also relate to the place of women in the wider Canadian society. Much more could be written, but the following will serve, once again, as a snapshot.

The Congregationalist Church, Unitarian Church, and the Salvation Army were among the first faith communities, in Canada, to include women in ordained ministry (beginning in the 1800s). However, even in these churches, there have been and continue to be restrictions—formal and largely informal—on the roles of women.

The United Church of Canada (a uniquely Canadian church formed by many Congregationalist, Presbyterian, and Methodist churches in 1925 and joined by the United Brethren in the 1960s) first ordained a woman in 1936. However, married women or women who might become married were not ordained until the 1960s, and, even then, women's ministry was associated more with children and youth. Today, women in ministry continue to be viewed with suspicion, trivialized, or dismissed. Lois Wilson (1927–), a prominent United Church ordained minister and now a Canadian senator, reflects on her groundbreaking experiences as a woman in the United Church and parts of the wider Canadian Christian community:

> I was elected the first woman as President of the Canadian Council of Churches, and Moderator of my church 1980–82, which is its highest elected office. In 1983 I was elected as one of seven Presidents of the World Council of Churches.... What frustrates me still is the obvious surprise with which one is greeted after service with the comment, "That was a very good sermon." I get very tired of having to be constantly alert to the subtle ways in which women clergy are sidelined, ignored, or fawned over. My main learning has been to act in the knowledge that I, too, am made in the image of God, and that acts or attitudes of discrimination and prejudice are the problem of the other person, not mine. I hope that the Spirit will enlighten them soon. (Bays, 160)

The Anglican Church ordained women for the first time in Canada on November 30, 1976. Women such as Thora Wade Rowe agonized over her desire to remain in the Anglican Church and her call to ordained ministry: "[S]omehow I could not leave my roots.... Yet sometimes in desperation I prayed, 'Lord, if I can't be ordained, please remove the call.' Seemingly, God was deaf" (Bays, 22). Thora's struggle continued from the mid-1950s to 1986 when she was ordained to the Anglican diaconate. Many women in other churches, such as the Roman Catholic Church, continue to feel torn between a call to ordained ministry and a desire to stay in their faith community.

For many of the same reasons that women in ordained ministry or those who are excluded from ordained ministry are marginalized, laypeople in general and laywomen in particular are also marginalized. This hierarchical valuing of ordained over lay is reflective both of clericalism and of sexism. If we believe that women are made in the image of the One/s we worship, then this theological claim needs to be brought into dialogue with any conflicting claims: If everyone is equal before the Holy, then why do our religions often fail to reflect that claim? These are questions that some women (and some men) continue to ask about organized religion and about the rest of society.

There are many women's groups in organized religions. At times the main role of such groups concerns the domestic dimension and hospitality of the faith community such as providing after-worship refreshment or planning and hosting craft sales and teas. The importance of these functions is not to be ignored or downplayed; the gift of hospitality is essential to the faithfulness and well-being of religious organizations. There are also women's groups that focus on spirituality, outreach, mission, social justice, and the study of theology or holy text. However, sometimes these latter groups are not as valued as much or taken as seriously within religious organizations as are those dedicated to hospitality functions. This skewed valuing is connected to systemic gender-role stereotyping and must be challenged.

Embodiment

Many women's religious issues are related to embodiment, including but not limited to sexual orientations, physical abilities, reproductive technologies and choice, and violence against women. Organized religion has tended to mirror social norms; those who do not conform to heterosexual norms, those who are differently abled, have a color of skin that differs from the (almost always) white norm, those who are too young or too old are, among others, marginalized in most areas of Canadian society, including organized religion. Women are doubly marginalized in these ways because of their gender.

Many women struggle to be more aware and inclusive of each other. For example, at Daring Hope, the Canadian festival conference to end the Ecumenical Decade of the Churches in Solidarity with Women in Church and Society (1988–1998) in Guelph (Ontario, Canada), African Canadian women *dared* to raise questions regarding their lack of inclusion in the Decade's work. Their challenges sparked discussion, evoked distress, concern, and greater awareness among the approximately 600 women and 25 men gathered. Out of these emotionally charged discussions also emerged the Ecumenical Network of Women of African Heritage.

Sexual Orientation

The United Church of Canada passed a very controversial motion at their 1988 General Council meeting in Victoria, British Columbia, that sexual orientation, in and of itself, is not a barrier to ordained ministry. Churches and faith groups, including the United Church, continue to wrestle with, avoid, and suffer much division regarding sexual orientation. By contrast, the Metropolitan Community Church and most Wiccan groups welcome people of differing sexual orientations. For those who have decided to remain with traditional faith groups, the fit can be painful. As Irshad Manji writes regarding her life as a Muslim and lesbian, "Forgive the morbid thought, but I often wonder if, in nervous anticipation of meeting the Divine One, I'll renounce my lesbianism on my death bed. . . . Problem is, every day is Judgement Day for the likes of me. As a semi-practicing Muslim and a full-practicing lesbian, I'm constantly asked how I reconcile my spiritual orientation with my sexual one" (Lake, 22).

Reproductive Technologies

The questions of reproductive technologies and choice also attract passionate energy on all sides of the debate. Issues related to our bodies and our faiths are among the most volatile; religion and faith claims are invoked, for instance, to justify so-called pro-life and pro-choice claims in the abortion debate. Women's authority over our in/ability to reproduce is passionately questioned, defended, or rejected by women and men.

Violence Against Women

Violence against women also continues to be a reality. For Canadians, the Montreal massacre in which fourteen women were killed on December 6, 1989, is not forgotten. Artist Almuth Lutkenhaus sculpted *The Crucified Woman*, which now stands in the garden behind Emmanuel College, the United Church College at the University of Toronto, to symbolize a call for justice and solidarity with all women crucified through abuse and violence. Every year, on the anniversary of the Montreal massacre, there are memorial vigils, usually ecumenical or secular, held at the foot of *The Crucified Woman* and in many other places across Canada to remember these fourteen and all other women who are violated by men.

Some understand such violence as individual tragedy, while others understand it as a systemic manifestation of sexism. One might expect conservative groups of self-identified religious women to be less interested or to adopt a blame-the-victim stance regarding abused women. However, a recent study in which ninety-four Canadian evangelical Christian women were interviewed showed that these women were well aware of violence against women and, as part of their faith commitment, offered support both spiritually and concretely to women experiencing violence. Most organized religions in Canada have yet to respond adequately, particularly at an institutional level, to violence against women, including abuse by religious leaders. On a secular level, things have not been much different. For example, it was not until 1983 that it was declared illegal for a husband to rape his wife.

Poverty

Violence against women and poverty were the two main issues around which women rallied in the World March of Women 2000. Many Canadian women's groups, including faith-based collectives, participated in this march. The value of the march was not only in addressing poverty but also in creating and strengthening community support and hope.

Poverty was the rallying issue for the women of St. Columba House. The community of Point St. Charles, which gave birth to St. Columba House and other socially active groups, is one of Montreal's most impoverished neighborhoods. St. Columba House is home to a number of social action groups including, for example, the Point Adult Centre for Education (PACE). PACE, an English adult education center, began in 1985 as a response to a door-to-door survey of the neighborhood. In the face of demoralizing government cutbacks in social programs, the collective draws strength and hope from biblical stories of God through Jesus representing the struggle for justice and from each other:

It is as though hope is what calls people out, perhaps gives encouragement with the accomplishments along the way, but then opens up new horizons or challenges. Hope is in what you are doing, but beyond. We began to understand that it is not hope "out there" in the sense of being an abstract ideal, or something unattainable, but the tough nature of hope that is both in the struggle itself and the hard, ongoing work one is called to. (Chamberlain et al., 3)

And in the hope and the struggle, our faiths and religious issues continue to unfold.

Vision and Hope

The Toronto-based Ecumenical Decade (of Churches in Solidarity with Women) Coordinating Group's vision statement expressed the hopes of many Canadian women:

To empower women to challenge oppressive structures in the global community, their country and their church; to affirm, through shared leadership and decision-making, the contributions of women in churches and communities; to give visibility to women's perspectives and actions in the work and struggle for justice, peace and the integrity of cre-

ation; to enable churches to free themselves from racism, sexism and classism and from teachings and practices that discriminate against women; to encourage churches to take actions in solidarity with women.

Moral vision enables us to discern what is not right in our world and compels us to act in response to this knowledge. Faith communities can provide a lens through which to interpret this vision. Some of the many justice issues that inform the moral visions of Canadian religious women include sexism, racism, classism, poverty and economic justice, day care, violence against women, biotechnology, ecology, the correctional system's response to women, just treatment of those who farm, and adequate representation of women in leadership positions.

Vision must be grounded in the reality of concrete experiences of suffering; otherwise, memory is not dangerous, and vision does not hold emancipatory potential but rather becomes nothing more than an empty wish. What feeds many Canadian women is their faith in a holy promise of justice and their work together in community.

SOURCES: Patricia Bays, ed., *Partners in the Dance—Stories of Canadian Women in Ministry* (1993). *Canadian Woman Studies/Les Cahiers de la Femme* 17.1 (Winter 1997). Joyce Carlson and Alf Dumont, eds., *Bridges in Spirituality—First Nations Women Tell Their Stories* (1997). Melissa Chamberlain, Elizabeth Garbish, Donna Leduc, Myrna Rose, and Faye Wakeling, *Hope Is the Struggle—A Community in Action* (1996). Sharon Doyle Driedger, "Soul Searchers," *Maclean's*, April 16, 2001, 42–47. Greta Hofmann Nemiroff, ed., *Women's Changing Landscapes—Life Stories from Three Generations* (1999). Ken Kilpatrick, "Still Hoping the Church Will Change—Women Feel the Challenge of the Last Decade Was Not Fully Met," *Toronto Star*, September 12, 1998, L16. Catherine Lake, ed., *ReCreations—Religion and Spirituality in the Lives of Queer People* (1999). Gertrude Lebans, ed., "Living and Changing on Carry the Kettle Reserve," *Gathered by the River—Reflections and Essays of Women Doing Ministry* (1994). Marilyn Legge, *The Grace of Difference—A Canadian Feminist Theological Ethic* (1992). Carolyn Sharp, "The Emergence of Francophone Feminist Theology," *Studies in Religion* 25.4 (1996): 397–407. Sharon Todd, "Veiling the 'Other,' Unveiling Our 'Selves': Reading Media Images of the Hijab Psychoanalytically to Move Beyond Tolerance," *Canadian Journal of Education* 23.4 (1999): 438–451.

INCLUSIVE LANGUAGE
Susan Thistlewaite

INCLUSIVE LANGUAGE IS a term that refers to the effort to transform English usage so that women and men, persons of color, the handicapped, and others traditionally excluded by accepted usage are represented fairly and equally in the words used to name them. The movement to change traditional usage to be more inclusive of women and others excluded is not confined to English-speaking peoples. Such efforts are under way on all continents in dozens of languages. The variety of changes proposed are extensive, depending on the history and construction of a particular language. In German, Spanish, or French, for example, where grammatical construction depends on a "masculine" or "feminine" case assigned to a word, often indicated by the ending, the work has focused on the invention of neutral (i.e., nongendered) endings. In Japanese, where the actual characters used to denote certain meanings can carry pejorative connotations for women (i.e., the word for *weakness* is based on a character meaning "woman"), there have been proposals even for new characters to form such words. Clearly these efforts are profound and complex.

The need for inclusive language arises from patriarchal patterns of language usage that take the male to be the normative human person. In English, the dominant language in North America, *man* and *men* are accepted and even stressed as representing all humankind; the pronouns *he* and *him* are taken to be generically human as well. This pattern of English usage is not accidental but depends on the social arrangements of patriarchy. Patriarchy is the social, legal, political, economic, and familial privileging of the male over the female.

> Patriarchy is the power of the fathers: a familial-social, ideological, political system in which men—by force, direct pressure, or through ritual, tradition, law, language, customs, etiquette, education and the division of labor—determine what part women shall or shall not play, and in which the female is everywhere subsumed under the male. (Rich, 56)

The Force of Religious Language

Religious language figures powerfully in the legitimating of patriarchy. As Marjorie Proctor-Smith says succinctly, "The critique itself is simple: exclusively or dominantly male language grants authority to men in patriarchal culture and religion" (24). Mary Daly has been even pithier: "When God is male, the male is God" (9).

Language is a key way that the very structure of patriarchy is communicated. This is a problem not exclusive to English or to the English-speaking West. In grammars that use gender as a metaphor for difference ("feminine" or "masculine" cases—see above), difficulties arise in separating grammatical gender from human, sexually based gender. As the Christian scriptures and the Hebrew Bible are translated from languages with gender-based grammars (Greek and Hebrew), grammatical gender has often been confused, especially in older translations, with sexual gender. The word *God* is a case in point. The word for *God* in Hebrew or Greek takes the masculine grammatical gender. The pronoun used for *God* has therefore been translated "He." Yet the grammatical case does not equal sexual masculinity.

The Inclusive Language Movement

Inclusive language in North America as a movement is related to the modern women's movement that began in the 1970s following the antiwar protests and the civil rights actions of the 1960s. Many women had been

In 1980, Claire Randall, then head of the National Council of Churches, announced that after almost three years of study and discussion, the NCC Christ's Division of Education and Ministry Task Force on Biblical Translation recommended a new translation of the scriptures used for worship. This committee was given the explicit mandate to address gender-specific language in translation.

strong leaders in these movements and found their efforts degraded and dismissed due to their gender. Like their abolitionist sisters in the nineteenth century, this effort on behalf of the rights of others began to include the rights of women per se. The "consciousness-raising" phase of this era, symbolized in such classics as Betty Friedan's *The Feminine Mystique* (1963), caused women to realize they were not included in the word *mankind*.

The Inclusive Language Movement in the Churches

The inclusive language movement in the Christian churches was related to the secular women's movement. The antiwar and civil rights movements were church-based religious arguments that used concepts of human equality and value to condemn racism and war. These same antiwar and antiracist activists, however, used religious arguments to keep women in the background of these struggles. Women activists, however, were able to cut through this double-think and make the connection between arguments for human freedom and equality and their own situation as oppressed persons under patriarchy.

The consciousness about the role of language in helping to keep women in a second-class status arose from these activist struggles. Women sought to be included in "the brotherhood of man" and quickly realized that the actual words *man* and *brother* did not mean all people. They actually just meant what they said, men and brothers. The language was part of their problem. When the religious movements against the war and against racism called for "The Brotherhood of Man under the Fatherhood of God," women quickly realized they had no place in that phrase.

In the churches, this insight translated into efforts to render liturgy and hymns more inclusively. In 1976 under pressure of many letters deploring the noninclusive language of the Revised Standard Version of the Christian Bible, the most commonly used translation in North America, the National Council of Churches of Christ's Division of Education and Ministry appointed a Task Force on Biblical Translation. In 1980 after almost three years of study and discussion, this task force recommended a new translation of the scriptures used for worship, the *Lectionary*, be commissioned. This committee was given the explicit mandate to address gender-specific language in translation. This was later expanded to include other types of discriminatory language. A translation team was assembled and produced *An Inclusive Language Lectionary, Years A, B and C. Readings for Year* A of the three-year lectionary cycle was published in October 1983, followed by *Years B* and *C* in subsequent years. *Year A* was later revised and reissued in a new translation.

The committee began with its mandate to address gender exclusivity but quickly expanded its work to include other types of exclusion. They became aware through the work on language about human beings that terms such as *the blind* and *the lame* for persons who have those conditions are pejorative. A person is more than his or her handicap. The language was changed to reflect this insight. A further insight was that language that equates darkness with sin, evil, ignorance, or misunderstanding tends to strengthen racism in a racist culture. "Where 'darkness' is set in contrast with 'light' and has a moral connotation, a substitute word for darkness is supplied—for example, 'The light shines in the deepest night' (John 1:5)" (*An Inclusive Language Lectionary, Year A*).

The most controversial changes by far were, of course, changes to God language. References to the post-Resurrection Christ use Christ as a substitute for the pronoun. This insight is based on the theological assertion that the risen Christ is one with God and God as infinite is beyond gender. References to the human Jesus retain the masculine pronoun. God as infinite was the basis for expanding the metaphor of God the Father to "God the Father [*and Mother*]" with italics and square brackets indicating the insertion into the text. The metaphor then connotes the parenthood of God in inclusive language.

Reactions were swift to follow. They ranged from the experience reported to the National Council by Reverend Len Freeman, pastor of University Baptist Church, Minneapolis, Minnesota, who wrote, "I have been trying for several years to do what I could with Scripture and your new lectionary is a great help. Some of the expressions like 'Human One,' for 'Son of Man' have opened up for us new depths of understanding in our work with the text." Other responses were very negative, calling the project "illegitimate theologically" and "appalling." The committee received threatening letters.

Many are surprised that mere translation from one language to another received such strong reactions. The very virulence of the responses reveals the power of language to tell us who we are. It also reveals the strong hold of exclusive God language on human imagination. Language changes to scripture are especially very threatening because interpretations of scripture have been an anchor for the worldview described above as patriarchy.

The inclusive language movement had strong roots in the churches: The United Church of Christ, the Presbyterian Church USA, the United Methodist Church, the Metropolitan Community Churches, the American Catholic Church, the Episcopal Church (USA), and others either passed resolutions supporting inclusive language and/or produced educational materials supportive of inclusive language use in liturgy and the common life of the church.

Backlash

The women's movement in the churches has been vital and strong for nearly three decades. Proof of its strength may be seen in the strong backlash to a conference held in 1994 called "Re-Imagining." This conference took place in Minneapolis, Minnesota, sponsored as part of the World Council of Churches celebration of the "Decade of Solidarity with Women." Several thousand women and men met over a number of days to hear presentations on newer advances in feminist, womanist, and *mujerista* (Hispanic women's) theologies from a very diverse group of presenters. Experimental liturgies were used to evoke many images for God under the "Re-Imagining" theme. Conservative Protestant publications reported distorted and exaggerated versions of "Goddess worship" and made much of the imagery of milk and honey used in one worship. The controversy became so visible that on May 24, 1994, Ted Koppel's *Nightline* program featured Dr. Rita Nakashima Brock explaining the purpose and actual content of the conference. Women in mainline denominations who had been instrumental in sponsoring the conference were vilified; some lost their positions; others resigned under pressure.

The image of "Sophia" or "wisdom" as used in the conference was confused with "Goddess worship" precisely because of the continuing equation of grammatical gender with sexuality. The term for *wisdom* or *sophia* takes the feminine case and therefore the female pronoun in English translation. The critics confused this translation with religious traditions where there are female deities. Ignorance of the Wisdom tradition particularly on the part of Protestants, coupled with the simplistic equation of sexual gender and grammatical gender, fueled the controversy. Some leaders such as the Reverend John Buchanan, then moderator of the Presbyterian Church USA and a prominent pastor and scholar, attempted to provide support in the form of biblical and historical accuracy. But such efforts were swept away in a tide of hysteria.

Continuing Efforts

Despite this backlash, efforts at strengthening inclusive language and its availability in Christianity have continued. It is clear from the reactions to the *Inclusive Language Lectionary* that biblical translation goes to the heart of the issue of inclusive language and its capacity to legitimate patriarchal religion. There is a need for a full-text inclusive language translation of the Bible.

In 1993 Oxford University Press commissioned a new biblical inclusive language project. Members of the earlier translation team for the National Council of Churches were approached and began work on a full-text translation of the New Testament and Psalms. A large number of these portions of the scriptures had already been translated in the earlier lectionary effort. But the assembled team did not merely duplicate earlier efforts. They attempted to create greater felicity in the text that would increase ease of use. Related issues such as handicapping conditions and racism were included in their work. In addition, efforts to address the seemingly pejorative reference to "the Jews," particularly in John, were addressed by using the clarification "the religious authorities" to indicate that the text is referring to the fact that it is certain Jews (a religious community) who are challenging other Jews who have authority in the Jewish community.

In 1995 *The New Testament and Psalms: An Inclusive Version* was published by Oxford. Again there were strong reactions to an inclusive language biblical translation, though these were less strident than in the 1980s. Oxford University Press had hired a consultant to manage the response of the press, and better, more accurate coverage resulted. Nevertheless, Oxford stopped short of commissioning the full text of the Hebrew Bible. There is currently no full-text inclusive language translation of the full Bible, Hebrew and Christian scriptures.

The inclusive language translation of the earlier project, the *Inclusive Language Lectionary*, has had influence beyond the Oxford translation as well. Between the publication of the *Inclusive Language Lectionary* and *The New Testament and Psalms: An Inclusive Version*, a separate committee, working under the auspices of the National Council of Churches in Christ in the U.S.A., the body who holds the copyright on the Revised Standard Version of the King James translation, published The New Revised Standard Version. The NRSV, as it is called, shows a strong influence of the work of the inclusive language translation committee, especially in regard to human gender. The NRSV, apart from substituting the term *God* for masculine pronouns for *God* added by the King James Version that are not in the original manuscripts, does not deal with the language for God or Christ at all.

Contested Issues

The most hotly contested issue in inclusive language work is the nature of language itself. Is the meaning of words fixed and immutable or is the meaning conveyed in language more fluid and evocative? Those who have opposed inclusive language, such as theologian Paul Holmer, have argued that there is a fixed "grammar" to faith that is not tied to history and culture. The core reality of faith continues to be expressed in this essential grammar, and any changes to specific words themselves are a threat to this core and a move away from faith.

Holmer's work is often cited by those who oppose inclusive language.

Feminist theologians such as Sallie McFague have provided critical theoretical underpinnings for the inclusive language movement in the churches and the religious academy. McFague's works such as *Metaphorical Theology* (1982) and *Models of God* (1987) have argued that these essentialist portrayals of language fail to take into account how language actually makes meaning. Words are deeply metaphorical. They make meaning in a wider social context. Religious language, in particular, is more evocative than essentialist. Religion builds a model of reality that is the evocation of possibility. In fact "reality is 'realities,' alternative ways that things might be." When words are essentialized, idolatry results.

The point of Christian religious language is not to simply utter the magic words like "Open Sesame." Rather, religious language is evocative of relationship with God and neighbor.

This conflict between essentialist and more metaphorical ways of looking at how language makes meaning underlies the whole of the inclusive language debates.

Man/Mankind

The question of whether women are "included" in the terms *man* and *mankind* is basic to inclusive language efforts. Essentialists claim that *man* and *mankind* are universals and that these terms include women. In a sense, they do. Patriarchal culture, best described in law by the famous *Blackstone's Commentaries* of 1752, considers that women have no legal existence apart from men. Whether of father or husband or other male relative, women can have no legal standing and no existence apart from a male to whom she is subordinate.

Looked at from this patriarchal perspective, then, and especially with an essentialist cast to linguistic theory, women have been considered to be "included" in *mankind* precisely because they have not been considered to exist apart from the men to whom society renders them legally, culturally, and religiously subordinate. The linguistic subordination is both an extension of these other realities and its confirmation in a false universalism.

Inclusive language, then, has a larger context of social and political struggle. The effort to render women visible in language in terms such as "men *and women*," "*humankind*," and "I now pronounce you *husband and wife*" (rather than "man and wife") has been called "linguistic visibility." Women can be and are discounted in religion and society precisely because they are invisible. When women are visible linguistically, they become visible as human actors and hence as human beings in their own right.

In inclusive language biblical translation related terms that denote the biologically male as the universal human are rendered differently. Terms such as *brethren* to address members of the church become *sisters and brothers*. *Sons of God* becomes *children of God* or, even more specifically, *Sons and Daughters of God*. Jesus as the "Son of God" is translated "Child of God" since Jesus' life is to be a model for all humanity.

God Language

The most frequently used metaphors for God are *Father* and *Lord*. *Father* is a male metaphor that is highly personal, connoting family intimacy, authority, care, and protection. With repetition metaphors lose their poetic connotations and begin to be understood as literal statements that define a fixed reality. In a literal reference to God as "Father" one begins to think of God as literally a male being. Those for whom *Father* has negative, rather than positive connotations, have great difficulty with that metaphor for God. But even for those for whom *Father* has a positive connotation, a literal reading or hearing of this word limits understanding of God to a narrow range of human understanding.

Occasionally in the Bible, the image of God is of a mother. With that textual basis, the Oxford *Inclusive Language* translation of the Bible introduced an innovative term. In order to in a sense "de-literalize" the image of God as a human father, that inclusive language translation sometimes renders "God the Father" as "God the Father-Mother" to deliberately create tension with essentialist human projections on to God. There are no literal "Father-Mothers," and the language is redeemed from an exclusively human connotation. The image projected of God, then, is more akin to "parent."

In addition to *Father*, the word *Lord* is used in the New Testament to designate either God or Jesus Christ. Because the word *Lord* is believed by some to be male oriented, but by others to be gender neutral, similar to the way in which *God* is usually understood, the inclusive language version retains *Lord* in some instances but makes substitution for it in others. The Greek word *kyrios*, translated "Lord" in English, has a number of meanings in the New Testament. For example, it can mean "owner"—of a vineyard, of a colt; and that meaning passed into *master*, or one who has control of something—of life, of one's own body, of a person who is enslaved. *Kyrios* is also used as a term of address to someone in a higher position than the speaker and sometimes is the equivalent of *sir*.

In the Septuagint, *kyrios* is one of the two most commonly used words to speak about God—the other is *theos* (God). In the New Testament both words are used for "God," but *kyrios* is also used for "Christ," and it is sometimes difficult to tell to whom (either Christ or

God) it refers. *Lord* is retained when referring to "the Lord Jesus Christ" and substituted when it is clear it refers to God.

Jesus Language

A distinction is made between Jesus the human and the post-Resurrection Christ, as pointed out earlier. Frequently in the New Testament, Jesus is referred to as "Son": Son of God, Son of Man, Son of the Blessed One, Son of the Most High, Son of David, and so on. When in the gospels the historical person Jesus is referred to as "Son, the word is retained. But when Jesus is called "Son of God" or "Son of the Blessed One," and the maleness of the historical person Jesus is not relevant, but the "Son's" intimate relation to the "Father" is being spoken about, the formal equivalent "Child" is used for "Son," and gender-specific pronouns are avoided. Thus readers are able to identify with Jesus' humanity.

If the fact that Jesus was a man, and not a woman, has no christological significance (i.e., makes no difference for how Jesus' life, death, and resurrection save humanity) in the New Testament, then neither does the fact that Jesus was a *son* and not a *daughter*. If Jesus is identified as "Son," believers of both sexes become "sons" of God, but if Jesus is called "Child," believers of both sexes can understand themselves as "children of God."

The title "son of man," found frequently in the gospels, has a complex history and is translated "the Human One" in the inclusive language. "The Human One" is clearly a title of a nonandrocentric form and is also open to the many nuances of interpretation that are possible in the original Greek term. No gender is ascribed to the term.

The continuing challenge of inclusive language is to raise consciousness among religious communities that the language we use for each other and for the divine is partial, incomplete, and constantly changing. This includes the recent history of inclusive language translation itself. It must be semper reformanda.

SOURCES: Mary Daly, *Beyond God the Father* (1973). Marjorie Proctor-Smith, *In Her Own Rite: Constructing Feminist Liturgical Tradition* (1990). Adrienne Rich, *Of Woman Born: Motherhood as Experience and Institution* (1976).

NEW RELIGIOUS RIGHT
Laura R. Olson

THE "NEW RELIGIOUS Right" commonly refers to the political movement of evangelical Protestants that began in the 1970s. Evangelicals, who believe that scripture is the revealed word of God and actively seek to convert others to Christianity, first attracted substantial attention from the national press in 1980 when they voted in large numbers for Ronald Reagan. The intense political mobilization of evangelical voters that attended the rise of the Religious Right marked a departure from the longstanding evangelical tradition of political avoidance. For generations, evangelical Protestant leaders had argued that politics was a dirty and sinful forum; Christians, they felt, would be better served by avoiding involvement in such a realm.

Events of the 1960s and 1970s brought about a sea change in evangelical opinions about the propriety of political participation. Many evangelicals felt threatened by the sweeping social changes of the 1960s. They lamented the U.S. Supreme Court's decisions that school prayer is unconstitutional and abortion constitutional. There was also great disappointment in evangelical circles with what were perceived as overly liberal policy initiatives during the presidency of Jimmy Carter, a professed born-again Christian. During the 1970s evangelical leaders came to feel that their political views were not being represented by what they viewed as an increasingly secular American government, and the Religious Right movement was born.

While the Religious Right's most visible leaders have been men such as Jerry Falwell, Marion "Pat" Robertson, and James Dobson, women have played important, if less obvious, roles as well. Particularly noteworthy are the multitudes of evangelical women across the United States who have supported the Religious Right despite the movement's rather conspicuous rejection of feminism. A central plank of the Religious Right's political and social agenda has been the preservation of the nuclear, heterosexual model of family. Evangelical women are discouraged from working outside the home and are expected to defer to their husbands. Female supporters of the Religious Right tend to embrace this notion of "male headship" and cherish their roles as mothers and homemakers.

Not surprisingly, relatively few visible female leaders have arisen within the Religious Right. Only two—Phyllis Schlafly and Beverly LaHaye—have attained national prominence. However, hundreds of thousands of women have worked to further the agenda of the Religious Right, both behind the scenes and at the grassroots level. Women played crucial roles in Pat Robertson's 1988 presidential campaign, and they have fought in key local-level battles over policy issues including the definition of family and education.

Phyllis Schlafly versus the Equal Rights Amendment

The first woman to appear on the national stage as a spokesperson for the Religious Right was Phyllis

The intense political mobilization of evangelical voters that attended the rise of the Religious Right marked a departure from the long-standing evangelical tradition of political avoidance. The notion of the nuclear, heterosexual family holds a place of special honor in the agenda of the Religious Right. *Copyright © Joan Biren.*

Schlafly. Schlafly stands as one of the most important figures—male or female—in the history of the Religious Right. Ironically, Schlafly herself is Catholic; nevertheless, her work has galvanized masses of evangelical Protestants. Schlafly first arose to political prominence in 1964 for two reasons: She vocally supported the presidential candidacy of Barry Goldwater, and she published a bestselling book, *A Choice, Not an Echo*. Even more significantly, she emerged in the 1970s as the principal leader of the "Stop ERA" movement, which was dedicated to defeating the proposed Equal Rights Amendment (ERA) to the U.S. Constitution.

The House of Representatives and the Senate passed the ERA in 1972, after which it needed to be ratified by thirty-eight states. Schlafly used her newsletter, *The Phyllis Schlafly Report*, to spread her view that the ERA posed a grave threat to American family structure. She actively questioned the ERA's implicit message that women do not need men to watch over them: "Women want and need protection. Any male who is a man—or gentleman—will accept the responsibility of protecting women" (Mansbridge, 69). The notion of women serving in the military, particularly on the front lines of combat, was especially repugnant to Schlafly, in part be-

cause she felt it would weaken the military. She shared this fear of women in combat with the homemakers she was attempting to mobilize; she also argued that the ERA would free men of their obligation to support their wives financially.

Because of Schlafly's efforts, the ERA became controversial in the mind of the American public, a development that marked its death knell. Twenty-two states had quickly ratified the ERA in 1972, but five later attempted to repudiate their support, and by 1977 the amendment was hopelessly stalled. Schlafly had led conservative women across America in both formal and symbolic protest against the ERA; many of her allies had taken to wearing red and white clothing as a visual symbol of the word *stop*. Unlike her counterparts in the National Organization for Women and other pro-ERA groups, Schlafly insisted upon using polite, "ladylike" lobbying tactics with lawmakers, even baking fresh bread for state legislators. In the court of public opinion, though, Schlafly played hardball by suggesting that passage of the ERA would lead to the legalization of gay marriage and the introduction of unisex public restrooms. Her strategies worked because evangelical women who participated in the Stop ERA effort felt particularly threatened by the women's movement and feminism, wishing to preserve and protect their roles as mothers and homemakers.

One of the key salvos in the war over the ERA took place in Houston. In recognition of the declaration of 1977 as the "International Women's Year," a federally funded National Women's Conference was convened there to discuss obstacles to women's equality. Opponents of this conference initiated a competing National Pro-Family Rally to protest the open discussion of abortion and gay rights taking place at the National Women's Conference. While Schlafly enthusiastically endorsed and participated in the National Pro-Family Rally, its key organizer was a woman named Lottie Beth Hobbs. Since 1974 Hobbs had been publishing an anti-ERA newsletter called *The Pink Sheet*, and she had also founded an antifeminist organization called Women Who Want to Be Women. Hobbs said she organized the Pro-Family Rally because "I'm a woman and they [the National Women's Conference] don't speak for me" (Martin, 165). The Pro-Family Rally magnified the growing division in American public opinion over the ERA and hastened its ultimate demise. To this day, the defeat of the Equal Rights Amendment ranks among the most significant policy victories achieved by the Religious Right—even though most histories trace the movement's roots only to the late 1970s.

The Eagle Forum

Phyllis Schlafly's importance to the Religious Right transcends her battle against the ERA. In 1975, she ran unsuccessfully for the presidency of the National Federation of Republican Women. Her views were seen as too extreme. In response to this defeat, Schlafly redoubled her efforts to build support for the Eagle Forum, an interest group she had founded three years earlier. Since its inception the Eagle Forum has promoted itself as an antifeminist organization, but it has embraced a wide variety of political goals in addition to the preservation of the nuclear model of family. In one memorable battle, the Eagle Forum fought against the Nuclear Freeze movement that aimed to slow or end the nuclear arms race in the 1980s.

The Eagle Forum was organized at both the state and national levels. Claiming 80,000 members in 2000, it placed particular focus on recruiting young people to its cause through its Teen Eagles and Eagle Forum Collegians organizations. It fights for school choice, tax cuts, "pro-family" policy, and private enterprise; it opposes abortion, gay rights, and national health care. The Eagle Forum also maintains a Congressional Scoreboard to measure support among members of Congress for its favored policy stands. Meanwhile, it endeavors to affect electoral outcomes nationwide through its own political action committee (PAC), Eagle Forum PAC, which channels campaign contributions to preferred candidates (nearly all of whom are Republicans). Schlafly herself continues to exert an important presence within the Religious Right. *The Phyllis Schlafly Report* is available on the Internet, and she writes a syndicated newspaper column that appears in over a hundred newspapers nationwide. She also tapes a radio talk show, *Phyllis Schlafly Live*, as well as additional radio commentary pieces that are nationally syndicated.

Concerned Women for America

In 1979, the same year in which Jerry Falwell attracted significant media attention for launching the Moral Majority, Beverly LaHaye quietly founded her own interest group, which she called Concerned Women for America. This group was designed primarily to appeal to evangelical women, promising to fight to preserve the nuclear model of family. Throughout the 1970s LaHaye had felt disenfranchised by the women's movement: "Betty Friedan was on Barbara Walters' [television] show, and she said, 'I'm representing the women of America.' [But] she was not representing *my* values at all, or any of the women that I knew" (Bates, 102). Concerned Women for America represented LaHaye's attempt to have her views represented.

Unlike Schlafly, LaHaye fit the more common model of female Religious Right leaders in that she arose to prominence alongside her husband, Tim LaHaye. Unlike other "Religious Right wives," however, Beverly LaHaye's popularity, effectiveness, and importance to the movement quickly came to eclipse that of her husband. She attracted attention for writing several influential books that dealt primarily with the "family issues" the Religious Right holds dear. For example, in *I Am a Woman by God's Design*, LaHaye argues that women should submit to men in marriage. In all of her writings LaHaye stresses her dual commitment to Christianity and political conservatism; for her the two are inextricably linked. Moreover, she conveys to evangelical women the mixed message that they can and should participate in the political process but that their lobbying should be done in most cases "from the kitchen table," a vivid illustration and reminder of her endorsement of male headship. Nevertheless, by 1985 LaHaye had become such a prominent Religious Right leader that Ronald Reagan appointed her to his Family Policy Advisory Board.

Compared to the Eagle Forum, Concerned Women for America's approach has been more explicitly rooted at the intersection between evangelical faith and politics. Its agenda is somewhat narrower than the Eagle Forum's, and its rhetoric is even more heavily steeped in religious metaphor. Like Schlafly, though, Beverly LaHaye was an important player in the fight against the Equal Rights Amendment. The two groups also have worked together and in coalition with other Religious Right groups such as the Moral Majority, the Christian Coalition, Focus on the Family, and the Family Research Council.

With over 700,000 members today, Concerned Women for America calls itself the nation's largest public policy women's organization. The organization works to defend the right of religious free exercise and the nuclear family model and to battle abortion, gay rights, pornography, and "secular humanism"—the notion that the United States is in the hands of leaders who do not respect Judeo-Christian moral standards. Concerned Women for America operates primarily through state and local chapters, all of which are networked with its national organization.

Women for Pat Robertson, 1988

Just as the women of the Religious Right have been involved in interest group lobbying and protest activity, so too they have been involved in electoral politics. Women played a remarkably important role in the 1988 race for the Republican presidential election through their support for the candidacy of Marion "Pat" Robertson. Before the 1988 presidential race, Robertson was best known as a religious broadcaster who hosted the popular *700 Club* television program. When he decided to challenge then–Vice President George H. W. Bush for the Republican presidential nomination, he forever changed both his image and his political significance. Something that is not commonly known about Robertson's ultimately unsuccessful presidential bid is that women were deeply involved at every level of his campaign organization. Constance Snapp was Robertson's campaign communications director, and Mary Ellen Miller was director of his field organization.

Among Pat Robertson's most devoted campaign workers was Marlene Elwell, a conservative Michigan homemaker who, like Phyllis Schlafly, is Catholic. When Elwell decided to become involved with Robertson's Freedom Council, a group that predated his campaign, she was initially met by discrimination. "In June of 1985 Pat came in to do a national news program. They needed organizing. I did it, the advance work. Pat was impressed and thought I might make a good state coordinator. That didn't happen . . . because I was a Catholic and a woman" (Hertzke, 141). However, Elwell soon proved her worth when she played an instrumental role in ensuring that Robertson would be competitive in the Michigan caucuses. This was not an easy task, as the Michigan Republican Party had explicitly planned to deliver the vast majority of votes in its primary to Bush.

After a contentious battle, Robertson won eight delegates to the Republican National Convention as a result of the Michigan caucuses. More important, he positioned himself, at least for a while, as a credible conservative challenger to the more moderate Bush. Elwell continued to work effectively for Robertson until he eventually dropped out of the race. She later became an activist in Robertson's Christian Coalition, the powerful Religious Right interest group he founded after his presidential campaign folded.

Fully 70 percent of the votes cast for Pat Robertson in 1988 primary elections came from women. The vast majority of these women were evangelical Protestants with whom Robertson's message of curbing family breakup and the "secularization" of public education resonated deeply. Female Robertson backers embraced very conservative views on gender roles and women's equality—they were more likely to agree that "women's place is in the home" than that "women and men should have an equal role in running business, industry, and government" (Hertzke, 217–219). In part, Robertson's great popularity among women may have been the result of his background in religious television. As Robert Wuthnow has shown, women are more likely than men to watch religious television programs, to contribute money to them, and to support the political perspectives discussed most frequently by religious broadcasters.

Women, the Religious Right, and Family Issues

The notion of the nuclear, heterosexual family holds a place of special honor in the agenda of the Religious Right. Evangelical Protestants worked in earnest to derail the Equal Rights Amendment, and they have been vocal critics of the gay rights movement for decades. Anita Bryant, a popular singer and former Miss America runner-up, led a highly publicized crusade against a proposed gay rights ordinance in Dade County, Florida, in 1977. Through the efforts of an organization she founded called Save Our Children, Bryant succeeded in convincing Dade County voters to overturn the ordinance. However, Bryant drew fire from the press and the gay community, lost her job as national spokesperson for the Florida Citrus Growers, and faded from the political stage.

Compared with Bryant, Connaught "Connie" Marshner was a less publicly visible but far more influential voice on family issues within Religious Right circles. As early as 1971, she was tapping into informal networks of evangelical women across the United States eager to fight to preserve "traditional family structures" and protect children. Marshner observed that "little clusters of evangelical and fundamentalist Moms' groups . . . were unstructured, they didn't have an organization; they were just in touch with each other, and they were beginning to be aware that there really was a problem [with liberal government policy toward families and children]" (Martin, 175). This early realization of the existence of a large potential block of evangelical voters who simply lacked organization was a precursor to the founding of marquee Religious Right interest groups like Jerry Falwell's Moral Majority and later Pat Robertson's Christian Coalition.

Long before even the Moral Majority appeared on the scene, Marshner was keeping evangelical women informed of her views on "family issues" through a newsletter called *The Family Protection Report.* Her most substantial contribution to the movement came later, when the Carter administration prepared to host a White House Conference on Families in the summer of 1980. Marshner led an effort to ensure that as many evangelicals as possible would be named as delegates, because she suspected that supporters of liberal welfare policies were set to dominate the conference's agenda. Moreover, she argued that the conference was not truly designed to address policy issues but rather to drum up support for Jimmy Carter's reelection bid.

Marshner was ultimately appointed to serve as a delegate to the White House Conference, but others—most notably Phyllis Schlafly—were not invited. Suspicion of the conference (and of Carter) continued to grow among evangelicals. In Beverly LaHaye's words, "[W]e came to realize that this White House Conference was really geared up toward changing the definition of the family. It wanted to include any two people who chose to live together, regardless of their sexual orientation" (Martin, 178). By noon on the second day of the conference, Marshner was leading her "pro-family" delegates in a mass walkout that attracted substantial media attention. Not long thereafter, Marshner joined with Schlafly, LaHaye, and the rising male stars of the nascent Religious Right for a rally they called the American Family Forum, held in Washington one month after the White House Conference. Nearly a thousand delegates representing more than 300 organizations attended. For many observers, this rally marked the beginning of the Religious Right movement, though clearly it also marked the culmination of at least a decade of ferment among evangelicals over family issues.

Women, the Religious Right, and Education Policy

In the early 1970s, Kanawha County, West Virginia, was not the sort of place that ordinarily attracted national attention. Nor was it the sort of place where women frequently arose to positions of political prominence. However, in the early 1970s a woman named Alice Moore, the wife of a fundamentalist pastor, came to play a highly significant role in the national battle over education policy. A grant from the federal govern-

ment had funded the development of a new sex education curriculum for the Kanawha County School District that was to be implemented in 1970. Moore was concerned that "this wasn't just a sex education course. . . . The stated purpose of the course was to teach children how to think, to feel, and to act. And it covered everything, from their relationship with their parents, to . . . sexual conduct" (Martin, 118).

Moore's concern led her to attempt to rally support from groups across the country against the curriculum. She received advice from a Texas husband-and-wife team, Mel Gabler and Norma Gabler, who were already well-known critics of "secular humanism" in school curricula. Moore came to feel she was not making sufficient headway, so she ran for—and won—a spot on the Kanawha County Board of Education. Her work on the board led to the abandonment of the sex education curriculum and the resignation of the superintendent of schools.

In 1974, Moore made even bigger news when she went to battle against a set of textbooks being considered for adoption by the board of education. Moore accused the books of overemphasizing racial and ethnic diversity, including profanity and explicit sexual contact, and promoting "moral relativism." Everywhere she and her allies searched for, and claimed to find, "non-Christian" messages in these textbooks. "I'm not talking about ignoring Christianity; I'm talking about attacking Christianity. . . . [In the books] Christians were always hypocrites. . . . Even Christ was mocked. It couldn't be by accident. It was by design" (Martin, 126).

The textbooks were eventually adopted at a highly contentious board meeting that was attended by over a thousand people. Undeterred, Alice Moore organized and led a school boycott that was soon joined by thousands in Kanawha County. It took only a few weeks before the board revisited its decision to adopt the textbooks, but by that point the conflict had turned violent. Parents who defied the boycott by sending their children to school had their homes and vehicles vandalized. Bombs, dynamite, and gunfire damaged school buildings. One opponent of the textbooks was killed, and many others on both sides of the debate were injured. Eventually the textbooks were restored as the official curriculum, and many of the perpetrators of violence were arrested and imprisoned. Moore continued to serve on the board of education, but she deeply regretted the violence that her crusade had inspired.

Nevertheless, the Kanawha conflict inspired evangelicals across the United States to challenge the use of "objectionable" textbooks and library books in public schools. Women have led many of these efforts, some through election to local school boards, others through grassroots activism. One example is Vicki Frost, a fundamentalist homemaker in Hawkins County, Tennessee.

As had Alice Moore before her, Frost turned in 1983 to Texans Mel Gabler and Norma Gabler for advice about fighting what she saw as "secular humanist" messages in her children's textbooks. The Gablers encouraged Frost to challenge the Hawkins County Board of Education, which she did, despite her view that "a woman is not supposed to be seen or heard in public" (Bates, 66). The ensuing battle attracted national attention and raged for years, finally ending in federal appeals court when the U.S. Supreme Court denied a hearing of the case.

Despite active assistance from Concerned Women for America, Vicki Frost's contingent lost their battle in court, and many of their children were expelled from Hawkins County schools for refusing to read the objectionable textbooks. However, as Jennie Wilson, an ally of Frost's, observed, "The world thinks we lost, but we won. . . . Our children are out [of the public schools]. They're getting a fine education [now], learning their heritage, how this great nation was built on Judeo-Christian principles" (Bates, 302). Today's burgeoning home school movement, which is fueled primarily by evangelicals who identify with the Religious Right, traces its roots to battles waged against school districts by women like Alice Moore and Vicki Frost.

Women in Today's Religious Right

Women continue to play important roles in various aspects of the Religious Right movement. Elizabeth Dole, who in 1999 became the first serious major-party female presidential candidate, is an evangelical with strong ties to the Religious Right. Both the Christian Coalition and the Family Research Council have been headed by women: Roberta Combs and Janet Parshall, respectively. Kay Coles James, one of relatively few African American women affiliated with the Religious Right, has held numerous governmental positions at the federal and state levels and for a time served as dean of the (Pat) Robertson School of Government at Regent University in Virginia Beach, Virginia. At the grassroots level, many evangelical women are deeply involved in fighting abortion by volunteering at the nationwide network of Crisis Pregnancy Centers. These centers oppose abortion. To encourage women not to choose abortions, they provide a variety of free services including pregnancy tests, counseling, medical referrals, and information about adoption and health insurance.

Women of the Religious Right also launched numerous organizations designed to be counterparts to Promise Keepers, the once visible evangelical men's movement. Among these counterpart groups were Women of Faith, Chosen Women, Promise Reapers, Heritage Keepers, and Suitable Helpers. The Promise Keepers movement has advocated the long-cherished view among evangelicals that men should be the heads of their households; along with that view comes the imperative for women to submit to the authority of their husbands. Counterpart organizations were designed to teach women how to surrender to male headship. Like Promise Keepers, these organizations have held mass meetings in stadiums and encourage women to live joyfully under God's domain.

Throughout its history, the Religious Right movement has structured the extent and nature of women's participation through its embrace of traditional gender roles. However, a small but vocal evangelical feminist movement does exist. Clyde Wilcox (*Onward Christian Soldiers?*) shows that only 16 percent of all white evangelicals oppose gender equality for women. While it has hardly been a champion of gender equality on paper, the Religious Right movement has incorporated women, and even given them the platform to speak as leaders, since its inception.

SOURCES: Important general sources on the Religious Right, and women's roles in it, include Allen D. Hertzke, *Echoes of Discontent: Jesse Jackson, Pat Robertson, and the Resurgence of Populism* (1993); James Davison Hunter, *Evangelicalism: The Coming Generation* (1987); Rebecca Klatch, *Women of the New Right* (1987); William Martin, *With God on Our Side: The Rise of the Religious Right in America* (1996); Clyde Wilcox, *God's Warriors: The Christian Right in Twentieth-Century America* (1992); and Clyde Wilcox, *Onward Christian Soldiers? The Religious Right in American Politics* (1996). On textbook controversies, see Stephen Bates, *Battleground: One Mother's Crusade, the Religious Right, and the Struggle for Control of Our Classrooms* (1993). Personal accounts by women leaders of the Religious Right include Beverly LaHaye, *I Am a Woman by God's Design* (1980); Phyllis Schlafly, *A Choice, Not an Echo* (1964); and Phyllis Schlafly, *The Power of the Christian Woman* (1981). Finally, for the definitive account of why the Equal Rights Amendment failed, see Jane J. Mansbridge, *Why We Lost the ERA* (1986). See also Robert Wuthnow, *The Restructuring of American Religion: Society and Faith since World War II* (1988).

SEXUALITY AND THE BLACK CHURCH
Kelly Brown Douglas

FUNDAMENTAL TO ANY discussion of the Black Church and sexuality is a clear understanding of two concepts: Sexuality and Black Church.

Sexuality

Christian ethicist James Nelson provides a comprehensive definition of *sexuality* that will be operative throughout this essay. He accurately clarifies that sexuality is about more than genitalia and sexual intercourse.

While sexuality is not the whole of what it means to be human, Nelson suggests that it is basic to being human. Sexuality compels emotional, affective, sensual, and spiritual relationships. Sexuality does not determine all human feelings, thought, and interactions, but it permeates and affects them all. Nelson explains that sexuality involves a person's self-understanding and way of relating in the world as a woman and a man. Nelson captures the meaning of *sexuality* best when he says:

> Sexuality is a sign, symbol, and a means of our call to communication and communion. This is the most apparent in regard to other human beings, and other body-selves. The mystery of our sexuality is the mystery of our need to reach out to enhance others both physically and spiritually. . . . [Sexuality] is who we are as body-selves who experience the emotional, cognitive, physical and spiritual need for intimate communion—human and divine. (17–18)

The Black Church

The Black Church is one of the most enduring black institutions. The contemporary Black Church is a multitudinous community of churches, diversified in origin, denomination, doctrine, worshiping culture, spiritual expression, class, size, and no doubt other less obvious factors. Though disparate, black churches share a unique history, culture, and role in black life that attest to their collective identity as the Black Church.

The history of the Black Church begins during the period of African enslavement in the United States. This church emerged as the enslaved rejected their enslavers' version of Christianity, a version that asserted God sanctioned slavery. The Black Church signified black people's resistance to an enslaving and dehumanizing white culture of slavery even as it testified to God's affirmation of freedom and blackness. The religious culture of the Black Church was shaped in large part by African traditional religions, Islam, African worldviews, and the Christian faith as that faith was encountered in the antebellum South and as some enslaved Africans may have brought it with them from their homeland. This culture is characterized by a unique spirituality that "honors personal experiences [with the Spirit] and fosters an ethic of comfort with diverse expressions of [a person's] interaction with the Spirit (Gilkes, 203). The Black Church is also distinguished by the pervasive role it has consistently played in the lives of black people. W. E. B. DuBois poignantly captured this role in his timeless description of the Black Church:

> The Negro church of to-day is the social centre of Negro life in the United States, and the most char-

acteristic expression of African character. . . . Various organizations meet [in Negro church buildings]. . . . Considerable sums of money are collected and expended here, employment is found for the idle, strangers are introduced, news is disseminated and charity distributed. At the same time this social, intellectual, and economic centre is a religious centre of great power. . . . Back of [its] more formal religion, the Church often stands as a real conserver of morals, a strengthener of family life, and the final authority on what is Good and Right. Thus one can see in the Negro church to-day, reproduced in microcosm, all the great world from which the Negro is cut off by color-prejudice and social condition. (214–215)

Though written at the turn of the twentieth century, DuBois's description remains apt as the Black Church continues to greatly influence the social and religious life of black women and men. Given the centrality of the Black Church within the black community, it is especially important to consider the Black Church in relation to matters of sexuality.

The Black Community and Concerns of Sexuality

The disproportionately high incidence of teenage births and HIV/AIDS (human immunodeficiency virus/acquired immune defiency syndrome) cases provide two examples of why the Black Church must give considered attention to matters of sexuality. While the birthrate among black teenage women has shown a decline, it remains much higher than the birthrate for white teenage women. Moreover, the percentage of black children who were born to teenage mothers (22 percent) was twice as that of children born to white teenage mothers in 1996. These black babies of teenagers also had higher incidence of birth-related problems than the babies born to teenage mothers of whites or any other racial group.

The high rate of HIV/AIDS infection within the black community reflects another point of concern. While black people comprised about 12 percent of the U.S. population in 1998, they represented 45 percent of all new AIDS cases reported during that same year and 62 percent of all the new cases reported among women and children. Since 1995 blacks have constituted a larger percentage of new cases than any other racial or ethnic group. The annual rate of 49.8 percent cases of AIDS among black women in 1998 was three times higher than that of Hispanic women and twenty times higher than that of white women. The annual rate for black men was twice that of Hispanics and seven times higher than white men. Cases among black children under thirteen were sixteen times that of white children, and the death rate was consistently higher for black people in all categories. Given these alarming statistics in regard to HIV/AIDS rates as well as teenage births, coupled with the Black Church's historical role in the life of black community, the Black Church would be expected to be in the forefront in addressing these sexual matters. That, however, has not been the case.

Sexuality a Taboo Issue

The Black Church has been characteristically conservative if not insular and unprogressive when it comes to matters of sexuality. No community problem has exposed the Black Church's unproductive stance toward sexuality more than the HIV/AIDS crisis. Silence or condemnatory attitudes typically have reflected the Black Church's response to this disease. Despite the fact that black men, women, and children clearly have been disproportionately impacted by this disease, the Black Church as a whole has been reticent to become involved in HIV/AIDS ministries and concomitant "sex" education. The Black Church thus has gained a reputation for being slow to respond to this crisis.

While the Black Church's response no doubt attests to the black community's general aversion toward homosexuality (as many in the Black Church community erroneously labeled HIV/AIDS a "gay disease") more significantly, this response reflects the black community's general reluctance to engage any sexual issues. This very disinclination typifies the Black Church attitude toward sexuality.

Various scholars have characterized sexuality as a "taboo" subject for the Black Church. Cornel West says that historically black institutions such as families, schools, and churches have refused to "engage one fundamental issue: *black sexuality*. Instead, they [run] from it like the plague" (86). Paula Giddings observes that discussions of gender *and* sexuality are the "last taboo" in the black community (442). Emilie Townes makes a similar point when she notes that while the black community is sexually active, it is also "sexually repressed," that is, unable to speak honestly about matters of sexuality (*In a Blaze of Glory*, chapter 4). How, then, does one understand such an aversion to sexual discourse?

White Cultural Exploitation of Black Sexuality

The Black Church's tacit refusal to forthrightly engage in sexual discourse reflects in large measure a history of white cultural manipulation and exploitation of black sexuality and black bodies. In an effort to dehumanize black people, white culture—that which supports and secretes white racist hegemony in the United States—has systematically mocked black sexuality. It has done so by stereotypically characterizing lascivious and passionate or denuded and asexual beings. Specifically,

the woman has been cast as a Jezebel or mammy, while the black man has been portrayed as a mandingo buck or sambo. Such dehumanizing depictions, particularly the lecherous images, have served as justifications for rapacious and brutal attacks upon black bodies by white society. Therefore, from the antebellum through post-Reconstruction period in the United States, black women were routinely molested by white male rapists, and black men were regularly victims of mob lynching and castration. Neither black women nor men had effective legal recourse and/or societal protection from these sexually violent crimes. The specter of white cultural sexual stereotypes and their concomitant brutality continues to haunt black people. Black sexuality is consistently caricatured in various media. Racial/sexual stereotyping has also impacted black people's treatment in the justice system. Two prominent examples of the continuing impact of sexual stereotypes on black lives are the cases of Anita Hill and O. J. Simpson.

When Anita Hill bought sexual harassment charges against then Supreme Court nominee Clarence Thomas, she became for many the personification of the black Jezebel. The October 1991 Thomas/Hill hearings were rife with racially and sexually loaded clichés and conventions—some admittedly selfishly introduced by Thomas himself—yet none stood out more than the Jezebel image surrounding Anita Hill. Thomas portrayed her as a vengeful woman whose flirtations were spurned and as one who was angry because of his interest in lighter complexioned women (i.e., white women, such as his wife). After all was said and done, Hill's charges of sexual harassment did not stand a chance of ever being taken seriously. Thomas, a man born black, had successfully undermined her by providing the bait necessary for others (the all-white male Senate panel) to see Hill as the typical black Jezebel. Thomas shamefully exploited the white cultural stereotype imposed upon black women. By stereotyping Hill, he made her the villain. That she could have been a victim of sexual harassment became impossible to accept. According to the "logic" of white culture, Jezebel asks for whatever sexual treatment she receives, from harassment to rape.

The 1994 O. J. Simpson saga revealed the continued prevalence of the sexual stereotyping of black men. Ironically, prior to the media spectacle made of the O. J. Simpson case, Simpson had successfully navigated the white world of glitz and power, virtually transcending his blackness and becoming one with that world. Yet the moment he was charged with killing his former white wife, his blackness became an issue for white society. This was evidenced by the June 27, 1994, *Time* magazine cover that featured a decidedly darkened illustration of Simpson on the cover. This treatment was reminiscent of a photo of a black man imprisoned for rape, Willie Horton, used in the 1988 presidential campaign to derail the bid of Michael Dukakis to become president. Both images were meant to viscerally reinforce the white cultural image of black men as violent, raping brutes. Both the Anita Hill hearing and the O. J. Simpson trial served as grim reminders of the sexual politics of white hegemony in the United States. With a black woman and man as its pawns, white culture sought to confirm its notion that black people are sexually perverse beings who pose a severe threat to the sanctity and morality of the white world.

The persistent ubiquity of black sexual stereotypes has had a profound impact on the way that the black Church has approached sexuality. A history of having black sexuality exploited and used as a weapon to support black oppression has discouraged the Black Church from freely confronting sexual issues. That such discourse might only affirm the stereotype that black people are obsessed with sexual matters or harbor a deviant sexuality fosters black people's reticence to openly confront concerns of sexuality, regardless of the profound necessity for doing so. One black churchwoman's comment made to me epitomizes the Black Church response. She said, "For Blacks to discuss sexuality publicly is like eating watermelon in front of White people. All you do is confirm their images of you." Essentially, the intrusion of white culture upon black sexuality has interfered with the black community's ability, in the main, to freely engage sexual concerns and thus respond to social/sexual matters. Making this point, Paula Giddings says, "It is [African Americans'] historical experience that has shaped or perhaps more accurately, misshaped the sex/gender issues and discourse in our community" (442).

Some black scholars have portrayed the Black Church's refusal to engage in public discourse about sexuality as a form of black cultural resistance to the corrupting influences of white culture, a survival strategy against white attacks. Cornel West makes this point when he says that "struggling black institutions made a Faustian pact with White America: avoid any substantive engagement with black sexuality and your survival on the margins of American society is, at least, possible" (86). Regardless of the reasons behind it, the black community's posture of public silence in regard to sexuality has greatly limited the Black Church's effectiveness in dealing with significant issues for black life. Consequently, various voices have emerged from within the black community demanding that the implicit moratorium on forthrightly discussing sexual matters be lifted.

In the book *Sexuality and the Black Church* womanist theologian Kelly Brown Douglas challenged the Black Church to engage in a sexual discourse of resistance. Douglas argues that a sexual discourse of resistance has two central goals: to penetrate the sexual politics of the black community and to cultivate a life-enhancing approach to black sexuality within that community. While these goals suggest several tasks to be carried out, Douglas contends that two are most fundamental. The first is to expose the manifold impact white culture has had on black sexuality. This discourse would examine the numerous and insidious ways in which this culture has caricatured and exploited black sexuality and variously impacted black self-perceptions, black relationships, and/or black spirituality. The second fundamental task for a sexual discourse of resistance is to provide a view of sexuality that is more reflective of the black faith tradition. Douglas argues that the African worldviews that most informed the enslaved crafters of the black faith tradition were those that did not make a precise distinction between sacred and secular realities. The very notion of secularity, she notes, had no place in many African cultures. According to many African traditions, all that was of the world was of God. Every aspect of life represented an opportunity for the manifestation of the divine presence. Douglas suggests that because of their traditional belief in the inherent unity between sacred and secular, enslaved Africans were able to grasp the radicality of God's disclosure in Jesus. They were able to testify to Jesus as one who understood their tears and pain, as one who walked with them, talked with them, and understood their grief. Most important, this belief in the sacredness of all life, she argues, allowed the enslaved Africans to celebrate sexuality as a divine gift and opportunity rather than renounce it as sinful.

Douglas contends that the Black Church must engage a kind of sexual discourse of resistance that will call black people back to their African religious heritage, the heritage that fostered a view of human sexuality as divine and resisted a view casting the body and sexuality as cauldrons of evil.

Douglas concludes by further suggesting that a sexual discourse of resistance would demand a transformation in the way the Black Church has traditionally conducted itself on sexually related matters, especially in regard to women and nonheterosexual persons. Again calling the church back to a faith tradition that witnesses to a Jesus who sides with the marginalized, enslaved, and oppressed, a sexual discourse of resistance would clarify that for the Black Church to be sexist, homophobic, and/or heterosexist is for that church to betray an understanding of Christianity shaped by its African heritage and crafted during enslavement. Essentially, Douglas argues that a sexual discourse of resistance would provide the opportunity for the Black Church to effectively respond to the various crises that have negatively impacted black life, such as the aforementioned teenage birthrate and HIV/AIDS epidemic.

Also recognizing the urgency of the situation within the black community, other religious leaders have acted to end the silence surrounding sexuality. Most prominent has been the Black Church Initiative program sponsored by the Religious Coalition of Reproductive Choice (RCRC). The president and chief executive officer of RCRC is black Baptist minister Carlton Veazey. The Black Church Initiative (BCI) was developed by RCRC to encourage black religious leaders, lay and clergy, to address sexual issues as those issues impact the black community. Since 1997 BCI has sponsored an annual National Black Religious Summit on Sexuality. During this summit black clergy and laity from across the United States discuss various topics confronting black America such as teenage pregnancy, HIV/AIDS, male/female relationships, and domestic violence. National leaders such as former U.S. Surgeons General David Satcher and Joycelyn Elders have participated in the summits. They too have called upon the Black Church community to become proactive in addressing the sexual concerns within the black community. The 2000 summit drew a record number of participants and offered a separate program for youth in attendance. This summit also included for the first time the participation of young people from South Africa. BCI also sponsors regional and local conferences on sexuality throughout the year. Beyond the conferences, Black Church Initiative provides two faith-based curriculums to be used in local congregations. "Keeping It Real" is a nine-week curriculum designed specifically for youth. "Breaking the Silence" is another nine-week course of study developed for local Black Church congregations.

The Kelly Miller Smith Institute at Vanderbilt Divinity School (Nashville, Tennessee), under the leadership of the Reverend Forest Whitaker, has initiated programs with local black congregations on sexuality issues. Two-day conferences are regularly held for national black religious leaders and scholars to come together to discuss the theological and biblical mandate for engaging matters of sexuality.

While historically the Black Church has been introverted on matters of sexuality, the dawning of the twenty-first century reveals a changing disposition. Unsettled by disturbing trends within the black community, various segments of the community have introduced sexual discourse within the Black Church. This breakthrough in regard to frank and transformative discourse on sexuality indicates that the Black Church has taken the necessary first step toward becoming more responsive to sexually related concerns.

SOURCES: Kelly Brown Douglas, *Sexuality and the Black Church* (1999); W. E. B. DuBois, *The Souls of Black Folk* (1903); Paula Giddings, "The Last Taboo," in *Race-ing Justice, En-Gendering Power*, ed. Toni Morrison (1992); Cheryl Townsend Gilkes, "Some Folks Get Happy and Some Folks Don't: Diversity, Community, and African American Christian Spirituality," in *The Courage to Hope: From Black Suffering to Human Redemption*, ed. Quinton Hosford Dixie and Cornel West (1999); James Nelson, *Embodiment: An Approach to Sexuality and Christian Theology* (1978); Emilie Townes, *In a Blaze of Glory: Womanist Spirituality as Social Witness* (1995); and Cornel West, *Race Matters* (1993).

GIRLFRIEND THEOLOGY: ADOLESCENT GIRLS AND FAITH COMMUNITIES
Dori Grinenko Baker

GIRLFRIEND THEOLOGY IS a method of religious education that helps adult women translate tenets of feminist and liberation theologies to adolescent girls within faith communities. Girls are invited into religious practices that honor feminine imagery of God and help them voice their indigenous knowledge of the holy. It grows out of the impulse of religious feminists in the latter half of the twentieth century to explicitly impart the traditions, values, and epistemologies of feminist theologies to younger audiences.

The Emergent Concern for Adolescent Girls

Across cultures, the adolescent girl's journey to adulthood is often characterized by abuse, violence, exploitation, and more subtle demeaning factors. At certain moments within U.S. history, women concerned about girls saw religion as a primary resource in addressing these violations. However, adolescent girls were largely absent from much of the early work of feminists in religion in the 1970s and 1980s. Earlier generations of women had formed organizations such as the Young Women's Christian Association (YWCA) to improve living and working conditions for young women who fled to the cities during the Industrial Revolution. Born of the 1850s religious awakenings, the YWCA grew out of an alliance of Protestant women concerned about the physical and spiritual well-being of girls. In later decades, it engaged women and girls in addressing issues of equality and social justice, especially the elimination of racism and the provision of sex education for working-class girls. As the second wave of feminism crested, concern for the lives of adolescent girls shifted from the religious impetus of the YWCA to more secular fields such as education and psychology, where researchers began to paint a picture of the perilous journey girls traverse on the way to maturity. In time, this work attracted the attention of feminists with religious commitments who turned to faith communities as resources to support girls' healthy development.

In the early 1980s, Carol Gilligan brought women's

Girlfriend Theology is a method of religious education that draws on the vast resources of the Judeo-Christian heritage to help women engage in practices that support the flourishing of girls. Like many feminist theologies, it begins with women's autobiographical reflection. Akin to "homeplace" as described by womanists, grassroots retreats led by *mujerista* and Asian-feminist theologians, and white women's consciousness-raising groups in the 1970s, it requires the creation of safe, hospitable gatherings. © *Gale Zucker/ www.gzucker.com.*

psychological development into view by critiquing developmental theories as constructed solely from observations of men's lives. In a later work Gilligan and collaborator Lyn Mikel Brown began to draw attention to the particular pitfalls confronting girls coming of age after the women's liberation movement of the 1970s. Especially noteworthy was the observation that formerly outspoken girls began to silence their inner selves in order to appear "nice and kind" as adolescence approached (Gilligan and Brown, 53). This dynamic was posited as a potential precursor to adult women's depression and, at the very least, a culturally approved thwarting of fulfillment of girls' and women's lives. Research supported by the American Association of Uni-

versity Women documented ways in which the classroom operated to subtly hinder girls' development, such as encouraging girls to hide their intelligence in mixed-gender settings and to fail to excel in typically male-dominated subjects like math.

The concern over adolescent girls became popularized with the 1996 publication of the bestseller *Reviving Ophelia: Saving the Selves of Adolescent Girls.* Reflecting on her practice as a clinical psychologist, author Mary Pipher detailed the demise of girls in their early teens, pointing to increase in drug and alcohol abuse, self-inflicted wounds known as cutting, eating disorders, and other harmful ways girls resist dominant culture. Pipher only briefly touched on resources of faith and spirituality as she outlined potential remedies for a "girl-poisoning" culture. Claiming that girls were only being heard through the filter of adult interpretation, a teen by the name of Sara Shandler published *Ophelia Speaks* (1999) in which girls spoke back to the adult world in unfiltered, first-person narratives about their lives from their particular social locations. Although examples of girls' bravery and healthy forms of resistance surfaced, these adolescent voices confirmed much of the research portraying female adolescence as a minefield laden with toxic forces such as eating disorders, rape, sexually transmitted disease, violence, and loss.

An accurate picture of girls' adolescent life had not yet emerged, however. These works, while careful to analyze gender issues, were not cognizant of race and class as factors that multiply oppression. Most of the research was done in populations of white, middle-class girls, belying the reality that other forces such as poverty and racism create a completely different set of obstacles for girls of color or those from working-class backgrounds. To some African American women, research conclusions about silencing and losing voice appeared askew. As African American educator Beverly Jean Smith writes, psychological research on women leaves out the experiences she had as a young woman, which taught her not to be passive but to resist oppressive forces of dominant culture. Later work addressed this gap, showing how girls of color and working-class white girls are more likely to risk confrontation and speak out in an effort to construct their emerging identities. This resilience was underscored by Lyn Mikel Brown's study of working-class white girls that showed girls actively resisting dominant cultural norms of femininity. Despite many examples of healthy resistance, harmful patterns of resistance among girls of color, of immigrant status, and of working-lower-class backgrounds emerged as well. The white standard of beauty marketed through pervasive media images, poor girls' lack of hope for access to meaningful employment, and other characteristics of dominant North American culture operate to skew girls' visions of themselves, thus increasing the burdens of maturing.

These writings added divergent meanings to popularized notions of girls' development. Supporting these multiple layers of meaning were the voices of women of color writing within the religious academy, who began to distinguish themselves from white feminist theologians with the emergence of womanist thought in the early 1980s. Within womanist writings, adolescent girls emerge as agents shaping identities of resistance and resilience on the way to adult spirituality. Womanists wove autobiography into their theory as a basis for theological reflection. In so doing, they pointed to ways in which their mothers, aunts, and other-mothers intervened on behalf of their wholeness as they came of age in a racist and patriarchal world. The result was the introduction of concern about adolescent girls into women's religious thought. For women of color, spiritual identities were often fashioned in the midst of struggles to secure physical and emotional needs and were thus inseparable from material and relational surroundings. By reflecting on this dynamic, womanists provided a model of women taking seriously the embodied spiritual needs of adolescent girls.

Fashioning a Feminist Theological Response

Alerted by this growing body of literature, feminist women in faith communities began to consider more explicitly the needs of contemporary girls in their midst. These generations of young women were coming of age in a church where some things had changed: Women's voices spoke from the pulpit and lectern; when used, inclusive language chipped away at the centuries of patriarchal imagery contained in Christian tradition; feminine imagery for God occasionally entered mainstream liturgy; and rituals created for and by women began to provide alternative religious experiences. But the didactic content of the mainline church had rarely been altered to equip girls with the tools of feminist consciousness. In what ways was the church as an institution continuing to impart patriarchal ways of knowing and experiencing God to girls? What interventions would allow girls to confront patriarchal portions of the Judeo-Christian heritage even as they redeemed other portions of it to confront patriarchy in society at large? In answer to questions such as these, feminists with religious commitments began to fill in gaps left by the vast psychological literature on girls' lives.

In the field of practical theology, feminists began to fashion a theological response to the social science research on girls' development and to call on churches to explicitly support girls' development. Carol Lakey Hess drew attention to the importance of transforming Christian community so that it might aid in the moral development of girls and women. Hess pointed out that dominant theologies of self-sacrifice thwart the development of women by negating necessary self-assertion. Reflecting on her own adolescent struggles with anorexia nervosa, Hess posited that eating disorders emerge out of a girl's attempt to carve out a separate self in the midst of an identity-repressing environment. Hess envisioned churches in which women retrieve the hidden texts of the faith tradition to provide alternative understanding of the self in relation to God and others. Thus, rather than colluding with sexist culture, churches might instead become alternate spaces that would affirm and challenge girls as they grow into adult voice. Through careful retrieval of biblical texts, Hess argued, communities of faith are poised to help foster healthy development in girls and women, but she stopped short of offering practical means of achieving that end.

Patricia Davis's work on counseling adolescent girls provided a first attempt at assessing the particularities of spiritual health for adolescent girls and guiding pastoral caregivers in substantive differences between girls' and boys' development. In a subsequent work, Davis reported the results of qualitative research with more than 100 girls across the United States. She urged adults in churches to listen to girls' pleas to "drop the niceness code" and courageously listen to their difficult questions around violence, financial problems, and sexuality. She argued that girls want adult woman role models who will embody spirituality and relationship styles that reveal integrity between true emotions and actions.

Others echoed the call for churches to engage in mentoring relationships and rites of passage programs for girls. Positing church as a "womb of hope," Evelyn Parker reflected on her life as an African American teen coming of age in rural Mississippi during the civil rights movement (1).

The church was a place that helped African American youth claim their role in God's covenant and encouraged human flourishing for all people. Armed with this formative experience, Parker investigated themes of loyalty that surfaced in the lives of the African American girl gang members she interviewed. Parker views contemporary girls' desire for loyalty through the lens of exemplary leaders in the civil rights movement whose lives embodied loyalty. The life of Daisy Bates, who strategized for the safety of a group of teens known as the Little Rock Nine through the turbulent events surrounding racial integration, becomes a model for the church as nurturing, protecting community in the midst of struggles against oppression. Parker envisions girls receiving protection and nurture from communities of faith, even as they struggle to make sense of the evils of racism and learn to resist it. In an ongoing work, Parker is editing a volume of essays investigating the spirituality of girls through the lens of race, class, and gender. Written by Native American, Latina, Asian, African American, and white feminist authors, this will be the first attempt to hear voices from girls in diverse settings in U.S. culture talk about their experiences of God through the thick description of critical ethnography.

The feminist theologians described above realized that psychological research calling attention to the lives of girls was missing a critical component. If girls internalize voices that limit their potential to be active agents forming and transforming their world, they are living less than human lives. This has not only psychological, emotional, and political implications but religious implications as well. A secular framework alone is not adequate to foster healthy development of girls. Faith traditions bring vital resources to the task of getting girls across the threshold of adolescence. These vital resources include the hidden strands of women's stories in Judeo-Christian scripture and tradition; the collected wisdom of women's stories of emancipation from various homelands and cultural contexts; and communities of living women engaged in their own feminist becoming who are willing to enter into mentoring circles with younger women. Girls coming of age in a historical era giving them more freedom than ever to construct their ways of being in the world stand to benefit from these resources. In the late 1990s, the time was ripe for feminist theologies to be contextualized to adolescent worlds.

Transforming Concern into Practice

Girlfriend Theology is one method of religious education that draws on the vast resources of the Judeo-Christian heritage to help women engage in practices that support the flourishing of girls. Like many feminist theologies, Girlfriend Theology begins with women's autobiographical reflection. Akin to "homeplace" as described by womanists, grassroots retreats led by *mujerista* and Asian feminist theologians, and white women's consciousness-raising groups of the United States in the 1970s, it requires the creation of safe, hospitable gatherings. In these spaces, the stories of girls are told, heard, honored, and reflected upon. Participants view those stories in light of the Judeo-Christian canon, the often hidden tradition of faithful women mystics and saints, the legends of women whose stories have been only scantily recorded, and the wider corpus of texts that shape the postmodern world.

Girlfriend Theology is a four-step method that begins with a person telling a story from her life to a group of four or five others, one of whom is a facilitator with theological or pastoral training. In advance of each session the facilitator has prompted the storyteller to prepare, in writing, a story to be read aloud. The stories vary widely in content and intensity. They reflect diversity of life experience and might be about anything: the suicide of a friend, the end of a relationship, an experience of abuse, or a shining moment when all is right with the world. The group listens as the prepared story is read aloud. The group then reflects upon the story in two ways, "experience near" and "experience distant" (Burbank, 151).

During experience near, group members share feelings and associations that the story evoked in them. Related stories and memories surface as the women and girls begin to engage the story from their own life experiences. Embodied clues such as tears, deep sighs, changes in breathing, or goose bumps lead to expression of feelings. Participants ask and answer questions as they tease out of the story the range of emotions and associations it suggests. Central symbols, themes, or images may arise. They are named, and the process then moves to its third step, experience distant.

During experience distant, conversation turns explicitly to themes, theological concepts, and issues embodied in the story. Participants may voice related stories from scripture or myth, or they might respond to the facilitator's prompting question, "Where is God present (or absent) in this story?" Although this method grew out of a Christian context, it has proven fruitful in interfaith dialogue when the facilitator is careful to explicitly name the conversation as interfaith and use language welcoming of diverse religious traditions. During this part of the method, the adult women give priority to the voices of girls, jumping in occasionally to underline theological insights the girls articulate. Often teachable moments arise when a woman, steeped in feminist theological understanding, is able to offer a new way of thinking about God for the younger women to test, accept, or reject. Likewise, the girls often become the teachers, allowing the adults to entertain fresh perspectives through the lens of adolescent experience. As the girls and women play with the story and its accompanying images, they arrive at new understandings about their lives in connection to the larger faith story. Classic religious themes such as grace, forgiveness, and prayer come into focus and are reinterpreted in light of the story's context and the group's reflection on it.

"Going Forth" is the final stage of the process. Here participants wonder about how this story and its interpretations might change their ongoing Christian practice. The aim of the process is not to end with grand conclusions but to have each participant leave with her own awareness or set of conclusions, some of which may be communally agreed upon and some of which may be individual. The final step of naming a potential change completes an action/reflection educational model and helps reinforce portions of the story/conversation that stood out as particularly meaningful.

Four key concepts undergird this method and provide guides for the adult women who participate. The first is Nelle Morton's concept of "hearing into speech." Morton describes a moment in her educational career when a student brought her to a new understanding of hearing. Several days into a workshop that spanned the course of a week, a reserved woman hesitantly began to speak, relating a painful story. "No one interrupted her. No one rushed to comfort her. No one cut her experience short. We simply sat. We sat in powerful silence. The women clustered about the weeping one went with her to the deepest part of her life as if something so sacred was taking place they [dare] not withdraw their presence or mar its visibility." Afterward, when the

woman described this experience, she said, "You heard me to my own story. You heard me to my own speech." Morton relates the recurrence of such liminal moments on different occasions where women gathered to accompany one another "into the depths . . . where sound is born." She tells of a "depth hearing that takes place before speaking—a hearing that is more than acute listening. A hearing that is a direct transitive verb that evokes speech—new speech that has never been spoken before. The woman . . . had indeed been heard to her own speech" (Morton, 205–206).

Morton goes on to affirm, "Hearing to speech is political. Hearing to speech is never one-sided. Once a person is heard to speech she becomes a hearing person" (206). A commitment to this kind of depth hearing, whenever it is possible, is foundational to Girlfriend Theology. When women and girls gather to hear each other's stories, they enter a space where they learn to sit in powerful silence and listen in ways that evoke new speech. Naming this as sacred space affirms God's presence in the act of holy listening. Being called forth into speech is not a solitary act of personal devotion but a political one—it names a new reality and creates a community with the potential to effect change. This community resembles the "community of resistance" described by Sharon D. Welch. Being grounded in a community of resistance, Welch writes, enables and sustains transcendence of the multiple oppressions that cripple human life. Stories of renewal and transformation written to "save ourselves" emerge from such communities of resistance (Welch, 18). In Girlfriend Theology, women and girls tell stories and hear one another to speech. These stories and this speech hold potential transformation for the speaker, the hearers, and the world.

The second concept informing Girlfriend Theology is Carol Lee Flinders's understanding of women's usable past. Flinders writes that as an indirect response to her awareness of deeply ingrained misogyny she began to pull together for herself a "body of evidence and imagery" to support her belief in feminine strength and beauty (Flinders, 45). This process crosses borders of art and religion, as girls deprived of relevant faith traditions find in literature an "adequate substitute for religion" (Norris, xvii). Flinders maintains that each woman of feminist consciousness has a usable past. Some of it is highly individual and particular, but some of it is shared among communities of mutuality and support. This usable past is a body of evidence and imagery, gleaned from poetry, art, scripture, quilts, dance, and other sources. It is this body of evidence that Girlfriend Theology invites into the conversation, sometimes introduced by the adults, sometimes by the girls, who are themselves immersed in the process of building their usable pasts. The "experience near" step of the Girlfriend Theology method stays close to the lived experiences of individual participants. It focuses on feelings, memories, and real-life encounters. The "experience distant" step, however, turns directly toward stories and images. As adults enter conversations with girls, no one is a silent partner. Adults have something to offer girls—a usable past girls hunger to explore but for which they may not know how to ask. The usable past is like a treasure chests full of images and stories giving girls and women reason to rejoice that they are female. The usable past thus becomes an essential resource in the feminist education of girls.

The third guide for Girlfriend Theology is the ancient practice of female clusters, reinterpreted as mentoring circles. Historian Gerda Lerner traces the first written documentation of an individual woman's life to the seventh century c.e. when the beginning of a long tradition of "sister books" emerged. In these books, younger nuns paid homage to their predecessors through written biographies. This could not have happened, Gerner argues, without female clusters—pockets of history where women's intellectual activity flourished, despite patriarchy. For women to think, to write, and to enter the marketplace of ideas, female audience was required. Women mystics and cloistered nuns were the first to achieve that audience. It is no accident that these female clusters supporting women of notoriety were often religious: During many different historical moments, the argument for women's equality often rested on theological and biblical grounds. Evidence of women thinking, writing, and publishing throughout history—work done against formidable odds and in order to claim their worth and autonomy—is available to contemporary women as a result of cumulative feminist movements across history and cultures. A primary goal of those movements has been to retrieve and reinterpret these hidden strains of women's thought and activity—to make of it a usable past. Armed with that usable past, women of today have potential for what women of past generations only sporadically achieved: the ability to move from private realms to transform public spheres. Female clusters on the fringes of the church became centers for the flourishing of women's theological capacities. From that fringe, they contributed to the slow but inevitable building of voices that could finally be heard at the centers of power and authority. Women in those female clusters were not all adults. Girls entered convents, cloisters, and monasteries at young ages. Although they may be difficult to hear, girls' voices entered that chorus as well.

Contemporary mentoring circles revive and reinterpret the ancient tradition of female clusters. In mentoring circles, adults share responsibility with each other and with the girls for the relationships that form and the content of the sessions. Mentoring circles are mutual and reciprocal, acknowledging that women need the companionship and insight of girls as much as girls need the companionship and insight of women. The life story that each participant brings determines the content of the conversations. As girls and women take turns bringing their stories, they take turns setting the agenda. In mentoring circles, adults are not trying to fix adolescent problems. Instead, they are willing to open the texts of their lives as potential windows for cross-generational conversation and reciprocal transformation.

If, as psychologists of women's experience maintain, North American culture sometimes silences girls and marginalizes their existence, Girlfriend Theology faithfully addresses the silence and marginalization with potential for healthy resistance. It invites girls to tell the stories of their lives out loud to a circle of mentoring friends within a Christian community. It is a contemporary expression of the ancient Christian practice of testimony, providing opportunity for girls to seek, articulate, and share the sacred truths of their lives as they come of age. At heart, it is a way of saving hidden, neglected, and silenced testimonies. In a communal process, a person finds a portion of her testimony, practices it within a safe space, harvests it for meaning, and returns to lived experience with that reflected-upon story as a new companion on the journey.

In the decade since its inception, Girlfriend Theology has been practiced with diverse communities of girls and women in churches, YWCAs, interfaith retreats, denominational workshops, and ad hoc faith communities, such as seminary-hosted summer youth academies. The themes that repeatedly arise serve as a corrective to traditional neo-Orthodox depictions of God. Seven particular theological assertions bear reporting, as they reflect girls and women constructing theology together. Those assertions include: First, God is mysteriously omnipresent but not magically omnipotent. Although humans cannot explain it, God is at work within human tragedies to create healing potential. God may not fix things, but neither does God abandon us. Second, God feels our pain and cries with us. Third, we have direct access to God through our bodies. Fourth, our lives are like fifth gospels, sacred texts through which, with the help of communities of accountability, God continues to reveal God's self. Fifth, we go to church to "share God, not find God" (Walker, 176). Religious institutions affirm our hunches about God but do not usually introduce us to God for the first time. Sixth, God is most fully alive or incarnated in us when our eyes are open to the pain of others. And seventh, church, at its best, is a community of compassion, a resource in our healing, and a potential agent of change in the world.

In summary, Girlfriend Theology fashions a feminist theological response to the psychological literature drawing attention to the sometimes perilous journey adolescent girls traverse on the way to adulthood. It uses the collected wisdom of women's stories of emancipation from various homelands and cultural contexts. This usable past enters conversation with stories of contemporary girls' lives and results in hearing into speech the theological voice of girls. Mentoring circles reminiscent of ancient female clusters live out feminist commitments in both form and content, thus transforming faith communities so that they might become "wombs of hope" nurturing the healthy development of adolescent girls.

SOURCES: Important works that map the intricacies of girls' relational lives include Carol Gilligan's *In a Different Voice* (1982) and her collaboration with Lyn Mikel Brown, *Meeting at the Crossroads* (1992). The collection *Women, Girls and Psychotherapy* (1991), ed. Carol Gilligan, Annie Rogers, and Deborah Tolman, widens earlier work to include discussions of race and ethnicity. Especially important is Beverly Jean Smith's article "Raising a Resister," found in that collection. Mary Pipher's book *Reviving Ophelia: Saving the Selves of Adolescent Girls* (1996) and Sara Shandler's collection *Ophelia Speaks* (1999) provide narrative accounts of the oppressive forces affecting adolescent girls in the late twentieth century. Two stud-

ies by the American Association of University Women, *Girls in the Middle* (1996) and *How Schools Shortchange Girls* (1995), bring to light the world girls negotiate in school. Three works deal specifically with the spiritual development of adolescent girls. They are Patricia Davis's *Beyond Nice* (2001), Carol Lakey Hess's *Caretakers of Our Common House* (1997), and Evelyn L. Parker's *Trouble Don't Last Always* (2003). Several works of feminist theology, especially those written by women of color, can be extrapolated to inform those who attend to the spiritual lives of adolescent girls. Among them are Carol Lee Flinders's *At the Root of This Longing* (1998), bell hooks's *Yearning* (1990), Ada María Isasi-Díaz's *En la Lucha/In the Struggle* (1993), and Chung Hyun Kyung's *Struggle to Be the Sun Again* (1990). The work of Beth Burbank, especially her article "Reflecting on Stories as a Way of Doing Theology in Clinical Pastoral Education" in *Journal of Supervision and Training in Ministry* (9 [1987]: 147–157) is foundational to the method of Girlfriend Theology. Nelle Morton's *The Journey Is Home* (1985), Gerda Lerner's *The Creation of Feminist Consciousness* (1993), Alice Walker's *The Color Purple* (1982), and Sharon D. Welch's *A Feminist Ethic of Risk* (1990) also inform the method. See also Kathleen Norris, *The Cloister Walk* (1996); and Dori Grinenko Baker, *Doing Girlfriend Theology: God-Talk with Young Women* (2005).

Index to Entries

African Americans: conversion to Christianity, 226–227; conversion to Islam, 622; education of, 255, 257; as evangelicals, 451–452; Great Migration of, 165–166; healing in nineteenth-century, 1261; intermarriage with Native Americans, 114; Lutheran Church and, 310–311; in Pentecostal denomination, 432; Protestantism and, 240–241; Puritan Christianity and, 232; settlements of, 1065; women: Catholic, 160–168; denominations for, 250–262; Muslims, 607, 608–615, *610*; as slaves, 231; in United Church of Christ, 370–371; women's club movement in, *865*; women's ordination and denominations, 945–946

African Caribbean religions: Christian thought and, 121; traditions in, 116; women's roles in, 122–123

African immigrants, 111, 112, 115

African Methodist Episcopal (AME) Church, 253, 262, 321, 431, 437, 451; hymnbooks of, 997; ordination of women in, 945; women leaders in, 839, 968, 1266, 1270

African Methodist Episcopal Zion (AMEZ) Church, 255, 258, 262, 433, 868, 1167; Daughters of Conference of, 258; hymnbooks of, 997; women leaders in, 969; Women's Home and Foreign Missionary Society in, 839

African Methodists, missionaries and, 837

African Mission School, 272

African Orthodox Church, 1077

The African Queen (film), 1014–1015

African Universal Church and Commercial League, 1081

African women, introduction into Caribbean region, 116

African-derived religions, 117–119; feminine conceptions of divine in, 119–121; as Obeah, 119

Afro-American Arts Institute, 995

Afro-Brazilian religion, 1165

Afro-Carribean religion, 1165

Afrocentricity, 1171–1172

Afro-Christian tradition, 117

Afshar, Haleh, 606

After Patriarchy: Feminist Transformation in World Religion (Gross), 40

Agassiz, Elizabeth Cabot Cary, 192

The Age of Innocence (Wharton), 1009

Age of Reform, 1021

Aglow International, 1263

Agnes of God (film), 1014

Agnes Scott College (Georgia), 917, 922

Agnes Whistling Elk, 103

Agnew, Mary, 782

Agudas N'Shei U'bnos Chabad (Organization of Women and Daughters of Chabad), 562–564

Aguilar, Grace, 898

Agunah, Inc., 587

Agus, Arlene, 1221

Ahlstrom, Sydney, 738

Ahmadiyyah movement, 611–612, 614

Ahmed, Gulam, 612

Ahmed, Leila, 606

Aidala, Angela, 788

AIDS, 52, 1093

Aitken, Robert, 641, 642

Ajiv, 690

Akers, Doris, 990

Alabama Lutheran Academy, 316

Alabama Union State, 999

Alabaster Box, 995

An Alarm Sounded to Prepare the Inhabitants of the World to Meet the Lord in the Way of His Judgements (Bowers), 233

Alberni Indian Girls Home, 348

Albrecht, Gloria, 57

Alcoholics Anonymous, 1236

Alcott, Bronson, 636

Alcott, Louisa May, 976, 1007–1008

Alemany, Bishop Joseph, 876

ALEPH: Alliance for Jewish Renewal, 797–798, 799, 802, 803

Alexander, Agnes, 779, 780, 786

Alexander, Cecil Frances, 455

Alexander, Lillian Hurt, 358

Alexander, Mary, 234

Alexander, Mrs. Cecil Francis, 975

Alexander VI (Pope), 94

Alexandra House (Vancouver), 1068

Ali, Mirza Husayn, 776

Ali, Noble Drew, 611, 613

Ali, Pearl, 611

Ali Baba and the Forty Thieves (film), 1015

Alicéa, Elisa, 481

Alimboyoguen, Sally, 184

Aliquot, Marie-Jeane, 165

All Nations Pentecostal Church, 258

All of Us: Beset by Birth, Decay and Death (Vihara), 650

All Peoples Mission, 1067

All Saints' Day, 171

All Souls' Day, 171

All the Way Home (Pride), 893

All We're Meant to Be: A Biblical Approach to Women's Liberation (Hardesty and Scanzoni), 16, 469, 472, 474

Allah's Temple of Islam, 749

Allebach, Ann J., 268

Allegany Franciscan Sisters, 844

Allen, Ethan Otis, 428

Allen, Paula Gunn, 19, 90, 110, 1111

Allen, Prudence, 788

Allen, Richard, 945, 987, 997, 998

Allen Street Methodist Episcopal Church (New York City), 322

Alliance for Progress, 847

Alliance of Unitarian and Other Liberal Christian Women, 388

Allin, John, 278

Allione, Tsultrim, *655,* 656

Allison, Margaret, 994

Alone in His Presence (album), 995

Aloysius, Sister, 161

Alpern, Sara, 70

Alpert, Rebecca, 43, 553, 1215, *1216,* 1218–1219, 1222, 1225

Alpert, Richard, 646

Alpha and Omega Pentecostal Church of America, 433

Alphabet raps, 768

An Alphabetical Compendium of the Various Sects (Adams), 636

Alphonsa, Mary, *188,* 191

Alredge-Clanton, Jann, 986

Alsdurf, James, 471

Altar Guilds, 283
Altar Society, 189
Alternative faith traditions, interfaith marriage and, 1273
Alternative medicine, 1265
Altgeld, John, 861
Altner, Joyce, 70
Alumni Association of Wycliffe College, 827
Alvare, Helen, 1106
Alverno College (Michigan), 888
Amana, Iowa, 708
Amana Inspirationists, 714
Amatu'l-Baha, 779, 784
Ambivalence, women's creative use of, 49
AME Zion Hymnal, 997
AMEC Bicentennial Hymnal, 997
American, Sadie, 1120
American Academy of Religion (AAR), 3, 59, 604, 816, 1169
American and Foreign Anti-Slavery Reporter, 1043
American and Foreign Anti-Slavery Society, 334
American Anti-Slavery Society, 334, 1044
American Association of Spiritualists, 775
American Association of University Graduates, 608
American Association of University Women (AAUW), 936, 1305
American Baptist Churches/USA, 286, 483
American Baptist Convention, 286; women leaders in, 15
American Baptist Home Mission Society, 290
American Baptist Woman's Home Missionary Society, 837
American Baptist Women in Ministry, 294
American Bible Society, 979
American Board of Commissioners for Foreign Missions (ABCFM), 346, 372–373, 374
American Buddhism, 710
American Catholic Women Missionaries, 843–850
American Catholics for African Americans, 844
American Christian Missionary Society, 301, 302
American Colonization Society, 256, 370
American Council for Jerusalem, 608
The American Experience (series), 989
American Family Forum, 1299
American Federation of Catholic Societies (AFCS), 843
American Federation of Jewish Women, 1090
American Federation of Labor, 130
American feminism, role of religion in, 13
American films, 1010–1017; Bible in, 1012–1014; religion, race, and ethnicity in, 1015–1016; social reform and censorship in, 1010–1012; women as religious leaders in, 1014–1015; women behind the camera in, 1016–1017
American Friend, 338
American Friends Service Committee (AFSC), 338–339, 1033, 1036
American Indian Movement (AIM), 1264
American Indians: appropriation of religious traditions, 102–109; children: in adoptive homes, 98–99; boarding schools for, 97–102, 99; in foster care, 98–99; hygiene and, 100; medical neglect and starvation of, 99–100; Church of England and, 270; conversion of, to Christianity, 1026; creation stories of, 83–89, 90; Episcopal women and, 275; gendered images in, 26; organization into Dorcas Societies, 245; removal of, 114–115; resistance by, 100–101;

treatment of, 1026–1027; women: Christian colonization and, 91–92; Christianity and, 89–97; response of, to Christianity, 96–97; status of, prior to Christianity, 90–91
American Jewish Committee (Chicago), 1280
American Legion, 1054
American Lutheran Church (ALC), 311, 315, 317
American Lutheran Church Women, 318
American Lutheran Church Women Missionary Federation, 313
American Mass Program, 998
American Methodism, 319, 320
American Missionary Association (AMA), 370–371, 372, 837
American Missionary Association of the United Church Board for Homeland Ministries, 503
American Peace Society, 1050–1051, 1053
American Protective Association, 128, 155
American Protestant Women in World Mission (Beaver), 346
American Reform movement, 533, 543
American Religious Identification Survey (ARIS), 1271–1272
American Revolution, 242
American School Peace League, 1053
American Sisters of Charity, 152
American Society of Muslims, 752
American Sunday School Association, 909
American Sunday School Union, 979, 983
American Telugu Association (ATA), 660
American Tract Society, 979
American Unitarian Association, 387
American Vajrayana, 657
American War Cry, 410, 412
American Woman Suffrage Association, 14
American Women for Peace (AWP), 1056
American-Arab Anti-Discrimination Committee, 608
Americanist Controversy, 158
Americanization, 31; films on, 1015–1016
Americans for Israel and Torah (AMIT), 560, 1125–1126
America's evangelical women, 447–457
America's Freedom of Religion Act, 681
Ames, Jessie Daniel, 1034
Amish, 262, 263, 269; in Colonial Pennsylvania, 230; families of, 264; in Mid-Atlantic colonies, 231
Amistad Committee, 1043
Amistad incident, 1042–1043
AMIT Women, 559, 566, 1125
Amritanandamayi, 661, 664
An Appeal for the Indians (Child), 1026
An Appeal in Favor of That Class of Americans Called Africans (Child), 1038
An Appeal to the Christian Women of the South (Grimké), 1044
An Appeal to the Coloured Citizens of the World (Walker), 1042
Anabaptists, 266–267, 707; belief in adult baptism, 232; in Colonial Pennsylvania, 230; institutional roles of, 268–269; migration of, 264–265; nonconformity of, 265–266; opposition to slavery, 1039; pacifism and, 266–267, 1050; "Quiet in the Land," 267–268; religious beliefs and historic background, 263–264; women of, 262–269
Anandamayi Ma, 30
Ancient One, 83, 85

Andal (poet), 664

Anders, Anna Rosina, 234

Anderson, Adisa, 1016

Anderson, June, 1287

Anderson, Myrtle, 1013

Anderson, Rachel, 611

Anderson, Robert, 992

Anderson, Robert Mapes, 402

Anderson, Tenshin Reb, 643

Anderson, Victor, 815

Andolsen, Barbara, 58

Andover Newton Theological Seminary, 1269

Andrews, Barbara, 317

Andrews, Edward G., 325

Andrews, Fanny Fern, 1053

Andrews, Inez, 992, 993

Andrews, Jedediah, 235

Andrews, Lynn, 103, 106

Androcentrism, 5–6, 7, 8, 39, 931; bias and, 41; Buddhism and, 11; as model of humanity, 3–4, 5; presuppositions in, 7; recordkeeping practices and, 5

Androgynous deity, 13, 711–712

Anekantvada, Jain principle of, 692–693

Angelic Gospel Singers, 994

Angelines, 212

Angier, Mary, 221

Anglican Church Women's Association, 283

Anglican method, 239

Anglican Women's Training College, 283, 829

Anglicans: in Canada, 217, 279–285; Catholicism and, 221; in Colonial New England, 226; deaconess program and, 831; differences between New Light Presbyterians and Orthodox, 239; infant baptism for, 232; ordination of women and, 1288; perception of, as Loyalists, 228; slaves as, 240. *See also* Church of England

Angyo, Sandra Jisshu, 1094

Animism, 185, 810

Anishnaabe (Ojibwe) people, 83

Annan, Kofi, 1108

Annunciation, 1171

Anointed Pace Sisters, 994

Ansa, Tina McElroy, 1167

Anshe Emeth, 533

Antebellum period: Episcopalians in, 272; laywomen in, 149–150; reforms in, 1021

Anthems, 995–996; contemporary hymns and, 995–996

Anthony, Susan B., 14, 289, 391, 722, 744, 839, 1024–1025, 1051, 1266

Anthony, Susan B. Coven (Los Angeles), 19, 815

Anthropology: of religion, 9; theological, 527–528

Anthropomorphic Figurines of Predynastic Egypt and Neolithic Crete with Comparative Material from the Prehistoric Near East and Greece (Ucko), 1204

Anti-Defamation League, 1277

Antifeminism, 21–23; Catholic women and, 200, 203–205

Anti-Judaism in Feminist Religious Writings (Kellerbach), 1282

Antinomianism, 224, 940

Antioch College, 882

Antiochian Women, 509

Anti-Saloon League, 158

Anti-Semitism, 557; feminism and, 595–597; Judaism and, 588–597, *593*; racialization of, 591–594; sexism and, 21

Anti-Slavery Convention of American Women (1837), 334, 1038, 1045–1047

Antislavery movement. *See* Abolitionist movement

Anti-Slavery Standard, 1047, 1051

Antisuffragists, 158

Antiwar movement, 1201

Anway, Carol Anderson, 731

Anzaldúa, Gloria, 489, 1140, 1198

Aonetta, Marie, 145

Aoyama, Shundo, 645

Apocalypse Now and Then: A Feminist Guide to the End of the World (Keller), 1180

Apocryphal/Deuterocanonical Books, 42

Apolinar Zapata, Maria, 494

Apolinaris, Yamina, 482

Apostolic Assembly of the Faith in Christ Jesus, 493

The Apostolic Faith, 398

Apostolic Faith Churches of God, 438

Apostolic succession, 947

An Appeal to Christian Women of the South, 334

Aquarian Minyan, 799

Aquinas Institute of Theology, 928

Aquino, María Pilar, 20, 1196, 1197–1198

Arabian Nights (film), 1015

Aranoff, Susan, 1228

Arbella, 223

Arbour, Frances, 1146

Arcane School, 762, 763

Archbishops' Western Canada Fund, 284

Archdeacon, John, 878

Archetypes, 66

Archibald, Adella, 345

Archios Mizrachi, 559

Arens, A. J., 757

Argue, Zelma, 403

Arians, 250

Arirao, Vickie, 185

Armenian Apostolic Church, Oriental Orthodox traditions and, ordination of women and, 520–523

Armenian Congregationalists, 372

Armer, Elizabeth, 876

Armer, Robert, 876

Arminian Magazine, 320

Armstrong, Alice, 293

Armstrong, Annie, 288, 289, 293

Armstrong, Annie, Easter Offering for Home Missions, 288, 291

Armstrong, Hannah Maria Norris, 287, 288

Armstrong, Louis, 167

Armstrong, Vanessa Bell, 260

Arnoul, Nadine, 515

Arnson, Pauline, 730

Aron, Isa, 905

Asatru, 810

Asbaje, Pedro Manuel de, 137

Asbury, Francis, 320

Asceticism, 29

Asch, Mrs. Sholem, 589

Beecher, Catharine Esther, 35, 452, 890, 913, 1021–1025, 1039, 1044, 1045
Beecher, Henry Ward, 14, 913, 977
Beecher, Lyman, 151, 890, 976, 977, 1039
Beechick, Ruth, 893
Beginning Anew: A Woman's Companion to the High Holy Days, 1226
Behr-Sigel, Elisabeth, *510*, 512, 513, 514, 515, 516, 525, 528
Beijing Women's Summit, 619
Being Bodies: Buddhist Women on the Paradox of Embodiment (Friedman), 1095
Being church, 1243
Being Nobody, Going Nowhere (Vihara), 650
Being with Dying (Halifax), 1096
Beissel, Conrad, 231, 234, 235, 707
Beit Shekhinah, 799
Bel Canto Foundation, 167
Belgic Confession, 342
Bell, Mary, 1067
Bellamy, Edward, 709
Belloc, Hilaire, 195
The Bells of St. Mary's (film), 1014
Belonick, Deborah, 524
Beloved (Morrison), 1172
Benderly, Samson, 901–902
Benderly girls, 902
Bendroth, Margaret Lamberts, 456
Benedictines, 154, 707; Swiss, 153
Benedictsson, Margaret, 391
Benevolence, female societies for, 154, 246, 248, 534, 557, 565, 590
Benevolent Hebrew Female Society of Congregation She'arith Israel, 557
Benezet, Anthony, 252
Ben-Gurion, David, 1124
Benjamin, Metuka, 904
Bennage, Dai-en, 640, 645
Bennett, Anne McGrew, 55
Bennett, Belle Harris, 327, 825, 840, 1034
Bennett, Dennis, 457, 459, 464
Bennett, Emma F., 981
Bennett, John, 76
Bennett, Katharine Jones, 354, 355–357, 1267
Bennett, Rita, 457, 464–465
Bennett College (N.C.), 916, 922
Benson, Ezra Taft, 726
Benzamin-Masuda, Michele, 644
Berenson, Bernard, 426
Berg, David, 714, 792–795
Berg, Deborah, 793
Berg, Faith, 793
Berg, Jane, 793
Berg, Virginia Brandt, 792–793
Berger, Sophia, 900
Bergeron, Yvonne, 218
Bergman, Ingrid, 1014
Berkeley, Lucy, 238
Berkson, Isaac, 902
Berkson, Libbie, 902

Berle, Milton, 404
Berlin, Meir, 559
Berman, Phyllis, 799, 801, 804
Bernard, Pierre, 638
Bernardin, Joseph, 953
Berrin, Susan, 1288
Berruecos, Antonia, 135
Berry, Modena Lowery, 292
Berry, Selisse, 1218
Bertell, Rosalie, 1111
Bertrand, Nicole, 796
Besant, Annie, 755–756, 761, 762, 763, 767
Bess, Ginney, 252
Besse, Joseph, 331
Bessere, Eugenie, 1016
Besson, Luc, 1014
Best, Marion, 367
Betanzos, Dominigo de, 94–95
Beth Din of America (RCA), 587
Bethlehem Centers, 327
Bethune, Joanna Graham, 453, 906
Bethune, Mary McLeod, 260, 434, 456, 870–871
Bethune Program Development Center, 871
Bethune-Cookman Institute, 871
"Better Films Committees," 1012
Bevilacqua, Anthony, 1104
Beynon, Francis Marion, 54
Beyond God the Father (Daly), 18, 392, 1174–1175, 1176, 1246
Beyond Sex Roles (Bilizekian), 473
Bhagavad-gita, 28, 660, 667
Bhairavi, 667
Bhakti yoga, 666
Bhangra folk dances, 698
Bharata Natya Sastra, 663
Bharata Natyam, 663
Bharati, Baba Premananda, 660
Bhiksuni Pema Chodron, 656
Bhog ceremony, 697
Biale, Rachel, 576
Bias: androcentric, 41; gender, 37; of historians, 6; secular, 14
Bibi Bhani, 695
Bibi Jagir Kaur, 702–703
Bible, 27; Adam, Eve, and Serpent story in, 35; American Standard Version (RSV), 36; depatriarchalizing and, 39–41; elimination of reading from state schools, 890; on film, 1012–1014; interpretation of: evangelical feminism and, 472–473; feminist, 37–39; in the round, 44; task of, 36; King James Version (KJV), 36; New International Version (NIV), 474; New King James Version (NKJV), 36; New Revised Standard Version (NRSV), 37; New Testament, 36, 39, 40–41, 42, 821; references to deacon/deaconess in, 821, 852; Revised Standard Version, 36–37; Scofield Reference, 428. *See also* Scriptures
Bible Belt, 242
Bible Christian Society, 245
Bible commonwealth, efforts to create, 223
Bible Presbyterians, 350

Bonds, Margaret, 988
Bonhoeffer, Dietrich, 1174
Bonner, Marita, 1168
Book clubs, Islamic, 617
The Book of Blessings: New Jewish Prayers for Daily Life, the Sabbath, and the New Moon Festival (Falk), 1223
Book of Common Prayer, 276
Book of Concord, 307
The Book of Medicine (Hogan), 51
Book of Mormon, 718
Book of Shadows (Curott), 817
Books Children Love (Wilson), 893
Boone, John, 100
Boone, Shirley, 460
Boorstein, Sylvia, 648, 1275
Booth, Ballington, 408, 409, 412, 426, 837–838
Booth, Catherine Mumford, 407, 412, 415, 425, 426, 442
Booth, Emma Moss, 412, 415, 426
Booth, Evangeline Cory, *408,* 412, 413, 415, 426, 982, 1015
Booth, Linda, 731
Booth, Maud Ballington, 837–838
Booth, Maud Charlesworth, 408, 409–410, 411, 412, 415, 426
Booth, William, 407, 413, 425
Booth-Clibborn, Catherine, 945, 982
Booth-Tucker, Frederick St. George, 413, 426
Booth-Tucker, Louise, 982
Bora, Katherine von, 311
Borderlands: defined, 1134–1135; life, 1135–1137; religion in, 1137–1140
Borthwick, Jane, 975, 976
Bosch, John, 782
Bosch, Louise, 782
Bostick, Mancil Mathis, 302
Bostick, Sarah Lue, *110,* 302
Boston Female Anti-Slavery Society, 1043, 1045
Boston Female Society for Missionary Purposes, 287, 293, 372, 835
Boston Missionary Training School, 440–441
Boston Pilot, 157
Boston Women's Trade Union League, 192
Boston's Children's Hospital, 273
Both Riches and Honor (Militz), 760
Boucher, Sandy, 20, 53, 642, 1099
Boukman (*houngan*), 121
Boulding, Elise, 268
Bounds, Elizabeth, 58
Bourgeoys, Marguerite, 144–145, 211
Bourget, Ignace, 212, 213
Bowden, Artemisia, 273
Bowe, Barbara, 1281
Bowen, Catherine Drinker, 69
Bowen, Louise DeKoven, 1072
Bowers, Bathsheba, 233
Bowles, Eva Del Vakia, 279, 1131–1132
Bowman, Thea, *161,* 167–168
Boyarin, Daniel, 1227
Boyer, Horace, 991
Boyle, Elizabeth, 152
Boys, Mary C., 1283
Boys' Missionary Clubs, 283

Bozyk, Reizl, 1016
Brackenridge, R. Douglas, 358
Bradbury, William, 983
Braden, Anne, 1084–1085
Braden, Carl, 1085
Bradlaugh, Charles, 755
Bradley, Marion Zimmer, 19, 816
Bradstreet, Anne, 368; writings of, 224
Brady, Mary A., 153
Braght, Thieleman J. van, 264
Brahma Sutras, 660
Brahma-Kumaris, 30
Brahman, 666
Brahmanas, 670
Brahmo Samaj, 667
Braille Torah, 561
Brainstorming, 1171
Brainwashing, 790
Bram, Emily, 433
Branch Davidians, 710, 714
A Brand Plucked from the Fire in Andrews, 868
Brando, Marlon, 1015
Branham, William, 458
Brant, Beth, 1236
Brant, Mary, 234
Brant, Roxanna, 466
Braschi, Romulo Antonio, 1108
Brasfield, Alice, 360
Braude, Ann, 769
Braun, Eunice, 782
Bray, Michael, 1101
Bray, Thomas, 252
Breaking the Fine Rain of Death: African American Health Issues and a Womanist Ethic of Care (Townes), 1172
Breen, Joseph I., 1012
Breitling, Marilyn, 375, 376
Breitman, Barbara, 801, 802
Brenau University (Georgia), 917, 922
Brennan, William, 104
Brenner, Athalaya, 42
Brent, Giles, 147
Brent, Margaret, *142,* 147; Suffrage Guild and, 192
Brent, Mary, 147
Bres, Guido de, 341
Bresee, Phineas, 427
Brethren (Dunkers): in Colonial Pennsylvania, 230; opposition to slavery, 1039; peace movements and, 1050, 1055
Brethren in Christ, 262
Breton, Albert, 181
Brevis, Anna Bear, 549
Brewster, Mary, 1062
Brice, Adele, 149
Brickner, Barnett, 540
Brickner, Rebecca Aaronson, 901
Bridges (periodical), 1220
Brigden, Beatrice, 1076
Briggs v. *Elliott,* 1084
Brighid's Day, 813
Bright, Bill, 445
Bright Jewels (hymnal), 983

Brightman, Edgar, 73–74
Bringle, Mary Louise, 986
B'rit Milah, 1224
British North America (Canada): Protestantism in, 242–249.
  See also Canada
British North American Act (1867), 1141
British Salvation Army "lassies," 837
British Society for the Propagation of Christian Knowledge
  (SPCK), 309
Brittingham, Isabella, 779, 784
Broadway Methodist Episcopal Church (Ohio), *824*
Brock, Rita Nakashima, 504, 933, 1293
Brocksopp, Joan, 331
Brodie, Jane, 249
The Broken Cord (Dorris), 1238
Broner, E. M., 21, 1224
Brontë, Charlotte, 974
Brook Farm, 150, 708
Brooke Medicine Eagle, 103
Brooklyn Deaconess House, 311
Brooklyn Tabernacle Choir, 986
Brooks, Nona, 757, 758–759
Brooks, Richard, 1015
Brooten, Bernadette, 42–43, 1217, 1282
Brotherhood of the Angels, 231
Brotherhood of the Carpenter, 1070
Brotherhood of the New Life, 711
Broughton, Virginia, 257, 295
Brown, Antoinette, 35, 347, 349, 350, 376, 969
Brown, Catherine, 96
Brown, Charlotte Hawkins, 456, 1035
Brown, Dorothy, 888
Brown, Elsa Barkely, 20
Brown, Este Virginia, 276–277
Brown, Hallie Quinn, 437, 456
Brown, John, raid on Harper's Ferry, 1039
Brown, Karen McCarthy, 733, 735
Brown, Lyn Mikel, 1305, 1306
Brown, Marie, 406
Brown, Mary, 982
Brown, Olympia, 385, 969; ordination of, 942
Brown, Robert, 400–401, 406
Brown, W. Gertrude, 1066
Brown v. Board of Education, 1081, 1083, 1084
Brown-Douglas, Kelly, 1237
Browning, Elizabeth Barrett, 976
Brownson, Josephine Van Dyke, 190, 874, *875,* 877
Brownson House, 190, 876, 1067
Brownsville, Texas, 1136
Brubaker, Pamela, 58
Bruce, Elizabeth, 385
Bruce, Ferne Isabel, 403
Brun, Carol Joyce, 376
Brunner, Pia, 958
Brunson, L. Madelon, 728
Brush, Ida, 778
Brush arbors, 113–114
Bryan, Catherine, 239
Bryan, William Jennings, 443
Bryant, Anita, 1298

Bryce, Mary Charles, 873, 881
Bryn Mawr College, 335, 913, 915, 922
Bucer, Martin, 341, 343
Buchan, Jane, 293
Buchan, Margaret, 293
Buchanan, John, 1293
Buchenholz, Gretchen, 1151, 1154, 1159–1160
Buck, Pearl S., 921
Buckingham, Jamie, 462
Buckingham (Mass.) Female Anti-Slavery Society, 1045
Buckminster, Joseph, 386
Budapest, Zsuzsanna, 19, 808, 809, 815, *815,* 1201, 1206,
  1264
Buddha Haus, 650
Buddhafield, 791
Buddha's Light International Association (BLIA), 676
Buddha's Light Mountain, 676
Buddhism, 6, 49, 185, 633–658, 677, 680, 1275; American,
  710; androcentric imagery for, 11; Asian forms of, 634,
  1207; Chan, 676; choice of ascetic or monastic life in, 29;
  devotional and meditative forms of, 675–676; Engaged,
  676, 1093–1099; Euro-American, 636–638, 1211; feminism
  and, 1211; Fo Guang Shan, 676; gender and, 26, 28, 40;
  lesbians in, 1210; Mahayana, 29, 639, 676, 684; meditation in, 1211, 1275, 1276; North American, 1095–1096;
  origins of, 633–639; Shin, 634, *635,* 637, 680–681, 683–
  684, 685, 686; Theravada, 29, 646–651, 676; Tibetan, 652–
  658, 686, 1096, 1213; Vajrayana, 29, 676, 1213; women's
  issues in contemporary, 1207–1214; women's status in, 9,
  11; Zen, 639–646, 685–686, 1211, 1212–1213
Buddhism after Patriarchy (Gross), 1098
Buddhist Alliance for Social Engagement (BASE), 1097
Buddhist Churches of America, 634, 681, 684–685, 686
A Buddhist Life in America: Simplicity in the Complex (Hali-
  fax), 1096
Buddhist Lodge, 638
Buddhist Peace Fellowship (BPF), 1094, 1097
Buddhist Society of America, 640
Buikema, Gertrude, 782, 783
Buisson de Saint-Cosme, Jean-François, 146
Bull, Sara, 668
Bullitt-Jonas, Margaret, *270*
Bultmann, Rudolf, 40–41
Bunch, Charlotte, 18
Büninger, Martha, 234
The Burden of Christopher (Converse), 1071
The Burden of the City (Horton), 1071
Bureaucracies for protestant church societies, 1265–1270
Burgess, Alice, 730
Burgess, Faith Rohrbaugh, 316–317
Burgess, Marie, 400–401
Burke, Bishop Barbara, 123
Burks, Mary Fair, 260
Burlage, Rob, 1091
Burleigh, Celia, 385; ordination of, 942
Burnet, Elizabeth, 320
Burnouf, Eugene, 636
Burns, Gene, 208
Burns, Lucy, 192–193, 196
Burr, Aaron, 344

Burroughs, Catherine, 654
Burroughs, Nannie Helen, 258, 260, 290, 291, 292, 456, 857–
    858, 863, 1031, 1073–1074, 1075, 1076, 1082, 1266
Burroughs, Nannie Helen, School, 292
Burrows, Lansing, 291
Burton, Richard, 1013, 1015
Burwell, Lucy, 238
Bush, George H. W., 1298
Bushman, Claudia, 16
Butler, Clementina Rowe, 324
Butler, Elizur, 114
Butler, Margaret, 363
Butterfield, Fanny, 322
Buttrick, Daniel, 113
Butts, Magnolia Lewis, 993
Bynum, Juanita, 457, 460, 465–467
Byrne, Elizabeth, 877
Byrne, Lavinia, 957

Cabet, Etienne, 708
Cabeza de Baca, Fabiola, 1196
Cabot, Jody, 816
Cabot, John, 1284
Cabot, Laurie, 816
Cabot tradition of witchcraft, 816
Cabrini, Frances Xavier, 156, 190–191, 843
Cabrini (Philadelphia), 888
Cadwallader, Priscilla, 333
Cady, H. Emilie, 758, 760
Cady, Linell Elizabeth, 933
Caesar, Shirley, 260, 433, 434, 992, 993–994
Cagle, Henry Clay, 427
Cagle, Mary Lee Wasson Harris, 418, 419, 423, 426–427
Cahan, Abraham, 1016
Cairo Conference on Population and Development, 1108
Cakes for the Queen of Heaven (Ranck), 19, 392
Calhoun, Robert, 76
California Civil Liberties Union, 1036
California Synod of the General Synod, 313
California-Pacific United Methodist Annual Conference
    Commission on the Status and Role of Women, 503
Calisch, Edith, 902
Call to Action, 133, 956
Call to Action Conference (Detroit), 953
Callahan, Sydney, 18
Callahan, William R., 952, 953, 957
The Callahans and the Murphy (film), 1015
Called Out, 1218
Called to Break Bread (Ferder), 954
Callen, Cathie, 516
Caller-response style of preaching, 451
Calling, 72–79
CALPULLI, 1186
Calvert, Cecilius, Lord Baltimore, 147
Calvert, George, Lord Baltimore, 147
Calvert, Leonard, Lord Baltimore, 147
Calvin, John, 223, 341–342, 771, 942, 975; predestination
    and, 285
Calvinist Baptists, 285, 348
Calvinist theology, 223, 769

Cambridge Buddhist Association, 638
Cambridge Buddhist Society, 641
Cameron, Donaldina, 347, *838*
Cameron, Kate, 983
Cameron Park, Texas, 1136
Camp meetings, 113, 323, 419–420, 425, 981; hymns and,
    976
Campbell, Alexander, 296, 298, 299–301, 303, 348
Campbell, Jane, 158
Campbell, Joan Brown, 1158, 1160, 1268
Campbell, Joseph, 766
Campbell, Lucie Eddie, 455, 990–991, 994, 995, 997
Campbell, Selina Huntington Bakewell, 298, 301
Campbell, Thomas, 298
Campnhey, Alan, 107–108
Campus Crusade for Christ, 445, 510
Canaanite Temple, 611
Canada: aboriginal, 1285–1287; Anglican Church in, 217, 279–
    285; Catholic women in, 143–146, 210–212, 218; deacon-
    ess movement in, 827; ecumenical, 1285; embodiment,
    1289–1290; Mennonites in, 265; Methodism in, 244;
    multicultural and multifaith, 1284–1285; new rituals, 1288;
    poverty, 1290; Presbyterians in, 345; Protestantism in, 242–
    249; public policy in, 1141–1149; Reformed Churches in,
    350; reproductive technologies, 1289; residential school
    system in, 100; settlement houses in, 1067–1068; sexual
    orientation, 1289; soul hunger, 1287; United Church in,
    361–368; violence against women, 1289–1290; vision and
    hope, 1290; wearing *hijad* in, 626–627; women in leader-
    ship, 1288–1289; women's ordination movement in, 216,
    218, 959; women's religious issues in, 1283–1290
Canada Assistance Plan (CAP), repeal of, 1148
Canada Bill 101 (1977), 1284–1285
Canada Bill C-31, 1286
Canadian Abortion Rights Action League (CARAL), 1143
Canadian Baptist "Female Mite Society," 287
Canadian Bill of Rights, 1142
Canadian Catholic Organization for Development and Peace,
    217
Canadian Catholics for Women's Ordination, 959
Canadian Charter of Rights and Freedoms, 1143, 1147
Canadian Christian-Jewish Consultation (CCJC), 1285
Canadian Churches and Foreign Policy, 1148
Canadian Conference for Women's Ordination, 216, 218
Canadian Conference of Religious, 217
Canadian Girls in Training (CGIT), 283, 365
Canadian Maritime Baptist Foreign Mission Board, 287
The Canadian Missionary Link, 293
Canadian National Defence Act, 1146
Canadian Network for Women's Equality, 216
Canadian Religious Conference, 216
Canadian Society for Study of Religion (CSSR), 59
Canadian Women's March (2000), 1148
Canavarro, Marie deSouza, 637
Candlemas, 813
Candon, Elizabeth, 1104
Cannon, Harriet Starr, 273
Cannon, Katie Geneva, 20, 56, 261, 1165, 1168, 1169, 1171,
    1231
Cantor, Aviva, 1221, 1224

Cantors Institute, 551–552
Caodism, 185
Cape Breton mission, 245
Capitalism, industrial, 1127
Capps, Annette, 466
Capra, Frank, 1014, 1015
Captivity narratives, 225, 1000–1001, 1007, 1009
Caravans, 993
Carbajal de Valenzuela, Romanita, 493–494
Carbury, Cardinal John, 207
Carder, Muriel Spurgeon, 294
Cardijn, Joseph, 199, 215
Cardin, Nina Beth, 1227
Carey, Alice, 976
Carey, Emma Forbes, 150
Carey, Lott, 256
Carey, Phoebe, 976
Caribbean region, 116; African women introduced into, 116
Caribbean religions, 732–738; African, 116–123; Christianity
    and, 737–738; Santería, 736–737; spiritism, 735; Vodou,
    733–735, 734
Carlebach, Shlomo, 801
Carlisle boarding school, 98, 101
Carlsson, Emmy, 308
Carlyle, Thomas, 1060
Carmelites, 206; Discalced, 138
Carmen, Arlene, 1101
Carnegie, Andres, 916
Carnegie, Louise, 343
Caro, Joseph, 577
Carothers, Warren Fay, 397
Carpenter, Bill, 995
Carpenter, Delores, 999
Carpenter, Dennis, 816
Carr, Anne E., 202, 203, 953
Carroll, Austin, 192
Carroll, Elizabeth, 953
Carroll, George M., 848
Carroll, Janet, 847
Carroll, John, 874
Carse, Matilda, 1075–1076
Carson, Rachel, 918, 921
Carson, Sara Libby, 1067
Carter, Jimmy, 464, 799, 1295, 1299
Carthage College, 316
Cartier, Jacques, 143; journals of, 1256
Cartwright, Harriet Dobbs, 246
Cartwright, Robert, 246
Carus, Paul, 637, 781
Cary, Emma Forbes, 192
Cary, Mary Ann Shadd, 371, 1039
Cary, Maude, 841
La Casa de San Gabriel, 478, 482–483
Casazza, Letha R., 294
Case, Adelaide Teague, 277, 910
Case, William, 245
Casgrain, Thérèse, 214
Cash, Rosalind, 1013
Cashman, Nellie, 154
Cason, Ann, 1097

Cason, Sandra, 1086
Castañeda, Margarita, 1185
Caste, Hinduism and, 660
Castillo, Noemi, 185
Castillo de Graxeda, José, 140
Castro, Fidel, 847
Catarina de San Juan, 135, 139–140
Catawba people, 112
Catechesis, 873
Catechesis Tradendae (document), 880
Catechetics: higher education and, 880; new, 878–880; in Ro-
    man Catholic tradition, 873–881
Catechetics and Prejudice: How Catholic Teaching Materials
    View Jews, Protestants, and Racial Minorities (Pawli-
    kowski), 1277
Catechism, age of, 874–876
Catechism and Examples (Sadlier), 874
Catechism of the Catholic Church (publication), 880
The Cathedral of Faith Choir, 994
Cather, Willa, 1009
Catherine of Siena, St., 30, 134
Catholic Action, 130, 131, 195–196, 215, 886
Catholic Anecdotes (Sadlier), 874
Catholic Association for International Peace, 196
Catholic Educational Association, 883
Catholic Evidence Guild of Rosary College, 195, 846
Catholic Family Movement (CFM), 131
Catholic Female Benevolent Society of Detroit, 150
Catholic feminism: legacy of, 208–209; theology of, 133
Catholic Foreign Mission Society, 845
Catholic Foresters, 190
Catholic Home Journal, 157
Catholic Hospital Association, 193
Catholic immigrants, 127–128, 145–148, 154–156, 178–180;
    outreach of nuns to, 155–156
Catholic Indian Missions, Bureau of, 843
Catholic Instruction League (Detroit), 874, 877, 878
Catholic Interracial Councils, 166
The Catholic Interracialist, 197
Catholic lay movements, 130
Catholic motherhood, spiritual promotion of, in Ontario,
    212–213
Catholic Network for Women's Equality, 959
Catholic New York, 879
Catholic Organizations for Renewal, 1243
Catholic orphanages, 155–156
Catholic Religious Right, 217
Catholic Settlement (Toronto), 1068
Catholic sisters: traditional teaching about women and, 207–
    208; women's movement and, 205–207. See also Nuns;
    specific orders
Catholic Students Mission Crusade, 196, 846
Catholic Summer School of America (New London, Conn.),
    157
Catholic Theological Society of America (CTSA) Conference
    (1989), 170
Catholic Total Abstinence League, 129–130
Catholic Total Abstinence Union, 158, 190
Catholic Truth Guild, 420
Catholic University (Washington, D.C.), 129, 883, 886

Catholic women: African American, 160–168; in age of progress, 156–158; American, 187–200; in American West, 153–154; in antebellum period, 149–152; antifeminist, 200; Asian and Pacific American, 178–187; in Canada, 210–212, 218; in Civil War, 152–153; colleges for, 129; in Colonial Mexico, 133–141; conservative, 205; ethnic diversity and, 131; Filipino American, 184–185; as immigrants, 154–156, 178–180; from Jacksonian period to Progressive Era, 148–159; Latina popular, 168–178; in New England, 141–148; in New France, 127, 141–148; in New Spain, 127, 160; in nineteenth century in Canada, 209–218; North American, 127–133; in Quebec, 209–218; since Vatican Council II, 200–209; slavery and, 160–161, 163; at turn of the century, 158–159; in twentieth century, 187–200; in Canada, 209–218; Vietnamese American, 185–186. *See also* Catholicism

Catholic women religious, before 1860, 150–152

Catholic Women's Association of Brooklyn, 159

Catholic women's colleges, in United States, 881–889

Catholic Women's League, 159

Catholic Worker, 130, 196, 1055, 1056

Catholic Worker (newspaper), 196, 1055, 1056

Catholic World, 157

Catholicism, 10, 16–17, 22, 127–218; African American hymnbooks of, 998; African American women in, 160–168; antiabortion movement and, 1106; Asians and, 131; in British North America, 244; in Colonial Mexico, 133–141; in Colonial New France and New England, 141–148; in Colonial Pennsylvania, 230; Communion of Saints in, 50; Counter-Reformation and, 135; development of education, 874, 875, 882–883; English, 127, 141–142; Haitian, 734; healing and, 1261; identification of calling in, 78; inclusive language and, 1292; interfaith marriage and, 1273; from Jacksonian period to Progressive Era, 148–159; Latina, 168–178, 1193–1200; monastic life in, 707; nuns in films, 1014; participation in charismatic movement, 459; positions of, on sexuality and reproduction, 1100; reproductive rights and, 1103; Santería and, 736; scientific medicine and, 1260–1261; settlements and, 1065; women missionaries and, 843–850; women in North American, 127–133; women-church movement in, 1243–1249; women's ordination movement in, 951–960, 1243; women's religious orders and, 16–17; YWCA and, 1133. *See also* Catholic women

Catholics for a Free Choice (CFFC), 58, 132, 133, 204, 1104–1105, 1105, *1107,* 1107–1108, 1245, 1246, 1248

Catholics for the Right to Decide, 959, 1108

Catholics Speak Out, 956, 958

Católicas por el Derecho a Decidir (Catholics for the Right to Decide), 959, 1108

Catt, Carrie Chapman, 192, 805, 1033, 1053, 1054

Causes of Unrest among Women of the Church (Hodge), 360

Cavalcanti, Tereza, 1197

Cayuga nation, 83

Cayuse people, 346

Cedar Crest College (Pa.), 918, 922

Celebration, 1171

Celeste, Dagmar, 959

Celestial marriage, 720

Celibacy: Christian, 712–713; deaconess movement and, 827

Cenacle, 190

Censorship, film, 1010–1012

Centenary Translation of the New Testament (Montgomery), 293

Center for Christian Education, 306

Center for Ecumenism, 1280–1281

Center for Emerging Female Leadership (CEFL), 482

Center for Jewish Women's and Gender Studies, 554

Center for Non-Traditional Religion, 816

Center for Pan Asian Community Services Inc., 504

Center for Women and Religion, 55

Center of Concern, 205–206

Central Conference of American Rabbis (CCAR), 539, 540, 541, 543, 962

Central Neighbourhood House, 1067

Centre for Christian Studies, 283, 365

A Century of Dishonor (Jackson), 1027

Cercles de fermières, 214–215

A Ceremonies Sampler, 1225

Ceremony (Silko), 1232

Cervantes, Carmen, 1196

César, Rev., 482–483

Cessation of formal religious activity, interfaith marriage and, 1274

Chadha, Gurinder, 703

Chai, Alice Yun, 500, 503

Chair of Unity Octave, 849

Chakko, Sara, 76

The Chalice and the Blade (Eisler), 19

Challah, ritual of, 569

Chamberlain-Taylor, Debra, 648

Champlain, Samuel de, 143–144

Champsee, Lata, 691

Chan Buddhism, 676

Chan Hon Fun, 500

Chan Khong, 1093, 1094

Chandler, Elizabeth Margaret, 334

Chang, Patricia Mei Yin, 972

Changing of the Gods (Goldenberg), 1202

Channing, William Ellery, 382

Channing, William Henry, 382

Chant, Laura Ormiston, 985

Chanukah songs, 553

Chapel Shrine of the Immaculate Conception (Robbinsonville), 149

Chapell, Frederick L., 396

Chapin, Augusta, 385; ordination of, 942

Chapman, J. Wilbur, 441–442

Chapman, Maria Weston, 1043, 1051

Chappell, Winifred, 1030, 1071–1072

Chapter One (album), 994

Charisma, 767

Charismatic healing, 1263

Charismatic movement, 457–467; Catholic participation in, 459; history of, 458–460; influential women in, 461–467; origin of, 457; views of women and gender, 460–461

Charity of the Immaculate Conception, 211

Charity of the Incarnate Word, 128

Charles E. Smith Day School (Washington, D.C.), 904

Charles, George B., 757

Collier, John, 106, 107
Collins, Addie Mae, 1089
Collins, Amelia, 777, 779
Collins, Anna, 877, 953
Collins, Joseph, 878
Colonial and Continental Church Society, 284
Colonial period: ending of, 248–249; protestant women in: in Mid-Atlantic colonies, 228–236; in New England colonies, 221–228; in Southern colonies, 236–242; Quakers in, 331–333; religious leadership by women in, 940–941
Colonial Teachers' Scheme, 284
Colonization, 256
Color, Ebony (Day), 196
The Color Purple (Walker), 1172
Colored Methodist Episcopal Church, 327
The Colored Sacred Harp (Jackson), 999
Colored Social Settlement (Washington, D.C.), 1066, 1074
Colored Young Women's Christian Association, 1131–1132
Columbia Bible Institute, 455
Columbia College, 882, 886; in Missouri, 922; in South Carolina, 922
Columbian Reading Union, 157
Columbus, Christopher, 118
Colvin, Claudette, 1089
Combs, Roberta, 1300
Comeouterism, 1047–1048
Commission for a New Lutheran Church (CNLC), 315, 316
Commission for the Study of the Ordination of Women as Rabbis, 965
Commission on Christian Marriage and Divorce, 367
Commission on Holy Matrimony, 276
Commission on Interracial Cooperation (CIC), 1034
Commission on Jewish Continuity (Boston), 906
Commission on the Gainful Employment of Married Women, 366
Commission on the Life and Work of Women in the Church, 1268
Commission on Women in Ministry (COWIM), 1269
Committee for Purity of the Press, 592
Committee for the Study of the Ordination of Women as Rabbis, 551
Committee on Christian Literature for Women and Children, 840
Committee on Jewish Law and Standards of the Conservative movement, 550, 583
Committee on Pastoral Research and Practices of the National Conference of Catholic Bishops (NCCB), 951
Committee on Religious Freedom, 608
Committee on the Cause and Cure of War (CCCW), 1033
Common schools, 890, 907
Commonality, recognition of, 65
Commonweal, 199
Communion, 797
Communitarian societies, women in, 707–718; androgynous divinity and new humanity, 710–712; founders and leaders, 714–716; gender equality and work roles, 716–717; sexuality and family, 712–714
Community Miracles Center, 765
Community of Christ, 721
Community of Saint Mary, 273

Community of St. Andrew, 826
La Compagnie des Indes, 146
Compartmentalization, 1156
Complex marriage, in Oneida community, 713
Compost, 815
Comstock laws, 1100
Conan, Laure, 213
Concerned Women for America, 21, 446, 464, 891, 1101, 1297–1298, 1300
Concilio Peña de Horeb, 497
Concordia College (Seward, Nebr.), 316
Concordia Theological Seminary, 947
Concordia University (River Forest, Ill.), 312, 316
Conde-Frazier, Elizabeth, 483
Conditae a Cristo, 159
Condoms4Life campaign, 1109
Cone, James, 261, 1236
Conference for Catholic Lesbians (CCL), 1218
Conference of Catholic Charities, 194
Conference of Major Superiors of Women (CMSW), 17, 132, 198, 199, 205, 207
Confession of Geneva, 342
Confraternity of Christian Doctrine (CCD), 874, 875–876, 878; National Congress, 876; Office of, 879
A Confraternity School Year Religion Course, the Adaptive Way, 879
Confrontation, 47–48
Confucianism, 185, 674–675, 677; doctrine of, 182
Confucius, birthday of, 675
Confucius Center (Chicago), 675
Confucius Church (Stockton, Calif.), 675
Congrégation de Notre-Dame de Montréal, 144, 211
Congregation for the Doctrine of the Faith, 216, 957
Congregation of Propaganda, 158
Congregation of the Lovers of the Holy Cross, 186
Congregation Shearith Israel (New Amsterdam, N.Y.), 554
Congregation Yeshuat Israel (Newport, R.I.), 554
Congregational Christian Churches: hymnals of, 998; women ministers in, 969
Congregational religious schools, 535, 537
Congregational Way, spread of, throughout New England, 224
Congregational Woman's Boards of Mission, 374
Congregationalist Training School, 829
Congregationalists, 348, 368–369; in Colonial New England, 225–226, 227; missionaries and, 837; opposition to slavery, 1039; orientation of women for, 1288
Congregationality, gospel hymns and, 982
Congregionalist American Board, 836; founding of, 835–836
Congress of American Women (CAW), 1056
Congress of Industrial Organizations (CIO), 1035
Congress of Racial Equality (CORE), 260, 870, 1083, 1086, 1091
Congress of Social Sciences and the Humanities, 59
Congressional Union for Woman Suffrage, 192–193
Conjuring, 1261
Connectedness, 64–65
Connecticut Anti-Slavery Society, 1047, 1051
Connelly, Marc, 1013
Conrad, Juana, 786

Daughters of Conference of the African Methodist Episcopal Zion (AMEZ) Church, 258
Daughters of Hadassah, 1124
Daughters of Isabella, 154
Daughters of Liberty, 228, 851
Daughters of Sarah (magazine), 16, 22, 467, 470, 471–472, 473, 474, 475
Daughters of Temperance, 452, 1024
Daughters of the American Republic, 1012
Daughters of the Dust (film), 1016
Daughters of the King, 275
Daughters of Utah Pioneers, 724
Daum, Annette, 1279
Davaney, Sheila Greeve, 932
Daviau, Pierrette, 218
David and Bathsheba (film), 1013
Davidek, Felix, 957
Davidson, Carrie Dreyfuss, 547
Davidson, Mrs. A. L., 985
Davies, Samuel, 239, 240
Davis, Addie, 21–22, 294
Davis, Allen F., 1061
Davis, Andrew Jackson, 770, 774
Davis, Bill, 1147
Davis, Cortwright, 121
Davis, Elizabeth Gould, 1201
Davis, Henrietta Vinton, 1080
Davis, Mary, 785
Davis, Patricia, 1307
Davis, Rebecca Harding, 1007
Davis, Ruth Lomax, 997
Davison, Helenor M., 325
Davison, Sarah Martin, 247
Da'wa, movements of, 622–623
Dawes Allotment Act (1887), 93, 101
Dawidowicz, Lucy, 1282
Dawson, Dorothy, 1086, 1091
Day, Cora Lee, 1016
Day, Dorothy, 130, 166, 196, 1055, 1056
Day, Helen Caldwell, 166, 196
Day, Sarah, 320
Day school, 904
Daya, Sister, 669
Dayton, Donald, 16, 470
Dayton, Lucille Sider, 16, 470
De Carlo, Yvonne, 1013
De Luna, Anita, 1200
De Mena, Maymie, 1080
Deaconess, 863; duties and rules for, 827–830
The Deaconess Advocate, 825
Deaconess Advocate (publication), 1032
Deaconess Association of the Diocese of Alabama, 826
Deaconess Bureau of the Woman's Home Missionary Society of the Methodist Church, 825
Deaconess Home and Hospital, 311–312
Deaconess Home for Colored People, 825
Deaconess movement, 274–275, 326, 821–833, 852–853, 863; connections to ancient world and New Testament, 821; duties and rules for deaconesses, 827–830; early-twentieth-

century, 830–832; initial developments in North America, 822–827; Kaiserwerth precedent, 822
Deaconess Organization of the Diocese of Maryland, 826
Deaconess Training School of the Pacific (Berkeley, Calif.), 274
Deaconesses in Europe and Their Lesson for America (Robinson), 826
Deaconesses (publication), 832
Dead Man Walking (film), 1014
Dead Man Walking (Prejean), 1152–1153
Dead Sea Scrolls, 1281
Death: Islamic preparation for burial and, 618; in Mid-Atlantic colonies, 233–234; Sikh women and, 700–701
The Death of Nature (Merchant), 1110
Death penalty, abolition of, in Canada, 1145–1146
D'Eaubonne, Françoise, 1110
Declaration of Independence (1776), 13, 1021, 1024
Declaration of Sentiments and Resolutions (Stanton), 13, 1024
Dedicated to Serve (Phillips), 731
Deepavali (festival of lights), 661
Deering, Marie, 1011
Defecting in Place, 203
Defensive Shield, 603
Definite Synodical Platform, 310
Deities: androgynous, 711–712; displacement of female, 92–93; rejection of patriarchal, 13
Del Duca, Gemma, 1278–1279
Del Pozzo, Teresa, 1091
Del Tufo, Alisa, 1153–1154
Delaney, Emma B., 259, 288, 289
Delaney, Joan, 849
DeLee, Victoria Way, 1087, 1089, 1090
Delille, Henriette, 163, 164, 165, 843, 844
Deloria, Vine, Jr., 83, 90, 105, 1229–1230, 1231, 1236
Delphi (Greece), 812
DeMille, Cecil B., 1012, 1013, 1015
Democracy, radical, 1081
Democratic National Convention (DNC), 1088
Democratization of American Christianity, 309
Democrats, temperance movement and, 1028
Demonarchy, 1168
Demystification, 50
Dengel, Anna, 194, 846, 849
Denison, Edward, 1060
Denison, Ruth, 646–647, 648, 1099
Denison House (Boston), 1064, 1070, 1072
Dentiere, Marie, 341
Deol, Monica, 703
Depatriarchalizing, 39–41
Der-McLeod, Doreen, 501
Derricotte, Juliette, 456
DeSalvo, Louise, 70
Descriptive women studies in religion, 5
The Desolate City: Revolution in the Catholic Church (Muggeridge), 205
Despair and Personal Power in the Nuclear Age (Macy), 650
The Destiny of the Mother Church (Knapp), 745
Destructiveness, 67
Detroit Women's Ordination Conference, 953–954
Detzer, Dorothy, 1054, 1055
Deutsch, Celia, 1281

Devamata, Sister, 668–669
Developmental patterns in religions, 9
Devi, Gayatri, *668*
Devi, Sri Sarada, 667
Devi, Sudha Puri, 669
Devine, Annie Bell Robinson, 261, 1089
DeVos, George, 1198
Devotional associations, 213
Dewey, John, 902, 910
DeWitty, Virgie Carrington, 995–996, 997
Dhaliwal, Daljit, 703
Dhamma Dena Desert Vipassana Center, 646–647
Dhamma Dena Meditation Center, 648
Dharma, 666
Dharma, Karuna, 640, 644
Dharma, Sarika, 644
Dharma Rain: Sources for Buddhist Environmentalism (Kaza and Kraft), 1095
Dharmapala, Anagarika, 637
Dhayani Yahoo, 103
Dhindsa, Gurvir, 703
Día de los Muertos: Day of the Dead, 130, 171–173
Diaconal ministers, 832
DIAKONIA, 312, 832
Diakonia News, 832
The Dial (periodical), 382, 385, 633, 636
Diamant, Anita, 1225
Diamond, Irene, 1112
Diamond Sangha, 642
Diaries, keeping of, by Protestant women, 233–234
Diary of a Witch (Leek), 814
Díaz, Zoila, 1196
Díaz Bolet, Esther, 483
Díaz-Stevens, Ana María, 847, 1200
Dickinson, Jennie, 407
Dickson, Sarah, 357
Dienemann, Max, 961
Dierks, Sheila, 1247
Digambara sect of Jainism, 689, 692, 693
Diksitar, 662
Dilling, Elizabeth, 594
Dim Sum (film), 1016
Dimity Convictions (Welter), 1004
Diné (Navajo) people, 85
Diner, Hasia, 905
Diner, Helen, 1201
Dingman, Maurice, 955
Diouf, Sylvaine, 610
Dipa Ma, 647
Dirks, Elisabeth, 268
Discalced Carmelites, 138
Disciples of Christ, 296–297, 343, 348; conservative years in, 303–305; missionaries of, in borderlands, 1139; missions in, 301–302; opposition to slavery, 1039; postfeminism, 305–306; preaching in early Christian Church movement, 297–298; reforms and, 302–303; rise of feminism, 305; Silena Holman and, 300–301; women in, 296–307, 299; as deaconesses, 300; loss of autonomy, 303; motherhood and education, 298–299; in worship service, 299–300
Discipleship, 893

Discipleship of equals, 202, 1243
Discipline of the Methodist Church, 830
Disco dandiya, 662
Discourses on Religion, Morals, Philosophy, and Metaphysics (Hatch), 771
Discovering Kwan Yin (Boucher), 1099
Discovering the Bible in the Non-Biblical World (Pui-lan), 42
Dispensational premillennialism, 439–440
The Distaff, 730
District of Columbia, abolition of slavery in, 1044
Divali (Indian festival of lights), 699
Divine, gendered images of, 26
Divine healing, 427–430, 1262
Divine Principle (Oon Young Kim), 789, 790
Divine Science, 757, 758–759, 1259
Divorce: Jewish, 585–586; in Qur'an, 625
Dix, Dorothea, 153
Dixie Hummingbirds, 994
Dixon, A. Y., 411
Dixon, John, 238
Dixon, Lucy, 238
Doane, William, 982, 983
Dober, Anna, 975
Dober, Regina, 233
Dobson, James, 405, 464, 1295
Doctor, Ginny, 278
Doctor, Rena Thomas, 278
Doddridge Farm, 197
Dodge, David Low, 1050
Dodge, Grace Hoadley, 1033, 1129–1130, 1131, 1133
Dodge, Jamie, 817
Dodson, Jualynne, 867
Doering, Sara, 648
Doherty, Austin, 18
Doherty, Edward ("Eddie"), 197
Doherty, Martha, 195
Doi, Connie, 681, 683
Doi, Kiyono, 681, 686
Doi, Saroku, 681
Dole, Elizabeth, 1300
Domestic and Foreign Missionary Society, 272, 281, 282; Board of Management of, 283
Domestic novels, 1004–1008
Domestic violence shelters, 156
Dominican Congregation of St. Rose of Lima, 150, 191
Dominican Sisters, 185, 878
Dominion Women's Enfranchisement Association, 391
Donaldina Cameron House, 501
Donatists, 250
Donato, Denise, 958
Donnelly, Dorothy, 953
Donnelly, Eleanor C., 157, 158, 159
Donnelly, Ignatius, 591
Donohue, John, 954
Donovan, Jean, 847
Donovan, Mary, 274, 276, 277
Don't Get Off the Train (Meyer), 466
Don't Just Do Something, Sit There (Boorstein), 648
Dooley, Kate, 881
Dorcas Societies, 245

Ecological disasters, 1113

Ecological-Feminism (Warren), 1112

Economic and Entrepreneurial Development Center, 871

Economy: racism and, 98–99; village of, 708; women in, 57–58

Ecumenical Association of Third World Theologians (EATWOT), 1197

Ecumenical Coalition for Economic Justice (ECEJ), 1144

Ecumenical Decade of the Churches in Solidarity with Women in Church and Society, 59, 517, 1285, 1289, 1290

Ecumenical Network for Women's Justice, 1285

Ecumenical Network of Women of African Heritage, 1289

Ecumenical Women's Caucus, 20

Ecumenism, 20, 1102

Eddy, Asa Gilbert, 739–740, 763

Eddy, Mary Baker, 26, 48, 50, 444, 711, 715, 738–746, *741*, 757, 970, 1259–1260

Edelman, Marian Wright, 917

Edelman, Rose K., 1054

Eden, Elana, 1013

Edes, Ella B., 158

Edmonds, John, 772

Edmunds-Tucker Act (1887), 723

Edson, Emily, 275

Education, 873–939; of African Americans, 255, 257; *Brown v. Board of Education* and, 1081, 1083, 1084; Catholic: catechetics and higher, 880; Catholic, 873–881; in Catholic women's colleges in United States, 881–889; development of, 882–883; colonial, 889; conservative Christian strategies in, 889–896; family, 905–906; Jewish, 896–906; Lutherans and, 889; Muslim, 616; pluralism and, 889; Protestant: colleges, 912–923; Sunday School and, 906–912; Quakers and, 889; reform in, 1021–1022; theological, 483, 923–930; women classroom teachers in, 930–939. *See also* Schools

Education Covenant of Partnership, 920

Educational Alliance, 900, 1063

Educational Conference of Seminary Faculties, 883

Educational Ministries for American Baptist Churches/USA, 482

Edwards, Esther, 344

Edwards, Henrietta, 1141

Edwards, J. Gordon, 1015

Edwards, Jonathan, 227, 344, 370, 416, 421, 771, 835, 967, 976, 979

Edwards, Lena, 167

Edwards, Phyllis, 278, 948

Edwards, Sarah, 344

Effendi, Shoghi, 776–780, 784

Egalitarianism, 10, 802; destruction of sociopolitical structures and, 93

Egbe Orisha Ile Wa, 122

Eggleston, Helen, 782

Eggleston, L. W., 782

Eicher, Anna, 231

Eicher, Maria, 231, 234

Eid festivals, 618

1801 hymnal (Allen), 998

Eighteenth Amendment, 1032

Eighteenth century, female preaching in, 966–968

Eighth Day Center for Justice, 956

Eilberg, Amy, 551, 552, 965

Eilberg-Schwartz, Howard, 1227

Eisenbaum, Pamela, 1281

Eisenhower, Dwight D., 1057

Eisenstein, Judith Kaplan, 553, 902

Eisler, Riane, 19

Ekklesia gynaikon, 1244

Ellen Cushing Junior College, 292

El Bethel (MacIlvary), 401

El Morya, 763

Elaborative imagination, 48–51

Elaw, Zilpha, 433, 451, 969

Elementary Forms (Durkheim), 1230

Elgenaidi, Maha, 618

Elhanan, 430

Eliach, Yaffa, 1282

Eliade, Mircea, 1201

Eliot, Charles W., 913, *914*

Eliot, Elisabeth, 405

Eliot, John, 97

Eliot, Margaret Dawes, 384

Eliot, Samuel A., 387

Eliot, T. S., 384

Eliot, Thomas Lamb, 384

Eliot, William G., 383

Elizabeth, Princess Palatine of Rhine, 231

Elizabeth College, 918

Elizondo, Santos, *486*

Elizondo, Virgilio, 173, 1196, 1198

Ellacuria, Ignacio, 1197

Eller, Cynthia, 1204

Ellington, Duke, 167

Elliott, Charlotte, 455, 975

Ellis, Marc, 1280

Ellis, Wilma, 786

Elmer Gantry (Lewis), 1015

Elmira College (New York), 917, 922

Elmira Female College, 882

Elster, Shulamith, 904

Elwell, Marlene, 1298

Elwell, Sue Levi, 543, 1221

Emancipation Proclamation (1863), 256

Emancipatory historiography, 1171

Embracing the Spirit: Womanist Perspectives on Hope, Salvation, and Transformation, 1170

Embroidery Guilds, 283

Embury, Philip, 235, 244, 319

Emergence narratives, 83, 85–87

Emergency Peace Campaign, 1055

Emerson, Ellen Tucker, 383

Emerson, Mary Moody, 382

Emerson, Ralph Waldo, 382, 383, 636, 659, 667, 739, 1008

Emery, Julia Chester, 274

Emery, Margaret Theresa, 274

Emigration, 256

Émile (Rousseau), 881

Emma, Queen of Hawaii, 273

Emma Willard Seminary, 354

Emmanuel College (Boston), 884
Emotional violence, against Indian children, 100
Employment Division v. *Smith*, 106
Emunah College, 561–562
Encuentros, 1184
Engaged Buddhism, 676, 1093–1099
Engels, Friedrich, 805, 1201
Engendering Judaism: An Inclusive Theology and Ethics (Adler), 43, 588, 1222
England, settlement houses in, 1060
English Catholics, 127, 141–142
English Dissenters, 975
English Independents, hymns and, 975–976
English Salvationists, 407
Enlightenment, 27, 1021; European, 3; rationalism and, 226; religious toleration and, 227
Enmanji, 685
Ennis, Caroline, 1142
Enough Is Enough: Aboriginal Women Speak Out (Goeres), 57
Enslaved women, as antislavery activists, 1040–1041
Entire Devotion to God: A Present to My Christian Friend, 424
Environmental Network, 1235
Ephrata Cloister, 231, 234, 235, 707
Episcopal General Convention, *948*
Episcopal Women's Caucus (EWC), 278
Episcopalians: African American hymnbooks of, 998; in antebellum period, 272; deaconess program and, 826, 827–828; General Division of Women's Work of, 15; inclusive language and, 1292; missionaries and, 837; ordination of women in, 18, 97, 947–949, 971; women in, 269–279
Epp, Helen, 265
Epstein, Helen, 1282
Epstein, Judith, 1124
Equal Rights Amendment (ERA), 16, 17, 21, 31, 206, 305, 375, 378, 470, 718, 725, 726, 891, 951, 1121, 1295–1297
Equal to Serve: Women and Men in the Church and Home (Hull), 473
Era Club, 1031
Erauso, Antonio, 140
Erauso, Catalina de, 135, 140–141
Erickson, Joyce, 470
Erickson, R. L., 400
Errett, Isaac, 302
Erskine, Noel, 121
Esbats, 814
Esperanto, 786
Espin, Orlando, 169–170
Espinoza, Carmelita, 1184
Essay on Slavery and Abolitionism (Beecher), 1044
Essenes, 707
Essentialist feminism, 931
Esteban, 160
Estrella, Julia Matsui, 502
Eternal femininity, 1176
Eternal masculinity, 1176
Ethan Frome (Wharton), 1009
Ethics: black womanist, 54; Christian, 52; feminist, 54–61; social, 52–61; *Mujerista*, 57; religious, 52
Ethnic diversity, among Catholics, 131
Ethnic healing, 1262

Ettenberg, Sylvia, 903
Etter, Marie Woodworth, 1262
Etter, Willie, 418
Ettlinger, Jacob, 572
Etz Chaim, 566
Eubanks, Rachel, 988
Eubanks Conservatory of Music, 988
Eucharist, 50
Euro-American Buddhism, 636–638
Euro-American colonists, healing among, 1257–1258
Euro-American Evangelical feminism, 467–476
Euro-American feminist theology, 1173–1181, *1175*
Euro-Catholicism, 117
European enlightenment, 3
European fascism, 1036
Evald, Emmy Carlsson, 313, 919
Evangelia (Toronto), 1067
Evangelical and Ecumenical Women's Caucus (EEWC), *468*, 472, 475
Evangelical Christianity, 104–105
Evangelical Churchman, 827
Evangelical Covenant Church, 16
Evangelical feminism: biblical interpretation and, 472–473; history of, 469
Evangelical Friends International, 340
Evangelical Lutheran Church in America (ELCA), 308, 315, 947; hymnals of, 998; women of, 318
Evangelical Lutheran Church in Canada, 317, 318
Evangelical Methodism, 253
Evangelical Orthodox Church, 510
Evangelical Protestantism, African American women and, 252–253
Evangelical revivalism, 1021
Evangelical United Brethren Church, 328, 944; merger with Methodist Church, 75
Evangelical Women's Caucus (EWC), 16, 467–468, *468*, 469–471. See also Evangelical and Ecumenical Women's Caucus
Evangelical Women's Union, 374
Evangelicalism, 1295; African Americans in, 451–452; flapper, 403; German, 371–372, 373; nineteenth-century reform, 452–455; Northern, 449–450; Southern, 450–451; in twentieth century, 455–457
Evangelicals for Social Action, 469, 470, 471
Evans, Carlton, 748
Evans, Elizabeth Hicks Morrell, 444–445
Evans, Jane, 539, 541, 542
Evans, Joseph, 444
Evans, Mary, 473
Evans, Mary Lue, 749
Evans, Quartus, 748
Evans, Rosalie, 748
Evans, Sara, 18
Evans, Walter, 762
Evanzz, Karl, 752
Evdokimov, Paul, 528
Everett, Edward, 638
Everett, Ruth Fuller, 640–641
Everyday Zen (Beck and Packer), 644
Evolution, Darwinian, 805–806
Ewing Street Congregational Church, 860

Executive Order 9066, 180
Existentialism, Christian, 18
Experiential feminism, 931
Experiment in Congregational Education (ECE), 905
Exponent II (newspaper), 16, 726
Extase (film), 1013
Extending the Call: Testimonies of Ordained Women, 731
Eynon, Elizabeth Dart, 245
Ezrat Nashim, 1221, 1222

Fabella, Virginia, 1197
Fabian Society, 755
Facing Death and Finding Hope (Longaker), 1096
Facing History and Ourselves National Foundation, 1282
Fair, Christine, 702
Faith and Fratricide (Ruether), 1278
Faith and Its Effects, 424
Faith and Order Commission of the National Council of
    Churches, 1278
Faith Corps, 677
Faith healing, 1262–1263
Faith homes, 429
Faith missions, 840–841
A Faith of One's Own, 1218
Faith Rest Cottage, 428
Faith Work under Dr. Cullis (Boardman), 429
*Faithful and Fearless: Moving Feminist Protest Inside the
    Church and Military* (Katzenstein), 209
A Faithful Narrative of the Surprising Work of God (Edwards),
    227
Falcon García, Ana María, 481
Falis, Sophia, 910
Falk, Marcia, 802, 1223, 1224
Fall, P. S., Academy (Ky.), 299
Fall Equinox, 814
Falun Dafa Information Center (New York), 678
Falun Gong, *678,* 678–679
Falwell, Jerry, 446, 464, 1295, 1299
Families: among African American Catholic women, 163;
    Amish, 264; celebration of, in Hinduism, 665; concern for
    maintaining ties, dual-career, 1125; education and, 905–
    906; Mennonite, 264; in Pentecostalism, 398–400; purity
    of, 570; woman's role in, 29–30, 793–795
The Family. *See* Children of God (COG)
Family History Libraries, 727
Family pew, introduction of, in Reform Judaism, 533, 534–
    535
The Family Protection Report (Marshner), 1299
Family Research Council, 1298, 1300
Family Violence Project of the Urban Justice Center, 1153–
    1154
Family Voice (magazine), 21
Famous Ward Singers, 992
Faraday, Michael, 772
Farajaje-Jones, Elias, 1237
Fard, Wallace D., 746, 747, 749
Farkas, Mary, 638, 641
Farley, Margaret, 55, 932, 953, 1103
The Farm, 710, 713, 717
Farmer, Irene, 215–216

Farmer, James, 1086, 1091
Farmer, Sarah Jane, 780–781
Farrakhan, Khadijah, 613
Farrakhan, Louis, 607, 613, 622, 746, 752
"Fa-sol-la" singing, 999
Father Divine Peace Mission, 710
Fatiman, Cécile, 121
Faurot, Randall, 300
Favela, Guadalupe, *169*
Fedde, Elizabeth, 311–312, 823, 827
Federal Council of Churches, 76, 1033, 1034, 1035. *See also*
    National Council of Churches (NCC)
Fédération nationale Saint-Jean-Baptiste (FNSJB), 214
Federation of Deaconess Associations, 832
Federation of Islamic Associations, 601
Federation of Jewish Charities, 1120
Federation of Temple Sisterhoods, 536, 542
Federation of Woman's Boards of Foreign Missions, 840
Federation of Women's Clubs, 1053
Feinstein, Moses, 581, 584
Feld, Merle, 1227
Feldman, Christina, 648
Feldman, David, 583
Felician sisters, 156
Feliciano, Dionicia, 495
Feliciano, Solomon, 495
Fell, Margaret, 27, 230, 233, 330
Fell, Nellie A., 429
Fell, Thomas, 330
Feller, Henriette Odin, 245
Fellman, David, 1273
Fellowes, Rockliffe, 1011
Fellowship of Reconciliation (FOR), 1033, 1055
Fellowship of the Maple Leaf, 284
Fellowship of the Spiral Path, 816
Female Academy (Warrenton, Virginia), 898
Female Anti-Slavery Convention (1837), 1044
Female Association, 1118
Female Association of Philadelphia for the Relief of Women
    and Children in Reduced Circumstances, 835
Female benevolent societies, 154, 246, 248, 534, 557, 565,
    590
Female biological primacy, theory of, 806
Female Building Society, 452
Female deities, displacement of, 92–93
Female Hebrew Benevolent Society, 590, 898, 968, 1118–
    1119, 1120
Female homoeroticism, 43
Female Literary Association, 1048
Female Ministry (pamphlet), 425, 945
Female missionaries: in films, 1014–1015; orders of, 129
Female Power and Male Dominance (Sanday), 1204
Female preaching: in seventeenth century, 966–968; in eigh-
    teenth century, 966–968; in nineteenth century, 968–970;
    in twentieth century, 970–973
Female Relief Society of the City of Nauvoo, 719
Female Religious and Moral Societies, 452–453
Female Society for Propagating the Gospel and Other Reli-
    gious Purposes, 246
Female submission, 467; doctrine of, 461

Fish, Leah Fox, 771, *772*
Fisher, Annie May, 423, 427
Fisher, Betty, 782
Fisher, Elizabeth, 392
Fisher, Mary, 224, 244, 331
Fisher, Violet, 328
Fishman, Sylvia Bank, 1122, 1125
Fishman, Y. L., 559
Fisk Jubilee Singers, 988–989
Fisk School, 988
Fitzgerald, John F., 192
FitzGerald, Kyriaki Karidoyanes, 514–515, 516, 517, 524
Fitzgerald, Osie M., 425
FitzGerald, Thomas, 516
Fitzpatrick, Ruth, 955, 958
Fitzpatrick, William Heard, 910
The Five Books of Miriam (Frankel), 1225–1226
Five Civilized Tribes, 113. *See also* Cherokee people; Chickasaw people; Choctaw people; Mvskoke people; Seminole people
Five Nations, 112
Five o'clock shadow, 595
Five Points Mission, 323, 430, 836
Flaliff, Cardinal George B., 216
Flam, Nancy, 542
Flanner House (Indianapolis), 1066
Flapper Evangelism, 403
Flashes of insight, 47–48
Fleischner, Eva, 1278, 1279–1280
Fleming, Alexie Torres, 482
Fleming, Bishop, 211
Fleming, Louise "Lulu" C., 259, 289
Fleming, Victor, 1014
Fliedner, Friederike, 311, 822
Fliedner, Theodor, 311, 822
Flinder, Carol Lee, 1308
Flirty fishing, 793, 794
Florence Kelley and the Nation's Work: The Rise of Women's Political Culture (Sklar), 859
Flores, Father Patricio, 1182
Florida Union State, 999
Flower, Alice Reynolds, 401–402
Flower, J. Roswell, 496
Fo Guang Shan Buddhism, 676
Focus on the Family (Dobson), 464, 1298
Foley, Margaret, 192
Foley, Nadine, 17
Fonda, Jane, 1014
Fools Crow v. *Gullet*, 105
Foote, Julia A. J., 433, 451–452, 868–869, 945, 969, 1167
For My People (Cone), 1236
For the Children's Sake (Schaeffer), 893
For the Soul of the People: Protestant Protest against Hitler (Barnett), 1283
Foraging societies, 9
Forbes, Mrs. John, 248
Ford, Ita, 847
Ford, John, 1015
Ford, Mary Hanford, 779
Ford, Sallie Rochester, 293

Fordham, Druecillar, 294
Foreign Mission Sisters of St. Dominic, 191
Foreign Missions Conference of North America, 840
Forest Lawn Cemetery (Los Angeles), 679
Forester, Fanny, 293
Formal religious leadership, 31–32
Forman, James, 1086
Fornication, 238
Forster, Gisela, 958
Forsyne, Ida, 1013
Forten, Charlotte, 257
Forth, Elizabeth Denison, 272
Fortune, Katie, 466
Foster, Abby Kelley, 340
Foster, Durwood, 78
Foster, Ebenezer J., 740
Foster, Esther, 783
Foster, Lawrence, 788
Foster, Martha Jane, 425
Foster, Mary Elizabeth Mikahala, 637
Foster care, Indian children in, 98–99
Foundation for Mind Research, 765–766
Fourier, Charles, 708
Fourierites, 716
The Fourth World of the Hopis (Courlander), 87
Fowler, James, 1198
Fox, Emmet, 759
Fox, Ethel, 902
Fox, George, 27, 233, 252, 329, 331
Fox, Katherine, 768, 769, 771, *772*, 773, 969, 1259
Fox, Margaret, 744, 768, 769, 771–772, *772*, 773, 969, 1259
Fox, Selena, 809, 816, 817, 969
Frame, Esther, 337
Francis, Ed, 764
Francis, Emma, 312
Francis I, King of France, 143
Franciscan Handmaids of the Most Pure Heart of Mary, 163, 165
Franciscan Missionaries of Mary, 846
Franciscan Sisters of Perpetual Adoration, 167
Franciscan Sisters of the Atonement, 849
Frank, Jerome, 1198
Frank, Ray, 960
Frankel, Ellen, 1225–1226
Frankenthaler, Helen, 66
Frankfurter, Felix, 862
Franklin, Aretha, 260, 992
Franklin, Benjamin, 770; death of, 234
Franklin, C. L., 992
Franklin, Deborah, 234
Franklin, Ursula, 1111
Frauen Kirchen groups, 1248
Fred, Randy, 101
Fred Victor Mission, 1067
Freda, Ezili, 120
Frederick Douglass Center (Chicago), 389, 1066
Fredriksen, Paula, 1281
Free African Society, 255
Free Baptist Woman's Missionary Society, 857

Free Church polity of Congregationalism, 942
Free Forever Prison Ministries program, 482
Free Love movement, 774
Free Methodist Church, 427, 454
Free Produce resolutions, 1043
Free Produce stores, 1049
Free Reformed Churches of North America, 350
Free Will Baptists, 285, 286, 287, 294, 1039; revivalism and, 417; Woman's Missionary Society of, 287; women leaders in, 968
Freed, Josh, 790
Freedman's Commission, 273
Freedmen's Aid, 1025
Freedom Council, 1298
Freedom Movement, 1091
Freedom rides, 260, 1081
Freedom Singers, 1091
Freedom Summer (1964), 1081, 1091
Freehof, Lillian, 903
Freeman, Jo, 18
Freeman, Len, 1292
Freemasons, 770, 1203
Freemen's Aid and Southern Education Society of the Methodist Episcopal Church, 916
Freiberg, Stella, 538–539
Freidenreich, Fradle, 904
Freire, Paulo, 935
Frelinghuysen, Theodore, 416
Fremont, Helen, 1282
French, Marilyn, 808
French Daughters of Charity, 152
Fresh Air Fund, 564
Freud, Anna, 426
Freud, Sigmund, 64
Friday Night Stories (Schechter), 546
Friedan, Betty, 14–15, 21, 357, 391, 469, 964, 1292
Friedman, Debbie, 542, 1224
Friedman, Lenore, 642, 1095
Friendly Aid House (New York City), 1065
Friendly visiting, 535
The Friendly Woman, 339, 340
Friends Committee on National Legislation, 339
Friends General Conference, 868
Friends to Liberia, 336–337
Friends World Committee on Consultation, 339
Friendship, 1083
Friendship Houses, 130, 196, 198–199
Frishman, Elyse, 543
Fritz, Maureen, 1281
Froebel, Friedrich Wihelm August, 909, 910
From Baca to Beulah (Smith), 429
From the Manger to the Cross (Olcott) (film), 1012
Frost, Gavin, 814
Frost, Vicki, 889, 891, 1299–1300
Frost, Yvonne, 814
Frothingham, Ebenezer, 227
Frow, Jennie, 841
The Frugal Housewife (Child), 1038
Fry, Susan M. D., 823
Fry, Theodore, 993

Frye, Mariella, 879
Frye, Theodore R., 993
Frymer-Kensky, Tikva, 588, 1226, 1277, 1282
Fuchs, Esther, 41
Fuchs-Kreimer, Nancy, 553
Fugitive Slave Law, 1006
Fujimoto, Rindo, 641
Fulkerson, Mary McClintock, 933–934
Full Gospel Business Men's Fellowship International (FGBMFI), 458–459, 462, 1263
Full Gospel Voice (magazine), 458
Fuller, Charles, 445, 456
Fuller, Grace, 456
Fuller, Jennie, 841
Fuller, Marcus, 841
Fuller, Margaret, 382, 387–388, 976
Fuller, W. E., Sr., 998
Fuller Theological Seminary, 455
Fundamentalism, 31, 439–447, 440, 970
Fundamentalism and Gender (Stratton), 31
Fundamentalist gospel tabernacles, hymns and, 986
Fung Loy Kok Institute of Taoism, 675
Fung Loy Kok Temple (Denver), 678
Funk, Annie, 269
FutureChurch, 956
Futures Process, 1097

Gaard, Greta, 1113
Gable, Clark, 1015
Gabler, Mel, 891, 1299, 1300
Gabler, Norma, 891, 1299, 1300
Gaffney, Margaret Haughery, 153
Gag rule, 1043–1044
Gage, Matilda Joslyn, 35–36, 805, 806, 1201, 1205
Gail, Marzieh, 783
Gaines, George, 290
Gakkai, Soka, 1209
Gallagher, Carol Joy, 278
Gallagher, Leah, 232
Gallant, Corinne, 216
Gallardo, Gloria, 1181
Galphin, George, 114
Galphintown, 111
Galvin, Edward, 845, 848
Gamble, Eliza Burt, 806
Gamoran, Emanuel, 903
Gamoran, Mamie, 903
Gampo Abbey (Nova Scotia), 30, 656
Gandhi, Mahatma, 669
Gandhi, Mohandas, 756
García, Catarina, 495
Garcia, Nicolasa de, 494
Garcia, Sixto, 170
Garcia Cortese, Aimee, 480, 481
García Peraza, Juanita, 496–497
Gardner, Freda A., 1270
Gardner, Gerald, 809, 1201, 1203–1204, 1264
Gardner, Pearl, 730
Gardnerian Wicca, 809, 810
Garfiel, Evelyn, 549

Garner, Erroll, 991
Garrett Evangelical Theological Seminary, 986, 1280
Garrison, William Lloyd, 1038, 1044, 1051, 1054
Garvey, Amy Ashwood, 1077–1078
Garvey, Amy Jacques, 1077, 1078–1079, 1080
Garvey, Marcus, 1076–1077, 1079–1080; "back to Africa" movement of, 260
Garveyism, 1076–1081
Gaskin, Stephen, 710
Gast, Mary Susan, 376
Gates, Ellen, 859–860
The Gates Ajar (Phelps), 1007
Gates of Prayer, 542
Gaudet Normal and Industrial School, 273
Gaudet-Joseph, Frances, 273
Gaudin, Juliette, 164, 165
Gauntier, Gene, 1012
Gautama, 29
Gavin, Theresa, 150
Gay Men's Health Crisis, 1096
Gayatri Devi, Srimata (Reverend Mother), 669
Gays: civil union of, 217; Hinduism and, 665–666; rights movement of, 1216, 1298. *See also* Lesbians
Gearhart, Sally Miller, 1216, 1219
Gebara, Ivone, 1197
Gelassenheit (yieldedness), 267
Geller, Laura, 542, 1221
Gellis, Audrey, 18
Gelug school, 652
Gender: analysis of, 43; boarding school abuses and, 101–102; Buddhism and, 26, 28, 40; in Christianity, 28; distinguishing between sex and, 23; evidence of injustice, in religion, 48; Hinduism and, 26, 28; images of, 26; Islam and, 26, 28; Judaism and, 26, 28; in Latina experience, 484–492; religious beliefs and practices and, *24;* social roles and, 23–33; women's ordination and, 949–950
Gender bias, 37
Gender jihad, 607
Gender relations, 52
Gender-inclusive core teachings, 10–11
Gender-inclusive language, 10–11
Gender-neutral core teachings, 10–11
Gendler, Everett, 801
General Catechetical Directory (publication), 880
General Directory for Catechesis (publication), 880
General Division of Women's Work (GDWW), 277
General Federation of Women's Clubs (GFWC), 870, 1010, 1012, 1027, 1028, 1033
General Missionary Convention of the Baptist Denomination in the United States for Foreign Missions, 286
Generation X Asian American Catholic women, 186–187
Generative women's voices, 53–54
Genesis Farm, New Jersey, 717, 1111–1112
Genius of Universal Emancipation, 334
Genocide, 105–106
Gentleman's Agreement Act (1907), 179, 681
Gentleman's Agreement (Hobson), 594
George, Cassietta, 992
George, Dan, 94
George, Margaret, 152

Georgetown College, 883
Georgia, 309; New Light Presbyterians in, 239; prohibition of slavery in, 237–239
Georgia Conference of the Methodist Episcopal Church, 916
Georgia Female College, 916
Gérin-Lajoie, Marie Lacoste, 213–214
Germaine, Saint, 1264
German Congregationalists, 372
German Evangelicals, 371–372; women as, 373
German Liberal Protestantism, 1282
German Pietists, 708; in Colonial Pennsylvania, 230–231
German Reform Judaism, 533, 961
German Reformed Church, 369–370, 374
German Sisters of St. Francis, 153
Germans, Lutheran Church and, 308–309
Germantown (Pa.) Protest (1688), 252, 1039
Geshe Tashi Namgyal, 655
Gestefeld, Ursula, 744, 757
G.e.t., Inc., 587
Getsinger, Lua, 777, 779, 783
Gezari, Temima, 902
Ghost Dance, 106
Ghost sickness, 1257
Gibbes, Emily V., 17, 37, 1269
Gibbs, Lois, 1112
Gibel, Inge Lederer, 1279
Gibson, Christine, 399
Gidda folk dances, 698–699
Giddings, Paula, 1302
Gilbert, Arthur, 1277
Gilded Age, 1027
Giles, Harriet, 292, 917
Gilkes, Cheryl Townsend, 20, 261, 867, 1169
Gill, Gillian, 746
Gill, Kathleen, 921
Gill, Sam, 1230
Gillespie, Angela, 157
Gillespie, Catherine, 347
Gillespie, Dizzy, 167
Gillespie, Joanna, 279
Gillespie, Lorraine, 167
Gillespie, Williams, 167
Gilligan, Carol, 54, 1304–1305
Gilman, Charlotte Perkins, 158, 806, 1009, 1053
Gilman, Nicholas, 227
Gilson, Bathurst, 932
Gilson, Etienne, 195
Gimbutas, Marija, 19, *807,* 808, 1201–1202, 1204–1205
Gingaskin people, intermarrige with blacks, 114
Ginneken, Jacques van, 197
Ginsberg, Allen, 1201
Ginzberg, Adele, 546–547, 549
Ginzberg, Louis, 545, 546, 1123
Girl Guides, 283, 284
Girlfriend Theology, 1304–1310, *1305*
Girls' Auxiliary, 281
Girls' Friendly Society, 275, 281–182
Giroux, Jeanne Brady, 938
Gladden, Washington, 1071
Glanzam, Louis, painting by, *142*

Glasgow Colonial Society, 245; Edinburgh Auxiliary of, 244–245

Glaspell, Susan, 1009

Glassman, Bernard Tetsugen, 643, 676, 1094, 1096

Gleason, Linus, 1277

Glendon, Mary Ann, 788, 1106

Glenn, Laura Franklin, 668–669

Gliedman, John, 816

Gliedman-Adler, Alexander, 816

Global Celebration for Women, 460

Global ecofeminism, 1112–1113

Global Recordings Network, 842

Glorious Revolution (1688), 332

Glover, George Washington, 738–739

Glover, George Washington, Jr., 739

Glueck, Nelson, 541, 962

Glynn, Mary Theresa, 1104

Gnostics, 250

God and the Rhetoric of Sexuality (Trible), 37

God Is Red (Deloria), 83

God language, 1292, 1294–1295

Goddaughters, 141–148

Goddess religion, rebirth of, 1200–1207

Goddess Spirituality, 712, 810

Goddesses: archeological records of, 19; data about, 8; as exotic and primitive, 7–8; religious movements centered around, 1288; worship of, 1293

Godmothers, 141–148

Godparents, 161

Gods and Goddesses of Old Europe (Gimbutas), 19, 808, 1201

"God's Light upon the Mountain," 288

God's Paintbrush (Sasso), 553

Godseed: The Journey of Christ (Houston), 766

Goenka, 647

Goeres, Mavis, 57

Goggin, Catherine, 155

Gohr, Glenn, 398

Gold, Shefa, 802, 803

Gold Flower Lady, 674

Goldberg, Whoopi, 1014

Golde, Marion, 589

Golden Chain (Bradbury), 983

Golden Dawn, 1203

Golden ghetto, 595

Golden Mother, 677

Goldenberg, Naomi, 1202

Golder, Christian, 824–825, 827, 853

Goldstein, Adela, 559

Goldstein, David, 420

Goldstein, Elyse, 1226

Goldstein, Joseph, 647, 651, 1097

Goldstein, Rose, 549

Goldwater, Barry, 1296

Golinkin, David, 584

Gone with the Wind (Mitchell), 1005

Gonzáles, Delores (Lolita) de, 494

Gonzales, Susan, 183–184

González, Fela, 497

Gonzalez, Michelle, 1198

González-Tejera, Awilda, 483

González-Wippler, Migene, 736

Good, Deirdre, 1281

Good, Martha Smith, 268

Good News for Women: A Biblical Picture of Gender Equality (Groothuis), 473

The Good News Yesterday and Today (Jungmann), 878

Good Samaritan Sisters, 452

Goodman, Susan, 905

Goodyear, Imogene, 730

Gordon, A. J., 396, 440

Gordon, Anna, 985

Gordon, Eleanor, *381*, 386, 390

Gordon, Jean Margaret, 390

Gordon, Kate, 390

Gordon, Maria Hale, 441

Gordon, Mary, 1108

Gordon College, 440–441, 444

Gordon Divinity School, 444

Gordon-Conwell Theological Seminary, 441

Goreh, Ellen Lashmi, 982

Goreh, Nehemiah, 982

Gornick, Vivian, 21

Gospel Advocate (newspaper), 301

Gospel Hall of Fame, 995

Gospel Hymns (Sankey), 977, 981

Gospel Light Publications, 445

Gospel Missionary Union, 841

Gospel music and musicians, 989–995

Gospel Music Hall of Fame, 992

Gospel Music Workshop of America (GMWA), 992, 993, 996

The Gospel Pearls, 990, 997, 998

Gospel recordings, 842

Gospel stars, 993

Goss, Ethel, 395, 397

Goss, Howard, 397, 401

Goss, Millicent, 397

Gotham Records, 994

Gothard, Bill, 446

Goto, Rosemary, 686

Gotsfeld, Bessie Goldstein, 559–560, 1125, 1126

Gotsfeld, Mendel, 559

Gotta Have Faith (album), 994

Gottheil, Gustav, 535, 900–901

Gottlieb, Lynn, 801, 803, 1222, 1223–1224

Gottschalk, Alfred, 541

Goucher College (Md.), 882, 916, 922

Government Nannies: The Cradle-to-Grave Agenda of Goals 2000 and Outcome Based Education (Duffy), 893

Grace, James, 790

Grace School for Deaconesses, 826

Graceland College, 731

Grady, Narayan Liebenson, 648

Grafstein, Ayla, 801, 802, 803, 804

Graham, Billy, 416, 445, 451–452, 456, 462, 469, 986

Graham, Isabella, 453, 835

Graham, Julia, 353

Graham, Leah (Demarest), 1065

Graham, Ruth Bell, 451, 462

Grail Institution for Overseas Service, 846

Grail International, 846–847

Grail (renewal movement), 132, 197–198, 199, 202
Grail Women Task Force, 1245
Grajeda, María, 496
Grand cosmogonic stories, 83
Grant, Amy, 986
Grant, Jacquelyn, 261, 1169
Grant, Ulysses S., 153; peace policy of, 98
Grassroots ministries, 482–483
Gratz, Rachel, 1118
Gratz, Rebecca, 565, 580, 590, 898, 899, 903, 968, 1118–1120, *1119*, 1124
Gratz, Sarah, 1118
Gratz College, 901
Graves, Ann, 287, 293
Graves, Mary H., 385, 942
Graves, Robert, 1201
Gray, Victoria, 261
Gray Panthers, 357
Greaser Act, 487
Great Awakening, 226–227, 235, 287, 344, 347, 351, 370, 941, 966, 976, 999; evangelical fervor of, 227; in Southern colonies, 239. *See also* First Great Awakening (1730–1760); Second Great Awakening (1800–1830)
Great Joy (Crosby), 984
Great Migration of African Americans, 165–166
The Great Physician (Boardman), 429
Great White Brotherhood of the Ascended Masters, 1262
The Greatest Story Ever Told (film), 1012–1013
Greek Orthodox Philoptochos Society, 509, 513
Greeley, Andrew, 954
Greeley, Horace, 772
Green, Ashbel, 346
Green, Carol Hurd, 888
Green, Joyce, 671
Green, Lear, 1040
Green, Paula, 1095
Green, Rayna, 105–106
Green, Tova, 1094
Green Acre, 780–782
The Green Egg (magazine), 817
Green Gulch Farm, 643
The Green Pastures (film), 1013
Green Spirituality, 810
Greenberg, Betty, 548
Greenberg, Blu, 583, 588, 1227, 1228, 1279
Greenburg, Dan, 595
Greene, Bonnie, 1145
Greene, Emily, 1054
Greenhow, Rose O'Neal, 152–153
Greenleaf, Elizabeth, 779
Greenwich House (New York City), 275, 1065, 1067, 1072
Greer, Jonathan, 994
Gregory, Wilton, 1109
Grey, Mary Martin de Porres, 847
Grey Nuns, 211, 212, 1111
Griffin, Bessie, 992
Griffin, Susan, 1112, 1202
Griffith, D. W., 1015
Griffith, Gwyneth, 367
Griffitts, Hannah, 233

Grimké, Angelina Emily, 35, 54, 334, 1023, 1044–1046, 1048, 1050, 1051, 1058
Grimké, Sarah Moore, 13, 35, 54, 334, 1023, 1044–1046, 1048, 1050, 1051, 1058
Grof, Stanislav, 1096
Groothuis, Rebecca Merrill, 473
Gross, Rita, 40, 50, 53, 684, 703, 1098, 1223, 1275
Group for the Rabbinical Ordination of Women, 551
Gruchy, Lydia, 349, 363, 364
Grudem, Wayne, 468–469
Gruel, Chevalier de, 144
Grumm, Christine, 316
Grupta, Lina, 40
Gua, Pierre de, 143
Guadalupe Hidalgo, Treaty of, 487, 1195, 1196, 1199
Guan Yin (Bodhisattva of Compassion), 26, 29, 634, 643, 674, 1264
Guandi, 673
Guangong, 673, 675
Guanyin. *See* Guan Yin
Guardiola Saenz, Leticia, 483
Gudorf, Christine, 60
Les Guérillères (Wittig), 19
Guerin, Theodore, 152
The Guide to Holiness (publication), 424, 980
Guillen, Patricio, 1186
Gujarati Samaj, 660
The Gujarati Society, 660
Gulko, Judith, 802
Gundersen, Joan, 272
Gundry, Pat, 472
Gurdwara Joti Sarup, 696, 697–698
Gurdwara Mata Gujari, 696
Gurney, Joseph John, 336
Gurney, Marion, 190, 1067
Gurneyite Friends, 336
Guru Amar Das (Nanak III), 695
Guru Angad (Nanak II), 695
Guru Arjan, 695
Guru Gobind Singh, 695, 696, 698, 699–700
Guru Granth, 695, 696–697, 698, 699, 700, 701, 702
Guru Har Krishan, 695
Guru Har Rai, 695
Guru Hargobind, 695
Guru Nanak, 695–696, 697, 698, 699
Guru Ram Das, 695
Guru Tegh Bahadur, 695, 696
Gurukula, 670
Gurumayi, 670–671
Guthrie, Lizzie M., 325
Gutiérrez, Gustavo, 847, 1174, 1197
Gutman, Sharon Weissman, 1283
Guyart, Marie, 144
Guys and Dolls (film), 1015
Gvosdev, Ellen, 517
Gwynedd-Mercy, 888

Hadassah, 545, 903, 1122, 1123–1125
Hadassah International Research Institute on Jewish Women, 1125

Hawaii Association of International Buddhists, 686

Hawaii Sugar Planters Association, 681

Hawkins, Tramaine, 260

Hawkins, Walter, 994

Hawthorne, Nathaniel, 150

Hawthorne, Rose, 191

Hayashi, Susanna, *179*, 181

Hayden, Casey, 18, 1056, 1086, 1091

Hayden, J. Carleton, 273

Hayden, Tom, 1091

Hayes, Diana, 847, 1171

Hayes, Patrick Cardinal, 165–166

Haynes, Elizabeth Ross, 1131

Hays, Will H., 1012

Hayward, David, 1013

Hayward, Susan, 1013

Hazon, Eshet, 803

Healing, 50, 1255–1265; African American, in nineteenth
century, 1261; among Euro-American colonists, 1257–
1258; charismatic, 1263; Christian Science, 1259–1260; divine, 427–430, 1262; eclectic witchcraft and, 1264–1265;
Ellen White's medical ministry, 1260; ethnic, 1262; faith,
1262–1263; imaginative interpretations of, 51; male, scientific medicine, 1258; Native American, 1256–1257; neopaganism and, 1264; neoshamanism and, 1264–1265; New
Age and, 1264–1265; New Age eclecticism and, 1264; recent immigrants and, 1263–1264; Santería and, 1264; scientific medicine, female acceptance of, 1260–1261; spiritualism, 1259; theosophy, 1262; twentieth-century
immigrants and, 1261–1262; Vodou and, 1264

Healing the Wounds: The Promise of Ecofeminism (Plant),
1112

Health Protection and Reproductive Health Initiative, 871

Healthy, Happy, Holy Organization (3HO), 693

Hearst, George, 777

Hearst, Phoebe, 777, 781, 782

Heart of Flesh: A Feminist Spirituality for Women and Men
(Chittister), 22

Heart-to-Heart, 420

The Heathen Helper (Osborne), 293

The Heathen Woman's Friend (journal), 324, 855

Heathenism, 810

Heaton, Hannah, 226

Heaven Knows, Mr. Allison (film), 1014

*Heavenly Pearls Set in a Life: A Record of Experiences and La-
bors in America, India and Australia* (Drake), 429

Heaven's Gate, 789

Hebden, Ellen, 397

Hebden, James, 397

Hebert, Louis, 143

Hebert, Marie (Rollet), 143–144

Hebrew burial societies, 557–558

Hebrew Education Society, 547

Hebrew Free School Association, 900, 901

Hebrew Industrial School for girls, 899

Hebrew Ladies' Benevolent Societies, 570–571

Hebrew Literary Society, 899

Hebrew Sunday School (Philadelphia), 898, 1118, 1119, 1120,
1126

Hebrew Teachers Training Institute for Girls, 561

Hebrew Technical School, 899

Hebrew Union College (HUC), 535, 536, 538, 539, 960

Hebrew Union College–Jewish Institute of Religion (HUC-
JIR), 541, 543, 544, 581, 962. *See also* Jewish Institute of
Religion (JIR)

Hebron, 234

Hecht, Lina, 899

Heck, Barbara, 235, 244, 253, 319

Heck, Fannie E. S., 290, 293

Heck, Paul, 244

Heck, Samuel, 941

Heeg, Aloysius, 874

Heidelberg Catechism, 342, 369

Height, Dorothy I., 871

Heilbrun, Carolyn, 70–71

Heineman, Barbara, 714

Heinzelmann, Gertrud, 199, 951

Heisey, Nancy Ruth, 268

Helene of Freyberg, 264

Helpers of Holy Souls (HHS), 879

Henderlite, Rachel, 350, 359

Henrichsen, Margaret, 328

Henry, Carl F. H., 445

Henry, Linda, 994

Henry IV, King of France, 143

Henry Street Settlement (N.Y.), 1062–1063

Henry VIII, King of England, 221

Hentz, Caroline, 1007

Hepburn, Audrey, 1014

Hepburn, Katharine, 1014

The Herald of Progress, 774

Herbart, Pestalozzi, 910

Heretic's Heart (Adler), 816

Heritage Keepers, 1300

A Heritage of Violence, 217

Heritage USA, 463

Herlacher, Sarah, 345

Las Hermanas (The Sisters), 17, 20, 133, 847, 1181–1188,
1183, 1244

Hermeneutics, feminist, 40, 41

Hernandez-Avila, Ines, 1233

Heroic medicine, 1258

Heroic motherhood, in Quebec, 213

Herrad of Hohenburg, 883

Herrera, Marina, 1196, 1200

Herring, Annie, 986

Herron, Sarah, 777

Herschel, Susannah, 40

Hershey, Barbara, 1013

Herzberger, Friedrich, 312

Heschel, Abraham Joshua, 801

Heschel, Susannah, 1221, 1282

Heschel School (Los Angeles), 904

Hess, Carol Lakey, 1306

Hestenes, Roberta, 470

Hester Street (film), 1016

Hevra kadisha, 557–558

Hewitt, Eliza, 980

Hewitt, Emily Clark, 953

Hewitt, J. N. B, 83, 84

Homan, Ken, 936
Home altars, Latina popular Catholicism and, 177
Home and Foreign Days, 839–840
Home Mission Monthly (magazine), 353
Home Missionary Society, 856
Home School Digest (magazine), 893
Home schooling, 889, 891–896
Homes of Truth, 758, 760–761
Homeschooling Today (magazine), 893
Homo religiosus, 25
Homoeroticism, female, 43
Homophobia, 1210
Homosexuality, 16. *See also* Lesbians
Honanie, Delbridge, *84*
Honi, Satomi, 681
Honor, Leo, 901
Honor killings, 951
Honpa Hongwanji Mission of Hawaii, 681, 685, 686
Hood, Margaret Scholl, 918
Hood College (Maryland), 918, 922
Hoodoo doctors, 1261
hooks, bell, 1095, 1169
Hoomi, Koot, 762
Hooten, Elizabeth, 331
Hoover, Theressa, 15, 17
Hop, The Devil's Brew (film), 1011
Hope, Bob, 765
Hope, Daring, 1289
Hope, Lugenia Burns, 1035, 1074, 1075, *1075*
Hopfe, Lewis, 761
Hopi people: emergence narratives of, 85, 87; use of cultural traditions by outsiders, 103
Hopkins, Emma Curtis, 744, 757–760, 761, 763, 970, 1259
Hopkins, George Irving, 757
Hopkins, Mattie, 279
Hopkins, Pauline, 1168
Hopkins, Samuel, 227, 941
Hopkins Metaphysical Association, 758
Hopkinson, Deborah, 642
Hopko, Thomas, 514, 528
Horan, Ellamay, 880
Horne, Martha J., 928
Horner, I. B., 637
Horner, R. C., 400
Hornstein Program in Jewish Communal Service, 905
Horowitz, Barbara Ostfeld, 541
Horticultural societies, 9
Horton, Isabelle, 829, 854, 1071
Horton, Myles, 1083, 1090
Horton, Willie, 1302–1303
Horton, Zilphia, 1083
Hoskens, Jane Fenn, 230, 966
Houdini, Harry, 775
Housa people, missionary efforts among, 112
House of God Church (HGC), hymnals of, 997
House of God Which Is the Church of the Living God, Pillar and Ground of the Truth, Inc., 432, 436
The House of Mirth (Wharton), 1009
House of Recovery, in British North America, 246
House Un-American Activities Committee, 1085

Household Saints (film), 1016
Household Saints (Prose), 189
Householders, 231
Houselander, Caryll, 195
Houses of Hospitality, 130, 196
Houston, Jean, 763, 765–766
Houston, Mary, 765
Hovsepian, Vatché, 521
How to Be a Jewish Mother (Greenburg), 595
How to Eat to Live, 613
Howard, Adelyn, 275
Howard, Chonita Morgan, 495
Howard, Joyce, 276
Howard, Lloyd, 495
Howard, Victoria, 1096–1097
Howe, Julia Ward, 158, 390, 391, 949, 977, *978*, 979, 1052–1053
Howell, Nancy, 1113
Howland, Emily, 335
Hrafnar, 816
Hsi Lai Temple (Hacienda Heights, Calif.), 676
Hsing Yun, 676
Hsuan Hua, 641
Huber, Jane Parker, 986
Hudson, Dovie, 1088–1089
Hudson, Mary Geraldine Guinness, 444
Hudson, Winson, 1088–1089
Hudson Bay Company, 249
Hueck, Catherine de, 130, 197
La Huelga, 1196
Huerta, Delores, 1183, 1198, *1199*
Hughes, Archbishop John, 162
Hughes, Langston, 992
Hughes, Sarah Ann, 258
Hughs, Mary, 150
Huguenots: infant baptism for, 232; women in Mid-Atlantic colonies, 229
Hui Kahea Pono, 502
Huitzilopochtli, 1195
Huizenga, Annette Bourland, 471
Hull, Gretchen Gabelein, 471
Hull House (Chicago), 130, 190, 275, *859*, 919, 1030, 1059, 1064–1067, 1072, 1074
Hull House Maps and Papers (publication), 1063
Hultin, Ida, 390–391
Human account of religion, 7
Human civilization, sociological theory of origins of, 1052
The Human Encounter with Death (Halifax), 1096
Human potential movement, 765
Human rights in Canada, 1146
Humanae vitae (Paul VI), 132, 199, 216, 1100
Humanism, secular, 889, 890–891, 1298, 1299; *Declaration of Sentiments and Resolutions*, 960
Hume, Sophia, 966
Humez, Jean, 1165–1166
Hung Ch'ih, 641
Hungarian Reformed churches, 372
Hunt, Alma, 293
Hunt, Dorothy, 635–636
Hunt, Ernest, 635–636

Hunt, Helen, 1156, 1158
Hunt, Mary, 59, 1108
Hunter, Fannie McDowell, 427
Hunter, James Davison, 890
Hunter, Jean Ross, 249
Huntington, Sarah, 836
Hunton, Addie Waite, 870, 1131
Hunton, George, 197
Hurley, James, 473
Hurley, Ruby, 1090
Hurston, Zora Neale, 65, 432, 434, 1167–1168, 1171
Husbands-Hankin, Shonna, 802–803
Huseth, Anna, 312
Hussey, Patricia, 1105
Huston, John, 1014
Hutchinson, Anne, 33, 36, 46, 48, 223–224, 230, 331, 347, 351, 368, 447–448, 940, 966, 967
Hutchinson, Beverly, 765
Hutchinson, Charles, 337
Hutchinson, Jean, 366, 367
Hutchison, Moira, 1147
Hutter, Jakob, 707
Hutterites, 262, 263, 264, 707, 712
Hutton, David, 400
Hutton, Ronald, 1203, 1204–1205
Huxley, Aldous, 646
Hyang, Seong, 644
Hybridity, 733
Hyde, Henry, 1104
Hyde Amendment, 1103
Hygiene, Native children and, 100
Hyman, Paula, 18, 571, 576, 905, 1221, 1226
Hymn Society, 986
Hymn writers, women, 974–987
Hymnal of the F. B. H. Church, 998
The Hymnals of the United Church of Christ, 998
Hymnody: African American, 987–1000; defined, 987
Hymns from the Land of Luther (Winkworth and Borthwick), 976
Hypatia: A Journal of Feminist Philosophy, 20
Hypnosis, 769
The Hypocrites (film), 1011

I, Mary Magdalene (Thompson), 783
I Am a Woman by God's Design (LaHaye), 460, 1297
I AM Movement, 763, 1264
I Believe in Miracles (television series), 421
Iberian Catholicism, 477
Iberville, Pierre LeMoyne d', 146
Icaza, Rosa María, 1200
Icelandic Women's Suffrage Association, 391
Icon of Sophia—Divine Wisdom (McGuckin), 63
Identity, religious feminists and, 20–21
Iglesia Cristiana Pentecostal, Inc., 481
Iglesias, María, 1184
Ikuta, C. Nozomi, 502
Ilaloo, Sister, 123
Illinois Factory Acts (1893), 861
Illinois Immigrants Protective League, 861
Illinois State Sunday School Association, 853

Imagination, women's religious, 45–52
Imago Dei, implications of, in theological anthropology, 527–528
Imamura, Jane Matsuura, 634–635, 638, 683, 684, 686
Imamura, Kanmo, 683, 684
Imamura, Ryo, 634
Imamura, Yemyo, 635
Imbolc, 813
Immaculata (Philadelphia), 888
Immanence, women's imaginative elaboration of, 49–50
Immediatist abolitionism, 1051
Immigrants: African, 111, 112, 115; Asian, 178–180; Catholic, 127–128, 145–148, 154–156, 178–180; outreach of nuns to, 155–156; Filipino, 179; healing and, 1261–1264; Jewish, 554–556; new, 154–155; Pacific, 178–180; religions of Chinese, 673–679, *678;* religions of Japanese, 680–687, *682;* Sephardic, 554–555; Sikh women as, 190, 693–695
Immigration, religion as reason for, 221, 231–232
Immigration Act (1924), 535, 674
Immigration Act (1952), 674
Immigration Act (1965), 180, 186, 500, 685
The Immigration and the Community (Abbott), 1065
Immigration Restriction Act (1921), 535
Imperialism, cultural, 837
In a Blaze of Glory: Womanist Spirituality as Social Witness (Townes), 1172
In God's Name (Sasso), 553
In Good Faith, 1148
In His Steps (Sheldon), 1071
In loco parentis, doctrine of, 886
In Memory of Her: A Feminist Theological Construction of Christian Origins (Fiorenza), 38, 202, 1246
In Search of Our Mothers' Gardens: Womanist Prose (Walker), 1166–1167
In Stewardship (document), 920
In Woman, Church, and State (Gage), 1201
Inaya, 689, 692–693
Incidents in the Life of a Slave Girl (Jacobs), 1001
Inclusive language, 1290–1295; gender, 10–11; in relation to biblical translation, 37
An Inclusive Language Lectionary, 37, 1269, 1292, 1293
Inclusivity, 64, 1171
Indentured servants, women as, 236
Independent Christian Churches, 296
Independent Fundamental Churches, 444
India, religions of, 8. *See also* Hinduism
Indian Affairs, Bureau of (BIA), 106
Indian Child Welfare Act (1978), 99
Indian festival of lights, 699
"Indian Guide" programs for youth, 102
Indian Peace Commission, 1026
Indian Placement Program, 725
Indian Religious Crimes Code, 93
Indian Reorganization Act (1934), 93
Indigenous religions, 103, 761; African Caribbean traditions and, 116–123; South American, 94–96. *See also* Aframerindians; Native Americans
Indirection, 45–46
Industrial capitalism, 1127; rise of, 1027
Industrial justice, responsibility for, 1035

Infant damnation, Calvinist policy of, 769
Infant mortality, in colonies, 236
Ingall, Carol, 905
Inglis, Charles, 280
Ingram, Rex, 1013
Initiation, Human and Solar (Hoomi), 762
Inner Light, 940
Insider/outsider status, women's, 45–52
Insight meditation, 646–647
Insight Meditation Society, 646–647, 651
Inskip, John, 425
Inspirationists, 708, 712
Institute for Black Catholic Studies at Xavier University of
    Louisiana, 167
Institute for Religious Life, 207, 208
Institute of Buddhist Dialectics, 656
Institute of Buddhist Studies, 685
Institute on Religion and Democracy, 460
Institutes of the Christian Religion (Calvin), 341
L'Institution Catholique des Orphelins Indigens, 162
Institution of Protestant Deaconesses, 822, 823
Intelligent design in science classes, 890
Inter Insigniores, 216, 528, 954, 957
Inter-Church Committee on Human Rights in Latin America
    (ICCHRLA), 1146
Intercommunity Justice and Peace Center, 1246
Interdenominational Theological Center, 343
Interfaith Center on Corporate Responsibility, 206
Interfaith marriage, 624, 1272–1274
Interlingua, 786
Intermarriage, 94, 113; between blacks and Native Ameri-
    cans, 114
International Association of Settlements, 1061
International Association of Women Ministers, 949
International Association of Women Preachers, 949
International Baha'i Bureau, 786
International Bible Society, 474
International Buddhist Mediation Center (Los Angeles), 644
International Buddhist Progress Society, 676
International Catholic-Jewish Historical Commission, 1280
International Church of the Foursquare Gospel, 404, 406,
    420, 456, 1263
International Committee of Women for Permanent Peace,
    1054
International Conference on Women and Orthodoxy, 1228,
    1228
International Congress of Religious Liberals, 669
International Council of Christians and Jews, 1277
International Council of Women (ICW), 1031, 1032, 1053
International Covenant on Civil and Political Rights, 1142–
    1143
International Development Center, 871
International Federation of Settlements and Neighbourhood
    Centres (IFS), 1059, 1061
International Fellowship Program in Coexistence, 1095
International Glove Workers Union, 189
International Healing Tao Centers, 678
International Human Rights Watch, 587
International Institute for Islamic Thought, 604
International Moshiach Congress for Women, 562

International Network of Engaged Buddhists, 1093
International New Thought Alliance, 759, 760
International Order of Good Templars (IOGT), 1024
International Orthodox Christian Charities, 509
International Peace Congress, 1053
International Raelian movement, 795–796
International Society for Krishna Consciousness, 664, 667,
    670
International Union of Superior Generals, 216
International We Are Church Movement (1997), 957
International Women's Year (IWY), 305, 726, 1297
Internment camps, relocation of Japanese Americans to, *179,*
    179–180
Inter-Orthodox Theological Consultation, 514
Interracial Cooperative Committee, 1065
Interreligious Affairs for the Union of American Hebrew
    Congregation, 1279
Interreligious collaboration, 1113–1114
Introducing Thealogy (Raphael), 1206
Inuit creation myth, 88–89
Inversion, 47–48
Invisible institutions, 254
An Invitation to Prayer (Labowitz and Gulko), 802
Inward Light, 224
Ireland, Patricia, 1134
Irenaeus of Lyons, 527
Iroquois Confederacy, 83
Iroquois people, legends of, 92
Irvin, Dorothy, 473–474
Irving, Amy, 1016
Irving, David, 1282
Irving College, 918
Is the Homosexual My Neighbor? Another Christian View
    (Mollenkott), 1217
Isabella, Queen of Spain, 118
Isasi-Díaz, Ada María, 20, 42, 56, 57, 489, 932, 955, 1185,
    1186, 1187, 1194, 1196, 1230
Isenberg, Nancy, 453
Ishibashi, Joan, 684, 685, 686
Ish-Kishor, Shulamith, 902
Isis Unveiled (Blavatsky), 755
Islam, 10, 601–629; African Americans in, 608–615, *610;* Ah-
    madiyyah movement in, 611–612, 614; gender and, 26, 28;
    male-female relationships in, 623; marriage in, 28, 31, 623–
    625; interfaith, 1273; mosques in, 615–619; oppression of
    women and, 31, 49; pilgrimages to Mecca in, 610; Qur'an
    as center of, 609–610; religious alternatives to woman's
    primary domestic role, 28–29; status of women and, 9;
    struggle for identity for North American women, 601–608;
    Sufi tradition of, 30; violence associated with, 603;
    women's issues in, 619–629. *See also* Muslim women;
    Qur'an
Islamic book club, 617
Islamic Center of Washington, D.C., 604
Islamic Circle of North America (ICNA), 621
Islamic feminism, 603
Islamic Foundation of Greater St. Louis, 616
Islamic law, 20–21
Islamic literature, role of women in, 604
Islamic Networks Group (ING), 618

of, in United States, 1118–1120; Zionist groups as, 1122–1126

Jewish-Christian relations, women's contributions to, 1276–1283

Jewison, Norman, 1014

Jews: agricultural colonies established by, 709–710; in Colonial Pennsylvania, 230. *See also* Judaism

Jews College Library, 545

Jim Crow laws, 14, 259, 1074, 1075

Jimenez, María, 497

Jinfa, 674

Jiv, 690

Jñana yoga, 666

Joan of Arc (Fleming), 1014

Jocks, Christopher, 1230

Jodo Shinshu (Shin [or Pure Land] Buddhism), 634, 637, 680–681, 683–684, 685, 686; temples of, *635,* 635–636

Jogues, Isaac, 145

Johannisstift, 822

John XXIII (Pope), 16, 199, 200, 1174, 1278

John F. Kennedy Commission, 963–964

John of the Cross, Saint, 206

John Paul II (Pope), 132, 145, 177, 182, 200, 204–205, 955, 957, 1106

John Street Methodist Chapel, 941

Johns, Altona Trent, 995

Johnson, Andrea, 955, 957, 958

Johnson, Carrie Parks, 1035

Johnson, Elizabeth, 50, 202, 203, 1198

Johnson, Hannah, 320

Johnson, Janis, 1145

Johnson, Jennie, 290, 294

Johnson, Marilyn, 1286

Johnson, Sonia, 16

Johnson, William, 107, 234, 1216

Johnson-Reed Act (1924), 188

Johnston, Bella, 348

Johnston, Julia, 980

Joint Commission on Social Service, 275–276

Joint stock company, 708

Jolliet, Louis, 146

Jolson, Al, 1015–1016

Jonas, Regina, 961–962

Jones, Absalom, 998

Jones, Adrienne Lash, 1131

Jones, Charles Price, 438, 989, 997

Jones, Christine, 814

Jones, Eli, 336–337

Jones, Jennifer, 1014

Jones, Jim, People's Temple of, 714

Jones, Mary Harris ("Mother"), 155, 189

Jones, Mary Jane Done, 721

Jones, May C., 294

Jones, Rebecca, 335

Jones, Ruth, 991

Jones, Shirley, 1015

Jones, Sybil, 336–337

Jonestown mass suicide, 710, 787

Jonquest, Anne, 143

Joseph, Norma Baumel, 1228

Joshin-san, 643

Joubert, Jacques Hector Nicolas, 164

Journal of Feminist Studies in Religion (JFSR), 1169, 1218, 1234, 1281

The Journal of Religious Instruction (Walsh), 879

Journey of Human Spirit (Kabotie and Honanie), *84*

The Joy Luck Club (film), 1016

Juana Inés de la Cruz, Sor, 45–46, *134,* 134–135, 137–139, 1195, 1198

Juárez, Benito, 141

Judah, J. Stillson, 753

Judaism, 3, 6, 8, 533–597, 1226; abortion and, 587; anti-Semitism and, 588–597, *593;* gender and, 26, 28; healing and, 1262; interfaith marriage and, 1273; Jewish law and gender, 576–588; marriage and, 31; normative, 568; ordination of women in, 960–965; religious alternatives to woman's primary domestic role, 28–29; rituals and, 568–576; status of women and, 9, 21; woman's education in religious matters, 28. *See also* Conservative Judaism; Orthodox Judaism; Reconstructionist Judaism; Reform Judaism

Judaism of the Golden Mean, 545

Judaism-in-the-Home project, 549

Judd, Carrie, 428, 429

Judeopagans, 1275

Judge, Thomas Augustine, 190

Judge, William Q., 709, 756

Judson, Adoniram, 248, 286, 287, 293

Judson, Ann Hasseltine, 248, 286, 287, 293, 453, 836

Judson College (Ala.), 922

Judson Female Institute (Ala.), 915, 917

Julia Ward Howe Peace Band, 1053

Julian of Norwich, 30

Jung, Carl, 1201

Jungmann, Josef, 878

Junior Hadassah, 1124

Jurigian, Paula, 522

Jury, Dan, 107

Jury, Mark, 107

Just a Sister Away: A Womanist Vision of Women's Relationship in the Bible (Weems), 1168–1169

Juster, Susan, 449

Justice, 57; *mujerista* account of, 1191–1193

Juteau, Danielle, 218

Juvenile Court system, 1072

The Juvenile Miscellany (Child), 1038

Kabbalism, 710, 802

Kabotie, Michael, *84*

Kaddish, recitation of, 565

Kaestle, Carl, 890

Kagyu school of Tibetan Buddhism, 652, 655, 656

Kahawai Journal of Women and Zen, 642

Kahle, Eleanor, 953

Kahn, Hazrat Pir Inayat, 1276

Kaiserwerth, 826, 827, 828, 830; deaconesses program and, 823, 826

Kaiserwerth Deaconess Institution, 822

Kalberlahn, Martin, 242

Kalemkerian, Louise, 521

Kim Le, 182
Kimball, Sarah M., 722
Kin, 71
Kind Words, 293
Kindergartens, 825
King, Barbara K., 752
King, Martin Luther, Jr., 166, 260, 389, 456, 752, 990, 1083, 1089, 1090, 1098; liberationist understanding of Christianity by, 261
King, Mary, 1056
King, Ynestra, 1112
The King of Kings (film), 1012
King Philip's War (1675–1676), 225
The Kingdom Darkness (Crouch), *222*
Kingfisher, Pame, 1235
King's Daughters, 189–190
Kingsbury, Joanna W., 1042
Kingsley, Bathsheba, 227, 421, 941, 967, 968
Kingsley House (New Orleans), 1066
Kingston's Female Benevolent Society, 246
Kinnan, Mary, 1001
Kinship, 71, 110; vocational, 71, 72, 79
Kirk, Martha Ann, 958
Kirk-Duggan, Cheryl A., 1173
Kirkjan, Kvenna, 1248
Kirtan, 697
Kirtland, Ohio, Mormon settlement of, 719
Kirwan, Mary Bernard, 210
Kissling, Frances, 1108
Kita-demanbre, 121
Kitahata, Stacy D., 503
Kitomaquund, Mary, 147–148
Kituwah, 111
Kleintop, Hazel, 403
Klevnick, Linda Sujata, 640
Knapp, Bliss, 745
Knapp, Joseph Fairchild, 980
Knapp, Phoebe Palmer, 426, 980, 982, 983
Knapp, Susan, 274–275
Knater, Rosabeth Moss, 797
Knight, Gladys, 260
Knight, J. Z., 763, 766–767
Knights of Labor, 155, 1073
Knight-Weillet, Renee, 783
Knobloch, Fanny, 779, 780
Knoche, Grace F., 757
Knoerle, Jeanne, 888
Knott, J. Proctor, 427
Knott, Lucy Pierce, 427
Knowing by heart, 933
Know-Nothing Party, 151
Knox, John, 341, 942
Koenig, Emilie Lohmann, 311
Kofey, Laura, 1081
Kohler, Kaufman, 572
Kohn, Barbara, 643
Kohn, Jacob, 545
Koho, Chisan, 641
Kohut, Alexander, 545
Kohut, Rebekah, 538, 580, 897, 903

Ko-i Bastis, Madeline, 644, 1096, *1097*
Koller-Fox, Cherie, 904
Kolodny, Debra R., 1219
Koltun, Elizabeth, 1221
Kolvig, Eric, 648
Kongo, 733
Korean American Presbyterian Church (KAPC), 350
Korean Association of Voluntary Agencies, 848
Korean Conflict, 259
Korean Ladies' Organization, 500
Korean War, 1056
Koresh, David, 710, 714
Koreshans, 709
Koreshan Unity, 711, 713
Kornfield, Jack, 647, 648
Kosher food, 556, 561
Kraemer, Ross S., 42, 43, 1282
Kraft, Charles, 77
Kraft, Kenneth, 1095
Krasner-Davidson, Haviva, 965
Kriege, Matilda, 909
Krieger, Delores, 761
Krishna, 667
Krishnamurti, J., 756, 762
Krody, Nancy, 1216
Kroeger, Catherine Clark, 471, 473, 474
Kroon, Ellen de, 462
Ku Klux Klan (KKK), 128, 750, 1032, 1077, 1234; women's, 592
Kuan Yin. *See* Guan Yin
Kubic, Lillian, 877
Kugler, Anna Sarah, 314
Kuhlman, Kathryn, 418, 420–421, 457, *458,* 460, 461–462, 495, 1263
Kuhn, Margaret E. (Maggie), *353,* 357
Kumamoto Band, 503
Kumina tradition, 119, 122
Kunz, Dora, 761
Kwan Um School of Zen, 644
Kwiat, Cecilie, 655
Kwok, Pui-Lan, 42, 504
Kyriarchy, 40, 1247
Kyrios, 1294–1295

La Flesche, Susette, 1026–1027
La Salle, Robert, Cavalier de, 146
Labadie, Jean de, 231, 707
Labadist society, 231
LaBelle, Patti, 992
Labor, division of, 24
Labor Zionism, 1126
Labowitz, Shoni, 799, 802, 803
Labrovitz, Helen, 593–594
Lacoste, Justine, 213
Ladd, Emma C., 396
Ladd, William, 1050–1051, 1051
Ladies' and Pastors' Christian Union, 323–324, 325, 823
Ladies' Association of the Colonial and Continental Church Society, 284
Ladies' Benevolent Society in British North America, 246

Ladies Catholic Benevolent Association, 154
Ladies Christian Association, 1128
Ladies Dime Savers Program, 313
Ladies' Hebrew Seminary, 901
Ladies' Home Missionary Society, 323
Ladies of the Royal Court of Ethiopia, 1078
Ladies' Physiological Societies, 1258
Ladies Repository, 823
The Ladies Repository, 321
Ladies Social Circle, 272
Ladies' Willing Worker Band, 405
Ladner, Dorie, 1091
Ladner, Joyce, 1091
LaDuke, Winona, 1233
Lady Liberty League, 816, 817
Laetare Medal, 874
Lafitau, Joseph François, 804
Lague, Micheline, 218
LaHaye, Beverly, 21, 446, 457, 460, 464, 465, 891, 1295, 1297–1298, 1299
LaHaye, Tim, 464, 1297
Lahoz, Puri, 185
Laird, Rebecca, 427
Laity rights, granting of, to Methodist women, 326–327
Lake, Leonora Barry, 158, 190
Lakota people, use of cultural traditions by outsiders, 103
Lakshmi, 661–662
Lalemant, Jerome, 144
Lalita Sahasranama, 663
Lamarr, Hedy, 1013
Lamberville, Jacques de, 145
Lambeth Conference of Bishops, 279, 831, 947–948
Lamson, Maude, 777
Lancaster, Burt, 1015
Lancaster, Ruth, *824*
Land Grant College Act (1862), 882
Land nationalism, 1234–1235
Landazuri, Elena, 1133–1134
Landi, Elissa, 1013
Landmann, George, 714
Lane, Emma Erskine Hahn, 638
Lane, Mary, 261
Laney, Lucy Craft, 257, 354, 456
Lange, Elizabeth Clarisse, 164
Langer, Ruth, 1283
Language: force of religious, 1291; gender, 10–11; God, 1292, 1294–1295; inclusive, 1290–1295; inspiration of feminism, to transform religious, 12; Jesus, 1295; power relationship and, 47–48; in relation to biblical translation, 37
The Language of the Goddess (Gimbutas), 808
Lankenau, John D., 312
Lankford, Sarah, 322, 422, 424
Lapson, Dvora, 902
Larson, Agnes, 316
Larson, April Ulring, 317
Larson, Nella, 1168
Las Casas, Bartolomé de, 485
Lasch, Christopher, 792
Lasch-Quinn, Elisabeth, 1061

Laska, Vera, 1282
Lasso de la Vega, Luis, 173
The Last Temptation of Christ (Kazantzakis), 1013
Lasyrenn, 120
Lathbury, Mary, 985
Lathrap, Mary, 1266
Lathrop, George, 191
Lathrop, Julia, 859, 861–862, 1065, 1072
Lathrop, Rose Hawthorne, 150, 159
Latin America, liberation theology in, 16, 36, 121, 130, 155, 932, 1174, 1185–1186
Latin American Bible Institute, 496
Latin American Conference of Religious Congregations (CLAR), 1184
Latin American Council of Christian Churches, 493
Latina experience, race and gender in, 484–492
Latina popular Catholicism, 168–178
Latina religious feminism, 20
Latina Roman Catholic theologies, 1193–1200; feminist, 1194, 1197–1199; gender-conscious, 1197–1199; pastoral, 1194–1195, 1199–1200; sociohistorical origins, 1195–1197
Latina/o Protestant church, 488–489
Latinas and religious/political activism, 1181–1188
Latinas in Ministry, 482, 484
Latinas in Theology, 483
Latino Oneness movement, 493
Latino Pastoral Action Center, 482
Latino Trinitarian Pentecostal Movement, 494–497
Latter-day Saints (LDS), 15
Laud, William, 222
Lauer, Rosemary, 199
Laughing Sinners (film), 1015
Laughter of Aphrodite (Christ), 808
Laughton, Charles, 1013
Laurin, Nicole, 218
Law, Bernard Cardinal, 1246
Lawrence, Margaret, 275
Law(s): Comstock, 1100; Hindu, 28; Islamic, 20–21; Jewish, 576–588; Jim Crow, 14, 259, 1074, 1075; Pakistani rape, 619; rape shield, 1144–1145
Laws, Curtis Lee, 443
Lawson, James, 1086
Lay Catholic feminists, *201,* 201–203
Lay Mission Helpers (Los Angeles), 846
Laywomen: in Antebellum period, 149–150; working-class Catholic, 154–155
Lazarus, Emma, 590, 899
Leacock, Eleanor, 808
Lead Me, Guide Me: The African American Catholic Hymnal, 998
Leadbeater, Charles W., 755
Leadership Conference of Women Religious (LCWR), 132, 205–206, 207, 209, 955
Leadership Council of Women Religious (LCWR), 17
Leadership Training Fellowship, 903
League for the Protection of Colored Women, 858
League of Colored Women, 865, 869
"The League of Isis," 807

League of Jewish Youth, 902

League of Nations, 1055; United States' refusal to join, 1032; Women's Charter, 1054

League of Women Voters (LWV), 1032, 1033, 1034

Leake, Annie, 247

Leaming, Marjorie, 391

Lear, Norman, 891

Leard, Elinor, 364

Leary, Timothy, 646

Leatherman, Lucy, 405

Leaven, 59

LeBar, Lois, 456, 910, 911

LeBar, Mary, 456, 910, 911

Lebsock, Suzanne, 452

Lectionary, 1292

Lee, Ann, 48, 235, 236, 708, 711, 714–715, 768, 835, 941, 967, 979–980, 1262

Lee, Clara G., 500

Lee, Dora A., 502

Lee, Hyapatia, 107

Lee, Jarena, *251*, 253, 321–322, 433, 451, 945, 946, 970, 1042, 1167

Lee, Linda, 328

Lee, Luther, 942

Lee, Martha A., 430

Lee, Sara, 903–904, 905

Lee, Sara S., 1283

Lee, T. L., 500

Leek, Sybil, 814

Lees, Carol, 1144

Leeser, Isaac, 898–899

A Legacy for Children (Hill), 233

Legal determination, 576

Legends of the Jews (Ginzberg), 545

Lehman, Edward, 32

Lehmann, Katherine, 313

Leibowitz, Nechama, 560

LeJeune, Olivier, 143, 144

Lekshe, Karma, 656

Lema'an Bnos Yisrael International, 587

LeMoyne, Jean-Baptiste, 146

LeMoyne, Simon, 145

Leo XIII (Pope), 189, 214, 843

Leonard, Ellen, 218, 959

Lepin, Mark, 1144, 1145

Lerner, Gerda, 14, 48, 1309

LeRoy, Susanna, 233

Lesbian Buddhist Sangha, 648

Lesbian Feminist Issues and Religion Group at American Academy of Religion, 1219

Lesbian Rabbis (Abrams), 543

Lesbians: achievements and future directions, 1219–1220; in Buddhism, 1210; civil union of, 217; defined, 1214; Hinduism and, 665–666; history of theological perspectives, 1215–1219; issues in religion, 1214–1220; Jewish, 1218; in North American Buddhist communities, 1098–1099; rights of, 1037; terminology in flux, 1214–1215; theology, 1219; who's who?, 1215

Lesch, Mary, 782

Lessons in Truth (Cady), 758, 760

Letters on the Equality of the Sexes (Grimké), 13, 1051

Letters to Catherine [sic] E. Beecher, 1045

Levine, Amy-Jill, 1281, 1282

Levinger, Elma Ehrlich, 903

Levinger, Lee, 903

Levinson, Sara, 1097–1098

Levinthal, Helen, 539, 961, 962

Levinthal, Israel, 961

Levison, Stanley, 1083

Levitt, Joy, 553

Lewis, Alice, 412

Lewis, Augusta, 155

Lewis, David, 336

Lewis, Dean, 18

Lewis, Edith, 1009

Lewis, Lucy Biddle, 338

Lewis, Rebecca Mendenhall, 336

Lewis, Sinclair, 1015

Lewis, Warren, 788, 792

Lhamo, Ahkön, 654

Lhamo, Jetsunma, 657

Li, Hongzhi, 678

Li, (Florence) Tim-Oi, 270, 277, 278, 284

Liberal Catholicism, 761

Liberal feminism, 22, 931, 1116

The Liberating Word, 37, 40, 1269

Liberation: national, 596; personal, 596

Liberation music, 1186

Liberation theology, 16, 36, 121, 130, 155, 479, 932, 1174, 1185–1186, 1195, 1197

Liberation Theology (Ruether), 1176

Liberationist feminism, 931

Liberator (newspaper), 114, 1038, 1042–1043, 1044, 1051

Liberia, Episcopal missionary colony in, 272

Liberian mission field, 256

Library of Tibetan Works and Archives, 656

Lichtenstein, Morris, 1259

Lichtenstein, Tehilla, 1259, 1262

Lieberman, Saul, 550

Lieberman clause, 550

Lieder ohne Worte (Mendelssohn), 977

Lief, Acharya Judy, 1096

Liele, George, 118

Lieu Quang school of Zen (Thien), 644

Life, Work and Experience of Mrs. M. B. Woodworth-Etter, Evangelist (Woodworth-Etter), 430

The Life, Work and Experiences of Maria Beulah Woodworth (Woodworth-Etter), 430

Life Ablaze: A Woman's Novena (Chittister), 23

The Life and Religious Experience of Mrs. Jarena Lee, a Coloured Lady (Lee), 970

Life in the Word (Meyer), 465

Life of a Martyr: To the Memory of Martin Luther King (Moore), 995

Life of Hester Ann Rogers, 424

The Life of Mrs. (Mary Bosanquet) Fletcher, 424

Life-cycle rites, 584, 1272–1273

Lifestyle of Learning (magazine), 893

Lutheran Church in America (LCA), 315, 317; orientation of women in, 15, 946
Lutheran Church–Canada, 318
Lutheran Church–Missouri Synod, 308, 310, 311, 312, 314, 315, 316, 317, 318, 947; hymnals of, 998; on women's leadership, 1270
Lutheran College for Women, 315
Lutheran Daughters of the Reformation, 314
Lutheran Deaconess Association, 312, 827
Lutheran Deaconess Conference, 311
Lutheran Home and Services Ministry to the Aged, 313
Lutheran Immigration Service, 316
Lutheran Reformation, 975
Lutheran Theological Seminary, 317
Lutheran Woman Today, 318
Lutheran women, 307–318; associations for, 312–314; Augustana (Scandinavian) Synod, 310, 315; Buffalo Synod, 313; Caribbean Synod, 317; in Colonial period, 308–309; Deaconess ministry in, 311–312; in education ministries, 316–317; feminism in, 317–318; Frankean Synod, 312; General Synod, 310, 311, 313, 315; Iowa Synod, 310, 313; in Mid-Atlantic colonies, 229; ministries of leadership in, 315–316; Minnesota (German) Synod, 310; in mission, 314; Missouri Synod, 310, 311, 312, 314, 315, 316, 317, 318; in nineteenth century, 309–311; Ohio Synod, 313; ordained ministry of, 317; roots, 307–308; Saskatchewan Synod, 317; Tennessee Synod, 310; in twentieth century, 314–315; United Synod, 313; Wisconsin Synod, 310, 314, 315, 317; Woman's Synod, 314. *See also* Lutherans
Lutheran Women's Caucus (LWC), 317–318
Lutheran Women's Leagues, 313
Lutheran Women's Missionary League (LWML), 314, 316
Lutherans, 823, 827; African American hymnbooks of, 998; colleges for women, 918; in Colonial Pennsylvania, 230; deaconess program and, 829; education and, 889; hymns and, 975, 976; infant baptism for, 232; in Mid-Atlantic colonies, 229, 231; in Southern colonies, 241; women's ordination and, 946–947. *See also* American Lutheran Church (ALC); Lutheran Church in America (LCA); Lutheran women
Lutkenhaus, Almuth, 1289
Lwa, 120
Lyman, Amy Brown, 724
Lynch, Mary B., 952, 1243
Lynch, Xaverius, 210
Lynching, 1035, 1074
Lyng v. *Northwest Indian Cemetery Protective Association*, 106
Lyon, Mary, *449*, 453, 836, 913, 914–915, 919, 1021, 1022, 1025
Lyons, Helen Levinthal, 962
Lyons, John, 877
Lyttle, Charles, 384

Ma Jaya Sati Bhagavati, 664, 671–672
Macartney, Clarence, 444
Macaulay, Susan Schaeffer, 893
MacColl, Christina Isobel, 1067
MacDonald, Kay, 1281
MacGillivrary, Janet, 363
Machado, Daisy L., 483

Machar, Agnes Maule, 1071
Machen, J. Gresham, 443
MacIlvary, Cora, 401
MacIntosh, Maria, 1007
Mackay, Isabella Gordon, 244–245
MacLaughlin, R. S., 1068
MacVicar, Elizabeth, 348
Macy, Joanna, 650, 676, 1094
Madison, Martin, 167
The Madonna of 115th Street (Orsi), 189
Maezumi, Hakuyu, 641, 1096
Magazine of the Children of the Kingdom (Robarts), 782–783
Magidson, Beverly, 551
Magnes Museum, 905
Magnetic sleep, 769–770
Magnetism, malicious animal, 739
Magnus, 91
Magsaysay Award, 677
Maguire, Daniel, 1105, 1108
Magyar Synod for Hungarian churches, 372
Maha Prajna Paramita, 643
Mahabharata, 27
Mahapraphu, Chaitanya, 670
Maharshi, Ramana, 671
Mahasaya, Lahiri, 669
Mahayana Buddhism, 29, 639, 676, 684
Mahayana Buddhism (Suzuki), 638
Mai Bhago, 696
Maidens of Brahma, 30
Maier, Judy, 959
Maimonides, 582, 583
Maine, University of, 882
Major, Sarah Righter, 423
Making Friends with Death: A Buddhist Guide to Mortality (Lief), 1096
The Making of a Moonie: Choice or Brainwashing (Barker), 790
Maksoud, Hala Salam, 608
Malaco Records, 993
Malaco's Mississippi Mass Choir, 994
Malakebu, Daniel, 289
Malcolm X, 261, 752
Maldonado, Angel de, 136
Maldonado Pérez, Zaida, 483
Male, scientific medicine, 1258
Male dominance, 8–10
Male-female relationships in Islam, 623
Malicious animal magnetism, 739
Maline, Judith, 1017
Malka of Belz, 803
Mallett, Sarah (Boyce), 424
Mallory, Kathleen, 290, 293
Malone, Mary, 217
Maloney, Elizabeth, 189
Maloney, Mary Xavier, 210
Malpeque, Prince Edward Island, Presbyterians in, 246
Mama Leo, 480
Mama Lola: A Vodou Priestess in Brooklyn (Brown), 735
Mamiya, Lawrence, 435
Man and Woman in Biblical Perspective (Hurley), 473

MAN as Male and Female (Jewett), 474
A Man Called Peter (Marshall), 344–345
Mance, Jeanne, 144, 211
Manifest Destiny, 485, 488, 1195–1196
Mankiewicz, Joseph L., 1015
Mankiller, Wilma, 1233
Manley, Joanna, 517
The Man-Made World or Our Androcentric Culture (Gilman), 806
Mann, Horace, 890
Mann, Vivian, 905
Manna Publishing Company, 990
Mansbridge, Jane, 21
Mansour, Agnes Mary, 1104
Manual of the Mother Church, 741–742
Manusmriti, 27
Manzanar War Relocation Center, 179, 181
Mary Baker Eddy Library for the Betterment of Humanity, 746
Maquiladora industry, 1136–1137
Maracle, Lee, 1238
Al-Marayati, Laila, 608, 619
March, Frederick, 1013
March on Washington (1963), 1081
Marcum, Jack, 359
Marcus, Beth, 349
Marder, Janet, 543
Marginalized communities, 1174
María de Jesús Tomelín, 137, 139
María de San José (nun), 135–137
Maria Shall Shine, 793
Marianismo, 95
Marie Big Pipe, 1238
Marie de l'Incarnation, 144
Marielitos, 488
Marinèt-limen-difé, 121
Marion College for Women, 918
Maritain, Jacques, 195
Markley, Mary, 315
Marks, Miriam, 878
Markstrom, Paul, 481
Marple, Dorothy, 316
Marquette, Jacques, 146
Márquez, Brixeida, 482
Marrant, John, 112
Marriage: celestial, 720; complex, in Oneida community, 713; Hindu, 661, 662; inter-, 94, 113, 114; interfaith, 624, 1272–1274; Islamic, 28, 31, 623–625; Jewish, 572, 585; as lesbian issue, 1219–1220; in Mid-Atlantic colonies, 232–233; polygamy, 709, 713, 718, 721, 722–723, 774; Quaker, 226; Sikh women and, 700
Marsden, George, 455
Marshall, Catherine, 344–345, 351
Marshall, John, 1104
Marshall, Martha Stearns, 240, 294
Marshall, Paule, 1172
Marshall, Peter, 344–345
Marshner, Connaught "Connie," 1298–1299
Marsot, Afaf Lutfi al-Sayyid, 606
Martell Otero, Loida, 483–484

Marthens, Catherine Louisa, 311, 822
Martin, Anna, 151
Martin, Clarice, 42, 261
Martin, Faith, 471
Martin, Gene, 994
Martin, Joan, 17, 58, 1173, 1270
Martin, Miriam, 218
Martin, Roberta, 455, 991–992
Martin, Sallie, 435, 455, 990, 991, 993
Martin, Steve, 992
Martin and Morris Music Company, 455, 991
Martin de Porres Grey, Sister, 166
Martinez, Margarita, 317
Martínez, María Inez, 1187
Martin-Wagner, Linda, 70
The Martyrs' Mirror (van Braght), 264
Marx, Karl, 805, 1201
Mary Baldwin College (Va.), 917, 922
Mary Crow Dog, 1233, 1235
Mary Joseph, Mother, 844
Mary Lou's Mass, 167
Mary Mary, 260
Mary the Mother of Jesus, 1264
Mary Two Axe, 1142
Marygrove College (Detroit, Mich.), 888
Maryknoll, 129, 191, 194, 845, 846, 847
Maryland, Catholic women in colonial, 147–148
MaryMartha, International Orthodox Women's Network Journal, 515, 529–530
Mary-Marthian Society, 150
Mary's Peace, 206
Marywood College (Scranton, Pa.), 888
Mason, Charles H., 436–437, 438, 997
Mason, Charlotte, 893
Mason, Lucy Randolph, 1035
Mason, Mary Morgan, 835
Mason, Otis T., 805
Masonic movement, 1205
Masorti movement, 549
Mass baptisms, 240
Massachusetts Association Opposed to the Further Extension of Suffrage to Women, 192
Massachusetts Bay Colony: Baptists in, 285; founding of, 223; Quakers in, 224–225
Massachusetts Peace Pagoda, 1095
Massachusetts Peace Society, 1050
Massachusetts Woman Suffrage Association, 192
Massachusetts Women-Church, 1246
Master Mind (periodical), 760
Masters, Kamala, 648
Masters, Robert, 766
Mata, Sri Daya, 1275
Mata Jitoji, 696
Mata Khivi, 695
Mater dolorosa, 67
Materialism, 31
Maternal Associations, 452
Maternity homes, 156
Mather, Cotton, 225, 448
Mather, Leo, 1106

Matheson, George, 981
Mathewes-Green, Frederica, 511, 516
Mathews, Donald G., 450
Mathews, Mark, 441
Mathews, Shailer, 1076
Mathiessen, Peter, 1096
Mathis, Father Michael, 846
Mathis, Marie, 293–294
Matriarchal cultures, 1281
Matriarchal prehistory, reality of, 8
Matriarchal superego, 63–64
Matriarchal theory, 808
Matsumoto, Irene, 686
Matsunaga, Yasuko, 682–683, 686
Matsuoka, Fumitaka, 1234
Matsuura, Shinobu, 634
Mattaponi people, intermarriage with blacks, 114
Matter, E. Ann, 1217
Matthews, Marjorie, *320, 328*
Mature, Victor, 1013
Matusiak, Father John, 516
Maultsby, Portia K., 987
Maurin, Peter, 130, 196
Mauriac, François, 195
Maxis, Almedie Duchemin, 164
Maxwell, May, 780, 783
May, Melanie, 1180
May Day rallies, 1056
Mayan people, 95
Ma'yan Seders, 1224
Mayflower, 222
Mayr-Lumetzberger, Christina, 958
Mazu, 673
Mbiti, John, 111
McBeth, Kate, *90*
McBrien, Richard, 953
McCandless, Amy, 916
McCarthyism, 37, 1056, 1085
McCauley, Deborah, 1279
McClain, William, 989
McClaren, Agnes, 846
McClellan, Mimi, 785
McCloud, Aminah, 607, 747–748
McClung, Nellie, 54, 363, 1073, 1076, 1141–1142, *1142*
McClurken, Frances Rye, 427
McClurken, J. O., 427
McCormick, Cyrus, 343, 1072
McCormick, Nettie, 343
McCormick Seminary, 343
McDade, Carolyn, 59
McDermott, Duffy, 955
McDonald, Jean A., 744, 745
McDonald, Lynn, 1146
McDonald-Smith, Michele, 648
McDonough, Fidelis, 955
McDowell, Mary Eliza, 1065, 1072
McEnroy, Carmel, 957
McFague, Sallie, 526, 1111, 1113, 1178, 1179–1180, 1235, 1294
McGaughey, Janie, 357–358

McGee, Kerr, 1235
McGill University (Toronto), 926; admission of women to, 214; Faculty of Religious Studies, 926
McGillis, Miriam Therese, 1111–1112
McGinnis, Marie Teresa, 717
McGrath, Mary Elizabeth Blake, 158
McGroarty, Julia, 156
McGuckin, Eileen, *63*
McGuire, Dorothy, 1012–1013
McGuire, George Alexander, 1077
McIntee, Harold, 101
McIntyre, Shelley, 106
McKeever, Jane, 298–299
McKeever's academy, 299
McKenna, Kevin, 958
McKenzie, Vashti, 966, 973, 1270
McKinley, William, 756
McKinney, Edna, 783
McKinney, Florence, 441
McKinney, Louisa, 54
McKinney, Nina Mae, 1015
McKissich, Sarah, 993
McLain, Melinda V., 1218
McLennan, John Ferguson, 805
McLeod, Mary Adelia, 948
McLin, Lena Johnson, 988, 995, 996
McMahon, Bernadette, 959
McMahon, Patricia, 1108
McMaster, Helen, 293
McMaster, Susan Moulton, 287, 292
McMurray, Frank, 910
McMurray, W. Grant, 731, 732
McNair, Denise, 1089
McNeil, Bhiksuni (Anila) Ann, 655–656
McNeill, John, 1215
McPherson, Aimee Semple, 394, 399–400, 403, 404, 416, 418, 420, 421, 423, 430, 442, 456, 460, 461, 495, 497, 971, *972,* 986, 1015, 1262–1263
McPherson, Harold, 399–400, 1262
McPherson, Jeanie, 1012
McPike, Sara, 192
McQuillan, Patricia Fogarty, 1107, 1108
McWhirter, Martha, 430, 709, 715, 716
McWilliams, Joanne, 217
Meacham, Joseph, 715
Mead, Lucia Ames, 1053
Mead, Margaret, 766
Mears, Henrietta, 445, 456
Mecca, pilgrimage to, 610
Medellín, Juana, 495
Medical Mission Sisters, 846
The Medical Missionary (magazine), 846
Medical neglect and starvation, of Indian children, 99–100
Medicine Woman (Andrews), 103
Meditation: Buddhism, 1211, 1275, 1276; insight, 646–647; Zen, 638
Mediumship, 770–773
Meehan, Brenda, 517
Meetings with Remarkable Women: Buddhist Teachers in America (Friedman), 642

Meir, Golda, 1126
Mejores Días/Better Days, 482
Melamed, Deborah M., 547–548
Melamed, Raphael, 547
Melançon, Louise, 218, 959
Melano Couch, Beatríz, 478–479
Melick, Emma C., 783
Mellenbruch, Laura, 314
Melton, Florence, 905
Melton, J. Gordon, 788
Melton Mini-Courses in Jewish studies, 905
Memoirs of the Life, Religious Experience, Ministerial Travels and Labours of Mrs. Zilpha Elaw, an American Female of Color (Elaw), 969
Mena, María Cristina, 1196
Mendelssohn, Felix, 977
Mendez Arceo, Sergio (Cuernavaca), 130–131
Mendoza, Roberto, 1230
Mengel, Gail, 731
Mennonite Central Committee, 269
Mennonite Nurses' Association, 267
Mennonite Women's Missionary Society, 269
Mennonite World Conference, 268
Mennonites, 262, 266, 268; in Colonial Pennsylvania, 230–231; families of, 264; opposition to slavery, 1039; as peace church, 1055; peace movements and, 1050; women in Mid-Atlantic colonies, 229
Menotti, Gian Carlo, 991
Men's club, 69
Mentoring circles, 1309
Merchant, Carolyn, 1110
Mercier, Evangeline, 195
Mercy College (Detroit, Mich.), 888
Meredith College (Raleigh, N.C.), 917, 922
Merici, Angela, 212, 883
Merrill, Lucy, 72
Merrill, Stephen M., 325
Mesley, Blanche Edwards, 730
Mesmer, Franz Anton, 769
Mesmerism, 769, 770
The Message, 825
The Message to the Blackman, 613
The Messenger (film), 1014
The Messenger: The Rise and Fall of Elijah Muhammad, 752
Messner, Roe, 463
Mestizo Catholicism, 477
Metaphorical Theology (McFague), 1294
Metaphysical movement, 753
Methodist Deaconess Association, 854
Methodist Deaconess Home, 825
Methodist Deaconess Society, 825
Methodist Episcopal Church, missionaries of, 840
Methodist Episcopal Church, North, women's ordination and, 944
Methodist Episcopal Church, South, 322, 325, 327, 426, 450, 454
Methodist Episcopal Women's Foreign Missionary Society, 855
Methodist Federation for Social Services, 1030, 1072
Methodist Hymnbook, 997

The Methodist Magazine, 320
Methodist Protestant Church, 454
Methodist Student Movement, 18, 1086
Methodists, 322, 325, 327, 443; African American hymnbooks of, 998; African American women as, 253; in borderlands, 1138, 1139; in British North America, 244–247; Canadian, 244, 248; Colonial and early American, 319–321; deaconess movement and, 827; deaconess program and, 823–825, 828–829; fight for coestablishment, 245–246; hymns of, 975, 976, 997; leaders of, 970–971; merger with Evangelical United Brethren, 75; in Mid-Atlantic colonies, 235; missionaries of, 836, 837; in Newfoundland, 243; in nineteenth century, 321–327; opposition to slavery, 1039; ordination of women and, 97, 943–944, 1288; revivalism and, 417; slaves as, 241; support for temperance, 255; in twentieth century, 327–329; women, 319–329. *See also* Southern Methodist Church; United Methodist Church; Wesleyan Methodist Church
Metoyer, Claude, 163
Metoyer, Coincoin, 163
Metropolitan Church (Baltimore, Md.), *1244*
Metropolitan Community Churches, inclusive language and, 1292
Metta Vihara (Germany), 650
Metzerott, Shoemaker (Woods), 1071
Mevo Satum: The Dead End, 587
Mexican-American War (1848), 1135
Mexican Mission for the Board of American Mission of the Joint Synod of Ohio, 314
Mexican Young Women's Christian Association (YWCA), 1134
Mexican-Hindus, 694
Mexico: religious women in colonial, 133–141; women's ordination movement in, 959
Meyer, Josiah Shelly, 852, 853, 854, 863
Meyer, Joyce, 457, 460, 465, 466
Meyer, Lucy Rider, 326, 824, 825, 828, 838, 841, 852–855, 985, 1071
Meyer, Marie, 318
Meyers, Carol, 40, 41, 42, 1226–1227
Meyers, Joel, 552
Meytzinger, Anna Margareth, 233
Michael, Lorraine, 1144
Michel, Virgil, 878
Michigan, University of, 882
Michigan Freedmen's Aid Commission, 1026
Mickelson, Alvera, 471
Mickelson, Berkeley, 471
Mid-Atlantic colonies, Protestant women in, 228–236
Middle colonies: Lutherans in, 308–309; Methodists in, 319
Middle East Studies Association of North America, 606
Middle Passage, 116, 251, 988
Midway College (Ky.), 917, 922
Mies, Maria, 1115
Migration of Anabaptists, 264–265
Mikve Israel, 571
Mildmay House, 826
Mildmay Training (London), 827
Miles, Mary, 273
Miles, Sylvia, 1016

Milhaven, Giles, 1105, 1108
Military-industrial complex, 1057
Militz, Annie Rix, 758, 760–761
Militz, Paul, 760
Mill, John Stuart, 1060
Millennial Harbinger (journal), 299, 301
Millennialism, 761
Miller, Earlean, 317
Miller, Elizabeth, 293
Miller, Frances, 441
Miller, H. L., Cantorial School, 552
Miller, Marian, 777
Miller, Susanna, 232
Miller, Verna, 77–78
Miller, William, 1260
Millerites, 420, 969
Mills, Cyrus, 919
Mills, Hayley, 1014
Mills, Susan, 919
Mills College Association for Community Work, 919
Mills College (Calif.), 919, 922
Milne, Mary, 293
Mind Cure movement, 757, 758
Mind Games (Houston and Masters), 766
Ministerium of Pennsylvania, 309
Ministries: exclusion of women from, 222; grassroots, 482–483; pastoral, 480–482; recording, 941
The Ministry of Deacons (publication), 832
Mink, Patsy Takemoto, 686
Minnesota, University of, 886
Minoan Sisterhood and Covenant of the Goddess, 817
Minogue, Kuya, 644
Minor, Pauline Oberdorfer, 434, 437–438
Mintz, Steven, 889
Miracle Distribution Center, 765
The Miracle of Our Lady of Fatima (film), 1014
The Miracle Woman (film), 1015
Mirenda, Rosalie, 888
Miriam's Cup, 575
Miriam's Well (Adelman), 1224
Miscegenation, 477
Mishnah, 576, 1222
Misogyny, 10
Missing Connections: Public Perceptions of Theological Education and Religious Leadership, 1150, 1154
Missio ad gentes, 849
Mission Helpers of the Sacred Heart, 877, 878
Missionaries, 834–850; in British North America, 248; Catholic women, 843–850; in civilization of southeastern Indians, 112–113; female orders of, 129; in films, 1011, 1014–1015; Muslim, 607; Native Americans, 834; Protestant women, 834–843
Missionary "box work," 274
Missionary Catechists of Our Lady of Victory, 877
Missionary Confraternity of Christian Doctrine, 877
Missionary Helper, 857
The Missionary Link, 857
The Missionary Monthly, 365
Missionary movement, 602
Missionary Servants of the Most Holy Trinity, 877

Missionary Sisters of the Sacred Heart, 190–191, 843
Missionary Society of the Church of England, 281
Mission-based Christianity, 118
Missions Room, 293
Mississippi Democratic Party, 1088
Mississippi Freedom Democratic Party (MFDP), 261, 1087–1088, 1091
Mississippi Masala (film), 1016
Missouri Compromise (1820), 333
The Mists of Avalon (Bradley), 19
Mita Congregation, Inc., 496–497
Mitchell, Elsie, 638, 641
Mitchell, Emily, 161
Mitchell, Joan, 66
Mitchell, John, 161, 641
Mitchell, Margaret, 1005
Mitchell, Priscilla, 161
Mitchum, Donie, 427
Mitchum, Robert, 1014
Mite Society, 248
Mix, Sarah Freeman, 428, 429
Mixed blood, 114
Miyamoto, Grace, 680, 683, 686
Mizrachi Women's Organization of America (AMIT Women), 559, 566, 1125
Models of God (McFague), 1294
Modern Thought (periodical), 759
Modern Times, 713
Modernism, 785
Modernist Controversy, 970
Modesty, 64
Modin, Camp, 902
Modoc people, 91
Moffett, Ruth, 779
Mohammed, Warith Deen, 607, 622, 625, 749, 752
Mohawk people, 83; matrilineal organization of, 90
Mohorter, James, 303
Moise, Mary, 401
Moise, Penina, 803
Mokcsay, Zsuzsanna, 815
Mollenkott, Virginia Ramey, 470, 472, 473, 474, 1215, 1217, 1269
Monasticism, 29; Protestant Christianity's general rejection of, 29
Monastics, women, 516–517
Mongoven, Ann Marie, 881
Monk, Maria, 151
Monophysites, 250
Monroe, Irene, 1215
Montagnais, Charité, 143–144
Montagnais, Espérance, 143–144
Montanists, 250
Montesinos, Antonio de, 94–95
Montez, Maria, 1015
Montgomery, Carrie Judd, 396–397, 401, 402, 409, 495
Montgomery, George, 396, 428, 429, 495
Montgomery, Helen Barrett, 14, 289, 291, 293, 294, 839, 1266
Montgomery, Judd, 428
Montgomery Bus Boycott, 260, 1081, 1083

Mudd, Rita, 1277
Mudge, Lewis S., 357
Mueller, Bertha, 827
Mueller, Iris, 958, 959
Mueller, Samuel, 233
Muggeridge, Anne Roche, 205
Muhammad, Ava, 613, 752
Muhammad, Clara Evans, 607, 612–613, 746–753, *747*
Muhammad, Elijah, 612, 613, 614, 622, 746, 748, 752–753
Muhammad, Emmanuel, 751
Muhammad, Fard, 612, 613
Muhammad, Halimah, 752
Muhammad, Laila, 752
Muhammad, N'Gina, 752
Muhammad, Tynetta, 613
Muhammad, Warithudeen, 614
Muhammad, Zakiyyah, 614
Muhammad ibn Abdullah (prophet), 609, 612, 615, 616, 625
Muhlenberg, Henry Melchior, 233, 309, 826
Muhlenberg, William A., 826
Mujeres por el Dialogo (Women for Dialogue), 959
Mujerista: social ethics, 57, theology, 1185–1186, 1191–1193, 1194, 1307
Muktananda, 670–671, *671*
Mulberry Street Methodist Episcopal Church (New York City), 322
Mulherin, Gabriella, 848
Mulkey, John, 348
Mulkey, Nancy, 348
Mulkey, Philip, 348
Müller, Friedrich Max, 636
Mulliken, Frances Hartman, 731
Multicultural animistic traditions, 810
Multicultural Shamanism, 810
Multidenominational movements, 821–1017; Deaconess movement as, 821–833; missionary movement as, 834–850; music and the arts as, 974–1017; ordination movement as, 940–973; religious education as, 873–939; women's societies in, 851–872
Multidialogics, 57
Multnomah Friends Meeting, 340
Multrain, George, 121
Multwood Group, 340
Mundelein College (Chicago), 884, 888
Munindra, 647
Murcott, Susan, 642
Murphy, Alexina, 959
Murphy, Elizabeth Blanch E., 158
Murphy, Joseph, 434, 736
Murray, Charlotte, 429
Murray, Grace, 424
Murray, Jane Marie, 878
Murray, John, 382
Murray, Judith Sargent, 35, 381–382, 384–385, 1021
Murray, Linda Haju, 640
Murray, Margaret, 1203, 1205
Murray, Pauli, 18, 71, 279
Murray, Shirley Erena, 986
Muschal-Reinhardt, Rosalie, 953, 955
Muscogee people, 88

Musgrove, Sara M. C., 429
Music, 974–1000; African American hymnody, 987–1000; women hymn writers, 974–987
Musical Society, 452
Muslim feminists, 20–21
Muslim Girls Training classes, 613
The Muslim Journal, 614
Muslim missionary activity, 607
Muslim women: African American, 607, 608–615, *610;* American Public Square and, 608; discourse on, in North America, 604–606; dress of, 31, 609, 618, 626–627, 1284; identity of, in America, 601–608; immigration of, 602–603; portrayal of, in American press, 603. *See also* Islam; Qur'an
Muslim Women's League (MWL), 619
Muslim Youth of North America (MYNA), 624
Mustapha, Ayesha, 614, 752
Mutual submission, 461, 467
Mutuality, 64
Mutuality (newsletter), 16
Mveng, Engelbert, 1236
Mvskoke people: African immigrants and, 111, 115; intermarriage and, 114; kinship ties and, 110; landed elite of, 113; missionary efforts among, 112; "Red Stick Revolt" among, 113
My Neighbour (Woodworth), 1063
My Purpose (my album), 994
Myers, Minnie, 411
Mystical Body of Christ, 195
Mystical religious, 761
Mystici Corporis (Pius XII), 195
Mythic Images, 817
A Mythic Life (Houston), 766
Mythopoetic traditions, 111–112
Myths, 6. *See also* Narratives

Na'amat (Women Working and Volunteering), 1126
Nachamson, Jennie, 1124
Nadell, Pamela, 905
Nadieh, Hadassah, 549
Nagaratnammal, Bangalore, 663
Nagasaki, U.S. bombing of, 1036, 1056
Nahalat Shalom, 803
Nahuas, 1195
Nahuatl people, botanical elements in world of, 175–176
Nair, Mira, 1016
Najimy, Kathy, 1014
Najmabadi, Afsaneh, 606
Nakade, Mary Beth, 686
Nakao, Wendy Egyoku, 640, 642, 643, 644, 645, 686
The Nakedness of the Fathers (Ostriker), 1225
Nako, Carmen, 1200
Name reality, 4
Name-giving, Sikh women and, 699
Nanda, Sister, 649
Nantucket Island, as Quaker stronghold, 226
Nanye-hi, 112
Naqshabandiyya Order, 614
Naropa University, 1094
Narraganset people, women leaders of, 91

National Organization for Women (NOW), 15, 17, 18, 21, 305, 357, 446, 725, 1057, 1296; Ecumenical Task Force on Women and Religion, 18; Muslim women and, 603

National Peace Conference, 1055

National Pro-Family Rally, 1297

National Religious Leadership Roundtable, 1219

National School of Social Service on the Catholic University, 193

National Secular Society, 755

National spiritual appropriation, 102–103

National Student Association (NSA), 1086, 1087; Race Relations Project, 1091

National Student Council of the Young Women's Christian Association, 18

National Sunday School Teacher, 909

National Trade and Professional School for Women and Girls, 292

National Training School for Women and Girls, 1074, 1266

National Travelers Aid Association, 1133

National Union of Evangelical Women, 374

National Urban League, 858, 1063, 1074, 1075

National Woman Suffrage Association, 1027

National Women's Conference, 1297

National Women's Party, 193

National Women's Studies Association Conference, 596

National Youth Administration, Division of Negro Affairs in, 260

Native American Graves Protection and Repatriation Act (NAGPRA), 87

Native American Love Techniques (Lee), 107

A Native American Theology (Tinker, Kidwell, and Noley), 1230, 1237

Native Americans: appropriation of religious traditions, 102–109; boarding schools and, 97–102, *99;* Christianity and women, 89–97; creation stories of, 83–89; healing and, 1256–1257. *See also* American Indians

Native Americans for a Clean Environment (NACE), 1235

Native liberation theology, 1229–1239; anthropological poverty, 1236–1239; healing, 1235–1236; land nationalism, 1234–1235; relationship to tradition, 1231–1234; spiritual/cultural appropriation, 1234

Native spiritual appropriation, 102–103

Native spiritualities, 104–105

Nativism, 128, 150, 151, 154, 155, 590–591

Natural law theory, 55

Nature Religions Scholars Network, 816

Nature/nurture assessment of gender roles spectrum, 25

Nautilus, 758

Nauvoo, Illinois, 708, 709, 713; Mormon settlement of, 719–720

Navajo people, 85

Navaratri, 661–662

Naylor, Gloria, 1167

Nazareth College (Ky.), 884

Neal, Marie Augusta, 953

Needham, Elizabeth, 442

Needham, George C., 442–443

Negro Baptist Church, first, 114

Negro Community Centre, 1068

The Negro World (newspaper), 1077, 1078, 1079

Neighborhood Guild (New York City), 1064

Neighborhood Union, 1035, 1074, 1075

Neighbourhood House, 1068

Nellas, Panayiotis, 527

Nelson, Betty, 998

Nelson, Dorothy, 778

Nelson, James, 1300–1301

Nelson, Peter C., 403

Neoevangelicals, 467

Neo-Hasidism, 20

Neopaganism, 10, 1264, 1271, 1274–1275

Neo-Pentecostalism, 435

Neo-Shamanism, 667, 1264–1265

Nerinckx, Father Charles, 152, 164, 845

Nersoyan, Hagop J., 520–521

Nestor, Agnes, 189

Network: A National Catholic Social Justice Lobby, 17, 205, 206

Network for Women's Issues, 1246

Network of Western Buddhist Teachers, 1275

Neu, Diann, 59, 1247

Neufeld, Elizabeth B., 1067

Neumann, Erich, 1201

Neumann College, 888

Neumark, David, 960

Neumark, Martha, 539, 960, 961, 964

New Age, 103, 104, 105, 106, 108, 667, 710, 753, 761–767

New Age eclecticism, 1264

A New Catechism of Sacred History (Sadlier), 874

The New Century Hymnal, 998

New Christian Right, 31, 464

New Deal, 1034

New Democratic Party, 1284

New Echota, Treaty of, 114

New England and the American Anti-Slavery Societies, 334

New England Deaconess Home and Training School, 825

New England Fellowship, 445

New England Non-Resistance Society, 1051

New England Woman's Suffrage Association, 390

The New Family and the New Property (Glendon), 788

New Family Reunification policy, 694

New feminism, 1106

New France, Catholic women in, 127, 143–147

New Group of World Servers, 762

New Harmony, 708

New immigrants, 154–155

New Jersey, Protestant Church in, 230

New Jerusalem, 235–236, 709, 713–714

New Left, 18, 710, 714, 717, 1083

New Light Baptist, 714

New Light Congregationalists, 226, 227, 241; in Mid-Atlantic colonies, 235

New Light Presbyterians: differences between orthodox Anglicans and, 239; in Georgia, 239; in Virginia, 239

New Menorah, 798

The New National Baptist Hymnal, 997

New Netherland: cosmopolitan community in, 228; Walloons in, 228

Northern Students' Movement (NSM), 1091
Norton, Eleanor Holmes, 71
Norton, Lydia, 226
Norwegian Lutheran Church in America (NLCA), 311
Norwegian Lutheran Deaconess Association, 827, 828
Norwegian Lutheran Home and Hospital, 312
Norwegian Relief Society, 311
Norwood, Dorothy, 260, 992, 993, 994
Nostra aetate (In Our Time), 1277
Nothing Special (Beck), 644
Notre Dame, College of (Maryland), 156
Notre Dame, School Sisters of, 191
Notre Dame, University of (South Bend, Ind.), 129, 883, 884, 886
Nott, Roxanna, 836
Nottoway people, intermarriage with blacks, 114
Nova Scotia, colonial settlement in, 244
Novels: domestic, 1004–1008; sentimental, 1007, 1009; women's, and religion, 1000–1010
Novick, Leah, 799, *800*, 803
Nowak, Susan, 1283
Noyes, John Humphrey, 708, 713, 717, 768
Noyes, Mrs. Eli, 287
Nuclear Guardianship Project, 650
Nugent, Agnes, 211
Nugent, Maria, 211
Nun in the Modern World (Cardinal Suenens), 198
Nun Zen-shin, 681
Núñez de Miranda, Antonio, 137–138
Nuns, 128–129; choir, 212; in films, 1014; outreach of, to immigrant Catholics, 155–156; service of, during Civil War, 128. *See also specific nuns*
The Nun's Story (film), 1014
Nuval, Terisita, 185
Nyabinghi House, 118
Nyack Bible Institute, 440
Nyingma, 652

Oates, Mary, 887
Obeah, 117; African-derived religion of, 119
Oberlin College, 882, 918–919, 924, 942, 986
Oberon, 817
Object teaching, 909
Oblate Sisters of Providence, 150, 161, 163, 164, 165, 968
Obrecht, Margaret, 1283
O'Brien, Mrs. John, 190
Ocapeoda, 1286
Ockenga, Harold, 445
O'Connell, William, 192, 193, 420
O'Connor, Cardinal, 1104, 1106
Odinism, 810
Odyssey House, 480–481
Oedipal conflict, 64
Oesterlein, Elizabeth, 915–916
Of Woman Born (Stone), 1202
Ofrendas, 172
Oh, Sandra, 1016
O'Hara, Bishop Edwin, 878
O'Hara, Pat Enkyo, 1096, *1212*
Ohr Torah Legal Aid Program, 587

Oikumene, 58
Oilmec, 813
Oionhaton, Theresa, 145
Ojibwe people, 83
Okawara, Miya, 502–503
O'Kelly, James, 297, 298
Oland, Warner, 1015–1016
Olazábal, Francisco, 496
Olcott, Henry Steel, 637, 709, 754–755
Olcott, Sidney, 1012
Old Lights, 226, 227; in Mid-Atlantic colonies, 235
Old Lutherans, 310, 311
Old Order, 263, 265, 266, 269
Old Side Presbyterians, in Mid-Atlantic colonies, 235
Old St. Mary's Church (San Francisco), 181
Old-Fashioned Revival (Fuller and Fuller), 456
O'Leary, Catherine, 155
Olenska, Ellen, 1009
Oliner, Pearl, 1282
Oliner, Samuel, 1282
Oliver, Anna, 325, 943, 946
Oliver, Edmund, 363
Oliver, Mary Eunice, 276
Olmstead, Mildred Scott, 1055
Olokun, 120
Ompan, Jerusha, 33, 35, 36
On a Positive Note, Her Joyous Faith, Her Life in Music, and Her Everyday Blessings (Winans), 995
On Being a Jewish Feminist (Heschel), 1221
On Our Way Series, 879
On the Crest of the Present (McGaughey), 357–358
On the Education of Christian Youth (1929) (Pius XI), 194
On Women and Judaism (Greenberg), 1227
One Million for Peace, 1148
One Woman's Liberation (Boone), 460
Oneida Community, 768, 774; complex marriage in, 713
Oneida nation, 83
Oneida Perfectionists, 708, 716–717, 792
O'Neill, Sara Benedicta, 195
Oneness, 405
Ono, Antoinette Yae, 181
Onondaga, 83
Ontario, spiritual promotion of Catholic motherhood in, 212–213
Oon, Young Kim, 790
Open Bible Standard Churches, 404
Open Court, 637
Ophelia Speaks (Shandler), 1306
Ordained Women in the Church of the Nazarene: The First Generation (Cagle), 427
Ordaining Women, 949
Order of Buddhist Contemplatives, 641
Order of Raël's Angels, 795–796
Order of the Star, 756
Ordinary Mind Zen School, 644
Ordinatio Sacerdotalis, 957
Ordination movement, 15, 32, 97, 940–973, 1288–1289; in African Methodist Episcopal (AME) Church, 945; Alliance of Baptists and, 942; Anglicans and, 1288; Armenian Apostolic Church and, 520–523; in Canada, 216, 218, 959;

Pacific American Catholic women, 178–187
Pacific and North American Asian Women in Theology and Ministry (PANAAWTM), 505
Pacific immigrants, 178–180
Pacifist Action Committee, 1055
Pacifist Quakers, 228
Packard, Sophia, 292, 917
Packer, Toni, 640, 644
Padres Asociados para Derechos Religiosos, Educativos Sociales (PADRES), 1182–1183, 1184, 1185
"Pagan Baby" money, 848
Paganism, 809
Page, Ann Randolph, 271
Page Act (1875), 178
Paik, Mary, 503
Paine College (Augusta, Ga.), 327
Paiute people, 91
Pak, Carmen, 78
Pak, Harry, 78
Pakistani rape laws, 619
Palache School for Jewish Girls (New York City), 898
Palacios, Luis, 135
Palafox y Mendoza, Juan de, 141
Palatines, 308
Pali canon, 27
Palmer, Phoebe Worrall, 322–323, 418, 419, 422, 424–425, 425, 454, 836, 969, 980
Palmer, Walter, 322, 419, 424, 980
Palo tradition, 117
Pamela (Richardson), 1000
Pamunkey people, intermarriage with blacks, 114
Pan-African principles, 1077
Panetta, Leon E., 1104
Pan-Protestant Deaconess Society of Dayton, Ohio, 830
Papal Volunteers for Latin America, 846, 847
Paramananda, Swami, 668–669
Parappuduwa Nuns Island (Sri Lanka), 650
Pardo, Mary, 1185
Pardy, Marion, 367
Parham, Charles Francis, 400, 401, 743
Parham, Kitty, 992
Parish School Conference, 883
Parker, Alice, 986
Parker, Arthur C., 84–85
Parker, Evelyn, 1307
Parker, Lois Stiles, 324
Parker, Mary, 1045
Parker, Mrs. Edwin, 856
Parker, Theodore, 382
Parks, Rosa, 1085, 1089, 1090
Parmentier, Adele, 150
Parmentier, Andre, 150
Parmentier, Posine, 150
Parmentier, Sylvia, 150
Parshall, Janet, 1300
Parsons, Agnes, 777, 785
Parsons, Sally, 294
A Particular Relation of the American Baptist Mission to the Burman Empire (Judson), 293
Partners for the Common Good, 206

The Partnership Way (Eisler), 19
Paryushan, 691
Pascal mystery, 173
Passavant, William, 311, 316, 822, 828
Passover, 6, 538, 575
Passover Seder, 1224
Pastoral Letter on Women's Concerns, 956
Pastoral ministries, 480–482
Patch, Penny, 1091
Patinkin, Mandy, 1016
Patriarchal religion, authority of, 1099
Patriarchy, 5, 1057; in feminist theory, 39–40; pernicious power of, 1215
Patriots' Rebellion (1837–1838), 211, 212
Patterson, Daniel, 739
Patterson, Mary Jane, 1102
Paul, Alice, 192–193
Paul (Apostle), exclusion of women from ministry and, 222, 227
Paul II (Pope), 951
Paul IV (Pope), 199
Paul VI (Pope), 131, 132, 953, 954; *Humanae vitae,* 132, 199, 216, 1100
Pauley, Frances, 1084
Pauline Epistles, 13, 16
Paulist Fathers, 181
Paulomi, 689, *690,* 691–692
Pawlikowski, John, 1277
Paxson, Diana, 816
Payne, Daniel, 436
Payton, Catherine, 332
Peabody, Elizabeth Palmer, 636, 909, 1027
Peabody, Francis Greenwood, 52
Peabody, Lucy Waterbury, 294, 444, 839
Peace, William, 917
Peace College (N.C.), 917, 922
Peace Mission, 716
Peace movements, 1033, 1050–1059
Peaceful Dwelling: Meditations for Healing and Living (Ko-I Bastis), 1096
Peaceful Dwelling Project, 1096
Peacemaker Order, 1094, 1096
Peacemaker Villages, 1094
Peake, Edith Livingston, 355
Pearce, Hannah, 322
Pearre, Caroline Neville, 302
Peavy, Frances, 1094
Peck, Gregory, 1013
Peck, Mary Gray, 1010, *1011*
Peel, Robert, 738
Peete, Nan, 279
Peirce, Deborah, 970
Peisley, Mary, 332
Peixotto, Rachel, 898
Peixotto, Simha, 898
Pelham, Joseph, *270*
Pelikan, Jaroslav, 525
Peltier, Leonard, 1238
Peltrie, Madame de la, 211
Pendleton, William, 299–300

Pleasant, Mary Ellen, 1039
Pleasant Hill Seminary, 298
Plessy v. *Ferguson,* 864
Plunkett, Mary, 757
Plural religious identities, 1274–1276; households and, 1270–1276, *1271*
Pluralism: cultural, 1130–1131; educational, 889; interfaith marriage and, 1273; Protestant, 889
Plymouth Brethren, 428
The Plymouth Collection (Beecher), 977
P'nai Or Religious Fellowship, 797
Poale Zion (Workers of Zion), 1126
Pocomania, 117
Poems of the Passing (Amatu'l-Baha), 784
Poethig, Kathryn, 1218
Pogrebin, Letty Cottin, 21, 596, 1223
Point Adult Centre for Education (PACE), 1290
Polen, Suzanne, 957
Polish Women's Alliance, 130, 154
The Politics of Prayer: Feminist Language and the Worship of God (Hitchcock), 205
Polle, Lillian, 427
Polyamory, 817
Polyandry, 30
Polygamy, 13–14, 709, 713, 718, 721, 774; opposition to, 722–723
Polygyny, 30, 720; in Qur'an, 624–625
Pomerleau, Dolly, 954, 955, 957, 958
Ponder, Annell, 1087
Pontellier, Edna, 1008
Pontifical Biblical Commission, 953
Pontifical Commission for Contemplative Religious, 207
Poochutal ("adorning with flowers"), 661
Pool, Tamar de Sola, 1124
Poole, Myra, 958
Pop-bhangra, 662
Popular Protestantism, 478
Popular religion, 169–171
Populist movement, 591, 864
Positive Magic (Weinstein), 817
The Possible Human (Houston), 766
Post, Amy, 774
Postfeminism, 305–306
Postmillennialism, 769
Postmodern feminism, 1116
Postmodernism, 5, 8, 785, 934; conditioning of power and difference and, 56–57
Poststructuralism, 934
Potomac Synod of the Reformed Church, 918
Powell, Lois, 376, 380
Power: distinction between authority and, 8; language and, 47–48; *mujerista* understanding of, 1192; postmodern conditioning of, 56–57
Powers, Mary, 786
Powhatan Confederation, 114
Powhatan people: African immigrants and, 111; intermarriage with blacks, 114
Powlas, Annie, 314
Powlas, Maud, 314
Poyen, Charles, 739

Prabhupada, A. C. Bhaktivedanta, 670
Practical Homeschooling (magazine), 893
Prager, Marcia, 797, 799, 801, 803, 804
Praise Keepers, 460
Praise songs, 987
Praise the Lord/People That Love (PTL), 400, 463
Praisesong for the Widow (Marshall), 1172
Prajnaparamita, 26
Pratilekhna, 690
Pratt, James, 636
Pratt, Renate, 1147
Pratt, Richard, 98–99
Pratt, Sunya, 636
Prayer, elimination from state schools, 890
A Prayer for the Earth (Sasso), 553
Prayer of Faith (Trudel), 429
Predestination, doctrine of, 223, 285
Prejean, Helen, 1014, 1152, *1153,* 1157
Premillennialism, 314–315
Preminger, Otto, 1014
Prendergast, Father John, 876
Prentiss, Elizabeth Payson, 977–978, 979
Prentiss, George L., 977
Presbyterian Board of Home Missions, 346
Presbyterian Church in America (PCA), 349, 350
Presbyterian Church in the United States of America (PCUSA), 357, 361; women's ordination and, 943
Presbyterian Church in the United States (PCUS), 349
Presbyterian Church USA, inclusive language and, 1292
Presbyterian Historical Society (PHS), 354; archives of, 353
Presbyterian Hymnal: Hymns, Psalms, and Spiritual Songs, 998
Presbyterian Life (magazine), 15
The Presbyterian Magazine, 355–357
Presbyterian Women in America, 352–366
Presbyterian Women's Foreign Mission Society (WFMS), 347
Presbyterians, 343; in borderlands, 1138; in British North America, 244; in Canada, 345; education and, 889; fight for coestablishment, 245–246; missionaries of, 837, 840; opposition to slavery, 1039; in Southern colonies, 241; women in America, 352–366; women ministers in, 971; women's colleges and, 917, 920; women's ordination and, 943. *See also* New Light Presbyterians; New Side Presbyterians; United Presbyterian Church; United Presbyterian Church in the USA; United Presbyterian Church of North America
Presbytery, Leitchfield, 355
Presbytery, Nolin, 355
Preston, Ruth Irish, 384
Prettyshield, Jessie, 1286–1287
Price, Rebecca, 911
Price, Thomas F., 845, 848
The Priceless Pearl (Amatu'l-Baha), 784
Pride, Mary, 893
Priesand, Sally Jane, 541, 573, 905, 963, *963*
Priestess, Mother, Sacred Sister (Sered), 1202
Priests, service of, during Civil War, 128
Priests for Equality, 952, 956
Primate's Theological Commission, 217
Primavesi, Anne, 1111, 1113
Princeton, 924

Printz, Armegat, 229–230
Prior, Jerilynn, 1147
Prior, Margaret, 968
Priscilla Papers (journal), 16, 471, 472, 473
Privatization, 57
Pro Ecclesia et Pontifice, 877
Proctor-Smith, Marjorie, 1252, 1291
Professional reformers, 1031
The Progress of Religious Ideas through Successive Ages
     (Child), 636
Progressive Era, 414, 1033, 1061
Progressive movement's social uplift agenda, 1123
Progressive National Baptist Convention (PNBC), 258, 262,
     431; hymnbooks for, 997; ordination of women and, 945;
     women's ordination and, 945
Progressive Party, 1065, 1085
Prohibition Era, 1032
Project People Foundation, 1159
Project Priesthood, 954
Pro-Life Action Plan, 1101
Promise Keepers, 446, 459, 460, 1300
The Promise of the Father (Palmer), 323, 969
Promise Reapers, 460, 1300
The Promulgation of Universal Peace (Straun), 783
Propaganda Fide Office, 848
Prophet, Elizabeth Clare, 763–764, 767, 1264
Prophet, Mark, 763–764, 1264
Prose, Francine, 189, 1016
Prosperity theology, 465
Prostitution, 1024; attitudes toward, 1023; cultural, 106;
     elimination of, 1021
Protestant American Sunday School Union, 898
Protestant church societies, bureaucracies for, 1265–1270
Protestant Church Women United, 202
Protestant Episcopal Church Board of Missions, 826
Protestant Episcopal Theological Seminary (Virginia), 928
Protestant female preaching, in United States, 965–973
Protestant missionaries, in borderlands, 1137–1140
Protestant Orphan Asylum, 246
Protestant pluralism, 889
Protestant Reformation, 221–222, 307
Protestant Sunday Schools and religious education, 906–912
Protestant women: in Colonial New England, 221–228; lead-
     ership and community building by, 851–864; in Mid-At-
     lantic colonies, 228–236; as missionaries, 834–843; in
     Newfoundland, 242–243; ordination movement and, 940–
     950; in Southern colonies, 236–242. *See also specific Prot-
     estant groups*
Protestant women's colleges, 922; issues faced by, in twenty-
     first century, 919–921; roots of, 913–914; in United
     States, 912–923
Protestantism, 221–505; African American denominations,
     240–241, 250–262; Anabaptists, 262–269; Anglicans in,
     279–285; Asian, 498–505; Baptists in, 285–296; Charis-
     matic movement in, 457–467; Christian Church/Disciples
     of Christ in, 296–307; in Colonial period, 221–249; Can-
     ada, 242–249; Mid-Atlantic, 228–236; New England, 221–
     228; Southern, 236–242; Episcopalians in, 269–279; Euro-
     American evangelical feminism and, 467–476; evangelicals
     in, 447–457; fundamentalism in, 439–447; Hispanic, 477–

497; Holiness movements in, 424–430; Lutheranism in,
     307–318; Methodists in, 319–329; Pentecostalism in, 394–
     407; Pentecostals, 492–497; Presbyterians in, 352–361;
     Quakers in, 329–341; race and gender in Latina identity,
     484–492; Reformed Churches in, 341–352; revivalism in,
     416–424; Salvation Army in, 407–416; Sanctified Church
     in, 430–439; Unitarian Universalist movement in, 380–
     393; United Church of Canada, 361–368; United Church
     of Christ in, 368–380; U.S. Latina evangélicas, 477–484;
     volunteeristic spirit of American, 830. *See also specific de-
     nominations*
Providence Vedanta Society, 669
Providentia Providebt, 164
Provincial Freeman (newspaper), 1039
Provincial Synod of the Church of England and Ireland
     (Canada), 280
Psalm singing, 976
Psychology, of women's religious experience, 62–68
Psychology and religion, 509
Psychotherapy, 1276
Public policy in Canada, 1141–1149
Public Universal Friend, 235
Puja, worship of, 664, 665
Pukkumina, 117
Pulpit ministry, African American women and, 257–258
Puranas, 27
Pure Gold (Lowry), 983
Pure Land Buddhism. *See* Jodo Shinshu
Purgatory: Doctrinal Historical and Poetical (Sadlier), 874
Puritan ideal, 224–225
Puritanism, 912; Northern, 447–448; women's role under,
     223
Puritans, 27, 368; African American women as, 252; charac-
     teristics of, 221–222; in Colonial New England, 222–224,
     225; Great Migration of, 222–223
Pusey, Edward, 826
Puysegur, Marquis de, 769
Pyke, Rachel Peixotto, 1119

Qi, 675, 678
Qigong, 675, 678
Quadragesimo Anno (Pius XI), 194–195
Quaker humanitarianism, 1021
Quaker Religious Thought, 339
Quakers, 13, 234, 329–341, 347; African American freedom
     and, 252; aftermath of Richmond Conference, 337–339;
     in British North America, 247–248; colonial beginnings
     of, 331–333; division/unity in, 339–340; education and,
     889; era of expansion, 333–334; feminism and, 339–340;
     hymns and, 979; in Mid-Atlantic colonies, 228–229, 231–
     232, 233; in New England colonies, 224–225, 226, 227–
     228; opposition to slavery, 1039; pacifist, 228; as peace
     church, 1055; peace movements and, 1050; revivalism
     and, 417–418; social reform movements and, 334–335; in
     Southern colonies, 241; theological/cultural splits, 335–
     336; turning point, 336–337; understanding of the inner
     light, 940; women as, 226; women missionaries of, 835;
     women's leadership in, 941–942
Qualified nondualism, 666
Quebec: heroic motherhood in, 213; reorganization of

French-speaking church in, 211–212; research on women and Catholicism in, 218; wearing *hijab* in, 626–627; women and social Catholicism in, 213–215

Queen Isabella Association, 758

Queen's Daughters, 189

Quevedo, Juan de, 95

Quiet Revolution, 213, 215

Quigley, Archbishop, 877

Quimby, Phineas Parkhurst, 739, 757, 758, 1259

Quinn, Donna, 1105

Quinn, Mary, 1043

Quintana, Gloria, 1146

Quito, Mariana de, 137

Quixote Center, 954

Quraishi, Asifa, 619

Qur'an, 6, 27, 28, 36; as center of Islam, 609–610, 612; descriptions of human creation in, 40; education of women and, 604; equality between men and women and, 604; Muslim marriage in, 624–625; reinterpretation and, 605–606; view of womanhood in, 609. *See also* Islam

Rabbinical Assembly, 965; Committee on Jewish Law, 550, 574

Rabbinical curriculum, offering of, to undergraduates, 962–963

The Rabbi's Letter, 563

Rabbis' Manual, 553

Rabin, Yitzhak, 1125

Rabinowitz, Jakie, 1015–1016

Raboteau, Albert, 525

Race: as factor in foundation of religious communities, 163; as issue for women's societies, 291; in Latina experience, 484–492

Race Amity Day (later changed to Race Unity Day), 785

Race motherhood, ideology of, *1080*

Race riots, 1032

Racial discrimination, linkage of slavery and, 1048

Racial egalitarianism, abolition and, 1048–1049

Racial Justice Award banquets, 1132

Racism, 75; African American Catholic women and, 162, 167–168; economic, 98–99; white, 1026–1027

Radcliffe Catholic Club, 192

Radcliffe College (Mass.), 882, 886, 915, 922

Radha devi dasi, 670

Radical abolitionists, 1038

Radical Christianity, 1284

Radical communitarian societies, 233

Radical democracy, 1081

Radical feminism, 22

Ragland, Margaret, 326

Ragsdale, Katherine Hancock, 1103

Rahima Foundation, 628

Rahman, Jamila Abdur, 611

Rahner, Karl, 203, 954

Railton, George Scott, 407

Rainbow Center, 1150–1152

Rainbow Coalition, 57

Rainey, Ma, 260

Raja Yoga, 756–757

Rajneesh, Mohan Chandra, 791

Rajneesh Movement/Osho Commune, 789, 791–792

Rakhmana, 1223

Ramabai, Pandita, 841

Ramadan, 610

Ramakrishna Brahma-Vabin, 669

Ramakrishna Mission of the Ramakrishna Order, 666–668

Ramakrishna monastic order, 660

Ramayana, 27

Ramaz School (Manhattan), 566

Ramerman, Mary, 958

Raming, Ida, 958, 959

Ramírez, Isabel, 137

Ramírez, Julie, 481–482

Ramon Magsaysay Award, 677

Ramona (Jackson), 1027

Ramos, Alonso, 139

Ramsay, Martha Laurens, 271, 448

Ramshaw, Gail, 45, 1283

Ramtha, 766–767

Ranck, Shirley Ann, 19, 392

Randall, Claire, 1268–1269

Randolph, Florence Spearing, 258, 433

Randolph, Paschal Beverly, 774

Randolph-Macon Woman's College (Va.), 916, 921, 922

Rangel, Nellie, 493–494

Rankin, Jeannette, 1054, 1055

Rankin, Melinda, 1139–1140

Ransom, Reverdy C., 1075

Rape laws, Pakistani, 619

Rape Shield Law (1992) (Canada), 1144–1145

Raphael, Geela Rayzel, 801, 802, 803, 1224

Raphael, Melissa, 1206

Rapp, George, 708, 711, 715–716

Rapp, Gertrude, 715–716

Rappard, Dora, 975

Rappite Harmonists, 712, 716

RAPPORT, 956

Rapture, 428

Rashad, Amatullah, 752

Rasmussen, Knud, 88, 89

Rastafarians, 118–119, 123

Rationalism, Enlightenment and, 226

Ratisbonne, Alphonse, 1280

Ratisbonne, Theodore, 1280

Ratzinger, Joseph, 957

Rauf, Muhammad Abdul, 604

Rauhes Haus, 822

Rauschenbusch, Walter, 838, 1069–1070, 1071, 1075

Raysheet Chochmah Bet Midrash, 798, 803

La Raza, 17, 1182

Read, Joel, 18

Reagan, Ronald, 1057, 1295, 1297

Reagon, Bernice Johnson, 1091

Realist, social commentary fiction, 1009

Reaper and Gleaner Circle of King's Daughters of the Twin Cities, 869

The Reappearance of the Christ (Bailey), 762–763

Rebbe MH"M, 562

The Rebbetzin's Letter, 563

Rebecca the Jewess (Baker), 591

Resacralization, 50

Réseau oecuménique des femmes du Québec/Women's Ecumenical Network (ROF/WEN), 1285

Residential school system, in Canada, 100

Resistance, by Indian children, 100–101

Response (magazine), 1221

Responsibility, 1171

Responsum Ad Dubium, 957

La respuesta (Sor Juana Inés de la Cruz), 45

Restoration Studies, 731

Retrospection and Introspection (Morse), 738

Reuter, Anna Catherina Antes Kalberlahn, 242

Reuter, Christian, 242

The Revelation of Baha-Ullah in a Sequence of Four Lessons (Brittingham), 784

Revised Standard Version of the Christian Bible, 1292

Revival Hymns and Plantation Melodies (Echols), 999

Revivals, 113, 117, 118, 122, 123, 416–424, 941–943, 976; automobiles and, 420; Christian Connections and, 417; defined, 416; Free Will Baptists and, 417; Holiness movement and, 418; Methodists and, 417; Pentecostalism and, 417, 418; Quakers and, 417–418; songs at, 981; spread of, 252; women hymn writers and, 979–982; women in, 422–423

Reviving Ophelia: Saving the Selves of Adolescent Girls (Pipher), 1305–1306

Reweaving the World: The Emergence of Ecofeminism (Diamond and Orenstein), 1112

Rexford, Orcella, 779

Rhea Hirsch School of Education at Hebrew Union College, 903–904, 905

Rhetorical criticism, 41

Rhine, Alice Hyneman, 590

Rhode Island, establishment of, 224

Rhodes, Barbara, 642, 645

Rhodes, Mary, 152, 845

Rhys-Davids, Caroline, 636, 637

Rhys-Davids, T. W., 636

Ricci, Mateo, 182

Rice, John R., 446, 971

Rice, Luther, 286

Rich, Adrienne, 792, 1202

Richards, Emma, 268

Richardson, Samuel, 1000

Richelieu, Cardinal, 141

Richman, Julia, 900, 903

Richmond, University of, 917

Richmond African Baptist Missionary Society, 256

Richmond Declaration of Faith, 337

Richmond Female Institute, 292

Ridderhof, Joy, 841–842, 842

Rider, Lucy Meyer, 828, 863

Riegert, Peter, 1016

Riggio, Ursula, 496

Riggs, Marcia Y., 1170–1171

Riggs, Ralph M., 401

Right and Wrong in Boston (Chapman), 1051

Righteous Discontent: The Women's Movement in the Black Baptist Church (Higginbotham), 857

Riley, W. H., 825

Riley, William Bell, 441, 443, 445

Ring shout, 987

Ringe, Sharon, 41, 473

Ringelheim, Joan Miriam, 1282

Rinpoche, Chögyal Namkhai Norbu, 656, 657

Rinpoche, Chögyam Trungpa, 1097

Rinpoche, Dezhung, 655

Rinpoche, Penor, 654

Rinpoche, Sakyong Mipham, 656

Rinpoche, Sogyal, 1096

Rinzai Zen, 681, 685

Rio Conference on Sustainable Development, 1108

Rio de Llano colony, 709

Río Grande Female Institute, 1139

Ríos, Elizabeth D., 482

Ripley, George, 382–383

Ripley, Sarah Alden Bradford, 382, 383, 384

Ripley, Sophia Dana, 150

Rise Up and Call Her Name: A Woman-Honoring Journey in Global Earth-Based Spiritualities (Fisher), 392

Risso Koseikai, 686

Ritchie, Nelly, 1197

Ritching, Edna Rose, 716

The Rite of Christian Initiation of Adults, 880–881

Rites of passage: Islamic celebration of, 617–618; Sikh women and, 699–701

Rituals, 171; feminist, 1249–1255, *1251;* in Hinduism, 661, 662–664; Judaism and, 568–576; women's religious issues in Canada and, 1288

Rivera, Socorro Favela, *169*

Rivers, Clarence Joseph, 998

Rivier College (Hudson, New Hampshire), 884

Rix, Harriet Hale, 760

Rizzetto, Diane Eishin, 640

Roath, Mary Wada, 683, 686

Robarts, Ella, 782

Robb, Carol, 58

Robbins, Jane E., 1064

Robbins, Tim, 1014

The Robe (film), 1013

Roberson, Lizzie Woods, 433

Roberta Martin Singers, 260

Roberts, Abigail, 298, 299, 370, 941

Roberts, B. H., 724

Roberts, B. T., 427

Roberts, Benjamin, 945

Roberts, Oral, 457, 458, 461, 465

Roberts, Phoebe McCarty, 247

Robertson, Carole, 1089

Robertson, Pat, 463, 464, 1295, 1298, 1299

Robinette, Gusta A., 328

Robinson, Ida, 258, 418, 421, 423, *431,* 432

Robinson, Jane Bancroft, 825

Robinson, Jo Ann Gibson, 1082

Robinson, Ruby Doris Smith, 1086, 1091

Roblin, Rodmond, 1073

Rochambeau, Donatien, 121

Rochester, University of, women students at, 289

Rockefeller, John D., 917
Rockefeller, Mrs. John D., 917
Rockefeller, Nelson, 496
Rockford College (Ill.), 921, 922
Rockford Female Seminary, 919
Roddy, Clarence, 445
Rodeph Shalom (Pa.), 537
Rodgers, Elizabeth Flynn, 155
Rodney, Lyalorisha Melvina, *117,* 122
Rodríguez, Baldemar, 494
Rodríguez, Jeanette, 1196, 1198
Rodriguez de Lizárraga, Angelita, 482–483
Roe v. *Wade,* 21, 204, 1100–1102, 1106
La Rogativa, 484
Rogell, Sharda, 648
Rogers, Alva, 1016
Rogers, Mary Josephine, 191, 845
Rogers, Samuel, 337
Rogow, Faith, 1120, 1224
Roitinger, Adelinde Theresia, 958
Roland Graeme, Knight (Machar), 1071
Rollet, Claude, 143
Rolling Stones, 993
Roman Catholic Legion of Decency, 1012
Roman Catholic seminaries, 926
Roman Propaganda Fide (Propagation of the Faith) Office, 845
Roman Synod on catechesis, 880
Romans 16:1–2, deacon/deaconess in, 821, 852
Rood, Helen, 77
Rood, Wayne, 77
Rooney, Andy, 107
Roosevelt, Eleanor, 70, 260, 279, 766, 1036–1037, 1084, 1085
Roosevelt, Franklin D., 106, 1055; New Deal and, 260
Roosevelt, Theodore, 1054
Root, Martha, 779, 784, 786
Rosa of Lima, 134, 137
Rosado Rousseau, Leoncia, 480, 481, 496
Rosales, Diego de, 140–141
Rosary College Catholic Evidence Guild, 195–196
Roscoe, Will, 107
Rose, Andy, 1218
Rose, Marcia, 648
Rosemont (Philadelphia), 888
Rosenbaum, Joan, 905
Rosenberg, Ellen, 542–543
Rosewell, Pam, 462
Rosh Chodesh, 801, 1288
Rosh Hashanah, 577, 960
Rosh hodesh, 575, 1224
Rosh Hodesh Exchange (newsletter), 1224
Rosicrucianism, 1203
Rosie the Riveter, 1055
Ross, Jean, 641
Ross, John, 94
Ross, Rosetta, 748
Rossetti, Christina, 976
Rossi, Mary Ann, 956
Rotary Club, 313

Roth, Joel, 551, 582
Roth, John, 1282
Rounsefell, Carrie, 982
Rousseau, Jean-Jacques, 881
Rousselon, Father Etienne, 164, 165
Roussy, Louis, 245
Rowe, Hannah, 241
Rowe, Maureen, 123
Rowe, Thora Wade, 1288
Rowland, Clara May, 760
Rowland, Henrietta, 1060
Rowlandson, Mary, 225, 1000–1001
Roy, Marie-Andrée, 218, 959
Royal Commission on the Status of Women, 216
Royal Service, 293
Royce, Josiah, 1199
RSV Bible Committee, 1269
Ruach HaAretz, 799
Ruch, Velma, 731
Rudd, Violet, 293
Ruddick, Sara, 70
Ruether, Rosemary Radford, 3, 202, 703, 788, 924, 953, 955, 1105, 1108, 1111, 1113, 1115, 1174, 1175, 1176–1179, 1197, 1204, 1215, 1235, 1247, 1278, 1280
Ruffin, Josephine St. Pierre, 865–866
Ruiz, Vicki, 1185
Runnalls, Donna, 926, *927*
Ruskin, John, 1060, 1064
Russell, Alys, 426
Russell, Bertrand, 426
Russell, Letty, 33, 38, 937, 1168
Russell, Mary Baptist, 152
Russell, Mrs. Alexander, 638, 640
Russell, Rosalind, 1014
Rustemeyer, Rosanne, 847
Rustin, Bayard, 1083
Rutgers University, 918
Rutherford, Gertrude, 367
Ryan, Bertha, 268–269
Ryan, Joan Marie, 845–846
Ryan, Martin L., 399
Ryan, Mary, 774
Ryan, Mary Perkins, 881
Ryan, Tim, 1146
Rynders, Isaiah, 771
Ryo, Juhi, 187

The Sabbath Journal of Judith Lomax, 271
Sabbath kiddush, 546
Sabbath Lake, Maine, Shaker community in, 708
The Sabbath-School Bell, 983
Sabia, Laura, 1144
Sabu, 1015
Sacks, Karen, 808
Sacred Calf Pipe Woman, 93
Sacred Congregation for Religious, 207
Sacred Harp singing, 999
The Sacred Harp (songbook), 999
Sacred Heart Review, 157

Sauer, Maria Christina, 231
Saulteaux, Bernice, 1287
Saulteaux, Jessie, 367, 1287
Savage, Mary, 294
Savannah River Ebenezer, 309
Save Our Children, 1298
Saving Work: Feminist Practices of Theological Education (Chopp), 937
Savoca, Nancy, 1016
Savoy Records, 993, 994
Saxe, Grace, 441
Sayadaw, Mahasi, 647
Sayadaw, U Pandita, 647, 1097
Sayle, Iris, 284
Scalabrini Sisters, 185
Scanlon, James Edward, 916
Scanzoni, Letha Dawson, 16, 469, 470, 472, 474, 1217
Scarritt Bible and Training School, 326
Schaar, Sophie, 1122
Schachter, Lifsa, 905
Schachter-Shalomi, Zalman, 798
Schaeffer, Francis, 893
Schauffler College of Religious and Social Work, 373
Schechter, Frank, 545
Schechter, Mathilde Roth, 545–546, *547*
Schechter, Solomon, 545
Schell, Elizabeth, 1252
Schenirir, Sarah, 566–567, 581
Schillebeeckx, Edward, 1244
Schisms, women's role in, 234–236
Schlafly, Phyllis, 21, 891, 1295–1297, 1298, 1299
Schmidt, Ruth A., 469
Schmucker, Samuel Simon, 310
Schneider, Susan Weidman, 1221
Schneiders, Sandra, 206
Schofield, Martha, 335
Scholer, David, 471, 472, 475
School for Girls, 901
School for International Training (Vt.), 1095
School of Biblical Instruction (Brooklyn, N.Y.), 901
School of Enlightenment, 767
School prayer, 1295; elimination of, from state, 890
Schoolman, Albert, 902
Schoolman, Bertha, 902
Schoolproof (Pride), 893
Schools: American Indian boarding, 97–102, *99*; Bais Yaakov, for Orthodox girls, 567; Bible reading elimination from state, 890; Catholic parish, 874, 875, 882–883; Christian day, 889, 893; common, 890, 907; Congregational religious, 535, 537; day, 904; home, 889, 891–896; normal, 900; residential, in Canada, 100; women as classroom teachers in, 930–939. *See also* Education
Schopflocher, Lorol, 779
Schorsch, Ismar, 551
Schrager, Susan, 669
Schucman, Helen, 763, 764–765, 767
Schucman, Louis, 765
Schuller, Eileen, 1281
Schurz, Carl, 98
Schurz, Margaretta, 909

Schwartz, Jacqueline, 642, 647
Schwenkfelders, in Colonial Pennsylvania, 230
Science and Health with Key to the Scriptures (Eddy), 741, 743–744, 745
Scientific American Journal, 775
Scientific medicine, 1258, 1263; female acceptance of, 1260–1261
Scientific Mental Practice (Hopkins), 758
Scobie, Ingrid, 70
Scofield, Cyrus, 440
Scofield Reference Bible, 428
Scopes, John, 443
Scopes trial, 455, 970
Scorsese, Martin, 1013
Scots Confession, 342
Scott, Anne Firor, 860
Scott, Catherine, 294
Scott, E. Jane, 825
Scott, Maylie, 644
Scott, Walter, 1120
Scottish Common Sense philosophy, 1021
Scottish Presbyterian sect, 1039
Scottsboro Boys, 870
Scripps College (Calif.), 922
A Scriptural Vindication of Female Preaching (Peirce), 970
Scriptures: authority of, 39; interpretation of, by North American women, 33–45; searching, 41–43. *See also* Bible
Scudder, Harriet, 346
Scudder, Ida, *342*, 346
Scudder, John, 346
Scudder, Vida Dutton, 275, 1030, 1064, 1070, 1071, 1072, 1076
Searching the Scriptures (Seim), 42, 474
Second Coming, 415, 439, 1260
Second Coming (film), 1013
Second Coming of Christ to Theosophy, 1262
Second Great Awakening (1800–1830), 113, 253, 271, 347, 452, 589, 768, 773, 835, 912, 941, 976, 977, 979, 1118
Second Helvetic Confession, 342
Second National Havurah Institute, 800
Second Plenary Council (Baltimore), 874
Second Seminole War, 114
Second Vatican Council. *See* Vatican II (1962–1965)
Second wave of feminism, 3, *4*, 12, 20, 51, 472, 931; Anabaptists and, 268; in religious organizations, 14–17
The Secret Doctrine (Blavatsky), 755
Secular bias, 14
Secular feminism, 606
Secular humanism, 889, 890–891, 1298, 1299
Secular reproductive rights movement, 1100
Secular women's movement, *952*, 1292
Seder, 538; Feminist, 21, 575; Ma'yan, 1224; Passover, 1224
Sedillo, Sylvia, 1184
Seekers, in Colonial Pennsylvania, 230
Segale, Blandina, 128, 154, 190, 843
Segovia Hoeferkamp, Suzanne, 483
Seifferly, Crystal, 817
Seim, Turid Karlsen, 474
Selective Training and Service Act (1940), 1055
Self-Realization Fellowship, 667, 669–670, 1275
Seligsberg, Alice, 1123–1124

Shimano, Eido, 641, 642

Shin Buddhism, 634, 637, 680–681, 683–684, 685, 686; temples of, *635*, 635–636

Shingon Buddhism (Shingon-shu), 681, 686

Shinto, 680, 686

Shipp, Ellis, 722

Shirdi Sai Baba, 671

Shirley, Eliza, 407

Shiva, 664

Shiva, Vandana, 1115

Shoah, 1277–1278, 1282

Shoemaker, Mary, 429

Shoemaker, Nancy, 91

Shomea, Lev, 801

Shortchanging Girls, Shortchanging America (study), 936

Shouter Baptists, 118, 122–123

Shouting, 1261

Showalter, Shirley, 268

Showalter, Winifred Mason Moore, 305

Shree Gurudev Siddha Peeth, 670

Shromani Gurdwara Prabhandak Committee (SGPC), 703

Shulhan Arukh, 577

Shum, Mina, 1016

Sibbitt, Mary, 340

Sick visitors, Methodist Church and, 319

Siddha Yoga, 667, 670–671, 686

Siddha Yoga Dham, 671

Sider, Ron, 470, 471

Siegel, Daniel, 802, 803, 804

Siegel, Hanna Tiferet, 801, 802, 803

Sierra Leone, relocation to, 256

Sigal, Philip, 550, 583

The Sign of the Cross (film), 1013

Signs and Wonders (Woodworth-Etter), 430

Sikh Centennial Foundation, 703

Sikhism, 693–703, *694; amrita* initiation, 699–700; Christmas celebration and, 699; Code of Conduct in, 701; death, 700–701; Ethical Code in, 699; heritage, 695–696; immigration and, 190, 693–695; name-giving, 699; rites of passage, 699–701; status of, 701–703; weddings, 700; worship, 696–699

Silber, David, 567

Silberz, Katherine, 151

Silent Unity, 759, 760

Silko, Leslie Marmon, 89, 1232, 1233–1234

Silkwood, Karen, 1235

Siller-Acuña, Clodomiro, 1198

Sillery, 144

Sills, Anna Peck, 859–860

Silman, Janet, 1142

Silver, Joan Micklin, 1016

Silver Bluff Baptist Church, 118; origin of, 253

Silver Raven Fox, 1265

Silverman, Althea Osber, 548

Silverman, Rabbi, 781

Silvestro, Marsie, 955

Simantam ("parting of the hair"), 661

Simhat bat ceremony, 575

Simhat Torah, 583

Simhat-Bat: Ceremonies to Welcome a Baby Girl, 552

Simkhovitch, Mary (Kingsbury), 275, 1063, 1065, 1067, 1072

Simkins, Modjeska Monteith, 1084, 1090

Simmer-Brown, Judith, 656–657, 1094

Simmons, Dorothy, 990

Simmons, Jean, 1013, 1015

Simmons, John K., 741

Simmons, Ruth, 65

Simmons-Akers Singers, 990

Simms, Florence, 1033

Simon, Abram, 536

Simon, Carrie Obendorfer, 536, *537*

Simone, Louise Manoogian, 519

Simonian, Seta, 521

Simons, Menno, 262

Simos, Miriam, 19, 815. *See also* Starhawk

Simpkinson, Anne, 685

Simpson, Albert B., 396, 428, 440, 454

Simpson, Cynthia, 817

Simpson, O. J., 1302–1303

Sims, J. Marion, 1258

Sims, Mary, 1132

Sinclair, Gordon, 404

Singer, Isaac Bashevis, 1016

Singh, Harbhajan (Yogi), 693

A Singing Something: Womanist Reflections on Anna Julia Cooper (Baker-Fletcher), 1172

Sinsinawa Dominican Women's Network, 1246

Sircar, Rina, 650–651

Sisson, Elizabeth, 429

Sister Act (film), 1014

Sister Act 2: Back in the Habit (film), 1014

Sister Formation Colleges, 884

Sister Formation Movement, 16, 132, 198

Sister Kay (film), 1281

Sister Rose Thering Endowment for Jewish-Christian Studies at Seton Hall University (South Orange, N.J.), 1280

Sisterhood Is Global Institute, 628

Sisterhood of the Congregation Orach Chaim, 558

Sisterhood of the Holy Communion, 273, 826

Sisterhood Sabbath, 539

Sisterhood Shabbat, 573–574

Sisters against Sexism (SAS), 1245

Sisters' Educational and Professional Standards Commission, 198

Sisters in Islam, 628

Sisters in the Wilderness: The Challenge of Womanist God-Talk, 1169–1170

Sisters of Charity, Baltimore, 883, 884

Sisters of Charity, Maryland, 843

Sisters of Charity (Halifax), 153, 211, 212, 215, 216

Sisters of Charity of Providence, 1277

Sisters of Charity of St. Vincent de Paul, 1184

Sisters of Charity of the Blessed Virgin Mary, 1245, 1260, 1282

Sisters of Dust, Sisters of Spirit: Womanist Wordings on God and Creation (Baker-Fletcher), 1172

Sisters of Earth, 717

Sisters of Good Shepherd, 156

Sisters of Loretto, 152, 154, 164, 211, 843, 845, 848, 1184, 1279

Society for Christian Ethics, 59
Society for Creative Anachronism, 816
Society for the Advancement of Judaism, 550, 552–553, 573
Society for the Propagation of the Faith, 191
Society for the Propagation of the Gospel (SPG), 240, 252, 281
Society of African Missionaries, 165
Society of Christian Socialists, 1070
Society of Companions of the Holy Cross, 275
Society of Friends, 27. *See also* Quakers
Society of Jesus, 957. *See also* Jesuits
Society of Jewish Science, 1262
Society of Medical Mission Sisters, 846
Society of St. Columban, 845
Society of St. Margaret, 273
Society of Tamil, 660
Society of the Companions of the Holy Cross (SCHC), 1070–1071, 1072
Society of the Holy Family, 162
Society of the Sacred Heart, 152, 195
Society of the Woman in the Wilderness, 231
Society of Women of Nazareth, 197
Sociology, 1031–1032
Socioreligious movement, club movement as, 865–867
Soelle, Dorothee, 56
Soen, Sa Nim, 642
Soeurs grises, 211
Soeurs de la Charité de Saint-Hyacinthe, 212
Soeurs de Notre-Dame du Bon Conseil, 214
Sohappy, Cindy Gilbert, 101
Sojourner Truth, 35, 54, 253, 255, 418, 421, 867, 1001, 1167
Sojourners Community, 456
Sola Scriptura, Puritan teaching of, 224
Soldiers Aid Association of Philadelphia, 153
Solidarity, 57
Solomon, Hannah, 899, 960, 1120
Soloveitchik, Joseph B., 581
Some Answered Questions (Dreyfus-Barney), 783
Somerset, Isabel, 430
Somogie, Beverly, 891–896, 892
Sonbol, Amira, 606
Song in a Weary Throat (Murray), 71
The Song of Bernadette (film), 1014
Songs of Love and Mercy, 997
Songs of Zion (Douroux), 996, 997
Sons of Temperance, 1024
Soto, Hernando de, 109
Soto Zen, 634, 641, 681, 685, 686
Soul Echoes (Tinley), 999
Soule, Caroline A., 388
Soule, Ida, 274
South American indigenous women, Christianity and, 94–96
South Carolina, slavery in, 237
South Carolina Association of Independent Home Schools, 894
South Carolina State Democratic Party, 1089
South Carolina Tuberculosis Association, 1084
South End House (Boston), 1074
Southard, M. Madeline, 949
Southard, Naomi, 503

Southeast Asians, immigration to United States, 180
Southern Association of Women's Colleges, 916
Southern Baptist Convention, 286, 291, 446, 454–455, 842; response to feminism in, 21–22; women leaders, 1270; women's ordination and, 942; women's subordination and, 27
Southern Baptist Women in Ministry, 22, 294
Southern Baptist Women's Missionary Union, 288, 290
Southern California Community Choir, 993
Southern Christian Leadership Conference (SCLC), 18, 260, 261, 870, 1083, 1087, 1090–1091
Southern colonies, Protestants in, 236–242
Southern Conference Educational Fund (SCEF), 1085
Southern Conference for Human Welfare (SCHW), 1084
Southern Frontier religion, 448–449
Southern Methodist Church, 825
Southern Patriot, 1085
Southern Protestantism, American Revolution and, 242
Southern sentimental novel, 1007
Southern Sociological Congress, 290, 1034
Southern Student Organizing Committee (SSOC), 1091
Southey, Robert, 974
Southwestern Bible Institute (Enid, Okla.), 403
Sovereignty, Inc., 767
The Sovereignty & Goodness of God, Together with the Faithfulness of His Promises Displayed: Being a Narrative of the Captivity and Restoration of Mrs. Mary Rowlandson (Rowlandson), 225
Soyen, Shaku, 640
Spafford, Belle, 725
Spahr, Jane Adams, 1218
Spalding, Eliza, 346–347
Spalding, Henry, 346
Spalding, John, 158
Spanish American War, 130; opposition to, 1053
Spanish Assemblies of God, 481
Spanish Inquisition (1492), 554
Sparling, Olive, 365
Spaulding, Martha, 294
Spellmire, Verona, 876–877
Spelman, Lucy Henry, 917
Spelman College (Atlanta), 916–917, 922
Spelman Seminary, 917
Spence, Peter, 998
Spencer, Aida, 473
Spencer, Gary, 596–597
Spencer, Geoffrey, 730
Spencer, Herbert, 742
Spertus Museum, 905
The Spiral Dance (Starhawk), 19, 815, 1202
SPIRIT, 103
Spirit baptism, 459
The Spirit of Judaism (Aguilar), 898
Spirit photography, 775
Spirit Rock Meditation Center, 648
Spirit-centered movements, 418
Spiritism, 637, 732–733, 735, 736, 737
Spiritual Baptists, 117, 118, 122–123
Spiritual Care for Living and Dying, 1096
Spiritual egalitarianism, 321

Streisand, Barbra, 1016
Strelley, Kate, 791
Strong, Josiah, 1071
Stuart, Maurine, 641, 642
Student Christian Movement, 18, 1086, 1087
The Student (magazine), 22
Student Nonviolent Coordinating Committee (SNCC), 260, 1056–1057, 1083, 1086, 1087, 1090–1091, 1092
Student Volunteer Movement, 73, 1129
Students for a Democratic Society (SDS), 18, 1091
Study circles, for Muslim women, 616–617, *617,* 627
Study Group on Jewish-Christian Relations, 1278
Stuhlmueller, Carroll, 953
Stull, Ruth, 444
Sturgeon, Noël, 1112
Sturges, Maria, 1043
Suárez, Pedro, 139
Submission: female, 461, 467; mutual, 461, 467
Subversion, 45–46
Suchocki, Marjorie, 50
Suchoff, Libbie, 902
Suddarth, Fannie, 427
Suenens, Léon-Joseph Cardinal, 198, 459
Suffering, feminine mode of approach to, 67
Suffrage Guild, 192
Sufi Order in the West, 1276
Sufism, 607, 614, 623, 627, 1276
Sugg, D. Adeline, 496
Suicide, Jonestown mass, 710, 787
Suitable Helpers, 1300
Sullivan, John, 198
Sullivan, Margaret Buchanan, 158
Sulpician Seminary, 164
Summer, Myrna, 994
Summer Institute of Linguistics, 841
Summer Solstice, 813
Summers, Jennie Bloom, 316
Summer's End, 813
Summit Lighthouse, 763–764, 1264
Sun Bear, 103
Sun Dance, 106, 1233
Sun Myung Moon, 789–791, *790*
Sunday, Billy, 416, 419, 441, 986
Sunday, Helen "Ma," 419, 441
Sunday School Motor Caravans, 284
Sunday School Movement, 272, 453, 976–977; hymns and, 982–984
Sunday Schools, 825, 873, 876; for American Muslim children, 616; in Baptist churches, 291–292; Protestant, 906–912; role of women in, 248; teaching at, *900, 908*
Sunim, Samu, 640, 641
Sunna, 605–606
Sunna, Karen, 640, 644
Sunni Islam, 622
The Sunshine Hour, 420
Surbey, Edith, 1066
Surrogate motherhood, 1109
Suzuki, Beatrice Erskine Hahn Lane, 637–638
Suzuki, Daisetsu (D. T.), 637, 638, 641

Suzuki, Shunryu, 641, 643
Svetambara sect of Jainism, 689, 692, 693
Swain, Clara, 325, 837
Swaminarayan, 660
Swartley, Willard, 472–473
Swartout, Mary, 348
Sweden, settlements in Delaware Valley, 229
Swedenborg, Emanuel, 710, 711, 739, 760, 769, 770
Swedish Separatists, 708
Sweeney, Anna, 877
Sweeney, Elizabeth, 196
Sweet Briar College (Va.), 918, 922
Sweet Selections, 997
Swidler, Arlene, 953
Swidler, Leonard, 472
Swift, Elizabeth, 409
Swift, Suzie, 409
Swiney, Frances, 806–807
Swiss German Reformation, 369
Sylvester, Nancy, 206
Synagogue auxiliary associations, emergence of, 536
Synagogue life, validation of women's participation in, 538
Syncretism, 117, 733
Syracuse Zen Center, 643
Szold, Benjamin, 1122
Szold, Henrietta, 545, 580, 581, 899, 903, 1122–1123, 1124

Tacoma Buddhist Society, 636
Tadoussac, 143
Tafari-Ama, Imani, 123
Tagore, Rabindranath, 669
Tahirih, 784
Tahirih Justice Center, 786
Tai chi, 678, 679
Tait, Bishop, 826
Tajima, Kengo, 501
Tajima-Peña, Renee, 501–502
Take Back the Night: Women and Pornography, 1165
Talbot, Eliza, 777
Taliban rule in Afghanistan, 619
Tallmadge, Nathanial, 773
Talmud, 576, 577, 1222
Tambourines to Glory (Hughes), 992
Tamez, Elsa, 1197
Tamil Sangam, 660
Tan, Amy, 1016
Tanenbaum, Marc, Center for Interreligious Understanding, 1280
Tantaquidgeon, Gladys (medicine woman), *1256,* 1257
Tanzer, Sara, 1281
Tao, 678
The Tao of Physics, 678
The Tao of Pooh, 678
Taoism, 185, 675, 677; Fung Loy Kok Institute of, 675
Taos people, 107
Tapestry, 1287–1288
Tara Mandala (retreat center), 656
Tarahan, Anastasia, 211
Tarango, Yolanda, 20, 1181–1185

Utley, Uldine, 423, 442
Utopian movements, 717

Vacation Bible School, 292
Vajrayana Buddhism, 29, 676, 1213
Vala kappu ("bracelets and amulets"), 661
Valenzuela, Genaro, 493
Valiente, Doreen, 809
Valley of Baca: A Record of Suffering and Triumph (Smith),
    429
Van Cleef, Paul, 345
Van Cott, Maggie Newton, 325, 969
Van der Meer, Haye, 951
Van Dyke, Mary Louise, 986
Van Kleeck, Mary, 275
Van Leeuwen, Mary Stewart, 456
Van Norden, Emma, 409
Van Waters, Miriam, 279
Varalakshmi Vrata (votive ritual), 662
Vargas, Julia, 497
Vargas, Matilde, 497
Vargas Seín, Teófilo, 497
The Varieties of Psychedelic Experience (Houston and Mas-
    ters), 766
Vasanthakumar, Nirmala, 43
Vasconcelas, Andre de, 109
Vasquez, Dinora, *330*
Vassar, Mathew, 915
Vassar College (New York), 882, 915, 922
Vatican, change in status at United Nations, 1108
Vatican Congregation for the Propagation of the Faith, 191
Vatican Declaration against the Ordination of Women, 959
Vatican II (1962–1965), 16, 459, 1174, 1181; American Cath-
    olic women since, 200–209; church music and, 167;
    church renewal and, 131; impact of, 189, 199; interfaith
    marriage and, 1273; on lay participation in Church, 887;
    Mexican women and, 130; on model for missions, 849;
    on Mystical Body, 846; on ordination of women, 951, 953–
    954; reforms in catechetorical field, 880; restoration of
    permanent diaconate, 832; women's religious orders fol-
    lowing, 1103–1104
Veazey, Carlton, 1102, 1304
Vedanta philosophy, 659–660, 666–667, 669
Vedanta Society, 660, 666–668, 1275
Vedas, 27
Vegetarian societies, 30
Veils, Islamic practice of, 609, 617–618
Venite Seorsum, 207
Veverka, Fayette, 1283
Via, E. Jane, 1105
Victoria Buddhist Dharma Society, 655
Vidya arambha ("the beginning of learning"), 661
Vietnam, 1057; American involvement in, 1057
Vietnamese American Catholic women, 185–186
The View of Judaism in German Christian Theology since 1945
    (Fleischner), 1278
Vignos, Alice, 876
Vilhalmsdottir, Audur Eir, 1248
Villa Valdéz, Susie, 492–493

Villafañe, Ana, Way Out Ministries, 482
Villard, Fanny Garrison, 1054
Vinaya (monastic) rules, 649
Violence, sexual/physical/emotional, 100
Violence against women, 1289–1290
Violet, Arlene, 1104
Vipassana movement, 646–647, 648, 651
Vira Saiva, 661
Virgin of Guadalupe, veneration of, 130
Virginia: Colonial settlement in, 221; New Light Presbyteri-
    ans in, 239; Protestant women in, 236–237; slavery in,
    237
Virtuous womanhood, 864
Vischer, Lukas, 343
Vishnu Sahasranama, 663
Visitation House of Ministries, 1181
Visitation Sisters, 161
Visiting Nurse services, 1072, 1123
Vivekananda, Swami, 659, 660, 666–668, 781, 1275
Vlk, Cardinal Miroslav, 957
Vocation, 71
Vocational kinship, 71, 72, 79
Vodou, 65, 117, 119, 120–121, 122, 732, 733–735, *734*, 736,
    737, 1156, 1165, 1264
Vodou Lwa, 121
Voices of the Matriarchs (Weissler), 1227
Volunteeristic spirit, of American Protestantism, 830
Volunteers of America, 412, 838
Von Sydow, Max, 1012–1013
Voorhees College (Denmark, S.C.), 273
Vorilhon, Claude, 795
Vote, women's right to, 1024
Voth, Heinrich (Henry), 87

Wachovia, North Carolina, Moravian settlement at, 241
Waddy, Henrietta, 992
Wade, Andrew, 1085
Wade, Dorothea, 424–425
Wade, Henry, 424–425
Wage Earning Women (study), 1033
Wagner, Jon, 788
Waite, Louise, 784
Wald, Lillian, 1062–1063
Waldo, Miss S. E., 668
Walker, Albertina, 260, 992, 993
Walker, Alice, 20, 261, 1165–1167, *1166,* 1172, 1173, 1216
Walker, David, 253, 1042
Walker, James, 945
Walker, Madame C. J., 1079
Walker, Marietta, 729–730, 731
Walker, Wyatt Tee, 987
Walker River Agency School, 100
Walking in balance, 1231
Wall, Jeffrey, 107
Wallace, Lew, 303
Wallace, Zerelda, 303
Walloons, 228
Walsh, James A., 191, 845

Western settlement, Catholic women in, 153–154
Western Women in Eastern Lands: An Outline Study of Fifty Years of Woman's Work in Foreign Missions (Montgomery), 14, 293
Western Women in Eastern Lands (Montgomery), 839
Westhampton College (Ga.), 917
Westhampton College (Va.), 922
Westminster Confession of Faith, 348
Westtown, 335
Westwood, Kathryn, 730
Wetamoo, 91
Wetherhead, Mary, 229
Weyanoke, 111
Whalen, Philip, 683
Wharton, Edith, 1009
Wharton, Edward, 1009
Wharton, Lulie P., 289–290
What Ever Happened to Good Old "Women's Work?" (Young), 277
What the Body Remembers (Baldwin), 703
Wheatley, Phillis, 368
Wheaton College (Ill.), 455, 910, 911
Wheel of Dharma (newsletter), 685
Wheel of the Year, 813
Wheeler, Winona, 108–109
When God Was a Woman (Stone), 19, 1202
When the Iron Eagle Flies (Vihara), 650
Where Angels Go, Trouble Follows (film), 1014
Where Are My Children? (film), 1011
White, Alma, 418–419, 423, 427
White, Andrew, 147
White, Anna, 712
White, Arthur, 418
White, Charles, 878
White, Clara, Mission, 1066
White, Eartha, 1066
White, Elizabeth, 336
White, Ellen Gould Harmon, 48, 969, 971, 1260
White, Evelyn D., 998
White, George, 989
White, Nathan, 336
White, Ray, 418
White, Wilbert W., 911
The White Book, 766
White cultural exploitation, of Black sexuality, 1302–1304
"White Path's Rebellion," among Cherokee people, 113
White racism, 1026–1027
White Ribbon Army, 985
White Savage (film), 1015
White slavery, 592
White Woman of the Seneca, 231
White Women's Christ and Black Women's Jesus: Feminist Christology and Womanist Response (Grant), 1169
Whitefield, George, 112, 226, 227, 239, 240, 241
Whitement, Lurana Mary, 849
Whitfield, Archbishop, 164
Whitman, Marcus, 346
Whitman, Narcissa, 346–347
Whitt, Laurie, 105
Whittaker, James, 715

Whittemore, Emma M., 430
Whittier, John Greenleaf, 781
Whittle, D. W., 982
Who Is My Self? (Vihara), 650
Wicca, 19, 712, 742, 761, 1201, 1203, 1264, 1288; ceremonial tools, 812; contributions of individual, 814–817; divine forms, 811–812; forms, 810; history, 809–810; legacies, 817–818; life passage rites, 812–813; lunar cycle, 814; sacred symbols, 812; sacred year, 813–814; sexual orientation and, 1289; spiritual practices, 812; values, 810–811; women in, 809–818, 810
Wichern, Johannes, 822
Widening Circles (Macy), 1094
Wider Church Ministries, 684
Widows Mite Society, 302
Wigger, Winand M., 156
Wilbur, John, 336
Wilcock, John, 814
Wilcox, Clyde, 1300
Wilcox, Ella Wheeler, 758
Wilkerson, Dave, 462
Wilkes, Eliza Tupper, 389
Wilkinson, Jemima, 235–236, 714, 835, 941, 967, 969
Willard, Emma, 35, 882, 890, 913, 1021–1022
Willard, Frances E., 14, 15, 18, 54, 396, 414, 425, 430, 453, 966, 969–970, 985, 1028–1030, 1032, 1053, 1073, 1076, 1150, 1158
Willey, Diane, 1280–1281
William and Mary, College of, 332
William Smith College (New York), 918, 922
Williams, Anita Rose, 166
Williams, Arné, 894–896
Williams, Barbara, 165
Williams, Caroline, 312
Williams, Delores, 20, 40, 51, 57, 261, 1111, 1168, 1169, 1231, 1234
Williams, E. Louise, 312
Williams, Emily H., 866
Williams, Fannie Barrier, 389, 866
Williams, Frank, 994
Williams, Lewin, 121
Williams, Lucinda, 294
Williams, Lucy, 856
Williams, Marion, 992, 993
Williams, Mary Lou, 167, 301–302
Williams, Nolan E., Jr., 999
Williams, Roger, 224, 225, 285, 294
Williams, W. H., 302
Williamson, Marianne, 765
Willie, Charles, 278
Willing, Jennie Fowler, 417, 418, 855–856, 856–857, 863
Willing, William, 856
Willis, Janice Dean, 1098
Willson, David, 247
Wilson, Bertha, 1143
Wilson, Cairine, 1141
Wilson, Carol, 648
Wilson, Elizabeth, 893
Wilson, Jennie, 891
Wilson, Lois, *362*, 363–364, 367, 1148, 1288

Women: African American denominations and, 250–262; in African Caribbean religion, 116–123; in American Episcopal Church, 269–279; of Anabaptist traditions, 262–269; in Baha'i community, 776–787; Baptist, 285–296; in British North America, 242–249; in Canadian Anglican Church, 279–285; in Caribbean religions, 732–738, *734;* Christian Church/Disciples of Christ tradition and, 297–307; in Christian Science, 738–746; in Colonial New England, 221–228; in Communitarian societies, 707–718; creative use of ambivalence and, 49; in economy, 57–58; exclusion from ministry, 222; feminist thought and, 804–809; generative voices of, 53–54; insider/outsider status of, 45–52; interpretation of scripture by, 33–45; issues of, in American Islam, 619–629; in Jewish Renewal, 797–804; Lutheran, 307–318; Methodist, 319–329; in Mid-Atlantic colonies, 228–236; Mormon, 718–727, *720;* in Nation of Islam, 612–613, 746–753, *747;* New Age movement and, 761–767; in new religious movements, 787–797; New Thought and, 757–761; oppression of, in Islam, 31, 49; in Orthodox Christian traditions, 509–518; as pastoral counselors, 66; primary roles in home and family, 29–30; in Protestant Church societies and bureaucracies, 1265–1270; psychology of religious experience, 62–68; Quaker, 329–341; Qur'anic view of, 609; in Reformed Churches, 341–352; religion and, *4;* religious imagination of, 45–52; in Reorganized Church of Jesus Christ of Latter-day Saints, 728–732, *729;* role of, in schisms and church scandals, 234–236; in Southern colonies, 236–242; spiritual biography and autobiography of, 68–79; spiritualism and, 768–776; status of, and Buddhism, 9, 11; suffrage of, 14; Theosophy and, 753–757; in Wiccan religion, 809–818, *815*

Women, A Resource in the Church (Winston), 316

Women, Environment, Education and Development (WEED), 1113

Women and Authority: Re-emerging Mormon Feminism, 16

Women and Christian Origins (Kraemer and D'Angelo), 43

Women and Jewish Law (Biale), 576

Women and Men and the Bible (Mollenkott), 474

Women and religion: fields of, 3, 11; methods of study and reflection, 3–11; subfields of, 3

Women at the Altar (Byrne), 957

Women Caught in the Conflict: The Culture War between Traditionalism and Feminism (Groothuis), 473

Women Church Convergence, 1105

Women for Dialogue, 131

Women for Faith and Family (WFF), 204

Women for World Peace, 790

Women Healing Earth: Third World Women on Ecology, Feminism and Religion (Ruether), 1115

Women hymn writers, 974–987; alternative movements, 986; American beginnings, 976–977; background, 975–976; literary women as, 977–979; revivals and, 979–982; social reform and voluntary associations, 984–985; Sunday School movement and, 982–984

Women in America: Being an Examination into the Moral and Intellectual Condition of American Female Society (Graves), 293

Women in Islam (WII), 619

Women in Mission Partnership program, 379–380

Women in New Worlds (Thomas and Keller), 453

Women in Orthodoxy, 511

Women in Scripture: A Dictionary of Named and Unnamed Women in the Hebrew Bible, 42

Women in the Catholic Workers, 198

Women monastics, 516–517

Women of Faith, 460, 1300; public leadership of, 1149–1161

The Women of Methodism (Stevens), 425

Women of Reform Judaism, 542

Women of the Church Coalition, 1244

Women of the Church Convergence, 133

Women of the ELCA (WELCA), 318

Women of the Restoration (Phillips), 731

Women of the Wall, 584

Women on the Border, *1138*

Women Priests in the Catholic Church (van der Meer), 951

Women revivalists, 422–423

Women Strike for Peace, 1057

Women Volunteers for Africa, 846

Women Working and Volunteering, 1126

Women-centered theology, 1165–1239; Buddhism, 1207–1214; Euro-American feminist, 1173–1181; Goddess, 1200–1207; Jewish, 1220–1229; Las Hermanas, 1181–1188; Latina Catholic, 1193–1200; Lesbian issues, 1214–1220; *Mujerista,* 1188–1193; Native women's, 1229–1239; womanist, 1165–1173

Women-church, 1243–1249; convergence, 1245; ecclesiology of, 1247; future of, 1248–1249; international/ecumenical expression of, 1248; liturgies of, 1247–1248; practice of, 1245–1246; theological dimensions of, 1246–1247

Women-Church Convergence, 1247

Women-connected, 1214–1215

Women-identified, 1214–1215

Women's Aglow Fellowship International (Aglow), 456, 459, 464, 465, 1263

Women's Alliance for Theology, Ethics and Ritual (WATER), 59, 133, 1244, 1246, 1247, 1248

Women's American Baptist Foreign Mission Society, 1266

Women's American Baptist Home Mission Society, 917

Women's American ORT (Organization for Rehabilitation and Training), 1122

Women's Auxiliary of Hebrew Educational Society, *899*

Women's Baptist Foreign Mission Society East, 287

Women's Baptist Foreign Mission Society West, 287–288

Women's Bible Commentary (Sakenfeld), 41–42, 473

Women's Board of Missions, 1266

Women's burial societies, 570

Women's Centenary Aid Association (WCAA), 388

The Women's Church, 1248

Women's clubs, black, 14, 17, 259, 1167, 1170

Women's College Coalition, 920–921

Women's Convention of the Church of God in Christ, 437

Women's Convention of the National Baptist Convention, 290, 1031

Women's Dharma Monastery, 649

Women's Division of Shaare Zedek Medical Center, 562

Women's Division of the National Democratic Party, 1084–1085

Women's Division of the United Methodist Church, 1102

Women's Division of Young Israel, 562–563

Women's Environment and Development Organization (WEDO), 1113

World AIDS Day (December 1) 2001, 1109
World Anti-Slavery Convention (London), 335
World as Love, World as Self (Macy), 1094
World Call (magazine), 304
World Council of Churches (WCC), 279, 367, 512–515, 525, 529, 832, 840, 849, 986, 1113, 1287; Ecumenical Decade: Churches in Solidarity with Women, 20; Madras meeting of, 76; Oxford meeting of, 76; Program to Combat Racism, 1147; Programme on Justice, Peace and the Integrity of Creation, 513
World Court, creation of, 1055
World Day of Prayer, 294, 345
World Day of Prayer for Missions, 839–840
World Friends, 365
World March of Women, 59, 1290
World Parliament of Religions (Chicago), 159, 659, 666–667, 671
World Service Greetings, 327
World Student Christian Federation, 1146
World War I, 259, 1033, 1055; outbreak of, 1053
World War II, 259, 1055–1056
World Zionist Organization, 1123
World's Christian Fundamentals Association, 443
World's Columbian Exposition (Chicago), 159, 637, 1120
World's Woman's Christian Temperance Union, 430
Worldwide Pictures, 462
Worman, "Aunt Teresa," 444
Wounded Knee, 106
The Wrath of Jonah: The Crisis of Religious Nationalism in the Israeli-Palestinian Conflict (Ruether), 1278
Wright, Alice Spearman, 1084
Wright, Elizabeth Evelyn, 273
Wright, Faye, 669
Wright, Frances, 708, 713, 715
Wright, J. Elwin, 445
Wright, J. Leitch, 111
Wright, Joel A., 445
Wright, Rachel, 333
Wright, Susannah, 231–232, 233
Writing a Woman's Life (Heilbrun), 70
Wu, Rose King Yoak Won, 278
Wuthnow, Robert, 208, 1298
Wycliffe Bible Translators, 841

Xavier University (New Orleans), 191, 844; Institute for Black Catholic Studies at, 167

Yakima women, Christianity and, 96–97
Yale University, 886, 924; founding of, 226
Yama Craw Baptist Church, 118
Yampolsky, Philip, 638
Yanait, Rathel, 1126
Yancy, Elyse, 992
Yarmouth (ocean liner), 1077
Yasutani, Ryoko, 641, 642
Yee, Gale, 504–505
Yenoja, 120
Yentl (film), 1016
Yeomans, Lilian, 400, 404
Yes, Lord! Church of God in Christ Hymnal, 998

Yeshiva Etz Chaim, 566
Yeshiva of Flatbush (Brooklyn), 566
Yeshiva University (NYC), 561, 566
Yiddishkeit, 1126
Yiguandao (I-kuan tao), 677–678
Yin Shun, 676
Yin-yang theory, 674
Yitzchak, Levi, 801
Yockey, Elvira, 374
Yoder, Barbara, 231
Yoga traditions, 1275
Yogananda, Paramahansa, 660, 667, 669–670, 1275
Yom Kippur, 960
Yoruba, 119, 733, 736, 1165
Yoshimachi, Bernadette, *179,* 181
You Can't Keep a Good Woman Down (Walker), 1165
Youmans, Letitia, 248
Young, Brigham, 709, 713, 720–721, 722, 728
Young, Francis, 277
Young, Rosa, 316
Young Buddhist Association, 683–684
Young Catholic Workers, 215
Young Christian Workers, 199
Young Feminist Network, 958
Young Judea, 1124
Young Ladies Charitable Union, 900
Young Ladies Seminary, 919
Young Men's Christian Association (YMCA), 871, 1128; hymnals of, 985
Young Men's Hebrew Association, 900
"Young Moravian Girl" (Hardt), *237*
Young People's Moorish League, 611
Young Woman's Auxiliary (YWA), 281, 283
Young Women's Christian Association (YWCA), 17, 281, 283, 762, 840, 871, 916, 918, 1027, 1028, 1030, 1033, 1034, 1063, 1082, 1127–1134, *1128,* 1304; of Canada, 1129; *Interracial Character* pledge, 1132; Mexican, 1134; National Training Institute, 1130
Young Women's Hebrew Association (YWHA), 900
Young Women's Settlement, 1067
Young Women's Union, 547, 899
Youngman, Henny, 765
Younkin, Sarah Matilda Hart, 303
Your Daughters Shall Prophesy: Feminist Alternatives in Theological Education, 934
Youth, Jan, 685–686
Youth Aliyah, 1124
Youth Ministries for Peace and Justice, 482
Youville, Marguerite d', 211

Zalman, Reb, 798–800, 801, 803–804
Zanotti, Barbara, 1218
Zapata, Dominga, 1200
Zárate, Rosa Martha, 1185–1186, 1187
Zavella, Patricia, 491
Zawatsky, Carole, 905
Zeligs, Dorothy, 902
Zell, Katherine, 341, 344
Zell, Matthew, 344